lonely planet

Sicily

Sally O'Brien
Fionn Davenport

W9-AGB-591

LONELY PLANET PUBLICATIONS
Melbourne • Oakland • London • Paris

SICILY

ELEVATION

4000m
2000m
1000m
500m
200m
0

National Parks

PALERMO
Beautiful and belligerent, decayed and decadent, this wonderful city is like no other

MONREALE
The glittering mosaics in the Cattedrale di Monreale may well be the world's most impressive

FAVIGNANA
The traditional annual mattanza, or tuna kill, draws big crowds and much blood

SELINUNTE
The many temple ruins are as captivating today as they were impressive in the 6th century BC

AGRIGENTO
The Valley of the Temples, Goethe's 'splendid valley', is one of the world's most important Hellenistic sites

Tyrrhenian Sea

To Cagliari
To Naples, Livorno & Genoa

Ustica
Ustica

Sferracavallo
Capo Gallo
Mondello
Mt Pellegrino (606m)
PALERMO
Soluto

Falcone-Borsellino
A29 Carini
Montelepre
Monreale
Bagheria

San Vito lo Capo
Riserva Naturale dello Zingaro
SS187
Scopello
SS186
Partinico
Piana degli Albanesi
Misilmeri
SS113
Mt Cofano (659m)
Términi Imerese
A19

Mt Calògero (1326m)
Himera
SS120

Marèttimo
Lèvanzo
Tràpani
Érice
Valdèrice
SS187
Castellammare del Golfo
SS113
Àlcamo
SS118
SS121
SS285
Paceco
A29d
Segesta
SS119
Birgi
SS187
SS115
Mòzia
A29
SS624
Corleone

Favignana
Favignana
Lo Stagnone
Salemi
Ruderi di Gibellina
SS188c
Lercara Friddi
SS188
SS189

Egadi Islands
Marsala
Capo Boeo
SS188
SS119
Partanna
SS188

Mazara del Vallo
Castelvetrano
SS386
SS118
Sant'Angelo Muxaro
SS189

Campobello
Menfi
Sciacca
SS115
Ribera

Cave di Cusa
Selinunte

Eraclea Minoa
Raffadali
Aragona
Racalmuto
SS640
Canicattì

Vulcanèlli di Macalube
Agrigento
Favara
Naro

Porto Empèdocle
Valley of the Temples
SS115
Palma di Montechiaro

Pelagic Islands

Linosa

To Porto Empèdocle (150km)

Lampedusa
Lampedusa

Same Scale as Main Map

MEDITERRANEAN SEA

To Tunis, Tunisia (150km)

0   15   30km
0   10   20mi

To Pelagic Islands (80km) (See Inset)

Pantelleria
Pantelleria
Montagna Grande (836m)

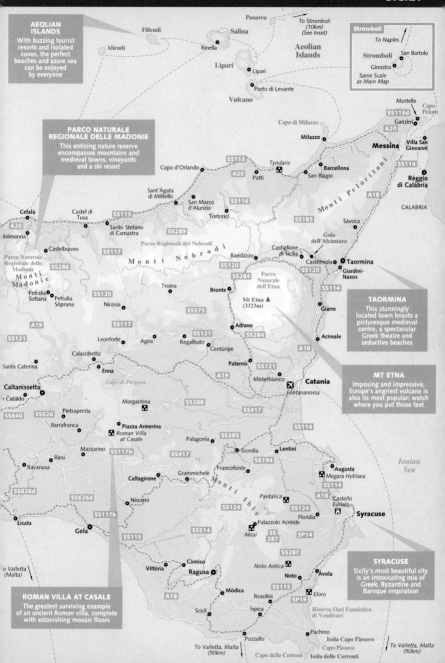

SICILY

AEOLIAN ISLANDS
With buzzing tourist resorts and isolated coves, the perfect beaches and azure sea can be enjoyed by everyone

PARCO NATURALE REGIONALE DELLE MADONIE
This enticing nature reserve encompasses mountains and medieval towns, vineyards and a ski resort

TAORMINA
This stunningly located town boasts a picturesque medieval centre, a spectacular Greek theatre and seductive beaches

MT ETNA
Imposing and impressive, Europe's angriest volcano is also its most popular; watch where you put those feet

SYRACUSE
Sicily's most beautiful city is an intoxicating mix of Greek, Byzantine and Baroque inspiration

ROMAN VILLA AT CASALE
The greatest surviving example of an ancient Roman villa, complete with astonishing mosaic floors

Panarea
To Stromboli (10km) (See Inset)

Stromboli
To Naples
Mortelle
Strombuli · San Bartolo
Ginostra
Same Scale as Main Map

Filicudi
Salina
Alicudi
Rinella
Aeolian Islands
Lìpari
Lipari
Porto di Levante
Vulcano

Capo di Milazzo
Capo Peloro
SS113d
Ganzirri
A20
Villa San Giovanni
Milazzo
Messina
SS114
Capo d'Orlando
SS113
A20
Tyndaris
Barcellona
Règgio di Calabria
Patti
San Biàgio
Sant'Àgata di Militello
San Marco d'Alùnzio
SS116
Monti Peloritani
A18
Cefalù
Castel di Tusa
SS113
Tortorici
SS185
Sàvoca
CALABRIA
ibilmanna
A20
Santo Stefano di Camastra
SS289
Parco Regionale dei Nebrodi
Gola dell'Alcàntara
Parco Naturale Regionale delle Madonie
Castelbuono
SS117
Monti Nebrodi
Castiglione di Sicilia
Castelmola
Taormina
Monti Madonie
SS286
Randazzo
SS120
Giardini-Naxos
Petralia Sottana
Petralia Sòprana
SS120
Troina
SS284
Parco Naturale dell'Etna
SS120
SS114
Nicosia
SS575
Bronte
Mt Etna (3323m)
Giarre
SS121
A19
SS117
Leonforte
Agira
SS121
Regalbuto
Adrano
SS284
Acireale
Calascibetta
Centùripe
Santa Caterina
Enna
Lago di Pergusa
Paternò
A18
Caltanissetta
Misterbianco
SS121
n Cataldo
Morgantina
Fontanarossa
Catania
SS640
SS626
Pietraperzia
SS288
Barrafranca
SS417
SS114
Piazza Armerina
Roman Villa at Casale
Palagonia
SS385
Mazzarino
SS117b
Scordia
Lentini
Ionian Sea
Ravanusa
Riesi
Caltagirone
Grammichele
Francofonte
SS194
Augusta
Megara Hyblaea
SS626d
SS626d
Niscemi
Monti Iblei
SS114
Pantalica
Castello Eurialo
Licata
SS117b
SS124
SS124
Syracuse
Gela
Palazzolo Acrèide
Floridia
SS115
Akrai
SP14
SS287
Vittòria
Còmiso
SS514
SS287
Noto Antica
SYRACUSE
To Valletta (Malta)
Ragusa
Mòdica
Noto
Avola
A18
SS115
Eloro
Rosolini
SP19
Scicli
Ìspica
Riserva Oasi Faunìstica di Vendicari
Pàchino
To Valletta, Malta (90km)
Pozzallo
Ìsola Capo Pàssero
Capo Pàssero
To Valletta, Malta (90km)
Capo delle Correnti
Ìsola delle Correnti

Sicily
2nd edition – September 2002
First published – August 2000

Published by
Lonely Planet Publications Pty Ltd ABN 36 005 607 983
90 Maribyrnong St, Footscray, Victoria 3011, Australia

Lonely Planet offices
Australia Locked Bag 1, Footscray, Victoria 3011
USA 150 Linden St, Oakland, CA 94607
UK 10a Spring Place, London NW5 3BH
France 1 rue du Dahomey, 75011 Paris

Photographs
Many of the images in this guide are available for licensing from
Lonely Planet Images.
Web site: www.lonelyplanetimages.com

Front cover photograph
Sicily's splendid scenery: lush countryside along the northeast coast
(Ionas Kaltenbach)

ISBN 1 74059 031 7

Printed by The Bookmaker International Ltd
Printed in China

Although the authors
and Lonely Planet try
to make the informa-
tion as accurate as
possible, we accept
no responsibility for
any loss, injury or
inconvenience sus-
tained by anyone
using this book.

Contents – Text

THE TYRRHENIAN COAST

THE AEOLIAN ISLANDS

THE EASTERN COAST

SYRACUSE & THE SOUTHEAST

CENTRAL SICILY

THE SOUTHERN COAST

WESTERN SICILY

Contents – Maps

MAP INDEX

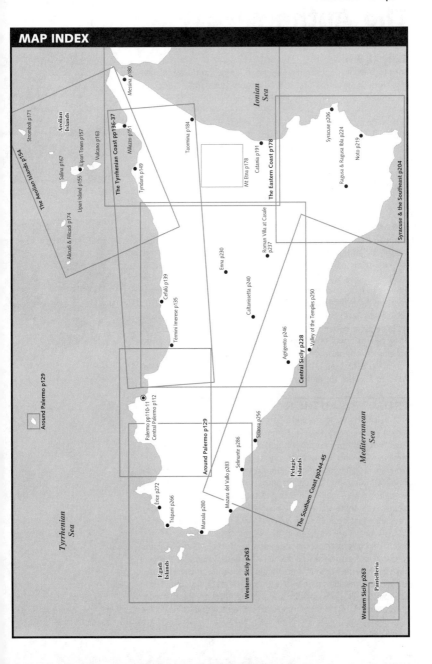

The Authors

Sally O'Brien

Born in Melbourne, raised in Seoul and Sydney and a keen traveller from the time she first shoved a toothbrush and a camera in a handbag as a child, Sally joined Lonely Planet in 1998 as an editor on Southeast Asian titles. She jumped the fence to update LP's guide *Sydney* and the Sydney chapter of *Australia*. She has visited Italy numerous times, and a lazy stint as a student in Umbria gave her sufficient Italian language skills to wander around the country and realise that the Mezzogiorno was where the *really* good food, coffee and anecdotes came from. Subsequent visits to Sicily have led her to understand why so many Sicilian emigrants return home – or long to.

Fionn Davenport

Fionn was born and raised in Dublin – an idyllic youth interrupted only by jarring moves to Buenos Aires, Geneva and New York (thanks to his dad's job). He stayed in Dublin long enough to complete a degree in French and History at Trinity College before moving to Paris and then New York. A series of odd jobs and adventures eventually landed him behind a desk editing other people's travel experiences for a travel publication. These days he splits his time between New York, Dublin and wherever the call of work and travel takes him. He has written about many destinations throughout the world and has previously written or contributed to Lonely Planet's *Spain*, *Dublin*, *Ireland*, *Britain*, *England* and the 1st edition of *Sicily*.

FROM THE AUTHOR

First of all, thanks to Amanda Canning and Tim Fitzgerald for my dream job. Thanks also to Fionn Davenport for his great first edition of this book and for his generosity with travel tips. A great big thank-you to Jenny Lansbury and Ian Stokes for their hard work and grace under pressure during a difficult and unpredictable time. In Melbourne, Lara Morcombe and Jody Fenn provided the best airport taxi, mail-collecting and plant-watering service possible. In Sicily, there are so many people to thank that it could make a separate book but I'll start with a general thanks to the many Sicilians who, every day and in every way, prove the cliched and often downright insulting stereotypes of their island untrue. Naming names: thanks to Jacqui Alio and Rosalba, Palermo's 'intrepid lady bus driver', for a magnificent time in the Madonie mountains; Rosalba's dad, who supplied the station wagon; Nic in Palermo for all the hospitality and sterling hotel gossip; the wonderful Michele Gallo, who made the ancient world come to life with his knowledge, wit and fortitude on one of the hottest days of the year; the Gallo family, who reminded me what it was like to eat dinner while a conversation took place; the *unbelievable* Signor Caviezel in Catania, who turned a potential nightmare into a great week with his kindness, contacts, efficiency and great conversation; to Romeo, for the nervous laughs on a still smokin' Mt Etna and for the snorkelling at Acicastello; to the delightful Giallongo family in Syracuse for making me feel like I was at home; crazy Max and Sergio in Syracuse for their uproarious descriptions of the way crazy young Sicilians live; Diana Brown for her kindness and the lowdown on the Aeolian Islands; Sam on Filicudi for his local knowledge; and the Palermitani film-makers who sympathised with my desire to stay in Palermo for as long as possible.

Finally, eternal thanks to my favourite Sicilian-American and old room-mate from my misspent student days on Via del Verzaro, Leslie Rodgers. Your photos and stories of your travels while searching for your grandfather's history in Sicily served as a call for me to travel there and your warmth, humour, generosity and friendship over the years have shown me just how Sicilian you are. *Mille grazie, e forse ci vediamo in giro, mia amica.*

This Book

This is the 2nd edition of Lonely Planet's *Sicily*. It was written by Sally O'Brien. Fionn Davenport wrote the 1st edition.

From the Publisher

This edition of *Sicily* was produced in Lonely Planet's London office. Jenny Lansbury was the coordinating editor and Ian Stokes was responsible for mapping, design and layout. Jenny was assisted by Imogen Franks, Michala Green, Francesca Parnell and Arabella Shepherd; Imogen helped produce the index. Ian was assisted by Rachel Beattie, Fiona Christie and David Wenk. Liam Molloy designed the chapter ends, Annika Roojun designed the cover and Lachlan Ross drew the back-cover map. Lonely Planet Images provided the photographs, and the illustrations were drawn by Jane Smith. Thanks to Finola Collins and Leonie Mugavin for help with the Getting There & Away chapter, and to Emma Koch and Quentin Frayne for checking the Language chapter. Thanks to Paul Piaia and James Timmins and especially to Tim Ryder and Amanda Canning for their all-round expertise and support throughout production. Finally, thanks to Sally O'Brien for her hard work despite other travel and writing commitments!

The quotation on page 114 is taken from *The Normans in Sicily* by John Julius Norwich (Penguin Books, 1992), copyright © John Julius Norwich, 1967, 1970. Reproduced by permission of Penguin Books Ltd.

Thanks

Many thanks to the travellers who used the last edition and contacted us with helpful hints, advice and interesting anecdotes: Myriam Alexowitz, Philip Angel, Corinne Balducci, Susanne Blumaeur, Lynn Broomfield, Henry Brownrigg, Annelies Burema, Michela Caldara, John Ciappetta, Hilary Clarke, Kylie Cox, Pascale Dodin, Joe Ehrl, Ivar Ekman, Rob Ferrara, Bruno Ghise, Ewan Girvan, Daphna Gutman, Martin Guy, David Harbin, Lynn Highland, Tammy Hippisley, Nick Hobbs, Andreas Jakobsson, Ylva Jakobsson, Herbert Kniep, Wietske Koen, Jo Lane, GW Lari, Christophe Liekens, Alison Lovell, Salvatore Maniscalco, Veit Marx, Kevin McIntyre, Sean Mitchell, Mia Montello, Thomas Morling, Hans Onkiehong, Lynn Osgood, RF Parsons, Stina Persson, Ivan Poom, Janice Potten, Mary Rice, Ralph Rozema, Jacqui Shoffner, Jaap Smit, Coby Stork, Lorena Tadori, Maurits van Achterberg, Chris Van Court, Wim Van De Water, Anneke van Luxemburg, Jan van Luxemburg, Georgette Van Schothors, Marko Vidrih, Charmaine Weeks, John Willemsens, Jim Young, Magda Zupancic.

Foreword

ABOUT LONELY PLANET GUIDEBOOKS

The story begins with a classic travel adventure: Tony and Maureen Wheeler's 1972 journey across Europe and Asia to Australia. There was no useful information about the overland trail then, so Tony and Maureen published the first Lonely Planet guidebook to meet a growing need.

From a kitchen table, Lonely Planet has grown to become the largest independent travel publisher in the world, with offices in Melbourne (Australia), Oakland (USA), London (UK) and Paris (France).

Today Lonely Planet guidebooks cover the globe. There is an ever-growing list of books and information in a variety of media. Some things haven't changed. The main aim is still to make it possible for adventurous travellers to get out there – to explore and better understand the world.

At Lonely Planet we believe travellers can make a positive contribution to the countries they visit – if they respect their host communities and spend their money wisely. Since 1986 a percentage of the income from each book has been donated to aid projects and human rights campaigns, and, more recently, to wildlife conservation.

> Although inclusion in a guidebook usually implies a recommendation we cannot list every good place. Exclusion does not necessarily imply criticism. In fact there are a number of reasons why we might exclude a place – sometimes it is simply inappropriate to encourage an influx of travellers.

UPDATES & READER FEEDBACK

Things change – prices go up, schedules change, good places go bad and bad places go bankrupt. Nothing stays the same. So, if you find things better or worse, recently opened or long-since closed, please tell us and help make the next edition even more accurate and useful.

Lonely Planet thoroughly updates each guidebook as often as possible – usually every two years, although for some destinations the gap can be longer. Between editions, up-to-date information is available in our free, quarterly *Planet Talk* newsletter and monthly email bulletin *Comet*. The *Upgrades* section of our website (W www.lonelyplanet.com) is also regularly updated by Lonely Planet authors, and the site's *Scoop* section covers news and current affairs relevant to travellers. Lastly, the *Thorn Tree* bulletin board and *Postcards* section carry unverified, but fascinating, reports from travellers.

Tell us about it! We genuinely value your feedback. A well-travelled team at Lonely Planet reads and acknowledges every email and letter we receive and ensures that every morsel of information finds its way to the relevant authors, editors and cartographers.

Everyone who writes to us will find their name listed in the next edition of the appropriate guidebook, and will receive the latest issue of *Comet* or *Planet Talk*. The very best contributions will be rewarded with a free guidebook.

We may edit, reproduce and incorporate your comments in Lonely Planet products such as guidebooks, websites and digital products, so let us know if you don't want your comments reproduced or your name acknowledged.

How to contact Lonely Planet:
Online: e talk2us@lonelyplanet.com.au, W www.lonelyplanet.com
Australia: Locked Bag 1, Footscray, Victoria 3011
UK: 10a Spring Place, London NW5 3BH
USA: 150 Linden St, Oakland, CA 94607

Introduction

'The deepest mystery is always hidden in the midday sun,' wrote Nietzsche, 'not in the darkness.' He may not have had Sicily in mind when he wrote this but he would have struggled to find a more compelling example of his theory. Today, the cloak of insularity is being cast aside and the Sicilians, who for centuries spoke loudest through their enduring silence, have begun to open up to the outside world. Yet deep into the island's mountainous interior, away from the bustling cities and trendy beach resorts, change is not so evident, and that all-embracing shroud of mystery lives on. Hardly surprising considering that the burden of 6000 years of invasion and occupation weighs heaviest here.

Since prehistory Sicily has attracted the attention of outsiders, who recognised its plentiful natural resources and extraordinary potential to sustain even the most developed civilisation. And of those there were plenty, including the Greeks, the Romans, the Arabs, the Byzantines, the Normans, the French and the Spanish, who came, saw and conquered – and in their wake left a trail of impressive ruins, monuments and buildings that draw ever-increasing gasps of admiration for their stunning beauty. Basking under the hot sun amid lush, subtropical vegetation, Sicily is one of the garden spots of the Mediterranean, a garden where you can come to play and learn about three millennia of European history.

Yet so much beauty has a price, and Sicily is heavily in debt. Each occupier mercilessly stripped the island's wealth, leaving her inhabitants to struggle with endemic poverty, mass emigration and an almost crippling dependency on outside aid which has left the island isolated and marginalised only 3km from the shores of its latest 'occupier', Italy. Since WWII the government in Rome has poured trillions of lire (and now the EU is adding plenty of euros) into the island in the hope of kick-starting its moribund economy, but a huge

percentage has been siphoned off through kickbacks and protection payments to a home-grown oppressor: the Mafia. A rash of ill-conceived and often illegal construction projects during the boom years of the 1950s and '60s has scarred parts of the landscape with some phenomenally ugly buildings and stretches of industrial wasteland that stand in stark relief to the island's natural and man-made splendours. In the

name of island-wide progress, these modern developments only benefited a powerful, self-interested few. Such myopic greed, coupled with problems that were not of its own making, has led many Italians to dismiss Sicily as an albatross around Italy's neck. The island has slumped even further into isolation and growing resentment of the government in Rome, which is as foreign to many Sicilians as the emperors of ancient history, and not that different from the oppressive Spanish, whose 500-year rule ended with Italian unification.

Despite its many problems, the island has plenty to offer the visitor. No matter where you are in Sicily there's always something to see, a little town to poke around or a beach to stretch out on. For all of its unifying elements, the island throws up an equal amount of diversity and contrast, from the decayed grandeur of the capital, Palermo, to the high-flying resorts of Taormina and the Aeolian Islands, both home to a chunk of Italy's glitterati during the summer – the have-yachts in the land of the have-nots. The more exotic west has a distinctly Tunisian feel about it, a stark contrast to the cosmopolitan, European flavours of Catania to the east. If traces of antiquity are what you seek, then you've come to the right place – Sicily's wealth of archaeological finds will have you planning a return visit before you've even left. The stunning Baroque architecture of the southwest alone is worth making the trip for, while walkers will find plenty of paths in the island's nature reserves and on Sicily's most prominent natural feature, the ever-active but always-popular Mt Etna.

Fittingly, the last say goes to a Sicilian – the island's most famous modern painter, Renato Guttuso:

'In Sicily you can find dramas, pastorals, idylls, politics, gastronomy, geography, history, literature... in the end you can find anything and everything, but you can't find truth.'

Facts about Sicily

HISTORY

Strategically located at the heart of the Mediterranean basin, Sicily has been the target of colonisers and settlers from all sides of the sea for over 6000 years. Eager to establish their primacy over the rich waters of the Mediterranean, invaders from two continents – Africa and Europe – turned Sicily into a defensive bulwark intended to support their commercial and military interests in the region. Each conqueror has undoubtedly contributed to the make-up of modern Sicily, some leaving a rich cultural heritage still in evidence today. Yet foreign occupation has also deeply scarred the island, whose inhabitants have always borne the brunt of the suffering heaped upon it by one coloniser after another. Even today, despite being part of a unified Italy, many Sicilians still feel that they are living through the latest cycle of occupation.

Earliest Settlers

The most compelling evidence of Sicily's first human settlers is found in a series of cave etchings that date from around 12,000 BC, located along the coastal areas of the western seaboard, most notably in the Grotta del Genovese on Levanzo and the Grotta dell'Addaura on Mt Pellegrino. Other than their ability to draw, little is known about these first settlers other than that they may have come from Africa in the late Pleistocene. The island was so far south as to make irrelevant the effects of the Ice Age, so it has proven difficult for palaeontologists to distinguish between the peoples of the successive prehistoric ages, from the Mesolithic to the Palaeolithic.

The first real evidence of an organised settlement familiar with rudimentary tools and the basic functions of farming, including animal husbandry and crop plantings, belongs to the Stentillenians, who originated from the Middle East and settled on the island's eastern shores sometime between 4000 and 3000 BC. They founded small colonies at Stentinello, Megara Hyblaea and on Lìpari, where they began the highly lucrative business of trading crafted obsidian, a hard, glassy stone that served as an adequate substitute for metal.

According to the Athenian historian Thucydides (c.460–404 BC), the island's prime location on the Mediterranean trading routes and the relative success of the Stentillenians in developing commerce made it a much sought-after prize for prehistoric colonists. Consequently, from the middle of the second millennium BC, new waves of settlers began appearing on its shores. From Hiberia (the Iberian peninsula) came the Sicanians, who settled around the coast; they were soon followed by the Elymians – thought by some historians, including Thucydides, to be refugees from Troy, although it is more likely that they were from Anatolia – who occupied the territory in and around Eryx (Èrice) and Segesta. Trade with Mediterranean powers such as Mycenae and Minoa grew and brought prosperity to the island, resulting in the fortification of settlements and their transfer to inaccessible higher ground as they sought to protect their wealth from marauding pirates. The settlement on Filicudi's Capo Graziano dates from this period.

Around 1250 BC the first Siculians (or Sikels) arrived from the Calabrian peninsula, forcing settlers on the eastern coast to pack up and move inland. The Siculians (from whom the island takes its name) were particularly successful in establishing working colonies that engaged in agriculture and trading – the vast necropolis of Pantalica near Syracuse was created during this period.

The last of the pre-Hellenic colonists were the Phoenicians from the eastern Mediterranean, who established a number of trading posts along the western coast. According to Thucydides, the Phoenicians filled the gap left by the demise of the Mycenaean trading empire. Here they laid the foundations for a number of cities including Mòzia, just off

The Symbol of Sicily

Triskele, the name for the ceramic bowl with three legs, stems from the ancient Greek word *thrinakrie* (*trinacria* in Italian), meaning trident-shaped, the name given to the island by Homer in the *Odyssey*. Sicily is also known as 'the island of the three promontories' – Capo Peloro, north of Messina; Capo Boeo, near Marsala; and Capo delle Correnti, south of Noto – which represent the island's extremities. Sicily's symbol, visible throughout the island, features three bent legs protruding outward from a central sun. Souvenirs of this symbol are available almost everywhere, especially in towns with a reputation for producing ceramics.

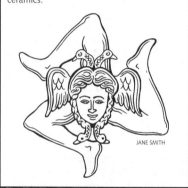

JANE SMITH

the coast from present-day Marsala. Eager to increase the potential for trading, they welcomed the arrival of the Greeks.

The Hellenisation of Sicily

There was no organised invasion of Sicily, nor did the Greeks who settled here all come from the one place. As the great city-states of Greece began flexing their imperialist muscles, so it seemed natural that they would try to carve up the Mediterranean pie between them. A group of Chalcidians landed on Sicily's eastern coast in 735 BC and founded a small settlement at Naxos. The following year a group of Corinthians followed suit and built their colony on the southeastern island of Ortygia, calling it Syracoussai (Syracuse).

In 729 BC the Chalcidians founded a second town south of Naxos called Katane (Catania) – and so it went until three-quarters of the island was in Hellenic hands. In 728 BC Megara Hyblaea was founded, in 689 BC Gela and in 628 BC both Selinus (Selinunte) and Zankle (Messina) – the latter on the site of a Siculian settlement. The last of the great cities to be founded was Akragas (Agrigento), established on the southern coast in 581 BC as a subcolony of Gela.

Initially, the Hellenic colonies lived pretty much at peace with their Phoenician and Elymian neighbours to the west, but the growing strength of Carthage in North Africa soon put an end to good relations. The Carthaginians were keen to establish a foothold in Sicily and, during the 7th century BC, created a string of alliances with the Phoenicians, which naturally aroused the suspicions of the island's Greek powers. By the middle of the next century, however, the Hellenisation of the island was complete. The sole exception was the northwestern corner, still in the hands of the Phoenicians and the Elymians, whose continued presence was bolstered by a powerful Punic army sent from the ancient city of Carthage (on the north African coast), now a formidable force in the western Mediterranean. They created a network of small cities intended to halt the eventual advance of the Greeks.

Still, the colonies of Magna Graecia (Greater Greece) were in the ascendant. Close ties with mainland Greece assured them of profitable trading routes while the plentiful resources of Sicily – supplemented through the introduction of the grape and the olive – were certain guarantees that the colonies would always have something lucrative to trade. The cities they built were a testament to the architectural sophistication and cultural elegance they had brought with them from the Greek mainland, but as the settlements grew in size and importance the colonists sought to outdo the cities in the motherland. As the colonies became wealthier, however, so greed and disaffection increased. Bitter rivalries, often reflecting those of the Greek city-states themselves, resulted in endless squabbling between the different cities. This sometimes spilled out into open warfare and led some of the more powerful colonies to seek a break from the political hold that the mother country had over them. Furthermore, in a pattern that would sadly become the norm for Sicily over the next 2500 years, the ordinary citizens (mostly Siculians who had been co-opted into working for their new Greek overlords) began to question the oligarchies that ruled them with almost no concern for their general welfare, leaving them in conditions of absolute squalor. In the midst of such upheaval and turmoil, the era of the tyrants began.

The Tyrannies

Obliged to expand to stay afloat in an increasingly competitive market and troubled by popular uprising at home, Hippocrates of Gela (498–491 BC) decided in 494 BC that the only way of ensuring his city's continued prosperity was to establish a totalitarian regime with him as autocrat, or tyrant. A few years later Theron of Akragas followed suit, whereupon he decided that what the city really needed was not just the firm rule of law, but an outlet to the Tyrrhenian Sea. Consequently he sought a temporary alliance with Hippocrates and they led their combined forces into Phoenician-Punic territory and annexed the colony at Himera. The death of Hippocrates brought Gelon to power in Gela, and he also seized Syracuse and made it the capital of his dominion.

Deeply concerned by the developments in Hellenic Sicily, the Carthaginians were quick to initiate a counter-offensive. They formed a rapid alliance with a number of city-states alarmed by the expansionist tendencies of Syracuse and Agrigento and in 480 BC sent a massive army led by Hamilcar to Himera. On 4 September the Carthaginians met the combined armies of Theron and Gelon and were convincingly defeated. Although this didn't spell the end of Carthage's involvement in Sicilian affairs, it marked the dramatic rise in importance of Syracuse, which soon came to be the dominant power on the island.

The meteoric rise of Syracuse under successive tyrants stirred another of the Mediterranean's great powers into action, but this time the foe was mighty Athens herself. One hundred years earlier it would have been unthinkable for a Sicilian colony to challenge the hegemony of mainland Greece, but under the tyrants all the rules had changed. Syracuse was now a direct rival to Athenian power; in 415 BC Athens decided to punish the Sicilian 'upstart' by deploying the largest fleet ever assembled, to subdue Syracuse. The Great Expedition, as it was known, resulted in a crushing defeat for Athens two years later. Seven thousand soldiers were captured and imprisoned in Syracuse's notorious limestone quarries, where many died or were sold into slavery.

The victory over Athens marked the zenith of Syracusan power on the island. The rest of Sicily, however, was in a constant state of civil war, which provided the perfect opportunity for Carthage to seek its revenge for Himera. In 409 BC a new army, this time led by Hamilcar's bitter but very brilliant nephew Hannibal, wreaked havoc in the Sicilian countryside, completely destroying Selinunte, Himera, Agrigento and Gela. In 405 BC the Syracusan tyrant Dionysius I (405–367 BC) launched a counter-offensive which resulted in the complete destruction of the Phoenician city of Mòzia between 398 and 397 BC.

Needless to say, Sicily was nothing short of a bloody battlefield throughout this period, and peace was very much in demand.

The Romans in Sicily

Although the Corinthian Timoleon (ruled 345–336 BC) did much to bring peace to the island, rebuilding cities and repopulating the island with a fresh wave of settlers from Greece and the Italian mainland, the days of Greek domination in Sicily were numbered. Under Agathocles (317–289 BC) Syracuse once again went on the rampage, fighting virtually everyone who stood in her way. Hieron II (265–215 BC) attempted to restore some order by forming an alliance with mainland Italy's newest power, Rome, but other than protect Syracuse during the First Punic War (264–241 BC), the alliance did little to stop the Roman tide that was sweeping its way across the Mediterranean basin. The end drew near in 213 BC when the Syracusans – caught between a rock and a hard place – made the disastrous mistake of siding with Carthage during the Second Punic War. Rome was unforgiving in victory and in 211 BC completed the conquest of Sicily which had begun in earnest after their victory in the First Punic War.

Under Roman rule Sicily was treated as a sub-colony whose inhabitants were not granted the right of citizenship. Consequently they were a largely dispossessed people whose only maintenance came from their service as indentured peasants and slaves on the large *latifondi* (landed estates) set up by their conquerors from the Italian mainland. The vast majority of Sicilians – most of them still Greek-speaking – were kept in conditions of such abject poverty that the rule of the most vicious Syracusan tyrants seemed like a golden age. In 135 BC the first slave revolt occurred, led by Eunus of Henna (Enna) and involving tens of thousands of men, women and even children. No sooner had the Romans suppressed the first revolt than the Second Servile War broke out (104–101 BC), with the rebellious slaves supported by a large chunk of the island's peasant class. This too was suppressed with great severity.

As the need to feed an ever-expanding Rome grew, Sicily's forests were felled to make way for the plantation of grain, which then became the island's main export – with the vast majority of the profits being channelled directly into the pockets of the Romans themselves. Under the praetorship of Verres (73–71 BC) Sicily's temples (or, at least, those that were still standing) were stripped of all their treasures, an act which so provoked Cicero that he prosecuted the praetor, successfully condemning him in two orations delivered in the Senate in Rome.

Although treated as little more than the Roman breadbasket, Sicily was to play a key role in the final days of the Roman republic. Following the political vacuum that was created by the murder of Julius Caesar in 44 BC, the popular and successful general Pompey sought to gain an advantage over his rivals to the seat of power – the triumvirate of Mark Antony, Lepidus and Octavius – by seizing the island and blocking all transfer of grain to the Italian mainland. Pompey held on for eight years, supported by a majority of Sicilians, but in 36 BC Octavius defeated his rival in a naval battle off the coast of Milazzo. Not forgetting Sicily's support of Pompey throughout the civil war, Octavius exacted a bloody retribution on the island which only ended when he was finally crowned as the emperor Augustus in 27 BC.

With the demise of the Republic, Sicily underwent a period of peace and relative prosperity as it once again became an important centre of trade within the Roman Empire. Syracuse experienced a partial rebirth as an important commercial centre, and the period coincided with the construction of some of the finer monuments of the Roman occupation, including the Roman villa at Casale. In the 3rd century AD Sicilians were finally granted the right to citizenship, but the end was already in sight for the greatest empire the world had ever seen. The Barbarians were knocking at the door and were keen to come in.

The Byzantine Interlude
After Rome fell to the Visigoths in AD 410 Sicily was occupied by Vandals from North Africa, but their tenure was relatively brief. In 535 the Byzantine general Belisarius landed an army and was welcomed by a population that, despite over 700 years of Roman occupation, was still largely Greek, both in language and custom. The Byzantines had great plans for the island, and were eager to use it as a launching pad for the retaking of Saracen lands with a view towards building a Christianised empire under the rule of Rome and the papacy. In 663 Syracuse temporarily supplanted Constantinople as the capital of the empire, but dreams of Byzantine greatness were not to be realised. A new power was emerging in the Mediterranean and its sights were firmly set on Sicily.

Saracen Sicily
By AD 700 the Moors were already in control of the North African coast and Spain, and considered Sicily a strategic stepping

stone in their territorial expansion and consolidation of the Mediterranean trading routes. Although Sicily had been subjected to repeated raids and Pantelleria, an island off the southern coast, had fallen under Arab control, it was not until 827 that a full-scale invasion took place. A combined army of Arabs, Berbers and Spanish Muslims – collectively termed Saracens – landed at Mazara del Vallo at the invitation of a Byzantine general rebelling against the emperor. In 831 Palermo fell, followed by Syracuse in 878, the latter's resistance punished by the wholescale massacre of its citizens and the stripping of all its wealth. Yet despite this the Saracen occupation of Sicily can be considered one of the better periods of its history, a time when a substantial section of the Sicilian population reaped a share of the rewards accrued from the renewed prosperity.

First and foremost, the Saracens introduced widespread agrarian reform. The large estates were broken up and the lands put under the direct control of the peasants with a view towards encouraging free trade. New crops were introduced, including citrus trees, date palms and sugar cane. More importantly, the Saracens developed and perfected a system of water supply and irrigation that was based on the maintenance of large tracts of woodland in the interior and marshlands along the coast, thereby preserving a moist micro-climate from which water could be drawn. Existing bridges and aqueducts were reinforced and new ones built, while the Saracens applied their skill in urban planning to redraw and redesign the layouts of cities and towns.

Sicily became an important centre for the expansion of Islam, but a policy of religious tolerance towards non-Muslims was also exercised. This was largely down to the taxation system which, although more equitable than at any other time in Sicily's history, was designed so that non-Muslims would pay higher taxes than Muslims. Consequently, it was not in the Saracens' interest to convert the population – though many Sicilians converted of their own accord to avoid paying higher taxes.

After the invasion, Palermo was chosen as the capital of the emirate and, over the next 200 years, became one of the most splendid cities in the Arabic world, a haven of culture and commerce rivalled only by Córdoba in Spain.

The Norman Invasion

By 1040, however, Arab Sicily was in crisis. The Kalbidi (or Aghlabid) dynasty of Tunisia, which had ruled the emirate without interruption since 947, was replaced by the Egyptian Fatimid clan who chose Cairo as their new capital, once more leaving Sicily on the periphery of power. Meanwhile, the Normans had begun a steady campaign of conquest and expansion in southern Europe, primarily through the efforts of the Hauteville brothers; the eldest, William 'Bras de Fer' (Iron Arm; c.1009–46), defeated the Byzantine Greeks who controlled Apulia (a region in southeast Italy) in 1042, whereupon he was elected count of Apulia. Four years later, he was succeeded by his brother Drogo (c.1010–51). Norman activity in southern Italy aroused the fears of the papacy who, although eager to be rid of the Byzantines, were equally suspicious of the Normans – they were considered by Pope Leo IX to be little more than destabilising anarchists establishing a foothold along the southern frontier of the papal territories. The arrival in 1047 of William and Drogo's half-brother Robert Guiscard (c.1015–85) eventually settled matters in favour of the Normans. For six years he wreaked havoc in Calabria and southern Campania, burning, looting and holding the people to ransom. Such mercenary activity, however, disguised a shrewd and capable military mind, and in 1053 he comprehensively defeated the combined forces of the Calabrian Byzantines, the Lombards and the papal forces at Civitate.

Robert's control of southern Italy, however, was threatened by internal strife bought on by the deaths of his brothers William, Drogo and the recently arrived Humphrey (c.1011–57), so Robert returned to Apulia in 1057 to wrest control of the territory from Humphrey's sons. Having established his supremacy, Robert turned his attentions to expanding the territories under his control. To achieve this, however, he had to deal with the Vatican.

Up to this point, the Normans (as mercenaries) had fought for and against the papacy as their needs had required. But Robert's relationship with the Vatican underwent a radical turn following the Great Schism of 1054, which resulted in the complete break between the Byzantine and Latin churches and forced the papacy into an uncertain alliance with the Normans. In 1059 Pope Nicholas II and Robert signed a concordat at Melfi (in the southern Italian region of Basilicata), which invested Robert with the titles of duke of Apulia and Calabria. In return, Robert agreed to chase the Saracens out of Sicily and restore Christianity to the island; as backup he summoned his younger brother Roger (c.1031–1101) from Normandy in 1060. Roger landed his troops at Messina in 1061 and captured the port after a siege lasting several months. In 1064 he tried to take Palermo but was repulsed by a well-organised Saracen army; it wasn't until Robert arrived in 1071 with substantial reinforcements that the city fell into Norman hands.

Roger was never willing to play second fiddle to his older brother but after their joint capture of Palermo he recognised Robert's role as supreme overlord in return for the title of count of Sicily and Calabria in 1072. Eager to make the most of this new role, Roger set about conquering the entire island, although it was to be another 20 years before the conquest of Sicily was complete. In the meantime, he began to reform the areas under Norman control, beginning with Palermo. The city was fortified, its streets were widened and a number of building projects undertaken. Lacking the personnel to completely replace the Arab system of government, Roger wisely went for a policy of partial assimilation between the two cultures, adopting elements of the efficient Saracen bureaucracy and encouraging the employment of Arab engineers and architects to aid in his construction projects. Roger's dalliance with the Arabs notwithstanding, the Normans did introduce a policy of Latinisation. By

1200 Christianity had replaced Islam as the official religion and Italian and French had supplanted Arabic as the island's language.

Roger ruled Sicily with a firm hand, maintaining a permanent army and a fleet at the ready in case there was any opposition to his rule. Robert's death in 1085 conveniently removed him as a potential rival to Roger's control of the island, though in fact Robert had had his sights on larger fry – the capture of the Byzantine throne.

Roger's death in 1101 brought his nine-year-old son Roger II (c.1105–54) to the seat of power after a short interregnum which saw the island ruled by the young Roger's mother, Adelaide of Savona. Unlike his father, Roger was a Mediterranean lord brought up in a cosmopolitan environment. He spoke Greek and Arabic, and was – despite assuming power at a young age – supremely gifted in the art of diplomacy. He used the skill with great success in fending off the local barons, who considered the Hautevilles little more than upstarts attempting to usurp total authority in Sicily. When his cousin William, duke of Apulia, died in 1127 he laid claim to the duchy against the wishes of the barons. He sought the support of Pope Honorius II, who duly invested him with the duchies of Apulia, Calabria and Sicily in 1128. The pope's death in 1130 resulted in a dispute between two rivals to the papal throne. Pope Innocent II was supported by most of Europe, but Roger supported the antipope Anacletus II; in return Anacletus crowned him king of the Two Sicilies, the kingdom of Naples and Sicily. Eight years later Anacletus died and a brief war between Roger and Innocent II resulted in the pope's capture (1139) at Galluccio in Calabria, whereupon Roger forced his captive to confirm his title of king.

The Two Sicilies

Roger II was a brilliantly gifted monarch, a keen intellectual who studied the science of government and built an efficient civil service that was the envy of Europe. He assigned key posts to a number of non-Norman advisers; his finances and army were controlled by Arabs while his increasingly powerful navy was controlled by a Greek, George of Antioch. His court was unrivalled for exotic splendour and learning, while Roger flaunted his multicultural heritage by wearing Arabic and Byzantine robes and even keeping a substantial harem. His enlightened rule was remarkable not only for his patronage of the arts but also for the creation of the first written legal code in Sicilian history and his success in enlarging his kingdom to include Malta, most of southern Italy and even parts of North Africa.

His death in 1154 left the kingdom in the hands of his son William I (1108–66), known as 'William the Bad', who had none of his father's attributes save a propensity for self-indulgence. During his rule the pope managed to organise the election of his English ally Walter of the Mill (Gualtiero Offamiglia) as archbishop of Palermo, a move that would prove to be a thorn in the side of the Hautevilles for over 20 years. William's successor to the throne in 1166 was William II (1152–89), who issued a direct challenge to the growing power of the pope on the island when he ordered that a second archbishopric be created at Monreale, only 10km from Palermo. The cathedral he ordered was decorated with some of the finest mosaics ever seen and to this day a visit remains one of the main highlights of a trip to Sicily (see the boxed text 'William vs Walter' in the Palermo chapter for details). It is perhaps fitting that his moniker was 'William the Good'.

William's premature death at the age of 36 left the throne in the hands of his illegitimate son Tancred (c.1130–94), who was elected king by an assembly of barons. His rule was challenged by the German (or Swabian) king Henry VI (1165–97), who laid claim to the throne by virtue of his marriage in 1186 to Roger II's daughter Constance, born after Roger's death. Tancred had a pretty torrid time of it all: apart from resisting the claims of the Hohenstaufens (Swabians), he had to deal with the barons' decision to purge the island of all Arabs, which forced many of them to leave Sicily for good, and the sacking of Messina in 1190 by the English king Richard I ('the Lion-Heart'), who stopped here on his way to the Third Crusade.

Tancred died in 1194. No sooner had his young son William III been installed as king than the Hohenstaufen fleet docked in Messina. On Christmas Day of that year Henry declared himself king and young William was imprisoned in the castle at Caltabellotta in southern Sicily, where he eventually died (in 1198).

Sicily under the Hohenstaufens

As Holy Roman Emperor, Henry chose to pay scant attention to his Sicilian kingdom, and he died prematurely of malaria in 1197. The previous year Henry had attempted to convince the German barons to make the emperor's crown hereditary, but to no avail. His young heir Frederick (1194–1250) had to make do with the Sicilian crown in 1196 and that of Germany in 1212. It wasn't until 1220 that the pope crowned him Holy Roman Emperor. To complicate matters, references to Frederick in history books name him both Frederick I of Sicily and Frederick II of Hohenstaufen.

Frederick's rule has been the subject of much debate in recent years, with some historians arguing that he was an enlightened and gifted ruler who managed to impose order on the kingdom after years of uncertain rebellion, while others insist that he was little more than a totalitarian despot who filled his court with some of Europe's great minds. Frederick was certainly a tough and unforgiving ruler, but he had also inherited many of his grandfather's qualities and, like Roger II before him, had a keen intellectual mind and a penchant for political manoeuvring.

In 1231 he issued the antifeudal Constitution of Melfi, which stripped the feudal barons of much of their power in favour of a more centralised authority – his own. He drew up the Liber Augustales, which created a unified legal system based on the legal code promulgated by the Roman emperor Augustus 1200 years earlier. This guaranteed certain rights to the citizenry while reinforcing the unquestionable authority of the monarch. He became an avid patron of the arts and the first official champion of vernacular Italian. In *The Divine Comedy*,

Dante (1265–1321) devoted an entire canto to the glory of Frederick's court and the marvellous poetry produced therein – to this day Sicilians will insist that the dialect that was the basis for Italian was not Tuscan in origin but Sicilian.

In the latter years of his reign Frederick took to calling himself Stupor Mundi, 'Wonder of the World', a none-too-humble recognition of his successful rule which had brought glory and stability to the island. Sicily had become a homogenised, centralised state which played a key commercial and cultural role in European affairs. Throughout the 13th century Palermo was recognised as the continent's most important city, a centre of learning that was unrivalled in the Western world. Yet Frederick's rule left substantial scars on the island, most notably in the restriction of free trade, the supplanting of rural settlements in favour of massive landed estates, and a heavy tax burden brought on by the pressures of maintaining the empire. Frederick's death in 1250 left the disaffected barons and their foreign allies, most notably the pope, in open rebellion against the Hohenstaufens. Frederick's son Manfred (1231–66) tried desperately to hold on to power, but his rule was seriously challenged when in 1255 the pope surreptitiously offered the throne to Prince Edmund of Lancaster, who adopted the title of king of Sicily despite the fact that he had never actually set foot on the island – and never would.

The Sicilian Vespers

The French pope Urban IV decided that Edmund was not the right man for the job and in 1263 offered the crown to Charles of Anjou, brother of the French King Louis IX (later St Louis). In 1266 the Angevin army defeated and killed Manfred at Benevento on the Italian mainland. Two years later, another battle took the life of Manfred's 15-year-old nephew and heir Conradin, who was publicly beheaded in a final attempt to end the Hohenstaufen line.

Under the Angevins Sicily was weighed down by an onerous tax burden (to pay for the expensive business of defeating the Hohenstaufens) and their rule was marked by the general oppression of the average Sicilian (mainly agricultural labourers), who had sided firmly with the Germans in the war of succession. Many of the baronial fiefs were awarded to French aristocrats, much to the chagrin of the Norman barons, but the breaking point drew near when Naples was made the capital of the kingdom over Palermo.

The story goes that it was the rape of a Sicilian girl by a gang of French troops on Easter Monday 1282 that sparked a popular revolt, known as the Sicilian Vespers, by the people of Palermo, who lynched every French soldier they could get their hands on. The revolt spread to the countryside and was supported by the barons, who had formed an alliance with pro-imperial Peter of Aragon, who landed at Tràpani with a large army and was proclaimed king. For the next 20 years the Aragonese and the Angevins were engaged in the War of the Sicilian Vespers, but it was almost immediately clear that the Angevins had permanently lost their foothold in Sicily. The island was to remain in Spanish hands for nearly all of the next 500 years.

The Spanish Occupation

Once the war between the pro-imperial Aragonese and the pro-Vatican Angevins was concluded with the Peace of Caltabellotta in 1302, the Kingdom of the Two Sicilies was divided with the Spaniards taking Sicily and the French retaining control over the mainland territories. Until 1458 Sicily was ruled directly by the Aragonese kings, but their general lack of interest in the island's welfare coupled with the strength of the barons meant that Sicily reverted to a pre-Hohenstaufen feudal regime, with a largely ineffectual central government in Palermo and all the real power concentrated in the hands of the Sicilian nobility, who maintained huge estates on the island. The Sicilian peasantry, which had borne the brunt of most of the fighting of the previous 100 years, suffered greatly, and the decimating effect of the Black Death in 1347–48, which was brought by ships to Messina, along with chronic periods of starvation hastened their descent into a state of desperate poverty.

By the end of the 14th century Sicily was marginalised with no commercial or political allies except Spain. The eastern Mediterranean was sealed off by the Ottoman Turks, while the Italian mainland was off limits on account of Sicily's political ties with Spain. The Spanish king Alphonse II (1416–58) attempted to regain a foothold in Italy by retaking Naples from the Angevins, but after his death the city was recaptured by the French and Sicily slid once more into semi-isolation. Even Spain began to lose interest in the island as it concentrated its efforts on the Reconquista (Reconquest) of the south of Italy from the Arabs, and started to turn its attentions away from the Mediterranean to the Atlantic as a preferred channel of trade. After 1458 the Spaniards ruled the island through viceroys – the only king to set foot on the island over the next 200 years was Charles V of Germany (a Habsburg), who docked here for a few days in 1535 on his way home from a crusade.

Culturally, Sicily was almost completely barren and the Renaissance that was sweeping throughout the republics and kingdoms of Italy was barely noticed in this feudal backwater. There were, however, some exceptions, not least in the Catalan-Gothic style that arrived in the 15th century and became all the rage in architecture and the fostering of some good local artistic talent, most notably Antonello da Messina (c.1430–79).

Sicily's isolation was to continue unabated for another 300 years. By the end of the 15th century Spain had discovered America and was no longer a major participant in the affairs of the Mediterranean, now the preserve of the Ottomans to the east and the great naval republics of Pisa, Genoa and Venice to the west. The viceroy's court was a den of corruption and mismanagement, serving only the interests of the favoured nobility at the expense of everyone else. With the expulsion of Jews from all Spanish territories in 1492, the era of religious tolerance was at an end. The most influential body on the island became the Catholic Church (whose archbishops and bishops were mostly Spaniards), which exercised draconian powers through a network of Holy Office tribunals, otherwise known as the Inquisition.

The Rise of Brigandry

Faced with restricted commercial opportunities, even the feudal nobility were forced to make changes in order to survive. They initiated a policy of resettlement that forced thousands of peasant families off the land and into new towns, with a view towards streamlining crop growth on their terrain. Many others moved to the big cities such as Palermo and Messina, leaving their estates in the hands of *massari* or *gabellotti*, bailiffs who were charged with collecting ground rents. The first murmurs of discontent gave way to sporadic uprisings against the overlords, but the most widespread protest against Spanish rule came in the form of brigandry, where small gangs of armed peasants began robbing from the large estates and generally causing mayhem, from burning crops to butchering livestock and killing bailiffs. The local authorities were usually inept at dealing with the brigands, who would disappear into the brush only to re-appear and strike again. These bands struck a mixture of fear and admiration into the hearts of the peasantry, who supported any efforts to destabilise the feudal system and were often willing accomplices in protecting the outlaws. Their revolutionary fervour, however, was held in check by the conservative Church, who declared every outlaw an enemy of Christianity. Although it would be another 400 years before crime became 'organised', the 16th and 17th centuries witnessed a substantial increase in the activities of brigand bands, who were referred to by the name 'mafia'. They protected themselves from prosecution by what was to become the modern Mafia's most important weapon, the code of silence.

The 17th & 18th Centuries

The 17th century brought nothing but disaster to Sicily in the form of plague, cholera and two cataclysmic natural disasters: the eruption of Mt Etna in 1669 and the devastating earthquake of 1693, which destroyed most of the cities on the eastern coast and killed more than 5% of the island's population. Reeling under the weight of natural destruction and state oppression, ordinary Sicilians demanded reform and the major cities, particularly Palermo and Messina, became centres of protest and unrest. The Spanish suppressed every attempt at revolt, but international politics were about to play a part in dislodging the Spanish from Sicily. In 1713, following the death of Charles II of Spain, the island passed into the hands of the House of Savoy (a noble Italian family that ruled an area of southeast France) as a result of the Treaty of Utrecht, but was traded to the Austrians in exchange for Sardinia in 1720. The Spanish reclaimed the island in 1734, this time under the Bourbon king Charles I of Sicily (1734–59), whose meagre attempts at reform through his viceroy (in keeping with tradition, Charles only ever visited the island once) were cut short when he gave up the Sicilian throne to become King Charles III of Spain. Under the reign of his successor Ferdinand IV – who ruled Sicily indirectly as Ferdinand IV of Naples until 1806 and directly as Ferdinand I of the Two Sicilies from 1816 to 1825 – the landed gentry vetoed any attempts at liberalisation and turned the screws even tighter on the peasantry. The spread of the revolutionary spirit after the demise of France's *ancien régime* in 1789 stopped well short of Sicily's shores, as the island's aristocracy and parasitic bourgeoisie sought to maintain their privileged position through increased repression.

The Napoleonic Wars & the End of Feudalism

Although Napoleon never occupied Sicily, his capture of Naples in 1799 forced Ferdinand to move to Sicily under the protection of the British, troops of whom had been sent in to thwart inclusion by Napoleon. Ferdinand returned to Naples in 1802 but was forced out again in 1806, when Napoleon awarded the crown to his brother Joseph. Spanish domination of Sicily was becoming increasingly untenable and Ferdinand's ridiculous tax demands were met with open revolt by the peasantry and the

more far-sighted nobles, who believed that the only way to maintain the status quo was to usher in limited reforms. After strong pressure from Lord William Bentinck, commander of the British forces, Ferdinand reluctantly agreed in 1812 to the drawing up of a constitution modelled on the British one. A two-chamber parliament was formed, feudal privileges were abolished, the king was forbidden to enlist foreign troops without the permission of parliament and a court was set up in Palermo that was to be independent of the one in Naples.

Revolution & Unification

With the final defeat of Napoleon in 1815 Ferdinand returned to Naples and annulled the constitution. He united the two states into the Kingdom of the Two Sicilies and took the title Ferdinand I, but the writing was on the wall. The first real uprising against Bourbon rule occurred in Palermo between 1820 and 1821. It was suppressed but followed by another in Syracuse in 1837, when citizens rose up during a cholera epidemic they believed had been spread by Bourbon officials. On 12 January 1848 conspirators in Palermo launched a new uprising which spread around the entire island. On 13 April they declared a provisional government but it soon collapsed under international pressure when Ferdinand of Savoy refused the crown that was offered to him. For the next 12 years the island was divided between a minority who sought an independent Sicily and the reactivation of the old Norman line of kings (one of Roger's descendants was involved in the provisional government, where he took the name Roger VII), and a majority who believed that the island's survival could only be assured as part of a unified Italy.

On 4 April 1860 the revolutionary committees of Palermo gave orders for a widespread revolt against the tottering Bourbon state. News of the uprising reached Giuseppe Garibaldi, who decided that this was the perfect moment to begin his war for the unification of Italy. He landed in Marsala on 11 May 1860 with about 1000 soldiers – the famous *mille* – and set about conquering

Sicily. His brilliant command of tactics coupled with a friendly peasantry assured his success: he defeated a Bourbon army of 15,000 at Calatafimi, 45km southwest of Palermo, on 15 May and took Palermo two weeks later. His victory at Milazzo on 20 July more or less completed his Sicilian campaign. Incredibly, the island was free of the Spanish for the first time since 1282.

If the Sicilian peasantry held high hopes of finally getting their hands on the land that had been denied them for so long they were sorely disappointed. Despite the revolutionary fervour, Garibaldi was not a revolutionary in the social sense, and his soldiers blocked every attempt at a land grab on the part of the ordinary worker. On 21 October a referendum was held which – amazingly – saw Sicily opt for unification with Savoy by a staggering 99%. According to many Sicilians (most of whom didn't have the right to vote), the island had a new foreign occupier.

From Unification to Fascism

Sicily struggled to adapt under the Piedmontese House of Savoy. Despite unification, Sicily still laboured under a system that was imposed on it by outsiders. Under the new constitution only one percent of the population had the right to vote, as voting rights were linked with property holdings, of which the majority of Sicilian people had none. The old aristocracy by and large maintained all of their privileges and land rights. All hopes of social reform were soon dashed as the new government was either too poor or too ignorant of the situation to affect any real change. Its efforts to centralise power, accompanied by burdensome taxes and military conscription – never before introduced to Sicily – intensified resentment. In 1866 a popular uprising in Palermo was brutally crushed by the Turin authorities who were wrongly convinced that what Sicily needed was a firm dose of law and order to bring it into line.

What the island needed, however, was a far-reaching policy of agrarian reform, including a redistribution of land. The large estates had been partially broken up after the abolition of feudalism but the only beneficiaries were the bailiffs – the traditional gabellotti – who leased land from the owners and then exacted prohibitive ground rents from the peasants who lived and worked on it. To assist them with their rent collections the bailiffs enlisted the help of local gangs, who then took on the role of intermediaries between the tenant and the owner, sorting out disputes and regulating affairs in the absence of an effective judicial system. These individuals were called *mafiosi* and were organised into small territorial gangs drawn up along family lines. They were able to fill the vacuum that existed between the people and the state; the new government was largely ignorant of Sicilian affairs and did not have the means at its disposal to reorganise Sicilian society from a grassroots level. Although evidence of the Mafia's early rise to power is sketchy, it is believed that by 1890 the Sicilian countryside had two distinct authorities: the legitimate forces of law and order, whose presence was largely inconspicuous and ineffectual – as well as grievously resented by most of the peasantry – and a rural Mafia, who comfortably slotted into the role of local power brokers in a land that was well used to taking the law into its own hands.

In 1894 the government (which had moved from Turin to Rome in 1870) responded to the growing threat of an agrarian trade union movement – a loose collection of representative groups known as *fasci* – with the imposition of martial law. What was particularly galling to the Sicilians was that the prime minister who made the decision was Francesco Crispi, himself a Sicilian and a one-time leader of the island's independence movement. Crispi sent 15,000 troops to Palermo to suppress any attempt at revolt on the part of the fasci. His repressive tactics were followed by an offer of mild reform, but this was eventually discarded by the ruling gentry, who felt that the government was meddling in their affairs.

By the turn of the 20th century the gap between the south and the north of Italy was wider than ever. Emigration was draining

Sicily and the rest of the south of millions of its inhabitants, and despite localised efforts at land reform the situation was going from bad to worse. In 1908 the Messina earthquake left the city in ruins, over 80,000 people dead and tens of thousands of others homeless. By the time Italy entered WWI in 1915 the island was on its figurative knees.

Sicily under Mussolini

In 1925 Benito Mussolini addressed the problem of Sicily by despatching his prefect Cesare Mori to Palermo with orders to crush lawlessness and insurrection on the island once and for all. Nobody was yet willing to admit openly that the Mafia held any kind of power in Sicily, but his intent was clear: upon his arrival, he ordered the round-up of thousands of individuals suspected of involvement in 'illegal organisations'. Free from the constraints of democratic law, Mori's roughhouse tactics were brutally effective, forcing the once ever-present Mafia to run for cover. To help him in his efforts, Mori drew on the support of the landed gentry, who were rewarded for their help with the reversal of all agrarian reforms achieved in the previous 50 years. Incredibly, Sicily in the late 1920s was still feudal in all but name.

Mussolini, the Italian Fascist dictator, was forced to resign after the Allies invaded Sicily in 1943.

In the 1930s, however, things began to change. Mussolini's drive to gain a foothold in Africa resulted in a massive increase in the demand for grain, and Sicily was declared by the propaganda machine as instrumental to Italy's quest for empire. As the whole island was prodded and encouraged to do its bit for Fascist glory, promises were made (but never kept) of widespread reform that would return land to its rightful owners. WWII put an end to all that. Sicily fell under German occupation and suffered greatly – many people were killed by heavy bombing during the Allied invasion and the subsequent German retreat back to the mainland. With the Mafia's help the US (under General Patton) was able to take Sicily in 1943; the liberation coincided with the freeing of the Mafia from the constraints of Fascist authority. The Mafia played a key role in the Allied landings, guiding the troops through the mountains and generally ensuring that their passage through the island was relatively untroubled. The fact that Sicily was taken from the Germans in only 39 days was testament to the Mafia's influence in the countryside. After the war, the prisons were emptied of all those unfairly convicted under Fascism, and Mafia activity picked up (and gradually became more powerful over the next 45 years) where it had left off.

Post-War Sicily

Following the war Sicily was in a state of upheaval. There was widespread support for the separatist movement, which called for a totally independent Sicily. The Communist Party was also extremely active on the island, organising discontented labourers and peasants into protest groups that called for radical reforms and a total redistribution of land. In response to demands for change, the government decided to grant partial autonomy to Sicily in 1946, but while the new status was met with general approval at a bureaucratic level, it did little to resolve the island's age-old problems. The Mafia, freed from the oppressive attentions of the Fascist regime, were enlisted by the ruling classes to help suppress the spread of left-wing ideologies in the countryside. On 1 May 1947, a May Day celebration at Portella della Ginestra, near Palermo, was fired upon by a gang of bandits led by Salvatore Giuliano, recently defected from the separatist movement – 11 people were killed and 65 wounded in what became a powerful symbol of the Sicilian tragedy.

The most powerful force in Sicilian politics in the latter half of the 20th century was the Democrazia Cristiana (DC; Christian Democrats), a centre-right Catholic party that appealed to the island's traditional conservatism. Allied closely with the Church, the DC promised wide-ranging reforms while at the same time demanding vigilance against Europe's latest threat, godless communism. They were greatly aided in their efforts by the Mafia, whose grassroots control of the countryside had been firmly re-established. They were thus in a position to ensure that the local DC mayor or councillor would always top the poll. In return, the system of *clientilismo*, or political patronage, that became a key feature of Sicily's political activities, guaranteed that Mafia business interests would be taken care of through the granting of favourable contracts in the massive reconstruction projects undertaken after 1950. Inevitably, much of the funding poured into the new Cassa del Mezzogiorno (Southern Italy Development Fund; Mezzogiorno is a name for the south of Italy) found its way into Mafia pockets, never to be seen again.

Sicily today is better off than at any other time in history, but the island still has enormous economic, social and political problems. The Mafia, despite an all-out campaign by the government in the 1980s and 1990s, is still a powerful presence and the system of political patronage lives on, irrespective of the demise of the DC (see Government & Politics later in this chapter). Feudal society may be a thing of the past, but the scars it left are still visible: the countryside is dominated by large estates, and small towns depopulated through emigration struggle to make ends meet in the face of a demanding economy and the constant presence of the Mafia.

GEOGRAPHY

Extending over 25,708 sq km, triangular-shaped Sicily is the largest island in the Mediterranean. It occupies a central and strategic location, about halfway between Gibraltar and the Suez Canal. Sicily's position just off the western tip of the Calabrian peninsula (Italy's 'toe') has likened it to a football being 'kicked' by the large Italian boot. Physically, the largely mountainous island (83% of the total surface can be described as either hilly or mountainous) straddles two continental shelves: the northern and eastern half of the island is considered to be an extension of the Calabrian Apennines while the southern and western half is topographically similar to the Atlas mountains of North Africa. Scholars have cast some doubt over the popular theory that the island was once part of the Italian mainland and that a rise in the level of the sea caused its separation. Despite being only 3km from the Calabrian tip at its closest point, an alternative theory has suggested that the island was formed immediately following the split between the European and African land masses between 80 and 90 million years ago; as evidence they point to the fact that Sicily is inching its way *closer* to the mainland, not farther away.

The topography of the island is a combination of mountain, plateau and fertile coastal plain. In the northeast, the mountains are made up of three distinct ranges: the Nebrodi and Madonie ranges, which skirt along virtually the entire length of the Tyrrhenian coast up to Palermo; and the Peloritani, which rise above the length of the eastern coast. The interior is mostly hills and plateaux that extend and slope downwards to the southern coast. Sicily's population is concentrated mainly on the fertile coastal plains, largely due to the island's historical importance as a centre of maritime trade. The coasts are an alternating panorama of rugged cliffs and low sandy shores that make up some of the island's most beautiful scenery.

Of the several island groups that are also contained within Sicilian territory the largest is the Aeolian archipelago, off the northeastern coast. Off the western coast are the three Egadi Islands of Favignana, Lèvanzo and Marèttimo, while 60km north of the coast of Palermo is the island of Ustica. The islands off the southern coast – Pantelleria and the Pelagic archipelago – are even further away, closer to Tunisia than they are to Sicily.

GEOLOGY

Sicily is renowned for its volcanic activity and the eastern half of the island is dominated by the imposing cone of Mt Etna (3323m), Europe's largest active volcano. There have been over 135 recorded eruptions. There were spectacular eruptions (the biggest in 40 years) in July 2001, which dazzled spectators and destroyed much of the infrastructure on Etna's southern side. Although the annals of Sicilian history are littered with tales of the volcano's destructive capabilities, the last devastating eruption occurred in 1669, when Catania was engulfed in lava. Sicily's two other active volcanoes are in the Aeolian archipelago. Although both Stromboli (924m) and Vulcano (500m) appear to be smaller than Mt Etna, they are actually roughly the same size: both are rooted at a depth of about 2000m below sea level, with only their cones breaking the surface of the sea.

Sicily's precarious position over two continental plates has resulted in the island being a major centre for seismic activity. Although most of the Italian peninsula is at risk, earthquakes largely strike the southern half of the country, including Sicily. The most recent quake occurred in 1968, when the western Belice valley was flattened by a powerful tremor. Before that, a cataclysmic quake followed by giant tidal waves levelled Messina and half of Calabria in 1908.

CLIMATE

Sicily is deemed to have a mild Mediterranean climate, which in layman's terms can be defined as hot, dry summers followed by mild winters with light rainfall. Even the intermediate seasons – spring and autumn – are usually characterised as an extension of the summer, so short is the Sicilian winter. This,

however, is far from the whole picture, as the island has a surprising variation of climatic conditions. The finest weather is usually found around the coast, where summer temperatures hover around the mid-30s and in even the coldest winter the thermometer never falls below 7°C, maintaining an average of between 10° and 13°C. The southern and western coasts, however, due to their proximity to Africa, are hotter than anywhere else on Sicily, and for six months of the year are affected by the sirocco wind that carries Saharan sand onto the island. In the most uncomfortable months, July and August, the wind is reputed to make visitors and locals alike tired and cranky. The Tyrrhenian coast is usually shielded by the mountainous interior from the worst effects of the sirocco, while the eastern coast is considered to have the best weather of all, with manageably hot summers and relatively dry winters.

In summer, the cities can be a nightmare, especially Palermo and Catania where the oppressive heat combines with smog to make conditions uncomfortable at best and downright insufferable at worst. Although the 'true' temperature taken at the weather station may be in the mid-30s, the traffic and tall buildings in the cities trap the heat and push the mercury up a few degrees; it

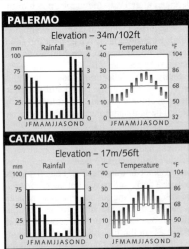

is not unusual to get a reading of 40°C or more in July and August. Like almost anywhere else, the best place to be in high season is on the quieter stretches of coastline, where a sea breeze usually takes the edge off the worst of the heat.

Sicily's interior presents a different story. Summer days are extremely dry and hot, with little or no respite until sundown, when an evening breeze cools the land – at altitude it can even get quite nippy. During the short winters (December to February, with the coldest month being January), the weather can be bitterly cold, especially after dark. There are two winter resorts on the island, in the Madonie mountains and on Mt Etna, both of which can see substantial snowfall in January.

ECOLOGY & ENVIRONMENT

Sicily is a dramatically beautiful country, with some of the most splendid scenery to be found anywhere in Europe. Yet humans seem to have done their level best to spoil the natural legacy of the island, both on land and off it. Throughout most of the 20th century industrialisation and urbanisation resulted in pollution problems that have yet to be dealt with adequately. In Palermo and Catania car emissions poison the atmosphere with carbon monoxide and lead that on a summer's day is clearly visible as a yellow pall of smog floating in the skies above. The seas surrounding the island, and therefore many of the beaches, have been fouled to some extent, particularly in the industrialised areas around Gela, Porto Empèdocle, Augusta and Tràpani, where it is inadvisable to go swimming. Aesthetically, these areas represent shameful scars on the island's otherwise pristine coastlines, industrial eyesores that stand in stark relief to the countryside around them.

Sicilians as a whole do not help matters greatly. Although deeply proud of their island, they have an extraordinarily lax attitude towards discarding rubbish where and when they please, something that will undoubtedly alarm most litter-conscious visitors.

Since the end of WWII, another major problem on the island has been that of illegal construction, known here as *case abusive*

(literally 'abusive houses'). It is widely believed that the Mafia are involved in most construction projects, which are used to launder ill-gotten money from the drugs trade. Many of the more modern houses built throughout the island, including most of the ugly suburbs that plague Sicily's cities, were constructed illegally. Once the authorities got around to checking whether the builders had permits or not, they were presented with a *fait accompli* and thus could do nothing about the situation. Perhaps the most appalling example of this is in the famed Conca d'Oro valley around Palermo, which at one time was thought of as a type of Eden, overflowing with citrus trees and olive groves. Today many of the trees have disappeared and the valley is ruined by overdevelopment.

Throughout the rural interior you will undoubtedly see plenty of houses that look half-built, with exposed brick and large metal girders jutting out through the top of the roof. Plaster facades are intentionally left off to avoid incurring taxes on 'finished' houses, while the ugly girders exist in the eventuality that the owner's children might need an extension when they decide to marry: a second floor is added to the house and the newlyweds simply move upstairs. Although these practices spoil the environment, it must be remembered that they are often born of necessity. Sicilians are by and large not a wealthy people so they make do with what they have, especially in the poorer rural communities.

The government's record on ecology is frankly a poor one. The Ministry for the Environment was only created in 1986, and many environmental laws are either badly enforced or ignored altogether. Recycling is almost completely unheard of in Sicily, although in the larger cities you will find the occasional bottle bank – far too few to make any considerable difference, however. The one bright spot is in the recent creation of national parks and nature reserves. See that section under Flora & Fauna for details.

FLORA & FAUNA

The long presence of humans in Sicily has had a significant impact on the island's environment, most notably in the widespread deforestation of the territory that began during Roman times. Enormous tracts of forest – important humid micro-climates that provided water for the land – were stripped to make way for the large-scale cultivation of grain, particularly in the interior, where virtually all of the land was divided up into massive estates to produce wheat for Rome. Along the western coast you will see plenty of vineyards. These were introduced by the Greeks, along with the olive tree, which grows throughout the island. You will also see plenty of citrus groves and – in the west – palm dates, both of which were brought here by the Arabs. Along the length of the southern coast the terrain is characterised by the presence of a North African brush, or *maquis*, interspersed with the occasional vineyard or olive grove. Throughout the island there are eucalyptus trees, introduced to Sicily by the Florio family in the 19th century in order to combat malarial marshlands. The slopes of Mt Etna are extremely fertile on its lower regions, with large tracts of land given over to the cultivation of olives, grapes, citrus and other fruits. The tree spurge *(Euphorbia dendroides)* is a common wild plant on the lower slopes. From 500m up, you can find nut plantations of pistachio, walnut, almond and chestnut, along with numerous pine, birch and oak trees.

Sicily's dense population, coupled with deforestation, has had an adverse effect on the island's fauna. Outside the nature reserves it is most unlikely that you will see any creatures other than sheep on your travels, while the coastlines are home to a regular selection of birds, mostly seagulls and cormorants. Sicily's only poisonous snake, the viper, can be found slithering around the undergrowth throughout the south of the island – watch out for it at archaeological sites. Even the great schools of tuna, which for centuries were to be found off the western coasts, are fast disappearing into the nets of large Japanese trawlers far offshore.

National Parks & Nature Reserves

Despite their poor track record on the environment, Sicilian authorities have gone to great lengths to protect large tracts of land from the bulldozer through the designation of specially protected nature reserves. The two coastal reserves of Zingaro, northwest of Palermo (see the Western Sicily chapter) and Vendicari on the southern coast (see the Syracuse & the Southeast chapter) are areas of extraordinary beauty that are well run and easily accessible on foot. Here you will find a plethora of bird life, including, in Zingaro, the rare Bonelli eagle, the Imperial crow and a species of wild dove; and in Vendicari, black-winged stilts, slenderbilled gulls and Audoin's gulls.

The Parco Naturale Regionale delle Madonie was set up in 1989 to protect a vast area of mountainous woodland east of the capital (see The Tyrrhenian Coast chapter). It is the only reserve on the island where people actually live, in small towns dotted throughout the hills. Farther west is the Parco Regionale dei Nebrodi (see The Tyrrhenian Coast chapter), where the San Fratello breed of horses, unique to Sicily, can be found roaming free along with all kinds of farmyard animals including sheep, pigs and cattle.

The island's only national park is the Parco Naturale dell'Etna (see The Eastern Coast chapter), which was set up to protect

JANE SMITH

The rare Bonelli eagle is to be found safe and sound in Sicily's nature reserves.

the volcano from the spread of development threatening its slopes up to the late 1980s. Although there is still a sizable amount of unwelcome construction on the mountain, the area appears to be in good hands.

The saltpans of Tràpani and Marsala are partially protected by the Regione Sicilia, while the long beach at Capo Bianco, near Eraclea Minoa, was purchased by the World-wide Fund for Nature (WWF) in 1991.

Visit W www.parks.it for further information on Sicily's parks (in Italian and English).

GOVERNMENT & POLITICS

In 1946, Sicily was declared an autonomous region within the Italian state, one of five to be granted partial or complete autonomy under the post-war constitution (the others are Sardinia, the mostly German-speaking Trentino-Alto Adige, Friuli-Venezia Giulia and Valle d'Aosta). The local parliament is known as the Assemblea Regionale Siciliana and is made up of 89 deputies and led by a regional president (in 2002 this is Salvatore Cuffaro). The president selects the cabinet *(giunta)* from the deputies, who in turn are responsible for the various departments of state, such as health, the environment and finance.

Sicily is split into nine provinces that take the name of their capital town or city. Each region is known by its two-letter code: Palermo (PA; includes Ustica), Messina (ME; includes the Aeolian Islands), Catania (CT), Enna (EN), Syracuse (SR), Ragusa (RG), Caltanissetta (CL), Agrigento (AG; includes the Pelagic Islands) and Tràpani (TP; includes the Egadi Islands and Pantelleria).

At the time of writing the leading force in Italian politics was media magnate and Italian president Silvio Berlusconi's Forza Italia (meaning 'Go Italy'), a centre-right party that more or less picked up where the DC (Democrazia Cristiana) left off after they were dismantled following the Tangentopoli scandal of the early 1990s (see Political Skulduggery later in this section). Apart from Forza Italia, the biggest parties are the neo-Fascist Alleanza Nazionale (a more public-friendly version of the old Movimento Sociale Italiano, the direct successors to Italian Fascism) and the Partito Popolare Italiano, a populist, centrist collection of disaffected socialists and the DC. It is difficult to tell the difference between the other parties represented; even their names tend to consist of the same key words but in different combinations (for example: Cristiani Democratici, Cristiani Democratici Uniti and Democratici di Sinistra). The Left has never held much sway in traditional Sicily, hence parties such as the Rifondazione Communista (Refounded Communists; formerly the old guard of the Italian Communist Party), Gruppo Communista (Communist Group) and even the Partito Socialista Sicilia (the Sicilian branch of the Italian Socialist Party) figure towards the bottom of the representative scale.

Political Skulduggery

Since WWII and autonomy the political system of Sicily has been mired in corruption, graft and cronyism. Dozens of books have been written on the multilayered webs of scandal and intrigue that have plagued the island over the last 50 years, and it would take more than a couple of paragraphs to begin to sift through the quagmire that is Sicilian politics. Simply put, the two main players in the island's affairs over the last 50 years have been the Mafia and the driving force behind Italy's political oligarchy, the DC, which dominated every Italian government from 1948 to 1994.

More so in Sicily than in the rest of Italy did the one-party domination of the political system, known in Italian as *partitocrazia*, play such a decisive role. It is widely believed that there existed between the Mafia and the island's most influential party, the DC, a Machiavellian pact whereby the Mafia would play its part in ensuring that the electorate would vote for the 'right' candidate come election time and, in return, they would largely leave the Mafia alone. Most of the island's governments adopted a 'hear-no-evil, see-no-evil' approach to Mafia affairs. On the few occasions that the authorities decided to curb the organisation's activities, their willingness soon faded and the situation carried on as before.

The Day of the Fox

Giulio Andreotti's troubles with the law started in 1993 when Baldassare Di Maggio, driver to Sicily's Mafia godfather Totò Riina, testified to the anti-Mafia commission that he had witnessed Andreotti and Riina exchanging a kiss on the cheek in the familiar style of two men who know – and trust – each other well. This remarkable statement shook the very foundations of Italian politics, for it was the first time that Andreotti, for decades the untouchable embodiment of the Italian political system, was directly implicated in the Mafia's affairs. Without needing an explanation, most Italians and Sicilians recognised the symbolic importance of *il bacio* (the kiss): if Di Maggio's statement was true, then there could be no doubt about it – Andreotti was indeed in league with the Mafia.

Andreotti was arrested and charged with Mafia association, and in 1994 went on trial in Palermo. Throughout the five-year trial Andreotti displayed an extraordinary forgetfulness about meetings and events at which he was shown to be involved, yet the wily old man – whose nickname was *la volpe* (the fox) because of his ability to manoeuvre himself and his party through the most difficult situations relatively unscathed – never once crumbled under the barrage of interrogation. His most damning admission was that of course he had had dealings with the Mafia – it was impossible to maintain a career in Italian politics without doing so – but that he had never knowingly helped the Mafia in any way nor did he serve as their political godfather in Rome.

Over the course of the trial Andreotti's lawyers did much to destroy Di Maggio as a credible witness, which raised key questions about the policy of pursuing the Mafia through the confessions of its former members, the so-called *pentiti* (literally the 'repented'); after all, argued Andreotti's counsel, why would the court take the word of a convicted murderer and gangster over that of a respected international politician? In a sense, the prosecution didn't just have Andreotti in the dock but the course of Italian history over the previous 50 years, and considering that the country was only beginning to recover from the widespread revelations of the Tangentopoli scandal, most commentators felt that the country could not stomach the possibility of the charges being proven. On 23 October 1999 the court returned a verdict of 'not guilty' and Andreotti walked out a free man.

Things, however, are beginning to change. The Tangentopoli (Bribesville) scandal (the institutionalisation of kickbacks and bribes which had been the country's *modus operandi* since WWII) that broke in Milan in early 1992 eventually implicated thousands of politicians, public officials and business-people, many of whom were charged with a host of criminal activities ranging from bribery, making illicit political payments and receiving kickbacks to blatant theft. Although largely focused on the industrial north of Italy, the repercussions of the widespread investigation into graft (known as Mani Pulite, or Clean Hands) were inevitably felt in Sicily, where politics, business and the Mafia were long-time bedfellows. The DC never really lost the 'taint' of all the corruption.

Palermo's outspoken former mayor *(sindaco)*, Leoluca Orlando, has been the most vocal political opponent of the Mafia's activities for many decades. Though he is no longer mayor and failed in his bid to be elected as the president of the Sicilian region, he remains a popular figure, having sponsored a wide-ranging programme of reform and restoration in the capital.

The demise of the DC has thrown the cosy arrangement between political parties and the Mafia – known as Il Terzo Livello, the Third Level – into disarray, as witnessed by the Mafia's wild attempts to assert their illicit authority over the island's affairs in 1992 by murdering the former DC mayor of Palermo, Salvatore Lima (who despite serving as a Euro MP was later revealed to have been a sworn-in member of the Mafia), and anti-Mafia magistrates Giovanni Falcone and Paolo Borsellino. For more details see The Mafia later in this chapter.

Italy's most important post-war politician was DC leader Giulio Andreotti, whose brilliant political mind and extraordinary capacity to survive even the most damning scandal will assure him a place alongside Machiavelli in the pantheon of Italian political strategists and thinkers. In 1993 he was charged with Mafia association and in 1995 put on trial in Palermo. In October 1999 he was sensationally acquitted, bringing an end to a trial that had electrified the entire country for five years (for more details see the boxed text 'The Day of the Fox').

ECONOMY

There are two commonly held opinions on the state of the Sicilian economy. While both concur that it is nothing short of a shambolic mess, one view – widely held in the more prosperous north of Italy – is that Sicily is an endless black hole of corruption, laziness and mismanagement that has swallowed without trace the trillions of lire (and now euros) that have been poured into the island via a plethora of development funds. The second view, more common in the poorer south, is that ordinary Sicilians have always been the victims of outsiders' narrow-minded greed, and while the industrialised north may have poured money into reviving the south's economy, there are no 'quick-fix' solutions to a problem that has been 2500 years in the making.

The truth of the matter lies somewhere in between. Of all the southern Italian regions, Sicily is the most troubled economically, mostly because it is so populous. Unemployment stands at an alarming 27%, which is more than double the Italian national average and triple that of the industrialised north. The average wage is just over half of the national average, and less than 40% of the wage earned north of Florence. Poverty is endemic, making Sicily the poorest of all Italian regions and one of Europe's most glaring economic black spots. With Sicily lagging so far behind economically, it comes as a surprise that the island is second only to the United States as a producer of sulphur; that one quarter of Italy's fishing vessels operate out of the island (most of them out of Mazara del Vallo, home to Italy's largest fishing fleet); and that the petrochemical industry is one of Sicily's biggest enterprises, operating huge plants along the southeastern and eastern coasts, at Catania, Syracuse, Ragusa and Gela.

Despite the growing importance of the tourist and services industries, Sicily remains a largely agricultural region, with wheat the most important crop. Cereal grains are grown on the larger estates in the interior and along the southern coast, while smaller holdings are devoted principally to the cultivation of olives, almonds, grapes, citrus fruits, beans and sumac, which is used as a dye in the tanning industry.

Smaller industries are given over to a variety of other enterprises, including canning and the production of wine and olive oil. In the larger urban centres you will find a thriving cottage industry engaged in the creation of glassware, metalware, ceramics and even matches (thanks to the presence of sulphur).

Such limited industrial activity, coupled with the age-old reliance on agriculture as a source of income, has spelled certain disaster for Sicily. Despite continuous efforts to modernise the island's economy, Sicily remains tied to the economic model created by the Romans over 2000 years ago. For almost its entire history of occupation the island has been methodically stripped of all its wealth, and whatever profits were generated in Sicily were almost always spirited abroad, with little or no money being reinvested back into the economy.

After WWII the government in Rome began to make serious efforts to address the enormous economic gap between the prosperous north and the poor south. In 1950 the Cassa del Mezzogiorno was set up with a view towards rebuilding the south's pitiful economy. Sicily was one of the main beneficiaries of the fund, which poured gigantic amounts of state money into all kinds of projects – from road building to the development of the petrochemical industry – aimed at kick-starting an economic recovery. Enormous amounts of money also came from the European Economic Community's (EEC; now the European Union) regional development fund, which helped finance a road-building project that saw the construction of

Sicily's limited network of motorways. In response to the growing northern frustration with the disappearance of so much of the cash into the pockets and bank accounts of the Mafia, the government decided to scrap the Cassa del Mezzogiorno in 1992 and leave most subsidies in the hands of the EU.

At the beginning of the 21st century Sicily remains in deep economic trouble. The petrochemical industry suffered an enormous collapse in the 1970s due to the oil wars that resulted from the Organisation of Petroleum Exporting Countries' (OPEC) landmark decision to raise oil prices in 1973. The citrus industry has imploded in the face of increased competition from Spain, Israel, South Africa and even the United States, who have flooded the Italian markets with cheaper produce. The once-powerful fishing fleets that provided much of Europe's tinned tuna have been challenged by the more efficient and mass-producing Japanese, whose nets now catch the majority of the Mediterranean's schools of tuna fish, leaving the local fleets with almost nothing. To add insult to injury, the tuna is taken to Japan where it is canned and then sold back to Sicily.

Although all of these factors play a key role in determining the state of Sicily's economy, the picture is far from complete without a mention of the island's single most powerful economic, political and social force: the Mafia (see The Mafia later in this chapter).

POPULATION & PEOPLE

According to 1998 estimates the population of Sicily is 5.19 million, 9% of the national population. The birth rate was put at 12.35 per thousand the same year, a little more than the European Union (EU) average of about 12 per thousand – surprising given the Sicilians' preoccupation with children and family.

Most of the island's population lives on or near the coast. Palermo is by far the largest city, with 750,000 inhabitants (over a million if one includes the surrounding hinterland), followed by Catania (376,000), Messina (270,000), Syracuse (125,900), Marsala (80,800) and Tràpani (72,500). The largest city in the interior is Caltanissetta, with a population of 61,300. The rest of the interior is relatively unpopulated.

Since the end of the 19th century Sicily has suffered an enormous drain of human resources through emigration. Between 1880 and 1910 over 1.5 million Sicilians left for the United States, and in 1900 the island was the world's main area of emigration. In the 20th century, Sicilians in their tens of thousands moved northwards to work in the factories of Piedmont, Lombardy and farther afield in Switzerland and Germany. Even today emigration continues to be a problem, with over 10,000 people leaving the island for pastures greener each year.

Despite an economy in often dire straits, Sicily is a popular port of call for thousands of *extracommunitari* (immigrants from outside the EU) that have flooded into Italy. Mazara del Vallo is home to a substantial Tunisian population (around 9000), most of whom work in the fishing industry. Palermo has a large number of African, Pakistani and Bangladeshi immigrants. It's not unknown for large boats to drop many illegal immigrants off at various locations, once the seas are calm (spring is a busy time).

EDUCATION

Sicily's educational system is the same as the rest of Italy's, consisting of a state-school system divided into several levels. Attendance is compulsory from the ages of six to 14 years, although children can attend a *scuola materna* (nursery school) from the ages of three to five years before starting the *scuola elementare* (primary school) at six. After five years they move on to the *scuola media* (secondary school) until they reach the age of 14.

The next level, the *scuola secondaria superiore* (higher secondary school), is voluntary and lasts a further five years until the student is 19 years old. It is, however, essential if young people want to go on to university. At higher-secondary level there are several options: four types of technical school, four types of liceo (humanities-based school), and teacher-training school.

[continued on page 39]

Sicily's spectacular coastline takes in everything from the historic harbour of Cefalù to windmills at Mòzia and Favignana's rocky beaches and crystal-clear water.

Top: Taormina's stunningly located 3rd-century-BC Greek theatre was turned into a gladiators' arena by the Romans.

Bottom: Room with a view: the well-preserved Doric temple at Segesta has never possessed a roof.

SICILIAN ARCHITECTURE & ART

BETHUNE CARMICHAEL

It is no exaggeration to claim that Sicily is a living museum of nearly 10,000 years of Mediterranean architecture and art. Its location as the meeting place of Mediterranean Europe, North Africa and the East brought waves of occupiers, traders and craftsmen to its shores, who in turn left some of the most spectacular buildings and works of art – from cave paintings to Doric temples to the glory of the Sicilian Baroque – to be found anywhere in Europe. While the particular styles of the colonisers are ever-present, it is also possible to detect the influences of local craftsmen, architects and painters who hung on to their own techniques while absorbing foreign styles, creating an artistic hybrid that is unique to the island. The problem is that while Sicily is indeed a rich museum, it is a very badly maintained one. A series of devastating earthquakes, volcanic eruptions and a spate of bombing in WWII has left many of Sicily's more noteworthy buildings and artworks in an alarming state of disrepair. Although in recent years the relevant authorities have initiated a number of restoration projects, there is still much work to be done, such as finding effective means to curb the pilfering of works of art – a favourite Mafia cash cow – which are smuggled abroad or disappear into dubious private (and sometimes public) collections.

Architecture

Hellenistic Sicily Although Sicily has plenty of examples of early Hellenistic architecture – including the rock-cut chamber tombs at Sant'Angelo Muxaro and a plethora of pottery on view in most of the island's archaeological museums – it was the founding of Syracuse in 735 BC that marked the beginning of the Hellenistic world's extraordinary contribution to Sicily's artistic patrimony. Undoubtedly, the apogee of their creative talents is the Doric temple, splendid examples of which can be seen at Selinunte, Segesta, Syracuse and at Agrigento's Valley of the Temples, one of the most breathtaking repositories of Greek architecture in the world.

Traditionally, the Doric temple was built to a rectangular plan with a divided interior, often with an end space which was occupied by the main altar. Most were colonnaded, although variations can be seen at Agrigento, such as the now ruined Temple of Jupiter (Tempio di Giove), where you can still make out the half columns and telamons (oversized human figures) which once topped them and supported the roof. The unusual temple at Segesta is a peristyle (a court surrounded by a columned portico), at the centre of which is an altar (although experts disagree on whether it was ever finished). The temple's slightly stunted appearance was an aesthetic choice, made with its location atop a hill in mind.

The best examples of the Sicilian Doric style, however, can be seen at Selinunte, whose temples show a break with the classic Greek model. The imposing Temple C once featured sculpted reliefs on the metopes (spaces along the frieze) and a Gorgon's head on the tympanum (the area above the main doorway), additions that were rare in Greece and not present on any of Sicily's other Doric temples (these can now be viewed in the Museo Archeologico Regionale in Palermo). Furthermore, the architects designed it so that the spacing of the columns at both the sides and the ends is the same, an aesthetic deviation from the standard model where the side columns are usually built closer together.

Greek theatres are another highlight of Hellenistic architecture, even though most of them were either modified or completely rebuilt during the Roman occupation. The best example of an original temple is at Segesta. It is relatively intact and benefits from the most spectacular natural setting on the island, with panoramic views of the valley below and the sea acting as a breathtaking backdrop to the stage. Other outstanding examples are the theatres of Syracuse and Taormina, although both were heavily altered to allow the Romans to stage gladiatorial battles instead of plays.

FIONN DAVENPORT

The Romans The Romans were less interested than the Greeks in enhancing Sicily's artistic wealth and most of their contributions were public buildings, such as the theatre in Catania and the aqueduct at Tèrmini Imerese. One outstanding exception is the Roman villa at Casale, just outside Piazza Armerina. This fantastic complex, made up of four separate groups and totalling 50 rooms, galleries and corridors, once belonged to the co-emperor Maximian, who ruled jointly with Diocletian in the 3rd century AD. The villa's ruins are mightily impressive but the real draw are the extensive polychrome floor mosaics. These finely executed mosaics testify to the wonderful skill of the craftsmen (almost certainly brought over from North Africa) in creating a variety of realistic and natural episodes in minute detail, from an exhaustive portrayal of a great hunt to scenes from Greek mythology to ten female figures clad in what must be the world's first bikinis.

Above: High upon a mountain, the 3rd-century-BC Greek theatre at Segesta has spectacular views out to sea.

Byzantine & Saracen Sicily

The Byzantines limited themselves to converting some of Sicily's Doric temples to Christian basilicas. The best example of this crossover can be seen in Syracuse's cathedral, which clearly shows both styles. Ironically, it would be another 300 years before the Byzantines, invited back to Sicily by the Normans, left their indelible mark on the island's architectural treasures.

Little too remains of Arab rule on the island. Their contribution was mainly to urban planning: they developed the 'branching tree' style of street grid, with main roads having minor offshoots that ended in blind alleys. Similarly, Arab ar-

BETHUNE CARMICHAEL

chitecture did not truly flourish until Norman times, when the Arab craftsmen and designers were actively encouraged to express themselves as part of a grander, symbiotic style that was particular to Sicily. This Arab-Norman collaboration perhaps represents its greatest period of artistic development.

The Normans

The Normans were a clever bunch and by the middle of the 11th century their domination of Sicily was virtually complete. The early stages of their rule were characterised by an intense period of artistic creativity and construction that resulted in the Sicilian Romanesque style, an intoxicating fusion of Byzantine, Arabic and Norman design and building. The wisdom of the Normans in not turning their backs on the substantial skills and aesthetic sense of the defeated Arabs, coupled with the return of many Byzantine craftsmen who had fled the island during the Arab occupation, created an exciting, multicultural atmosphere. This was actively encouraged and patronised by the clergy who, along with the Norman barons, were responsible for commissioning the period's most important buildings – the cathedrals. Indeed, it is in ecclesiastical architecture that we can see the best of what the Normans had to offer.

Although there are myriad fine examples of Norman cultural expression in Sicily, including plenty of fortified strongholds and a plethora of churches, the apotheosis of the Hauteville rule can be seen in the cathedrals at Monreale and Cefalù, along with the Palazzo dei Normanni in Palermo. The first great cathedral was commissioned by Roger II (c.1105–54) at Cefalù in classic Romanesque style (with a chevron pattern and a Latin-cross plan made up of a long, tall nave, a deep choir stall and two flanking chapels) although typically Sicilian touches can be detected, such as the use of pointed arches and angled columns. The decoration of the interior, however, stands out as one of the finest anywhere in Europe. The extensive mosaics – with the dominant figure of the long-faced Christ Pantokrator (All-Powerful) at the centre – were created in classical style by Byzantine craftsmen. Yet despite their beauty they fall somewhat short of the mosaics at Monreale, which represent Sicily's greatest contribution to European art in the Middle Ages. It is the sheer scale of the decoration that at first overwhelms, but the closer one

Above: The glorious mosaics of the Roman villa at Casale

examines them the more one appreciates their unsurpassed beauty and profound spiritual effect. Here, unlike the mosaics at Cefalù, one can detect a break with the rules of Byzantine representative art: the stories of the Bible are executed starting at the church's main entrance and proceed in chronological order from the Creation to the Last Judgement – a tacit indication of the Norman barons' desire to see the Roman west become dominant over the Orthodox east. Their iconography was also influenced by contemporary events, hence the appearance of the recently canonised Thomas à Becket as one of the key saints.

The third building of this magnificent trio is the enormous Palazzo dei Normanni in Palermo, the stronghold of Norman power in Sicily and the seat of the Hauteville dynasty. The palace was originally built by the Arabs in the 9th century but was enlarged by the Normans in 1132–40. The real attraction at the heart of this monolithic structure is the exquisite Cappella Palatina (Palatine Chapel), which features an Egyptian-style cupola and a wooden honeycomb ceiling that is undoubtedly inspired by Arabic screen designs. The chapel itself is devoted to Christian worship though decorated with scenes from a variety of sources, including Greek, Persian and Indian myths as well as visual representations of key moments in the Bible. It was largely designed, constructed and decorated by local workers and is a perfect example of the fusion of styles that sets the Sicilian Romanesque apart from other forms used in mainland Italy.

The key buildings of secular architecture can be found in and around Palermo, and include the graceful palace of La Zisa, summer residence of the Hauteville kings. Again the Arab influence is noteworthy and it is fitting that today the palace serves as the city's museum of Arabic art. It is likely that the palace was also decorated with mosaics but these have largely disappeared.

With the demise of the Hautevilles and arrival of the Hohenstaufen (Swabian) dynasty in the 13th century, the emphasis shifted from the creative arts to erecting mighty castles and fortifications. It would be another 400 years before Sicily witnessed as rich a period of architectural genius and then it was only in response to a devastating earthquake that flattened half the island.

The Renaissance In sculpture and architecture, the dominant school of the 15th and 16th centuries was founded by Domenico Gagini (1420–92), a student of the Quattrocento (1400s) Florentine style who almost single-handedly dragged Sicilian architecture out of the Middle Ages and created a style that fused local designs with those more popular on the Italian mainland. Traditional styles persisted, particularly in the construction of fortified homes, which copied the Arab-Norman model – which was medieval in appearance, with plenty of rustication and squinches (a narrow slit window at a corner) – rather than contemporary forms. The 15th century also saw the arrival of the Catalan-Gothic style, a blend of influences that featured horizontal lines and large, flat bare surfaces and is most obvious in Palermo's cathedral and in the Chiesa di San Giorgio Vecchio in Ragusa Ibla.

Above: The intricately decorated doors of the 12th-century Norman cathedral at Monreale

Sicilian Baroque The most important artistic and architectural development since the early Middle Ages was the explosion of the Baroque style, which became widespread throughout the southeast of the island following the devastating earthquake of 1693. Towns that were almost entirely destroyed were rebuilt in this elegant new style, including Noto, Mòdica, Ragusa, Catania and large parts of Syracuse. The dominant figure at this time was Rosario Gagliardi (1700–70), the engineer and architect considered to be the father of Sicilian Baroque. He was the designer of the splendid Cattedrale di San Giorgio at Ragusa Ibla as well as the Chiesa di San Giorgio in Mòdica. GB Vaccarini (1702–68) introduced the Roman Baroque to Catania and his work shows the distinctive influence of Francesco Borromini. In Syracuse, Andrea Palma (1664–1730) designed the wonderful facade of the city's cathedral, adding yet another cultural layer to the church and its history.

The 19th & 20th Centuries Art Nouveau took off in Palermo thanks to the talent of Ernesto Basile (1857–1932) who designed the Villa Igiea for the Florio family. His father, GB Basile, was responsible for the monumental Corinthian Teatro Massimo in Palermo.

The less said about the ugly Sicilian architecture of the 20th century the better.

Art

Prehistoric Sicily Of all the important prehistoric art discovered in Sicily, the most extraordinary examples are on the island of Lèvanzo, off the western coast. In 1949, in the Grotta del Genovese, locals uncovered a series of cave paintings and incised outlines made up of 32 separate animal figures depicted in a lifelike style, including cattle, deer and horses. The paintings are thought to date to the Neolithic period (c.4000–2400 BC) and the incisions to the Upper Palaeolithic (c.40,000–12,000 BC). On Mt Pellegrino (606m), just north of Palermo, the Grotta dell'Addaura is home to another set of incised drawings dating from the Upper Palaeolithic period. They are remarkable for the presence of human figures as well as the usual representations of animals. There are some fine examples of art from the Neolithic period, including finds of pottery and basic tools made on Lìpari and in the Megara Hyblaea area, north of Syracuse.

Hellenistic Sicily The artistic achievement of the Sicilian Greeks was not limited to architecture alone, for they produced a phenomenal amount of pottery, including the particularly beautiful red-and-black kraters (vases) which came from Gela. The world's most important collection of these vases is exhibited at the archaeological museum in Gela.

The Normans The Norman period saw a fantastic burst of artistic creativity. In the cloister of the cathedral at Monreale is the largest collection of Norman sculpture in Sicily, consisting of over 200 slim columns with twin capitals and each featuring a singular composition, with discernible influences from the Byzantine, Arabic, French and central Italian styles. See The Normans under Architecture for details on the mosaics created during this period.

The Renaissance Although Sicily did not figure too much in the new learning and aesthetic principles that swept first through Italy and then Europe during the Renaissance, Sicilian painting and sculpture was very much in the ascendancy; however, its influences were mostly Spanish and Flemish. The first of the great Sicilian artists was Antonello da Messina (c.1430–79), most famous for his beautiful portraits, who trained in the Flemish style but later allowed his paintings to show influences of the Italian Piero della Francesca (c.1420–92), one of the earliest luminaries of Renaissance art.

An important sculptor was Francesco Laurana (c.1430–1502), who hailed from Italy and was heavily influenced by the early Renaissance. Although Laurana spent only a brief period of his prolific career in Sicily, his influence on Sicilian artists was considerable.

Sicilian Baroque In the 17th century, Sicily benefited artistically from the presence of two non-Sicilian artists. Caravaggio (1571–1610), whose turbulent life led him from Italy to Sicily in the late 1600s, created some important works here. Messina's Museo Regionale has two very fine Caravaggio paintings. The Flemish painter Anthony Van Dyck (1599–1641) was in Sicily in 1624 and you can see his altarpiece of the Virgin with San Domenico in the Oratorio del Rosario, behind the Chiesa di San Domenico in Palermo.

The 19th & 20th Centuries There is an alarming dearth of good modern art in Sicily. The island's greatest modern painter, Renato Guttuso (1912–87), was renowned for painting in a visceral style that reflected his Sicilian 'nature': his paintings burst with colour and portray the island and its personalities in all their harshness and beauty.

Below: Byzantine craftsmen created the beautiful classical mosaics at Monreale's Norman cathedral.

BET-IUNE CARMICHAEL

[continued from page 32]

The government is in the process of re-forming the education system. The standards of education in the state-run system compare well with those in other countries, although the system does have its problems, compounded by relatively low standards in teacher training and poor government management. Officially at least, only 3% of Sicilians over the age of 15 cannot read or write, although the real figure is probably closer to 5%.

University courses usually last from four to six years, although students are under no obligation to complete them in that time. In fact, students often take many more years to fulfil their quota of exams and submit their final thesis. Attendance at inevitably over-crowded lectures is optional and for scientific courses practical experimentation is rare. Students therefore tend to study at home from books. All state-school and university examinations are oral, rather than written. There are universities in Palermo, Catania, Syracuse and Messina.

ARTS
Literature
Until the 19th century, there was a relative dearth of great Sicilian literature. It all began so promisingly in the 13th century, however, with the birth of the Sicilian school of poetry at the court of Frederick II of Hohenstaufen, which predated Dante and Petrarch in the use of Italian rather than the more accepted language of high literature, Latin. It is a little-known fact (but one acknowledged by Dante) that the first official literature in Italian was born in Palermo. Its authors were the jurists, notaries, captains and officials of the court, who sought relief from their roles as state functionaries in the composition of poems essentially about courtly love, using the traditional Provençal lyric and fitting it to a new metric model.

One of the earliest exponents of the new school was Jacopo da Lentini (c.1215–90), known as Il Notaro (The Notary), who wrote the earliest extant sonnets in the Italian language, the school's most important

and original metric innovation. Other notables included Guido delle Colonne (1210–80), a judge, and Rinaldo d'Aquino, whose splendid *Lamento dell'Amante del Crociato* (Lament of the Crusading Lover) is about the only thing we know of him. Unfortunately, the school petered out with the death of Frederick in 1250.

With few exceptions, such as Antonio Veneziano (1543–93), whose style was a worthy imitation of Petrarch's, there were no truly great authors writing in Sicily until the 19th century, when the literary colossus that was Giovanni Verga (1840–1922) emerged onto the scene. His early novels gave little indication of the impact he would later have on Italian literature. It is worth mentioning that his timing was certainly spot on, as he lived and wrote through some of the most intense historical vicissitudes of modern Italy: the unification of Italy, WWI and the rise of Fascism. His greatest novel is *I Malavoglia* (1881), the first novel of the Realist school, the Italian equivalent of the French Naturalists, whose greatest success was Emile Zola. Verga's classic, essentially a story about a family's struggle for survival through desperate times in Sicily, is a permanent fixture on every Sicilian school-child's reading list.

The 20th century has been kind to Sicilian literature. Playwright and novelist Luigi Pirandello (1867–1936) was awarded the Nobel Prize for Literature in 1934 for a substantial body of work that included *Sei Personaggi in Ricerca di un Autore* (Six Characters in Search of an Author) and *Enrico IV* (Henry IV). Poet Salvatore Quasimodo (1901–68) won the award in 1959 for his exquisite lyric verse, which included delightful translations of works by Shakespeare and Pablo Neruda. Elio Vittorini (1908–66) captured the essence of the Sicilian migration north in his masterpiece *Conversazione in Sicilia* (1941), the story of his return to the roots of his personal, historical and cultural identity.

Sicily's most famous novel of the 20th century was a one-off by an aristocrat whose intent was to chronicle the social upheaval caused by the end of the old regime and the unification of Italy. Giuseppe Tomasi di Lampedusa (1896–1957) published *Il Gattopardo* (The Leopard) in 1957 and it was an immediate success with both critics and the public. Though strictly a period novel, it is of great relevance to the modern day, as its insightful observations into every stratum of Sicilian society prove the old French adage: *plus ça change, plus ça reste la même chose* ('the more things change, the more they stay the same').

Leonardo Sciascia (1921–89), born in Racalmuto (see The Southern Coast chapter), used contemporary themes for the body of his work and is recognised as one of the great writers of the latter half of the 20th century (see the boxed text 'A Sicilian Iconoclast'). Another contemporary writer worth

mentioning is Gesualdo Bufalino (1920–96), whose novel *Le Menzogne della Notte* (Night's Lies) won the prestigious Strega Prize in 1988. It tells the story of four condemned men in a Bourbon prison who spend the eve of their execution recounting the most memorable moments of their lives.

Readers of Italian might be interested in the crime fiction of Andrea Camilleri (b.1925), who comes from the Agrigento province. His immensely popular books feature smatterings of dialect, Sicilian characters and gripping plot twists. All bookshops will stock his work.

Music

Vincenzo Bellini (1801–35) reigns supreme in the pantheon of great Sicilian composers

A Sicilian Iconoclast

Acclaimed and criticised throughout his life, Leonardo Sciascia (1921–89) is one of the most important Italian writers of the 20th century. He proudly claimed to have been the first Sicilian writer to directly tackle the contentious subject of the Mafia (in *The Day of the Owl*, 1961), a subject that fascinated and tormented him until the day he died. Although radically opposed to the activities of organised crime, he was sensitive to the paradoxical nature of Cosa Nostra, which he considered to be against Sicily yet an intangible part of its social and cultural fabric.

In his later years, he developed an almost irrational dislike for the activities of Giovanni Falcone's anti-Mafia commission, accusing the magistrate of being vainglorious and nothing more than a headline chaser. A committed left-winger, he dallied with the extremist elements during the 1970s and in 1979 published a famous pamphlet called *Il Caso Aldo Moro* (The Aldo Moro Affair) in which he subtly accused the ruling Democrazia Cristiana (DC; Christian Democrats) of collusion in the kidnapping of the Italian prime minister Aldo Moro by the Red Brigades. Although the popular press derided him at the time, much of what he believed was subsequently proven to be at least partially true, and Sciascia consolidated his position as a hero of the anti-establishment opposition.

Despite his vocal political activities, Sciascia is still best remembered as one of the most extraordinary writers to have emerged from Sicily. His other great novels include *A Ciascuno il Suo* (To Each His Own; 1966), *Il Consiglio d'Egitto* (The Council of Egypt) and *Todo Modo* (One Way or Another), both published in 1974. His simple and direct approach to narrative marked him as one of *the* great stylists of the 20th century, while his often black humour made him one of the most widely read authors of his generation.

JANE SMITH

The power of the pen: Leonardo Sciascia confronted Sicily's most volatile issues.

(see the boxed text 'The Master of Song' in The Eastern Coast chapter), but before him came the versatile Alessandro Scarlatti (c.1669–1725). Along with the Venetian Apostolo Zeno and the Roman Pietro Trapassi (or Matastasio), Scarlatti is credited with creating the kind of lyrical opera that later became known as the 'Neapolitan' style. He wrote more than 100 works, including the oratorios *Il Trionfo dell'Onore* (The Triumph of Honour; 1718) and *La Griselda* (1721).

In contemporary terms, there are virtually no writers of good music in Sicily. Aldo Clementi (b.1925) is a classical composer whose name will be unknown to all but serious students of the avant-garde.

Cinema

Sicily has not produced any directors of note with the exception of Giuseppe Tornatore (b.1956). Tornatore followed up on the incredible success of *Cinema Paradiso* (1990) with *La Leggenda del Pianista sull'Oceano* (The Legend of the Pianist over the Ocean; 1998), a quirky tale of a genius piano player born and raised in the bowels of a huge ocean-going liner. His most recent release was *Malèna* (2000), starring Monica Bellucci in a coming-of-age story set in Sicily in the 1940s.

Puppet Theatre

Sicily's most typical form of traditional entertainment is the puppet theatre, which was first introduced to the island by the Spanish in the 18th century. It provided ordinary people with a chance to attend a 'theatre' of sorts as nearly everything else was closed off to them. The puppeteers re-enacted the old tales of knights and damsels within a modern context, and despite their names – such as Angelica, Orlando, Rinaldo and Astolfo – the characters represented Sicilians in everyday life. The puppets themselves were the creation of a number of extraordinary artisans; in Palermo there was Gaetano Greco, the first of a long line of puppeteers; in Catania there was Giovanni Grasso and his lifelong rival Gaetano Crimi. The last of the great puppeteers was

Emanuele Crimi, who died in 1974. Nowadays it's something of a dying art, though you can still see performances in Palermo and Cefalù (see the relevant regional chapters for details).

SOCIETY & CONDUCT

It is difficult to make blanket assertions about Sicilian culture, if only because there are huge differences between the more modern-minded city dwellers and those from the traditional, conservative countryside.

Stereotypes

Foreigners may think of Sicilians as passionate, animated people who gesticulate wildly when speaking, love to eat, drive like maniacs and never forget a grudge. There's a little bit more to it than that, however.

Coming closer to the truth than the traditional stereotype is the journalist Luigi Barzini's (1908–84) description of Italians as a hard-working, resilient and resourceful people, optimistic and with a good sense of humour. Sicilians are also passionately loyal to their friends and families – all-important qualities, noted Barzini, since 'a happy private life helps people to tolerate an appalling public life'.

Yet initially Sicilians can seem mistrustful of strangers, particularly those who ask a lot of questions. At first meeting they may appear guarded and somewhat taciturn – a common attribute in the countryside – regarding the newcomer with suspicion and responding to queries with a shrug of the shoulders and a monosyllabic grunt. Remember that this is the land where silence is ingrained in the very character of the people, an understandable response (or lack of!) to centuries of foreign intrusion. Once the ice has broken, however, Sicilians are as friendly and embracing as any people in Europe, and it is not uncommon to be invited into their homes to share in a family meal.

Sicilians have a strong distrust of authority and, when confronted with a silly rule, an unjust law or a stupid order (and they are regularly confronted with many of them), they do not complain or try to change it, but rather try to find the quickest way around it.

The Sicilian Stereotype

Think 'Sicilian' and a variety of images springs to mind – from the black-clad widow, bent double with hard work and age, to the menacing mafioso in a dark suit and sunglasses. Almost all images of Sicilians tend to be of the 'short and dark' variety, as if Sicily is populated by the human form of espresso. However, due to its Norman heritage, Sicily has a lot of tall, fair-haired people, and even a number of redheads throughout the island – you'll spot them easily with their flaming red hair and, in summer, beetroot-red faces.

Another image people have of Sicily is of a poverty-stricken island, ravaged by centuries' worth of invading forces who took all the food. This may have been the case, but like in other poor countries the locals made the best of the basic ingredients they had and refined their cookery to the delicious dishes they have today. Sicilian cuisine is highly regarded and so easy to enjoy – it seems that everyone in Sicily can cook extremely well. Every second person will tell you that their mother makes the best *caponata* – a sweet-and-sour dish made with tomatoes, aubergines, olives and anchovies – and the sheer number of portly boys of primary-school age in need of a good support bra would seem to signify that in this day and age there's plenty to go around!

Family

The family remains of central importance in the fabric of Sicilian society. Young Sicilians tend to stay at home until they marry, a situation partly exacerbated by the lack of affordable housing. At the centre of the family is *la madre*, the mother, the most venerated of all Sicilians. She is considered second only to the Virgin Mary, who many jokingly believe must have been an islander; after all, the son she adored lived with her until he was 30 and when he was killed by the authorities she maintained an air of dignified composure as she mourned!

Still, modern attitudes have begun to erode the traditions. In the larger cities such as Palermo and Catania you will find a vibrant youth culture that has rejected many traditional values as antiquated and out-of-date, although the sexual revolution that has gripped northern Italy is looked upon with more than a mild hint of suspicion.

Dos & Don'ts

Sicilians tend to be tolerant but, despite an apparent obsession with (mostly female) nakedness, especially in advertising, they are not excessively free and easy. Women, for instance, are sure to be verbally harassed if they wear skimpy or see-through clothing.

Topless sunbathing, while not uncommon on some Sicilian beaches (especially on the islands), is not always acceptable and can often offend. Take your cue from other sunbathers. Walking the streets near beaches in a bikini or not much clothing is also best avoided.

In churches you are expected to dress modestly. This means no shorts (for men or women) or short skirts, and shoulders should be covered. Churches that are also major tourist attractions, such as the cathedrals at Monreale and Palermo, will often enforce strict dress codes. If you visit one during a service (which preferably you should refrain from doing), try to be as inconspicuous as possible.

The *polizia* and *carabinieri* (see Police under Legal Matters in the Facts for the Visitor chapter) may well be used to handling brusque Sicilians, but they don't take kindly to discourteous treatment by foreigners (and have the power to arrest you if they feel you have insulted them) so be diplomatic in your dealings with them!

THE MAFIA
Origins

There is no other word in Italy as contentious as 'mafia'. It took over 110 years of common usage before it was officially acknowledged as referring to an actual organisation. Although formally recorded by the Palermitan prefecture in 1865, the term was not included in the Italian penal code until 1982.

The origins of the word have been much debated. The author Norman Lewis has suggested that it derives from the Arabic *mu'afah* or 'place of refuge'. Nineteenth-century etymologists proposed *mahjas*, the Arabic word for 'boasting'. Whatever the origin, the term *mafioso* existed long before the organisation known as the Mafia and was used to describe a character that was elegant and proud, with an independent vitality and spirit.

Although mafiosi had been involved in sporadic acts of brigandry since the 13th century, their role did not become defined until after 1812 and the abolition of feudalism, when local mafiosi were used as bailiffs or *gabellotti* by landowners to strong-arm ground rents out of the peasantry.

Up to WWII the Mafia operated almost exclusively in the countryside, controlling rents and extorting a percentage of each crop yield in return for protection. Their role and presence was never spoken of publicly, with every small town and village under their control adhering steadfastly to the ancient code of *omertà*, which means 'manliness' and – in this context – a need to take care of one's own problems without talking. Much to the frustration of the authorities, Sicilians kept quiet about every aspect of the Mafia's activity, due to fear and suspicion.

It is reputed that Sicily's first real 'godfather' was Don Vito Cascio Ferro, who developed close ties with the American Black Hand, the earliest form of Italian Mafia (operating from New York at the turn of the 20th century). It would be another 50 years, however, before US-Sicilian cooperation was to radically change the make-up and goals of the Sicilian mob.

The 'New' Mafia

In 1982 a leading mafioso named Tommaso Buscetta was arrested in Brazil and extradited to Italy, where he was charged with a litany of Mafia-related crimes, including murder, money-laundering, extortion and drug trafficking. A Palermitan magistrate called Giovanni Falcone (see the boxed text 'Palermo & the Mafia' in the Palermo chapter) led Buscetta's interrogation and, after nearly four years, the impossible occurred: Buscetta broke the code of silence and decided to talk. His revelations shocked and

fascinated the Italian nation, as he revealed the innermost workings of La Società Onorata ('The Honoured Society', the Mafia's chosen name for itself), including how it was organised and who its main characters were. In response to his confession Buscetta was given a new identity and relocated in the US by the witness protection programme. He died, aged 71, in April 2000.

Buscetta told of how the Mafia began its expansion into the cities after WWII. It took over the construction industry, channelling funds into its bank accounts and creating an elaborate network of kickbacks and pay-offs that were factored into every project undertaken on the island. In 1953, a meeting between representatives of the US and Sicilian Mafias resulted in the creation of the first Sicilian Commission, or Cupola, on which were represented the six main Mafia families (or *cosche*, literally meaning 'artichoke') so as to efficiently run their next expansion into the extremely lucrative world of narcotics. At the head of the commission was Luciano Liggio from Corleone, whose 'family' had played a vital role in developing US-Sicilian relations. The 1953 meeting was something of a one-off and US and Sicilian Mafia families have since worked separately.

Throughout the 1960s and '70s the Mafia earned billions of dollars from the drugs trade (or *narcodollari*), the profits of which were laundered through a variety of sources, including real estate and urban development projects. Inevitably, the raised stakes made the different Mafia families greedier for a greater share of the spoils and from the late 1960s onwards Sicily was awash with vicious feuds that left hundreds dead.

In 1982 Pio La Torre, Regional Secretary of Sicily's Communist Party, was gunned down in Palermo as a punishment for having proposed a law in parliament that would have allowed prosecutors greater access to private bank accounts. Three months later, the recently appointed chief prefect of police, General Dalla Chiesa – fresh from his successful pursuit of Italy's Red Brigade terrorist group – met his death, along with his wife, when they were ambushed in the heart of the capital. In his diary, the contents of which became public after his death, Dalla Chiesa had revealed he felt that the government in Rome was 'isolating' him in Sicily without the effective means to tackle the Mafia. During his tenure he had uncovered evidence of corruption at the highest levels of government and suspected that the Mafia's interests were being protected by the upper echelons of the political system. He reserved judgement about the real intentions of prime minister Giulio Andreotti (see the boxed text 'The Day of the Fox' earlier in this chapter), whom he suspected of having other agendas with regard to crime-fighting in Sicily. These revelations, along with a long list of admissions by Mafia informers, raised the question of what is commonly termed Il Terzo Livello (The Third Level: the arrangement between the Mafia and government), an issue that is as contentious today as it was scandalous when first revealed.

Dalla Chiesa's brutal murder was only one in a long line of *cadaveri eccellenti* (excellent corpses). His death led to prosecutors and magistrates being granted wider powers of investigation and, in 1986, 500 top mafiosi were put on trial in the first *maxi-processo* (super-trial) in a specially constructed bunker near Palermo's Ucciardone prison. The trial resulted in 347 convictions, of which 19 were life imprisonments and the others jail terms totalling a staggering 2065 years.

The Mafia responded to the convictions with typical brutality. The murder of Salvatore Lima in 1992 (see Political Skulduggery under Government & Politics earlier in this chapter) was treated in informed circles as a warning to the government to curb the prosecuting magistrates' vigour.

The tidal wave of disgust and anger that followed these savage murders is arguably the most important development in the fight against the Mafia. For the first time ordinary people spoke out against organised crime in powerful public displays of emotion. The funerals attracted tens of thousands of mourners and all around Sicily there was a tangible sense that the people had reached the end of their tether. In January 1993 the authorities arrested Totò Riina, who had been living openly in Palermo

since 1969. He was charged with a host of murders, including those of the anti-Mafia magistrates Giovanni Falcone and Paolo Borsellino, and sentenced to life imprisonment for all of them.

The Mafia Today

Since Riina's conviction, other top mafiosi have followed him behind bars, most notably his successor Leoluca Bagarella, arrested in 1995, and the vicious killer Giovanni Brusca, arrested in 1996. In 1998 top bosses Vito Vitale and Mariano Troia were arrested and prosecuted, as well as Mafia accountant Natale d'Emmanuele, thought to be the main number-cruncher for Catania's mob. The authorities proudly declared that the Mafia was on the run and that its organisation was permanently damaged.

Yet many questions remain, particularly about the circumstances of the arrest of Totò Riina. Journalists and commentators alike have wondered how was it possible for the most wanted man in Italy, one of the most dangerous criminals in the whole world, to live so openly in Palermo without benefiting from some kind of official protection? When he was finally revealed to the world in court, it startled many to observe that this criminal mastermind was actually a diminutive figure with a hesitant command of Italian, much in the tradition of the typical, old-style Sicilian peasant. Furthermore, the arresting officers found a dog-eared notebook in his pocket full of sums and figures roughly scribbled in with a pencil. Is it possible, people asked, that the world's largest drug syndicate could be efficiently run by a semi-literate man whose accounts were kept in a schoolchild's notebook? Surely, they proclaimed, there was somebody (or bodies) behind him?

Nobody has been able to answer these questions convincingly one way or the other. The Mafia, however, is far from dead and buried. An English journalist once noted: 'Everyone knows that the Mafia and the establishment are intertwined, and that this marriage is one of the pillars of political life in Italy. The Mafia is not only omnipotent, it is omnipresent.' Recent works on the Mafia, such as Norman Lewis' *In Sicily*

(2000) and Alexander Stille's *Excellent Cadavers* (1995), have reported the presence of a rival organisation known as *Stidda* (meaning 'Star') that has been making its presence felt in the south of Sicily (Agrigento, Gela and Caltanissetta) since the 1990s. It's believed that the Stidda is comprised of mafiosi who left the Mafia during the turbulent 1980s.

RELIGION

Religion is a big deal in Sicily. With the exception of the small Muslim communities of Palermo and the larger community of Tunisian Muslims in Mazara del Vallo, the overwhelming majority of the islanders consider themselves practising Roman Catholics. Even before the 1929 Lateran Treaty between the Vatican and the Italian state, where each recognised the legitimacy of the other and Roman Catholicism became the official religion of the land, Sicily was incontrovertibly Catholic, mostly due to 500 years of Spanish domination. In 1985 the treaty was renegotiated whereby Catholicism was no longer the state religion and compulsory religious education was dropped, but this only reflected the reality of mainland Italy north of Rome. In the south, the Catholic Church remains strong and extremely popular. Most young people – usually the first to fall away from the Church – still attend Mass once a week.

Some of the older traditions, such as a widow wearing black for a full year after her husband's death, have been largely confined to the small communities of the interior. Here too you will also find that the mix of faith and superstition that for centuries dictated Sicilian behaviour is still strong, and that the local curate is still considered the most important person in the community. Pilgrimages remain a central part of the religious ritual, with thousands of Sicilians travelling to places like the Santuario

Stray Flock

Most Sicilians claim to be Catholic, but ask them about the *malocchio* (evil eye) and see what happens. Most will make a simple hand movement (index and little finger pointing down, with the middle and ring fingers folded under the thumb) which is designed to ward off evil spirits. Others, if pressed, might admit to wearing amulets. A pregnant woman might wear a chicken's neck hanging around her own to ensure that her child is not born with the umbilical cord around its neck. Insurance agents can have difficulty discussing life insurance policies with clients, as many of them don't want to discuss their eventual death, or the possibility of suffering serious accidents. This phenomenon is known to sociologists as Catholic paganism.

Helen Gillman

della Madonna Nera at Tyndaris or the church at Gibilmanna in the Madonie mountains. The younger, more cosmopolitan sections of society living in the cities tend to dismiss their elders' deepest expressions of religious devotion, but mostly everyone still maintains an air of respect.

LANGUAGE

The official language is Italian, which is spoken by everyone except a minority in the backwaters of the interior. Most Sicilians also speak Sicilian dialect, a rich patois comprising words of Arabic, Greek, French, Italian and Spanish origin – basically a linguistic amalgam of 3500 years of history. When speaking to outsiders, Italian is used, but when speaking among themselves, Sicilians largely revert to dialect. For more information about the Italian language and the Sicilian dialect, some useful words and phrases and a food glossary, see the Language chapter later in this book.

Facts for the Visitor

SUGGESTED ITINERARIES

You could cover quite a bit of ground in a week, especially if you have your own vehicle, but you will still probably have to limit yourself to a handful of towns and sights. Two weeks is plenty of time to acclimatise yourself and get the most out of Sicily. If you plan a longer stay (say, a month), you can explore the island at your leisure and really begin to understand the often contradictory nature of this extraordinary place, which can infuriate and charm at the same time. Below are three itineraries that might help you organise your trip.

One Week

Devote at least one day to exploring Palermo. Make sure you put a few hours aside to get to the Cattedrale di Monreale. Your next objective should be Agrigento, within easy striking distance of the capital, from where you could head east along the coast to Syracuse. Once you're done with the Baroque southeast, Mt Etna is next. From there, make the short trip up the coast from Catania to the resort town of Taormina. Alternatively, you could go inland from Catania towards Enna, and on to Piazza Armerina and the Roman villa at Casale. From the capital you can also travel along the Tyrrhenian coast to Milazzo and the Aeolian Islands.

Two Weeks

Two weeks allows you to explore the island's less touristy areas. From Palermo a westerly arc will take you to small coastal resorts and the Riserva Naturale dello Zingaro. From there, move south to Tràpani, a good base for visiting the province. The medieval hill town of Èrice, near Tràpani, is most picturesque. While in the west, you shouldn't miss Segesta and Selinunte, which – along with the Valley of the Temples in Agrigento – are Sicily's premier ancient Greek sites. Next travel to Agrigento itself, perhaps stopping at Eraclea Minoa to relax on the gorgeous beach. If you're interested in all things classical, visit

the top-notch archaeological museum in Gela, further along the coast. From there you can either head into the interior or continue east. If you do the latter, spare a day for Catania then pay a visit to Mt Etna. Taormina and the Aeolian Islands are the next obvious destinations. From Cefalù you can visit the hill towns to the south and the Parco Naturale Regionale delle Madonie, one of the most impressive landscapes on the island.

One Month

A month will give you plenty of time to really explore Sicily. Devote a few days to Palermo and its surrounding area before heading west to Tràpani province to take in the Riserva Naturale dello Zingaro, the Egadi Islands and Èrice, and the cities of Tràpani, Mazara del Vallo and Marsala (about four days). From there, head to the southern coast, visiting Sciacca, Caltabellota and the countryside of the Belice valley. Spend a couple of days in Agrigento, devoting at least one day to the Valley of the Temples. From Agrigento, you can explore the Pelagic Islands and the coastal/archaeological areas of Eraclea Minoa and Selinunte for a few days. After this, pop into Gela to see the archaeological museum, and explore the countryside and coast on the way to the southern-most area of Sicily – the Baroque splendours of Ragusa and Syracuse provinces. From Syracuse, head to Catania for a few days, exploring the rich culture of the city and its excellent food and nightlife. You can use Catania as a base for exploring the Etna region, before heading into Central Sicily and the towns of Enna, Caltanissetta, Nicosia plus the Parco Naturale Regionale delle Madonie. From here, travel along the Tyrrhenian coast to the delightful resort of Cefalù, where you can head to the Aeolian Islands for some sun (or wind, depending on the season!). Then make time for Messina and the magnificent resort of Taormina – probably the best way to finish up a month of travel.

PLANNING
When to Go

The best time to visit Sicily is in the low season, between April and June and September and October, when the weather is usually good, prices are lower and there are fewer tourists. Late July and August are the times to avoid the place: the sun broils, prices are inflated and the island's top attractions are awash with a tide of holiday-makers. Most of Italy goes on holiday in this period and a chunk of the population chooses Sicily as its preferred destination.

The beaches and offshore islands warm up relatively early, usually around mid-April, and stay hot well into October, so you can still enjoy the sunshine when the rest of Italy is dusting off heavy sweaters. The same is true of the natural parks, particularly Madonie and Mt Etna – these are best visited in the months surrounding July and August. The dramatic effect of climbing Mt Etna is somewhat spoiled by having to wait in a queue to board a 4WD or sharing the top with a crowd.

You may prefer to organise your trip to coincide with one of the many festivals that fill the Sicilian calendar – Easter is a particular highlight as the whole island celebrates. See Special Events later in this chapter for more information.

What Kind of Trip

There are several ways to organise your trip around Sicily besides simply touring the main towns and cities. If you fancy a sea-and-sun holiday, there are fewer places in the whole of Italy that are better – Sicily has plenty of resorts, beachfront towns and offshore islands expressly given over to that purpose. The island is rich in tradition and culture, and has a long and varied history, so you could easily organise your trip according to a theme.

An increasingly popular option is *la vacanza agrituristica* in the island's interior, which involves renting a house or lodging in a farming community in the countryside (see Agriturismo under Accommodation later in this chapter). In winter, you can even go skiing in the Madonie area or on Mt Etna, though the resorts here are small and it is difficult to predict how much snow there will be, especially during mild winters.

Maps
Small-Scale Maps The best map of Sicily is published by the Touring Club Italiano (TCI) at a scale of 1:200,000. It costs €6.20

and you can buy it in bookshops, airports and motorway cafes in Sicily. Michelin also has a very good multilingual fold-out map (No 432; €6.20) of Sicily and the offshore islands at a scale of 1:400,000.

Road Atlases The AA's *Road Atlas – Italy* (1:250,000), available in the UK for £13.99, includes Sicily. De Agostini's *Atlante Turistico Stradale della Sicilia* (1:250,000; €18.10) contains city plans and tourist itineraries. It is available in bookshops throughout the island.

What to Bring

Pack as little as possible. A backpack is an advantage since petty thieves have been known to prey on luggage-laden tourists with no free hands. Backpacks with straps and openings that can be zipped inside a flap are more secure than the standard ones.

Suitcases with portable trolleys may be fine in airports but you won't get far on foot with them. Remember that most everyday necessities (including medicine) can be found easily in Sicily – there is no need to stock up in advance and drag it all around with you. Prescriptions can be filled easily too.

A small pack (with a lock) for day trips and sightseeing is preferable to a handbag or shoulder bag.

Clothes Sicily is scorching hot in summer, with temperatures in the high 30°s or even low 40°s Celsius. Consequently, you should stick to the lightest fabrics, such as thin cotton T-shirts and shorts. If you plan on entering churches or other religious buildings – and sightseeing in Sicily involves a lot of them – be sure your clothes cover your shoulders and knees. Remember also a light cotton hat for sun protection. It is pleasantly warm in spring and autumn so you won't need anything other than a jacket or a light sweater for the cooler evenings. Winter is usually mild so a lined raincoat should suffice.

If you plan on travelling in the interior or walking in the mountains, make sure you bring the necessary clothing and equipment, in particular a pair of walking boots (lightweight and waterproof). Even in high summer you would be advised to have some warm clothing on long walks – it can get chilly at high-altitude spots such as Mt Etna.

Although not nearly as obsessive about their dress as on the mainland, Sicilians still like to make an effort when going out, and usually put on something that is casually dressy.

Unless you plan to spend large sums of money in dry-cleaners and laundrettes (which can be difficult to find), pack a portable clothes-line and get used to the idea that you'll be doing a lot of handwashing!

Useful Items In addition to any special personal needs, consider taking the following:

- under-the-clothes moneybelt or shoulder wallet, for your money and documents
- small Italian dictionary and/or phrasebook
- Swiss army knife – with a bottle-opener, for alfresco dining
- medical kit (see Health later in this chapter)
- padlock(s) to secure your luggage to racks and to close hostel lockers
- sleeping sheet to save on sheet rental costs in youth hostels (a sleeping bag is unnecessary unless you're camping)
- adapter plug for electrical appliances
- torch (flashlight)
- alarm clock
- sunglasses and a hat
- universal sink plug

For information on the availability of basic and more specific medication, see Medical Kit Check List under Health later in this chapter.

RESPONSIBLE TOURISM

It would be nice to see more travellers with an awareness of local sensibilities. Visitors all too often seem to leave manners and common sense at home. In the main tourist centres, locals are by now used to the sight of tourists wandering around in less than their Sunday best. Bear in mind that sweaty, sun-scorched flesh does not a pretty sight make, less still to a people known for their sense of style.

When visiting the many Greek and Roman ruins dotted throughout the island, don't go clambering where you are asked not to or have no need to. On an immediately practical level, if you're visiting the sites of ancient cities such as Selinunte, stay on the well-marked paths: there are snakes in the undergrowth whose bite, although not fatal, will require medical treatment.

Don't use a flash when photographing artwork in museums, churches and so on. The burst of light can damage the art.

Respect for tradition and religion is deeply rooted in Sicily, so when visiting churches be sure to show the proper decorum. If you must talk, do so in a whisper so as not to disturb those who have come to pray.

The moral of the story is, simply, respect the monuments and works of art, the towns and their people, as you would your own prized possessions.

TOURIST OFFICES
Local Tourist Offices

The quality of tourist offices in Sicily can vary quite dramatically. As you would expect, offices in popular destinations such as Palermo, Catania, Taormina, Syracuse and the Aeolian Islands are used to dealing with visitors from all over the world. They are usually well-stocked and staffed by employees with a working command of at least one foreign language, usually English but also French, German and others. As Sicilians are by nature a pretty friendly bunch, they will often go out of their way to help you no matter where you are.

The main tourist office for the entire region of Sicily is the Assessorato Regionale del Turismo, delle Communicazioni e dei Trasporti (ARTCT), which is generally concerned with promotion, budgeting and other projects far removed from the daily concerns of the humble tourist.

Otherwise, tourist offices in Sicily are divided into two tiers: regional and local. Regional offices are known as the Azienda di Autonoma Provinciale per l'Incremento Turistico (APT). They run efficient tourist offices with plenty of up-to-date information on both the province and its main town or city.

Local offices in Sicily are known by a variety of names that change according to

the town, but the most common are Azienda Autonoma di Cura, Soggiorno e Turismo (AAST) or Azienda Soggiorno e Turismo (AST). They only have information on the town in which they're based but are the place to go if you want specific information such as bus routes or museum openings. In many small towns and villages, the local tourist office is called a Pro Loco, often similar to the AAST or AST offices but on occasion little more than a room with a small desk.

Although most offices of the APT, AAST or AST respond to written or telephone requests for information, you can sometimes draw a blank with smaller bureaux that are off the tourist path, usually because they lack staff or funds.

Tourist offices generally open 9am to 12.30pm or 1pm and 3pm to 7pm Monday to Friday. Hours are extended during the summer (usually from May to September, but sometimes even Easter to October) when many of the offices in popular destinations are open part or all of Saturday and occasionally even Sunday.

All APT offices and most of the larger AAST and AST offices should be able to provide the handy accommodation guide called the *Guida dell'Ospitalità nella Provincia*. These are updated annually and include every hotel, camp site, hostel and other rented accommodation within each of Sicily's nine provinces.

Information booths at most major train stations and in locations throughout the bigger cities tend to keep similar hours but in most cases only operate during the summer. Here you can usually pick up a map *(pianta della città)*, a photocopied list of hotels *(elenco degli alberghi)* and information on the major sights *(informazioni sulle attrazioni turistiche)*.

The address and telephone number of local tourist offices are listed under towns and cities throughout this book.

Tourist Offices Abroad

Information on Sicily is available from the Italian State Tourist Office (ENIT; W www .enit.it) in the countries listed overleaf.

Australia
(☎ 02-9262 5744, fax 9262 5745) c/o Italian Chamber of Commerce, Level 26, 44 Market St, Sydney, NSW 2000
Austria
(☎ 01-505 1639, fax 505 0248, ⓔ enit-wien@ aon.at) Kaerntnerring 4, 1010 Vienna
Canada
(☎ 416-925 4882, fax 925 4799) Suite 907, South Tower, 175 Bloor St East, Toronto M4W 3R8
France
(☎ 01 42 66 03 96 or 01 42 66 66 68, fax 01 47 42 19 74, ⓔ enit.parigi@wanadoo.fr) 23 rue de la Paix, 75002 Paris
Germany
Berlin: (☎ 030-247 8397, fax 247 8399, ⓔ enit-berlin@t-online.de) Karl Liebknecht Strasse 34, 10178 Berlin
Frankfurt: (☎ 069-259126, fax 232894, ⓔ enit.ffm@t-online.de) Kaisertrasse 65, 60329 Frankfurt-am-Main
Munich: (☎ 089-531317, fax 5345227, ⓔ enit-muenchen@t-online.de) Goethestrasse 20, 80336 Munich
Netherlands
(☎ 020-616 8244, fax 618 8515, ⓔ enitams@ wirehub.nl) Stadhouderskade 2, 1054 ES Amsterdam
Spain
(☎ 91-559 9750, fax 559 8885, ⓔ italia turismo@retemail.es) Gran Via 84, Edifico Espagna, 28013 Madrid
Switzerland
(☎ 01-211 7917, fax 211 3885, ⓔ enit@ bluewin.ch) Uraniastrasse 32, 8001 Zurich
UK
(☎ 020 7355 1557, fax 7493 6695, ⓒ enitlond@ globalnet.co.uk) 1 Princes St, London W1R 9AY
USA
Chicago: (☎ 312-644 0996, fax 644 3019, ⓔ enitch@italiantourism.com) Suite 2240, 500 North Michigan Ave, Chicago, IL 60611
Los Angeles: (☎ 310-820 1898, fax 820 6357, ⓔ enitla@earthlink.net) Suite 550, 12400 Wilshire Blvd, Los Angeles, CA 90025
New York: (☎ 212-245 5095, fax 586 9249, ⓔ enitny@italiantourism.com) Suite 1565, 630 Fifth Ave, New York, NY 10111

Sestante CIT (Compagnia Italiana di Turismo), Italy's national travel agency, has offices worldwide (known as CIT or Citalia outside Italy). Staff can provide extensive information on travelling in Sicily and will organise tours, as well as book individual hotels. CIT staff can also make train bookings and sell Eurail passes and discount passes for train travel in Sicily. Offices include:

Australia
Melbourne: (☎ 03-9650 5510) Level 4, 227 Collins St, Melbourne 3000
Sydney: (☎ 02-9267 1255) Level 2, 263 Clarence St, Sydney, NSW 2000
Canada
Montreal: (☎ 514-845 9101, toll-free 800 361 7799) Suite 901, 666 Sherbrooke St West, Montreal, Quebec H3A 1E7
Toronto. (☎ 905-415 1060, toll-free 800 387 0711) Suite 401, 80 Tiverton Court, Markham, Toronto, Ontario L3R 0G4
France
(☎ 01 44 51 39 51) 5 blvd des Capucines, 75002 Paris
UK
(☎ 020-8686 0677, 8686 5533) Marco Polo House, 3–5 Lansdowne Rd, Croydon, Surrey CR9 1LL
USA
(☎ 212-730 2121) Level 10, 15 West 44th St, New York, NY 10036

Italian cultural institutes in major cities throughout the world have extensive information on the study opportunities available in Sicily.

VISAS & DOCUMENTS
Passport
Citizens of the 15 European Union (EU) member states plus Switzerland, Slovenia, Croatia, Malta and Turkey can travel to Sicily with their national identity cards alone. People from countries that do not issue ID cards, such as the UK and Ireland, must have a valid passport. All non-EU nationals must have a full valid passport.

If you've had your passport for a while, check that the expiry date is at least six months off, otherwise you may not be granted a visa (if you need one). If your passport is stolen or lost while in Sicily, notify the police and obtain a statement, and then contact your embassy or consulate as soon as possible (see Embassies & Consulates later in this chapter).

Visas

Italy is one of 15 countries that have signed the Schengen Convention, an agreement whereby all EU member countries (except the UK and Ireland) plus Iceland and Norway have abolished checks at common borders. The other EU countries are Austria, Belgium, Denmark, Finland, France, Germany, Greece, Luxembourg, the Netherlands, Portugal, Spain and Sweden. Legal residents of one Schengen country do not require a visa for another Schengen country. Citizens of the UK and Ireland are also exempt from visa requirements for Schengen countries. In addition, nationals of a number of other countries, including Canada, Japan, New Zealand and Switzerland, do not require visas for tourist visits of up to 90 days to any Schengen country.

Various other nationals not covered by the Schengen exemption can also spend up to 90 days in Sicily without a visa. These include Australian, Israeli and US citizens. However, all non-EU nationals entering Italy for any reason other than tourism (such as study or work) should contact an Italian consulate as they may need a specific visa. They should also insist on having their passport stamped on entry as, without a stamp, they could encounter problems when trying to obtain a *permesso di soggiorno* (resident permit; see Permits later). If you are a citizen of a country not mentioned in this section, you should check with an Italian consulate whether you need a visa.

The standard tourist visa issued by Italian consulates is the Schengen visa, valid for up to 90 days. A Schengen visa issued by one Schengen country is generally valid for travel in all other Schengen countries. However, individual Schengen countries may impose additional restrictions on certain nationalities. It is therefore worth checking visa regulations with the consulate of each Schengen country you plan to visit.

It is mandatory that you apply for a visa in your country of residence. You can apply for no more than two Schengen visas in any 12-month period and they are not renewable inside Italy. It's worth applying early for your visa, especially in the busy summer months.

Study Visas Non-EU citizens who want to study at a university or language school in Sicily must have a study visa. These visas can be obtained from your nearest Italian embassy or consulate. You will normally require confirmation of your enrolment, proof of payment of fees and adequate funds to support yourself before a visa is issued. The visa will cover only the period of the enrolment. This type of visa is renewable within Sicily but, again, only with confirmation of ongoing enrolment and proof that you are able to support yourself – bank statements are preferred.

Permits

EU citizens do not require permits to live, work or start a business in Sicily. They are, however, advised to register with a police station *(questura)* if they take up residence, in accordance with an anti-Mafia law that aims at keeping a watch on everyone's whereabouts in the country. Failure to do so carries no consequences, although some landlords may be unwilling to rent out a flat to you if you cannot produce proof of registration. Those considering long-term residence will eventually want to consider getting a work permit (see the following section), a necessary first step to acquiring an ID card *(carta d'identità)*. While you're at it, you'll need a tax-file number *(codice fiscale)* if you wish to be paid for most work in Sicily.

Work Permits Non-EU citizens wishing to work in Sicily will need to obtain a work permit *(permesso di lavoro)*. If you intend to work for an Italian company, the company must organise the permit and forward it to the Italian embassy or consulate in your home country; only then will you be issued with an appropriate visa.

If non-EU citizens intend to work for a non-Italian company, will be paid in foreign currency or wish to go freelance, they must organise the visa and permit in their country of residence through an Italian embassy or consulate. This process can take several months so look into it early.

It is in any case advisable to seek detailed information from an Italian embassy or consulate on the exact requirements before attempting to organise a legitimate job in Sicily. Many foreigners, however, don't bother with such formalities, preferring to try and work illegally (*al nero*, literally 'in the black'). See Work later in this chapter for details.

Permesso di Soggiorno If you stay at the same address for more than one week, you are technically obliged to report to a police station and obtain a permesso di soggiorno. Tourists who are staying in hotels do not need to do this as hotel owners must register all guests with the police.

A permesso di soggiorno is only necessary if you plan to study, work (legally) or live in Sicily. Obtaining one is never pleasant, although for EU citizens it is fairly straightforward and success is guaranteed. Other nationals may find it involves long queues, rude police officers and the frustration of arriving at the counter (after a two-hour wait) to find that you don't have all the necessary documents.

The exact requirements, such as documents and *marche da bollo* (official stamps), can vary from one place to another. In general, you will need a valid passport containing a visa stamp indicating your date of entry into Italy, a special visa issued in your own country if you are planning to study, four passport-style photographs and proof of your ability to support yourself financially.

It is best to go to the police station to obtain precise information on what is required.

Travel Insurance
A travel insurance policy to cover theft, loss and medical problems is a good idea. Some policies offer lower and higher medical-expense options; the higher ones are chiefly for countries such as the USA, which have extremely high medical costs. There is a wide variety of policies available carefully so check the small print.

Some policies specifically exclude 'dangerous activities', which can include scuba diving, motorcycling, and even trekking. A locally acquired motorcycle licence is not valid under some policies.

You may prefer a policy that pays doctors or hospitals directly rather than you having to pay on the spot and claim later. If you have to claim later make sure you keep all documentation. Some policies ask you to call back (reverse charges) to a centre in your home country where an immediate assessment of your problem is made.

Check that the policy covers ambulances or an emergency flight home.

Driving Licence & Permits
EU member states' driving licences are recognised in Sicily. If you hold a licence from other countries, you are supposed to obtain an International Driving Permit too. See Paperwork & Preparations under Car & Motorcycle in the Getting There & Away chapter for more information about car documents.

Hostel Cards
A valid Hostelling International (HI; W www.iyhf.org) hostelling card is required in all associated youth hostels (Associazione Italiana Alberghi per la Gioventù) in Sicily. You can get this in your home country or at youth hostels in Sicily. In the latter case you apply for the card and must collect six stamps on it at €2.60 each. You pay for a stamp on each of the first six nights you spend in a hostel. With six stamps, you are considered a full international member.

Student, Teacher & Youth Cards
The International Student Identity Card (ISIC), for full-time students, and the International Teacher Identity Card (ITIC), for full-time teachers and professors, are issued by more than 5000 organisations around the world – mainly those involved in (student) travel. The cards entitle you to a range of discounts, from reduced museum entry charges to cheap air fares.

Student travel organisations such as STA (Australia, the UK and USA), Council Travel (the USA) and Travel CUTS (Canada) can issue these cards. See Air in the Getting There & Away chapter for some addresses, phone numbers and Web sites.

Anyone aged under 26 can get a Euro<26

card. This gives similar discounts to the ISIC and is issued by most of the same organisations. The Euro<26 has a variety of names including the Under 26 Card in England and Wales.

Centro Turistico Studentesco e Giovanile (CTS) youth and student travel organisation branches in Sicily can issue ISIC, ITIC and Euro<26 cards. You have to join the CTS first, however, which costs €25.80.

Seniors Cards

Seniors aged over 60 or 65 (depending on the reductions they're seeking) can get many discounts simply by presenting their passport or ID card as proof of age.

Copies

All important documents (passport data page and visa page, credit cards, travel insurance policy, air/bus/train tickets, driving licence) should be photocopied before you leave home. Leave one copy with someone at home and keep another with you, separate from the originals.

You can also store details of your important documents in Lonely Planet's online Travel Vault, which is safer than carrying photocopies and is accessible at any time. It's the best option if you travel in a country with easy Internet access. You can create your own password-protected travel vault free of charge at W www.ekno.lonely planet.com.

EMBASSIES & CONSULATES
Your Own Embassy or Consulate

It's important to realise what your own embassy – the embassy of the country of which you are a citizen – can and can't do to help you if you get into trouble. Generally speaking, it won't be much help in emergencies if the trouble you're in is remotely your own fault. Remember that you are bound by the laws of the country you are in. Your embassy will not be sympathetic if you end up in jail after committing a crime locally, even if such actions are legal in your own country.

In genuine emergencies you might get some assistance but only if other channels have been exhausted. For example, if you need to get home urgently, a free ticket is exceedingly unlikely – the embassy would expect you to have insurance. If you have all your money and documents stolen, it might assist with getting a new passport but a loan for onward travel is out of the question.

Some embassies used to keep letters for travellers or have a small reading room with home newspapers but these days the mail-holding service has usually been stopped and even newspapers tend to be out of date.

Italian Embassies & Consulates

The following is a selection of Italian diplomatic missions abroad. As a rule, you should approach the consulate rather than the embassy (where both are present) on visa matters. Also bear in mind that in many of the countries listed below there are further consulates in other cities.

Australia
Embassy: (☎ 02-6273 3333, fax 6273 4223, e ambital2@dynamite.com.au) 12 Grey St, Deakin, Canberra, ACT 2601
Consulate: (☎ 03-9867 5744, fax 9866 3932, e itconmel@netlink.com.au) 509 St Kilda Rd, Melbourne, VIC 3004
Consulate: (☎ 02-9392 7900, fax 9252 4830, e itconsyd@armadillo.com.au) Level 45, Gateway, 1 Macquarie Place, Sydney, NSW 2000

Austria
Embassy: (☎ 01-712 5121, fax 713 9719, e ambitalviepress@via.at) Metternichgasse 13, Vienna 1030
Consulate: (☎ 01-713 5671, fax 715 4030) Ungargasse 43, Vienna 1030

Canada
Embassy: (☎ 613-232 2401, fax 233 1484, e ambital@italyincanada.com) Level 21, 275 Slater St, Ottawa, Ontario K1P 5H9
Consulate: (☎ 514-849 8351, fax 499 9471, e cgi@italconsul.montreal.qc.ca) 3489 Drummond St, Montreal, Quebec H3G 1X6
Consulate: (☎ 416-977 1566, fax 977 1119, e consolato.it@toronto.italconsulate.org) 136 Beverley St, Toronto, Ontario M5T 1Y5

France
Embassy: (☎ 01 49 54 03 00, fax 01 45 49 35 81, e ambasciata@amb-italie.fr) 7 rue de Varenne, 75007 Paris
Consulate: (☎ 01 44 30 47 00, fax 01 45 25 87

50, e italconsulparigi@mailcity.com) 5 blvd Emile Augier, 75116 Paris

Germany
Embassy: (☎ 030-25 44 00, fax 25 44 01 69, e ambitalia.segr@t-online.de) Dessauer-strasse 28/29, 10963 Berlin
Consulate: (☎ 069-7 53 10, fax 7 53 11 43, e italia.consolato.francoforte@t-online.de) Beethovenstrasse 17, 60325 Frankfurt-am-Main

Ireland
Embassy: (☎ 01-660 1744, fax 668 2759, e italianembassy@eircom.net) 63–65 Northumberland Rd, Dublin 4

Netherlands
Embassy: (☎ 070-302 1030, fax 361 4932, e italemb@worldonline.nl) Alexanderstraat 12, 2514 JL The Hague
Consulate: (☎ 020-550 2050, fax 626 2444, e consital@euronet.nl) Herengracht 581, 1017 CD Amsterdam

New Zealand
Embassy: (☎ 04-473 5339, fax 472 7255, e ambwell@xtra.co.nz) 34 Grant Rd, Thorndon, Wellington

Spain
Embassy: (☎ 91 423 3300, fax 575 7776, e segreamb@ambitaliamadrid.org) Calle Lagasca 98, Madrid 28006

Switzerland
Embassy: (☎ 031-350 0777, fax 350 0711, e ambital.berna@spectraweb.ch) Elfenstrasse 14, 3000 Bern 16
Consulate: (☎ 022-839 6744, fax 839 6745, e consulate.italy@ties.itu.int) 14 rue Charles Galland, Geneva 1206

UK
Embassy: (☎ 020-7312 2200, fax 7312 2230, e emblondon@embitaly.org.uk) 14 Three Kings Yard, London W1Y 4EH
Consulate: (☎ 020-7235 9371, fax 7823 1609) 38 Eaton Place, London SW1X 8AN

USA
Embassy: (☎ 202-612 4400, fax 518 2154) 3000 Whitehaven St NW, Washington, DC 20008
Consulate: (☎ 310-826 6207, fax 820 0727, e cglos@conlang.com) Suite 300, 12400 Wilshire Blvd, Los Angeles, CA 90025
Consulate: (☎ 212-7737 9100, fax 249 4945, e italconsulnyc@italconsulnyc.org) 690 Park Ave, New York, NY 10021

Embassies in Rome

Most countries have an embassy in Rome, and several also maintain consulates in Palermo (see the following section). Passport enquiries should be addressed to the Rome-based offices:

Australia (☎ 06 85 27 21) Via Alessandria 215, 00198
Canada (☎ 06 44 59 81) Via Zara 30, 00198
France (☎ 06 68 60 11) Piazza Farnese 67, 00186
Germany (☎ 06 49 21 31) Via San Martino della Battaglia 4, 00185
Ireland (☎ 06 697 91 21) Piazza Campitelli 3, 00186
Netherlands (☎ 06 322 11 41) Via Michele Mercati 8, 00197
New Zealand (☎ 06 441 71 71) Via Zara 28, 00198
Spain (☎ 06 87 26 84) Largo Fontanella Borghese 19, 00186
Switzerland (☎ 06 80 95 71) Via Barnarba Oriani 61, 00197
UK (☎ 06 422 00 001) Via XX Settembre 80a, 00187
USA (☎ 06 4 67 41) Via Veneto 119a, 00187

Consulates in Palermo

It may be handier for some to go to a consulate in Palermo. Office hours are 9am to 12.30pm and 2.30pm to 3.30pm Monday to Friday. Offices include:

France (☎ 091 58 50 73) Via Segesta 9, 90139
Germany (☎ 091 625 46 60) Viale Scaduto 2d, 90144
Malta (☎ 091 33 33 33) Via Principe Belmonte 55, 90139
Netherlands (☎ 091 58 15 21) Via Roma 489, 90139
Tunisia (☎ 091 32 12 31) Piazza Ignazio Florio 2, 90144
UK (☎ 091 58 25 33, fax 091 58 42 40) S Tagiavia & Co, Via Cavour 121, 90133
USA (☎ 091 611 00 20) Via Re Federico 18b, 90141

CUSTOMS

On 1 July 1999, duty-free sales within the EU were abolished. Under the rules of the single market, goods bought in and exported within the EU incur no additional taxes, provided duty has been paid somewhere within the EU and the goods are for personal consumption.

Travellers entering Italy from outside the EU are allowed to bring in duty free: 200

cigarettes, 1L of spirits, 2L of wine, 60mls of perfume, 250mls of toilet water, and other goods up to a total value of €175. Anything over this limit must be declared on arrival and the appropriate duty paid (it is advisable to carry all your receipts with you).

MONEY

A combination of travellers cheques and credit/cash cards is the best way to take your money.

Currency

On 1 January 2002, the euro became the currency of cash transactions in all of Italy and throughout the EU (except for the three foot-draggers: Denmark, Sweden and the UK). Until 1 March, both the lira (L) and the euro (€) were legal tender in Italy as all over the country the old currency was traded in for the new. Some people even had problems changing their L50,000 or L100,000 notes as a mass of old counterfeit notes was circulated Italy-wide so as not to let them go to waste!

The euro is divided into 100 cents. Coin denominations are one, two, five, 10, 20 and 50 cents, €1 and €2. The notes are €5, €10, €20, €50, €100, €200 and €500.

All euro coins across the EU are identical on the side showing their value, but there are 12 different obverses, each representing one of the 12 euro-zone countries. All euro notes of each denomination are identical on both sides. All euro coins and notes are legal tender throughout the euro zone. You don't need to change money at all when travelling to other single-currency members and prices in the member states are immediately comparable. And even EU countries not participating in the single currency may price goods in euros and accept euros over shop counters.

For more information on the euro check out the Web site w www.europa.eu.int/euro. A good Web site for exchange rates is at w www.oanda.com.

Like other continental Europeans, Italians indicate decimals with commas and thousands with points.

Prices Quoted

This book was researched during the transition period, when not all prices were available in euros. Prices quoted (for example, by hotels, restaurants and entertainment venues) in the national currency have been converted to euros at the fixed conversion rate (€1 is equal to 1936.27L). These may undergo further change.

Exchange Rates

country	unit		(€)
Australia	A$1	=	0.605
Canada	C$1	=	0.714
Japan	¥100	=	0.855
New Zealand	NZ$1	=	0.500
UK	£1	=	1.630
USA	US$1	=	1.135

Exchanging Money

You can exchange money in banks, at post offices or in currency exchange booths (a bureau de change or *cambio*). Banks are generally the most reliable and tend to offer the best rates. However, you should look around and ask about commissions. These can fluctuate considerably and a lot depends on whether you are changing cash or cheques. While post offices charge a flat rate of €0.52 per cash transaction, banks charge €1.29 or even more. Travellers cheques attract higher fees. Some banks charge a small fee per cheque while post offices charges a maximum €2.60 per transaction. Currency exchange booths often advertise 'no commission' but the rate of exchange is usually inferior to that of banks.

Cash Don't bring wads of cash from home (travellers cheques and plastic are much safer). Bag snatchers and pickpockets – a problem in Sicily's more crowded areas – prey on cash-flashing tourists, so your best bet is never to carry more than you need for a day or two. It is, however, an idea to keep an emergency stash separate from other valuables in case you should lose your travellers cheques and credit cards. You will need cash for many day-to-day transactions (many small guesthouses, eateries and shops do not take credit cards and cash is a necessity at markets).

Travellers Cheques These are a safe way to carry your money because they can be replaced if lost or stolen. They can be cashed at most banks and exchange offices. American Express and Thomas Cook are widely accepted brands. If you lose your American Express cheques, you can report your loss by phoning a 24-hour toll-free number (☎ 800 87 20 00) from anywhere in Italy.

Buying cheques in a different currency (such as US dollars if you are not coming from the USA) means you pay commission when you buy the cheques and again when cashing them in Sicily.

It's vital to keep your initial receipt, a record of your cheque numbers and the ones you have used, separate from the cheques themselves. Take your passport when you go to cash travellers cheques.

Credit/Debit Cards Carrying plastic is the simplest way to organise your holiday funds. You don't have large amounts of cash or cheques to lose, you can get money after hours and at weekends, and the exchange rate is sometimes better than that offered by travellers cheques or cash exchanges. By arranging for payments to be made into your card account while you are travelling, you can avoid paying interest.

Major cards, such as Visa, MasterCard, Eurocard, Cirrus and Eurocheque, are accepted throughout Sicily. They can be used for many purchases (including in some supermarkets) and in hotels and restaurants. Credit cards can also be used in ATMs displaying the appropriate sign or (if you have no PIN number) to obtain cash advances over the counter in many banks – Visa and MasterCard are among the most widely recognised for such transactions. Check charges with your bank but, as a rule, there is no charge for purchases on major cards and a minimum charge on cash advances and ATM transactions in foreign currencies. For larger withdrawals this charge rarely exceeds 1.5%.

It is not uncommon for ATMs in Sicily to reject foreign cards. Don't despair or start wasting money on international calls to your bank. Try a few more ATMs displaying your card's logo before assuming the problem lies with your card rather than with the local system.

If your credit card is lost, stolen or swallowed by an ATM, you can telephone toll-free to have an immediate stop put on its use. For MasterCard the number in Italy is ☎ 800 87 08 66; for Visa, phone ☎ 800 81 90 14.

American Express is also widely accepted (though not as commonly as Visa or MasterCard). There is no full-service office in Sicily as American Express is represented by a number of travel agents throughout the island. If you lose your American Express card you can call ☎ 800 86 40 46 in Sicily or contact the office in Rome on ☎ 06 7 22 82, which runs a 24-hour cardholders service.

International Transfers One reliable way to send money to Sicily is by 'urgent telex' through the foreign office of a large Italian bank, or through major banks in your own country, to a nominated bank in Sicily. It is important to have an exact record of all details associated with the money transfer. The money will always be held at the head office of the bank in the town to which it has been sent. Urgent telex transfers should only take a few days, while other means, such as telegraphic transfer or draft, can take weeks. It is also possible to transfer money through American Express and Thomas Cook.

A speedier option is to send money through Western Union (☎ toll-free 800 46 44 64 or 800 22 00 55, Ⓦ www.western union.com). The sender and receiver have to turn up at a Western Union outlet with passport or other form of ID and the fees charged for the virtually immediate transfer depend on the amount sent. For US$400, Western Union charges the sender US$34 from the US, with different fees from other countries; the money can supposedly be handed over to the recipient within 10 minutes of being sent. This service functions through many outlets in Sicily, including Incontri Internazionali, at Piazza Castelnuovo 35 and at

Maccorp Italiana Forexchange, both at Stazione Centrale in Palermo and Falcone-Borsellino airport (☎ toll-free 800 60 16 22 for both).

Another service along the same lines is MoneyGram, which operates mainly through Thomas Cook. Like Western Union they are expanding their network of agents.

Security

Keep only a limited amount of your money as cash and the bulk in more easily replaceable forms, such as travellers cheques or plastic. If your accommodation has a safe, you may feel more secure using it. If you have to leave money in your room, divide it into several stashes and hide them in different places.

For carrying money on the street, the safest thing is a shoulder wallet or under-the-clothes moneybelt. An external money-belt attracts rather than deflects attention from your valuables.

Costs

Sicily isn't as cheap as many travellers assume but it is one of the few destinations in Italy where the budget-minded can have a relatively comfortable time. You should bear in mind that Sicily is essentially a warm-weather destination and a key factor to consider is the often wild difference in costs between the major holidays and summer months (usually Easter and from May to September, with the highest prices in August) and the rest of the year. Even the most popular tourist resorts, such as Cefalù, the Aeolian Islands and Taormina drop their prices dramatically out of season; in effect the sunshine can often double your costs.

The less-visited areas of the island – the west and parts of the interior – generally offer cheaper accommodation and eating options; even prices in supermarkets are lower than in the tourist meccas. Admission fees to all the major archaeological sites and museums run by the Regione Sicilia are set at the same price, which at the time of research was either €2.05 or €4.15. Most offer a discount to students, OAPs and children.

A very prudent backpacker might scrape by on €30 per day but only by staying in youth hostels or camp sites, eating one simple meal per day, buying a sandwich or a pizza slice for lunch, travelling slowly to keep transport costs down and minimising visits to museums and galleries.

One rung up, you can get by on €50 per day if you stay in the cheaper guesthouses or small hotels and keep sit-down meals and museum visits to one a day. Lone travellers may find even this budget hard to maintain.

If money is no object, you'll find plenty of ways to get rid of it, especially in the cities and resorts where there's no shortage of luxury hotels, expensive restaurants and shops to wave wads at. Realistically, a traveller wanting to stay in comfortable lower-to mid-range hotels, eat two square meals per day, not feel restricted to one museum per day and be able to enjoy the odd drink and other minor indulgences should reckon on a minimum daily average of €90 (more if you have a car).

Ways to Save If you could, it would be nice to avoid paying the extra charged by many guesthouses for compulsory breakfast – a coffee and brioche in a cafe cost less and taste better. The sad reality is that many places only offer one price on rooms and that includes breakfast.

In bars, prices can double (sometimes even triple) if you sit down and are served at the table. Stand at the bar to drink your coffee or eat a sandwich.

Read the fine print on menus (usually posted outside eating establishments) to check the cover charge *(coperto)* and service fee *(servizio)*, which can be as high as 20% in some of the more touristy places.

Tipping & Bargaining

You are not expected to tip on top of restaurant service charges but it is common to leave a small amount. If there is no service charge, the customer might consider leaving a 10% tip, but this is by no means obligatory. In bars, Sicilians usually leave small change as a tip often as little as €0.05 or €0.10. Tipping taxi drivers is not common practice but you should tip the porter at higher-class hotels.

Bargaining or haggling is less common-place than it once was but it still goes on at Sicilian markets and is considered quite an art form. Most traders and stallholders work on the premise that the foreign tourist always has more money than the local, so if they spot you for an outsider (and they will!) you'll have a harder time of it than if you were a local. Never accept the first price quoted and counter-offer with half the amount. Don't be deterred by stallholders who dismiss you with a wave of the arm: the person at the next stall may well accept your offer after a brief (and obligatory) haggle. While bargaining in shops is not acceptable, you might find that the proprietor is disposed to give a discount if you are spending a reasonable amount of money.

It is quite acceptable (and advisable) to ask if there is a special price for a room in a guesthouse if you plan to stay for more than a few days.

Taxes & Refunds

A value-added tax (known as Imposta di Valore Aggiunto or IVA) of around 19% is slapped onto just about everything in Sicily. Tourists who are residents of countries outside the EU may claim a refund on this tax if the item was purchased for personal use and costs more than a certain amount (€154.94 in 2002). The goods must be carried with you and you must keep the fiscal receipt.

The refund only applies to items purchased at retail outlets affiliated to the system – these shops display a 'Tax-free for Tourists' sign. Otherwise, ask the shopkeeper. You must fill out a form at the point of purchase and have the form stamped and checked by Italian customs when you leave the country. You then return it by mail within 60 days to the vendor, who will make the refund, either by cheque or to your credit card. At major airports and some border crossings you can get an immediate cash refund or have your credit card credited at specially marked booths.

For more information call Global Refund Italia (☎ 0331 28 35 55, W www.global refund.com) or consult the rules brochure available in affiliated stores.

Receipts

Laws aimed at tightening controls on the payment of taxes in Italy mean that the onus is on the buyer to ask for and retain receipts for all goods and services. This applies to everything from a coffee to a haircut. Although it rarely happens, you could be asked by an officer of the fiscal police (guardia di finanza) to produce the receipt immediately after you leave a shop. If you don't have it, you may be obliged to pay a fine of up to €155. Generally, whoever is working the cash register will hand one over to you automatically.

POST & COMMUNICATIONS

Sicily's postal service is notoriously slow, unreliable and expensive. Stories abound of sacks of mail found dumped in rivers when post office workers couldn't be bothered dealing with them.

Stamps (francobolli) are available at post offices and authorised tobacconists (look for the official tabacchi sign, a big 'T', often white on black).

Main post offices in the bigger cities are generally open from around 8am to at least 5pm. Many open on Saturday mornings too. Tobacconists keep regular shop hours (see Business Hours later in this chapter for details).

Postal Rates

Postcards and letters up to 20g sent airmail (via aerea) cost €0.77 to Australia, New Zealand, the US, Africa, and Asia, and €0.62 to Europe. Aerograms are a cheap alternative; they can be purchased at post offices only.

Priority post (posta prioritaria) charges €0.62 for postcards and letters weighing up to 20g posted to destinations within Italy, the EU, Switzerland and Norway, which are supposed to arrive the following day. The cost increases to €8.06 for European mail weighing up to 2kg, €16.53 for Africa, Asia and the US, and €20.66 for Australia.

If you want to post more important items by registered mail (raccomandato) or by insured mail (assicurato), remember that they will take as long as normal mail. Registered mail costs €2.58 on top of the normal cost of the letter. The cost of insured mail depends on the value of the object being sent (€3.11 for objects up to €51.65 value) and is not available to the USA.

Sending Mail

If you choose not to use priority post (see the previous section), an airmail letter can take up to two weeks to reach the UK or the USA, while a letter to Australia will often take between two and three weeks.

The service within Sicily is not much better: local letters take at least three days to arrive and intercity letters take up to a week.

Parcels *(pacchetti)* can be sent from any post office. You can buy posting boxes or padded envelopes from some post offices. Stationery shops *(cartolerie)* and some tobacconists also sell padded envelopes. Don't tape up or staple envelopes – they should be sealed with glue (it's one of those old Italian rules). Your best bet is not to close the envelope or box completely and ask at the counter how it should be done. Parcels usually take longer to be delivered than letters and a different set of postal rates applies.

Express Mail Urgent mail (maximum 20kg for international destinations) can be sent by the post office's express mail service, known as *posta celere*. Letters up to 500g cost €15.49 within Europe, €23.76 to the USA and Canada and €35.12 to Australia. A parcel weighing 1kg will cost €17.56 within Europe, €27.89 to the USA and Canada, and €41.32 to Australia and New Zealand. Posta celere is not necessarily as fast as private services. It will take two to five days for a parcel to reach the USA, Canada or Australia and one to three days to European destinations.

Couriers Several international couriers operate in Sicily: DHL (☎ 199 19 93 45 Italywide or 091 58 87 22 in Palermo, W www .dhl.it) in Palermo is based at Agenzia Silvestri, Via Volta 44. Note that if you are having articles sent to you by courier in Sicily, you might be obliged to pay IVA of up to 20% to retrieve the goods.

Receiving Mail

Poste restante is known as *fermo posta*. Letters marked thus will be held at the counter of the same name in the main post office in the relevant town. Poste restante mail should be addressed as follows:

John SMITH
Fermo Posta
Posta Centrale
90100 Palermo
Italy

You need to pick up your letters in person and present your passport as ID.

American Express card or travellers-cheque holders can use the free client mail-holding service at American Express offices. Take your passport when picking up mail.

Telephone

The partly privatised Telecom Italia is the largest phone company in the country and its orange public pay phones are liberally scattered all over the place. The most common accept only telephone cards *(carte/ schede telefoniche)*, although you will still find some that accept both cards and coins. Some card phones now also accept special Telecom credit cards and even commercial credit cards.

Phones can be found in the streets, train stations and some big stores as well as in unstaffed Telecom centres, a few of which also have telephone directories for other parts of the country.

You can buy phonecards at post offices, tobacconists, newsstands and from vending machines in Telecom offices. To avoid the frustration of trying to find fast-disappearing coin telephones, always keep a phonecard on hand. They come with a value of around €2.50 to €7.75. Remember to snap off the perforated corner before using them.

Public phones operated by a new telecommunications company, Infostrada, can be found in airports and train stations. These phones accept Infostrada phonecards (available from post offices, tobacconists and newsstands), which have similar values to Telecom Italia's phonecards. Infostrada's rates are slightly cheaper than Telecom's for long-distance and international calls but you cannot make local calls from these phones.

Costs Rates, particularly for long-distance calls, are among the highest in Europe. A local call *(comunicazione urbana)* from a public phone will cost €0.10 for three to six minutes, depending on the time of day you call. Rates for long-distance calls *(comunicazione interurbana)* within Sicily depend on the time of day and the distance involved. At the worst, one minute will cost about €0.18 in peak periods. The peak time for domestic calls is 8am to 6.30pm Monday to Friday and from 8am to 1pm Saturday. Cheap rates apply 6.30pm to 8am Monday to Friday, on Saturday afternoon and on Sunday and public holidays.

For international calls, different times apply. Cheap rates to the UK apply from 10pm to 8am Monday to Saturday and all day Sunday, to the US and Canada from 7pm to 2pm Monday to Friday and all day Saturday and Sunday, and to Australia from 11pm to 8am Monday to Saturday and all day Sunday.

If you need to call overseas, beware of the cost. Even a call of five minutes to Australia after 10pm will cost around €5.15 from a private phone (more from a public phone). Calls to most of the rest of Europe (except the UK, which is cheaper) cost €0.64 for the first minute and €0.41 thereafter (it's closer to €0.61 from a public phone).

Domestic Calls Since July 1998 area codes have become an integral part of the telephone number. The codes all begin with 0 and consist of up to four digits. You must now dial this whole number, even if calling from next door. For example, any number you call in the Palermo area will begin with 091.

Toll-free numbers *(numeri verdi)* all begin with the prefix 800. The prefix 848 indicates a national number charged at a local rate.

Mobile-telephone numbers begin with a four-digit prefix, such as 0330, 0335 or 0347.

For directory enquiries, dial ☎ 12.

International Calls Direct international calls are easily made from public telephones by using a phonecard. Dial 00 to get out of Sicily, then the relevant country and city codes, followed by the telephone number.

Useful country codes are: Australia ☎ 61, Canada and the USA ☎ 1, France ☎ 33, Germany ☎ 49, Greece ☎ 30, Ireland ☎ 353, New Zealand ☎ 64, Spain ☎ 34 and the UK ☎ 44. Other codes are listed in Italian telephone books.

To make a reverse-charge (collect) international call from a public telephone, dial ☎ 170.

It is easier, and often cheaper, to use the Country Direct service in your country. You dial the number and request a reverse-charge call through the operator in your country. Numbers for this service include:

Australia (Optus)	☎ 172 11 61
Australia (Telstra)	☎ 172 10 61
Canada (AT&T)	☎ 172 10 02
Canada (Teleglobe)	☎ 172 10 01
France	☎ 172 00 33
Germany	☎ 172 00 49
Ireland	☎ 172 03 53
Netherlands	☎ 172 00 31
New Zealand	☎ 172 10 64
UK (BT)	☎ 172 00 44
UK (BT Automatic)	☎ 172 01 44
USA (AT&T)	☎ 172 10 11
USA (IDB)	☎ 172 17 77
USA (MCI)	☎ 172 10 22
USA (Sprint)	☎ 172 18 77

For international directory enquiries, call ☎ 176.

eKno Communication Service Lonely Planet's eKno global communication service provides low-cost international calls (local calls, you're usually better off with a local phonecard). eKno also offers free messaging services, email, travel information and an online travel vault, where you can securely store all your important documents. You can join online at Ⓦ www.ekno.lonelyplanet .com, where you will find the local-access numbers for the 24-hour customer-service centre. Once you have joined, always check

Taking Your Mobile Phone

Italy uses GSM 900/1800, which is compatible with the rest of Europe and Australia but not with North American GSM 1900 or the totally different system in Japan (although some North American GSM 1900/900 phones do work here). If you have a GSM phone, check with your service provider about using it in Sicily and beware of calls being routed internationally (very expensive for a 'local' call). The alternative is to link up with a local service provider.

the eKno Web site for the latest access numbers for each country and updates on new features.

Calling Sicily from Abroad Dial the international access code (00 in most countries), followed by the code for Italy (39) and the full number including the initial zero (for example – 00 39 091 555 55 55). If calling a mobile phone, you must drop the initial 0.

Telegram

These dinosaurs can be sent from post offices or dictated by phone (☎ 186) and are an expensive, but sure, way of having important messages delivered by the same or next day.

Fax

There is no shortage of fax offices in Sicily's cities and larger towns but the country's high telephone charges make it an expensive mode of communication. Some offices charge per page and others charge per minute, and still others charge for both! In all cases, prices vary considerably from one office to another. However, in general, to send a fax within Sicily you can expect to pay €2.60 for the first page and €1 for each page thereafter, or about €1.60 for the first minute and €1 for subsequent minutes. International faxes can cost from €4.20 for the first page and €2.60 per page thereafter, depending on the destination. Faxes can also be sent from some Telecom public phones. It usually costs at least €1 per page to receive a fax.

Email & Internet Access

Travelling with a portable computer is a great way to stay in touch with life back home but unless you know what you're doing it's fraught with potential problems. If you plan to carry your notebook or palmtop computer with you, remember that the power supply voltage in the countries you visit may vary from that at home, risking damage to your equipment. The best investment is a universal AC adapter for your appliance, which will enable you to plug it in anywhere without frying the innards. You'll also need a plug adapter for each country you visit – often it's easiest to buy these before you leave home.

Also, your PC-card modem may or may not work once you leave your home country – and you won't know for sure until you try. The safest option is to buy a reputable 'global' modem before you leave home or buy a local PC-card modem if you're spending an extended time in any one country. Keep in mind that the telephone socket in each country you visit will probably be different from the one at home so ensure that you have at least a US RJ-11 telephone adapter that works with your modem. You can almost always find an adapter that will convert from RJ-11 to the local variety. For more information on travelling with a portable computer, see Ⓦ www.teleadapt.com or Ⓦ www.warrior.com.

Major Internet service providers have dial-in nodes throughout Europe; it's best to download a list of the dial-in numbers before you leave home. If you access your Internet email account at home through a smaller ISP or your office or school network, your best option is either to open account with a global ISP or to rely on cybercafes and other public access points to collect your mail.

If you do intend to rely on cybercafes, you'll need to carry three pieces of information with you to enable you to access your Internet mail account: your incoming (POP or IMAP) mail server name, your account name and your password. Your ISP or network supervisor will be able to give you these. Armed with this information, you should be able to access your Internet mail account from any net-connected machine in the world, provided it runs some kind of email software (remember that Netscape and Internet Explorer both have mail modules). It pays to become familiar with the process for doing this before you leave home.

You'll find cybercafes throughout Europe: check out W www.netcafeguide.com for an up-to-date list. New cybercafes are opening all the time in Sicily (particularly in the well-visited spots; ask at the local tourist office for details) and, if there isn't a cafe, you can often find a business with a computer that offers Internet access. You can expect to pay about €5.15 an hour at a cybercafe.

DIGITAL RESOURCES

The World Wide Web is a rich resource for travellers. You can research your trip, hunt down bargain air fares, book hotels, check on weather conditions or chat with locals and other travellers about the best places to visit (or avoid!).

One of the best places to start your Web explorations is the Lonely Planet Web site at W www.lonelyplanet.com. Other sites you might like to surf include:

Best of Sicily (W www.bestofsicily.com – English) This detailed site has loads of useful links and tips for travelling throughout Sicily.
CTS Village (W www.cts.it – mostly Italian) This site provides useful information from CTS, Italy's leading student travel organisation.
Ferrovie dello Stato (W www.fs-on-line.com or W www.trenitalia.it – both multilingual) This is the official site of the Italian railways. You can look up fare and timetable information here, although it can be a little complicated to plough through.
Parks.it (W www.parks.it – multilingual) This is the place to look for basic information on all of Sicily's national and regional parks, along with any other protected areas.

BOOKS

Over the centuries Sicily has been a source of endless fascination to a stream of foreign visitors, who have come to soak up the beauty and express an opinion. Some of these are little more than uninformed,

prejudiced twaddle, but those who have taken the time to delve a little deeper have left us with some penetrating insights that are worth checking out, if only to aid your own interpretations. The Mafia is a red-hot subject that has spawned a thousand and one books, most of which are a thinly veiled attempt to get to the summit of the best-seller list, but there are a few that offer well-considered, informative and thoughtful analyses of a highly complex issue.

Most books are published in different editions by different publishers in different countries. Your local bookshop or library is best placed to advise you on the availability of the following recommendations.

Lonely Planet

Travellers planning to move around more widely should consider Lonely Planet's *Italy*. The *Italian phrasebook* lists all the words and phrases you're likely to need on your travels. *World Food Italy* is a full-colour book containing information on the whole range of Italian food and drink, including Sicilian cuisine and a useful language section with the definitive culinary dictionary.

Guidebooks

The ultimate guide is the red hardback 1004-page *Sicily* (€46.50), published in English and Italian by the Touring Club Italiano (TCI; W www.touringclub.it). There are also the small red guides *Agrigento & Siracusa* and *Palermo, Monreale, Cefalù* (both €20.70). The TCI also puts out a green soft-cover series divided by regions and provinces; look out for *Sicilia* (Italian; €18.10) and *Siracusa e Provincia* (Italian; €13). So far Syracuse is the only provincial guide for Sicily. In English, you can buy TCI's *Sicily* for €20.15.

Travel

The grand touring classic is Johann Wolfgang von Goethe's *Italienische Reise* (Italian Journey, 1786–88), with a substantial section on Sicily. Another interesting travel book is *A Traveller in Southern Italy* by HV Morton. Though written in the 1960s – Sicily has changed enormously since then – it remains a valuable guide to the island and its people.

The narrative of Vincent Cronin's *The Golden Honeycomb* (1959) is organised as a trip in search of Daedalus's legendary golden honeycomb but is actually an account of a sojourn in Sicily in the 1950s. Again it may seem out of date but the insight into the ways and attitudes of the Sicilians, especially in the interior, is still relevant today.

Sicily (1973) by Russell King, part of the *Islands* series, is well-written and contains informed chapters on all of Sicily's high- and low-lights, including architecture, ancient history and the Mafia.

Sicily: An Archaeological Guide (1977) by Margaret Guido is an in-depth guide to the island's network of prehistoric and classical sites. Be aware that it hasn't been revised since the late 1970s so all practical information is out of date, and unfortunately, it's out of print.

A great read about some of the island's towns and cities (although not strictly a travel guide) is Mary Taylor Simeti's *On Persephone's Island* (1986), which looks at the festivals, events and agriculture of the four seasons and makes considered observations (from a US expat perspective) on Sicilian culture and social mores.

History & Politics

Giuliano Procacci's *History of the Italian People* (1970) and Paul Ginsborg's *A History of Contemporary Italy* (1990) are absorbing and very well-written books with good sections on Sicily. *The Italians* (1968) by Luigi Barzini is an undisputed classic on the history and traditions of the Italian people, with an excellent chapter on Sicily and the Mafia. In *Frederick II: A Medieval Emperor* (1988), David Abulafia delves into the life and times of the greatest of the Hohenstaufen rulers of Sicily and finds that he did have chinks in his formidable armour. John Julius Norwich's *The Normans in Sicily* (1992; includes an earlier title, *Kingdom in the Sun*) is a fascinating, detailed account of the Norman takeover of the island. *The Sicilian Vespers* (1992) by Steven Runciman is the best book on the popular 13th-century uprising against the French Angevin dynasty.

The Mafia

Norman Lewis's *The Honoured Society* (1984) is a good introduction to the subject, even though his lack of confirmed sources makes the book a little dated. The best book on the subject is Gian Carlo Caselli's *A True History of Italy* which, with almost surgical precision, chronicles the rise of the Mafia and its nefarious influence on the apparatus of state. The author was one of Sicily's leading anti-Mafia magistrates and his book benefits from some extraordinary testimony by recalcitrant mobsters. *Men of Honour* (1993) by Giovanni Falcone is in a similar vein and is an essential read for anyone looking to understand the state of the Mafia today. Falcone, a top anti-Mafia prosecutor, paid for his knowledge with his life. A fascinating book about the work and untimely deaths of Falcone and Paolo Borsellino, an anti-Mafia judge, is Alexander Stille's *Excellent Cadavers* (1995).

Peter Robb's *Midnight in Sicily* (1998) is a well-written and immensely enjoyable treatise on the four pillars of Sicilian society: art, culture, food and the Mafia. Renate Siebert's *Secrets of Life and Death: Women and the Mafia* (1996) has been translated by Liz Heron and provides first-hand accounts of the role of women within this patriarchal structure.

Art & Architecture

Anthony Blunt's classic *The Sicilian Baroque* (1968) is the key read on the subject, containing a detailed and precise history of the style as well as illustrations and black-and-white photos of buildings and churches. The book is out of print in the US but you might find it in the public library.

Palazzi of Sicily (1998) by Angheli Zalapi, with photographs by Melo Minnella, is a look at the magnificent palaces still standing in Sicily and is particularly interesting for visitors to Palermo.

FILMS

Sicily has been the subject of a number of great Italian films, including Luchino Visconti's *La Terra Trema* (The Earth Trembles; 1948), which is a brilliant adaptation of

Giovanni Verga's *I Malavoglia*, and the wonderful *Il Gattopardo* (The Leopard; 1963), Visconti's take on Lampedusa's novel of the same name.

The Taviani brothers, Paolo (born 1931) and Vittorio (born 1929) brought Sicily to life in *Kaos* (1984), which was based on several of Luigi Pirandello's short stories. Nanni Moretti (born 1953), who first came to the silver screen in the late 1970s, has proven to be a highly individualistic actor-director. His *Caro Diario* (Dear Diary), a whimsical, self-indulgent, autobiographical three-part film largely set on the Aeolian Islands, won the prize for best feature film at Cannes in 1994.

Il Postino (The Postman; 1995), starring Massimo Troisi, was one of the most striking Italian films of the 1990s. It tells the story of a shy village postman on the island of Salina who comes in contact with the great Chilean poet Pablo Neruda, a meeting that opens the postman's heart to the beauty of poetry.

Of all the films with a link to Sicily, easily the best known is Francis Ford Coppola's epic trilogy *The Godfather*, based on Mario Puzo's bestseller of the same name. Excellent performances by a host of actors, among them Al Pacino, Marlon Brando, James Caan, Robert Duvall and Talia Shire, were awarded with a heap of Oscars, including two for Best Film (for the first two pictures). This largely romanticised tale of the rise to power of a New York Mafia crime family from its humble origins in the Sicilian town of Corleone is worth watching because it's an expertly crafted story but it will teach you very little about the Mafia itself. A chunk of each instalment is set in Sicily, including the famous wedding scene from the first film (set in Savoca on the eastern coast) and the opera scene from the third film (set in Palermo's Teatro Massimo).

Roberto Rossellini's *Stromboli* (1950, also known as *Stromboli, La Terra di Dio*) was filmed on the eponymous island and tells the story of Karen (played by Ingrid Bergman), a young refugee from a POW camp who marries a local fisherman (Mario Vitale) to escape imprisonment. The film's drama – a good example of the Italian neorealist school

of cinema – is played out against the ever-present threat of the volcano.

Woody Allen's *Mighty Aphrodite* (1995) is set in New York and has nothing to do with Sicily, but the scenes of the Greek chorus were shot in Taormina's Greek theatre.

A recent film, based on real events, is *I Cento Passi* (One Hundred Steps; 1999), which tells the story of Giuseppe Impastato, who established a pirate radio station in Cinisi in the 1970s, using it to broadcast diatribes against the corruption and dominance of Gaetano Badalamenti's Mafia clan in the area. Impastato was murdered in 1979; Badalamenti was imprisoned in the US in 1987 for his involvement with the US Mafia. In the film, Impastato is played by Palermo-born actor Luigi Lo Cascio, who won the Best Actor award at the 2001 Venice Film Festival for his role in *Luce dei Miei Occhi* (Light of My Eyes).

Lonely Planet produces the video *Corsica, Sicily & Sardinia*.

NEWSPAPERS & MAGAZINES

It can be difficult to find a selection of national daily newspapers from around Europe in Sicily. In larger tourist resorts you can usually pick up the *International Herald Tribune* and either the *Guardian* or the *Independent*, both at least one day old. In Taormina and Lìpari during the high season, a wider selection is usually available, including French and German magazines and newspapers.

The only Sicilian daily is *Il Giornale di Sicilia* (€1.30), which is sold everywhere. It is uncompromisingly tough on corruption and political scandals (an almost daily occurrence), and has a good (if limited) section on international news and a terrific listings page with details of all cinemas, theatres, festivals and other events. It is published in provincial editions.

So-called 'national' papers – actually important dailies published out of three major Italian cities – are also sold throughout Sicily. These include Milan's *Corriere della Sera* (€1.20), Turin's *La Stampa* and Rome's

[continued on page 70]

DALLAS STRIBLEY

DALLAS STRIBLEY

BETHUNE CARMICHAEL

ALAN BENSON

DALLAS STRIBLEY

Enough to make your mouth water: Sicily is renowned for its spicy cooking, tasty fish, delicious baking and luscious fresh vegetables.

DAMIEN SIMONIS

ALAN BENSON

ALAN BENSON

Slippery eels, *spaghetti alle vongole* and cold meats are some of the delicacies that may or may not tempt you!

DINING *ALLA SICILIANA*

Sicily is recognised throughout Italy for the high quality of its cuisine, which has evolved over 25 centuries of foreign occupation and influence. In a country where preparing even the simplest meal is treated as an art form and each region proudly proclaims its superiority over the others, Sicilian cuisine is granted a seat at the table of honour. As you would expect from an island, the emphasis is on fish – and in Sicily you will find the day's catch in virtually everything you see on a menu – but the meat options should not be ignored either. Their greatest achievement is the incredible variety of imaginatively created cakes and pastries: an ideal way to top off any meal.

The secret of Sicilian cuisine lies in the island's climate and history. Due to the warm weather, vegetables grow pretty much year round and they are usually fresher, juicier and more abundant than those grown in the seasonal climates up north – eat a Sicilian tomato and you'll notice the difference. You will also notice that the cooking is spicier than elsewhere in Italy: this is a legacy of the Arabs, who – more than any other foreign occupier – left their stamp on the Sicilian kitchen, particularly in the west, where a popular substitute for pasta dishes is couscous (a fish-based version, rather than the more common meat-based North African variety). Other cultures have also played their part: the Greeks introduced the olive and the vine, the Romans turned the island over to the wholesale planting of wheat, and Spanish rule saw an imaginative and varied approach to the preparation of fish.

Recommended further reading includes Lonely Planet's full-colour *World Food Italy*, which incorporates information on the cuisine of Sicily. For assistance deciphering the menu turn to the food glossary in the Language chapter later in this book.

For details of cooking courses see Cooking Tours under Organised Tours in the Getting There & Away chapter.

Antipasti

Sicilians aren't big on *antipasti* (literally 'before pasta'), or hors d'oeuvres, but in recent decades they have started making an appearance on the Sicilian table. In Palermo, the most common dish is *panelle*, chickpea fritters cooked in olive oil and flavoured with parsley. In the east a popular titbit is *olive fritte*, olives fried in olive oil, crushed garlic, vinegar and marjoram. The Spanish introduced the white bean to the island (appositely called *fagioli Spagnoli* here), which you will find boiled and flavoured with garlic, celery and chunks of mint leaves *(fagioli alla menta)*. Another popular dish is *caponata*, which can consist of a number of ingredients but seems to always include tomatoes, aubergines, olives and anchovies. The taste is best described as 'sweet and sour' and recipes are zealously guarded, with every Sicilian sure that only their mother makes the best caponata.

Pasta

Not surprisingly, many of the island's pasta dishes lean heavily on the use of fish and vegetables. The simplest of all pasta dishes – available on virtually every menu on the island – is *pasta a picchi pacchiu*, the Sicilian version of pasta with tomato and chilli sauce. Sicilian tomatoes are renowned through-out Italy for their rich, fulsome flavour and it is unlikely you'll eat a better version of the dish anywhere else in the country. Unlike the mainland, which uses parmesan almost exclusively, Sicilians like to spread liberal helpings of a strong cheese called *caciocavallo* on their pasta dishes (despite the name *cavallo*, which means horse, the cheese is actually made from cow's milk) – although you will find parmesan served in most restaurants.

The most famous and typical of all Sicilian pasta dishes is *pasta con le sarde* (pasta with sardines), which can be found most anywhere along the coast. It is a heavy dish that can look less than appetising, but the liberal use of wild mountain fennel (unique to Sicily), onions, pine nuts and raisins gives the sardines a wonderfully exotic flavour. Catania is home to *pasta alla Norma*, whose rich combination of tomatoes, aubergine and grated ricotta cheese was named in tribute to the city's most famous son, the composer of *Norma*, Vincenzo Bellini. High tribute indeed. In the interior you will find a dependency on meat (mostly mutton and beef) and cheese rather than fish. Baroque Mòdica is where the island's best lasagne *(lasagne cacate)* is made, with two kinds of cheese – ricotta and *pecorino* (sheep's cheese) – added to minced beef and sausage and spread between layers of home-made pasta 'squares'.

A Sicilian Classic

Many travellers leave Sicily with a desire to recreate the Sicilian dining experience for themselves at home. Here we've included a recipe for the ever-popular *primo piatto* (first course), *pasta con le sarde* – pasta with sardines, which will feed four people.

Pasta con le Sarde

2 onions (finely sliced)	a few strands of saffron
4 anchovy fillets	½ a wine glass of olive oil
1kg fennel	500g *bucatini* (long, hollow tubes
1kg fresh sardines (boned)	of pasta)
50g raisins (softened)	salt and pepper
50g pine nuts	

First, boil the fennel in a pot of well-salted water. After approximately seven minutes drain in a colander by pressing with the back of a spoon, squeezing out all the moisture. Keep the water in which you boiled it. Mince the fennel and set aside. Lightly fry the onions in the olive oil and add the anchovies. Next, chop the sardines (pilchards are the best type to use) into small pieces and add to the onions. Add salt, pepper and the fennel, and cook the lot for about five minutes. Then add raisins (first, let them soak in water for about 20 minutes to soften), pine nuts and some saffron thinned with a little water. Once you've done this, turn to your pot of boiling water and half-cook the bucatini (this should take no more than six or seven minutes; you can also use *penne*, *rigatoni* or any other type of short pasta), drain, and add to the sauce. Cook the mixture until the pasta is *al dente* (firm to the bite) and serve.

Fish

One could devote an entire book to the use of fish in Sicilian cuisine. The extensive development of underwater fishing and – until recent years – the widespread presence of bluefish (including sardines, tuna and mackerel) off the island's shores have ensured that fish is a staple of most meals, at least anywhere near a coastline. Each town and city has its own specialities, even though the tourist boom has seen a spread of local dishes onto menus throughout Sicily.

JANE SMITH

In Palermo, a local favourite is *sarde a beccafico alla Palermitana* (Palermitan-style stuffed sardines), which are best eaten in the fried-fish shops around the traditional Vucciria market. Here in the capital you can also try the *polpette di nunnata* (fishballs), made from fish that's pounded into a pulp and fried with parsley, garlic and grated pecorino cheese. In recent years the dish has been increasingly difficult to find due to the largely illegal use of freshly-hatched anchovies, sardines and red mullet. In Messina, *agghiotta di pesce spada* is a local classic which you will also see labelled as *pesce spada alla Messinese* (Messinese-style swordfish), a mouth-watering dish flavoured with pine nuts, sultanas, garlic, basil and tomatoes. The western Egadi Islands are home to two splendid fish dishes, *tonno 'nfurnatu* (oven-baked tuna with tomatoes, capers and pale olives) and *alalunga di Favignana al ragù*, fried albacore which is served in a spicy sauce of tomatoes, red chilli peppers and garlic; it is not uncommon to see the sauce appear as part of your pasta dish either. Finally, a popular food throughout the island is *calamari* and *calamaretti* (squid and baby squid), which are prepared in a variety of ways: stuffed, fried, or sautéed in a tomato sauce.

Meat

Above: Fish is a fundamental ingredient in the island's cuisine.

Although you can find a limited number of meat dishes along the coast, you won't see the best dishes until you move further inland. The province of Ragusa is renowned for its superb and imaginative uses of meat, particularly mutton, beef, pork and rabbit. Its most famous dish is *falsomagro*, a stuffed roll of minced beef, sausages, bacon, egg and pecorino cheese. Another local speciality is *coniglio all'agrodolce* (sweet-and-sour rabbit), which is marinated in a sauce of red wine flavoured with onions, olive oil, onions, bay leaves and rosemary. In the Madonie mountains, Castelbuono is the home of *capretto in umido* (stewed kid) and *agnello al forno all Madonita* (Madonie-style roast lamb). The latter is left to soak in a marinade of oil, lemon juice, garlic, onion and rosemary which gives it a particularly delicious flavour. Goat and kid dishes will often appear on the menu as *castrato* – don't be put off! It means the goat was castrated, giving the meat a tender quality, and doesn't refer to what's on your plate.

Desserts

Sicilians are justifiably proud of their desserts, which are perhaps the island's culinary highlight. Of the cakes, pride of place goes to the *cassata*, made with ricotta cheese, sugar, vanilla, diced chocolate and candied fruits. In a restaurant always ask if it is home-made *(fatto in casa)* to ensure that what you get isn't a supermarket imitation of the real thing. In the west you can find *cuccia*, an Arab cake made with grain, honey and ricotta. Most will have heard of the famous *cannoli* (cream horns), pastry tubes or horns filled with sweetened ricotta and sometimes candied fruit or chocolate pieces, which are found throughout the island but are best in Palermo. Also look out for *pasta di mandorle* (an almond pastry) and *pasta paradiso* (melting moments).

Sicily's extraordinary pastries – rich in colour and elaborately designed – may well be the best you'll ever find. Any decent *pasticceria* (pastry shop) will have an enormous spread of freshly made cakes and little pastries that are a perfect accompaniment to after-dinner coffee. It is very common for Sicilians to have their meal in a restaurant and then go to a pastry shop where they have a coffee and cake while standing at the bar. Chocoholics will salivate at the displays of little buns overflowing with rich chocolate cream.

Other Sicilian sweets to try are *gelso di mellone* (watermelon jelly), *buccellati* (little pies filled with minced fruit), *pupe* (sugar dolls made to celebrate the Festa dei Morti on 2 November) and *ucchiuzzi* (biscuits shaped like eyes, made for the Festa di Santa Lucia on 13 December).

If you are in Palermo around late October, before the festival of Ognissanti (All Saints' Day on 1 November) you will see plenty of stalls selling and displaying the famous almond confectioneries known as *frutti della Martorana* (fruit of the Martorana), named after the church which first began producing them. There's nothing fruity about them other than their appearance but this almond paste biscuit, shaped and decorated to resemble fruits (or whatever takes the creator's fancy), is part of a Sicilian tradition that dates back to the Middle Ages. Today the 'fruits' are sold all over the island pretty much throughout the year but only during the week preceding All Saints' Day will you see such a wonderful array of colour and shape.

JANE SMITH

Left: Sicily is heaven for the sweet-toothed – cassata and cannoli are specialities.

Wines

Sicily is not famous for its wines but there are a few that can compete with the more renowned wines of the Italian mainland, and the region is exporting more and more wine each year. Most wines are fairly cheap, though as for any wine, prices vary according to the vintage. The island's most prized producer is Regaleali, which produces robust reds and some delicious whites that go perfectly with almost any dish. The wine you'll see on most menus, however, is the Corvo di Salaparuta, a velvety red that is an ideal

LPP

companion to meaty falsomagro (see Meat earlier), while the whites are usually quite fresh and slightly fruity. The island's most popular white wine is Rapitalà from Àlcamo, a soft, neutral white that goes well with most whitefish dishes. If you're looking for something a little more flavoured you might try one of the Etna whites, whose mild fragrance of wine flowers sits well with the spicier bluefish dishes. Other excellent reds include Ceravasuolo (produced around Ragusa and Còmiso) and Donnafugata (ask for that produced at the Vigna di Gabri).

Messina produces the strong Faro red, which goes well with most meat dishes, and a good white called Capo Bianco. Grapes cultivated on the volcanic soil around Etna are used in the production of Etna reds, rosés and whites. Another good choice from the area is the rosé Ciclopi – it is known as the best wine to drink with rabbit dishes.

From the southwest, the best-known wines are the red Terreforti produced near Catania and the Anapo white, Eloro and Pachino reds, all produced near Syracuse. In recent years the three wines from the Agrigento region – Drepano, Draceno and Saturno – have made an impact on the American market. From the west, Belice (red and white) and Capo Boeo (white) are good choices. Segesta reds and whites are also popular for their well-balanced body and generous taste.

Sicilian dessert wines are excellent, and worth buying to take home. Top of the list is Marsala, the sweet wine from the western port city. Sweet Malvasia is a fruity wine whose best producer is Carlo Hauser – just look for his name on the bottle and you'll know you have a good one. Italy's most famous Muscat is the Moscato di Pantelleria, which also comes as a table red.

There are three main classifications of wine – DOCG (*denominazione d'origine controllata e garantita*), DOC (*denominazione di origine controllata*) and *vino da tavola* (table wine) – which will be marked on the label. A DOC wine is produced subject to certain specifications, although the label does not certify quality. DOCG is subject to the same requirements as normal DOC but it is also tested by government inspectors. While there are some table wines that are better left alone, there are also some of excellent quality, notably the Sicilian Corvo red and white, which is your standard plonk.

For hints on particular vineyards you might want to invest in a wine guide. Burton Anderson's hardback guide *Best Wines of Italy* is a handy little tool to have in your back pocket.

[continued from page 64]

La Repubblica (€0.90). This trio forms what could be considered to be the nucleus of a national press and each publish a Sicilian edition. Politically speaking, they range from establishment-right *(La Stampa)* to centre-left *(La Repubblica)*. Their prices tend to rise by about €0.50 when they contain a weekly magazine supplement *(inserto)*.

RADIO & TV

You can pick up the BBC World Service on medium wave at 648kHz, on short wave 6195kHz, 9410kHz, 12095kHz and 15575 kHz, and on long wave at 198kHz, depending on where you are and the time of day. Voice of America (VOA) can usually be found on short wave at 15205 kHz.

The three state-owned stations are: RAI-1 (1332 AM or 89.7 FM), RAI-2 (846 AM or 91.7 FM) and RAI-3 (93.7 FM). They combine classical and light music with news broadcasts and discussion programmes.

The three state-run TV stations, RAI-1, RAI-2 and RAI-3 are run by Radio e Televisione Italiane. Historically, each has been in the hands of one of the main political groupings in the country, although allegiances are less clear these days.

Of the three, RAI-3 tends to have some of the more interesting programmes. Generally, however, these stations and the private Canale 5, Italia 1 and Rete 4 (all owned by Berlusconi!) tend to serve up a diet of indifferent news, appalling variety hours and equally terrible game shows. Talk shows, some interesting but many nauseating, also abound. Infotainment channels, where a bewildering array of dubious anticellulite treatments and diet aids are advertised, are also clogging the dial.

Other stations include Telemontecarlo (TMC), on which you can see CNN if you stay up late enough (starting as late as 5am), and a host of local channels.

VIDEO SYSTEMS

If you want to record or buy video tapes to play back home, you won't get a picture if the image registration systems are different.

TVs and nearly all pre-recorded videos on sale in Italy use the Phase Alternation Line (PAL) system common to most of Western Europe and Australia, which is incompatible with France's SECAM system or the NTSC system used in North America and Japan.

PHOTOGRAPHY

A roll of 100 ASA Kodak film costs around €4.15/5.15 for 24/36 exposures. Developing costs around €6.20/7.75 for 24/36 exposures in standard format. A roll of 36 slides costs €6.20 to buy and €5.15 for developing.

TIME

Italy (and hence Sicily) is one hour ahead of GMT/UTC during winter and two hours ahead of GMT/UTC during the daylight-saving period (from the last Sunday in March to the last Sunday in October). Most other Western European countries have the same time as Italy year-round, the major exceptions being Britain, Ireland and Portugal, which are one hour behind.

When it's noon in Sicily, it's 3am in San Francisco, 6am in New York and Toronto, 11am in London, 9pm in Sydney and 11pm in Auckland. Note that the change-over to/from daylight saving usually differs from the European date by a couple of weeks in North America and Australasia.

ELECTRICITY
Voltages & Cycles

Electric current in Sicily is 220V, 50Hz, as in the rest of continental Europe. Several countries outside Europe (such as the USA and Canada) use 110Hz, which means that appliances with electric motors (such as some CD- and tape-players) from those countries may perform poorly. It is always safest to use a transformer.

Plugs & Sockets

Plugs have two round pins, as in the rest of continental Europe.

WEIGHTS & MEASURES

Sicily uses the metric system. Basic terms for weight include *un etto* (100g) and *un chilo*

(1kg). Like other continental Europeans, the Italians indicate decimals with commas and thousands with points.

LAUNDRY
Although laundrettes are uncommon on Sicily, there are a couple of coin laundrettes in Palermo where you can do your own washing. A load will cost around €5.15. The alternative is to wash your underclothes and T-shirts yourself and send your delicates to a dry-cleaner. Dry-cleaning *(lavasecco)* charges range from around €3.10 for a shirt to €6.20 for a jacket.

TOILETS
Public toilets are not exactly widespread in Sicily. Most people use the toilets in bars and cafes – although you might need to buy a coffee first!

HEALTH
Travel health depends on your predeparture preparations, your daily health care while travelling and how you handle any medical problem that does develop. While the potential dangers can seem quite frightening, in reality few travellers to Sicily experience anything more than an upset stomach.

Medical Services
The quality of medical treatment in public hospitals is not great in Sicily. Overcrowding, underfunding and staff shortages can all add up to a nightmare experience that you would do best to avoid if you can.

Private hospitals and clinics throughout the region generally provide excellent services but are expensive for those without medical insurance. That said, certain treatment in public hospitals may also have to be paid for and can be equally costly.

Your embassy or consulate in Italy can provide a list of recommended doctors in major cities; however, if you have a specific health complaint, it would be wise to obtain the necessary information and referrals for treatment before leaving home.

The public health system is administered along provincial lines by centres generally known as Unità Sanitarie Locali (USL) or

---

Medical Kit Check List

Following is a list of items to consider including in your medical kit – consult your pharmacist for brands available in your country. Basic drugs are widely available and indeed many items requiring prescriptions in countries such as the USA can be obtained easily over the counter in Sicily. If you require specific medication, it's easier to bring it with you. Condoms can cost between €6.20 and €13 for a dozen (supermarkets are generally cheapest).

☐ **Aspirin or paracetamol (acetaminophen in the USA) –** for pain or fever

☐ **Antihistamine –** for allergies, eg, hay fever; to ease the itch from insect bites or stings; and to prevent motion sickness

☐ **Cold and flu tablets, throat lozenges and nasal decongestant**

☐ **Multivitamins –** consider for long trips, when dietary vitamin intake may be inadequate

☐ **Antibiotics –** consider including these if you're travelling well off the beaten track; see your doctor, as they must be prescribed, and carry the prescription with you

☐ **Loperamide or diphenoxylate –**'blockers' for diarrhoea

☐ **Prochlorperazine or metaclopramide –** for nausea and vomiting

☐ **Rehydration mixture –** to prevent dehydration, which may occur, for example, during bouts of diarrhoea; particularly important when travelling with children

☐ **Insect repellent, sunscreen, lip balm and eye drops**

☐ **Calamine lotion, sting relief spray or aloe vera –** to ease irritation from sunburn and insect bites or stings

☐ **Antifungal cream or powder –** for fungal skin infections and thrush

☐ **Antiseptic (such as povidone-iodine) –** for cuts and grazes

☐ **Bandages, Band-Aids (plasters) and other wound dressings**

☐ **Water purification tablets or iodine**

☐ **Scissors, tweezers and a thermometer –** note that mercury thermometers are prohibited by airlines

Unità Soci Sanitarie Locali (USSL). Increasingly they are being reorganised as Aziende Sanitarie Locali (ASL). Through them you find out where your nearest hospital, medical clinics and other services are. Look under 'U' or 'A' in the telephone book (sometimes the USL and USSL are under 'A' too, as Azienda USL).

Under these headings you'll find long lists of offices – look for Poliambulatorio (Polyclinic) and the telephone number for Accetazione Sanitaria. You need to call this number to make an appointment: there is no point in just rolling up. Clinic opening hours vary widely, with the minimum generally being 8am to 12.30pm Monday to Friday. Some open for a couple of hours in the afternoon and on Saturday mornings too.

Each ASL/USL area has its own Consultorio Familiare (Family Planning Centre) where you can go for contraceptives, pregnancy tests and information about abortion (legal up to the 12th week of pregnancy, although quite expensive).

Medical Cover

Citizens of EU countries are covered for emergency medical treatment in Sicily on presentation of an E111 form. Treatment in private hospitals is not covered and charges are also likely for medication, dental work and secondary examinations, including X-rays and laboratory tests. Ask about the E111 at your local health services department a few weeks before you travel (the form is available at post offices in the UK). Australia also has a reciprocal arrangement with Italy so that emergency treatment is covered – Medicare in Australia publishes a brochure with the details. Advise medical staff of any reciprocal arrangements *before* they begin treating you. Most travel insurance policies include medical cover. See Travel Insurance under Visas & Documents earlier.

Pre-Departure Preparations

Make sure you're healthy before you start travelling. If you are embarking on a long trip, have a check-up to make sure your teeth are OK. If you wear glasses take a spare pair and your prescription.

If you require a particular medication take an adequate supply as it may not be available locally. Take part of the packaging showing the generic name rather than the brand, which will make getting replacements easier. It's a good idea to have a legible prescription or letter from your doctor to show that you legally use the medication (to avoid any problems).

Basic Rules

Stomach upsets are the most likely travel health problem but in Sicily the majority of these will be relatively minor and probably due to overindulgence in the local food. Some people take a while to adjust to the regular use of olive oil in the food.

Water Tap water is drinkable throughout much of Sicily although Sicilians themselves have taken to drinking the bottled stuff. The sign *acqua non potabile* tells you that water is not drinkable (you may see it in trains and at some camp sites). Water from drinking fountains is safe unless there is a sign telling you otherwise.

Environmental Hazards

Heat Exhaustion Dehydration and salt deficiency can cause heat exhaustion. Take time to acclimatise to high temperatures, drink sufficient liquids and do not do anything too physically demanding.

Salt deficiency is characterised by fatigue, lethargy, headaches, giddiness and muscle cramps; salt tablets may help but adding extra salt to your food is better.

Anhidrotic heat exhaustion is a rare form of heat exhaustion that is caused by an inability to sweat. It tends to affect people who have been in a hot climate for some time, rather than newcomers. It can progress to heat-stroke. Treatment involves removal to a cooler climate.

Motion Sickness Eating lightly before and during a trip will reduce the chances of motion sickness. If you are prone to motion sickness try to find a place that minimises movement – near the wing on aircraft, close to midships on boats, near the centre on buses. Fresh air usually helps; reading and cigarette smoke don't. Commercial motion-sickness preparations, which can cause drowsiness, have to be taken before the trip commences. Ginger (available in capsule form) and peppermint (including mint-flavoured sweets) are natural preventatives.

Prickly Heat Prickly heat is an itchy rash caused by excessive perspiration trapped under the skin. It usually strikes people who have just arrived in a hot climate. Keeping cool, bathing often, drying the skin and using a mild talcum or prickly heat powder or resorting to air-conditioning may help.

Sunburn In Sicily you can get sunburned surprisingly quickly, even through cloud. Use a sunscreen, a hat and some barrier cream for your nose and lips. Calamine lotion is good for soothing mild sunburn. You could also avail yourself of the soothing properties of aloe vera gel, especially since the plant is found almost everywhere on the island. Always protect your eyes with good-quality sunglasses.

Sexually Transmitted Diseases HIV/AIDS and hepatitis B can be transmitted through sexual contact. Other STDs include gonorrhoea, herpes and syphilis; sores, blisters or rashes around the genitals and discharges or pain when urinating are common symptoms. In some STDs, such as wart virus or chlamydia, symptoms may be less marked or not observed at all, especially in women. Chlamydia infection can cause infertility in men and women before any symptoms have been noticed. Syphilis symptoms eventually disappear completely but the disease continues and can cause severe problems in later years. While abstinence from sexual contact is the only 100% effective prevention, using condoms is also effective. The different sexually transmitted diseases each require specific antibiotics.

Insect-Borne Diseases
Leishmaniasis This is a group of parasitic diseases transmitted by sandflies and found in coastal parts of Sicily. Cutaneous leish-maniasis affects the skin tissue, causing ulceration and disfigurement, and visceral leishmaniasis affects the internal organs. Seek medical advice, as laboratory testing is required for diagnosis and correct treatment. Avoiding sandfly bites is the best precaution. Bites are usually painless, itchy and yet another reason to cover up and apply repellent.

Lyme Disease Lyme disease is a tick-transmitted infection, which can be acquired throughout Europe, including in the forested areas of Sicily. The illness usually begins with a spreading rash at the site of the tick bite and is accompanied by fever, headache, extreme fatigue, aching joints and muscles and mild neck stiffness. If untreated, these symptoms usually resolve over several weeks but, over subsequent weeks or months, disorders of the nervous system, heart and joints may develop. Treatment works best early in the illness. Medical help should be sought.

Bites & Stings
Jellyfish Sicilian beaches are occasionally inundated with jellyfish. Their stings are painful but not dangerous. Dousing in vinegar will deactivate any stingers that have not fired. Calamine lotion, antihistamines and analgesics may reduce the reaction and relieve the pain. If in doubt about swimming, ask locals if any jellyfish are in the water.

Snakes Italy's only dangerous snake, the viper, is found throughout Sicily. To minimise your chances of being bitten, always wear boots, socks and long trousers when walking through undergrowth where snakes may be present – especially at archaeological sites. Don't put your hands into holes and crevices and be careful when collecting firewood.

Viper bites do not cause immediate death and an antivenin is widely available in pharmacies. Keep the victim calm and still, wrap the limb tightly, as you would for a sprained ankle, and attach a splint to immobilise it. Then seek medical help, if possible with the dead snake for identification.

Don't attempt to catch the snake if there is even a remote possibility of being bitten again. Tourniquets and sucking out the poison are now comprehensively discredited.

WOMEN TRAVELLERS

Sicily is not a dangerous region for women but women travelling alone will often find themselves receiving unwanted attention from men and may find it difficult to remain alone. This attention usually involves staring, catcalls, hisses and whistles, and is more annoying than anything else. The following passage from Claire Rabe's novel *Sicily Enough* (1976) illustrates the sort of attention that lone women often encounter in Sicily:

'There, every woman who passes is judged. When they approve, 'buona' is uttered with a hoarse gusto... The face of a woman is looked at last. She must simply not be ugly. A robust body with abundant breast and rear and a fattish face is a fine 'cavallo' or 'vaca'. The inspection is continuous, noisy with smacks and hisses, an obvious need to make each opinion public, to share. They tell each other how they feel and how they would treat each case.'

It is not uncommon for Sicilian men to harass women in the street, while drinking a coffee in a bar or waiting for public transport. On an island where the sanctity of marriage is still held in the highest regard, a wedding ring is a great deterrent. Claiming to be pregnant (*'Sono incinta'*) is also very effective in getting rid of lotharios. Otherwise, position yourself near a family group or group of women, or tell them that you're waiting for your fiancé (*fidanzato*). Ignoring them and, if necessary, walking away will also do the trick. As frustrating and annoying as it may be, remember that no real harm is meant. Avoid becoming aggressive as this almost always results in an unpleasant confrontation. If all else fails, approach the nearest member of the police or *carabinieri* (military police).

Basically, most of the attention falls into the minor nuisance category. However, women on their own should use their common sense. Avoid walking alone on deserted and dark streets, and look for centrally located hotels within easy walking distance of places you can eat at night. Women should not hitch alone.

Standing on a Pedestal

The role of women in Sicilian society is a traditional and often conflicting one. The conflict is the product of two distinct cultures – Arab and Catholic – that for over 1000 years have seen women cast in the dual role of subservient homemaker and symbol of Catholic purity, worshipped as the embodiment of the Virgin Mary. To the modern thinker such attitudes smack of oppression – a woman on a pedestal can easily be torn down when she does not live up to the impossible ideals imposed upon her by Sicilian men.

You would be mistaken, however, to assume that women meekly perform this role. Even in the traditional interior, women are recognised as the central force of the family and have adapted to their constricted position with admirable strength and vigour. More often than not they have exploited the position that has been foisted upon them to their own advantage and it is they who dictate the course of a community's affairs.

Things are changing, albeit slowly. In the larger, more cosmopolitan cities, such as Palermo and Catania, a younger and better-educated generation has rejected traditional mores in favour of an attitude more in keeping with 21st-century western values and it is not uncommon to see groups of women sitting at the bar alongside everyone else. In the fight against the Mafia, women have taken a leading role, organising protest marches and generally involving themselves at every level in the struggle to rid the island of the nefarious influence of organised crime. Sicily is not Sydney, however, and while the struggle for equality of the sexes has come on in leaps and bounds, it still lags some way behind.

Recommended reading is the *Handbook for Women Travellers* (1995) by M & G Moss. It's actually out of print but you may be able to find a second-hand copy or borrow one from a library.

GAY & LESBIAN TRAVELLERS

Although homosexuality is legal in Sicily and the age of consent is 16, it is not particularly well tolerated anywhere. There are almost no gay and/or lesbian clubs and bars, and overt displays of affection by homosexual couples can attract a negative response. Yet physical contact between men (and women), such as linking arms and kissing on the cheek, is commonplace and very much part of Sicilian life. It is best to bear this strange dichotomy in mind when travelling throughout the island and – depressing though it may be – to avoid open displays that might incite locals. Again, as with attitudes to women (see the previous section), the views on homosexuality are changing, at least in cities such as Palermo and Catania, but progress seems to be even slower than it is with women's rights. Younger Sicilians are generally tolerant of same-sex relationships and often see them as no indication of homosexuality. However, as one young Sicilian man said to us: 'You can sleep with anyone when you're younger, as long as you eventually get married and have children...'!

The annual *Guida Gay Italia* is available at many newsstands in Palermo and Catania. If you want to track down the small (but growing) gay scene in Palermo, contact ArciGay (☎ 091 33 56 88, W www.malox.com/arcigay – Italian only) at Via Genova 7, which offers a basic contact point.

International gay and lesbian guides worth checking out are the *Spartacus International Gay Guide* (the Spartacus list also includes the comprehensive *Spartacus National Edition Italia*, in English and German), published by Bruno Gmünder Verlag, Mail Order, PO Box 11 07 29, D-1000 Berlin 11, Germany, and *Gay Travel A-Z: The World of Gay & Lesbian Travel Options at Your Fingertips*, published by Ferrari Publications, PO Box 37887, Phoenix, AZ 85069, USA.

DISABLED TRAVELLERS

The Italian State Tourist Office in your country may be able to provide advice on Italian associations for the disabled and the help available in Sicily (for contact details see Tourist Offices Abroad in the earlier Tourist Office section). It may also carry a small brochure, *Services for Disabled People*, published by the Italian state railway company, Ferrovie dello Stato (FS), which details facilities at stations and on trains. Some of the better trains, such as the ETR460 and ETR500 trains, have a carriage for passengers in wheelchairs and their companions.

The Italian travel agency CIT can advise of hotels with special facilities, such as ramps. It can also request that wheelchair ramps be provided on arrival of your train if you book travel through CIT.

The UK-based Royal Association for Disability & Rehabilitation (RADAR) publishes a guide called *Holidays & Travel Abroad: A Guide for Disabled People*, which provides a useful overview of the facilities that are available for disabled travellers throughout Europe. Contact RADAR (☎ 020-7250 3222, W www.radar.org.uk) at 12 City Forum, 250 City Rd, London EC1V 8AS.

You may also be able to get help on Sicily itself. Cooperative Integrate (Co.In.) is a national voluntary group with links to the government and branches all over the country. They publish a quarterly magazine for disabled tourists, *Turismo per Tutti* (Tourism for All; Italian and English) and have information on accessible accommodation, transport and attractions. Co.In. (☎ 06 232 67 505, W andi.casaccia.enea .it/hometur.htm) is at Via Enrico Giglioli 54a in Rome.

SENIOR TRAVELLERS

Seniors are entitled to discounts on public transport and on admission fees at some museums. It is always important to ask. The minimum qualifying age is generally 60 years. You should also seek information in your own country on travel packages and discounts through seniors organisations and travel agencies.

TRAVEL WITH CHILDREN

Discounts are available for children (usually under 12 years of age) on public transport and on admission to museums, galleries and other sites.

One great way to keep children entertained is with traditional Sicilian puppet theatre. Try the Museo Internazionale delle Marionette in Palermo and the Opera dei Pupi in Cefalù.

Always make a point of asking at tourist offices if they know of any special family or children's activities; these may come in handy if the children (and adults!) have had enough of museums and galleries. Also ask for details on the hotels that cater for kids. Families should book accommodation in advance, wherever possible, to avoid inconvenience.

Chemists *(farmacie)* sell baby formula in powder or liquid form as well as sterilising solutions, such as Milton. Disposable nappies (diapers) are widely available at supermarkets, chemists (where they are more expensive) and sometimes in larger stationery stores. A pack of around 30 disposable nappies costs around €10.30. Fresh cows' milk is sold in cartons in bars (which have a 'Latteria' sign) and in supermarkets. If it is essential that you have milk, you should carry an emergency carton of UHT milk, since bars usually close at 8pm. In many out-of-the-way areas in Sicily, the locals only use UHT milk. For more information, see Lonely Planet's *Travel with Children*.

USEFUL ORGANISATIONS

The Istituto Italiano di Cultura (IIC; Italian Cultural Institute), with branches all over the world, is an organisation sponsored by the government which promotes Italian culture and language worldwide. They put on classes in Italian and provide a library and information service. This is a good place to start your search for places to study in Sicily. The library at the London branch (see under UK in the list below) has an extensive reference book collection, with works on art and history, a range of periodicals and videos. IIC branches include:

Australia
Sydney: (☎ 03-9820 2054) 233 Domain Rd, South Yarra, Melbourne, VIC 3141
Melbourne: (☎ 02-9392 7939, W www .iicmelau.org) Level 45, Gateway, 1 Macquarie Place, Sydney, NSW 2000
Canada
Toronto: (☎ 416-921 3802) 496 Huron Street, Toronto, Ontario M5R 2R3
Montreal: (☎ 514-849 3473, W www.iicto-ca .org/istituto.htm) 1200 Penfield Drive, Montreal, Quebec H3A 1A9
France
(☎ 01 44 39 49 39, W www.italynet.com/ cultura/istcult) Hotel Galliffet, 50 rue de Varenne, 75007 Paris
Germany
Berlin: (☎ 030-261 78 75) Hildebrandstrasse 1, 10785 Berlin
Munich: (☎ 089-76 45 63) Hermann Schmidt-strasse 8, 80336 Munich
Ireland
(☎ 01-676 6662) 11 Fitzwilliam Square, Dublin 2
Switzerland
(☎ 01-202 48 46) Gotthardstrasse 27, 8002 Zurich
UK
(☎ 020 7235 1461, W www.italcultur.org.uk) 39 Belgrave Square, London SW1X 8NX
USA
(☎ 202-387 5261, W www.italcultusa.org) Suite 610, 2025 M St NW, Washington, DC 20036

Centro Turistico Studentesco e Giovanile (CTS; W www.cts.it) is the main Italian student and youth travel organisation. They act mainly as a travel agent but you can also obtain ISIC, Euro<26 and Youth Hostel cards at their branches. Note, however, that you will generally be obliged to pay a joining fee of €25.80. CTS has branches in the main centres across Sicily, including Palermo, Catania and Enna, Messina, Syracuse, Tràpani and Agrigento.

DANGERS & ANNOYANCES
Theft

This can be a problem for travellers in Sicily – groups of pickpockets and bag snatchers operate in the most touristy parts of the bigger cities and some of the coastal resort towns.

Prevention is better than cure. Wear a moneybelt under your clothing. Keep all important items, such as money, passport and tickets, in your moneybelt at all times. If you are carrying a bag or camera, wear the strap across your body and have the bag on the side away from the road to deter snatch thieves who operate from motorcycles and scooters, an all-too-common occurrence in Palermo. Many of the perpetrators are young teenagers whose sorry destiny is to be swallowed up into the lower ranks of the Mafia – if they haven't been so already.

Motorists are not immune to thieves either. If you're in traffic, make sure that your window is rolled up (and hope that you have air-conditioning!) and that all your valuables are out of view; a common ploy by assailants is to reach in and grab whatever is available before speeding off (some thieves even carry crowbars to smash the window if they see something of particular value).

Parked cars are the easiest prey for thieves, particularly those with foreign numberplates or rental company stickers. Naturally, *never* leave valuables in your car – in fact, try not to leave anything in the car if you can help it.

In the case of theft or loss, always make a report at the police station within 24 hours and ask for a statement, otherwise your travel insurance company won't pay out. For emergency numbers, see the boxed text 'Emergency Numbers' below.

Traffic

Sicilian traffic – particularly in Palermo – is second only to Naples as the most chaotic in Europe. The unprepared tourist is likely to be in for a shock when first confronted with the sheer lunacy of local motorists, who have seemingly never heard of the rules of the road. The honking of car horns is incessant and – for the most part – without purpose other than to make noise or greet pedestrian acquaintances passing by. Nearly every car you will see has a dent on it – these are battle scars, for driving here is truly like a war. If you must drive in the city, you'll need to develop nerves of steel pretty quickly and remember the golden rule: if there's a gap, go for it, because if you don't

someone else will and everyone behind you will start honking their disapproval.

Drivers are not keen to stop for pedestrians, even at pedestrian crossings. Sicilians simply step off the footpath and walk through the (swerving) traffic with determination – it is a practice that seems to work, so if you feel uncertain about crossing a busy road, wait for the next Sicilian. In the major cities, roads that appear to be for one-way traffic have special lanes for buses travelling in the opposite direction – always look both ways before stepping out.

EMERGENCIES

For emergency medical treatment, go straight to casualty *(pronto soccorso)* section of a public hospital, where you can also get emergency dental treatment. If you need an ambulance, call ☎ 118. Sometimes hospitals are listed in the phone book under Aziende Ospedaliere. In major centres you are likely to find doctors who speak English. Often, first aid is also available at train stations, airports and ports. See the boxed text 'Emergency Numbers' below for a list of services you can call, depending on your dilemma.

LEGAL MATTERS

For many Sicilians, finding ways to get around the law (any law) is a way of life. They are likely to react with surprise, if not annoyance, if you point out that they might be breaking the law. No-one bats an eyelid about littering or dogs pooping in the middle of the footpath – even though many municipal governments have introduced regulations against these things.

Emergency Numbers

Wherever you are in Sicily, these are the numbers to ring in an emergency:

Military Police (Carabinieri) ☎ 112
Police (Polizia) ☎ 113
Fire Brigade (Vigili del Fuoco) ☎ 115
Highway Rescue (Soccorso Stradale) ☎ 116
Ambulance (Ambulanza) ☎ 118

The average tourist will probably have a brush with the law only if robbed by a bag snatcher or pickpocket.

Drugs

Sicily's drug laws are lenient on users and heavy on pushers. If you're caught with drugs that the police determine are for your own personal use, you'll be let off with a warning – and, of course, the drugs will be confiscated. If, instead, it is determined that you intend to sell the drugs, you could find yourself in prison. It's up to the police to determine whether or not you're a pusher, since the law is not specific about quantities. The sensible option is to avoid illicit drugs altogether. Sicilian attitudes to drug use are very conservative for the most part.

Drink Driving

The legal limit for blood alcohol level is 0.08% and breath tests are now in use. Penalties for driving under the influence of alcohol can be severe.

Police

The police *(polizia)* are a civil force and take their orders from the Ministry of the Interior, while the *carabinieri* (military police) fall under the Ministry of Defence. There is a considerable duplication of their roles, despite a 1981 reform intended to merge the two forces.

The police wear powder-blue trousers with a fuchsia stripe and a navy-blue jacket, and drive light blue cars with a white stripe, with 'polizia' written on the side. Tourists who want to report thefts and people wanting to get a residence permit will have to deal with them. They are based at the *questura* (police station).

The carabinieri wear a dark-blue uniform with a red stripe and drive dark-blue cars with a red stripe. They are well-trained and tend to be helpful. Their police station is called a *caserma* (barracks). Although innocent queries are always dealt with politely, the carabinieri's role in Sicily is an especially sensitive and difficult one – as along with the regular army (recently confined to barracks) – they are the vanguard in the fight against the Mafia; consequently they have a reputation for being harsh and sometimes heavy-handed.

Other varieties of police in Italy include the *vigili urbani*, basically traffic police, and the *guardia di finanza*, who are responsible for fighting tax evasion and drug smuggling. Their role in Sicily is vastly inflated compared to the rest of Italy and they are given wide berth by many Sicilians; the ordinary tourist, however, will have almost no occasion to deal with them.

BUSINESS HOURS

Generally shops open from around 9am to 1pm and 3.30pm to 7.30pm (or 4pm to 8pm) Monday to Friday. Some stay closed on Monday mornings. Big department stores, such as Oviesse and Rinascente, and most supermarkets have continuous opening hours: 9am to 7.30pm Monday to Saturday. Some even open 9am to 1pm on Sunday. Smaller shops open on Saturday morning until about 1pm.

Businesses such as travel agencies usually open 9am to 12.30pm or 1pm and 4pm to 7pm.

Banks tend to open 8.30am to 1.30pm and 2.45pm to 3.45pm Monday to Friday, although hours can vary. They are closed at the weekend but it is always possible to find an exchange office open in the larger cities and in major tourist areas.

Major post offices open 8.30am to 6pm or 7pm Monday to Saturday. Smaller post offices generally open 8.30am to 2pm Monday to Friday and from 8.30am to noon on Saturday.

Pharmacies usually open 9am to 12.30pm and 3.30pm to 7.30pm. They are always closed on Sunday and usually on Saturday afternoon. When closed, pharmacies are required to display a list of pharmacies in the area which are open. Big cities, such as Palermo, Catania and Messina, have a 24-hour pharmacy.

Bars (in the Italian sense, that is, coffee-and-sandwich places) and cafes generally open 7am to 8pm, although some stay open after 8pm and turn into pub-style drinking and meeting places. Discos and clubs might open around 10pm but often there'll be no-one there until midnight. Restaurants open roughly from noon to 3pm and 7.30pm to 11pm. Restaurants and bars are required to close for one day each week (the day varies between establishments).

Museum and gallery opening hours vary although there is a trend towards continuous opening hours from around 9.30am to 8pm. Many close on Monday.

PUBLIC HOLIDAYS
Most Sicilians take their annual holiday in August, deserting the cities for the cooler seaside or mountains. This means that many businesses and shops close for at least a part of the month, particularly during the week around Feast of the Assumption (Ferragosto) on 15 August. The Easter break (Settimana Santa) is another busy holiday period for Sicilians. National public holidays in Sicily include the following:

New Year's Day (Anno Nuovo) Celebrations take place on New Year's Eve (Capodanno)

Epiphany (Befana) 6 January

Good Friday (Venerdì Santo) March/April

Easter Monday (Pasquetta/Giorno dopo Pasqua) March/April

Liberation Day (Giorno della Liberazione) Held on 25 April to mark the Allied victory in Italy and the end of the German presence and Mussolini.

Labour Day (Giorno del Lavoro) 1 May

Feast of the Assumption (Ferragosto) 15 August

All Saints' Day (Ognissanti) 1 November

Feast of the Immaculate Conception (Concezione Immaculata) 8 December

Christmas Day (Natale) 25 December

St Stephen's Day (Boxing Day, Festa di Santo Stefano) 26 December

Individual towns also have public holidays to celebrate the feasts of their patron saints. See the following section.

SPECIAL EVENTS
Sicily's calendar is full to bursting with events, ranging from colourful traditional celebrations, with a religious and/or historical flavour, through to festivals of the performing arts, including opera, music and theatre. Some appear in the following list.

January
Epiphany (Befana) The town of Piana degli Albanesi, near Palermo, celebrates the festival of *La Befana* with a colourful parade that culminates in a firework display.

February
Carnevale During the week before Ash Wednesday, many towns stage carnivals and enjoy their last opportunity to indulge before Lent (the name derives from the Latin for 'goodbye meat'). The popular festivities in Sciacca are renowned throughout Sicily for imaginative floats, which are usually made up along allegorical themes. The party in Taormina is also pretty good.

Feast of St Agatha (Festa di Sant'Agata) From the third to the fifth of the month, Catania celebrates the feast of its patron saint with the procession of the saint's relics amid food stalls, fireworks and all-round mayhem.

April
Easter (Pasqua) Holy Week in Sicily is a very big deal and is marked by solemn, slow-moving processions and passion plays. Tràpani's procession of *I Misteri* is the island's most famous but there are similar ones worth checking out in Enna and in towns throughout the island.

Motor Racing (Corsa Automobilistica) The circuit is around Lago di Pergusa near Enna. Racing begins its season on the last weekend of April and runs to the end of September.

July
Feast of St Rosalia (Festa di Santa Rosalia) From the 11th to the 15th, Palermo pulls out all the stops in the celebration of one of its patron saints. Amid the street celebrations – music, food, dancing and partying – the saint's relics are paraded from the city's cathedral.

August
Medieval Pageant (Palio dei Normanni) On the 14th and 15th of the month, Piazza Armerina is almost completely given over to a wonderful celebration of its Norman past as it commemorates Count Roger's taking of the town from the Arabs in the 13th century. There are costumed parades, a procession into the town and even a joust.

September
Pilgrimages (Pelegrinaggi) This is the month for many of Sicily's pilgrimages. The most important are on the 4th to Mt Pellegrino, north of Palermo, and to the church at Gibilmanna in the Madonie on the 8th.

ACTIVITIES

If the museums, galleries and sights are not enough for you, there are numerous options to get you off the beaten track.

Cycling

This is a good option for people who can't afford to hire a car but want to see some of the more out-of-the-way places, particularly in the interior. You'll need some serious stamina and a good bike to tame the mountains and hills, though. You can either bring your own bike or buy or hire one in Sicily. Bike hire costs between €5.15 and €15.50 per day.

Skiing

Strange as it may seem, Sicily has two winter ski resorts, in the Parco Naturale Regionale delle Madonie (see The Tyrrhenian Coast chapter) and on Mt Etna (see The Eastern Coast chapter). Skiing in Sicily tends to be cheaper than in northern Italy.

Walking

The serious walker will relish the chance to climb a volcano or two, both on the mainland and on the Aeolian Islands. The Nebrodi and Madonie nature reserves (see The Tyrrhenian Coast chapter) also have well-marked and challenging trails. If you plan on walking up Mt Etna, remember that this is an active volcano and walkers are strongly advised not to proceed beyond the safety zone (usually marked out with ropes). See the Mt Etna section in The Eastern Coast chapter for details, or pick up Lonely Planet's *Walking in Italy*, which has chapters on climbing both Stromboli and Mt Etna.

Water Sports

Scuba-diving, snorkelling, windsurfing and sailing are extremely popular at Sicily's beach resorts, where you will have no problem renting boats and equipment. On Lipari (see The Aeolian Islands chapter) you will find plenty of outfits willing to relieve you of your money in exchange for diving courses.

COURSES

Travelling through Sicily can be made easier if you know some Italian. The best and most fun way to learn the language is *in situ*. The University of Catania has a well-regarded school of language and culture (Scuola di Lingua e Cultura Italiana per Stranieri; ☎ 095 710 2264, W www.unict.it/flls – Italian only) at Piazza Dante 32, Catania 95100. It offers 50 hours of Italian language and culture classes for €258. If you fancy learning the language in beautiful Taormina, Babilonia (☎/fax 0942 2 34 41, W www.babilonia.it), at Via del Ginnasio 20, is a good school that offers classes in Italian language, literature, history and art history. Accommodation can also be arranged through the school. A one-week standard language course (five hours per day) costs €180, running up to the four-week intensive language course (six hours per day) at €1440.

For details of cooking courses, see Cooking Tours under Organised Tours in the Getting There & Away chapter.

WORK

It is illegal for non-EU citizens to work in Sicily without a work permit but trying to obtain one can be time-consuming. EU citizens are allowed to work in Sicily but they still need to obtain a residency permit from the main police station in the town where they have found work. See Work Permits under Documents earlier for more information. The main challenge, however, will not be bureaucracy but the economy – unemployment in Sicily is around 27%, the highest of any region in Italy. Frankly, other than being sent here by a company, teaching a little English or doing bar work at a summer resort, you won't have much luck securing employment.

English Tutoring

Virtually the only source of work available to foreigners in Sicily is teaching English but, even with full qualifications, an American, Australian, Canadian or New Zealander might find it difficult to secure even a temporary position. There are language schools in Palermo, Catania and a few larger towns but teaching positions don't often come up. Most of the more reputable schools will only hire people with a work permit and will require a Teaching English as a Foreign Language (TEFL) certificate. It is advisable to apply for work early in the year in order to be considered for positions that become available in October (language school years correspond roughly to the Italian school year: late September to the end of June).

Some schools hire people without work permits or qualifications but the pay is usually low (around €9 an hour). It's more lucrative to advertise your services and pick up private students (although rates vary wildly, ranging from as low as €7.75 up to €25 an hour). Most people get started by placing advertisements in shop windows and on university noticeboards. Although you can get away with absolutely no qualifications or experience, it might be a good idea to bring along a few English grammar books (including exercises) to help you at least appear professional.

To find a list of language schools, try the *Pagine Gialle* (Yellow Pages, available online at W www.paginegialle.it) under Scuole de Lingue (Language Schools) or try one of the following:

Kennedy School (☎/fax 091 22 54 40, e kennedyschool@tin.it) Via Sirtori 55/73, 90145 Palermo
International House Language Centre (☎ 091 58 49 54, fax 091 32 36 25, e ihpal@ gestelnet.it) Via Daita 29, 90139 Palermo
English Study Centre (☎ 095 722 23 93, fax 095 38 41 68, e englishstudycentre@ tiscalnet.it) Via Trieste 46, 95127 Catania
The English College (☎/fax 095 53 57 77) Via Cilestri 36, 95129 Catania

ACCOMMODATION
Prices for accommodation quoted in this book are intended as a guide only and reflect the cost of a room during high season (April to September). There tends to be a fair degree of fluctuation in hotel prices depending on the season and, sometimes, whim. It is not unusual for prices to remain fixed for years on end and, in some cases, they even go down. It is more common that they rise by around 5% or 10% annually. Always check room charges before putting your bags down.

Reservations
It's a good idea to book a room in advance if you are planning to travel during peak tourist periods. Hotels usually require confirmation by fax or letter, as well as a deposit. Tourist offices will generally send out information about hotels, camp sites, apartments and so on.

Camping
Camp sites in Sicily vary in terms of facilities: some are well organised and well laid out while others are simply an empty space where you can pitch a tent with facilities that comprise of little more than a toilet-and-shower block.

Even the most basic camp sites can be surprisingly dear once you add up the various charges but they generally still work out cheaper than a double room in a one-star hotel. Prices range from around €4.15 to €9.30 per adult, plus €4.15 to €9.15 for a site. You'll also often have to pay to park your car and there is sometimes a charge for use of the showers, usually around €1.30.

Independent camping is generally not permitted and you might find yourself disturbed during the night by the carabinieri. But, out of the main summer tourist season, independent campers who choose spots not visible from the road, don't light fires, and who try to be inconspicuous shouldn't have too much trouble. Always get permission from the landowner if you want to camp on private property. Camper vans are popular throughout Italy and Sicily.

TCI publishes an annual book which lists all the camp sites in Italy, *Campeggi e Villagi Turistici* (€16.50), and the Istituto Geografico de Agostini publishes the annual *Guida ai Campeggi in Europa*, which is sold together with *Guida ai Campeggi in Italia* (€18.10). These guides are in Italian only and are available in all major bookshops.

Hostels
Youth hostels *(ostelli per la gioventù)*, of which there are only a handful in Sicily, are run by the Associazione Italiana Alberghi per la Gioventù (AIG; W www.hostels-aig.org), which is affiliated to Hostelling International

(HI). You need to be a member but can join at one of the hostels. For details on how to get a card see Hostel Cards under Visas & Documents earlier. Nightly rates vary from €7.75 to €14.45 including breakfast. A meal will cost €7.75. Accommodation is in segregated dormitories although some hostels offer family rooms (at a higher price per person).

Hostels are generally closed from 10am to 3.30pm. Check-in is from 6pm to 10.30pm although some hostels will allow you a morning check-in before they close for the day (confirm beforehand). Curfew is 11.30pm or midnight. It is usually necessary to pay before 9am on the day of your departure, otherwise you could be charged for another night.

Guesthouses & Hotels

Hotels (albergi) and guesthouses (pensioni) are allowed to increase their prices twice a year but many don't. Travellers should always check on prices before deciding to stay. Make a complaint to the local tourist office if you believe you're being overcharged. Some proprietors employ various methods of bill-padding, such as charging for showers or making breakfast compulsory.

There is often no difference between a guesthouse and a hotel; in fact, some establishments use both titles. However, a hotel will generally be of one- to three-star quality while a guesthouse can be awarded up to five stars.

Inns (locande, similar to pensioni) and affittacamere (rooms to rent, also known as alloggi) are generally, but not always, cheaper. Inns and affittacamere are not included in the classification system.

The quality of accommodation can vary a great deal. One-star hotels and guesthouses tend to be basic and usually do not have an en-suite bathroom. Standards at two-star places are often only slightly better but rooms will generally have a private bathroom. Once you arrive at three stars you can assume that standards will be reasonable, although quality still varies dramatically between establishments. Four- and five-star hotels are sometimes part of a group of hotels and offer facilities such as room service, laundry and dry-cleaning.

A single room (camera singola) will always be expensive. Although there are a few pokey exceptions, you should reckon on a minimum of €20, while a double room with twin beds (camera doppia) and a double with a double bed (camera matrimoniale) will cost from around €30. It is much cheaper to share with two or more people. Proprietors will often charge no more than 15% of the cost of a double room for each additional person.

Prices are highest in Taormina, on the Aeolian Islands and in Cefalù.

Tourist offices have booklets listing accommodation, including prices (although they might not always be up to date).

Agriturismo

Agriturismo is a holiday on a working farm and is an idea that is gaining in popularity in Sicily. Traditionally families rented out rooms in their farmhouses and it is still possible to find this type of accommodation. However, more commonly now the term refers to a restaurant in a restored farm complex, which has rooms that are available for rent. All agriturismo establishments are operating farms and you will usually be able to sample the local produce.

They are becoming an increasingly popular choice with travellers wanting to enjoy the peace and quiet of the countryside. Generally you will need to have your own transport to get to and away from these places. Check with local tourist offices for information on agriturismo options available in the area.

Rental Accommodation

Finding rental accommodation in the cities can be difficult and time-consuming but not impossible. Rental agencies will assist, for a fee. A one-room apartment with kitchenette in Lipari will cost around €520 per month (long term). Renting in other towns can be considerably cheaper.

Short-term rental is inevitably more expensive but many locals are keen to rent to foreigners for brief periods. Tourist offices can be of help in giving you a list of possibilities.

FOOD

Eating is one of life's great pleasures for Sicilians and, though they have stiff competition from other Italian regions, they pride themselves (justifiably) on being at the top of the pile when it comes to dining well. See the earlier section 'Dining *alla Siciliana*' for information on Sicilian cuisine, including wine.

Lonely Planet's *World Food Italy* is a full-colour book with information on the whole range of Italian food and drink, including Sicily. It incorporates a useful language section, with the definitive culinary dictionary and a handy quick-reference glossary.

Vegetarian Food

Vegetarians will have few problems eating in Sicily, although vegans may have difficulties. While few restaurants are strictly vegetarian, vegetables are a staple of the Italian diet. Most eating establishments serve a good selection of vegetable *antipasti* (starters) and *contorni* (vegetable side orders prepared in a variety of ways). If you're a vegan, you're in for a tougher time, with many dishes featuring some sort of animal product (butter, eggs, animal stock).

Self-Catering

If you have access to cooking facilities, it is best to buy fruit and vegetables at open markets and salami, cheese and table wine at an *alimentari* (a cross between a grocery shop and a delicatessen). *Salumerie* sell sausages, meats and sometimes cheeses. For quality wine, search out an *enoteca*. For fresh bread go to a *forno* or *panetteria* (bakeries that sell bread, pastries and sometimes groceries) or an alimentari. Most towns also have supermarkets.

Meals

Sicilians rarely eat a sit-down breakfast *(colazione)*. They tend to drink a cappuccino and eat a pastry while standing at a bar.

Lunch *(pranzo)* is traditionally the main meal of the day and many businesses close for several hours every afternoon to accommodate the meal and a siesta. Lunch consists of a starter *(antipasto)*; a first course *(primo piatto)* of pasta or risotto; and a second course

(secondo piatto) of meat or fish. Italians often then eat a salad *(insalata)* or vegetable side dish *(contorno)*, and round off the meal with fruit, or occasionally dessert *(dolce)*, and coffee, often on the way back to work.

The evening meal *(cena)* used to be more simple but in recent years habits have changed because of the inconvenience of travelling home for lunch every day.

In general, Italians are not big snackers although they do sometimes have a quick bite (a sandwich, slice of pizza or cake) halfway through the morning or afternoon.

DRINKS
Nonalcoholic Drinks

Coffee The first-time visitor to Sicily is likely to be confused by the many ways in which the locals consume their caffeine. Sicilians take their coffee seriously; some say even more seriously than in the rest of Italy, which is quite a feat. It's said that you'll never get a dud coffee in Sicily, as any place that wasn't up to scratch would close very quickly – and it seems to be true.

First is the pure and simple *espresso* – a tiny cup of very strong black coffee. *Doppio espresso* is a double shot of the same. You could also ask for a *caffè lungo*, but this may end up being more like the watered-down version with which Anglos will be more familiar. If you want to be quite sure of getting the watery version, ask for a *caffè americano*.

Enter the milk. A *caffè latte* is coffee with a reasonable amount of milk. To most locals it is a breakfast or morning drink. A stronger version is the *caffè macchiato*, basically an espresso with a dash of milk. Alternatively, you can have *latte macchiato*, a glass of hot milk with a dash of coffee. The *cappuccino* is basically a frothy version of the caffè latte. You can ask for it *senza schiuma* (without froth), in which case the froth is scraped off the top. It tend to comes lukewarm so ask for it *molto caldo* if you want it hot.

In summer, the local version of an iced coffee is a *caffè freddo*, served in a long glass and sometimes helped along with ice cubes.

To warm up on those winter nights, a *corretto* might be for you – an espresso 'corrected' with a dash of *grappa* (grape liqueur) or some other spirit. Some locals have it as a heart-starter.

After lunch and dinner it wouldn't occur to Italians to order either caffè latte or a cappuccino – an espresso, macchiato or corretto is perfectly acceptable. Of course, if you want a cappuccino there's no problem but you might have to repeat your request a couple of times to convince disbelieving waiters that they have heard correctly.

An espresso or macchiato can cost from an island-wide standard of €0.60 or €0.75 standing at a bar to €2 sitting outside at the Teatro Massimo in Palermo – or even €3.10 in glitzy Taormina.

Granita Sicily's greatest contribution to summer thirst-quenchers is *granita*, a drink made of crushed ice with fresh lemon or other fruit juices, or with coffee topped with fresh whipped cream. Like the Irish with Guinness, Sicilians treat it as the creation of a skilled artisan and will be glad to recommend where the best *granite* are to be had in their town. It will generally cost €1.55.

Latte di Mandorla The cultivation of almonds is widespread throughout Sicily so the Sicilians have invented a delicious cold drink that is basically almond pulp and water. It is drunk mostly in the west, where you can also buy it in supermarkets, but the best place to get it is in a bar, where it is freshly made.

Tea Sicilians don't drink a lot of tea *(tè)* and, if they do, it's generally only in the late afternoon, when they might take a cup with a few *pasticcini* (small cakes). You can order tea in bars, though it will usually arrive in the form of a cup of warm water with an accompanying tea bag. If this doesn't suit your taste, ask for the water molto caldo or *bollente* (boiling). In places where there

is a substantial Arab influence (Mazara del Vallo, for instance), you might find *tè ai pinoli* (pine-nut tea), often spruced up with a mint leaf. You can find a range of herbal teas in herbalist's shops *(erboristeria)*, which will sometimes also stock health foods.

Soft Drinks The usual range of international soft drinks are available in Sicily although they tend to be expensive if bought outside a supermarket (anywhere between €1 and €1.50).

Water While tap water is reliable and safe throughout the country, most Sicilians prefer to drink bottled mineral water *(acqua minerale)*. It will be either sparkling *(frizzante)* or still *(naturale)* and you will be asked in restaurants and bars which you would prefer. If you want a glass of tap water, ask for *acqua dal rubinetto*, although simply asking for *acqua naturale* will also suffice.

Alcoholic Drinks

Beer The main domestic labels are Peroni, Dreher and Moretti, all very drinkable and cheaper than the imported varieties.

Sicily imports beers from throughout Europe and the rest of the world. Several German beers, for instance, are available in bottles or cans; English beers and Guinness are often found on tap *(alla spina)* in *birrerie* (bars specialising in beer).

Wine See the earlier section 'Dining *alla Siciliana*' for details of Sicilian wines.

Liqueurs Sicily's most famous dessert wine is Marsala, a heavy sweet wine which is made exclusively in and around the city of the same name (see the Western Sicily chapter for details). The best (and most widely known) label is Florio. After dinner try a shot of grappa, a strong, clear brew made from grapes. Or you could go with an *amaro*, a dark liqueur prepared from herbs or the delightful *limoncello*, a refreshing bittersweet lemon liqueur. For a sweeter liqueur, try an almond-flavoured *amaretto* or the aniseed *sambuca*.

ENTERTAINMENT
Bars & Pubs
Italians cannot be said to have a 'drinking culture' but, especially in the bigger cities, you'll find plenty of bars. You can get beer, wine or anything else at practically any bar where you can also get coffee. They range from work-a-day grungy to chic places-to-be-seen. Places operating first and foremost as nocturnal drinking establishments generally stay open until about 1am.

Perhaps one reason why Italians don't tend to wander out of bars legless is the price of a drink: a tiny glass of beer can start at around €2! For a pint you are looking at an average of €4. However, if you ask for a shot of something like whisky at a bar, you may well be bowled over not only by the cheap price (€3.10) but the generosity of the serving!

Discos & Clubs
Discos (what Brits think of as clubs) are expensive: entrance charges hover around €13, which may or may not include a drink. Sicily is not the most happening clubland but you'll find some reasonable places in Palermo and coastal spots such as Cefalù and Taormina. Some are huge, with several dance spaces catering to various tastes.

Outside the big cities and the summer resorts, the pickings are slim. Often the clubs are out in the countryside and if you aren't in the know and don't have wheels they can remain pretty much out of reach. The theory is that at least the city- and town-dwellers don't have their sleep ruined.

Jazz
The number of jazz fans is growing in Sicily and in summer there are quite a few jazz festivals in major towns and cities. A real treat is to see live jazz at the Chiesa di Santa Maria dello Spasimo in Palermo, a wonderful venue that is free to all (see Lo Spasimo under La Kalsa in the Palermo chapter for more details).

Classical Music
Palermo and Catania are great places for classical concerts, either at the Teatro Massimo or at the Teatro Politeama-Garibaldi (both in Palermo) or at Teatro Massimo Bellini in Catania.

Cinemas
There is no shortage of cinemas in Sicily but all foreign films are dubbed into Italian. It costs about €6.70 to see a movie although that can come down to €3.60 on the cheap day (often Wednesday).

Theatre
If you can understand Italian, you'll have several theatres to choose from in places such as Palermo, Syracuse, Catania and Enna. Performances in languages other than Italian are hard to come by; enquire in tourist offices.

One great way of keeping abreast of cultural festivals and events is the handy Lapis guide, which comes out fortnightly in Sicily's major towns and cities. It's a free publication, with extensive listings for jazz, electronic music, pubs, cabaret and plays.

SPECTATOR SPORT
Football
Il calcio (football) excites Sicilian souls more than politics, religion, good food and dressing up all put together. Unfortunately, no Sicilian team has been in the premier league (Serie A) for quite a while; Palermo are perennial strugglers around the middle of Serie C. Most Sicilians, though, are fanatical supporters of Italy's most successful team of the last 40 years: Juventus of Turin. On those rare occasions when they are forced to play a home match away from home (usually as a punishment imposed by soccer authorities on account of crowd trouble), Juventus always play in Palermo's La Favorita stadium. Tickets for matches at La Favorita can be bought from newsstands in Palermo.

SHOPPING
Shopping in Sicily is probably not what you are used to back home. Most shops are small businesses and large department stores and supermarkets tend to be thin on the ground.

If you need necessities such as underwear, tights, pyjamas, T-shirts or toiletries, head for one of the large retail stores such as Oviesse or Rinascente, found in most major cities. Otherwise, you can pick up underwear, tights and pyjamas in a haberdashery *(merceria)*, toiletries and condoms in a pharmacy or sometimes in an alimentari, and items such as T-shirts in a normal clothing store. Supermarkets also stock toiletries and condoms. For stationery such as airmail paper, notepads, pens, greeting cards and so on, try a paper-goods shop *(cartoleria)*.

The most interesting places to shop in Sicily are at the markets and every town worth its salt has at least one. Palermo's La Vucciria is probably the most famous of all and many Palermitans also shop in one of the city's two other markets. Catania has an excellent produce market and Syracuse's is fine too. At most markets you can pick up virtually everything you need, from fish to frocks and all things in between. These are also the places to go to buy the best in imitation gear, as most Sicilians like to dress well but can't afford to buy the real McCoy.

Ceramics

Since the days of the ancient Greeks, Sicily has deservedly maintained a reputation for high-quality ceramics such as vases, ornaments and tableware. The best places to buy them are in Caltagirone, Santo Stefano di Camastra and Sciacca, the main centres of production.

Souvenirs & Handicrafts

Sicily does a roaring trade in souvenirs and handicrafts, particularly as most of the traditional crafts are fast disappearing, leaving the past in the hands of souvenir sellers. One of the most popular souvenirs is a miniature model of the traditional Sicilian cart, which once ruled the countryside before the advent of sealed roads. Painstakingly decorated with all kinds of colourful features, the originals are now collector's items in high demand. Also popular are Sicilian puppets from the island's most typical form of entertainment, the puppet theatre.

Getting There & Away

Sicily is not the easiest place in Europe to get to. The best (and fastest) way to get there is by air – it can often be cheaper than the long overland route, which involves travelling the length of Italy. If you're coming from outside Europe, competition between airlines on intercontinental routes means you should be able to pick up a reasonably priced fare to Rome or Milan, even if you are coming from as far away as Australia or New Zealand. It's no problem to pick up an onward connecting flight to Sicily once you're in Italy. If you live in Europe, there are a limited number of direct flights available as well as some interesting charter options and, if time is on your side, you can also travel overland by hopping on a train. Another alternative is to arrive by boat from Naples, Genoa or Livorno.

AIR
Airports & Airlines
Sicily has two main airports: Falcone-Borsellino (☎ 091 702 04 09, W www.gesap.it – Italian only) outside Palermo, and Fonta-narossa (☎ 095 34 05 05, W www.aeroporto .catania.it) in Catania. There is also a small airport at Birgi, near Tràpani, which is only used for domestic flights within Sicily (see the Getting Around chapter for details). The island is not served by intercontinental flights and only a limited number of airlines fly there. If you're coming from outside Italy you'll more than likely have to pick up a connecting flight (and probably change airlines) in either Rome or Milan; if you're coming from within Italy, Palermo and Catania are served by flights from a number of Italian destinations. Alitalia is the main carrier to and from Sicily, serving both Palermo and Catania. Another local airline is the Sardinian Meridiana, which has flights between mainland Italy and Sicily. During the summer months (usually May to October) both airports are served by a number of charter flights, although airline schedules can be restrictive.

Buying Tickets
With a bit of research – ringing around travel agents, checking Internet sites, perusing the travel ads in newspapers – you can often get yourself a good travel deal. Start early as some of the cheapest tickets need to be bought well in advance and popular flights can sell out.

Full-time students and people aged under 26 years (under 30 in some countries) have access to better deals than other travellers. You have to show a document proving your date of birth or a valid International Student Identity Card (ISIC) when buying your ticket and boarding the plane.

Generally, there is nothing to be gained by buying a ticket direct from the airline. Discounted tickets are released to selected travel agents and specialist discount agencies, and these are usually the cheapest deals going.

One exception to this rule is the expanding number of 'no-frills' carriers, which mostly sell only direct to travellers. Unlike the 'full-service' airlines, no-frills carriers often make one-way tickets available at around half the return fare, meaning that it is easy to put together an open-jaw ticket when you fly to one place but leave from another.

The other exception is booking on the Internet. Many airlines, full-service and no-frills, offer some excellent fares to Web surfers. They may sell seats by auction or simply cut prices to reflect the reduced cost of electronic selling.

Many travel agencies around the world have Web sites, which can make the Internet a quick and easy way to compare prices. There is also an increasing number of online agents, such as W www.travelocity.com and W www.deckchair.com, that operate only on the Internet. Online ticket sales work well if you are doing a simple one-way or return trip on specified dates. However, online superfast fare generators are no substitute for a travel agent who knows all about special deals, has strategies for avoiding layovers and can offer advice on everything from which airline has the best vegetarian food to the best travel insurance to bundle with your ticket.

You may find the cheapest flights are advertised by obscure agencies. Most such firms are honest and solvent, but there are some rogue fly-by-night outfits around. Paying by credit card generally offers protection, as most card issuers provide refunds if you can prove you didn't get what you paid for. Similar protection can be obtained by buying a ticket from a bonded agent, such as one covered by the Air Travel Organiser's Licence (ATOL; W www.atol .org.uk) scheme in the UK. Agents who accept only cash should hand over the tickets straight away and not tell you to 'come back tomorrow'. After you've made a booking or paid your deposit, call the airline and confirm that the booking was made. It's generally not advisable to send money (even cheques) through the post unless the agent is very well established – some travellers have reported being ripped off by fly-by-night mail-order ticket agents.

If you purchase a ticket and later want to make changes to your route or get a refund, you need to contact the original travel agent. Airlines issue refunds only to the purchaser of a ticket – usually the travel agent who bought the ticket on your behalf. Many travellers change their routes halfway through their trips, so think carefully before you buy a ticket which is not easily refunded.

For Sicily, the cheapest deals tend to be available out-of-season (between October and April) and when travelling on weekdays. Always ask about the route: it may be that the cheapest tickets involve an inconvenient stopover. Don't take schedules for granted either: airlines usually change their schedules twice a year, at the end of March and the end of October.

Travellers with Specific Needs

If they're warned early enough, airlines can often make special arrangements for travellers, such as wheelchair assistance at airports or vegetarian meals on the flight. Children under two years travel for 10% of the standard fare (or free on some airlines) as long as they don't occupy a seat. They don't get a baggage allowance. 'Skycots', baby food and nappies should be provided by the airline if requested in advance. Children aged between two and 12 can usually occupy a seat for half to two-thirds of the full fare, and do get a baggage allowance.

The disability-friendly Web site at W www .allgohere.com has an airline directory that provides information on the facilities offered by various airlines.

The Rest of Italy

Alitalia (☎ 800 05 03 50, W www.alitalia.it in Italian, W www.alitalia.co.uk in English) flies to Palermo from Rome at least a dozen times daily and from Milan (sometimes via Naples) at least 11 times daily. Specials are frequently available – for example, you can fly from Rome to Palermo for as little as €80 and Milan to Catania for €100.

The Italian domestic airline Meridiana (☎ 199 11 13 33, W www.meridiana.it – Italian only) has numerous regular flights between mainland Italy (Bologna, Milan, Florence, Pisa, Turin and Verona) and Palermo and Catania. A standard one-way

Air Travel Glossary

Alliances Many of the world's leading airlines are now intimately involved with each other, sharing everything from reservations systems and check-in to aircraft and frequent-flyer schemes. Opponents say that alliances restrict competition. Whatever the arguments, there is no doubt that big alliances are the way of the future.

Courier Fares Businesses often need to send urgent documents or freight securely and quickly. Courier companies hire people to accompany the package through customs and, in return, offer a discount ticket which is sometimes a bargain. However, you may have to surrender all your baggage allowance and take only carry-on luggage.

Fares Airlines traditionally offer 1st class (coded F), business class (coded J) and economy class (coded Y) tickets. These days there are so many promotional and discounted fares available that few passengers pay full fare.

Lost Tickets If you lose your airline ticket, an airline will usually treat it like a travellers cheque and, after enquiries, issue you with another one. Legally, however, an airline is entitled to treat it like cash and if you lose it then it's gone forever. Take very good care of your tickets.

Onward Tickets An entry requirement for many countries is that you have a ticket out of the country. If you're unsure of your next move, the easiest solution is to buy the cheapest onward ticket to a neighbouring country or a ticket from a reliable airline which can later be refunded if you do not use it.

Open-Jaw Tickets These are return tickets where you fly out to one place but return from another. If available, this can save you backtracking to your arrival point.

Overbooking Since every flight has some passengers who fail to show up, airlines often book more passengers than they have seats. Usually excess passengers make up for the no-shows, but occasionally somebody gets 'bumped' onto the next available flight. Guess who it is most likely to be? The passengers who check in late. If you do get 'bumped', you are normally offered some form of compensation.

Reconfirmation Some airlines require you to reconfirm your flight at least 72 hours prior to departure. Check your travel documents to see if this is the case.

Restrictions Discounted tickets often have various restrictions on them – such as needing to be paid for in advance and incurring a penalty to be altered or cancelled. Others are restrictions on the minimum and maximum period you must be away.

Round-the-World Tickets RTW tickets give you a limited period (usually a year) in which to circumnavigate the globe. You can go anywhere the carrying airlines go, as long as you don't backtrack. The number of stopovers or total number of separate flights is decided before you set off and they usually cost a bit more than a basic return flight.

Ticketless Travel Airlines are gradually waking up to the realisation that paper tickets are unnecessary encumbrances. On simple one-way or return trips, reservations details can be held on computer and the passenger merely shows ID to claim their seat.

Transferred Tickets Airline tickets cannot be transferred from one person to another. Travellers sometimes try to sell the return half of their ticket, but officials can ask you to prove that you are the person named on the ticket. On an international flight, tickets are compared with passports.

fare from Bologna to Palermo/Catania is €214/229, from Milan it's around €229 to both and from Florence €205/215.

Air Europe (☎ 800 45 40 00, reservations ☎ 079 285 44 00, W www.aireurope.it – Italian only) also flies from Milan to Palermo and Catania; a standard return fare is around €155 to both destinations.

Air One (☎ 06 48 88 00 in Rome, W www.air-one.it) flies from Rome and Milan to Pantelleria and Lampedusa. Various specials are always available (but do get booked up quickly) – you can fly from Rome to Pantelleria or Lampedusa for €170 return. From Milan to Pantelleria it costs from €210 return. Air One also has flights from Milan to Palermo and Catania (both around €200 one way), although there are also specials available for return flights.

Continental Europe

It's worth considering air travel between Sicily and other countries in continental Europe if you are pushed for time. Short hops can be expensive but good deals are available from some major hubs.

Several airlines, including Alitalia, Qantas and Air France, offer cut-rate fares on the European legs of long-haul flights. These are usually cheap, but often involve flying at night or early in the morning.

Keep an eye out for special deals which can bring prices down.

France A recommended discount travel agency is OTU Voyages (☎ 01 40 29 12 22, W www.otu.fr), 39 ave Georges-Bernanos, 75005 Paris, which has branches across the country and specialises in student travel. Other agencies include Voyageurs du Monde (☎ 01 42 86 16 00, W www.vdm.com), 55 rue Ste-Anne, 75002 Paris, and Nouvelles Frontières (☎ 08 25 00 08 25, W www.nouvelles-frontieres.fr), 87 blvd de Grenelle, 75015 Paris, with branches across the country.

Alitalia flies between Paris and Palermo and Catania. At the time of research a return flight cost around €320. There are regular flights between Paris and Rome or Milan. The train is generally an easier bet for Milan

(see Train under Land later in this chapter for details) but you can occasionally find good air deals to Rome – for example, a low-season return flight with Alitalia costs around €213 (cheaper than the train).

Germany If you're looking for a cheap deal, Munich is a haven of bucket shops and more mainstream budget travel outlets. Council Travel (☎ 089-39 50 22), Adalbertstrasse 32, near the university, is one of the best. In Berlin, a recommended agency is STA Travel (☎ 030-311 09 50, W www.statravel.de), Goethestrasse 73, 10625 Berlin, which has branches around the country. Germany also has a number of online travel agents that are worth checking out. Try W www.lastminute.de and W www.justtravel.de.

Alitalia flies from Munich to Palermo and Catania via Rome or Milan. At the time of research a flight to Rome cost €203. KLM-Royal Dutch Airlines flies from Munich to Rome from around €275 one way. Lufthansa flies direct to Milan and Naples for around €235 and €285 respectively.

The Netherlands There are plenty of discount travel agents along Amsterdam's Rokin, but shop around to compare prices before deciding. One recommended travel agent, Holland International (☎ 070-307 6307), has offices in most cities. Online, try W www.budgettravel.com or W www.airfair.nl.

Alitalia (☎ 020 470 01 18) flies to both Palermo and Catania via Rome; return flights cost around €445 in the high season.

Spain Recommended agencies include Barcelo Viajes (☎ 91-559 18 19), Princesa 3, 28008 Madrid, which has branches in major cities, and Nouvelles Frontières (☎ 91-547 42 00, W www.nouvelles-frontieres.es), which has an office at Plaza de España 18, 28008 Madrid, plus branches in major cities.

Alitalia flies from Madrid to both Palermo and Catania (via Rome and Milan) for around €420 return. Discount return flights to Palermo from Madrid cost about €300.

In Barcelona, Meridiana (☎ 93 487 57 75), Paseo de Gracia 55, flies to Palermo via major Italian cities. A return costs €390.

The UK & Ireland

Discount air travel is big business in London. Advertisements for many travel agencies appear in the travel pages of the weekend broadsheet newspapers, in *Time Out*, the *Evening Standard* and in the free magazine *TNT*.

For students or travellers under 26 years, a popular travel agency is STA Travel (☎ 020-7361 6262, **W** www.statravel.co.uk), which has an office at 86 Old Brompton Rd, London, and branches across the country. STA sells tickets to all travellers but caters especially to young people and students.

Other recommended discount travel agents include Trailfinders (☎ 020-7937 1234, **W** www.trailfinders.co.uk), 215 Kensington High St, London, and Flightbookers (☎ 020-7757 2000, **W** www.ebookers.com), 177–178 Tottenham Court Rd, London.

No-frills airlines (see Buying Tickets earlier) are increasingly big business for travel between the UK and Italy. While none fly directly to Sicily, you can fly to one of Italy's major hubs and take a domestic flight onto the island. Go (☎ 0870 607 6543 in the UK, ☎ 848 88 77 66 in Italy, **W** www.go-fly.com) flies to Rome and Naples, and Ryanair (☎ 0870 333 1231 in the UK, ☎ 199 11 41 14 in Italy, **W** www.ryanair.com) flies to Rome. Fares vary according to availability; book early and be prepared to travel mid-week to get the best deals.

The two principal airlines linking the UK and Italy are Alitalia and British Airways. Alitalia (☎ 0870 544 8259, **W** www.alitalia.co.uk), 4 Portman Square, London, has regular flights from London to both Palermo and Catania for approximately £220. British Airways (☎ 0845 7733 377, **W** www.british-airways.com), 156 Regent St, London, does not fly to Sicily but you can fly to Rome (a standard return costs around £200) and pick up a connecting flight with an Italian airline there.

Meridiana (☎ 020-7839 2222), 15 Charles II St, London, flies from London to Palermo and Catania, via various Italian cities, for around UK£230 return. LAI Travel (☎ 020-7837 1477, **W** www.laitravel.co.uk), 185 King's Cross Rd, London, has return flights to Palermo and Catania costing around £240.

At the time of writing a new airline, Ciao Fly (**W** www.ciaofly.com), was about to launch, offering flights from London to Catania. For more details check out its Web site.

There are no direct scheduled flights to Sicily from Ireland, so you will need to pick up a connection in Milan or Rome. It is worth comparing the cost of flying to Italy directly from Dublin with the cost of flying to London first and then on to Italy.

Aer Lingus (☎ 0818 365 000, **W** www.aerlingus.com) has regular daily flights to Rome from Dublin for approximately €510. Alitalia's office in Dublin (☎ 01-677 5171) is located at 63 Dawson St, Dublin 2.

The USA & Canada

Discount travel agents in the USA are known as consolidators (although you won't see a sign on the door saying Consolidator). San Francisco is the ticket consolidator capital of America, though some good deals can be found in Los Angeles, New York and other big cities. Consolidators can be found through the Yellow Pages or the major daily newspapers. The *New York Times*, the *Los Angeles Times*, the *Chicago Tribune* and the *San Francisco Examiner* all produce weekly travel sections in which you will find a number of travel agency ads. Watch out for their SOT number – if they have one of these they are probably legitimate.

Council Travel (**W** www.counciltravel.com) is America's largest student travel organisation. It has around 60 offices in the USA – its head office (☎ 800-226 8624) is located at 205 E 42 St, New York, NY 10017. STA Travel (☎ 800-777 0112, **W** www.statravel.com) has offices in Boston, Chicago, Miami, New York, Philadelphia, San Francisco and other major cities.

At the time of writing, a one-way high-season fare from New York to Rome cost around US$1000. The same fare from the West Coast cost an extra US$500. Note that these fares will involve one, or maybe two, connections. If you can't find a particularly good deal, it is worth considering a cheap transatlantic hop to London to trawl through the bargains there. See The UK & Ireland earlier for details.

Canadian discount air ticket sellers are also known as consolidators and their air fares tend to be about 10% higher than those sold in the USA.

Travel CUTS (☎ 800-667 2887, W www.travelcuts.com) is Canada's national student travel agency and has offices in all major cities.

Return fares from Toronto to Rome or Milan start from around C$1430 in the high season (around C$1050 in the low season).

Australia & New Zealand

For flights from Australia to Europe (and Italy), there are a lot of competing airlines and a wide variety of air fares. There are no direct flights between Australia and Sicily so you'll need to change planes at some point in Italy. Cheap flights from Australia to Europe generally go via Southeast Asian capitals or the Middle East. If a long stopover between connections is necessary, transit accommodation is sometimes included in the price of the ticket. If it's at your own expense, it may be worth considering a more expensive ticket.

Quite a few travel offices specialise in discount air tickets. Some travel agencies, particularly smaller ones, advertise cheap air fares in the travel sections of weekend newspapers such as the *Age* in Melbourne and the *Sydney Morning Herald*.

STA Travel (☎ 131 776 Australia-wide, W www.statravel.com.au) and Flight Centre (☎ 131 600 Australia-wide, W www.flightcentre.com.au) are major dealers in cheap air fares.

High-season return fares to Palermo (via Rome or Milan) cost from around A$2400 return; low season fares are about A$1000 cheaper.

In New Zealand, as in Australia, STA Travel (☎ 09-309 0458, W www.statravel.co.nz) and Flight Centre (☎ 09-309 6171, W www.flightcentre.co.nz) are popular travel agents. Ads for other agencies can be found in the travel section of the *New Zealand Herald.*

From New Zealand, Qantas or Alitalia flights from Australia are the most direct way to get to Palermo. Expect to pay around NZ$2200/2700 for a return flight in the low/high season.

LAND

Located at the southern extremity of the Italian peninsula, getting to Sicily overland involves travelling the entire length of the country, which can either be an enormous drain on your time or, if you have plenty to spare, a wonderful way of seeing Italy on your way to Sicily. There are plenty of options for entering Italy by train, bus or private vehicle, but at some point you are going to have to stop at a mainland port and travel over the water by boat (most people go from Villa San Giovanni or Règgio di Calàbria to Messina). Bus is usually the cheapest option, but services are less frequent and considerably less comfortable than the train.

If you are travelling by bus, train or car to Italy it will be necessary to check whether you require visas to the countries you intend to pass through.

Bus

There is no direct service to Sicily from outside Italy. Eurolines (W www.eurolines.com), a consortium of European coach companies, operates services across Europe but only goes as far as Rome. If you are sold on arriving by bus, you have to change buses (and carriers) in Rome.

Contact Eurolines in Rome (☎ 06 440 40 09) at Eurolines Roma, Circonvallazione Nomentana 574, Lato Stazione Tiburtina.

The Rest of Italy From Rome, Segesta/Interbus (☎ 06 481 96 76) at Saistours, Piazza della Repubblica 42, has two departures daily from Piazzale Tiburtina to

Messina (€31, 9 hours), Palermo (€35.65, 12 hours) and Syracuse (€34.60, 12 hours), all via Naples.

Sais Autolinee (☎ 051 24 21 50 in Bologna, ☎ 050 4 62 88 in Pisa) has buses from Bologna to Messina (€54.30, 14 hours, via Florence and Siena) and from Pisa to Messina (€54.30, 15 hours), Catania and all the way down the Eastern coast (via Florence, Siena and Perugia). Sais also has buses from Naples and Amalfi to Sicily.

Continental Europe The Eurolines network covers all of Europe. Check out the Web site (W www.eurolines.com) for details of offices, timetables and fares in each country. We've listed some of the main offices here.

Austria (☎ 01-712 04 53) Schalter 2, Autobusbahnhof Wien-Mitte, Hauptstrasse 1b, Vienna
France (☎ 01 49 72 57 80) 22 rue Malmaison, 93177 Paris
Germany (☎ 069-79 03 50) Am Romerhof 17, 60486 Frankfurt-am-Main
Netherlands (☎ 020-560 87 87) Julianaplein 5, 1097 DN Amsterdam
Spain (☎ 91-327 1381) Calle Alcalá 478, 28027 Madrid

The UK Eurolines (☎ 0870 514 3219, W www.eurolines.co.uk), 52 Grosvenor Gardens, Victoria, London SW1, runs buses to Rome (33 hours) at 8.30am on Monday, Wednesday and Friday with increased services from July to September. At the time of writing, under 26/adult return fares from London to Rome cost around £99/109, to Milan £89/99. Prices rise in the peak summer season (July and August) and in the week before Christmas.

Train

Not quite as tough-going as travelling by bus, one major advantage of getting to Sicily by train is the greater options you have en route, including more frequent departures and the possibility of breaking up your journey so that it isn't one long slog.

The *Thomas Cook European Timetable* is the trainophile's bible, giving a complete listing of train schedules, supplements and

reservations information. It is updated monthly and is available from Thomas Cook offices and agents worldwide.

On overnight hauls you can book a *cuccetta* (couchette) for around €15 to €23 on most international trains. In 1st class there are four bunks per cabin and in 2nd class there are six (see Types of Train later).

It is always advisable, and sometimes compulsory, to book seats on international trains to and from Sicily.

Some of the main international services include transport for private cars – an option worth examining to save wear and tear on your vehicle before it arrives in Sicily.

The Rest of Italy A one-way adult fare from Rome to Palermo on a EuroCity (EC) or InterCity (IC) train costs €79.50/55 for 1st/2nd class (11 hours, about nine daily). The equivalent from Milan costs €104/73 (19 hours, at least one daily). The *espresso* train from Rome to Messina costs €58.20/40.70 (about nine hours, five daily); from Milan to Messina with Eurostar (ES) costs €114/93.50 (14 hours, at least two daily).

See the following sections for details on types of trains, the Italian rail network and buying tickets.

Information For information on trains you can call ☎ 848 88 80 88 (in Italian) anywhere in Italy or visit W www.fs-online.com (in Italian, English, Dutch, French and Spanish).

Main train timetables generally display *arrivi* (arrivals) on a white background and *partenze* (departures) on a yellow one. Imminent arrivals and departures also appear on electronic boards. You will notice a plethora of symbols and acronyms on the main timetables, some of which are useful for identifying the kind of train concerned.

Types of Train A wide variety of trains circulate around Italy. They start with slow all-stops *locali*, which generally don't travel much beyond their main city of origin or province. Next come the *regionali*, which also tend to be slow but cover greater distances, sometimes going beyond their region of origin. *Interregionali* and *espresso* trains cover greater distances still and don't necessarily stop at every station.

From this level there is a leap upwards to InterCity (IC), faster long-distance trains operating between major cities and for which you generally have to pay a *supplemento* on top of the normal cost of a ticket. Services using top-of-the-range locos are now collectively known as Eurostar Italia (ES).

Notturne (night trains) are either old *espressi* or, increasingly, InterCity Notte (ICN) services. You generally have the option of a couchette (one of four or six fold-down bunkbeds in a compartment) or a proper bed in a *vagone letto* (sleeping car), which tends to be much more expensive. The international version is the EuroNight (EN).

Passes & Discounts Eurail, InterRail, Europass and Flexipass tickets are valid on the national rail network. Passes for travel within Italy, which allow you unlimited rail travel for varying periods of time, are listed below. These can all be bought in Italy (from any mainline station) or before you leave home. In the UK, contact Railchoice (☎ 020-8659 7300, **W** www.railchoice .co.uk).

Italy Railcard – eight, 15, 21 or 30 days' unlimited travel; prices range from €209 to €360 for 2nd-class tickets

Italy Flexicard – four, eight or 12 days' travel within one month; prices range from €160 to €280 for 2nd-class tickets

EuroDomino – three to eight days' unlimited travel; prices for those aged under 26/adults range from €109/145 to €174/226 (note that those under 26 are restricted to 2nd-class tickets)

Biglietto Chilometrico – valid for two months; allows up to five people (singly or as a group) to cover 3000km, with a maximum of 20 trips; costs €116.70 and you must pay supplements on InterCity trains

People aged between 12 and 26 can acquire the Carta Verde and people aged 60 and over the Carta d'Argento. Both cost €25.80, are valid for a year and entitle holders to 20% off ticket prices. Children aged between four

and 12 years are automatically entitled to a 50% discount; those under four travel free.

Tickets There are many ticketing possibilities. Apart from the standard division between 1st and 2nd class on the faster trains (generally you can get only 2nd-class seats on locali and regionali), you usually have to pay a supplement for travelling on a fast train.

As with tickets, the price of the supplement is in part calculated according to the length of the journey. You can pay the supplement separately from the ticket. Thus if you have a 2nd-class return ticket from Florence to Rome, you might decide to avoid the supplement one way and take a slower train but pay a supplement for the return trip to speed things up a little. Whatever you decide, you need to pay the supplement before boarding the train.

You can buy rail tickets (for major destinations on fast trains at least) from most travel agents. If you choose to buy them at the station, there are automatic machines that accept cash. If you queue at the windows, watch out for those displaying the Eurostar sign – they will only sell you tickets on ES trains.

It is advisable, and in some cases obligatory, to book long-distance tickets in advance, whether international or domestic. In 1st class, booking is often mandatory (and free). Where it is optional (which is more often, but not always, the case in 2nd class), you may pay a €2.60 booking fee. Tickets can be booked at the windows in the station or at most travel agencies. It is also possible to book tickets over the phone (☎ 199 16 61 77) with a credit card.

Rules & Fines When you buy a ticket you are supposed to stamp it in one of the yellow machines scattered about all stations (usually with a *convalida* sign on them). Failure to do so will be rewarded with an on-the-spot fine. This rule does not apply to tickets purchased outside Italy. If you buy a return ticket, you must stamp it each way (each end of the ticket).

The ticket you buy is valid for two months until stamped. Once stamped it is valid for 24 hours if the journey distance (one way) is greater than 200km, six hours if it is less. For a return ticket, the time is calculated separately for each one-way journey (that is, on a short return trip you get six hours from the time of stamping on the way out and the same on the way back).

All seats on ES trains on Friday and Sunday must be booked in advance. On other days wagons for unbooked seats are set aside. If you board an ES train on a Friday or Sunday without a booking, you pay a €5.15 fine.

Continental Europe If you're travelling to Sicily from anywhere outside Italy you'll have to change trains somewhere along the line in Italy; the handiest place is Rome, although there are also trains for Sicily that depart from Milan and Turin (and travel via Rome).

From Paris to Palermo your options include the overnight sleeper which goes via Naples (€156.65 return). Other sample fares include Vienna (€239.20 single, 26 hours), Amsterdam (€334.90 single, 36 hours) and Barcelona (€255.15 single, 36 hours).

The UK The Channel Tunnel allows for land transport links between Britain and continental Europe. The Eurostar passenger train service (☎ 020-7928 5163, Ⓦ www .eurostar.com) travels from London to Paris and Brussels. The Eurotunnel vehicle service travels between Folkestone and Calais; see the Car & Motorcycle section later in this chapter for details.

Alternatively, you can get a train ticket that includes the Channel crossing by ferry, SeaCat or hovercraft. After that, you can travel via Paris and southern France or by swinging from Belgium down through Germany and Switzerland. The journey from London to Palermo takes 35 hours and a return fare costs around £500.

For information on fares and schedules including the Eurostar, contact the Rail Europe Travel Centre (☎ 0870 584 8848, Ⓦ www.raileurope.co.uk) or European Rail (☎ 020-7387 0444).

Car & Motorcycle

Driving to Sicily is an expensive proposition, especially once you cross the border into Italy, which has the highest motorway tolls (from the French or Swiss borders to Naples it'll cost around €45) as well as the most expensive petrol in Europe (see Car & Motorcycle in the Getting Around chapter). Furthermore, it's quite a drive to get to the ferry embarkation point at Villa San Giovanni, from where you'll cross the Straits of Messina into Sicily: you might make the trip from the French or Swiss borders in around 17 hours but only if you keep to the motorways, drive flat out (remember that the speed limit in Italy is 130km/h) and avoid the worst of the traffic – during the holiday seasons it'll be a minor miracle if you do.

From the UK, you can take your car across to France either by ferry or the Channel Tunnel car train, Eurotunnel (☎ 0870 840 0046, Ⓦ www.eurotunnel.com). The latter runs 24 hours, with up to four crossings (35 minutes) each hour between Folkestone and Calais in the high season. You pay for the vehicle only and fares vary according to the time of day and season. A one-way fare between Folkestone and Calais in August costs £137.50.

The main points of entry to Italy are: the Mt Blanc tunnel from France at Chamonix, which connects with the A5 for Turin and Milan; the Grand St Bernard tunnel from Switzerland (SS27), which also connects with the A5; and the Brenner pass from Austria (A13), which connects with the A22 to Bologna. Mountain passes in the Alps are often closed in winter and sometimes in autumn and spring, making the tunnels a less scenic but more reliable way to arrive in Italy. Make sure you have snow chains in winter.

An interesting Web site loaded with advice for people planning to drive in Europe is at Ⓦ www.ideamerge.com/motoeuropa. If you want help with route planning, try Ⓦ www.euroshell.com.

Paperwork & Preparations Proof of ownership of a private vehicle (a Vehicle Registration Document for UK-registered cars) should always be carried when driving through Europe. All EU member states' driving licences (not the old-style UK green licence) are fully recognised throughout Europe, regardless of your length of stay. Those with a non-EU licence are supposed to obtain an International Driving Permit (IDP) to accompany their national licence. In practice, you will probably be OK with national licences from countries such as Australia, Canada and the USA. If you decide to get the permit, your national automobile association can issue them.

Third-party motor insurance is a minimum requirement in Italy and throughout Europe. The Green Card, an internationally recognised proof of insurance obtainable from your insurer, is mandatory. Also ask your insurer for a European Accident Statement form, which can simplify matters in the event of an accident. Never sign statements you can't read or understand – insist on a translation and sign that only if it's acceptable.

A good investment is a European breakdown assistance policy, such as the AA Five Star Europe Service (☎ 0870 600 0371, W www.theaa.co.uk) in the UK. Check what motoring assistance/insurance policies are available from your country's various automobile organisations. In Italy, assistance can be obtained through the Automobile Club Italiano. See Organisations under Car & Motorcycle in the Getting Around chapter for details.

Every vehicle travelling across an international border should display a nationality plate of its country of registration. A warning triangle (to be used in the event of a breakdown) is compulsory throughout Europe. A first-aid kit, a spare-bulb kit and a fire extinguisher are also recommended.

See Road Rules under Car & Motorcycle in the Getting Around chapter for details on driving in Italy.

Rental There is a mind-boggling variety of special deals, and terms and conditions attached to car rental. Here are a few pointers to help you through.

Multinational agencies – Hertz, Avis, Budget and Europcar – will provide a reliable service and good standard of vehicle.

However, if you walk into an office and ask for a car on the spot, you will always pay high rates, even allowing for special weekend deals. National and local firms can sometimes undercut the multinationals but be sure to examine the rental agreement carefully.

Planning ahead and pre-booking a rental car through a multinational agency before leaving home will enable you to find the best deals. Pre-booked and prepaid rates are always cheaper. Fly/drive combinations and other packages are worth looking into. You simply pick up the vehicle on your arrival in Italy and return it to a nominated point at the end of the rental period. Ask your travel agency for information, or contact one of the major rental agencies.

No matter where you hire your car, make sure you understand what is included in the price (unlimited kilometres, tax, insurance, collision damage waiver and so on) and what your liabilities are. Insurance can be a vexed issue. Are you covered for theft, vandalism and fire damage? Since the most common and convenient way to pay for rental is by credit card, check whether or not you have car insurance with the credit card provider and what the conditions are. The extra cover provided may pick up the slack in any local cover.

The minimum rental age in Sicily is 21 years. A credit card is usually required. Note that some car rental agencies will not let you take the car on the ferry to Sicily (due to insurance reasons).

The cost of hiring a car varies according to the type of car and how long you are renting it for. For example, a three-door Corsa hired in Rome for a week will cost £159 with UK-based W www.carhire4less.co.uk. There's an extra charge of around £25 for dropping it off in Sicily.

Purchase It is illegal for non-residents to purchase vehicles anywhere in Italy, including Sicily. The UK is probably the best place to buy second-hand cars (prices are not so competitive for new cars). Bear in mind that you will be getting a right-hand-drive car (with the steering wheel on the right, for driving on the left-hand side of the road).

If you want a left-hand-drive car and can afford to buy new, prices are relatively low in Belgium, the Netherlands and Luxembourg. Paperwork can be tricky wherever you buy.

SEA

Unless you're flying, you'll have to board a ferry or hydrofoil at some point to get to Sicily (usually to Messina). The easiest and most common point is at Villa San Giovanni, from where there are regular ferries connections, or from Règgio di Calàbria, 15 minutes farther south at the end of the A3, where you can pick up a hydrofoil as well as a ferry. You can, however, also board a ferry in Naples, Genoa or Livorno bound for Palermo.

Tirrenia (☎ 091 602 11 11, W www .tirrenia.it – Italian only) has ferry services between Tunisia and Tràpani and between the Italian mainland, Sicily and Sardinia. Virtu Ferries (☎ 095 53 57 11, W www .virtuferries.com) has services between Malta and Pozzallo, Catania and Licata, and Grandi Navi Veloci/Grimaldi (☎ 091 58 74 04, W www.grimaldi.it – Italian only) runs boats between Genoa, Livorno and Palermo. Siremar (☎ 091 58 24 03, W www .siremar.it), Snav (☎ 091 611 85 25, W www.snavali.com) and Ustica Lines (☎ 091 844 90 02, W www.usticalines.it) all run services from Naples to Sicily: Siremar to Milazzo and on to the Aeolian Islands, Snav to Palermo and Ustica Lines to Ustica.

Although boarding a ferry to Sicily is almost as easy as getting on a bus, you might want to consider pre-booking your passage if you are travelling in the high season, especially if you have a vehicle.

The following agencies handle ticket bookings in these countries:

Belgium
Tirrenia: Armando Farina (☎ 3-231 5650) Cuyckstraat 1, Antwerp
France
Tirrenia: SNCM (☎ 01 49 14 24 55) rue Godot de Mauroy 12, Paris
Germany
Tirrenia: Armando Farina (☎ 069-666 8491) Schwarzenwaldstrasse 82, 730309 Frankfurt-am-Main

Malta
Tirrenia: Mifsud & Sons (☎ 356-23 22 11) 311 Republic St, Valletta VLT 04
Virtu Ferries: (☎ 356-31 88 54) 8 Princess Elizabeth St, Ta'Xbiex, MSD 11
Spain
Tirrenia: Viajes Montesol (☎ 93 49 034 19) Calle Guitar 43/3, Barcelona
Grandi Navi Veloci/Grimaldi: (☎ 93 44 398 98) Muelle Poniente Norte, Barcelona
Switzerland
Tirrenia: Avimare (☎ 01-315 8060) Oelikoner-strasse 47, Zurich
Tunisia
Tirrenia: CTN (☎ 01-321 300) 122 rue de Yougoslavie, Tunis
UK
Tirrenia: SMS UK Travel & Tourism (☎ 020-7244 8422) 40 Kenway Rd, London SW5 0RA
Grandi Navi Veloci/Grimaldi: G&C Lines (☎ 020-7930 5683) 103–105 Jermyn St, London SW1Y 6EE
USA
Grandi Navi Veloci: (☎ 313-563 4838) #1903 Monroe St, Dearborn, Michigan 48124

From Villa San Giovanni

FS (☎ 090 67 52 34) operates between 20 and 25 car-and-passenger ferries daily between Villa San Giovanni and Messina (25 minutes, hourly). At the time of research, prices for a single ticket were €0.95 for foot passengers and from €13.95 for cars (depending on size).

Caronte (☎ 090 4 14 15) runs ferries to Messina every 10 to 20 minutes (every hour between midnight and 6am) daily; the journey takes 35 minutes. Cars cost the same as for the FS ferries but foot passengers travel for free. Tickets can be purchased at kiosks at the respective terminals by the ferry dock.

From Règgio di Calàbria

FS runs 20 hydrofoils a day from Monday to Saturday and 10 on Sunday. The 20-minute trip costs €3.10/4.65 single/return. Navigazione Generale Italiana (NGI; mobile ☎ 0335 84 277 84) has car ferries between Messina's port and Règgio di Calàbria every two hours from 12.20am to about 11.15pm. Car tickets start at €7.75; foot passengers pay only €0.50.

From Naples

Tirrenia (☎ 081 251 47 21), Stazione Marittima, has a daily service to Palermo departing at 8.45pm and arriving at 6.30am. Tickets cost from €34.35/40 in the low/high season (cabins are available). Car-and-driver tickets start from €66.85/85.45 in the low/high season.

Snav (☎ 081 761 23 48), Via Giordano Bruno 84, Naples, runs one ferry daily to the Aeolian Islands from mid-April to early October, departing at 5.30pm and arriving at 9.30pm. Tickets cost €51.65/77.45 in the low/high season; car-and-driver tickets cost from €108.45/160.10. The ferry terminal is at Mergellina, to the west of the city centre.

Ustica Lines (☎ 081 580 03 40) has hydrofoils from Naples to Tràpani (via Ustica, Favignana and Lèvanzo) at 3pm Monday, Thursday and Saturday between 15 June and 15 September. The journey to Tràpani takes seven hours and costs €82.65.

From Genoa

Grandi Navi Veloci/Grimaldi (☎ 010 58 93 31), Via Fieschi 17, in Genoa, runs ferries daily (except Sunday) to Palermo during the high season, departing between 8.30pm and 11pm, depending on the day. The 20-hour journey costs from €74.40/106.40 in the low/high season for a *poltrona* (airline type armchair) and €100.70/152.35 for a car (less for motorcycles and scooters). The ferries depart from the Terminal Traghetti at Via Milano 51.

From Livorno

Grandi Navi Veloci/Grimaldi (☎ 0586 40 98 04), Varco Galvali, Darsena 1 in Livorno, has three departures weekly (11pm on Monday, Wednesday and Friday) for Palermo. The trip takes 17 hours. Tickets for a poltrona cost from €62/100 in the low/high season; cars cost from €90.40/137 (less for motorcycles and scooters). There are also cabins (sleeping up to four) and suites available. The ferries depart from Stazione Marittima in Calata Carrara, northwest of the city centre. Ferries from Palermo to Livorno depart at 11pm on Tuesday, Thursday and Saturday.

From Malta

Virtu Ferries (☎ 356-31 88 54), 8 Princess Elizabeth St, Ta'Xbiex, has ferries departing Malta for Pozallo between 1 March and 7 October (schedules vary). Return tickets cost up to Lm37 and cars can be transported from 1 May to 7 October. Ferries from Malta to Catania depart between 1 March and 7 October (some can take cars). There are services to Licata from 19 July to 2 September.

From Tunisia

Tirrenia (☎ 01-321 300), at 122 rue de Yougoslavie in Tunis, has a weekly ferry departing Tunis for Tràpani at 9pm on Monday. The journey takes 10½ hours and poltrona tickets cost €43.65/51.40 in the low/high season.

ORGANISED TOURS

Options for organised travel to Sicily are increasing all the time. The Italian State Tourist Office (see Tourist Offices Abroad in the Facts for the Visitor chapter) can provide a list of tour operators, noting what each specialises in. Tours can save you a lot of hassle, but they rob you of independence and generally do not come cheap.

General

Sestante CIT (known as CIT or Citalia outside Italy), with offices worldwide (see Tourist Offices Abroad in the Facts for the Visitor chapter), organises a variety of tours.

A couple of big specialists in the UK are Magic of Italy (☎ 020-8939 5453, Ⓦ www.magictravelgroup.co.uk), 227 Shepherd's Bush Rd, London, and Alitalia's subsidiary, Italiatour (☎ 01883-621900, Ⓦ www.italiatour.co.uk), at 9 Whyteleafe Business Village, Whyteleafe Hill, Whyteleafe, Surrey CR3 0AT. Italiatour is based in Dublin at 4 Dawson St, Dublin 2 (☎ 01-671 7821). Italiatour's US operation (Ⓦ www.italiatour.com) has a couple of Sicilian tours, including the 'Magnificent Sicily' (nine days, US$1599 including air fare and accommodation). Between them all they offer a wide range of tours, city breaks and resort-based holidays covering most of the island.

Walking Tours

Several companies offer organised walking tours in selected areas. Ifyoutravel (☎ 020-7565 7575, **W** www.ifyoutravel.com), 27a Pembridge Villas, Notting Hill, London, has a week-long walking tour based in Poggi that covers walks around Mt Etna, the Alcantara Valley and the Nebrodi mountains. Tours costs around £600 (including air fare from the UK).

Vantaggio (☎ 212-784 0259, **W** www .vantaggio.com), 17th floor, 41 East 57th St, New York, has a Sicily Walking Tour, moving in eight days from Enna to Palermo and taking in some spectacular scenery in the Madonie mountains. Tours cost around US$1865 (air fare not included).

Another good tour is the 'Splendors of Sicily' tour (around US$2995 including accommodation and meals) organised by Italian Connection (☎ 1800 462 7911, **W** www .italian-connection.com), 11 Fairway Dr, Suite 210, Edmonton, Alberta, Canada T6J ZW4. Starting in Catania before transferring to Lago di Lentini, this trip involves day walks to places such as Taormina, Castelmola, Syracuse, Noto, Ragusa Ibla, Agrigento and Èrice.

Cooking Tours

Tasting Places (☎ 020-7460 0077, **W** www .tastingplaces.com), Unit 108, Buspace Studios, Conlan St, London, offers one-week trips led by cooking instructors, which are perhaps the best means of getting to the island's heart – through its stomach. You cook and eat your way to a better understanding at their base at Villa Ravida in Menfi, near Selinunte in the Agrigento province in Sicily's southwest. Prices start at £1125 per person (excluding flights).

Another cooking tour that gets good feedback is Cook Italy's (☎ 051 644 86 12 in Italy, **W** www.cookitaly.com) week-long cooking school in beautiful Syracuse, which relies on fresh local produce. The course costs around €2350 (and includes accommodation in a double room).

Other Tours

If you're looking to get right into Sicily's history, architecture and archaeology, Smithsonian Study Tours (☎ 202-357 4700, **W** www. smithsonianstudytours.org), 1100 Jefferson Dr SW, Washington, DC 20560-0702, has a 12-night 'Legacy of Sicily' trip, which includes time in Palermo, Segesta, Èrice, Selinunte, Agrigento, Piazza Armerina, Syracuse, Catania and Taormina. The tour costs about US$4765 per person (and includes the air fare from New York and accommodation).

Getting Around

You can reach all of the major – and most of the minor – destinations in Sicily by train or bus, but it always seems to take a lot longer than it should, especially considering the size of the island.

Trains are the most efficient means of public transport, linking all of the major cities and connecting most of the coastline, but they tend to chug along in no real rush to get to their destination. Some train stations in the interior are inconveniently located a bus ride or long walk out of town.

Bus travel can be a little more difficult to work out because there are so many different companies, but it is a cheap way to get around.

Your own wheels give you the most freedom, and you can stray off the main routes to discover out-of-the-way hill towns or deserted beaches. The limited motorway *(autostrada)* system is toll-free except for certain tracts between Messina and Catania and Palermo and Messina, which is a huge bonus, but the extensive network of state roads can be a traffic nightmare. You should also be aware that petrol is expensive and that the stress of driving and parking your car in the bigger Sicilian cities could easily ruin your trip.

AIR

Boat trips to Sicily's offshore islands are frequent and reliable, but you may want to catch planes for Pantelleria and the Pelagic Islands if your time is limited.

Flights can be bought at the airport or booked through any travel agency, including Sestante CIT (☎ 091 58 63 33), Via della Libertà 12, Palermo, and Centro Turistico Studentesco e Giovanile (CTS; ☎ 091 33 22 09), Via Nicolò Garzilli 28g, Palermo. For further addresses see Travel Agencies under individual cities in the regional chapters.

Air Sicilia (☎ 091 702 03 10 or toll-free 800 41 24 11) and Alitalia (☎ 848 86 56 41, Ⓦ www.alitalia.it) fly twice daily to Lampedusa from Palermo (€93 one way). There are also flights with Air One (☎ 091 702 01 11, Ⓦ www.air-one.it) between Palermo and Lampedusa. Gandalf Airlines (☎ 06 420 14 895, Ⓦ www.gandalfair.it) has departures for Pantelleria from Birgi airport, south of Tràpani, priced at about €77.

BUS

Bus services within Sicily are provided by a variety of companies and vary from local routes linking small villages to intercity connections. By utilising the local services, it is possible to get to just about any location on the island. Buses are usually a more reliable and faster way to get around if your destination is not on a main train line (trains tend to be cheaper on major routes).

You might get bus timetables for the provincial and intercity services from local tourist offices. In larger cities, most of the main intercity bus companies have ticket offices or operate through agencies. Details are provided in the individual town and city sections. In some smaller towns and villages, tickets are sold in bars – just ask for *biglietti per il pullman* – or on the bus. Note that in Sicily some minor bus routes are linked to market requirements and Sicily's early-morning habits: this can often mean leaving incredibly early or finding yourself stranded after 4pm!

It is not usually necessary to make reservations on buses, although it is advisable in the high season for overnight or long-haul trips. Phone numbers and addresses of major bus companies are listed throughout this book.

TRAIN

Travelling by train in Sicily may be slow, but it is simple, cheap and generally efficient. The Ferrovie dello Stato (FS) is the partially privatised state train system. There are five types of train. Intercity (IC) trains are the fastest (and a bit more expensive), stopping only at major stations (an example of this is the Palermo-Messina line, with the IC train stopping only at Tèrmini Imerese, Sant' Àgata di Militello and Milazzo between starting and ending the journey). The *diretto*, *interregionale* and *espresso* stop at all but the most minor stations, while the *regionale* (also called *locale*) is the slowest of all, making every stop on the line – to be avoided if at all possible. There is one private line in Sicily, the Ferrovia Circumetnea, which does a circuit of Mt Etna (see Around Mt Etna in The Eastern Coast chapter for details). Eurostar Italia (ES) does not run in Sicily.

Travellers should note that all tickets must be validated before you board your train. See Rules & Fines under Train in the Getting There & Away chapter for details.

There are left-luggage facilities at all train stations. They are often open 24 hours; if not, they usually close only for a couple of hours after midnight. Charges are from €2.60 per day per piece of luggage.

Call ☎ 848 88 80 88 (toll-free, Italian only) or visit Ⓦ www.fs-on-line.com or Ⓦ www.trenitalia.com (both multilingual) for information. To book tickets by telephone, call ☎ 199 16 61 77.

Reservations & Classes

It is recommended that you book train tickets for long trips, particularly if you're travelling at the weekend or during holiday periods (see Public Holidays in the Facts for the Visitor chapter for details), otherwise you could find yourself standing in the corridor for the entire journey. You can get timetable information and make train bookings at most travel agencies, including CTS and Sestante CIT, or you can simply buy your ticket on arrival at the station. If you are doing a reasonable amount of travelling, it is worth buying a train timetable. There are several available, including the official FS timetables, which can be bought at newsstands in or near train stations. A thinner Sicily-only booklet is available free at some major train stations and tourist offices: ask for the Orario Ufficiale dei Treni Siciliani (free). There's also the Vettro Nuovo Orari delle Ferrovie (€3.35), available at newsstands, which covers all the trains in Italy.

There are 1st and 2nd classes on all Italian trains, with a 1st-class ticket costing a bit less than double the price of 2nd class.

Costs

To travel on IC trains you are required to pay a *supplemento*, an additional charge determined by the distance you are travelling, usually between 20% and 25% of the ticket price. If you don't buy a supplement before you board you can get one from the conductor but it will cost you closer to 40% of the ticket price. See Bicycle later in this chapter for details of taking your bike by train.

Sample prices for one-way train fares are as follows (return fares are generally double):

from	to	fare (€)
Palermo	Agrigento	6.70
	Messina	16.30
	Syracuse	17.55
Catania	Messina	6.95
	Agrigento	10.05
	Palermo	15.50

It is not worth buying a rail pass if you are only travelling in Sicily, since train fares are reasonably cheap and the network isn't big enough to justify the expense.

CAR & MOTORCYCLE
Documents

If you want to hire a car or motorcycle, you will generally need to produce your driving licence. Certainly you will need to produce it if you are pulled over by the police or *carabinieri* (military police), who may also want to see an International Driving Permit (IDP) if it's a non-EU licence. For further details see Paperwork & Preparations under Car & Motorcycle in the Getting There & Away chapter.

Roads

Roads are generally good throughout the island and there is a limited network of motorways *(autostrade)*. The main west–east link is the A19, which extends from Palermo to Catania. The A18 runs along the eastern coast between Messina and Catania, while the A29d goes from Palermo to the

Road Distances (km)

	Agrigento	Caltanissetta	Catania	Cefalù	Enna	Èrice	Marsala	Mazara del Vallo	Messina	Palermo	Ragusa	Sciacca	Syracuse	Taormina	Tràpani
Agrigento	---														
Caltanissetta	58	---													
Catania	183	125	---												
Cefalù	158	100	180	---											
Enna	91	33	92	133	---										
Èrice	182	231	318	176	264	---									
Marsala	132	219	305	192	252	48	---								
Mazara del Vallo	91	190	324	211	223	67	19	---							
Messina	283	225	100	176	180	352	396	387	---						
Palermo	126	113	208	73	135	112	141	126	249	---					
Ragusa	124	137	101	237	130	308	256	215	201	250	---				
Sciacca	57	115	240	215	148	125	109	64	340	183	181	---			
Syracuse	218	165	60	331	140	378	350	309	160	268	94	275	---		
Taormina	230	172	47	229	205	365	362	321	53	255	157	287	107	---	
Tràpani	174	225	312	168	258	6	50	69	344	104	298	127	392	359	---

western coast, linking the capital with Tràpani and (through the western interior) Mazara del Vallo along the A29. The A20 runs from Palermo to Messina; at the time of writing it was still incomplete between Cefalù and Sant'Àgata di Militello. Drivers usually travel at very high speeds in the fast (left-hand) lane on motorways, so use that lane only to pass other cars.

There's a toll to use the A18 and A20 motorways, depending on the size of car (credit cards accepted).

To really explore the island, travellers need to use the system of state and provincial roads. *Strade statali* (state roads) are single-lane highways and are toll-free; they are represented on maps as 'S' or 'SS'. *Strade provinciali* (provincial roads) are sometimes little more than country lanes, but provide access to some of the more beautiful scenery and the many small towns and villages. They are represented as 'P' or 'SP' on maps.

Road Rules

Motoring organisations (the RAC etc) in various countries have publications that detail road rules for foreign countries. If you get an International Driving Permit, it should also include a booklet that explains the signs and road rules of Italy.

In Sicily, as throughout continental Europe, you drive on the right-hand side of the road and overtake on the left. Unless otherwise indicated, you must always give way to cars coming from the right. It is compulsory to wear seat belts if fitted to the car (there are front seat belts on all cars and rear seat belts on cars produced after 26 April 1990). If you are caught not wearing a seat belt, you will be required to pay an on-the-spot fine, although this doesn't seem to deter Sicilians, many of whom use them only on motorways.

Random breath tests now take place in Sicily. If you're involved in an accident while under the influence of alcohol, the penalties can be severe. The blood-alcohol limit is 0.08%.

Speed limits, unless otherwise indicated by local signs, are as follows: on motorways 130km/h; on all main, non-urban roads 110km/h; on secondary roads 90km/h; and in built-up areas 50km/h. Speeding fines follow EU standards and are proportionate with the number of kilometres that you are caught driving over the speed limit, reaching well over €260.

You don't need a licence to ride a moped under 50cc but you should be aged 14 or over; a helmet is compulsory for those aged under 18. You can't carry passengers or ride on motorways. The speed limit for a moped is 40km/h. To ride a motorcycle or scooter up to 125cc, you must be aged 16 or over and have a licence (a car licence will do). Helmets are compulsory when riding a motorcycle bigger than 50cc, although this is a rule that many Italians choose to ignore. For motorcycles over 125cc you need a motorcycle licence.

On a motorcycle you will be able to enter restricted traffic areas in Sicilian cities without any problems and traffic police generally turn a blind eye to motorcycles parked on footpaths. There is no lights-on requirement for motorcycles during the day.

City Driving & Parking
Driving in Sicilian towns and cities is quite an experience and may well present the unprepared with a few headaches. The Sicilian attitude to driving bears little similarity to the English concept of traffic in ordered lanes (a normal two-lane road in Sicily is likely to carry three or four lanes of traffic). Instead, the main factor in determining right of way is whichever driver is more *prepotente* (forceful). If you must drive in a Sicilian city, remain calm and keep your eyes on the road and you should be OK. Once you arrive in a city or village, follow the *centro* (city centre) signs. Most roads are well signposted.

Be extremely careful where you park your car, especially in major cities. If you leave it in an area marked with a sign reading *Zona Rimozione* (Removal Zone), it will almost certainly be towed away and you will pay a heavy fine to retrieve it. It is a good idea to leave your car in a supervised car park if you have luggage, but even then it is a risk to leave your belongings in an unattended car.

Car parks in major cities are indicated throughout the book. In Sicily they are denoted on signs by a white 'P' on a blue background. There are parking meters in most cities and even in the historic centres of

small towns. You are likely to have to pay in advance (anything from around €0.50 to €1.80 per hour) for the number of hours you think you will stay.

Petrol
The cost of petrol in Sicily is very high – ranging from around €0.98 to €1.03 per litre (slightly less for unleaded petrol). Petrol is called *benzina*, unleaded petrol is *benzina senza piombo* and diesel is *gasolio*. If you are driving a car that uses LPG (liquid petroleum gas), you will need to buy a special guide to service stations that have *gasauto* or GPL. By law these must be in non-residential areas and are usually in the country or on city outskirts, although you'll find plenty on the motorways. GPL costs around €0.52 per litre.

Rental
Rental agencies are listed under the major cities in this book. Most tourist offices can provide information about car or motorcycle rental; otherwise, look in the local *Pagine Gialle* (Yellow Pages).

Rental Warning

Be careful when signing a rental agreement in Sicily. Some travellers have reported that the charges on their credit cards far exceeded the sum they expected to pay (even on cars that were booked from home) and it is difficult to query the charges as they don't show up until after your return home. Sicilian operators – even representatives of internationally recognised firms – have been known to slap all kinds of unforeseen charges onto the agreed price, after the keys have been returned. To avoid any hassle, make sure you know exactly how much the price of the car is when you pick it up, as plenty of rental agencies do not factor in such charges as local taxes when quoting a price, and be sure to find out exactly how much will be charged to your credit card as you return the keys. Unfortunately, it's hard to insist on paying by cash or cheque as most companies want your credit card details as security.

Car It is cheaper to arrange car rental before leaving your own country, for instance through some sort of fly/drive deal. For more information see Rental under Car & Motorcycle in the Getting There & Away chapter).

You have to be aged 21 or over (23 or over for some companies) to hire a car in Sicily and you will find the deal far easier to organise if you have a credit card. Most firms will accept your standard licence, sometimes with an Italian translation (which can usually be provided by the agencies themselves), or IDP.

At the time of writing, Maggiore (☎ 848 86 70 67, W www.maggiore.it) budget prices were as follows: a Lancia Y with three doors, five seats, no stereo or air-conditioning cost €69.70/348.60 per day/week; a Fiat Nuova Punto with three doors, five seats, stereo and air-conditioning cost €77.45/387.35; and a Nissan Terrano with five seats, seven seats, stereo and air-conditioning cost €190/950.30. Prices include 100km per day, collision damages liability reduction, theft protection liability reduction and VAT. A high-season surcharge of 10% applies 15 July to 20 August; special weekend rates are available.

Motorcycle You'll have no trouble hiring a small motorcycle such as a scooter (Vespa) or moped. There are numerous rental agencies in the cities (where you'll also usually be able to hire larger motorcycles for touring) and at tourist destinations such as seaside resorts. The average cost for a 50cc scooter (for one person) is around €26/129 per day/week. For a 125cc (for two people) you will pay from around €31/194 per day/week. For a moped (virtually a motorised bicycle) you'll pay around €20.50/108.50 per day/week. Most agencies will not rent motorcycles to people aged under 18. Note that many places require a sizable deposit and that you could be responsible for reimbursing part of the cost of the bike if it is stolen. Always check the fine print in the contract.

See Road Rules earlier for more details about age, licence and helmet requirements.

Purchase

For information on purchasing cars in Sicily, see Purchase under Car & Motorcycle in the Getting There & Away chapter.

Organisations

The Automobile Club Italiano (ACI; W www.aci.it – Italian only) no longer offers free roadside assistance to tourists. Residents of the UK and Germany should organise assistance through their own national organisations, which will entitle them to use ACI's emergency assistance number (☎ 116) for a small fee. Without this entitlement, you'll pay a minimum fee of €77.45 if you call ☎ 116.

ACI has an office in Palermo (☎ 091 30 04 68), Via delle Alpi 6, and in Catania (☎ 095 53 33 80/1), Via Sabotino 3, plus others in Agrigento, Caltanissetta, Enna, Messina, Ragusa, Syracuse and Tràpani.

BICYCLE

Cycling can be a great way to see the countryside as well as get around busy town centres. There are no special road rules for cyclists. Helmets and lights are not obligatory but you would be wise to equip yourself with both. You cannot cycle on motorways.

If you plan to bring your own bike, check with your airline for any additional costs. The bike will need to be disassembled and packed for the journey.

Bikes can be taken very cheaply on trains (from €3.60 to €5.15, depending on the type of train), although fast trains will generally not accommodate them (the alternative is to send them as registered luggage, which can take a few days). Check with the FS (see Train earlier in this chapter for details) for more information. Bikes can be transported free on ferries to Sicily.

Make sure you bring tools, spare parts (including a puncture-repair kit and a spare inner tube), a helmet and a very solid bike lock – theft is a major problem in the big cities.

Rental

Bikes are available for hire in most towns and many places have both city and mountain bikes. Rental costs for a city bike start at €5.15/25.80 per day/week; a good mountain bike will cost around double the price. See Getting Around under the relevant cities in this guide for more information.

Purchase

If you shop around, you can pick up a ladies bike without gears from €100 and a mountain bike with 16 gears for up to €260, but you will pay a lot more for a very good bike.

Organisations

There are organisations that can help you plan your bike tour or through which you can organise guided tours. In England, contact the Cyclists' Touring Club (☎ 01483-417217, W www.ctc.org.uk), Cotterell House, 69 Meadrow, Godalming, Surrey GU7 3HS. The club can supply members with information on conditions, itineraries and cheap insurance. Membership costs £27 per year (£16.50 for seniors and the unemployed, £10 for those aged under 26).

HITCHING

Hitching is never entirely safe in any country and we don't recommend it. Travellers who decide to hitch should understand that they are taking a small but potentially serious risk. People who do choose to hitch will be safer if they travel in pairs and let someone know where they are planning to go. A man and a woman travelling together is probably the best combination. Women travelling alone should be extremely cautious about hitching anywhere.

In Sicily it can be pretty tough to get a lift, as most motorists tend to be mistrustful of anyone standing on the side of the road. It is illegal to hitch on Sicily's motorways but quite acceptable to stand near the entrance to the toll booths. You could also approach drivers at petrol stations and truck stops. Never hitch where drivers can't stop in good time or without causing an obstruction. Look presentable, carry as little luggage as possible and hold a sign in Italian indicating your destination.

BOAT

Sicily's offshore islands are served by *traghetti* (ferries) and *aliscafi* (hydrofoils).

Services for the Aeolian Islands run from Milazzo; for the Egadi Islands from Tràpani; for the Pelagic Islands from Porto Empèdocle near Agrigento; and Ustica is served from Palermo. See the Getting There & Away sections in the relevant regional chapters for details. (For details of services to the Italian mainland and other Mediterranean destinations, see Sea in the Getting There & Away chapter.)

On overnight services (such as to the Pelagic Islands), travellers can choose between cabin accommodation (men and women are usually segregated in 2nd class, although families will be kept together) or a *poltrona*, an airline type armchair. Deck class is available only in summer and only on some ferries, so ask when making your booking. Restaurant, bar and recreation facilities are available on the larger ferries. All ferries carry vehicles.

The following companies serve Sicily's offshore islands.

Siremar (W www.siremar.it – Italian only)
Services (ferry and hydrofoil) between Palermo and Ustica, Tràpani and the Egadi Islands, Porto Empèdocle and Lampedusa/Linosa, Milazzo and the Aeolian Islands.
Snav (W www.snavali.com)
Hydrofoils between Milazzo and the Aeolian Islands.
Ustica Lines (W www.usticalines.it)
Hydrofoils between Tràpani and the Egadi Islands, between Lampedusa and Linosa, and between Pantelleria and Tràpani.

LOCAL TRANSPORT

All the major cities and towns have good local (bus) transport systems; Palermo and Catania also have a metro.

Bus & Metro

City bus services are usually frequent and reliable. You must always purchase bus tickets before you board the bus and validate them once aboard. It is common practice among Sicilians and many tourists to ride on the buses for free by not validating their tickets – just watch how many people rush to punch their tickets when an inspector boards the bus. However, if you get caught with a non-validated ticket, you will be fined on the spot (up to €25.80 in Palermo and Catania).

The metro systems in Palermo and Catania are limited and don't service destinations of real interest to most tourists. You must buy tickets and validate them before getting on the train. You can get a map of the network from tourist offices in Palermo and Catania.

You can buy tickets at most *tabaccherie* (tobacconists), at many newsstands and at ticket booths. Tickets generally cost from €0.60 to €0.75 for one hour to 90 minutes (varies from city to city). Most cities offer 24-hour tourist tickets, which can mean big savings.

Taxi

Taxis in Sicily are expensive so, if possible, it's preferable to catch a bus. If you need a taxi, you can usually find them in taxi ranks at train and bus stations or you can telephone (numbers are listed in the Getting Around sections of the major cities). However, if you book a taxi by phone, you will be charged for the trip the driver makes to reach you. Taxis will rarely stop when hailed on the street and generally will not respond to telephone bookings made from a public phone.

Rates vary from city to city. A good indication of the average is Palermo, where the minimum charge is €3.10. After that it's €2.07 for the first kilometre, then €0.67 per kilometre thereafter. There are supplements

of €1.55 from 10pm to 6am and €1.29 from 6am to 10pm on Sunday and public holidays. No more than four or five people will be allowed in one taxi, depending on the size of the car.

Watch out for taxi drivers who take advantage of new arrivals and stretch out the trip – and consequently the size of the fare.

ORGANISED TOURS

People wanting to travel to Sicily on a fully organised package tour have a wide range of options and it is best to discuss these with your travel agency. See Organised Tours in the Getting There & Away chapter for more information.

Once in Sicily, it is often less expensive and usually more enjoyable to see the sights independently. If you are in a hurry or prefer guided tours, go to the Sestante CIT office in Palermo. They organise city tours for an average price of €23.25 and also offer an eight-day Sicily tour costing €760 (includes twin-share accommodation, transport and meals).

The CTS, which has offices in all of Sicily's major cities, offers six- or seven-day tours of the island for around €775. The price includes twin-share accommodation, half board, transport by bus and admission to museums and sites.

Tourist offices can generally assist with information on local agencies that offer tours.

Palermo

postcode 91100 • pop 750,000

Sicily's capital and largest city is a place of compelling contradictions. Difficult to define yet impossible to ignore, Palermo is bold, blaring and enticing. At one time an Arab emirate and seat of a Norman kingdom, and in its heyday regarded as the grandest city in Europe, Palermo today is in a remarkable state of decay in many parts. It's a city noted more for its crumbling buildings and crime-ridden neighbourhoods than its glorious past and cultural wealth. Noisy, intense and a feast for the senses, Palermo is a place that some first-time visitors to Sicily consider avoiding. They would be missing out. The capital demands a bit of effort but rewards those willing to give it the attention it deserves.

Behind the decay, Palermo is a beautiful city with a reserve of cultural, architectural and historical wealth to rival any of Europe's great capitals. With a long history of occupation by various Mediterranean powers, Palermo's role as a crossroads between east and west has resulted in an intoxicating cultural cross-fertilisation. This finds its best expression in the city's architectural mix, a fusion of diverse styles that include Byzantine, Arab, Norman, Renaissance and Baroque.

Severely criticised for allowing its architectural heritage to languish following the heavy bombing of WWII and their general disinterest during the post-war years, the authorities have recently begun a number of sizable restoration projects. Not least was that of the Teatro Massimo, which reopened to much fanfare in 1997. Some quarters of the historic centre, for years abandoned to the crime that turned them into night-time no-go zones, have been given a new lease of life with the opening of some great bars, cafes and restaurants. This has created a scene to rival the more established and up-market nightlife centred around the grander streets north of Piazza Verdi.

Palermo's most interesting attraction, however, is its populace. Like their city,

Highlights

- Dawdle around the Quattro Canti's atmospheric streets and alleys
- Visit the adjacent churches of La Martorana and San Cataldo, symbols of the city's multicultural past
- Let your strings be pulled at a traditional puppet show
- Eat, drink and make merry in one of the crumbling yet beautiful city piazzas
- Be dazzled by mosaic glitter at the Capella Palatina in Palermo or the cathedral in Monreale

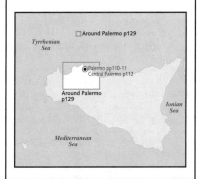

Palermitans can be a demanding lot. You will find that they are also warm and friendly, enthusiastic consumers of life's pleasures (both simple and sophisticated) and full of energy and passion.

Finally, a word on Palermo's most enduring shadow. Although still a powerful and ominous presence, the Mafia's activities took a substantial battering during the 1990s, especially following the 1992 killings (see Government & Politics in the Facts about Sicily chapter). The army, called onto the streets after the murders of anti-Mafia magistrates Giovanni Falcone and Paolo Borsellino (see the boxed text

'Palermo & the Mafia' later in this chapter), were removed in the summer of 1999 and the city has resumed an air of normality. Organised crime presents no real threat to the visitor save for the occasional incident of scooter-powered bag-snatching and the strong police presence throughout the city has deterred much petty crime.

HISTORY

Palermo's superb position by the sea at the foot of Mt Pellegrino (606m), with the fertile Conca d'Oro valley behind it, has long made it a rich prize for Sicily's colonisers. Around the 8th century BC the Phoenicians established the town of Ziz here, on the site of a prehistoric village. It remained a relatively minor town under Roman, and later Byzantine, control and it was not until AD 831, when it was conquered by the Arabs, that the city truly flourished and became a jewel of the Islamic world.

When the Normans took control in 1072, things only improved. The seat of the kingdom of Roger I of Hauteville, Palermo was hailed as one of the most magnificent and cultured cities of 12th-century Europe. However, for more than 50 years after Roger's death the monarchy foundered. It eventually passed to the German Hohenstaufens and the Holy Roman Emperor Frederick I, still remembered as one of Sicily's most enlightened rulers and a pioneer of the Italian language (Dante devoted an entire canto of his *Divine Comedy* to Frederick and his patronage of early Italian poetry). After Frederick's death, Palermo and all of Sicily passed to the French Anjou family, themselves later deposed following the Sicilian Vespers revolt (see The Sicilian Vespers in the Facts about Sicily chapter), which started in Palermo. Eclipsed by Naples, Palermo then sank into a long, slow decline, which continued right up to the 20th century.

Following WWII, the city expanded substantially as its population swelled through the influx of rural labourers looking for better-paid work. The old city sank into greater disrepair as Palermitans moved out from the centre into newly built housing estates that did little for Palermo's aesthetic charm (but

allegedly filled the Mafia's coffers). Violence once made the city a European pariah but the process of restoration and rehabilitation has begun. As Palermo begins the new millennium, things look brighter than they have done for centuries.

ORIENTATION

Palermo is a large but manageable city. The historic centre is divided into four quarters *(canti)* – La Kalsa, Albergheria, Il Capo and La Vucciria – which meet at the Quattro Canti crossroads of Corso Vittorio Emanuele and Via Maqueda. Quattro Canti is the centre of historic Palermo and a good marker for travellers. The historic centre – a maze of winding streets and minuscule alleyways – is relatively small in comparison with the expanse of the modern city. Bordered to the west by the Palazzo dei Normanni and the Porta Nuova, to the east by the old port of La Cala, to the south by the train station (Stazione Centrale) and to the north by Piazza Verdi, here you will find the bulk of Palermo's sights of interest as well as the most authentic taste of Palermitan life, including the all-important markets and some of the city's cheapest restaurants and hotels.

Most of the cheaper guesthouses and hotels are around the train station. It's a grimy and chaotic area but behind the decaying mansions lining the main streets is a fascinating maze of narrow lanes and tiny squares though you can also, unfortunately, get a better idea here of just how decrepit parts of Palermo still are. It's not nearly as bad as it was even a few years ago but visitors should be on their guard in the quieter, less-lit side streets late at night.

Traffic restrictions on Via Maqueda have gone some way towards helping the street to re-establish itself as one of the city's most elegant boulevards, ensuring that boutique-gazers and window-shoppers aren't choked by traffic fumes. Via Roma, home of the budget stores and snack bars, has had no such luck and continues to deal with the plague of gridlock that grips it from 8am to 8pm daily. At the time of research, traffic on Via Roma ran one way (north from the train station) and traffic on Via Maqueda ran one way (south to the train station), although locals tell us that this situation changes on a regular basis.

North of Piazza Verdi is the newer and more modish part of the city, a mixture of late-19th-century elegance and post-WWII development, some parts a little more eye-catching than others. From the modern Piazza Castelnuovo, Viale della Libertà cuts a swanky swathe north to the Giardino Inglese (English Gardens) and Villa Sperlinga; it's a wide avenue adorned with expensive apartment blocks, outdoor cafes and most of the city's boutiques and designer shops.

INFORMATION
Tourist Offices
The main APT office (☎ 091 58 38 47 or 091 605 83 51, Ⓦwww.palermotourism.com – Italian only) is at Piazza Castelnuovo 34. The

staff speak some English and you can pick up a map of the city and the free fold-out *Lapis Palermo* guide, with listings of cultural events. The office opens 8.30am to 2pm and 2.30pm to 6pm Monday to Friday, and 8.30am to 2pm on Saturday. There is a branch office (☎ 091 616 59 14) at the train station, which has the same opening times, and another at Falcone-Borsellino airport (☎ 091 59 16 98), that opens 8am to midnight Monday to Friday and 8am to 8pm at the weekend. There are also information kiosks at Piazza della Vittoria and Piazza Pretoria.

Money
The exchange office at the train station opens 8am to 8pm daily and there's another (Banca di Sicilia) at the airport, which opens 8.30am to 1pm and 2.45pm to 7.15pm daily. Otherwise, there is no shortage of banks in the city, generally open 8.30am to 1.15pm and 2.45pm to 4.15pm Monday to Friday. The majority have ATMs, including the Banca Nazionale del Lavoro, Via Roma 297 and the Monte dei Paschi di Siena on Piazza Bagnasco. American Express is represented by Ruggieri & Figli (☎ 091 58 71 44), Via Enrico Amari 40.

Post & Communications
The main post office is at Via Roma 322. It opens 8.30am to 6.30pm Monday to Saturday and has a fax service. There is a (pretty grotty) telephone centre virtually opposite the train station on Piazza Giulio Cesare. It opens 8am to 9.30pm daily.

One good central place to access the Internet and email is Aexis Telecom at Via Maqueda 347. Access costs €4.15 for one hour and you can also send faxes and moneygrams here.

At Stazione Marittima, on the first floor of the Vitorio Veneto jetty, you can access the Internet for €0.20 per minute. The connection here is both fast and secure. It opens 9am to 7pm on the days when boats are landing.

Free Internet access is available at Villa Trabia on Via A Salinas. Call ☎ 091 740 59 41 for reservations (essential).

La Dolce Vita

One Sicilian who has really made a mark on the women of the world is Domenico Dolce, one half of the coveted high-end fashion house Dolce & Gabbana. Born in August 1958 in Polizzi Generosa (Palermo province), he moved to Milan for work in the 1980s, meeting future partner Stefano Gabbana. Their influence away from the catwalks has seen many of the world's most famous women (Madonna for one) lining up to don a little something that reflects their unique mix of colour, cut and fabric, with more than a heavy nod towards the image of the 'Sicilian Black Widow' (albeit young and sexy). On an island where male-dominated institutions (the Mafia, the government and the Church) seem to rule, Dolce & Gabbana's Sicilian-inspired clothes remind us that there's always a strong woman behind it all and that Sicilian society is avowedly matriarchal.

Sadly, if you're in the mood to blow some cash at a Dolce & Gabbana boutique, you're out of luck. Dolce & Gabbana do not have an actual shop on Sicily – a situation that will hopefully be rectified in the future – although their clothes are stocked in the ritzy boutiques of Palermo's Viale della Libertà and in Sicily's other prosperous cities.

PALERMO

PALERMO

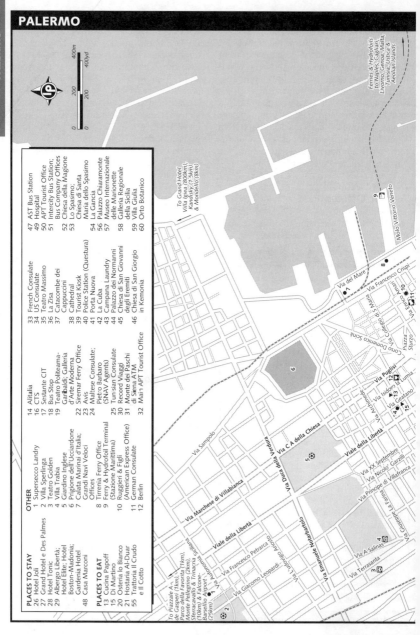

PLACES TO STAY
26 Hotel Joli
27 Grand Hotel e Des Palmes
28 Hotel Tonic
29 Albergo Libertà;
   Hotel Elite; Hotel
   Boston-Madonia;
   Gardenia Hotel
48 Casa Marconi

PLACES TO EAT
13 Cucina Papoff
15 Di Martino
20 Osteria lo Bianco
21 Hostaria Al-Duar
55 Trattoria Il Crudo
   e Il Cotto

OTHER
1 Supersecco Landry
2 Villa Sperlinga
3 Teatro Golden
4 Villa Trabia
5 Giardino Inglese
6 Prigione dell'Ucciardone
7 Calata Marinai d'Italia;
   Grandi Navi Veloci
   Offices
8 Tirrenia Ferry Office
9 Ferry & Hydrofoil Terminal
   (Stazione Marittima)
10 Ruggieri & Figli
   (American Express Office)
11 German Consulate
12 Berlin

14 Alitalia
16 CTS
17 Sestante CIT
18 Bus Stop
19 Teatro Politeama-
   Garibaldi; Galleria
   d'Arte Moderna
22 Siremar Ferry Office
23 Avis
24 Maltese Consulate;
   Pietro Barbaro
   (SNAV Agents)
25 Tunisian Consulate
30 Record Viaggi
31 Monte dei Paschi
   di Siena ATM
32 Main APT Tourist Office

33 French Consulate
34 US Consulate
35 Teatro Massimo
36 La Zisa
37 Catacombe dei
   Cappuccini
38 Cathedral
39 Tourist Kiosk
40 Police Station (Questura)
41 Porta Nuova
42 La Cuba
43 Campana Laundry
44 Palazzo dei Normanni
45 Chiesa di San Giovanni
   degli Eremiti
46 Chiesa di San Giorgio
   in Kemonia

47 AST Bus Station
49 Hospital
50 APT Tourist Office
51 Intercity Bus Station;
   Bus Company Offices
52 Chiesa della Magione
53 Lo Spasimo;
   Chiesa di Santa
   Maria dello Spasimo
54 La Gancia
56 Palazzo Chiaramonte
57 Museo Internazionale
   delle Marionette
58 Galleria Regionale
   della Sicilia
59 Villa Giulia
60 Orto Botanico

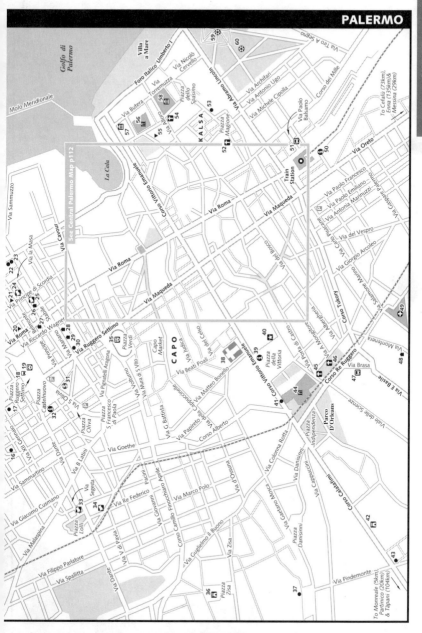

PALERMO

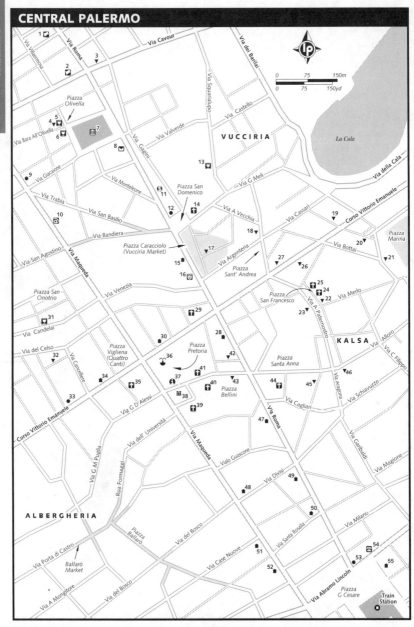

CENTRAL PALERMO

CENTRAL PALERMO

PLACES TO STAY
15 Hotel Moderno
28 Hotel Confort
30 Grande Albergo Sole
34 Centrale Palace Hotel
47 Albergo Corona
48 Hotel Sicilia
49 Hotel del Centro; Albergo Concordia
50 Albergo Rosalia Conca d'Oro
51 Albergo Orientale
52 Albergo Vittoria
55 Hotel Elena

PLACES TO EAT
3 Hostaria la Sella
4 La Traviata
17 Trattoria Shanghai
18 Sant'Andrea
19 Ristorante a'Vucciria
20 La Cambusa
21 Il Bagatto

22 Mi Manda Picone
23 Antica Focacceria San Francesco
26 Café Centro Storico
27 Casa del Brodo
32 Caffè Arabo
42 Hostaria da Ciccio
43 Trattoria da Massimo
45 Osteria dei Vespri
46 Trattoria Stella

OTHER
1 Netherlands Consulate
2 British Consulate
5 Bikers Bar; Soprintendenza
6 Fuso Orario
7 Museo Archeologico Regionale
8 Main Post Office
9 Feltrinelli
10 Aexis Telecom
11 Banca Nazionale del Lavoro

12 Gulliver Bookshop
13 I Grilli Giù
14 Chiesa di San Domenico
16 Teatro Biondo
24 Chiesa di San Francesco d'Assisi
25 Oratorio di San Lorenzo
29 Chiesa di San Matteo
31 I Candelai
33 Libreria Sellerio
35 Chiesa di San Giuseppe dei Teatini
36 Fontana Pretoria
37 Tourist Kiosk
38 Palazzo Pretorio
39 Chiesa di San Cataldo
40 La Martorana
41 Chiesa di Santa Caterina
44 Chiesa di Santa Anna
53 Lo Casico Pharmacy
54 Telephone Centre

Travel Agencies

Sestante CIT (☎ 091 58 63 33), where you can book travel tickets, is at Viale della Libertà 12. There is a CTS travel agency (☎ 091 611 07 13) at Via Nicolò Garzilli 28g. Record Viaggi (☎ 091 611 09 10) is at Via Mariano Stabile 168, between Via Ruggero Settimo and Via Roma.

Bookshops

Feltrinelli bookshop (☎ 091 58 77 85), at Via Maqueda 395, has a good foreign-language section. Gulliver, on the corner of Via Roma and Piazza San Domenico, also stocks a limited selection of foreign-language books. Libreria Sellerio, at Corso Vittorio Emanuele 504, is also worth checking out. It was founded by Leonardo Sciascia. Generally, bookshops open 9am to 8pm Monday to Saturday. Several stands around Piazza Verdi sell foreign newspapers.

Laundry

Like most places in Sicily, you will probably have to resign yourself to washing your clothes in the sink: there are only a couple of coin-operated laundrettes in Palermo. Campana, in the university district south-

west of the city centre, is at Via Cuba 2. Take bus No 105 from Piazza Indipendenza. A little closer to the centre, Supersecco is at Via Alfieri 25, just off Viale della Libertà.

Medical Services

The hospital (*ospedale*; ☎ 091 666 11 11) is at Via Carmelo Lazzaro. You can call for an ambulance on ☎ 091 30 66 44. There are several pharmacies that stay open until midnight, including Lo Cascio (☎ 091 616 21 17), near the train station at Via Roma 1.

Emergency

The central police station (*questura centrale*; ☎ 091 21 01 11), where you should go to report thefts and other crimes, is on Piazza della Vittoria. You can also call the foreigners office (*ufficio stranieri*; ☎ 091 651 43 30), which is inside the police station. If your car has been towed away, call ☎ 091 656 97 21 to find out where to collect it.

Dangers & Annoyances

Over the past 30 years Palermo deservedly earned itself a reputation as a dangerous city – and not just because of the alleged Mafia killings and gangland shootings, which have rarely troubled the foreign visitor. A strong police presence was deemed necessary to counter the widespread scourge of bag-snatchers, pickpockets and other petty-crime merchants who plagued the city. The problem still exists but it is nowhere near the scale of the 1980s and early 1990s. The police are largely responsible for the improvement but renewed efforts to clean up the decay of the historic centre have also played a significant role. Although not problem-free, Palermo's trouble areas – in particular the area from the Vucciria market towards the port and the Kalsa quarter northeast of the train station – are certainly not the no-go zones they have been in recent decades, and urban renewal and restoration programmes are making the areas more pleasant for residents and tourists alike.

Still, the visitor should remain cautious at all times, remembering that where there is poverty (and parts of Palermo are shamefully blighted) you should avoid wearing ostentatious jewellery and may wish to leave you bag at home. It's also a good idea to keep your valuables in a money belt. Stay away from poorly lit and deserted streets, particularly late at night or if you are alone. Keep an eye out for pickpockets around the main intercity bus station on Via Paolo Balsamo.

QUATTRO CANTI

The busy intersection of Corso Vittorio Emanuele and Via Maqueda marks the Quattro Canti (Four Corners) of Palermo, the centre of the oldest part of town. Also known as Piazza Vigliena or the Teatro del Sole (Theatre of the Sun), it was originally laid out in 1608 by Giulio Lasso and completed in 1620. In each corner the Spanish Baroque facade is decorated with three tiers: in the first, a fountain and a statue of one of the four seasons; in the second, a statue of the Spanish kings Carlos V and Felipe II, III and IV; and in the third, a statue of a patron saints of the city (Christina, Ninfa, Olivia and Agata). In the southwestern corner is the Baroque **Chiesa di San Giuseppe dei Teatini** *(free; open 9am-6pm daily)*, topped by a soaring cupola. The magnificent interior is dripping with marble,

lovingly restored after substantial damage suffered during WWII. At the time of writing, the scaffolding had just been removed from the Quattro Canti after a restoration and cleaning effort to take off the black grime that had coated the area for decades.

ALBERGHERIA
Piazza Pretoria

This square hosts the eye-catching **Fontana Pretoria**, created by Florentine sculptor Francesco Camilliani in 1554–55. At the time of its unveiling, the shocked populace named it the Fountain of Shame because of its nude motifs. Take time to study the numerous figures that decorate every corner. Closing off the eastern side of the square is the Baroque **Chiesa di Santa Caterina** (closed for restoration), while the **Palazzo Pretorio** or Muncipio (municipal offices), also known as the Palazzo delle Aquile because of the eagle sculptures that guard each corner of the roof, fronts the southern edge of the square. The fountains was being restored at the time of research but there were windows in the scaffolding, allowing people to still see the statues.

La Martorana

Perhaps Palermo's most famous medieval church, La Martorana *(☎ 091 616 16 92, Piazza Bellini 3; free; open 8am-1pm & 3.30pm-7pm Mon-Sat, 8.30am-1pm Sun & hols)* is a few steps south of Piazza Pretoria. Its original name was the Chiesa di Santa Maria dell'Ammiraglio (after King Roger II's chief admiral, George of Antioch, who paid for its construction in 1143) but was it renamed in 1433 when King Alphonse of Aragon presented it to a Benedictine order founded by Eloisa Martorana. Although the original 12th-century structure has been altered over the centuries, it still retains its Arab-Norman bell tower and the interior is richly decorated with Byzantine mosaics (the effect is somewhat spoilt by some unattractive Baroque additions, described by John Julius Norwich in *The Normans in Sicily* as '…those simpering cherubs and marzipan Madonnas that mark the real dark ages of European religious art…'). Mosaic portraits to

Palermo & the Mafia

It is an open secret that the Mafia exercised an all-pervasive control over Palermo's affairs for decades. From building contracts to the distribution of EU funds, the Mafia ensured that it received the lion's share of the cash. As a political pawnbroker the Mafia has determined the fortunes of city officials of all levels, from the lowliest clerk right up to the mayor's office. In Rome, the powers-that-be postured and made the appropriate noises but did little else to break the Mafia's vice-like grip on the island's affairs.

In the mid-1980s, however, the dogged and courageous determination of the Palermitan magistrature, led by Giovanni Falcone and Paolo Borsellino, began to turn the tide against the bosses. The first super-trial took place in Palermo in 1986, when 357 of the 500 accused were convicted and sentenced. The bloodshed that ensued was understood to be the Mafia's vicious reaction to such a blow but the magistrates were not to be deterred. In 1990 the then-

JANE SMITH

**Anti-mafia campaigner
Giovanni Falcone**

mayor, Leoluca Orlando, for years a luminary of the Sicilian Christian Democrats, was ejected from the party on account of his vocal anti-Mafia stance. Incredibly, Orlando resuscitated his seemingly moribund career and stormed back as the leader of his own political party, La Rete (The Network), and was re-elected mayor in 1991. Although Falcone and Borsellino were tragically eliminated by the unforgiving Mafia, the popular Orlando continued the fight against organised crime (even though his critics claim that he is more interested in his own glory than in defeating the Mafia). In 2001 he ran for the position of president of the Sicilian region but was unsuccessful. One of his greatest successes may well be the common usage of the phrase 'La Primavera di Palermo' (The Palermo Spring) by Palermitans, referring to the rebirth of civic hope and pride that has seen Palermo's cultural and architectural attractions getting the attention they have needed for so long.

note here are of Roger II being crowned by Jesus Christ, and George of Antioch, crouched behind a shield at the feet of the Virgin Mary. The exquisite details of his face and beard are a great achievement in mosaic art. Totally in keeping with the decoration, the Greek eastern-rite Mass is still celebrated here. Try to time your visit to avoid the many weddings and baptisms celebrated in the church.

Chiesa di San Cataldo

Next to La Martorana is this tiny, simple church *(free; open 9am-3.30pm Mon-Fri, 9am-12.30pm Sat & 9am-1pm Sun & hols)* dating from the period of the Norman domination of Sicily. Its battlements and red domes are another fusion of Arab and Norman styles. It was founded in the 1150s by Maio of Bari (William I's Emir of Emirs) but was not finished due to Maio's murder in 1160, hence the lack of adornment within.

Chiesa di San Matteo

On the northern side of Corso Vittorio Emanuele, this Baroque church *(☎ 091 33 48 33; free; open 9am-5pm Mon-Sat, 10am-11am Sun)* has a richly decorated interior. The four statues in the pilasters of the dome represent the Virtues and were carved by Giacomo Serpotta in 1728.

Palazzo dei Normanni

Across the Piazza della Vittoria and the gardens from the cathedral is the Palazzo dei Normanni, also known as the Palazzo Reale (Royal Palace). Built by the Arabs in the 9th century, it was extended by the Normans and restructured by the Hohenstaufens. It is now the seat of Sicily's regional government.

Enter from Piazza Indipendenza to see the breathtaking **Cappella Palatina** *(☎ 091 705 48 79; free; open 9am-noon & 3pm-5pm Mon-Fri, 9am-noon Sat, noon-1pm Sun)*, a magnificent example of Arab-Norman artistic genius, which was built during the reign of Roger II and decorated with Byzantine mosaics. The chapel is undoubtedly Palermo's most extraordinary treasure, a wondrous example of art at its most exalted (the enjoyment of which is only spoilt by the look-and-get-out attitude of some of its guardians – though, in fairness, the place does get pretty packed). The mosaics alone, rivalled only by those of Ravenna and Istanbul, make the chapel an absolute must on any tourist itinerary.

While the mosaics demonstrate the Byzantine influence on Palermitan art, the geometric tile designs are a clear reminder of Arab input. The carved wooden ceiling is a classic example of the intricate Arab-style stalactite design. There might be queues, as a guard stops the chapel from getting overcrowded, but any wait (usually quick) is worth it. The **Sala di Ruggero** (King Roger's Room), the king's former bedroom, is also worth visiting as it is decorated with 12th-century mosaics. It is only possible to visit the room with a guide (free of charge). Go upstairs from the Cappella Palatina and ask if it's open.

There are guided tours of the palace itself but you'll need to book a few days in advance (fax 091 705 47 37). Preference is given to groups and school trips so lone travellers can have difficulty booking, especially when the regional assembly is in session.

Porta Nuova

Next to the palace is the Porta Nuova, built to celebrate the arrival of Carlos V in Palermo in 1535 after a victory over the Tunisians. Designed in the Mannerist style, it was partially destroyed by lightning in 1667 and rebuilt with the addition of the conical top. More than 400 years later, it still serves as a demarcation line between the old and new city.

Chiesa di San Giovanni degli Eremiti

Just south of the Palazzo dei Normanni, this church (☎ 091 651 50 19, Via dei Benedettini; admission €4.15; open 9am-7pm Mon-Sat,

9am-1pm Sun), whose name translates as St John of the Hermits, is Palermo's best-known example of the Norman-Arab architectural mix. Built under Roger II, it is topped by five red domes and set in a pretty, tree-filled garden with cloisters that offer temporary respite from the chaos outside. The bare interior of the now deconsecrated church features some badly deteriorated frescoes including, on the left wall, the 12th-century *Madonna con Gesù Bambino e Santi* (Virgin Mary with Christ Child and Saints). Once the most privileged monastery in Sicily, today's visitor may find it difficult to imagine the former glory of this church, as there's not much left to see. If you're pinching pennies, save your €4.15 and visit the Chiesa di San Cataldo (see earlier in this chapter) instead or buy a cumulative €7.75 ticket here, which also entitles you to enter Monreale, La Cuba and La Zisa.

Next door is the 18th-century **Chiesa di San Giorgio in Kemonia**, rebuilt on the site

---

William vs Walter

King William II wasn't happy to see his archbishop and former teacher, the Englishman Walter of the Mill, consolidate his position from his basilica in the city centre. Walter was a steadfast ally of Pope Innocent II, who had been feuding with William's family since the pope's capture by Roger II in 1139. To break papal control over his city, William decided to upstage the archbishopric, firstly by endowing a new monastery outside his royal grounds and then, in 1174, by constructing a cathedral so magnificent that it would outshine Walter's new basilica in the city. William's cathedral at Monreale – built in less than 10 years – quickly became a sight to behold and the enraged Walter decided to stop at nothing to outdo the king. Consequently in 1185 he ordered that the basilica be torn down and a new, infinitely more splendid church be built. As a result of the rivalry Palermo had two outstanding churches but their construction had very little to do with their founders' piety or love of God. Still, they're not bad results for an ego-trip.

of an older structure. The rococo interior features the paintings of Giuseppe Tresca.

IL CAPO
The Cathedral

Despite its hotchpotch of styles and many alterations, Palermo's cathedral (☎ 091 33 43 76, Corso Vittorio Emanuele; cathedral free, treasury €0.50; cathedral open 7am-7pm Mon-Sat, 8am-1.30pm & 4pm-7pm Sun & hols; treasury open 9.30am-5.30pm Mon-Sat, for groups only Sun), southwest of the Quattro Canti, is certainly imposing. Construction began in 1184 on the site of an existing basilica at the behest of Palermo's archbishop, Walter of the Mill (Gualtiero Offamiglia), who was eager to challenge the supremacy of the cathedral at Monreale (see the boxed text 'William vs Walter').

The cathedral has been an architectural playground many times since, with bits added and removed according to whim. Such lack of aesthetic cohesion has been detrimental to the building, most disastrously between 1781 and 1801 when the architectural harmony of the building was radically affected through the construction of the dome (the brainchild of one Ferdinando Fuga). Not content with messing up the exterior, the delicate basilican plan inside was scrapped in favour of an in-vogue Latin-cross plan, including the addition of side aisles. The only original element is the apse, an impressive example of Norman architectural style. Arab influences in some of the geometric decoration are unmistakable and the graceful Gothic towers distract the eye from the unfortunate dome.

Despite the architectural mess, the interior is rich in works of art. The **Tombe Imperiali e Reali** (Imperial and Royal Tombs) are to the right of the main entrance. The four elegant porphyry sarcophagi contain the remains of Roger II (rear left, although he wanted to be buried at the cathedral in Cefalù), Frederick II of Hohenstaufen (front left), his mother Constance de Hauteville (rear right) and Henry VI of Hohenstaufen (front right). Also buried here (in the wall) are Duke William and Constance of Aragon. Halfway down the right aisle is a magnificent treasury, whose most extraordinary exhibit is a tooth

extracted from Santa Rosalia, one of the patron saints of Palermo. Her ashes are also kept here in a silver urn. For information about the Festa di Santa Rosalia, see Special Events in the Facts for the Visitor chapter.

ALONG VIA ROMA

Running north from the train station, Via Roma is one of Palermo's more interesting main streets. Not nearly as elegant as the parallel Via Maqueda, it embodies the mayhem and chaos that is Sicily's capital; the incessant noise of its traffic is merely a sideshow to the hubbub of its shops, bars and markets. It is here that you'll find many of Palermo's cheaper clothing outlets, a multitude of basic bars where Palermitans gather to drink coffee and exchange gossip and, in the side streets off the main drag, some of the city's most frequented markets, including the famed but run-down Vucciria. Via Roma is also home to the beautiful Chiesa di San Domenico and the Museo Archeologico Regionale.

LA VUCCIRIA

The most renowned of Palermo's four quarters, La Vucciria is a largely off-putting mess of dilapidated buildings and a confusing maze of alleyways. At night the streets are eerily empty and can seem quite intimidating, maybe for a good reason: a favourite robber's trick has been to throw something from a building to knock over a victim so that they can be robbed more easily. Still, the quarter attracts droves of visitors, most of whom come for its famous market, and if you visit the area during the day, you'll be fine.

Sicilian painter Renato Guttuso's most important work is a painting of the market and writer Leonardo Sciascia devoted many inches to describing its allure, calling it 'a hungry man's dream'. Every morning (and nowadays into the afternoon) except Sunday the stalls are opened in the small Piazza Caracciolo behind the Chiesa di Sant'Antonio and the vendors go to work. In *Midnight in Sicily*, Peter Robb describes the market as 'the belly of Palermo and the heart too'.

As markets go it is still an interesting place (and great for self-catering tourists) but unfortunately La Vucciria is no longer what it was. Today it can appear more of a tourist attraction, with many locals now using markets in other quarters of the historic centre.

To get there, take the steps off Via Roma that run alongside Chiesa di Sant'Antonio.

Museo Archeologico Regionale

A block north of the main post office (backing on to Via Roma), is the imposing Museo Archeologico Regionale *(☎ 091 611 68 05, Piazza Olivella 24; admission €4.15; open 8.30am-1.45pm daily plus 3pm-6.45pm Tues-Fri)*, one of the most important museums of its kind in Europe. Its vast collection includes Greek stone carvings from Selinunte, the Hellenistic *Ariete di Bronzo di Siracus* (Bronze Ram of Syracuse), the largest collection of ancient anchors in the world and finds from archaeological sites throughout the island. The most interesting room is the **Sala di Selinunte**, featuring all of the metopes (stone carvings) from the seven Greek temples uncovered at Selinunte. The best of these, recovered from Temple E, show Hercules fighting an Amazon, the marriage of Zeus and Hera, and Athena and the Titan. Also worth looking out for is the bronze 5th-century-BC statue of a boy known as the *Efebo di Selinunte* (Youth of Selinunte). The first floor also has an interesting 3rd-century mosaic on the floor.

Chiesa di San Domenico

About 200m south of the museum, off Via Roma, is this church *(☎ 091 58 48 72, Piazza San Domenico; free; open 9am-11.30am Mon-Fri, 5pm-7pm Sat & Sun)*, one of Palermo's most remarkable Baroque structures. It was built in 1640 following the design of architect Andrea Cirincione; the facade was added in 1726 after the buildings that once occupied the square were demolished to give the church some space. The church serves as the city's pantheon, housing the tombs and cenotaphs of some notable Sicilians, including former Italian prime minister Francesco Crispi.

Behind the church is the **Oratorio del Rosario** *(Via dei Bambinai; free; open 9am-1pm & 2pm-5.30pm Mon-Fri, 9am-1pm*

Sat), which has an altarpiece by Van Dyck of the Virgin with San Domenico.

Prigione dell'Ucciardone

Not so much a sight but a landmark, and impossible to visit (unless you're here to visit a 'guest'!), this Bourbon prison overlooking the water is Sicily's most notorious detention centre for the Mafia.

The place is shrouded in myth; it has been suggested that the inmates have a greater say in the running of the place than the authorities and that Mafia business is run from here (that is, when they are not eating meals delivered from Palermo's finest restaurants).

After the Falcone-Borsellino murders in 1992 (see the boxed text 'Palermo & the Mafia' earlier in this chapter) the more 'connected' inmates were transferred to prisons on the Italian mainland but it remains Italy's most Mafia-populated prison.

LA KALSA

Plagued by gob-smacking poverty and decay in some parts, La Kalsa – one of the city's original quarters, whose name derives from the Arabic word *khalisa* (meaning 'pure') – was heavily bombed in 1943 and more or less allowed to sink into squalor ever since. This is one of the city's most notorious neighbourhoods and, at least until a few years ago, most visitors were advised to keep away once the sun went down. Thankfully, things are starting to change, albeit slowly, quite noticeably and a number of the quarter's more important attractions are finally being given the attention they deserve after languishing in obscurity for decades. A few restaurants and bars have opened in the hitherto abandoned streets, bringing new life to a moribund quarter. The summer programme of free concerts and recitals in the magnificent ruins of the Chiesa di Santa Maria dello Spasimo is one of the city's best attractions (see Lo Spasimo later in this chapter). Nevertheless, visitors are advised to exercise caution in the area by keeping away from poorly lit or empty streets and, if possible, not walking alone.

Museo Internazionale delle Marionette

A must for puppet-lovers and those keen on Sicilian culture, this museum (☎ 091 32 80 60, Via Butera 1; admission €2.60; open 9am-1pm & 4pm-8pm Mon-Fri, 9am-1pm Sat) is well laid out with puppets from Sicily and around the world. Some of the craftsmanship on display here is extraordinary (check out the three-headed dragon), with suits of armour, expressive faces and all manner of Norman and Saracen characters. In July, puppet shows (€5.15) are staged here at 5.50pm Friday. As a repository of Sicily's oral and cultural history, now generally on the wane, it can't be beaten.

Oratorio di San Lorenzo

Near the old port of La Cala, just south of Corso Vittorio Emanuele, is the Oratorio di San Lorenzo (Via dell'Immacolatella; free; open 9am-noon Mon-Fri), built in 1569 by the Compagnia di San Francesco, a local Franciscan order. The church is worth visiting for the extraordinary stucco decoration by Giacomo Serpotta, his undoubted masterpiece, completed between 1698 and 1710. The work includes 10 symbolic statues and a series of panels with details from the lives of St Lawrence and St Francis, the best of which is the Martirio di San Lorenzo (Martyrdom of St Lawrence), on the far wall. Even the pews are works of art, laced with mother-of-pearl. A large Natività (Nativity) by Caravaggio once hung on the wall behind the altar but it was stolen in 1969 and has never been found.

Chiesa di San Francesco d'Assisi

Virtually next door to the oratory, this church (☎ 091 58 23 70, Piazza San Francesco; free; open 8am-6pm Mon-Fri, 8am-noon & 4.30pm-6pm Sat & Sun) was originally built (between 1255 and 1277) in tribute to St Francis of Assisi but was substantially altered over the centuries. The side chapels were added in the 14th and 15th centuries; the presbytery was elongated in 1589 and, following an earthquake in 1823, it was restored in neoclassical style. Damaged by Allied bombs in 1943, the restorers went to work on it once again after the war, removing some of the later modifications in an effort to return it to its original appearance. The facade – featuring a fine rose window and a flamboyant Gothic portal – dates from the 19th century and was thankfully left intact. Inside there are sculptures by the Gagini family.

Palazzo Chiaramonte

This imposing 14th-century palace near Piazza Marina is also known as the Steri (from the Latin word hosterium, meaning 'fortified building') and it is pretty obvious why. Sicily's most powerful baron of the day, Manfredi Chiaramonte, commissioned it in 1307 but it was not completed until 1380. Although it has been extensively altered since then, it still boasts an imposing facade that served as a model for many other buildings in Sicily. The Chiaramonte family, however, didn't have too many years to enjoy their palace: the last member, Andrea, was beheaded in the square in 1396 for his part in a rebellion against King Martino I of Aragon. Following the family's demise, the palace became the seat of the viceroys of Sicily and, in 1601, was made a tribunal of the Holy See, home of the infamous Grand Inquisition. Victims were jailed in the Carcere Filippine, a long area lined with cells; the walls are still decorated with their drawings and poems. At the end of the 18th century it was made the seat of the regular courts and continued in this role until 1960, when the courts were moved to a building in the newer part of the city. Today it serves as the administrative offices of the university and is only open to the public during exhibitions and other events.

Galleria Regionale della Sicilia

Sicily's most important art gallery (☎ 091 623 00 11, Via Alloro; admission €4.15; open 9am-1.30pm Mon-Sat, 3pm-7.30pm Tues & Thur, 9am-1pm Sun) is housed in the imposing Palazzo Abatellis, building of which began in 1490 by Matteo Carnelivari for the praetor of Palermo, Francesco Abatellis. The Catalan-Gothic building was badly damaged during WWII but underwent restoration by Carlo Scarpa in 1954, the year it opened as the gallery. Today it is home to an impressive collection of work, most notably sculpture and paintings dating from the 14th to 16th centuries but also including work from later years. The ground floor is devoted to sculpture, beginning with a remarkable 12th-century Arabic door frame and a painting of *Madonna con Santi* (Madonna with Saints) by Tommaso de Vigilia (Room 1). Room 2 is the palace's former chapel, and is now home to the *Trionfo della Morte* (Triumph of Death), a magnificent fresco that once hung in the Palazzo Sclafani. It is unclear who the author of the work was but some experts have attributed it to Pisanello. In the painting, Death is an archer on horseback piercing the wealthy and smug while the miserable (tellingly represented by a painter and his pupil!) pray for release. At the end of the corridor containing Arabic ceramics is Room 4, housing the gallery's most exquisite (and famous) piece: the white marble bust of *Eleonara di Aragona* (Eleonora of Aragon) by Francesco Laurana.

The 2nd floor is devoted primarily to Sicilian art, including Antonello da Messina's well-known panel of the *Assunzione* (Assumption). A number of Flemish paintings are also on show, perhaps to illustrate the influence of the Dutch school on Sicilian art; the most important of these is the *Malvagna* triptych by Jan Gossaert. The gallery is accessed through Via Alloro just off Piazza Abatellis.

La Gancia

Virtually next door to the gallery is the 15th-century Chiesa di Santa Maria degli Angeli (☎ *091 616 52 21, Via Alloro 27; free; open 9am-5pm Mon-Fri, 9am-1pm Sat, 10am-12.30pm Sun)*, better known as La Gancia. Palermo's oldest organ (1620) is over the main doorway (access, however, is through a side door), the work of Raffaele La Valle. Also worth checking out is the pulpit between the fifth and sixth chapels on the right, which is the work of the Gagini school. It's a lovely church, with a tranquil atmosphere. At the time of research, the front was under scaffolding but the interior was accessible.

Lo Spasimo

South of Piazza Marina, and along Via della Vetreria, this complex of buildings includes the **Chiesa di Santa Maria dello Spasimo** *(☎ 091 616 14 86; free; open 8am-midnight daily)*, a typical example of late-Gothic style, although it was actually built during the Renaissance. Building work on the church extended as far as the walls and the soaring apse, but it has stood for centuries without a roof and its interior is host to a couple of tall ailanthus trees. Restored and opened to the public in 1995, the complex is a wonderful venue for concerts, performances and exhibitions, which take place nightly from June to the end of September.

At the side of the church is a small building that houses the curator's office *(open 9am-1pm & 4pm-7pm Mon-Fri)*; in the foyer is an extraordinary model of historic Palermo. Outside opening hours you'll have to content yourself with staring at it through the window.

Chiese della Magione

Across Piazza Magione from Lo Spasimo is the Chiese della Magione *(☎ 091 617 05 96, Via Magione 44; free; open 9.30am-6.30pm daily)*, also known as La Magione. This fine Norman church was founded in 1191 by the Cistercians but was awarded to the Teutonic Knights by the Holy Roman Emperor Henry VI in 1197. They held on to it until 1492, when Pope Innocent VIII expelled them from Sicily. Like most other Palermitan churches it was victim to the fad of redecoration but, in this instance, didn't fare too badly. Inside, the floor contains the marble funereal slabs of a bunch of Teutonic Knights. To the east of the church are the remains of a 12th-century cloister with double-lintel arches set on twin columns adorned by two splendid capitals. They bear a similarity to those in the cloister at Monreale, which is hardly surprising considering they were made by the same artisans.

THE 19TH-CENTURY CITY

North of Piazza Verdi, Palermo takes on a less worn, more cosmopolitan look. Here, in *la Città del Ottocento* (the 19th-Century

City), are some glorious examples from the last golden age in Sicilian architecture. The most obvious examples are Teatro Massimo and the smaller Teatro Politeama-Garibaldi.

Not surprisingly, you will find most of the city's designer boutiques and elegant, outdoor cafes here. Viale della Libertà, which strides northwards from Piazza Castelnuovo, is as fancy a street as any you'd see in Rome, Milan or Florence – although the aesthetics of some of the modern apartment blocks leave a lot to be desired.

Teatro Massimo
Overlooking Piazza Verdi, the proud and haughty 19th-century Teatro Massimo *(☎ 091 605 35 15 or toll-free 800 65 58 58; admission €2.60; open 10am-3.30pm Tues-Sun except during rehearsals)* finally reopened in 1997 following a restoration programme that had been in progress for 20 years. Building commenced in 1875 when the original square was levelled to make way for Giovanni Battista Basile's masterpiece, which was eventually completed in 1897 by his son Ernesto. The monumental Corinthian structure was the pride of Sicily when it first opened (with a performance of Verdi's *Falstaff*); it boasted the third-largest stage in the world, after the Opéra Garnier in Paris and Vienna's Staatsoper.

High society and illustrious personages failed to prevent the theatre from falling into disrepair less than 100 years after it opened, and when it closed in 1973 few could have imagined that it would be 24 years before its doors were opened to the public once more. Palermo's ex-mayor, Leoluca Orlando, made its restoration a priority of his term in office (even though his critics argued that he delayed the opening for political motives) and today it has been returned to its previous lustre. In front of the theatre, two beautiful Art Nouveau kiosks designed by Ernesto have also been renovated.

See Entertainment later in this chapter for details of the box office and performances.

Teatro Politeama-Garibaldi
Dominating Piazza Ruggero Settimo, Palermo's second theatre (and the Teatro Massimo's substitute for the length of its closure) was designed in classical form by Giuseppe Damiani Almeyda between 1867 and 1874. It features a particularly striking facade that looks like a triumphal arch topped by bronze chariots. Apart from serving as a theatre (☎ 091 605 33 15 for bookings) it is also home to the **Galleria d'Arte Moderna** *(☎ 091 58 89 51; entrance Via Turati 1; admission €3.10; open 9am-7.30pm Tues-Sat, 9am-1pm Sun & hols)*, installed in 1910 with an array of modern and contemporary Italian art. The theatre itself is only open during performances.

OUTSIDE THE CITY CENTRE
Catacombe dei Cappuccini
Between the early 17th century and 1881, Sicilians of a certain social standing who didn't want to be forgotten on their death were embalmed by Capuchin monks. The catacombs in the Capuchin convent *(☎ 091 21 21 17, Piazza Cappuccini 1; bus No 327 from Piazza Indipendenza; admission €1.30; open 9am-noon & 3pm-5pm daily)*, about 1km west of the city centre, contain one of the city's most bizarre sights – the mummified bodies and skeletons of some 8000 Palermitans. Over the entrance, a sign states that a visit here has three levels of importance: historic, cultural and reflective. Inside, the skeletal remains of the 'lucky' dead line the dimly lit, damp corridors, divided into different categories according to gender and profession. The most disconcerting sight is the near-perfectly preserved body of Rosalia Lombardo (just follow the signs – in Italian and English – for '*bambina*/baby girl'), who died at the tender age of two in 1920. The doctor who embalmed her died soon after, taking a secret formula to the grave that would have been of use to those who struggled with the bodies of Lenin and, later, Chairman Mao. Gory and perturbing, the catacombs are one of the city's premier tourist attractions.

La Zisa
Just north of the catacombs is the 12th-century Arab-Norman castle *(☎ 091 652 02 69, Piazza Guglielmo il Buono; bus No 124*

from Piazza Ruggero Settimo; admission €2.60; open 9am-7pm Mon-Sat, 9am-1pm Sun) whose name derives from the Arabic '*el aziz*', which translates as 'the splendid'. The once-magnificent palace was built for William I and completed by William II, who used it as a seasonal residence. In its time, it was a magnificent oasis of gardens and water courses. After many years of neglect it was purchased by the government who undertook substantial restoration on it. Today it houses a museum of Arabic crafts of which the main features arc the superbly crafted screens (called *mush-rabbiya* in Arabic) and a gorgeous 12th-century bronze basin.

La Cuba

About 1km southwest of Porta Nuova is a marvellous example of Arab-Norman Fatimid architecture known as La Cuba *(☎ 091 59 02 99, Corso Calatafimi 94; admission €2.10; open 9am-7pm Mon-Sat, 9am-1pm Sun & hols)*. Built in 1180, the castle was once part of an enormous park, planned by William II, which also incorporated La Zisa. In the 14th century, Giovanni Boccaccio used the castle as the setting for a story of his *Decameron* (Day V, 6); two centuries later it was used as a leper colony before being converted into a cavalry barracks by the Bourbons. Apart from a model of it in its earlier days, there isn't much to see inside.

PUBLIC PARKS

Palermo has a number of pleasant parks. The most attractive is **Villa Giulia** *(☎ 091 740 40 28; free; open 8am-8pm daily)* in La Kalsa, reached along Via Abramo Lincoln. This 18th-century landscaped oasis has a bunch of welcome diversions from the city's chaos, including deer and a kid's train. Next door are the **Orto Botanico** *(Botanical Gardens; ☎ 091 623 82 41, Via Lincoln; admission €3.10; open 9am-6pm Mon-Fri, 9am-1pm Sat & Sun)*. To the north of the city centre, skirting along Viale della Libertà past Piazza Crispi are the **Giardino Inglese** (English Gardens). Once a pretty little park, in recent decades the gardens have became a seedy

hangout for drug addicts, though the city authorities have gone to immense efforts to clean it up in the past couple of years and it appears to be fine now.

One lovely park that's a great resting spot for sightseers is **Giardino Garibaldi** in Piazza Marina. With a huge shaded area under some wonderful large trees (including a particularly fine *Ficus magnolioides*), this park is an oasis in La Kalsa.

Farther north (about 3km from the city centre) is Palermo's biggest park, the **Parco della Favorita**. The Bourbon monarch Ferdinand purchased the land in 1799 and commissioned the original layout; he even lived here in a small palace (now closed) for a couple of years during his exile from Naples. Today, the park is home to Palermo's eponymous soccer stadium – where the city's main team plays – and a brand-new sports centre, as well as public tennis courts.

SPECIAL EVENTS

Palermo's biggest annual festival, the Festa di Santa Rosalia, takes place from 11 to 15 July. The saint's relics are brought through the city amid four days of fireworks and partying. It's a great time to be in the city, with all kinds of festivities going on throughout the medieval city, including music, food and fireworks. Actually, it's all-round pandemonium.

PLACES TO STAY

You should have little trouble finding a room in Palermo at whatever price you choose. The main tourist office will make recommendations but not bookings.

Head for Via Maqueda or Via Roma, between the train station and the Quattro Canti, for the bulk of the cheap rooms, some of which are in old apartment buildings. Rooms facing onto either street will be noisy. Women travelling alone should be wary if staying in the area near the train station. The area around Piazza Castelnuovo offers a higher standard of accommodation with fewer budget options (catch bus No 101 or 107 from the train station to Piazza Sturzo).

PLACES TO STAY – BUDGET
Camping
Trinacria *(☎ 091 53 05 90, Via Barcarello 25)* €4.15/7.50 per person/tent. Open year-round. This place by the sea at Sferracavallo is the best camp site near Palermo and has good facilities. Catch bus No 616 from Piazzale A de Gasperi (which can be reached by bus No 101 from the train station).

Hotels
Casa Marconi *(☎ 091 657 06 11,* e *casam arconi@iol.it, Via Monfenera 140)* Singles/doubles with bathroom €25.80/37.20. Palermo's only near-equivalent to a hostel is actually a hotel-cum-dormitory that operates as a B&B. Casa Marconi has very good rooms for cheap prices. To get there, take bus No 246 from the train station and get off at the hospital opposite Piazza Montegrappa, turn left onto Via Monfenera and walk for about 300m. Casa Marconi is on the left.

Albergo Orientale *(☎ 091 616 57 27, Via Maqueda 26)* Singles/doubles with bathroom €31/51.65. The building that houses this run-down but clean and basic hotel was probably quite beautiful many years ago, and the entrance via the courtyard certainly gives you an idea of its previous atmosphere. There's no heating in winter.

Albergo Rosalia Conca d'Oro *(☎ 091 616 45 43, fax 091 617 58 52, Via Santa Rosalia 7)* Singles/doubles with bathroom €23.25/36.15. Just around the corner from Albergo Orientale is this place, which has ancient but clean rooms.

Albergo Vittoria *(☎/fax 091 616 24 37, Via Maqueda 8)* Singles/doubles without bathroom €20.65/31. A clean but tired-looking place, the Vittoria is close to the train station and the owners are friendly.

Hotel del Centro *(☎ 091 617 03 76, fax 091 617 36 54,* e *hoteldelcentro@libero.it, Via Roma 72)* Singles/doubles €15.50/31, with bathroom €36.15/49. The clean rooms and friendly service make this a good central choice. Rooms have air-con, TV and phone.

Albergo Concordia *(☎/fax 091 617 15 14, Via Roma 72)* Singles/doubles €15.50/31, with bathroom €31/46.50. In the same building as Hotel del Centro, this place is also reasonable value, although the rooms are quite ordinary.

Albergo Corona *(☎ 091 616 23 40, Via Roma 118)* Singles/doubles without bathroom €18.10/36.15. The Corona has clean rooms, although the management can be quite brusque.

Hotel Confort *(☎ 091 32 43 62 or 091 33 17 41, Via Roma 188)* Singles/doubles with bathroom €23.25/40.30. Close to Corso Vittorio Emanuele, the Confort is a decent choice, although rooms can be noisy.

Hotel Sicilia *(☎/fax 091 616 84 60, Via Divisi 99)* Singles/doubles €25.80/41.30, with bathroom €38.75/62. The Sicilia has clean, large rooms, although they can be quite noisy as they face Via Maqueda. The management is friendly and helpful.

PLACES TO STAY – MID-RANGE
Hotel Elena *(☎ 091 616 20 21, fax 091 616 29 84, Piazza Giulio Cesare 14)* Singles/doubles with bathroom €41.30/54.30. Almost next door to the train station, the Elena isn't great value, but its location and the fact that the airport bus stops virtually at its front door make this a good choice for late night or early morning travellers. Rooms without a bathroom are available although the communal bathrooms are quite grotty.

Hotel Moderno *(☎ 091 58 82 60, fax 091 58 86 83, Via Roma 276)* Singles/doubles €43.90/59.40. Like most hotels in Sicily with the name 'Moderno', it's not, but the rooms have TV, phone and air-con, and it's within spitting distance of La Vucciria market.

Hotel Tonic *(☎ 091 605 53 38, fax 091 58 55 60,* e *hoteltonic@hoteltonic.com, Via Mariano Stabile 126)* Singles/doubles with bathroom €72.30/92.95. The friendly, English-speaking Tonic has good rooms with air-con, parking, TV and phone.

The following places are all located in the same modern building at Via Mariano Stabile 136, near Piazza Castelnuovo.

✸ ***Albergo Libertà*** *(☎/fax 091 32 19 11,* ✸ *Level 10, Via Mariano Stabile 136)* Singles/doubles €28.40/41.30, with bathroom €51.65/62. The Libertà is a great choice, with good rooms and a lobby that's all black marble, harbour views and a discount *Dynasty* vibe.

Hotel Elite (☎ 091 32 93 18, fax 091 58 86 14, Level 5, Via Mariano Stabile 136) Singles/doubles with bathroom €56.80/77.50. It's a bit overpriced here but the rooms have air-con, TV, phone and breakfast is included.

Hotel Boston-Madonia (☎ 091 58 02 34 or 091 611 35 32, fax 091 33 53 64, Via Mariano Stabile 136) Singles/doubles with bathroom €46.50/67.15. Actually two hotels (Boston on Level 5, Madonia on Level 3), the rooms here are decent enough, with TV, phone, air-con and parking but the management's a bit vague.

Gardenia Hotel (☎ 091 32 27 61, fax 091 33 37 32, e gardeniahotel@gardeniahotel .com, Level 7, Via Mariano Stabile 136) Singles/doubles with bathroom €51.65/ 72.30. This is a smart, pleasant place, with phone, TV, air-con and wheelchair access.

PLACES TO STAY – TOP END
Grande Albergo Sole (☎ 091 604 11 11, fax 091 611 01 82, Corso Vittorio Emanuele 291) Singles/doubles/triples €87.90/118.80/ 154.95. Right near the Quattro Canti, this 150-room hotel has swanky rooms, with all the usual fancy trimmings, plus very good discounts in the low season. Breakfast is included.

Grand Hotel e Des Palmes (☎ 091 602 81 11 or 091 58 39 33, fax 091 33 15 45, e des palmes@thi.it, Via Roma 398) Singles/ doubles with bathroom €118.80/175.60. The four-star Grand Hotel e Des Palmes, at the Piazza Castelnuovo end of town, is one of the ritziest hotels in Palermo and has beautiful rooms. Breakfast is included.

Centrale Palace Hotel (☎ 091 33 66 66, fax 091 33 48 81, e cphotel@tin.it, Corso Vittorio Emanuele 327) Singles/doubles/ triples with bathroom €136.85/196.25/ 260.80. This beautiful 63-room hotel is lavishly furnished and close to many of Palermo's attractions. Breakfast is included.

Hotel Joli (☎ 091 611 17 65, fax 091 611 17 66, e info@hoteljoli.com, Via Michele Amari 11) Singles/doubles with bathroom €77.50/103.30. Not far from Via Roma, the delightful rooms here are well equipped and

quite luxurious, with phone, TV, air-con and a nice communal terrace. Reservations are advised.

Grand Hotel Villa Igiea (☎ 091 54 37 44, fax 091 54 76 54, e villa-igiea@thi.it, Salita Belmonte 43) Singles/doubles with bathroom & breakfast €175.60/278.90. This magnificent five-star property, 3km north of the city centre in the suburb of Acquasanta, is the best hotel in town. Complete with a private beach and every other luxury, this sumptuous villa (designed by Ernesto Basile in 1900) was once the property of the Florio family (of tuna and marsala-wine fame) and is now a favourite of the elite. Prices drop by 50% in the low season, so check rates with the hotel.

PLACES TO EAT
With more than 300 officially listed restaurants and eateries to choose from in the city and surrounding area, you should have little trouble finding something to suit your taste and budget.

Palermo's cuisine takes advantage of the fresh produce of the sea and the fertile Conca d'Oro valley. One of its most famous dishes is the tasty *pasta con le sarde*, with sardines, fennel, onions, raisins and pine nuts. Swordfish is also served here, sliced into huge steaks. A reflection of Sicily's proximity to North Africa is the infiltration of couscous, basically a bowl of steamed dough grains usually served with a sauce.

Palermitans are late eaters and restaurants rarely open for dinner before 8pm. If you arrive at 9pm, you'll be eating with the locals, which really does make a difference to a restaurant's atmosphere.

Price estimates in this guide are for two courses with salad/vegetables or a dessert per person, plus some local wine.

Restaurants
Budget *Trattoria da Massimo* (☎ 091 616 75 20, Via Discesa dei Guidici 24) Meals around €13. Open daily. This nice-looking place offers good food, with fixed-price menus from €6.70 for two courses plus salad.

Hostaria la Sella (☎ 091 58 53 21, Via Cavour 97) Meals around €13. This eatery offers a good lunch and cheap pizza for under €5.15.

Antica Focacceria San Francesco *(☎ 091 32 02 64, Via A Paternostro 58)* Meals around €7.75. Closed Sun. If you want to try an age-old Palermo snack – a *panino* (bread roll) with *milza* (veal innards) and ricotta cheese – head here, one of the city's oldest eating-houses (established in 1834). It also serves great pizza and has a lovely outdoor area in Piazza San Francesco at night. Worth seeking out.

Ristorante a'Vucciria *(Via Chiavettieri 7)* Meals around €13. With standard Sicilian fare and a small outdoor area, this is a reasonable choice near La Vucciria market.

La Traviata *(☎ 091 32 88 61, Piazza Olivella 18)* Meals around €15.50. This good trattoria/pizzeria offers Italian and Tunisian dishes. There's a pleasant outdoor area and it's popular with a young crowd. Abu Nawas Pub, also on the premises, serves cold beer.

Osteria lo Bianco *(☎ 091 58 58 16, Via Enrico Amari 104)* Meals around €16. Osteria lo Bianco, off Via Roma at the Castelnuovo end of town, has a menu that changes daily. It's a simple, easy-going place.

Trattoria Shanghai *(☎ 091 58 97 02, Vico Mezzano 34)* Meals around €13. Closed Sun. In the heart of La Vucciria is this very basic and scruffy little trattoria with tables on a terrace overlooking the market. Despite its Chinese name, the restaurant serves typical (but not typically good) Sicilian food. You come here for the atmosphere, not the grub.

Hostaria Al-Duar *(☎ 0347 473 57 44, Via Ammiraglio Gravina 31a)* Fixed menu €9.30. Closed Mon. If you feel like a Tunisian night out, with couscous and other typical North African dishes, try this place on the first street south of Via Enrico Amari.

Mid-Range ***Hostaria da Ciccio*** *(☎ 091 32 91 43, Via Firenze 6)* Meals around €18. Just off Via Roma, Hostaria da Ciccio is a small restaurant with some good dishes (for example, the *involtini di pesce spada* – swordfish roulade, stuffed with breadcrumbs) and unenthusiastic service.

Mi Manda Picone *(☎ 091 616 06 60, Via A Paternostro 59)* Meals around €18.

Closed Sun. In a fabulous 13th-century building and with seating in beautiful Piazza San Francesco, this excellent restaurant has a great wine list and very good food. It's also open until 1.30am, if you fancy a late-night tipple.

Casa del Brodo *(☎ 091 32 16 55, Corso Vittorio Emanuele 175)* Meals around €20. Closed Tuesday. For more than 100 years this Palermitan institution has been serving up good Sicilian food, all much appreciated by locals. The *tortellini in brodo* (tortellini pasta in broth) is truly restorative after a hard day's sightseeing and the help-yourself antipasto buffet (€6.20) is good value.

Caffè Arabo *(Caffè d'Oriente; Piazza Gran Cancelliere 8)* Meals around €18. Next door to a mosque *(moschea)* and decorated with beautiful tiles, this place serves good North African/Middle Eastern food and great pine-nut tea *(tè ai pinoli)*. The piazza location here can't exactly be described as charmingly decrepit – just decrepit really.

Trattoria Stella *(☎ 091 616 11 36, Via Alloro 104)* Meals around €23. Stella is in the courtyard of the old Hotel Patria. In summer, the entire courtyard is filled with tables. The food is good and it's a friendly place.

La Cambusa *(☎ 091 58 45 74, Piazza Marina 17)* Meals around €20. Closed Mon. This popular eatery, near La Cala and on Piazza Marina, serves good, reasonably priced meals.

Trattoria Il Crudo e Il Cotto *(☎ 091 616 92 61, Piazza Marina 45)* Meals around €18. This is another popular eatery. It serves good fare and has a nice location on Piazza Marina.

Top End ***Cucina Papoff*** *(☎ 091 58 64 60, Via Isidoro La Lumia 32)* Meals around €26. Closed Sun & August. Papoff is a Bulgarian name but the food here is good, solid Sicilian. It's at the newer end of town in a nice setting.

Osteria dei Vespri *(☎ 091 617 16 31, Piazza Croce dei Vespri 6)* Meals around €26. Off Via Roma, past Chiesa di Santa Anna, this trattoria has outside tables and excellent food (the tuna dishes are highly recommended).

Il Bagatto (☎ *091 611 63 83, Piazza Marina 24*) Meals around €31. Open daily. This is a great little restaurant with a mouthwatering menu of excellent pasta and seafood dishes.

Sant'Andrea (☎ *091 33 49 99, Piazza Sant'Andrea 4*) Meals around €26. Closed Tues. This is a lovely restaurant in the heart of La Kalsa. It serves delicious and imaginative dishes and, although it is a little pricier than other places in the area, it's worth it. Try the antipasto of Sicilian dishes, which is a meal in itself.

Some of the posher restaurants are on the outskirts of Palermo or in the nearby town of Mondello (see Around Palermo later in this chapter), so you'll need your own transport or a taxi.

Cafes
On Via Principe di Belmonte (which is closed to traffic between Via Ruggero Settimo and Via Roma) there are numerous cafes with outdoor tables where you can linger over breakfast or lunch. If you want to spend less, buy a panino in one of the many bars along Via Roma.

Di Martino (☎ *091 58 59 90, Via Mazzini 54*) This is one of Palermo's nicest cafes. Its outdoor tables are thronged nightly with a good-looking crowd. The sandwiches are well worth trying.

Café Centro Storico (☎ *091 32 19 32, Corso Vittorio Emanuele 132*) In La Kalsa, this small place has been fitted out like an old-fashioned tea salon and is a good place for a *macchiato* (espresso with milk).

Markets
Palermo's historical ties with the Arab world and its proximity to North Africa are reflected in the noisy street life of the city's ancient centre, and nowhere is this more evident than in its markets.

Each of the four historic quarters of Palermo has its own market, *La Vucciria* being the most famous (see La Vucciria earlier in this chapter). Although it's popular with tourists, many Palermitans shop elsewhere these days, especially at *Il Ballarò* and *Capo* markets, which extend through the tangle of lanes and alleyways of the Albergheria and Capo quarters respectively. Here you can purchase anything your stomach desires (and several items it may recoil at – slippery tripe and all sorts of fishy things) as well as a host of off-the-back-of-a-truck-style bargains. Markets open 7am to 8pm Monday to Saturday (until 1pm on Wednesday). La Vucciria market winds down in the afternoon although some stalls hang around until early evening (around 6pm). Although great places in which to wander, you should keep an eye on your belongings while walking through the markets.

ENTERTAINMENT
After playing second fiddle to Catania for many years, Palermo is finally catching up and is great for nightlife and entertainment. A bunch of new bars have opened in the historic centre, bringing life to the once moribund quarters. The traditional arts have benefited from a much-needed injection of funding resulting in the reopening of the Teatro Massimo. The summer programme of concerts and recitals at Chiesa di Santa Maria dello Spasimo in La Kalsa is a definite highlight (for more information see Lo Spasimo earlier in this chapter).

Bars
Near the Quattro Canti, Via Candelai is packed with great bars that are doing a roaring trade with the Palermitan youth.

I Candelai (☎ *091 32 71 51, Via dei Candelai 65*) This great bar, a converted furniture shop, features live music and a booming sound system.

Fuso Orario (☎ *091 32 03 56, Piazza Olivella 2*) This is another great spot, with a range of bottled and draught beers to quench every thirst.

Bikers Bar (*Piazza Olivella 13*) Piazza Olivella itself is a great spot to check out as it is jammed with people virtually every night – and Bikers Bar has outdoor tables.

I Grilli Giù (*Piazza Valverde 9*) Across Via Roma in La Vucciria is I Grilli Giù, a trendy little spot where you can drink cocktails and listen to a DJ spin the latest sounds.

Berlin (☎ *0338 347 88 66, Via Isidoro la*

Lumia 21) In the newer city to the north, Berlin, at the corner of Via Isidoro La Lumia and Via Quintino, is an ultra-sleek bar popular with Palermo's gay community (who are a discreet bunch on a largely traditional island).

Kandisky ☎ 091 637 53 38, Discesa Tonnara 4) This is a great place to come for dancing, drinking and generally having a good time. It's stylish and gets great word of mouth from the locals.

Theatre

Teatro Massimo (☎ 091 58 95 75, W www .teatromassimo.it, Piazza Verdi 9) For opera and ballet, the Massimo is the main venue. Its programme runs from October to May and tickets cost from €13 to €26.

Teatro Biondo (☎ 091 58 23 64, Via Roma) If your Italian is up to it, you can see plays at the Teatro Biondo. The daily paper *Il Giornale di Sicilia* has a listing of what's on.

The *Teatro Politeama-Garibaldi (☎ 091 605 33 15, Piazza Ruggero Settimo)* and the *Teatro Golden (☎ 091 30 52 17, Via Terrasanta 60)* – take bus No 103 from the Politeama-Garibaldi – put on a pretty good year-round programme of music and plays. Tickets cost around €13.

GETTING THERE & AWAY
Air

Falcone-Borsellino airport is at Punta Raisi, 32km west of Palermo. Alitalia has an office (☎ 091 601 91 11) at Via Mazzini 59. For information on tickets and routes, both international and domestic, see under Air in the Getting There & Away and Getting Around chapters.

Bus

The main intercity bus station is on Via Paolo Balsamo, east of the train station.

Segesta (☎ 091 616 90 39), Via Paolo Balsamo 26, has a direct daily service to Rome (€35.65 one way). It also runs frequent buses to Tràpani (€6.70, two hours). SAIS Trasporti (☎ 091 617 11 41), Via Paolo Balsamo 20, runs buses to Cefalù (€4.65, twice daily) and Piazza Armerina (€10.35, 11 daily). SAIS Autolinee (☎ 091 616 60 28),

Via Balsamo 16, has services to Catania (€12.40, eight daily Monday to Saturday, four on Sunday), Enna (€5.95, 1¾ hours, six daily Monday to Saturday, four on Sunday) and Messina (€12.40, eight daily Monday to Saturday, four on Sunday). Interbus (☎ 091 616 60 28), Via Paolo Balsamo 16, runs to Syracuse (€13.95, four hours, six daily Monday to Saturday). For Marsala, go to Salemi (☎ 091 617 54 11), Via Rosario Gregorio 44. Cuffaro (☎ 091 616 15 10), Via Paolo Balsamo 13, operates buses to Agrigento (€6.70, five daily).

Away from the main terminal, AST (☎ 091 680 00 30), on Corso Ruggero, runs buses to Ragusa. It also operates services to Corleone, Cefalù, Palazzo Adriano and Montelepre.

Numerous other companies serve points throughout Sicily and most have offices in the Via Paolo Balsamo area. Their addresses and telephone numbers, as well as destinations, are listed in the *Agenda Turismo* booklet, available at the main APT tourist office and many hotels.

Train

Regular trains leave for Messina (via Milazzo; €16.30, 3½ hours, every 30 minutes), Catania (€15.50, 3½ hours, every hour), Syracuse (€17.55, change at Catania) and Agrigento (€6.70, two hours, 11 daily), as well as nearby towns such as Cefalù. There are also Intercity trains to Règgio di Calàbria, Naples and Rome. Train timetable information is available in English at the station. There is a Transalpino office inside the station, as well as baggage storage (open 6am to 10pm daily, €2.60 per 12 hours) and washing facilities (showers and basins).

Car & Motorcycle

Palermo is accessible on the A20 from Messina (only partially completed) and from Catania (A19) via Enna (this route is quicker). Tràpani and Marsala are also easily accessible from Palermo by motorway (A29), while Agrigento and Palermo are linked by the SS121, a good state road through the interior of the island.

Rental AVIS (☎ 091 58 69 40) is at Via Francesco Crispi 115 and at the airport (☎ 091 59 16 84). Maggiore (☎ 091 612 14 15) is at the ferry terminal and at the airport (☎ 091 59 16 81). All major rental companies are represented in Palermo.

Boat
Ferries use the ferry terminal (Stazione Marittima) on Molo Vittorio Veneto, off Via Francesco Crispi, for Cagliari (Sardinia), Naples, Livorno and Genoa. The Tirrenia office (☎ 091 602 11 11) is at the port in Palazzina Stella Maris, Calata Marinai d'Italia. Siremar (☎ 091 749 31 11), Via Francesco Crispi 118, runs daily ferries and hydrofoils to Ustica (€10.85 for foot passengers and from €20.65 for cars by ferry; €16 for foot passengers only by hydrofoil). Snav, represented in Palermo by the Pietro Barbaro agency (☎ 091 33 33 33) at Via Principe di Belmonte 55, runs a summer hydrofoil service to the Aeolian Islands. From 12 April to 8 October it also operates a daily ferry service to Naples, departing at 9am and arriving at 1pm (going the other way it leaves Naples at 5.30pm). *Poltrona* (airline type seat) tickets cost from €51.65 one way (€77.50 Friday to Monday 27 July to 3 September).

Grandi Navi Veloci (☎ 091 58 74 04), part of the Grimaldi Group at the port in Calata Marinai d'Italia, runs ferries from Palermo to Genoa and Livorno.

The baggage deposit facility (from €1) at the ferry terminal opens 7am to 8pm daily.

GETTING AROUND
To/From the Airport
Regular trains connect the Falcone-Boresellino airport at Punta Raisi with Palermo's central train station between 4.45am and 12.05am daily. The journey takes 45 minutes and costs €4.15 each way.

Regular blue buses run by Prestia e Comandé (☎ 091 58 04 57) will take you into town. They leave from outside the train station, in front of Hotel Elena, roughly hourly from 5am to around 10.45pm. Buses run from the airport to the train station from 6.45am to midnight (or until the arrival of the last flight). The timetable is posted at the bus stop outside the train station, to your right as you leave the station. Buses also stop on Piazza Ruggero Settimo, just near the Teatro Politeama-Garibaldi. The trip takes about one hour and costs €4.65.

Taxis to the airport cost upwards of €38. There is a taxi rank (☎ 091 59 16 62) at the airport. Alternatively you could try Autoradio Taxi (☎ 091 51 27 27 or 091 51 33 11).

Bus
Palermo's city buses (AMAT) are quite efficient and most stop in front of the train station. Tickets (€0.75 for 1½ hours, day pass €2.60) must be purchased before you get on the bus and are available from tobacconists or the booths at the AMAT bus station.

Metro
Most visitors will have little cause to use Palermo's metro system, as its 10 stations radiating out from the main train station are a good hike from any destination likely to interest the tourist. There is talk of expanding the system to Falcone-Borsellino airport, which would be useful, should it ever happen. A single trip ticket costs €0.75.

Car & Motorcycle
Do *not* drive in Palermo if you can avoid it. The city has a massive problem with gridlock, which makes getting from one side of the city to the other virtually an all-day affair. Also, Palermitans seem to have little respect for the rules of the road (though if you have dealt with Rome or Naples in your own vehicle, Palermo will present no difficulties). Theft of and from vehicles is a big problem, however, and you are advised to use one of the attended car parks around town if your hotel has no parking space. You'll be looking at paying around €1 per hour. Some hotels have small car parks but they are often full; check with your hotel proprietor.

Around Palermo

NORTH OF PALERMO
There are beaches northwest of the city at Mondello and Sferracavallo (see Golfo di

Mosaics at Palermo's market...

... and the Cappella Palantina

Palermo's cathedral is a striking hotchpotch of architectural styles.

The beautiful, Baroque Chiesa di San Domenico in Palermo

Palermo's Porta Nuova

Climb the towering crag of La Rocca for fabulous views over medieval Cefalù.

Massive fortress-like towers dominate the Duomo di Cefalù.

Anyone for a spot of fishing?

The temperature's rising... head for the coast to top up your tan.

AROUND PALERMO

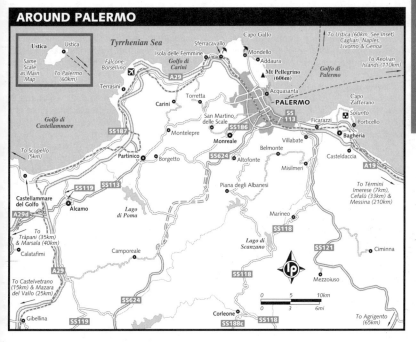

Sturzo; free; open 7am-7pm daily). One of Palermo's patron saints, St Rosalia, lived as a hermit in a cave on the mountain, now the site of a 17th-century shrine. The water, which is channelled from the roof of the cave into a large font, is said to have miraculous powers. Whatever your beliefs, this is a fascinating place to visit, but remember that it is a shrine and not a tourist haunt.

On the northern side of Mt Pellegrino, at Addaura, is the **Grotta dell'Addaura**, where several cave drawings from the Upper Palaeolithic and Neolithic periods have managed to survive into the 21st century. The cave generally opens to visitors 9am to midday on Friday and Saturday, by prior arrangement through the Soprintendenza Archeologica (☎ 091 696 13 19), next to the Museo Archeologico Regionale in Palermo. To get there head up the road above the beach at Addaura and follow the signposts (the caves are about 400m away). At the time of research, it was temporarily closed.

Carini & Around) but if you're really into spending some time by the sea you'd be better off heading farther afield, to Scopello, for example. Mondello is popular with Palermitans, who crowd the beachfront, Viale Regina Elena, during their evening strolls. There are numerous seafood restaurants and snack stalls along the avenue. Buses for Mondello and Sferracavallo leave from Piazza A Gasperi (north of Palermo town centre).

Le Terrazze Charleston (☎ 091 45 01 71, Viale Regina Elena) Meals around €46.50. Closed 7 Jan-10 Feb. One of the area's best-known restaurants, this *very* fancy place attracts a fashionable crowd. Reservations are advised.

La Barcaccia (☎ 091 45 15 19, Via Piano Gallo 4) Meals around €31. Closed Tues. For a seafood meal in ritzy Mondello, try this small place.

Between Palermo and Mondello is Mt Pellegrino and the **Santuario di Santa Rosalia** (☎ 091 54 03 26; bus No 812 from Piazza

CATTEDRALE DI MONREALE

At the heart of Monreale, a pleasant town on the top of a hill only 8km southwest of Palermo and easily accessible by city bus, is one of Europe's premier attractions – this cathedral (*☎ 091 640 44 13; bus No 389 from Piazza Indipendenza; cathedral free, treasury admission €2.10, cloisters €4.15; cathedral open 8am-6pm daily, treasury open 9.30am-12.30pm & 3.30pm-5.30pm daily, cloisters open 9am-7pm Mon-Sat, 9am-1pm Sun & hols)* should not be missed on any account.

Considered the finest example of Norman architecture in Sicily, the magnificent 12th-century cathedral in fact incorporates Norman, Arabic, Byzantine and classical elements and, despite renovations over the centuries, remains substantially intact. It was built for William II, whose motivations for ordering its construction were almost entirely political, stemming from his rivalry with the archbishop of Palermo, Walter of the Mill. Eager to curb the growing power of the papacy in Sicily (with whom the archbishop was closely allied), William made Monreale an archbishopric in 1183, thereby devaluing the prestige of Walter's cathedral in Palermo. When William died the cathedral lost much of its political importance; as a work of art, however, it is timeless.

The central doorway has bronze doors by Bonanno Pisano and the northern door is by Barisano di Trani. Although the exterior is both graceful and elegant, nothing can quite prepare you for the dazzling interior, one of the most impressive creations of the Italian Middle Ages and one of the most beautiful to be found anywhere in the world.

The walls of the aisles, sanctuary and apses are entirely covered in magnificent gilded mosaics – a total surface area of 6340 sq metres. The artists were local and Venetian mosaicists but the influence of the Byzantine style is all-pervasive. Completed in 1184 after only 10 years' work, the mosaics are the apogee of Norman-Arabic art, an articulate and fitting tribute to the grandeur of Sicilian culture of that time.

In the central apse is the dominating half-figure of Christ Pantokrator (All-Powerful) giving benediction and below him, the Virgin Mary and child, bearing the legend Panacrontas (All-Chaste). Beneath them again are the ranks of saints, each identified by name (look out for St Thomas à Becket between Silvester and Laurence; he was canonised in 1173, just before the mosaics were started). The side apses are dedicated to the martyrdoms of St Paul (east) and St Peter (west), whereas the central nave is a pictorial history of the early books of the Bible, beginning with the Creation and including a great depiction of Noah's Ark.

Outside the cathedral is the entrance to the cloisters, which were part of a Benedictine abbey once attached to the church. There are 228 twin columns with polychrome ornamentation. Each of the Romanesque capitals is different, depicting plants, animals and fantastic motifs. The capital of the 19th column on the western aisle depicts William II offering the cathedral to the Virgin Mary.

Visitors are advised to keep coins ready so they can turn on the large electric lights (even though the number of tourists passing through will ensure that the church will not stay dark for long).

AROUND MONREALE

Ten kilometres west of Monreale and over 500m above sea level, San Martino delle Scale is home to the massive Benedictine abbey of **San Martino** (*free; open 9am-6pm Mon-Sat, 9.30-11.30am & 5pm-7pm Sun & hols)*. According to some, the abbey was founded by St Gregory the Great in the sixth century. Things worth seeing here include some fine 18th-century paintings, a grand 18th-century staircase and a library. Take bus No 2 from Monreale.

GOLFO DI CARINI & AROUND

The Golfo di Carini makes a decent alternative to the crowds of Mondello if you want some sun and sea. There's a good *camp site* (see Camping under Places to Stay for Palermo earlier in the chapter) at Sferracavallo and if you want a fancy meal, try *Il Delfino* (*☎ 091 53 02 82, Via Torretta 80, Sferracavallo)*. Remember to wear your good clothes to this popular but pricey fish restaurant. Meals cost around €50.

Less than 10km from the coast is the town of **Carini**, with a ruin of a 16th-century castle, in need of some TLC. **Montelepre**, farther inland, is a fairly unattractive town of little interest to the visitor save for those who want to see the birthplace of the famous Sicilian bandit Salvatore Giuliano (1922–50), who hid out in the area and returned to the town under the cover of darkness. Very much a wanted man in his time, he captured the imagination of many Sicilians, who *love* a good bandit. Giuliano is a Robin Hood-type figure to many, even today, although his links with the Mafia and his involvement in the massacre of peasants at nearby Portella della Ginestra show that he was certainly no angel. Giuliano was killed in 1950 (his body was found in a courtyard in Castelvetrano), supposedly by his cousin and second-in-command Gaspare Pisciotta (who was subsequently poisoned in Ucciardone prison whilst on trial).

There are direct buses (€2.30) from Palermo to Montelepre with AST.

Partinico, 20km southwest of Palermo, is famous for its associations with social reformer Danilo Dolci (1924–97; Aldous Huxley called him 'the Gandhi of Sicily'), who spent many years in Partinico working with the desperately poor (and this was easily one of the worst areas in Sicily) and trying to break the entrenched attitudes to omnipresent and oppressive Mafia rule. Times have changed now and the town is not the grim slum it once was, nor is it much of a tourist attraction, although the Baroque fountain in Piazza Duomo is interesting.

You can get to Partinico with AST buses (€2.30) from Piazza Lolli in Palermo.

BAGHERIA

Once a summer retreat for Palermo's elite, Bagheria is little more than a satellite suburb of Palermo now (15km east, on the Palermo-Messina train line or the SS113), albeit with some fascinating (and generally crumbling) 18th-century villas. The suburb has been ruined by some shocking new developments but if you want to see something that's shocking in a good way, head to **Villa Palagonia** *(1715; ☎ 091 93 20 88, Piazza Garibaldi; admission €2.60; open 9am-1pm & 4pm-6.30pm daily)*. It's an extraordinary building decorated with some bizarre rooms and a collection of grotesque sculptures in the garden that were said to cause miscarriage in pregnant women. To get to Bagheria, take the train from Palermo (€1.55, about 20 minutes).

SOLUNTO

About 20km east of Palermo are the remains of the Hellenistic-Roman town of Solunto *(☎ 091 90 45 57; admission €3.10; open 9am-1hr before sunset Mon-Sat, 9am-1pm Sun)*. Although the ancient city is only partially excavated, it's well worth the trip to see what has been brought to light. Founded in the 4th century BC on the site of an earlier Phoenician settlement, Solunto was built in a particularly panoramic position – on Mt Catalfano, overlooking the sea. Wander along the main street, the Roman *decumanus*, and take detours up the steep, paved sidestreets to explore the ruined houses, some of which still sport their original mosaic floors. Take particular note of the theatre and the Casa di Leda (if you can find it), which has an interesting floor mosaic.

To get there, take the train from Palermo and get off at the Santa Flavia–Solunto–Porticello stop (€1.55, 15 minutes, every 30 minutes) and ask for directions. It's about a 30-minute uphill walk.

USTICA
postcode 91100 • pop 1100
Almost 60km north of Palermo lies the lonely turtle-shaped island of Ustica. In 1980, a passenger jet crashed near the island in mysterious circumstances, leaving 81 people dead. Investigators suspect the military was involved and a dozen Italian air-force officers stand accused of a cover-up.

Ustica is, otherwise, a tranquil place with barely more than 1000 inhabitants, most living in the mural-bedecked village of the same name. The best months to come are June and September; to visit during August is sheer lunacy due to the volume of tourists and the price hikes. Parts of the rocky coast have been declared a marine reserve and the limpid waters, kept sparkling clean by an Atlantic current through the Straits of Gibraltar, are ideal for diving and submarine photography.

Information

You'll find a tourist office (☎ 091 844 94 56) for the marine reserve on Piazza Umberto I, part of an interlocking series of squares in the centre of the village. It opens 8am to 1pm and 4pm to 6pm Monday to Friday and 8am to 2pm on Saturday and Sunday (to 9pm during the summer). The staff can advise on activities around the island and have a list of the dive centres.

Call the *pronto soccorso* (casualty; ☎ 091 844 92 48) for medical emergencies. For police, call the *carabinieri* (military police; ☎ 091 844 90 49).

Activities

Among the most rewarding dive sites are the Secca Colombara to the north of the island and the Scoglio del Medico to the west. Note that Zone A of the marine reserve, taking in a good stretch of the western coast north of Punta dello Spalmatore, is protected. Fishing, diving and even swimming without permission are forbidden in the area. The reserve's information office can organise sea-watch diving excursions into the zone. The dive hire outlet **Ailara Rosalia** *(☎ 091 844 91 62, Banchina Barresi)* operates during the summer. Otherwise, bring your own gear. The number for the hyperbaric chamber is ☎ 091 844 93 80 or 091 844 96 30.

You can also hire a boat and cruise around the island, visiting its many grottoes and tiny beaches. **Hotel Ariston** *(☎ 091 844 90 42, Via della Vittoria 5)* is one of several

Where Fact & Fiction Meet

Most readers will recognise Corleone as the name given to Mario Puzo's fictional Godfather, Vito Andolini, when he landed at New York's Ellis Island. Puzo's choice was no accident, as this small town has played a pivotal role in the bloody affairs of the Mafia since the American landing in Sicily in 1943. Two returning *Corleonesi* serving in the US Army, a Captain De Carlo and a 'Mr Vincent', arrived to negotiate the town's surrender to the Americans with the local Mafia boss – and later Democrazia Cristiana (DC; Christian Democrats) power-broker – Michele Navarra, who happened to be De Carlo's cousin. A bloody struggle between the different players ensued over who would actually control the local family, with De Carlo and Navarra winning out.

The demise of the old feudal Mafia and the possibility of huge profits from the blossoming drug trade meant trouble. Navarra (an old-fashioned don) was deemed superfluous by his greedy young deputy, Luciano Liggio. In 1958 Navarra was killed, sparking a five-year war that left hundreds dead. By 1963 Liggio was in charge but a belated strike by the authorities resulted in the arrest of thousands of mafiosi, including Liggio and his apprentice, a semi-literate farm boy called Totò Riina.

In 1968, the newly released Liggio was diagnosed as suffering from Pott's disease and was forced into early retirement. He appointed a killer named Bernardo Provenzano as his heir but his lack of intelligence meant that Riina soon became head of the family, despite being a fugitive from justice.

Over the next 24 years Riina intimidated and murdered his way to a position of supreme power, virtually eliminating the Sicilian Commission, or Cupola (a partnership of Mafia families in Sicily and America), and becoming the most feared man on the island. His totalitarian control, however, was to have unforeseen consequences: in 1986 Tommaso Buscetta, his life threatened by Riina's Corleonesi, became the first senior mafioso to give evidence, thus setting off a chain of events that would see hundreds more testify against their own. In 1993 Riina was eventually arrested (his driver told the authorities of his whereabouts) but not before he had ordered the brutal killing of Sicily's most heroic magistrates, Giovanni Falcone and Paolo Borsellino. In a scene straight out of *The Godfather*, Riina refused to speak during his many trials other than to wish one presiding judge peace, 'but not in this life; in the next one, which is far more important'.

agencies that can organise boat trips, diving and motorcycle rental. You could try **Scubaland** *(☎ 091 844 92 16, Via Petriera 7)* to hire a boat or dinghy.

Places to Stay & Eat

There are eight hotels and several *affittacamere* (rooms for rent) on Ustica.

Pensione Clelia (☎ 091 844 90 39, fax 091 844 94 59, e clelia@telegest.it, Via Magazzino 7) Singles/doubles with bathroom €41.30/69.70. Open 21 July-3 Sept. This is a decent place with a good little restaurant.

The town centre offers many other eating options, with a good selection of restaurants and bars.

Getting There & Around

From April to December there is at least one Siremar hydrofoil daily from Palermo (€16). A car ferry runs daily throughout the year (except Sunday during winter); high-season fares are €10.85 for foot passengers and from €20.65 for cars. The Siremar office *(☎ 091 844 90 02)* is on Piazza Capitano V di Bartolo in the centre of Ustica. During the summer you can also pick up the Tràpani-Favignana-Ustica-Naples hydrofoil run by Ustica Lines on Monday, Thursday and Saturday from 15 June to 15 September. The journey from Naples to Ustica takes four hours and costs €65.60 one way.

Orange minibuses make a round trip of the island, they leave from the town hall every 30 minutes (€1). Alternatively you could hire a moped at the Hotel Ariston (see Activities earlier for details) from around €25 per day.

CORLEONE

postcode 90034 • pop 11,260
elevation 550m

In the heart of a valley 60km south of Palermo is the farming town of Corleone, unremarkable in every respect but one: since WWII it has been the unofficial capital of the Sicilian Mafia (see the earlier boxed text 'Where Fact and Fiction Meet'). Centuries of poverty and natural disasters – including a particularly devastating landslide in 1418 – have taken their toll but the town has a lot of wealth, as evidenced by the impressive condition of the 14th-century **Chiesa Madre** and the 17th-century **Chiesa di Santa Rosalia**, which is home to a lovely canvas by Giuseppe Velasquez depicting *San Giovanni Battista sull'Isola di Palmos* (St John the Baptist on the Island of Palmos). Curiously, the town has in recent years become a location for Scandinavian weddings, with groups of couples trekking here from northern Europe to get hitched. Those wanting to see some Godfather-style action are going to be sorely disappointed – it's best to come here with the aim of seeing a well-maintained Sicilian town and some impressive countryside.

There is a tourist office *(☎ 091 846 11 51)* in the town hall, located on Piazza Garibaldi. The only place to stay in the area is *Belvedere (☎ 091 846 49 44, fax 091 846 40 00, Contrada Belverdere)*, where singles/doubles with bathroom cost €62/72.30. *Bentivegna (Piazza Vittorio Emanuele 1)* is a great pastry shop that creates delicious *cannoli* (cream horns).

There are regular AST buses from Palermo (€3.60, 1½ hours, four daily).

The Tyrrhenian Coast

Highlights

- Stroll through the hilltop town of Caccamo, with its imposing Norman castle
- Admire Cefalù's combination of sun, sand and sea but don't forget the magnificent mosaics in the cathedral
- Ski and hike in the Parco Naturale Regionale delle Madonie
- Drive through Sicily's largest nature park, the Parco Regionale dei Nebrodi
- Dig the Greek and Roman ruins at Himera, Tyndaris, San Marco d'Alunzio and San Biàgio

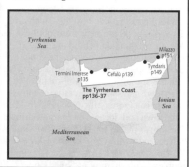

The stretch of coast between Palermo to the west and Milazzo to the east is an almost uninterrupted line of resorts, beaches and little towns pretty much entirely given over to the Italian tourist industry. Between June and September the well-worn roads carry a steady stream of foreign tourists and Italian holidaymakers to and from the coastline's manifold attractions. The best of these is the pretty town of Cefalù which, though advertising itself as a traditional fishing village, has developed into a resort second only to Taormina in popularity. Just behind Cefalù is the Parco Naturale Regionale delle Madonie, unlike other parks on the island in that it is dotted with small towns and an increasingly popular

ski resort. Farther east of Cefalù are the coast's best beaches: clean, unpolluted and relatively uncrowded (except at the height of summer). Here you will find some interesting ruins and a couple of hill towns that live in splendid semi-isolation. Starting behind Santo Stefano di Camastra and bordered by the towns of Mistretta, Cesaro and Randazzo, the massive Parco Regionale dei Nebrodi is another great spot for nature lovers. At the eastern end of the coast is Milazzo, an industrial port that serves as the main point of transit to and from the Aeolian Islands.

Tèrmini Imerese to Cefalù

If you're coming east from Palermo, the first stop of any interest beyond the capital's outer limits is the part-resort, part-industrial centre of Tèrmini Imerese. Not quite the beach resort *par excellence*, the town is surrounded by some pretty grim industrial development that is as bad as it gets until you reach the eastern end of the coast and Milazzo. Out of Tèrmini Imerese, the real attractions are inland, past the imposing peak of Mt Calògero (1326m) to the western edge of the Parco Naturale Regionale delle Madonie, where you'll find a couple of hill towns that are worth every effort to visit.

TÈRMINI IMERESE
postcode 90018 • pop 26,500

The town dates from prehistoric times, though its name is derived from the two neighbouring Greek settlements of Thermae and Himera. The latter was destroyed by the Carthaginians in 408 BC and its inhabitants moved to the former, which was then renamed Thermae Himerensis. The town flourished for another 150 years, ruled for a time by local boy Agathocles (who went on to bigger and better things as the first and most ferocious tyrant of Syracuse). It was taken by the Romans in 252 BC and became famous as a thermal spa for the treatment of urological diseases. Among those who came for the cure was the Greek poet Pindar, who praised the spa's therapeutic value. Traces of the old baths still remain. Until the 19th century Tèrmini Imerese was enclosed within a set of protective walls but it has since spilled out into the outlying countryside. Its growth, however, has been almost singularly industrial, due mainly to the establishment of a massive power plant after WWII and a number of petrochemical factories that have somewhat spoilt the town's overall appearance. Although for a time Tèrmini Imerese experienced some much-needed prosperity, in the last decade several plants have closed, causing widespread unemployment.

Orientation & Information

Like so many of Sicily's older settlements, Tèrmini Imerese has an upper and lower town. The upper half is where you'll find all of the sights of interest, whereas the lower half is home to the town's hotels and day-to-day activity. The train station is southeast of the town centre along the coast; all buses arrive and depart just in front of the train station.

The tourist office (☎ 091 812 82 53) is in the town hall *(municipio)* on the main square, Piazza del Duomo. It opens 9am to 1pm and 3.30pm to 6pm Monday to Friday. The community's Web site is at **W** www .comune.termini-imerese.pa.it.

Things to See

At the heart of the upper town is Piazza del Duomo, dominated by the 17th-century **cathedral** *(Piazza del Duomo; free; open 9am-7pm daily)*; it has been under continuous renovation since the mid-1980s and the four 16th-century statues that adorned it have been replaced by copies. The facade dates from 1912. Inside the church, the third northern chapel contains sculptures from the Gagini school and the four original statues from the facade. In the fourth southern chapel there is a wonderful relief by Ignazio Marabitti, *Madonna del Ponte* (Madonna of the Bridge).

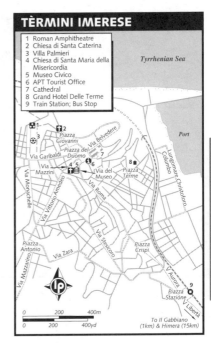

TÈRMINI IMERESE

1 Roman Amphitheatre
2 Chiesa di Santa Caterina
3 Villa Palmieri
4 Chiesa di Santa Maria della Misericordia
5 Museo Civico
6 APT Tourist Office
7 Cathedral
8 Grand Hotel Delle Terme
9 Train Station; Bus Stop

To the north of the cathedral, Via Belvedere affords great views of the town and the coast. Opposite the cathedral is the **Museo Civico** *(☎ 091 812 82 79, Via del Museo; free; open 9am-1pm & 3.30pm-5.30pm Tues-Sun)*, established in 1873. It has three different sections devoted to archaeology, art and natural history.

Backed up against the museum is the **Chiesa di Santa Maria della Misericordia** (Church of Our Lady of Mercy). The entrance is off Via Mazzini, west out of Piazza del Duomo. Inside is a marvellous triptych of the *Madonna con Santi Giovanni e Michele* (Madonna with Saints John and Michael; 1453), attributed to Gaspare da Pesaro.

To the northwest of the cathedral, down Via Ianelli, is the **Chiesa di Santa Caterina**, home to a very good fresco of the *La Vita della Santa Caterina d'Alessandria* (Life of St Catherine of Alexandria) by Giacomo Graffeo. The church keeps very irregular hours; check at the tourist office or at the

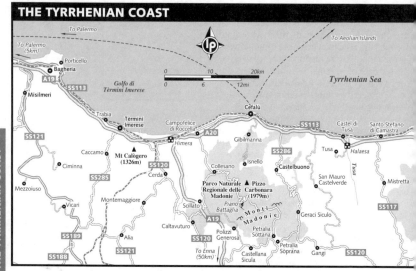

THE TYRRHENIAN COAST

Tyrrhenian Sea

church itself. From here there are some lovely views of the citrus groves and the sea beyond.

Just beyond the church are the public gardens of **Villa Palmieri**, laid out in 1845. Inside are the remains of a public building known as the Curia, which was built sometime during the 2nd century AD, and the faint traces of the town's Roman amphitheatre *(anfiteatro)*.

Special Events

The town celebrates Carnevale with a pa rade of allegorical floats in the week before the beginning of the Lenten period. Contact the tourist office for details.

Places to Stay & Eat

Himera (☎ 091 814 01 75, fax 091 815 92 06, SS113, Località Buonfornello) €5.15/14.45 per person/site. Open year-round. With a wide range of facilities (restaurant, pool, disco and so on), this two-star camp site, 15km south of town, is the pick of the bunch.

Il Gabbiano (☎ 091 811 32 62, fax 091 811 42 25, e hotelgabbiano@hotelgabbiano.it, Via Libertà 221) Singles/doubles with bathroom €46.50/72.30. South of the train station (just walk parallel to the tracks for about 15 minutes), this is the town's cheapest hotel. It

has good quality rooms; those in the main hotel are better-equipped.

Grand Hotel delle Terme (☎ 091 811 35 57, fax 091 811 31 07, Piazza Terme) Singles/doubles with bathroom €90.40/138.40. The only other option is in the heart of the upper town; the Grand Hotel delle Terme has fancy rooms with TV, fridge and phone. Rates include free use of the thermal baths which are on the property.

The selection of restaurants in Tèrmini Imerese is surprisingly poor for a resort town. The upper town has a number of bars and *paninoteche* (sandwich bars) where you can get a bite to eat.

Getting There & Away

SAIS Trasporti (☎ 091 617 11 41) runs buses between Tèrmini Imerese and Palermo (€1.80, 30 minutes, two daily) and Cefalù (€1.80, 30 minutes, one daily).

The best way to get to Tèrmini Imerese is by train. The town is a stop on the Palermo -Messina and Palermo-Agrigento lines; there are departures every 20 minutes or so from Palermo's central station (€2.30). The trip takes between 20 and 40 minutes, depending on whether you're on a *rapido* or the *diretto*.

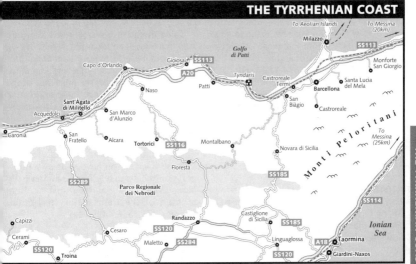

THE TYRRHENIAN COAST

The train station at Tèrmini Imerese also has a left-luggage facility (€2.60 for 12 hours), which opens 8am to 8pm daily.

CACCAMO
postcode 90012 • pop 8600
elevation 521m

Lorded over by its imposing **castle**, the hilltop town of Caccamo is a popular day trip out of Tèrmini Imerese. A Carthaginian stronghold that served as a constant thorn in Himera's side in the 5th century BC, the official founding of the town wasn't until 1093, when the Normans began building the castle on a rocky spur overlooking a cliff. Most visitors make a beeline for this imposing structure but, while the tour (free, but tips are appreciated) is relatively interesting (if you understand Italian), the castle itself is being slowly converted into a conference centre, which kind of ruins the overall effect. The best parts are the walls and original fortifications, which included some ingenious traps for any intruder who might have breached the outer perimeter.

From the castle there are some great views of the surrounding countryside, including the Rosmarina artificial lake which was created by a controversial dam built in 1993. Submerged within the lake is a stone bridge built in 1307 on the road that once linked the town with Palermo.

Since the 1950s, the town itself has suffered the loss of almost half of its inhabitants to emigration, but you'd never know it wandering through the traffic-filled streets. The attractive 11th-century **cathedral** was remodelled twice, in 1477 and 1614. Inside, the sacristy has some lovely carvings of the *Madonna con Bambino e Angeli* (Madonna and Child with Angels) and *Santi Pietro e Paolo* (Saints Peter and Paul) by Francesco Laurana.

On the left-hand side of the cathedral are two churches: the one farthest away from the cathedral is the **Chiesa dell'Anime del Purgatorio** (dedicated to the Souls of Purgatory), featuring some fine stucco work in the eastern end and an 18th-century organ. A local tour guide is almost always on hand to explain the history of the church and guide you downstairs to the musty catacombs, where the skeletons of a number of townspeople lie in niches along the wall, a burial practice that lasted from the 17th century up to 1863.

La Spiga d'Oro (☎/fax 091 814 89 68, Via Margherita 74) Singles/doubles with bathroom €33.60/56.80. This is the town's only hotel. Its 14 rooms are clean, if a little basic; there's also a restaurant.

Al Belvedere (☎ 091 814 94 26, Via Circonvallazione 23) Meals about €12.90. Closed Monday. This is a fine local restaurant serving dishes from the region, including pasta and *salsicce* (sausages).

To get to Caccamo, take the bus from in front of the train station in Tèrmini Imerese (€2.60, 30 minutes, 14 a day Monday to Saturday).

HIMERA

The town of Himera was founded in 648 BC by Greeks from Zankle (now Messina) and was named after the River Imera that flows nearby. It was the first Greek settlement on this part of the island and was a strategic outpost just outside the eastern boundary of the Carthaginian-controlled west. In 480 BC the town was the scene of a decisive battle between the two foes, with the combined armies of Theron of Agrigento and Gelon of Syracuse defeating a sizable Carthaginian army led by Hamilcar, who lost his life during the fighting. The Carthaginians had intended to take Himera and then move on to wrest control of the island from Greek hands, but the Greek victory put a temporary end to Carthaginian ambitions and consolidated the Greek position on the island. As for Himera itself, it paid the price for Carthage's defeat in 409 BC, when Hamilcar's nephew Hannibal completely destroyed the town in revenge for his uncle's death.

Compared with other Greek sites around the island, the remains here *(free; site open 9am-6pm daily)* are a little disappointing. The only recognisable ruin is the **Tempio della Vittoria** (Temple of Victory), a Doric structure supposedly built to commemorate the defeat of the Carthaginians (although scholars have recently come to doubt that hypothesis). Whatever its origin, Hannibal did a good job of destroying it. To the south of the temple was the town's **necropolis**. It is currently being excavated so, apart from

a few loose stones and the semblance of a structure, there is nothing much to see.

Some artefacts recovered from the site are kept in the small **antiquarium** (☎ 091 814 01 28; admission €2.05; open 9am-6pm Mon-Sat), about 100m west of the site's entrance (it's up a small lane off the other side of the main road). Although the more impressive displays are in Palermo's Museo Archeologico Regionale, you can see the well-sculpted lion-head spouts that were used to drain water off the temple's roof.

The ruins are 8km east of Tèrmini Imerese. Unless you have your own transport you'll have to rely on one of four daily buses (Monday to Saturday) that run from in front of the train station in Tèrmini Imerese (€1.55, 15 minutes).

CEFALÙ
postcode 90015 • pop 14,000

If Taormina is Sicily's resort town *par excellence*, then Cefalù is its eager younger sibling, desperately trying to catch up. Just over an hour by train or bus from Palermo, this attractive beachside town is now the premier destination on the Tyrrhenian coast. Its popularity is reflected in the number of tour buses that hit town daily during the summer months and the near-exorbitant prices. Still, the town's location on the sea, backed up against the towering mass of a crag known simply as La Rocca (The Rock), plus its relatively unspoilt medieval streets and historic sights, make this a wonderful place to spend a couple of days – just be prepared to feel the pinch! Cefalù is also an easy day trip from Palermo, if your time is limited.

History

A small Greek settlement existed here from the 5th century BC; its name, Cephaloedium, was derived from the Greek name for 'horse', after the shape of the crag above which (sort of) looks like a horse's head. In 307 BC the town was taken by Agathocles of Syracuse but it only really made its name in the following century when it was captured by the Romans, who used it as a key port in the control of the Tyrrhenian Sea. In AD 857 it was the Arabs' turn and

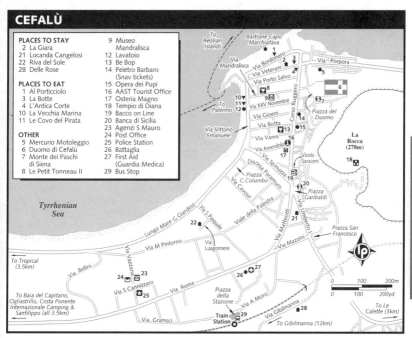

CEFALÙ

PLACES TO STAY
2 La Giara
21 Locanda Cangelosi
22 Riva del Sole
28 Delle Rose

PLACES TO EAT
1 Al Porticciolo
3 La Botte
4 L'Antica Corte
10 La Vecchia Marina
11 Le Covo del Pirata

OTHER
5 Mercurio Motoleggio
6 Duomo di Cefalù
7 Monte dei Paschi
   di Siena
8 Le Petit Tonneau II

9 Museo
   Mandralisca
12 Lavatoio
13 Be Bop
14 Peietro Barbaro
   (Snav tickets)
15 Opera dei Pupi
16 AAST Tourist Office
17 Osteria Magno
18 Tempio di Diana
19 Bacco on Line
20 Banca di Sicilia
23 Agenzi S Mauro
24 Post Office
25 Police Station
26 Battaglia
27 First Aid
   (Guardia Medica)
29 Bus Stop

THE TYRRHENIAN COAST

documentary evidence testifies to the
town's importance as an Islamic stronghold.
The Normans, however, set about destroying every trace of Eastern influence when
they captured Cefalù in 1064. Roger II
commissioned the town's impressive cathedral in 1131 and Cefalù became the seat of
one of Sicily's most powerful bishoprics.
The town's importance, however, began to
wane not long after Roger's death, and for
the next eight centuries Cefalù was little
more than a quaint fishing port with a few
elegant buildings and a magnificent cathedral from the Norman era.

Information

Tourist Offices The AAST tourist office
(☎ 0921 42 10 50, fax 0921 42 23 86,
ⓦ www.cefalu-tour.pa.it), along the main
road at Corso Ruggero 77, opens 8am to
2.30pm and 3.30pm to 7pm Monday to Friday, and 9am to 1pm and 3.30 to 7pm on
Saturday.

Money The Banco di Sicilia on Piazza
Garibaldi has an ATM, as does Monte dei
Paschi di Siena, at Piazza del Duomo 15,
which opens 8.20am to 1.50pm and 2.35pm
to 3.45pm Monday to Friday. Banks open
9am to 1.20pm and 2.45pm to 3.45pm
Monday to Friday. It's not a good idea to
exchange money at any of the *cambi* (exchange) booths around town as they generally charge higher commissions than
banks; those that say they don't charge
commission make up the difference in the
exchange rates. You can, however, change
money at the post office, where rates are
pretty good.

Post & Communications The unwieldy-
looking post office is at Via Vazzana 9, off
Via Roma. It opens 8.10am to 6.30pm Monday to Saturday. Agenzia S Mauro, across
the road from the post office at Via Vazzana
7, serves as the town's telephone exchange.
To access email, go to Bacco On Line, on

the corner of Vicolo Saraceni and Corso Ruggero. It charges €2.60 for 30 minutes.

Medical Services & Emergency There is a first-aid station (*guardia medica*; ☎ 0921 42 36 23) at Via Roma 15. Battaglia pharmacy, next door at No 13, opens 8am to 1pm and 4pm to 8pm Monday to Saturday.

The police station *(questura)* is at Via Vazzana 3, opposite the post office.

Duomo di Cefalù

According to the official version, Roger II ordered that a mighty church be built after he survived a violent storm off the shore of Cefalù. The origin of the cathedral *(☎ 0921 92 20 21; free, donations accepted; open 8am-noon & 3.30pm-6.30pm daily)*, however, is more likely the result of Roger's tempestuous relationship with the Palermitan archbishopric, which was busy consolidating its temporal power by constructing the Cappella Palatina in Palermo's Palazzo dei Normanni (see the Palermo chapter for details). Eager to curb the growing influence of the papacy in Sicily (with whom the archbishopric had close ties), Roger thought that building a mighty church so far from Palermo would prove an effective slap in the face. Built in a time of such hostility, it is hardly surprising that from the outside, the wonderfully sited cathedral looks more like a solid fortress than a place of worship – with two massive towers flanking the facade. This is where Roger II wished to be buried, although he ended up in Palermo's much less attractive cathedral.

The entrance is on the southern side, to the right of the facade. The interior is largely plain until you get to the apse and vault, which are decorated with some of the most beautiful mosaics in Sicily, if not all of Italy. The mosaics were completed sometime between 1150 and 1160 – some 20 to 30 years before the mosaics of Monreale – and feature (in the central apse) the gigantic figure of Christ Pantokrator (All-Powerful) holding an open bible bearing a Latin and Greek inscription from John 8:12: 'I am the light of the world; he who follows me shall not walk in darkness.' Easily the

best mosaic depiction of Christ in Sicily, the artist responsible has managed to capture a truly human expression on Christ's face – no mean achievement in the 12th century! Underneath is the Virgin Mary flanked by archangels; underneath again, in two rows of six, are the twelve Apostles. At the time of research the mosaics were being restored, but work should be finished by the time you read this.

Donations are much needed and greatly appreciated.

La Rocca

The massive crag that towers 278m above the town is a popular climb, especially in good weather when the panoramic views of the town and coast are splendid. Steps to the right of the Banco di Sicilia on Piazza Garibaldi mark the start of the clearly signposted, steep path up the cliff. It's a 20-minute climb to the **Tempio di Diana** (Temple of Diana), built sometime during the 4th or 5th century BC. Below it are the straggly remains of a set of fortified walls built during the Byzantine period. Apart from a few loose rocks, there is nothing left of the Norman castle that once crowned the rock's peak.

Other Things to See

Off Piazza del Duomo is the private **Museo Mandralisca** *(☎ 0921 42 15 47, Via Mandralisca 13; admission €4.15; open 9am-8pm daily)*. Its collection includes Greek ceramics and Arab pottery, as well as paintings, notably the *Ritratto di un Uomo Ignoto* (Portrait of an Unknown Man; 1465) by Antonello da Messina (1430–79). The unknown man's smile is almost as enigmatic and thought-provoking as the Mona Lisa's – without the attendant hype.

Turn left outside the museum and walk down Via Mandralisca towards the sea. On Via Vittorio Emanuele is the **lavatoio**, a 16th-century wash-house built over a spring which was well known in antiquity.

The town's other main sight is the **Osteria Magno**, on the corner of Corso Ruggero and Via Amendola. This imposing mansion built in the 14th century has been heavily renovated over the centuries and today is only open for temporary art exhibits. If you want to get a look inside at other times, ask for the keys at the tourist office.

Otherwise, the town is a splendid place for a walk or a swim. The lovely little port is lined with narrow fishing boats where you might find the occasional fisherman mending his nets (although the demise of the fishing industry makes such an occurrence less and less likely). The boardwalk along the beach is very popular for the evening *passeggiata*, or stroll; in summer the cafes and restaurants that line it are almost always full.

Swimming

Cefalù's crescent-shaped beach is one of the most popular along the whole coast. In summer it is always packed so be sure to get down early to get a good spot. If you want relief from the blazing sun, you can rent a beach umbrella (€2.60) from the bar on the beach. Deckchairs (€5.15) are also available. Again, if you want to rent either get here early as they tend to be snapped up pretty quickly. Some sections of the beach require a ticket, but you can swim and sunbake for free in the area closest to the old town.

Places to Stay

Cheap accommodation is like gold dust in Cefalù. Between June and August prices are exorbitant and there is no such thing as value for money. At the height of summer (mid-July to the end of August) you will have difficulty finding anywhere to stay at any price, so be sure to book early.

The good news is that out of season (between October and April) the hotels that remain open drop their rates substantially, some even by half. Unless otherwise indicated, the accommodation listed below is open year-round and all prices listed are for the peak season.

Camping There are several camp sites in the area.

Costa Ponente Internazionale Camping (☎ 0921 42 00 85) €5.95 per person. Four kilometres west of town at Contrada Ogliastrillo, this camp site has numerous facilities, including parking, disabled access and

sports. Take the La Spisa bus from Cefalù train station.

Sanfilippo (☎/fax 0921 42 01 84) €5.15 per person. Open 10 Apr-10 Sept. Next to Costa Ponente is Sanfilippo, which has reasonable facilities. To access both of these places by car, take the SS113 and follow the signs.

Hotels ***Locanda Cangelosi*** (☎ 0921 42 15 91, Via Umberto I 26) Singles/doubles without bathroom €20.65/36.15. This is the only cheap option in town and there are only four rooms so book in advance (although another four rooms are available nearby – ask the owner). Rooms are adequate.

La Giara (☎ 0921 42 15 62, fax 0921 42 25 18, Via Veterani 40) Singles/doubles with bathroom €54.25/80. Uphill from the beach and off Corso Ruggero is La Giara, where prices drop dramatically in the low season. It's not great value but the location is excellent.

Delle Rose (☎/fax 0921 42 18 85, Via Gibilmanna) Doubles with bathroom €59.40. A comfy option is the friendly Delle Rose, which is about a 10-minute walk from the centre on the road to Gibilmanna.

Riva del Sole (☎ 0921 42 12 30, fax 0921 42 19 84, Via Lungomare 25) Doubles with bathroom €77.45. This place, in a hideously ugly building, is conveniently near the beach. Thankfully, the rooms are good.

With only a couple of exceptions, you won't get good value for money in Cefalù's top-range hotels.

Le Calette (☎ 0921 42 41 44, fax 0921 42 36 88, Via Vincenzo Cavallaro 12, Località Caldura) Singles/doubles with bathroom €95.55/108.45. Le Calette is on the eastern side of the headland about 2km out of town. It's set in its own grounds, complete with swimming pool, buffet bar and restaurant, and is a very good-looking place.

Baia del Capitano (☎ 0921 42 00 05, Località Mazzaforno) Singles/doubles with bathroom €67.15/100.70. Baia del Capitano is in an olive grove near the beach at Mazzaforno, 4km out of town towards Palermo. It has pleasant rooms with TV and fridge, and a pool.

THE TYRRHENIAN COAST

Places to Eat

Although the town is packed with restaurants, the food can be surprisingly mundane and the tourist menus unimaginative. Still, there are a few spots that stay ahead of the crowd by offering well-prepared dishes at prices that don't make you feel like you're being ripped off, an all-too-common feeling during the high season in this tourist-driven town. Most restaurants fill up between 8.30pm and 10pm so, unless you want to find yourself dining at 11.30pm, book your table in advance (a few hours' notice is sufficient).

Le Covo del Pirata (*Via Vittorio Emanuele 59*) Meals about €10. A cheap spot for a quick lunch is this 'pirate's cove', which serves cheap sandwiches, a limited number of pasta dishes and filling salads. Ask for a seat on the tiny terrace overlooking the port. At night it turns into a club (see Entertainment later).

Al Porticciolo (*☎ 0921 92 19 81, Via Bordonaro 66*) Meals about €25, pizza €3-9. Closed Wed. With a good reputation and very good pizza, it's possible to eat here on a small budget –those wanting a blow-out can easily be accommodated too. The great wine list is highly tempting.

La Botte (*☎ 0921 42 43 15, Via Veterani 6*) Tourist menu €11.35. Closed Mon. This trattoria is just off Corso Ruggero. The *pasta con le sarde* (pasta with sardines, anchovies and fennel), a Sicilian speciality found on every menu in town, is particularly good. Credit cards are accepted.

L'Antica Corte (*☎ 0921 42 32 28, Corso Ruggero 193*) Tourist menu €11.90. This is one of the better restaurants in town and the prices reflect it if you stray from the well-priced tourist menu. In summer, the air-conditioning provides welcome relief from the heat of the day.

La Vecchia Marina (*☎ 0921 42 03 88, Via Vittorio Emanuele*). Tourist menu €18.10. Closed Tues. This is the best fish restaurant in town, serving an array of freshly caught beauties, which you can enjoy with a delightful view of the sea.

Otherwise, there are a few restaurants along the seafront that serve similar menus of fish and meat dishes as well as pastas, all priced around €7.75 for a main course. A cheap *al fresco* alternative is to grab some supplies and eat at Bastione Capo Marchiafava, off Via Bordonaro, which has great ocean views.

Entertainment

The *Opera dei Pupi* (*☎/fax 0921 42 22 30, Corso Ruggero 92; tickets €5.15; performances 6.30pm Wed, Sat & Sun*) shows traditional puppet plays by Teatro Arte Cuticchio. There is also a small puppet museum (€2.60), which opens 9am to 1pm and 4pm to 10pm daily.

Cefalù has a number of pretty good bars that are popular in summer.

Le Petit Tonneau II (*☎ 0921 42 14 47, Via Mandralisca 66*) Closed Tues. Just down from the Museo Mandralisca is this French-owned bistro (the name means 'little tuna') that's fun for a late-night drink. There's also another branch on Via Vittorio Emanuele.

Be Bop (*Via Botta 4*) This is another good spot with live music on summer weekends.

No summer resort is complete without its complement of discotheques, and Cefalù is no different.

Le Covo del Pirata (*see Places to Eat for details*) This is the town's version of an 'alternative' club, with soul, hip hop and beats played by DJs nightly throughout the summer (music from 10.30pm).

Ogliastrillo (*☎ 0921 42 05 78*) Open June-Sept. This venue, next to the Costa Ponente Internazionale camp site (see Places to Stay earlier), is a typical Italian summer disco.

Tropical (*Lungomare G Giardino*) Open June-Sept. The outdoor Tropical is similar to Ogliastrillo, with the usual house music selections and expensive drinks.

Getting There & Away

Buses run from outside the train station. SAIS (*☎ 091 617 11 41*) buses leave Palermo for Cefalù twice daily (€4.65, one hour). SAIS also runs a daily bus to and from Tèrmini Imerese (€1.80, 30 minutes).

The best way of getting here is by train. The line links Cefalù with Palermo (€3.60, just under one hour, every 30 minutes) and virtually every other town on the coast.

You can also get a hydrofoil from Cefalù to the Aeolian Islands from 1 June to 30 September. Snav hydrofoils depart Cefalù for Alicudi at 8.10am on Wednesday, Thursday and Friday (from €16). During the same period, there are hydrofoils to/from Palermo on the same days. You can buy tickets at Pietro Barbaro (☎ 0921 42 15 95), at Corso Ruggero 82.

Getting Around

Cefalù itself is small enough to walk around. If you find yourself heading farther afield, a taxi service (☎ 0921 42 25 54) operates out of Piazza del Stazione, next to the train station. Rates depend on where you want to go, but a 5km trip, for instance, should cost no more than €5. Be sure to fix the rate before you leave.

If you are driving, parking can be a problem though you should be able to find somewhere on the roads that run parallel to the long beach southwest of the town centre.

Mercurio Motoleggio (☎ 0921 92 38 08), at Via Candeloro 33, rents out 50cc Vespas for €25.80/162.70 per day/week.

PARCO NATURALE REGIONALE DELLE MADONIE

This 40,000-hectare nature reserve, between Palermo and Cefalù, incorporates the Madonie mountain range and some of the highest mountains in Sicily after Mt Etna (the highest peak is Pizzo Carbonara at 1979m). Instituted in 1989 by the Regione Sicilia, the park also takes in numerous small towns and villages and plenty of farms and vineyards. It is an area where people live, rather than simply a nature reserve – so you can combine walking with visits to some of its more interesting towns, such as Petralia Sòprana and Petralia Sottana. Also worth visiting is the

THE TYRRHENIAN COAST

The Targa Florio

Locals have enduring memories of Sicily's famous car race which was run almost every year from 1906 until its demise in 1973. The Targa Florio was created and sponsored by the Marsala wine and tuna-canning family and was contested on the twisting roads of the Madonie mountains, lined with what must have been every inhabitant of the region. In 1970 it was abundantly clear that Sicilian schoolteacher Nino Vaccarella, moonlighting as a Ferrari racing-car driver, was the hometown favourite. V-A-C-C-A-R-E-L-L-A was graffitied across every blank expanse of wall around the 72km length of the circuit, and at every corner (and there were over 700 of them!) crowds of Sicilians leaned dangerously out onto the track to watch for the arrival of the local hero.

During its life the Targa Florio was run on a variety of circuits before settling down to the Piccolo Madonie circuit, winding along the coast from the town of Campofelice di Roccella then climbing up into the mountains through Cerda, Caltavuturo, Scillato and Collesano before dropping back down to the coast. Revived after WWII, the Targa Florio continued as a major event through the 1950s and into the 1960s, and in the last few years became a straight fight between the smaller, more agile Porsches and Alfa Romeos and the powerful Ferraris, of which one in particular was cheered on by the roars of the partisan crowd. By the late 1960s motor racing faced greater demands for increased safety and the prospect of cars capable of over 300km/h (200mph) hurtling along stone-walled straights and into tiny villages, where spectators stood unprotected on the circuit perimeter, became completely intolerable. The Targa Florio was doomed.

Nino Vaccarella never made it in the big leagues of Formula One racing but in Sicily his knowledge of the local roads guaranteed that he would always challenge for the lead. As for the Targa Florio itself, it has been nearly 30 years since a racing V12 Ferrari 512 hurtled through Campofelice but the memory of the race survives in the Targa Tasmania rally run every year in the Australian island state, and with every Porsche 911 Targa to cruise the streets of Los Angeles or London.

Tony Wheeler

small town of Gibilmanna, where the 17th-century church is the object of pilgrimage.

In summer, Madonie is a popular destination for Palermitans armed with picnic baskets, who tend to make a day of just wandering or driving through the expanse of the park. In winter it is the only place, other than Etna, where you can go skiing (see Activities later).

Orientation & Information

The best way to visit the park is with your own transport; otherwise you'll have to rely on the limited public transport (see Getting There & Away later for details). From Tèrmini Imerese head east for 16km along the coastal SS113 to Campofelice di Roccella and then turn off for Collesano, 13km inland. From Cefalù it is even easier: just follow the directions for the Santuario di Gibilmanna (Sanctuary of Gibilmanna), 14km to the south.

The body responsible for the park, Ente Parco delle Madonie has a tourist office (☎ 0921 68 40 11) in Petralia Sottana at Corso Paolo Agliata 16. It has details about the park and several one-day walks, as well as information about transport and accommodation. A good map available is the Cefalù–Madonie map (1:50,000; free), with details on the towns and walking trails in the region.

Activities

More Swiss than Sicilian, the little **ski resort** at Piano Battaglia (around Pizzo Carbonara) is dotted with chalets that play host to an ever-growing number of Sicilian downhill skiers in winter. The Rifugio Giuliano Marini (see Places to Stay for details) rents out equipment; you should be able to get skis and boots for around €26 per day.

For details of a good half-day walk in the area, see the boxed text 'Meandering in the Madonie'.

Petralia Sòprana & Petralia Sottana

Beautifully positioned at the top of a hill above a tree line of pines, Petralia Sòprana (from the Italian word *sopra* meaning 'on' or 'above') is one of the best-preserved little towns in northern-central Sicily. Unlike in other Sicilian settlements, the stone houses have been left unplastered, thus preserving their medieval appearance. At the heart of the main square, Piazza del Popolo, is a WWI memorial built by Antonio Ugo in 1929. The most beautiful church in town is the 18th-century Chiesa di Santa Maria di Loreto at the end of Via Loreto, off the main square. Inside is an altarpiece by Gagini and a *Madonna* by Giacomo Mancini. The cathedral, off Piazza dei Quattro Cannoli, was consecrated in 1497 and has an elegant 18th-century portico.

Below Petralia Sòprana, the town of Petralia Sottana (from the Italian *sotto* meaning 'under') doesn't have any real sights to speak of but is a pretty place and nice for a stroll.

Polizzi Generosa

At the start of the Imera Valley, Polizzi Generosa (917m) is a charming town, given the nomenclature *generosa* (generous) by Frederick II in the 1230s. The town is riddled with churches and often shrouded in mist, and it's a lovely place to wander around or

> ### Meandering in the Madonie
>
> The Madonie mountains are many Sicilians' favourite place for hiking and there is an impressive array of signposted walks of varying degrees of difficulty. The following describes a scenic walk of around three hours from Piano Battaglia to Piano Sempria. From Rifugio Ostello della Gioventù Piero Merlino (see Places to Stay) in Piano Battaglia take path No 2, heading north to Pizzo Scalonazzo (1903m), where there is a nearby mountain refuge (unattended). The road then snakes northwest, passing Pizzo Carbonara (1979m) before continuing west to a forked path that marks the start of path No 1. Take the left path (heading north) and continue to another unattended refuge. The path then winds its way to the Rifugio Francesco Crispi (see Places to Stay) at Piano Sempria, an area wooded with oaks.

to start a trek through the Madonie from. One sight worth visiting is the **Chiesa Madre**, with a Flemish depiction of the *Madonna and Child with Angels* from the early 16th century and a *Madonna of the Rosary* by Guiseppe Salerno.

Pick up some pastries from **L'Orlando** *(Via Rampolla 1)* and satisfy your sweet tooth while you stroll.

Gibilmanna

If you're a casual tourist, the main reason for coming here is to appreciate the wonderful view from the belvedere in front of the 17th-century **church**, from where you can see the spread of the Madonie and the peak of Pizzo Carbonara. While here, you will probably mingle with visitors whose intent is a little more serious, as they come in pilgrimage to pray at the elaborately decorated Baroque **Santuario di Gibilmanna**, a shrine of the Virgin Mary. During the shrine's coronation on 17 August 1760 (which also marked the official consecration of the church), the Virgin is supposed to have shown signs of life, which restored sight to two blind worshippers and speech to a mute. The miracle was confirmed by the Vatican and the church has been one of Sicily's most important shrines ever since.

Places to Stay & Eat

Although there are a couple of hotels in the park, the more interesting accommodation is in a choice of *rifugi* (mountain chalets) or *agriturismi* (rooms in working farmhouses), a welcome change from the usual four walls and a bed.

The following rifugi are all handy for those wishing to ski.

Rifugio Ostello della Gioventù Piero Merlino *(☎ 0921 64 99 95, Località Piano Battaglia-Mandria Marcate)* Bed/full board €15.50/36.15 per person. Not quite a youth hostel in the proper sense, this place caters to all visitors and has eating and drinking areas.

Rifugio Giuliano Marini *(☎ 0921 64 99 94, Località Piano Battaglia)* Bed/full board €12.90/28.40 per person, with private bathroom. Right at Pizzo Carbonara, this rifugio has chalet-style rooms and good facilities.

Luigi Orestano *(☎/fax 0921 66 21 59, Località Piano Zucchi)* Bed/full board €15.50/31 per person, with private bathroom. Near Isnello, approximately halfway between Piano Battaglia and Cefalù, the Luigi Orestano is a little more expensive than the others but it's a good place to stay – plus it has a disco!

If you're looking for something with a little more character, try one of the following options.

Salaci *(☎ 0921 68 72 60, Contrada Salaci, Petralia Sòprana)* Singles/doubles with bathroom €31/62. This agriturismo has dining, dancing and swimming facilities.

Madonie *(☎/fax 0921 64 11 06, Corso Paolo Agliata 81, Petralia Sottana)* Singles/doubles with bathroom €46.50/67.15. This good hotel, in a late-19th-century building, has rooms with TV, phone and fridge, plus parking, disabled access and a lift.

Flugy Ravetto *(☎ 0921 67 41 28, fax 0921 67 41 28, **W** www.aziendeflugyravetto .com, Contrada Ogliastro)* Half-board €51.65 per person. About 2km outside San Mauro Castelverde on the road to Cefalù, Flugy Ravetto offers accommodation in small apartments. To get here from the A20 Palermo-Messina motorway, take the Castelbuono exit until you reach the Castelverde intersection, then follow the SP52.

Bel Soggiorno *(☎ 0921 42 18 36, Località Gibilmanna)* Singles/doubles with bathroom €25.80/43.90. This small two-star hotel in Gibilmanna is good value for money, plus it's clean and tidy.

If you're looking for something to eat, the hotels in the area generally have restaurants attached. Otherwise try the towns for a stand-up snack or sit-down meal.

Getting There & Away

Transport could be a problem in the Madonie unless you have a car. Gibilmanna is served by a local bus (20 minutes) from Cefalù's Via Umberto I, and most of the towns can be reached by SAIS and AST bus from Palermo and – to a lesser extent – Cefalù.

THE TYRRHENIAN COAST

East to Milazzo

The 83km stretch of coastline between Cefalù and Capo d'Orlando to the east is dotted with little coves, clean beaches and a couple of resorts that have become increasingly popular in recent years, including the ceramics centre of Santo Stefano di Camastra and Sant'Àgata di Militello. Beyond Capo d'Orlando the coast becomes more developed and industrialised the closer you get to Milazzo, the main point of departure for the Aeolian Islands. The highlights here, however, are the classical remains at Patti and Tyndaris. All places mentioned are on the main Palermo-Messina railway line, which is served by frequent trains throughout the day. Inland from this route lies the 85,000-hectare Parco Regionale dei Nebrodi, with numerous towns and villages offering a glimpse into traditional Sicilian country life.

CASTEL DI TUSA
postcode 98079 • pop 480
About 25km east of Cefalù, just inside the province of Messina, is this little resort village that doesn't attract quite as many tourists as other spots along the coast. Just above the town (at 600m) are the ruins of the **castle** that gave the resort its name. A small road (9km) leads inland to the parent village of **Tusa** (population 3400), where in the bed of the river of the same name are a number of modern sculptures that have been the subject of much litigation and argument over the years (see the boxed text 'Art in the River'). There's no bus between the two so you'll have to walk if you don't have your own transport. But don't feel that you have to – for the cynical, the works can easily be offered as proof that modern art needs to be put out of its misery.

Between the coastal resort and the village you'll see a signpost for **Halaesa**, a Greek city founded in the 5th century BC. Beautifully positioned on a hill commanding fine views of the surrounding countryside and – on a clear day – the Aeolian Islands, the most conspicuous remains are those of the *agora* (marketplace) and its massive rusticated

walls. Just down the hill are the barely recognisable remains of a small theatre. The site was first excavated in the 1950s and again in 1972, but nothing has been done since then.

Atelier sul Mare (☎ 0921 33 42 95, e ateliersulmare@nebro.net, Via C Battisti 4). Singles/doubles with bathroom cost €72.30/103.30. This hotel in Castel di Tusa is one of Sicily's most distinctive places to stay. Each room is fitted out like an artistic installation or on a certain theme. There's even a room kitted out in homage to the controversial artist Pasolini – the mind boggles! The owner has gone all out to make a stay here a memorable and comfortable one, and the restaurant is noteworthy too.

The town is a 25-minute train ride from Cefalù (€1.30) and is served by trains on the Palermo-Messina line hourly throughout the day; to Palermo €4.15 (1½ hours), to Messina €6.70 (three hours).

SANTO STEFANO DI CAMASTRA
postcode 98077 • pop 5100
About 8km east of Castel di Tusa, Santo Stefano di Camastra is a popular coach-tour stop on account of its bustling ceramics industry. The industry grew up as a result of

---

Art in the River

Inaugurated in 1986, *Fiumara d'Arte* (Art in the River Bed) is a controversial project conceived by contemporary artist Pietro Consagra, whose aim was to create art outside of the sterile confines of a gallery's four walls. Placed in the bed of the River Tusa, his pieces generated immediate dismay and opponents rushed to get a court order forcing him to remove them. The courts granted their wish in 1991 and again in 1993, but the work remains and installations by other artists such as Tano Festa, Antonio di Palma and Hidetoschi Nagasawa were set up in other river beds, caves and hills along the coast.

To get to the art (best by car), start from Santo Stefano di Camastra and head west towards Castel di Tusa, turning left just before the bridge over the River Tusa (signposted).

numerous clay quarries in the hills above the town. Indeed, until 1693 the town was farther up the hill and was called Santo Stefano di Mistretta; it was destroyed by a landslide in 1692 and a new town was built closer to the coast.

Other than ceramics (almost every second shop stocks them), the town doesn't offer all that much to the casual visitor. If you're interested in the process behind the manufacturing of ceramics, you can pop your head into the **Museo Civico delle Ceramiche** *(Civic Museum of Ceramics; Palazzo Trabia, Via Palazzo; free; open 9am-1pm & 4pm-8pm in summer, 9am-1pm & 3pm-7pm in winter)* in the Palazzo Trabia towards the sea.

If you're after a place to stay, try *La Plaja Blanca (☎ 0921 33 12 48, fax 0921 33 13 73, Via Fiumara Marina)* Doubles with bathroom & breakfast €72.30. This two-star hotel, with a restaurant, is a good choice, although it's popular with groups.

PARCO REGIONALE DEI NEBRODI

In the heart of the Nebrodi mountains, which span from the Peloritani range in the east to the Madonie range just east of Palermo, this nature reserve was set up in 1993 and constitutes the single largest forested area on the island. Cutting through the heart of the park is the SS289 which links Cesarò in the interior with Sant'Àgata di Militello. Along the way you'll come across a wide variety of trees, including oak, elm, ash, beech, cork, maple and yew, as well as varying landscapes that cater to different breeds of animals. In the uplands you will find farm animals grazing on the holly bushes, while lower down you can catch sight of the San Fratello breed of horses, unique to this area and recognisable by their oddly shaped noses.

Although ostensibly a protected area, hunters roam the woodlands looking for game. Some good news for the environment has been the recent announcement of the gradual reintroduction of the *grifone* (griffon), a species once threatened by poisonous fox-baits.

As a rule, you'll need your own transport to get around the park. The SS116 connects Capo d'Orlando with Randazzo, while the SS117 connects Santo Stefano di Camastra with Nicosia.

SANT'ÀGATA DI MILITELLO
postcode 98076 • pop 12,800

This relatively new town (founded in the 18th century), 30km east of Santo Stefano di Camastra, is a popular little resort along this stretch of coast, and makes a handy base from which to tour the coastline and the Parco Regionale dei Nebrodi. In summer it's usually crammed with Italian holidaymakers eager to make the most of the nice long stretch of beach. The only sight really worth mentioning is the **Chiesa del Carmelo** in the centre of town, which has a handsome 18th-century gable. If you're heading into the Nebrodi nature reserve, you may want to visit the **Museo dei Nebrodi** *(☎ 0941 72 23 08, Via Cosenz 70; free; open 9am-noon Mon-Fri)*, which has some information on the area, including maps.

Parimar (☎ 0941 70 18 88, Via Medici 1) Singles/doubles with bathroom €25.80/43.90. The Parimar is a nice enough two-star hotel and not so small that it's always booked out.

Za'Pippina (Via Cosenz 197) Meals about €18. Closed Tues in winter. If you fancy some fresh local seafood at reasonable prices, this long-running place is worth popping into.

You can get here by frequent trains from Milazzo (€3.60, about 50 minutes).

SAN MARCO D'ALUNZIO
postcode 98076 • pop 2300
elevation 540m

On the road to Capo d'Orlando from Sant'Àgata di Militello, the first turn-off inland (signposted) weaves its way uphill for 5km to this remarkable little town founded by the Greeks in the 5th century BC and later occupied by the Romans, who named it Aluntium.

San Marco d'Alunzio is definitely worth making the effort to visit, at least for a couple of hours. At its entrance is the spectacularly situated **Tempio di Ercole** (Temple of

Hercules), with terrific views over the sea. A now roofless Norman church was subsequently built on the temple's red marble base. Virtually all of San Marco's older buildings were constructed using this locally quarried marble, which is named after the town – Aluntium.

From the temple, Via Aluntina leads up to the town proper and a number of interesting churches, the best of which is the **Chiesa di Santa Maria delle Grazie**, where you can find a beautiful statue of the *Madonna con Bambino e San Giovanni* (Madonna and Child with St John), which has been attributed to Domenico Gagini. At the top of the hill are the scant remains of the **castle** built by Robert Guiscard in 1061, the first castle built by the Normans in Sicily.

Buses from Sant'Àgata di Militello make the 5km run to San Marco d'Alunzio (€0.75, 10 minutes) about 10 times a day Monday to Saturday (fewer on Sunday). Departures are from outside the train station.

CAPO D'ORLANDO
postcode 98071 • pop 12,000

The busiest resort town on the coast after Cefalù, Capo d'Orlando was founded – at least according to the legend – when one of Charlemagne's generals, a chap called Orlando, stood on the headland and declared it a fine place to build a castle. The ruins of the castle, including traces of the 14th-century masonry and ribbing, are still visible. In 1299 Frederick II of Aragon was defeated here by the rebellious baron Roger of Lauria, backed up by the joint forces of Catalonia and Anjou. Recent rebels were the town's shopkeepers and traders, who made a name for themselves in the 1990s with their firm stance against the Mafia's demands for the infamous *pizzo* (protection money) – sadly an all-too-rare bit of resistance against a racket that seems ingrained in Sicilian society.

Visitors come here for the beaches, both sandy and rocky, that are on either side of town. The best swimming is to the east. It's also the best option for accommodation seekers not wishing to make the trip to Cefalù or Milazzo. The tourist office (☎ 0941 91 27 84) is on Via Piave. It opens 9am to 1pm and 4pm to 7pm Monday to Friday, 9am to 1pm on Saturday.

Note that on Ferragosto (15 August), there is a procession of boats along the coast to celebrate the Assumption of the Virgin Mary.

Places to Stay & Eat
Nuovo Hotel Faro (☎ *0941 90 24 66, fax 0941 91 14 61, Via Libertà 7*) Singles/doubles with bathroom €31/62. This is the cheapest hotel in Capo d'Orlando, with comfortable rooms and balconies overlooking the sea.

La Meridiana (☎/fax *0941 95 77 13, Via Trassari 2*) Doubles with bathroom €72.30. La Meridiana is an elegant hotel with gracious and friendly management. Doubles have air-con, TV and phone.

La Tartaruga (☎ *0941 95 05 12, fax 0941 95 50 56, Lido San Gregorio*) Singles/doubles with bathroom €62/93. La Tartaruga, with well-appointed rooms, is to the east of town overlooking a wide, sandy beach. Prices drop after August and the hotel's restaurant is a great (though moderately expensive) place to eat.

There's no shortage of places to get a bite to eat.

Da Enzo (☎ *0941 90 17 00, Via Lo Sardo*) Meals about €13. This is a good pizzeria with a fine selection of pasta dishes.

Il Gabbiano (*Via Trazzera Marina*) Meals about €21. Right by the water, Il Gabbiano is a pleasant place to dine.

Á Uletta (☎ *0941 91 17 00, Piazza Duca degli Abruzzi 21*) Meals about €18. Closed Mon. With an ample buffet and a range of fish and meat dishes, you'll dine well here, even on a tight budget.

Getting There & Away
The best way to get here is by train from Palermo (€6.45, two hours) or from Milazzo (€3.10, one hour 10 minutes).

PATTI
postcode 98066 • pop 13,000
elevation 157m

This fairly attractive but not exactly thrilling town, 26km east of Capo d'Orlando, first developed when it was flooded with refugees from nearby Tyndaris after the latter's destruction by landslide in the 1st century AD.

In 1094, a Benedictine abbey (now replaced by the town's cathedral) was founded here by Roger II. Patti was created a bishopric in 1131 but was destroyed by Frederick II of Aragon after it sided with the French Anjou family during the revolt of the Sicilian Vespers in the 13th century. In 1554 it was plundered by the pirate Khaired-din Barbarossa, or Redbeard. At the top of the hill is the town's 18th-century **cathedral**, built on the site of the Norman church where Roger II buried his mother Adelasia (Adelaide), who died here in 1118. Her remains were later transferred to a fine Renaissance sarcophagus, which you can see in the right transept.

There is an AAPT tourist office (☎ 0941 24 11 36, **e** aastpatti@icatamail.com) at Piazza Marconi 11 in the centre of town, which opens 9am to 1pm daily.

Most visitors come here to visit the remains of the **Roman villa** (☎ 0941 36 15 93; admission €2.05; site open 9am-7pm daily Apr-Sept, 9am-5pm daily Oct & Mar, 9am-4pm daily Nov-Feb) on the eastern outskirts of town beneath the motorway viaduct. Built in the 4th century AD, it was destroyed by an earthquake 100 years later and was not uncovered until 1976. Sadly, the site is badly positioned, littered with cigarette butts and poorly maintained (please don't take photographs of these fragile remains), although an ugly plastic roof has been erected to protect the polychrome mosaics from the scorching sun and the fumes emanating from the motorway overhead. The mosaics are very faded and explanations of the site are pretty much non-existent. A small room near the ticket office houses some artefacts (labelled in Italian) found during renovations. You can buy a ticket (€3.10) here that also gives you entry to the site at Tyndaris.

To get to Piazza Marconi from Patti's train station, you can take a bus (€0.75) or walk for about 20 minutes (uphill, but signposted).

TYNDARIS
elevation 230m
About 6km east of Patti, at Capo Tindari, are the ruins of ancient Tyndaris (☎ 0941 36 90 23; admission €2.05; site open 9am-1hr before sunset daily), founded on a spectacular rocky promontory by Dionysius the Elder in 396 BC after a victory over the Carthaginians. It remained a close ally of Syracuse until 256 BC when it was taken by the Romans. The town was partially destroyed by a landslide in the 1st century AD, further damaged by an earthquake in AD 365 and finished off by the Arabs in the 10th century. Excavations of the site began in the 19th century but did not proceed in any cohesive manner until 1949.

The first thing you see when you get off the bus from Patti is the **Santuario della Madonna** (Sanctuary of the Madonna). Built in the 1960s, this enormous church houses the sacred relic that is the Madonna Nera (Black Madonna), thought to have been made in Asia Minor and to have come to Sicily by sea. Religious pilgrims flock here in droves to pray at her feet due to the miracles they believe she has performed. Interestingly, the inscription underneath the

THE TYRRHENIAN COAST

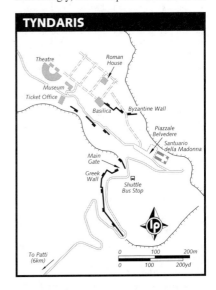

icon reads '*Nigra sum, sed hermosa*', which means 'I am black, but I am beautiful'.

From the sanctuary, a path leads to the site entrance. The majority of the ruins here are of Roman origin, including the **basilica** to the right of the entrance. In the 1950s the building was the subject of a controversial 'renovation' using modern materials (specifically concrete), which opponents protested were unrepresentative of its original appearance. Just beyond the basilica is a **Roman house** in remarkably good condition. The floor has some fine mosaics. At the far end of the town's main street is the **theatre**, originally a Greek structure but substantially modified by the Romans, who used it as a gladiators' arena. Part of the theatre was dismantled to build the city's **walls**, which are still in evidence around the perimeter.

To the left of the main entrance is a small **museum** containing finds from the site, including an impressive bust of the emperor Augustus. There's a tourist office (☎ 0941 36 91 84) on site at Via Teatro Greco 15.

Special Events
From mid-to late July to early September the theatre hosts a festival of Greek drama, ballet, cabaret, opera and music. For information ask at the ticket office at the entrance to the site, at the AAPT tourist office in Patti (see Patti earlier) or visit the Web site at W www.ilbotteghino.it/tindari. You can also call ☎ 090 34 38 18 for details about prices. However, you'll need a car to see the performances as buses only run in the morning.

Getting There & Away
There are five buses daily between 6.50am and 11.40am from Piazza Marconi in Patti to Tyndaris (€1.55). Buses run from a car park about 1km from the site itself; you can walk the rest of the way or get one of the shuttle buses which make the run every 10 minutes or so (€0.75).

VILLA ROMANA DI SAN BIÀGIO & CASTOREALE
A short drive east along the SS113 from Tyndaris, the **Villa Romana di San Biàgio** (*Roman Villa;* ☎ *090 974 04 88, Via*

Nazionale; admission €2.05; open 9am-1hr before sunset daily) is the site of the remains of a 1st century AD Roman villa, with black-and-white mosaics, one of which features an interesting fishing scene.

Castoreale (population 3126), 10km south of Milazzo, is a well-preserved medieval town with many churches. It was a favourite hunting spot of Frederick II of Aragon. His tower, **Torre di Federico II**, was built in 1324. Mostly in ruins now, it operates as a hostel for half the year (see below). Other sights include the **Chiesa Matrice**, with a painting of Santa Caterina d'Alessandria (St Catherine of Alexandria; 1534) by Antonello Gagini.

Ostello della Gioventù delle Aquile (☎ *090 974 63 98, fax 090 974 64 46, Via Federico II*) Dorm bed €7.75. Open 1 Apr-31 Oct. This small 24-bed hostel is situated in the tower, making it one of the more interesting cheap places to stay in Sicily.

You can get here by bus from Barcellona (about 7 buses a day until 6pm Monday to Saturday) or by car (take the SS113 and then turn off at Barcellona).

MILAZZO
postcode 98057 • pop 32,000
Hardly Sicily's prettiest town by day, Milazzo is shrouded in layers of industrial development that can make even the most determined visitor run for the nearest ferry or hydrofoil to the Aeolian Islands. Indeed, the prime reason for setting foot in this town is to get off the main island, as this is the main port for travel to the archipelago. Unless you arrive late in the evening or in the dead of winter, you should be sea-bound within the hour, as departures are very frequent. Still, you could do a lot worse than wander about the surprisingly pleasant streets of the old city, fronted by an elegant promenade lined with palm trees that runs along the water. At night, the lights of the industrial development on the outskirts of Milazzo are quite attractive, and the lively passeggiata is a highlight.

Orientation & Information
Everything of interest here is within walking distance of the ferry and hydrofoil port.

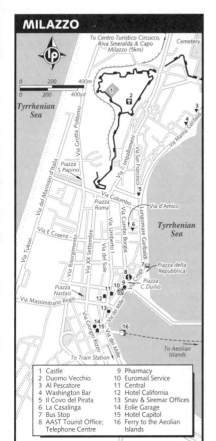

MILAZZO

1 Castle	9 Pharmacy
2 Duomo Vecchio	10 Euromail Service
3 Al Pescatore	11 Central
4 Washington Bar	12 Hotel California
5 Il Covo del Pirata	13 Snav & Siremar Offices
6 La Casalinga	14 Eolie Garage
7 Bus Stop	15 Hotel Capitol
8 AAST Tourist Office;	16 Ferry to the Aeolian
Telephone Centre	Islands

The train station is on Piazza Marconi, about 3km south of the port along the seafront. Orange AST buses run between the station and the quayside, departing every 20 minutes or so at busy times or every 30 to 40 minutes otherwise (between 5.30am and 8.40pm). Tickets (€0.75, valid for one hour 30 minutes) can be bought inside the train station or at the shop opposite the quayside bus stop with the AST sign.

The AAST tourist office (☎ 090 922 28 65), Piazza C Duilio 10, is behind Via Crispi. It opens 8am to 2pm and 4pm to 7pm Monday to Friday and 8am to 2pm on

Saturday (plus 8am to 2pm on Sunday from June to September).

There are public telephones at Associazione Pro Milazzo on Piazza Duilio, a couple of doors away from the AAST. It opens 8am to 1pm and 3pm to 8pm Monday to Saturday and 9am to 1pm on Sunday. All of the ticket agencies for travel to the islands are virtually next door to each other on Via dei Mille, near the ferry terminal.

The first-aid station can be called on ☎ 090 928 1158, the police on ☎ 090 928 1720 and the *carabinieri* (military police) on ☎ 090 928 6170. There's a 24-hour pharmacy near the port, at the corner of Via Luigi Rizzo and Via Cassisi.

At Euromail Service, Via dei Mille 7, you can check your email (€5.15 per hour) or send faxes. Photocopying is also available.

Things to See & Do
Milazzo's **castle** (☎ 090 922 12 91; free; open 10am-7pm daily June-Aug, 10am-5pm daily Mar-May & Sept, 10am-3.30pm daily Oct-Feb; guided tours at 10am, 11am & noon year-round, plus at 5pm, 6pm & 7pm June-Aug, at 3pm, 4pm & 5pm Mar-May & Sept, at 9am, 2.30pm & 3.30pm Oct-Feb) was originally constructed by Frederick II in 1239 but was enlarged by Charles V of Aragon in the 15th century. The Norman keep is still intact at the centre of the mostly Spanish fortifications. This interesting site is of massive proportions and also contains the city's *duomo vecchio* (old cathedral; closed).

There's good **swimming** to be had at Capo Milazzo, 6km north of the city centre, but the most easily accessible is a great, long stretch of pebbled beach that can be reached at the end of Via Colombo. Follow the signs to Baia del Tonno, then pass the ugly *stadio* (stadium).

Places to Stay
There are a couple of camp sites at Capo Milazzo, which is accessible by bus from the quayside bus stop at Piazza della Repubblica. Buses depart approximately every one hour 30 minutes between 5.40am and 8.10pm. Ask the bus driver to let you off at whichever camp site you want to stay at.

THE TYRRHENIAN COAST

THE TYRRHENIAN COAST

Centro Turistico Cirucco (☎ *090 928 47 46*) €7.75/3.60 per person/site, €25.80 per person per night in 2-bed bungalow. Open Apr-Oct. This is a huge camp site with good facilities.

Riva Smeralda (☎ *090 928 29 80*) €7.75/3.60 per person/site, €33.60 per person per night in 2-bed bungalow. Riva Smeralda is a smaller camp site than Centro Turistico Cirucco. While it's perfectly decent, the management can be a tad grumpy.

There are several hotels near the port if you get stuck for the night. Many of them involve sharing a bathroom.

Central (☎ *090 928 10 43, Via del Sole 8*) Singles/doubles without bathroom €25.80/46.50. The Central has basic rooms, best described as OK. It doesn't accept credit cards, but the staff are kind and considerate.

Hotel California (☎ *090 922 13 89, Via del Sole 9*) Singles/doubles without bathroom €20.65/41.30. Clean but dark, this place is nothing like the Eagles' song, although there is a midnight curfew.

Hotel Capitol (☎ *090 928 32 89, Via Giorgio Rizzo 91*) Singles/doubles €25.80/41.30, with bathroom €31/51.65. The Capitol is close to the hydrofoil dock and, though the rooms are quite plain, the hotel is kept scrupulously clean throughout. Credit cards are not accepted.

Places to Eat

For something to eat, you don't need to go far from Lungomare Garibaldi along the seafront.

La Casalinga (*Via d'Amico*) Meals about €16. La Casalinga is good for seafood dishes and has a nicely decorated dining area.

Al Pescatore (☎ *090 928 65 95, Via Marina Garibaldi 176*) Meals about €21. The seafood here is definitely recommended, as is the efficient service (the staff are used to dealing with hordes about to catch boats to the Aeolian Islands). The *involtini di pesce spada* (swordfish roulade, stuffed with breadcrumbs; €8.25) is delicious.

Il Covo del Pirata (☎ *090 928 44 37, Via San Francesco 1*) Meals about €34, pizza about €10. Closed Wed. One of Milazzo's best restaurants, the ground floor section is a very popular pizzeria at night and the service is as smooth as silk. Reservations are advised.

Washington Bar (☎ *090 922 38 13, Via Marina Garibaldi 94*) This very pleasant bar is a great spot to unwind with a drink while you watch the passeggiata go by. The excellent nibbles that accompany drinks orders only add to the charm. You can also get great *gelato* (ice cream) here.

Getting There & Away

Milazzo is easy to reach by bus or train from Palermo and Messina. Giuntabus (☎ *090 67 37 82*) runs an hourly service to/from Messina (€3.10, 50 minutes). All intercity buses run from Piazza della Repubblica along the quayside. Trains are more frequent, with two departures and arrivals hourly for both Palermo (€8.40, 2½ to three hours) and Messina (€2.05, 45 minutes). See The Aeolian Islands chapter for details of travel to and from the islands.

If you fancy leaving the car here while you island-hop, you can park long term at the Eolie Garage, next to Hotel Capitol (see Places to Stay earlier).

The Aeolian Islands

The seven islands of this volcanic archipelago (Isole Eolie in Italian) north of Milazzo make up one of the most popular tourist resorts in Sicily. In summer, all but the outlying western islands are awash with waves of day-trippers and holiday-makers, tempted by the near-perfect high-season weather. The islands are all different, ranging from the developed tourist resort of Lìpari and the understated jet-set haunt of Panarea, to rugged Vulcano, the spectacular scenery of Stromboli with its fiercely active volcano, the fertile vineyards of Salina, and the solitude of outlying Alicudi and Filicudi. Yet the Aeolian Islands all share one thing in common, at least in summer: the blazing sun warms a limpid, blue sea that laps the rocky shores and sandy beaches.

That same sea, however, can turn ferocious, especially in winter when high waves crash with awesome power against the coast. It is no coincidence that the ancient Greeks believed the islands to be the home of Aeolus (who gave the archipelago its name), the god of the wind (see the boxed text 'The Vulcan Winds' later in this chapter). Although the modern traveller may marvel at the islands' beauty, living here has almost always been a constant struggle. Between the 1930s and 1950s, many inhabitants emigrated to Australia (often called the eighth Aeolian Island by locals), leaving the outer islands virtually abandoned and only a small contingent on the others. The advent of tourism has helped avert disaster for five of the islands, but Alicudi and Filicudi are still suffering from the loss of so many human resources.

As with any popular place, the surge of tourism has its negative side. In July and August Lìpari can be mayhem, with even a nice spot on the beach very difficult to find. During this period you will need to book accommodation well in advance. The best time to come is in May and early June or late September and October, when the weather is still fine and the hordes are either yet to arrive or have been and gone. Ferries and hydrofoils

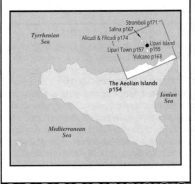

(aliscafi) operate year-round, but winter services are much reduced and sometimes cancelled due to heavy seas.

Salina was the setting for the Oscar-winning *Il Postino* (1995), directed by Michael Radford and starring Massimo Troisi and Philippe Noiret. Also filmed on the islands were the films *Stròmboli* (see Around the Island in the Stromboli section

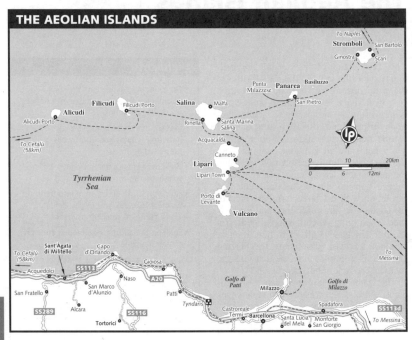

THE AEOLIAN ISLANDS

To Naples
Stromboli   San Bartolo
Ginostra   Scari

Punta   Panarea   Basiluzzo
Milazzese
San Pietro

Filicudi   Filicudi Porto   Salina   Malfa
Alicudi
Alicudi Porto   Rinella   Santa Marina
Salina
To Cefalù   Acquacalda
(58km)
Canneto
Lìpari
Tyrrhenian   Lìpari Town
Sea
Porto di
Levante
Vulcano

0   10   20km
0   6   12mi

Sant'Agata
di Militello   Capo
To Cefalù   d'Orlando   To
(58km)   Gioiosa   Messina
Acquedolci   SS113
Naso   A20   Golfo di   Golfo di
San Marco   Patti   Milazzo
San Fratello   d'Alunzio   Patti   Milazzo   Spadafora
Tyndaris   Castroreale   SS113d
SS289   Alcara   SS116   Termi   Barcellona   Santa Lucia   Monforte   To Messina
Tortorici   del Mela   San Giorgio

for details) and Nanni Moretti's *Caro Diario* (Dear Diary).

Getting There & Away
Hydrofoil Both Siremar and Snav (see Getting There & Away in the Lìpari section for contact details) run hydrofoils from Milazzo to Lìpari (€11.10, one hour five minutes) and on to the other islands. From 1 June to 30 September hydrofoils depart almost hourly (from around 7am to 7pm) to Lìpari, and also stop at Vulcano (€10.33, 45 minutes) and either Santa Marina Salina (€12.65, 1½ to two hours) or Rinella (€12.65, 1½ to two hours) on Salina. Services to the other islands are less frequent unless you change in Lìpari: there are a combined nine departures daily for Panarea (€13.15, two hours) and Stromboli (€16, 2½ hours). There are only two departures (one with each company) for Alicudi (€21.17, three hours) and Filicudi (€17.30, two hours 20 minutes).

From October to May the frequency of service is substantially reduced: there are only two departures daily to Vulcano, Lìpari and Salina and one daily to Panarea, Stromboli, Filicudi and Alicudi.

Ferry Siremar runs five ferries from Milazzo to Lìpari for about half the price of the hydrofoil (€6.45; motor vehicles from €17 to €40, depending on size), but they are slower and less regular. NGI Traghetti (☎ 090 928 40 91), at Via dei Mille 26, just near the Snav and Siremar offices in Milazzo, also runs a thrice-daily car ferry service for the same rates.

Getting Around
Regular hydrofoil and ferry services operate between the islands, but they can be disrupted, particularly to the outer islands, by heavy seas. Lìpari's two ports are separated by the citadel – hydrofoils arrive at and depart from Marina Corta, while Marina Lunga

(also known as Porto Sottomonastero) services ferries. Siremar and Snav have ticket offices in the same building at Marina Corta. Siremar also has a ticket office at Marina Lunga. Full timetable information is available at all offices. On the other islands, ticket offices are at or close to the docks.

Single fares and approximate sailing times from Lìpari are:

Alicudi
  €16, two hours (hydrofoil)
  €9, 3¾ hours (ferry)
Filicudi
  €11.10, 1½ hours (hydrofoil)
  €6.45, 2¾ hours (ferry)
Panarea
  €6.70, 50 minutes (hydrofoil)
  €3.90, two hours (ferry)
Salina
  €5.15, 35 minutes (Santa Marina, hydrofoil)
  €5.95, 45 minutes (Rinella, hydrofoil)
  €3.10, 45 minutes (Santa Marina, ferry)
  €3.60, 1½ hours (Rinella, ferry)
Stromboli
  €13.15, one hour (hydrofoil)
  €7.75, 3¾ hours (ferry)
Vulcano
  €2.30, 10 minutes (hydrofoil)
  €1.30, 25 minutes (ferry)

LÌPARI
postcode 98050 ● pop 11,000
● elevation 602m

The largest of all the islands – it measures 37.6 sq km and is 9.5km long – Lipari is also the most popular and developed in the archipelago. The main town, of the same name (called Lipari Town here for simplicity) is typically Mediterranean, with pastel-coloured houses huddled around its two harbours. The island is also home to four other towns – Acquacalda, Canneto, Pianoconte and Quattropani. Most activity begins and ends in Lipari Town, although Canneto (3km north) does have some restaurants and hotels. It is now a centre for mining pumice stone, a volcanic product, and is the best-equipped base for exploring the archipelago.

History
Lipari Island has been inhabited since the 4th millennium BC, when it was settled by

people of the Stentinello culture, named after the village near Syracuse where the first traces of this civilisation were found. The island bore the poetic name Meligunis, meaning 'gentle slopes', and its inhabitants were expert miners and traders of obsidian (see the boxed text 'Rough Trade'). In 580 BC it was settled by Greeks from Rhodes, who renamed it after the mythical first king of the island, Liparo. During the Punic Wars, Lìpari sided with Carthage and in 260 BC the Carthaginians defeated the Romans in a sea battle off the coast. Their control over the islands as a whole, however, only lasted another eight years until they were convincingly defeated by the Romans, who incorporated the entire archipelago into their Sicilian province, where it has remained ever since. They built the nucleus of their city on the ruins of the Greek acropolis, located between the two harbours where the remains of the Norman cathedral now stand.

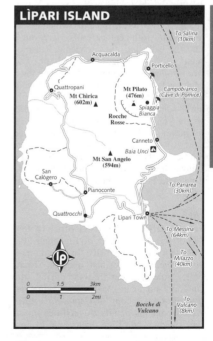

LÌPARI ISLAND

To Salina (10km)
Acquacalda
Porticello
Quattropani
Mt Pilato (476m)
Campobianco (Cave di Pomice)
Mt Chirica (602m)
Spiaggia Bianca
Rocche Rosse
Canneto
Baia Unci
Mt San Angelo (594m)
San Calògero
To Panarea (30km)
Pianoconte
Quattrocchi
Lipari Town
To Messina (64km)
To Milazzo (40km)
0   1.5   3km
0   1   2mi
Bocche di Vulcano
To Vulcano (8km)

THE AEOLIAN ISLANDS

Under the Normans in the 12th and 13th centuries, Lìpari Island entered a period of prosperity thanks to extensive mining of sulphur and alum and excavation of pumice. In 1544, however, the town was sacked. As many as 10,000 of its inhabitants were killed or sold into slavery by the pirate Khair-ed-din Barbarossa, or Redbeard, who despite the Arabic name was actually an Italian mercenary called Ariadeno. The Aragon king Charles V succeeded in repopulating the island with Spaniards and Calabrians soon after Barbarossa's death in 1546 and rebuilt the town, adding the solid walls visible today.

By virtue of a Fascist decree in 1926 Lìpari was declared an open prison for political enemies of the regime; not long after the arrival of the first prisoners – three communist activists – the locals helped them escape by boat to Tunisia.

Orientation

Tourists arrive at one of two ports in Lìpari Town: Marina Lunga and Marina Corta. They are situated either side of the cliff-top citadel (known as the *castello*), which is surrounded by 16th-century walls. Here you'll find the cathedral, the archaeological museum (Museo Archeologico Eoliano) and two run-down Baroque churches. The town centre extends between the ports. The main street, Via Vittorio Emanuele, runs roughly north–south to the west of the castle and is where you'll find banks, bars, offices and restaurants. Hydrofoils dock at Marina Corta, from where you should walk to the left across the square to Via Garibaldi and follow the 'centro' signs for Via Vittorio Emanuele. Ferries come and go from Marina Lunga.

Information

Tourist Offices The AAST office (☎ 090 988 00 95) is at Via Vittorio Emanuele 202. It is the main tourist office for the archipelago, although offices also open on Stromboli, Vulcano and Salina during the summer, and it can assist with accommodation. Pick up a copy of *Ospitalità in Blu*, which contains details of facilities on all the islands. The office opens 8am to 2pm

---

Rough Trade

As far back as 4000 BC, the island's first settlers – from the Stentinello culture – made up for the lack of metal by expertly working obsidian, a hard, glass-like rock found all over the island. They managed to develop a roaring trade throughout the known world. The crafted stone would be loaded into fast, light boats and shipped to markets in faraway places. Finds at the archaeological site of Pergamum, in present-day Turkey, have revealed fragments of raw and carved Liparese obsidian that was used in the treatment of the ill.

Nowadays, you can still buy chunks of obsidian on Lìpari, although it's more likely to be used for paperweights and door-stoppers. Lìpari's other 'rough trade' is pumice, which is still exported today. You can see the site of production at the Cave di Pomice, on the island's northeastern side.

---

and 4.30pm to 7.30pm Monday to Friday and 8am to 2pm Saturday.

Money There are several banks in Lìpari Town, including the Banca di Roma, directly opposite the AAST and with an ATM on Via Vittorio Emanuele. Outside banking hours, exchange facilities can be found at the post office and several travel agencies.

Note that banking facilities on the other islands can be limited.

Post & Communications The post office (☎ 090 981 13 79) is at Via Vittorio Emanuele 207 and opens 8.30am to 6.30pm Monday to Friday and 8.30am to 1pm on Saturday. Public telephones can be found throughout Lìpari Town.

For Internet access, Netnet (☎ 090 981 24 62), at Via Marte 1, charges €3.60 for 30 minutes and €5.15 for one hour.

Bookshops La Stampa, at Via Vittorio Emanuele 170, is a bookshop with a selection of foreign language newspapers, usually English, German and French, and some novels.

LÌPARI TOWN

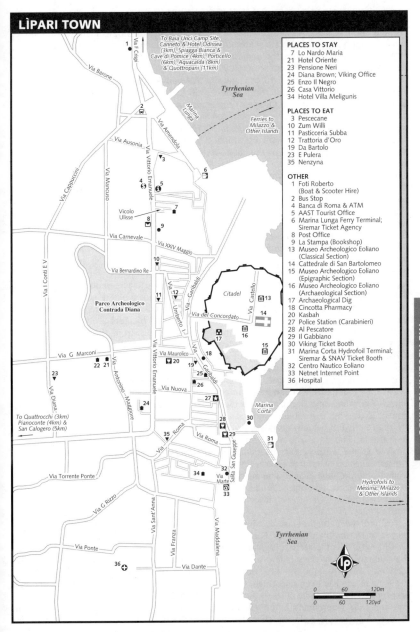

PLACES TO STAY
7 Lo Nardo Maria
21 Hotel Oriente
23 Pensione Neri
24 Diana Brown; Viking Office
25 Enzo Il Negro
26 Casa Vittorio
34 Hotel Villa Meligunis

PLACES TO EAT
3 Pescecane
10 Zum Willi
11 Pasticceria Subba
12 Trattoria d'Oro
19 Da Bartolo
23 E Pulera
35 Nenzyna

OTHER
1 Foti Roberto
   (Boat & Scooter Hire)
2 Bus Stop
4 Banca di Roma & ATM
5 AAST Tourist Office
6 Marina Lunga Ferry Terminal;
   Siremar Ticket Agency
8 Post Office
9 La Stampa (Bookshop)
13 Museo Archeologico Eoliano
   (Classical Section)
14 Cattedrale di San Bartolomeo
15 Museo Archeologico Eoliano
   (Epigraphic Section)
16 Museo Archeologico Eoliano
   (Archaeological Section)
17 Archaeological Dig
18 Cincotta Pharmacy
20 Kasbah
27 Police Station (Carabinieri)
28 Al Pescatore
29 Il Gabbiano
30 Viking Ticket Booth
31 Marina Corta Hydrofoil Terminal;
   Siremar & SNAV Ticket Booth
32 Centro Nautico Eoliano
33 Netnet Internet Point
36 Hospital

THE AEOLIAN ISLANDS

Medical Services & Emergency The hospital (☎ 090 9 88 51) and *pronto soccorso* (casualty; ☎ 090 988 52 67) are both on Via Sant'Anna. There are three pharmacies in town. Cincotta Pharmacy (☎ 090 981 14 72) is at Via Garibaldi 60 and opens 9am to 12.30pm and 3.30pm to 8pm Monday to Saturday from May to October, 9am to 12.30pm and 3.30pm to 7pm Monday to Saturday from November to April. The '*farmacie di turno*', a timetable showing which pharmacy is on night-duty, is on the noticeboard outside.

If you need a doctor in an emergency, call ☎ 090 988 52 26. The *carabinieri* (military police; ☎ 090 981 13 33) are on Via Garibaldi.

Citadel (Upper Town)

After Barbarossa's murderous rampage through the town in 1544, the Spaniards rebuilt and fortified Lipari in the area at the top of the small cliff between the two harbours. Although somewhat like closing the barn door after the horse has been captured, tortured and sold into slavery, the citadel's fortifications look impregnable enough and are still relatively intact. Inside the walls are substantial reminders of Lipari's troubled past. You enter the area via a set of steps (Via del Concordato) that leads up to the 17th-century **Cattedrale di San Bartolomeo** (check with the tourist office for opening times). It was built to replace the original Norman cathedral, which was destroyed by Barbarossa. The only original element to survive is the 12th-century Benedictine cloister. The reconstruction (1654) features a handsome Baroque facade. The interior is hung with chandeliers and features, in the northern transept, a silver statue of St Bartholomew (1728).

Around the cathedral are a couple of other ruined Baroque churches, but the real area of interest is the **archaeological dig** in the southern half of the citadel. A rich collection of finds from the Neolithic period to the Roman era has been unearthed, giving archaeologists invaluable clues to the civilisations that flourished in the Mediterranean. You won't make much sense of what's here, however, without visiting the town's archaeological museum, Museo Archeologico Eoliano, found within a number of buildings in the citadel.

Museo Archeologico Eoliano If you're at all interested in Mediterranean archaeology and ancient history, this museum (☎ 090 988 01 74; admission €4.15; open 9am-1.30pm daily; Archaeological & Epigraphic Sections open 9am-1.30pm daily, Classical Section open 9am-1.30pm & 3pm-7pm daily) is an absolute must, as it contains a collection of finds that is among the most complete in Europe. The **Archaeological Section** (Sezione Archeologica) of the museum is divided into two buildings. Just south of the cathedral, the former Palazzo Vescovile (Bishop's Palace) is devoted to artefacts found on Lipari, beginning with the Neolithic and Bronze Ages upstairs and continuing in chronological order to the Roman era downstairs. Amid the plethora of artefacts – pottery, flints and a variety of cutting tools – is some finely sculpted obsidian, telling evidence of the relative sophistication of prehistoric civilisation. Prehistoric finds from the other islands are housed in the small pavilion directly in front of the palace.

On the other side of the cathedral is the **Classical Section** (Sezione Classica), which houses finds from the island's 11th-century-BC necropolis. These are beautifully displayed, and include a sizable collection of burial urns as well as models of a Bronze-Age burial ground and Lipari's necropolis. Upstairs is an impressive array of decorated vases and the museum's most treasured items: the most complete collection of Greek theatrical masks in the world. There are also a number of statuettes of dancers and actors – the one of *Andromeda con Bambino* (Andromeda with Child) is particularly beautiful – and some elegant jewellery. The next room contains polychromatic vases decorated by an artist simply known as 'Il Pittore Liparoto' (the Lipari Painter; 300–270 BC).

The last part of the museum is the **Epigraphic Section** (Sezione Epigrafica), housed in a smaller building south of the Archaeological Section. Here you will find

JANE SMITH

Masking a turbulent past: Lipari has been home to pirates and prisoners.

a little garden of engraved stones and a room of Greek and Roman tombs.

Around Lìpari Town

The only worthwhile sight outside the citadel is the **Parco Archeologico Contrada Diana**, west of Via Vittorio Emanuele, which has revealed part of the original Greek walls (5th and 4th centuries BC) and Roman houses. At the southwestern end of the park is the necropolis, where the tombstones are still visible in the overgrown grass. The park, alas, is rarely open. All of the important finds, however, are in the archaeological part of the museum (see previous section).

Once you've satisfied your cravings for artefacts, there isn't much left to do except amble around the narrow streets of the town, sit at a port-side cafe or stretch out on the beach. There is an assortment of boutiques, dive shops, grocery shops and restaurants on Via Vittorio Emanuele.

Around Lìpari Island

Although Lìpari Town is so self-contained that you could easily spend your entire holiday there, the rest of the island is worth checking out, especially if you want to find the best swimming spots. The island is small enough that a grand tour of its perimeter should take no more than 30 minutes by car.

Canneto Only 3km north of Lìpari Town at the end of a short tunnel, Canneto is a relatively quiet village that serves as an accommodation overspill when the main town is booked out. There are a couple of bars, shops, hotels and supermarkets on the beachfront – a long, pebbled stretch that's OK for swimming and where you can hire deckchairs and umbrellas.

Just beyond the town, and a popular stop on the bus route, is **Spiaggia Bianca** (White Beach), the most popular beach on the island. Its name derives from the layers of pumice dust that once covered it. These have been slowly washed away by the rough winter seas, leaving it a darker shade of grey.

Cave di Pomice Between Spiaggia Bianca and Porticello lie these pumice quarries at Campobianco, where the pumice that is a mainstay of Liparese industry is extracted for uses from toothpaste to construction. This unlikely place is one of the better spots to splash into the sea, via one of the pumice chutes that allow you to slide from the hillside above directly into the azure water – a particularly brilliant version of blue due to the deposit of pumice dust. Such a scene features in the Taviani brothers' classic film *Kaos*, based on short stories by Luigi Pirandello. It's easiest to get to the chutes by boat. Most tours will stop here to allow you some time to slide.

Above Campobianco looms the ancient crater of **Mt Pilato** (476m), the source of all of the pumice found in the area. The last eruption occurred in AD 700. All around the crater are fields of solidified obsidian known as the **Rocche Rosse** (Red Rocks) due to the colour of the stone. You can reach the crater via a path from the northern end of Campobianco (about 1.2km).

The bus winds its way northwards to the little village of **Porticello**, which has a small stony **beach**, and then on to Acquacalda on the northern side of the island. There's nothing much to do here but savour the views of Salina, Alicudi and Filicudi from the rugged cliffs.

Northwest to Quattropani West of Lìpari Town (and accessible by bus from the Marina Lunga), through some lush vegetation, the road climbs for about 3km to the belvedere known as **Quattrocchi** (Four Eyes), although you'll only need two to appreciate the stunning views of Vulcano to the south. Less than 1km north is the small village of **Pianoconte**; a side road before the village proper veers off to the Roman baths of **San Calògero**, famous in antiquity for the thermal spring that flowed at a constant temperature of 60°C. The last stop on the bus route is at **Quattropani**, from where you can walk the 5km north to **Aquacalda** and catch a bus returning to Lìpari.

Activities
Scuba diving is popular on Lìpari. For information on courses, contact the **Centro Nautico Eoliano** (☎ 090 981 26 91, Salita San Giuseppe 8) or the AAST office.

Viking (☎ 090 981 25 84, Vico Himera 3; ticket booth at Marina Corta) conducts very good **boat tours** of all the islands, such as: Stromboli by night (€23.25, daily); Panarea (€15.50, daily); Vulcano (€12.90, daily); Alicudi and Filicudi (€25.80, Monday and Thursday); Lìpari and Salina (€18.10, Thursday, Friday and Sunday); and Panarea and Stromboli (the second island by night; €31, daily). You're often free to wander around the islands at your own pace, and the access to grottoes and coves, with time for swimming and snorkelling, is a boon for those not wishing to hire a boat of their own.

Places to Stay
Lìpari provides plenty of options for a comfortable stay. On arrival, you'll be approached by touts offering accommodation in a private house, where you have your own room (usually a double) with private bathroom and modest cooking facilities. Don't ignore offers: they are often ideal considering that there are no hotels in the budget category. In the high season you might have to commit to a multiday stay, or sometimes even a week.

Be warned that prices usually double during July and August and that accommodation can be very difficult to find, so book in advance. High-season prices are given here unless stated otherwise. If all else fails, tourist office staff will billet new arrivals in private homes. Prices tend to drop considerably in the low season.

For a list of rental apartments, contact the tourist office.

Camping *Baia Unci* (☎ 090 981 19 09, fax 090 981 17 15, e baiaunci@tin.it, Marina Garibaldi) Open 15 Mar-15 Oct. €7.75/13.95 per person/tent. The island's camp site is at Canneto, about 3km out of Lìpari Town, and accessible by Urso bus from near the Esso service station at Marina Lunga.

Private Homes *Casa Vittorio* (☎/fax 090 981 15 23, e casavittorio@netnet.it, Vico Sparviero 15) Room with bathroom €62, 1-bed apartment €72. This home off Via Garibaldi near Marina Corta. has small apartments in addition to rooms. There are two terraces with views. You can find the owner (unless he finds you first) at Via Garibaldi 78, on the way from Marina Lunga to the city centre.

Diana Brown (☎ 090 981 25 84, fax 090 981 32 13, e dbrown@netnet.it, Vico Himera 3) Singles/doubles with bathroom €62/67. Owned by a friendly and helpful South African expat who has lived on Lìpari for almost 30 years, the seven rooms here are spotlessly clean, with air-con, fridge and comfy beds. You can also borrow beach towels and hairdryers, and there are clothes-washing facilities. Prices plummet to around €26 between 10 October and 30 April. Definitely recommended and reservations advised.

Enzo Il Negro (☎/fax 090 981 31 63, e enzoilnegro@libero.it, Via Garibaldi 29) Singles/doubles & triples €39/85. Enzo Il Negro has clean, comfortable digs. All rooms have air-con, fridge and balcony, and the colourful tiles in some rooms really

A sublime sunset over the mounds of drying salt outside Mòzia

Rows of rusting anchors on Favignana, famous for its annual tuna kill

Favignana's dramatic tufa cliffs

Weatherworn but still vibrant

Favignana's pretty main square, Piazza Madrice

The lure of Mt Etna: fantastic, fiery, devastating

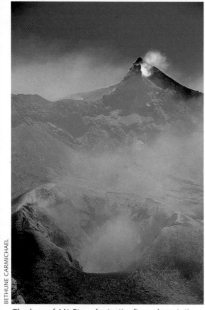
Contemplate Taormina's charming cathedral.

An aerial view of elegant and popular Taormina

Taormina as seen from its lofty Greek theatre

make you feel as though you're in something far more special than a 'room for rent'.

Lo Nardo Maria (☎ 090 988 04 31 or 090 981 20 54, 🖲 *pensionelonardo@netnet.it, Vicolo Ulisse 34)* Doubles with bathroom €51.65. Lo Nardo Maria has pleasant rooms complete with kitchen overlooking a narrow alleyway. There's a lovely terrace at the top of the house where the owner serves coffee and cold drinks in summer. You can also see if there's room at Via Vittorio Emanuele 216. Prices halve in the low season.

Hotels *Pensione Neri* (☎ 090 981 14 13, fax 090 981 36 42, 🖲 *htlneri@netnet.it, Via G Marconi 43)* B&B €56.80 per person. Off Via Vittorio Emanuele, Pensione Neri is in a lovely old, renovated villa. All rooms have bathrooms and the reception here is warm and welcoming. Prices drop by about €26 in the low season.

Hotel Oriente (☎ 090 981 14 93, fax 090 988 01 98, 🖲 *hoteloriente@netnet.it, Via G Marconi 35)* B&B singles/doubles/triples/quads €70/119/150/180. With all sorts of old objects adorning the walls and helpful management, the Oriente is a popular choice. In the low season, prices drop considerably.

Hotel Odissea (☎ 090 981 23 37, fax 090 988 07 21, 🖲 *hotelodissea@tiscalnet.it, Via Nazario Sauro 12)* Singles/doubles with bathroom €62/103. This charming, white-washed hotel is in Canneto and has good facilities. Credit cards are accepted too.

Hotel Villa Meligunis (☎ 090 981 24 26, fax 090 988 01 49, 🖲 *villameligunis@net net.it, Via Marte 7)* Singles/doubles with bathroom €180/260. This glorious 32-room 18th-century villa, on a hill overlooking Marina Corta, is Lipari's top hotel, with all the usual four-star amenities, and breakfast included.

Places to Eat

Try pasta with the island's excellent capers and be prepared to spend big to eat the day's sea catch. The waters of the archipelago abound in fish, including tuna, mullet, cuttlefish and sole, all of which end up on restaurant tables at the end of the day. Bear in mind that many places are open daily in summer, and shut down for winter. The local wine is the sweet, honey-coloured Malvasia, which you'll find on almost every wine list.

Although prices go up in the high season, you can still eat cheaply by sticking to the pizzerias along Via Vittorio Emanuele.

Pescecane (☎ 090 981 27 06, Via Vittorio Emanuele 223)* Tourist menu €12.40, pizzas €3.60-4.33. With vibrant young staff and very good pizza, this is a choice pick for an easy-going dinner or lunch.

Zum Willi (☎ 090 981 14 13, cnr Via Vittorio Emanuele & Via Umberto I)* Pizzas about €5.15. This place is basically a bar that serves pizzas.

Trattoria d'Oro (☎ 090 981 13 04, Via Umberto I 28–32)* Meals about €21. This is a good small restaurant with fresh seafood dishes.

Da Bartolo (☎ 090 981 17 00, Via Garibaldi 53)* Meals about €26. Pasta dishes are good here. It's one of the island's better trattorie and the fish is recommended, although it's a little overpriced.

Nenzyna (☎ 090 981 16 60, Via Roma 2)* Meals about €15.50. This is a no-nonsense trattoria with decent food.

E Pulera (☎ 090 981 11 58, Via Diana)* Meals about €33.50. Open June-Oct. A quick walk from the busy main drag, this beautiful restaurant has imaginative and excellent cooking, with great local ingredients.

Pasticceria Subba (☎ 090 981 13 52, Via Vittorio Emanuele 92)* Open since 1930, this is a great place to enjoy a coffee and a marvellous selection of mouth-watering Sicilian pastries and cakes.

You can buy supplies at the *grocery shops* along Via Vittorio Emanuele. There are also cafes and gourmet shops on this strip.

Entertainment

Most of the town's nightlife is concentrated in and around the Marina Corta, where there are a handful of bars with outdoor seating.

Il Gabbiano (☎ 090 981 14 71) and *Al Pescatore* (☎ 090 981 15 37) are both on

THE AEOLIAN ISLANDS

Marina Corta and have outdoor seating, making them popular places for people-watching, especially with a glass of Malvasia.

Kasbah (*☎ 090 981 10 75, Via Maurolico 25*) Open until 3am summer. The only late-night bar in Lìpari Town is the beautiful, Moroccan-themed Kasbah, which has live music and is a great place to enjoy a drink.

Getting There & Away
Siremar has two offices in Lìpari, for hydrofoils at Marina Corta (☎ 090 981 22 00) and for ferries at Marina Lunga (☎ 090 981 13 12). Snav (☎ 090 981 24 48) has an office at Marina Corta. NGI Traghetti is located near the Siremar office at Marina Lunga.

For details of ferry and hydrofoil departures for Milazzo and the other islands, see Getting There & Away and Getting Around at the beginning of this chapter.

Getting Around
Bus Urso buses (☎ 090 981 12 62 or 090 981 10 26), at Via Cappuccini 29, run an efficient and frequent service to every point of interest on the island, departing from just near the Esso service station at Marina Lunga. Pick up timetables from the office. There are frequent departures for Canneto (€1.30, daily, every hour between 8am and 9pm); there are also regular services to Acquacalda, Porticello and Quattrocchi. During July and August, the service increases. The company also offers special round trips of the island, which are a good way of seeing the sights if your time on Lìpari is limited. These trips (€3.10, one hour 10 minutes) depart at 9.30am, 11.30am and 5pm daily from 1 July to 30 September.

Boat Touring the island's waters by boat is the best way to get in some crowd-free swimming, especially in summer. Boats are available for hire at Foti Roberto (☎ 090 981 23 52), at Via F Crispi 31, to the right as you leave Marina Lunga. A three-seater motorised rubber dinghy costs around €52 per day and a 14-seater costs around €260.

Scooter Foti Roberto (see Boat earlier) also rents out scooters (about €30 per day) and mopeds (about €20 per day).

VULCANO
postcode 98050 ● pop 800 ● elevation 500m
Just south of Lìpari, and the first port of call for ferries and hydrofoils from Milazzo, Vulcano actually boasts three volcanoes – Vulcano Piano, Vulcanello and Fossa di Vulcano (or Gran Cratere, 'Large Crater'). Only the last of these is still active, although it is in its death throes. It constantly emits a thin fumarole, and expels an obnoxious stench of sulphurous gases, reminiscent of the after-effects of a hastily eaten curried egg sandwich washed down with off-beer. You get a nasty whiff of it as you approach the dock by boat, but rest assured that (surprisingly) everyone gets used to it pretty quickly. Mind you, if you're allergic to sulphur, this island may well play havoc with your sinuses and digestion.

Although uninhabited for millennia on account of the volcanic activity, the island today is a favourite playground of the Italian jet-set, with a number of fancy villas and exclusive hotels that cater to those with plenty of credit. Though you may want to give overnighting here a miss on account of the prices, the island is still an excellent destination for a day trip from Lìpari, or even from Milazzo on the Tyrrhenian Coast (see that chapter earlier). In addition to the volcano, the island has one of the best beaches in the archipelago. The thermal baths are also renowned for their curative powers.

History
To the ancient Greeks, the island of Thermessa, Terasia or Hiera – as Vulcano was variously known – must have inspired great respect, if not downright fear. The god of fire and war, Vulcan (Hephaestus to the Greeks), had his workshop here, where he was assisted by the cyclops, and Aeolus, the god of the wind, also swirled about.

Still, the island's activity was a source of curiosity to the scientists of antiquity, including Thucydides, Xenofon, Strabo and the Roman writer Pliny, who chronicled the 'birth' of the youngest of the three volcanoes, Vulcanello, in 183 BC. The Romans established a working colony here as they sought to exploit the island's subsoil, rich in alum and sulphur.

In the Middle Ages, the island was regarded as the 'antechamber of hell', an assessment you might agree with if you arrive on August weekends or in the week before or after Ferragosto (15 August) when the island is packed to capacity.

Under the Bourbons the island was used as a working farm populated by convicts from Lipari, but the enterprise collapsed with the decline of the French dynasty. At the beginning of the 19th century, a Scot named Stevenson purchased the northern part of the island with a view towards exploiting its resources (sulphur, alum and boric acid), much as the Romans had done, but his plans were shot due to a violent volcanic eruption. The most recent period of serious activity occurred between 1888 and 1890, and volcanologists have assured us that it was most likely the last, although a live volcano is still a live volcano...

Information

Tourist Offices The tourist office (☎ 090 985 20 28) is a mobile stand in the port area. It usually opens 8am to 2pm Monday to Saturday from June to late September. It has lists of accommodation as well as a couple of informative brochures on the island.

Money The Banco di Sicilia (☎ 090 985 23 35) in the port area has an ATM. It opens 8.30am to 1.30pm and 2.45pm to 3.45pm Monday to Friday between June and September only. You can change money at the Thermessa agency, which is also the Snav ticket office (☎ 090 985 22 30), also in the port area.

Post & Communications The post office (☎ 090 985 30 02) is in Piano. There are public telephones to your right as you leave the ferry or hydrofoil, on the approach road to the *fanghi* (mud baths).

Medical Services & Emergency If you need a doctor, call ☎ 090 985 22 20. The Bonarrigo pharmacy (☎ 090 985 22 44) is at Via Favoloro 1.

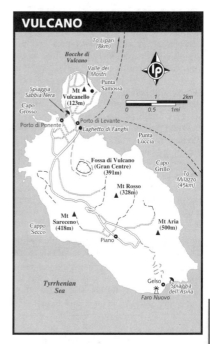

The *carabinieri* (police) can be reached on ☎ 090 985 21 10.

Things to See & Do

Porto di Levante & Around Once you've disembarked, head over to Vulcano's famed mud baths, the **Laghetto di Fanghi** *(admission €0.77; open 6.15am-8.30pm).* They're adjacent to the dock at the bottom of a *faraglione* (stack), a long stone finger jutting up into the sky. The fanghi are actually one large mud pit of thick, hot, smelly, sulphurous gloop that has long been considered an excellent treatment for all kinds of rheumatic pains, skin diseases and 'various gynaecological disorders', as a sign at the mud baths says.

Rolling around in the mud can be a tantalising experience, even if the smell is atrocious. Remember to remove all watches and jewellery, as the mud will often ruin anything it comes in contact with. Also, wear something that you don't mind destroying, because once the smell is in you'll never get rid of it. Experts have advised that prolonged immersion can be bad for you on account of the pit's slight radioactivity; consequently, you should not stay in for more than 10 or 15 minutes and pregnant women should avoid it altogether. Finally, don't let any of the mud get in your eyes as the sulphur stings. Other than that, hold your nose.

When you're done, you can clean off in the nearby sea – a natural Jacuzzi with hot, bubbling water, it's perfect for relaxing in.

Fossa di Vulcano (Gran Cratere) The island's other main attraction is climbing Fossa di Vulcano (391m). Follow the intermittent signs for 'Al Cratere' (or ask for directions) which take you left (south) out of

---

The Vulcan Winds

In Homer's *Odyssey* Vulcano is the realm of the wise and benevolent King Aeolus, who inherited the island by marrying Cyane, the daughter of the island's first king, Liparo.

On their return from the 10-year war against Troy, Ulysses and his crew docked at Vulcano, where Aeolus welcomed them as his guests. On their departure, Aeolus presented Ulysses with a bag holding all of the Mediterranean winds that would further delay Ulysses' epic journey home to the island of Ithaca. Left out of the bag was Zephyr, the only wind guaranteed to speed the ship onwards. Aeolus' parting words to Ulysses were to keep the bag closed until he had arrived home. But things were never that easy for the poor voyager. Just as they were within sight of Ithaca, curiosity got the better of Ulysses' crew, who were convinced that the bag contained a fabulous treasure that their captain was keeping from them. Before Ulysses knew what was happening, the bag was opened and the enraged winds flew out, blowing the ship away from shore and back to Vulcano. Stunned at their greed and stupidity, Aeolus threw his former guests off the island and they once more resumed their journeys. It would be years before they would see Ithaca again.

---

the port area along Via Provinciale. About 500m farther on a track slopes off to the left (not well signposted; look out for a gravel track on your left) which leads up to the crater. It's about one hour's scramble over some pretty tough ground that is totally exposed to the sun, so make sure you wear strong, closed shoes and bring plenty of water. When you've reached the top, you can lean over a ledge and look into the main crater, the source of the nasty smell you've had in your nose the whole way up! From the top there are splendid views of all of the other islands (weather permitting).

Porto di Ponente & Around On the far side of the peninsula from Porto di Levante at Porto di Ponente is **Spiaggia Sabbia Nera** (Black Sand Beach), a smooth, sandy beach, and one of the nicest in the archipelago, with faraglioni jutting into the sky. Paddle boats are usually available for hire on the beach (around €7.75 for one hour).

The isthmus on the island's north is Vulcanello, which contains the interestingly named **Valle dei Mostri** (Valley of the Monsters), a group of wind-eroded dark rocks that have formed grotesque shapes.

Gelso On the island's southern coast is Gelso, where you'll find paddle boats for hire. Nearby, approached by a signposted steep dirt track (pedestrians only) that branches off before Gelso, is the crescent-shaped sweep of black sand and inviting waters known as **Spiaggia dell'Asina** (Donkey Beach). There's a rudimentary bar/cafe here, where you can also hire sun lounges (€7.75) and umbrellas (€5.15). One of the great things about the beach is that it's often uncrowded, even in the summer months. To get to both Gelso and the beach, Scaffadi has buses that leave Porto di Levante at 10.15am, 11.35am and 4.30pm from 15 June to 15 September (€1.80). Buses from Gelso leave at 11am, 12.10pm and 5pm. Boat tours of the island also call in here.

Piano & Capo Grillo Piano is the plain where most of Vulcano's population lives, and from there you can get to Capo Grillo, where there are breathtaking views of the coast and out to sea. Scaffadi has seven buses from Porto di Levante to Piano and Capo Grillo between 8am and 6pm Monday to Saturday (two on Sunday and public holidays). From Piano, seven buses go to the port between 7.30am and 5.15pm Monday to Saturday (two on Sunday and public holidays).

Activities

Pino & Giuseppe (☎ 090 985 24 19, Via Comunale Levante, nr Porto di Levante) in front of the tobacconist organises **boat trips** around the island (€10.35) and to Stromboli crater (€51.65, approximately eight hours).

The proprietor of **Gioielli del Mare** (☎ 090 985 21 70, Porto di Levante) organises **bus tours** (€10.35 per person, about two hours) around the island for groups of about 12 people. Make a booking and hope a large enough group will form.

Places to Stay & Eat

Hotel Torre (☎ 090 985 23 42, Via Favaloro) Doubles with bathroom €46.50. Simple, clean and cheap for Vulcano, this small hotel is close to Porto di Levante and the mud baths.

Pensione La Giara (☎ 090 985 22 29, Via Provinciale 18) B&B €56.80 per person. Open late Apr-early Oct. The pleasant *pensione* has good rooms with bathroom and staggering discounts outside August.

Rojas Bahja Hotel (☎ 090 985 20 80, e hotelrojas@netnet.it, Porto Levante) B&B €69.70 per person. Open June-Sept. Near the mud baths, this beautiful, lavishly tiled hotel is a good spot to stay, with bathroom, TV, phone and air-con in every room.

Hotel Arcipelago (☎ 090 985 20 02, fax 090 985 21 54, Vulcanello) Singles/doubles with bathroom €62/103. The Arcipelago enjoys a beautiful position on the northern coast of Vulcano (signposted), and has many facilities, on top of TV, phone, air-con and fridge in its rooms.

Hotel Conti (☎ 090 985 21 51, fax 090 985 21 53, e conti@netnet.it, Via Porto di Ponente) Singles/doubles with bathroom €88/124. The three-star Conti is on the Porto di Ponente side of the island and has

lovely views from its public areas, plus a pizzeria.

Meals are invariably fish-based and often overpriced.

Da Maurizio (☎ 090 985 24 26, Via Porto di Levante) Tourist menu €15.50. This is a pleasant restaurant in an attractive setting. Anything but the tourist menu sends the bill sky-high though.

Da Vincenzino (☎ 090 985 20 16, Via Porto di Levante) Meals about €26. Just near Da Maurizio, this place is close to the port and OK for lunch or dinner.

La Piazzetta (☎ 090 985 33 77, Via Porto di Levante) Meals about €18. With a nice outdoor area (no real view, though), this place has good pizzas.

There are also small bars and cafes near the main port – none are particularly good, but they are convenient and reasonably priced.

At Gelso, on the south side of the island, there are a couple of good, small trattorie, **Pina** (☎ 0368 66 85 55) and **Da Tony** (☎ 0337 95 31 76), which are open for lunch (both about €18).

Getting There & Away

Vulcano is an intermediate stop between Milazzo and Lipari and a good number of vessels go both ways throughout the day. See the Getting There & Away section at the beginning of this chapter for details.

All boats and hydrofoils dock at Porto di Levante, on the northwest of the island. To your right as you disembark is the small peninsula of Vulcanello.

Getting Around

You can hire boats on the island. One company that offers this service is Centro Nautico Baia di Levante (☎ 0339 337 27 95 or 0338 497 36 06). Boat prices start at over €51.65, so a group booking is best.

If you want to hire a mountain bike or scooter, da Paolo (☎ 090 985 21 12) has plenty, from €5.15/25.80 respectively in the high season, less at other times. You'll find it about 25m from the port, on the way to Pensione La Giara.

See the earlier Gelso and Piano & Capo Grillo sections for details of travel on Scaffadi

THE AEOLIAN ISLANDS

buses. Call ☎ 0339 600 57 50 (24 hours) if you need a taxi.

SALINA

postcode 98050 • pop 2400
elevation 962m

Although it owes its modern name to the *saline* (saltworks) of Lingua, Salina is defined and shaped by the two volcanoes that gave it its ancient Greek name of Dydime, meaning 'double'. Although extinct since antiquity, previous eruptions combined with plenty of water have rendered the island the most fertile in all the archipelago. The famous Aeolian capers grow plentiful here, as does the grape used to make Malvasia wine. Only on Salina are you assured of drinking the genuine article, as much of the Malvasia on other islands is imported from the Sicilian mainland.

With the exception of Alicudi and Filicudi, this is the least visited of all the islands, though the number of tourists is growing every year, and there's a strong Australian presence due to returning emigrants and their families. Consequently, the island isn't geared exclusively to the tourist industry; you can get a partial impression of what the islanders' daily lives are actually like, with most people going about their business – farming and fishing – as they have done for centuries.

History

Salina has been inhabited since the Bronze Age, but the first real settlement dates back to the 4th century BC at Santa Marina Salina. The town was important throughout Hellenistic and Roman times as a centre for farming, and it continued to grow up to the 8th century AD, its population swelled by Liparese looking to avoid volcanic activity on Vulcano. Under the Arabs the island was stripped of its wealth and much of the populace was forced to leave; it was only during the 17th century that it began to thrive once more.

Orientation & Information

Boats dock at Santa Marina Salina, where you will find most accommodation, or at Rinella, a fishing hamlet on the southwest coast. The other main villages on the island are Malfa, on the northern coast, and Leni, slightly inland from Rinella.

In summer there are AAST booths in Rinella, Malfa and Santa Marina Salina. There are two branches of Banca Antonveneta (with ATMs) on the island, at Via Provinciale 2, Malfa, and close to the port of Santa Marina at Via Lungomare Notar Giuffrè, open 8.40am to 1.20pm Monday to Saturday.

There is a post office (☎ 090 984 30 28) on Via Marina Garibaldi in Santa Marina Salina, where you can also change money. There are a couple of public phones in Bar Rago (☎ 090 980 90 55), Via del Risorgimento 182, also in Santa Marina Salina, and other public phones at the island's ports.

For medical assistance, call ☎ 090 984 40 05. For the *questura* (police), phone ☎ 090 984 30 19 or 090 984 30 42.

Santa Marina Salina

Santa Marina Salina is Salina's main port, and the busiest spot on the island when the hydrofoil or ferry docks. The main street here is Via Risorgimento, where there are some bars/cafes, the odd souvenir shop and a few *alimentari* (grocery shops). It's one block back from the *lungomare* (seafront promenade) at the port. If you turn right from the docking area and head along the lungomare, you can swim off the stone beach. The road left from the port leads to Lingua (see under the following section).

Around Salina

Lingua Only a 3km walk or bus ride from Santa Marina Salina, Lingua is a small, pleasant town with some hotels and trattorie and a small beach. You can also head from Lingua by path up to Monte Fosse delle Felci (follow the signs for Brigantino). Corn and barley are the main crops around Brigantino, but as soon as you start climbing (take the path to the right), you'll see plenty of olive trees that eventually give way to vineyards. A century ago the hilltops were covered in vine, but local industry has suffered greatly at the hands of

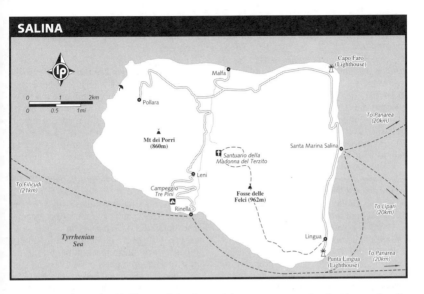

SALINA

Capo Faro (Lighthouse)
Malfa
To Panarea (20km)
Pollara
Mt dei Porri (860m)
Santa Marina Salina
Santuario della Màdonna del Terzito
To Filicudi (21km)
Leni
Campeggio Tre Pini
Fosse delle Felci (962m)
Rinella
To Lipari (20km)
Tyrrhenian Sea
Lingua
To Panarea (20km)
Punta Lingua (Lighthouse)

competition from the Sicilian mainland, leaving only a few cultivators of the famed Malvasia wine.

Malfa Malfa is located on the northern side of Salina, accessible by the road leading from Santa Marina. It's the largest town on the island and you can swim here at the good beach.

In Palazzo Marchetti, you can visit the **Museo dell'Emigrazione Eoliana** *(Emigration Museum;* ☎ *090 984 43 72; free; open 9am-1pm Mon-Fri June-Sept)*, which gives visitors an idea of the scale and effect of emigration from the Aeolian islands.

Madonna del Terzito & Monte Fosse delle Felci At Valdichiesa, in the valley separating the two volcanoes, is the Santuario della Madonna del Terzito (Sanctuary of the Madonna of Terzito), which is a place of pilgrimage, particularly around Ferragosto on 15 August. From the church, you can follow the track (signposted) all the way to the peak of **Fosse delle Felci** (962m) and visit the very well-managed **nature reserve** *(riserva naturale)*. Along the way you'll see plenty of colourful flora, including wild

violets, asparagus and a plant known locally as *cipudazza* (Latin *Urginea marittima*), which was sold to the Calabrians to make soap but used locally as mouse poison! Once you've reached the top (the last 100m are particularly tough), you have unparalleled views of the entire archipelago. You can get to the sanctuary by taking a bus from Santa Marina Salina to Rinella or Leni, and asking the driver to let you off at the sanctuary.

Rinella Rinella is a popular underwater spearfishing spot, and there's also swimming from the rocks near the Tre Pini camp site. It's a lovely, though quiet, spot to visit or stay on the island, and seems quite removed due to the steepness of the road to the rest of the island. Without transport of your own, you'll have to rely on buses.

Pollara Don't miss a trip to the beach near Pollara, the setting for much of Massimo Troisi's last film, *Il Postino*. The climb down is a bit tricky but the beach itself with its backdrop of cliffs is absolutely unbeatable. You can get here by bus from Santa Marina Salina.

Places to Stay & Eat

Santa Marina Salina *Mamma Santina* (☎ *090 984 30 54, fax 090 984 30 51,* e *mammasantina@ctonline.it, Via Sanità 40)* Singles/doubles €31/57, doubles with bathroom €72.30, half-board with bathroom €77.45 per person. To get to this pleasant pink-and-white pensione, head for Via Risorgimento (the narrow main street) and walk north for a few hundred metres. The guesthouse is uphill along a winding lane to your left and also has a restaurant.

Hotel Bellavista (☎/fax 090 984 30 09, Via Risorgimento 8) Singles/doubles with bathroom €82.65/144.60. Open Apr-late Sept. The Bellavista has panoramic views of the sea and three-star facilities.

There are several restaurants clustered around the docks.

Portobello (☎ 090 984 31 25, Via Bianchi 1) Meals about €26. This is probably the best restaurant in town, with a good range of Aeolian-style dishes on offer.

Lingua *Il Delfino (☎ 090 984 30 24, fax 090 984 32 98, Via Garibaldi 19)* Doubles/triples with bathroom €41.30/51.65. With good simple rooms and a restaurant, this place is worth a stay.

A Cannata (☎/fax 090 984 31 61, e *cannata@netnet.it, Via Umberto)* Doubles €51.65, with bathroom €72.30. With an excellent restaurant and less than 10 rooms, you'd be advised to book in advance in summer. In the low season, room prices halve.

Il Gambero (☎ 090 984 30 49, Via Manzoni 2) Meals about €23. For fish dishes, the Gambero is a great choice.

Malfa *Residence Santa Isabel (☎ 090 984 40 18, fax 090 984 43 62,* e *santaisabel @isole-eolie.it, Via Scalo 12)* Doubles/triples with bathroom €89/103. Open Apr-Oct. The furnished apartments here are good value for Malfa, which is the most expensive part of Salina. There's also a restaurant.

Punta Scario (☎ 090 984 41 39, fax 090 984 40 77, e *htlscario@netnet.it, Via Scalo 8)* Half-board with bathroom €82.65 per person. The very comfortable Punta Scario has stylish rooms with phone and terrace, and some of the views are spellbinding. There's also a restaurant on the premises.

Rinella *Campeggio Tre Pini (☎ 090 980 91 55, Rinella Beach)* €7.25/17.55 per person/ tent. The island's only camp site (and easily the best of the two in the Aeolian Islands) has good amenities and plenty of shaded areas for camper vans and tents. You can get here by ferry or hydrofoil (walk up and left from the port for about 100m), or by regular buses from Santa Marina.

Hotel L'Ariana (☎ 090 980 90 75, fax 090 980 92 50, e *lariana@netnet.it, Via Rotabile 11)* Singles/doubles with bathroom €51.65/92.95, half-board €80 per person. The delightful L'Ariana is in a late-19th-century villa overlooking the sea at Rinella. It has terraces and a pleasant bar (easily the best spot to sip a glass of Malvasia at sunset), and the restaurant here is the best place to eat in this part of the island. Low season prices make this great value.

Getting There & Away

Hydrofoils and ferries service Santa Marina Salina and Rinella. There are at least eight hydrofoil connections between Santa Marina Salina and the other islands daily from 1 June to 30 September; service is reduced at other times. There are at least four hydrofoils daily between Rinella and the other islands. Siremar has ticket booths at the harbours (Santa Marina Salina ☎ 090 984 30 04, Rinella ☎ 090 980 91 70) as does Snav (Santa Marina Salina ☎ 090 984 30 78, Rinella ☎ 090 980 92 33). For information on arrivals and departures from Milazzo, see the Getting There & Away section at the beginning of this chapter.

Getting Around

Regular Citis buses (☎ 090 984 41 50) run from Santa Marina Salina to Lingua, Malfa, Rinella, Pollara, Valdichiesa and Leni (€1.80). Timetables are posted at the ports and around the island.

Motorcycles and scooters (around €21 per day) can be hired from Antonio Bongiorno (☎ 090 984 34 09), at Via Risorgimento 240,

Santa Marina Salina. If you feel like hiring a scooter in Rinella (and given the steepness of the road from here to the rest of the island, it's a good idea), check out Eolian Service (☎ 090 980 92 03) at the port, where you can hire a scooter from €15.50 per day.

Boats are available for rent from June to August at Nautica Levante (☎ 090 984 30 83) on Via Lungomare, Santa Marina Salina.

PANAREA

postcode 98050 ● pop 320 ● elevation 421m

Easily the most picturesque of the Aeolian Islands, tiny Panarea is 3km long and 2km wide. In recent decades it has taken on an air of exclusivity akin to Vulcano, as northern Italians buy summer homes here to make the most of the fabulous swimming and good rocky beaches. Consequently, finding accommodation can be an expensive nightmare in the high season of July and August. Out of season, however, everything quietens down considerably and the prices drop accordingly.

The island's population lives almost exclusively on the eastern side of the island, in one of the three former hamlets of Ditella, San Pietro and Drauto, although you'll hardly notice the difference between them as they have all merged into one strip of tangled lanes and pretty seafront houses. Addresses here are approximate as the intimacy of the place makes it unnecessary – everyone knows everyone else by name, history and quirky habits, and even the *forestieri* (outsiders) who spend their summers here are known by their place of origin ('oh, you mean that fellow from Turin who owns the fancy villa up past Piero's?').

All boats dock at San Pietro, where you'll also find most of the accommodation, plus an ATM and public phones.

In a medical emergency call ☎ 090 98 30 40. The Sparacino pharmacy (☎ 090 98 31 48) is on Via Iditella. You can call the carabinieri, between June and September only, on ☎ 090 98 31 81.

Around the Island

Head south to Punta Milazzese, about a 30-minute walk past a couple of beaches, to see the **Bronze-Age village**, made up of 23 huts, which was discovered in 1948. It is reckoned that the headland here was inhabited as far back as the 14th century BC, while pottery found at the site shows distinctly Minoan influences, lending credence to the theory that there were ties between the islanders and the Cretans. The artefacts found here are on display in the Museo Archeologico Eoliano at Lipari.

From the Punta Milazzese a set of steps leads down to the **Cala Junco**, a stunningly beautiful little cove where the swimming is excellent and the water a deep aquamarine. The island's other beach is to the north of Ditella, at the end of a track – just follow the signposts for **Spiaggia Fumarola**. The 'Stone Beach' here is isolated and a perfect place for a quiet swim, except in July and August, of course, when the ringing of mobile phones is incessant.

Offshore

Panarea's own little archipelago consists of six tiny islets off the eastern shore which can only be reached by boat (see Getting Around later in this chapter). The largest island, **Basiluzzo**, is also the farthest away, and is given over to the cultivation of capers. At the back of the island, visible from land, is the impressive wreck of a Roman ship.

Nearest to Panarea is **Dàttilo**, which has a pretty little beach called **Le Guglie**. Of the three little islands south of Dàttilo, you should make for **Lisca Bianca**, the one farthest away, where you can indulge in your own little spot of wreck-hunting (although you won't find any treasure), if you're equipped with scuba gear. Contact **Amphibia** *(☎ 090 98 33 11, Via Iditella on Panarea)* to hire gear. Crossing the narrow channel from the islet of **Bottaro** (actually nothing more than a protruding rock) to Lisca Bianca, you will notice there is a small white beach on Lisca Bianca's southern side. Proceed left past the beach and continue around the sharp point of the island. Here, at a depth of perhaps 40m or 50m, you will find the wreck of an old English ship that sank in the 19th century.

Places to Stay & Eat

Locanda Rodà (☎ 090 98 32 12, fax 090 98 30 03, Via San Pietro) Singles/doubles with bathroom €51.65/82.65, half-board €82.65 per person. The closest you'll come to a cheap hotel here is the Locanda Rodà, which is uphill from the port and to the left. It has a pizzeria/trattoria that charges average prices.

Lisca Bianca (☎ 090 98 30 04, fax 090 98 32 91, e liscabianca@liscabianca.it, Via Lani 1) Doubles with bathroom €186. Prices drop by over 50% in the low season. This is one of the loveliest places to stay on Panarea. With whitewashed walls, sea views, a terrace and a great Arabic-themed bar, you may find it hard to leave.

La Sirena (☎/fax 090 98 30 12, e studio barca@netnet.it, Via Drauto 4) Half-board with bathroom €87.60 per person. Prices plummet in the low season. This is on the way to the Bronze-Age village. It has a pleasant trattoria but only four rooms.

Trattoria da Pina (☎ 090 98 30 32) Meals about €23. In the same area as La Sirena is this trattoria, with a terrace overlooking the sea.

Da Francesco (☎ 090 98 30 23) Meals about €21. With good views from the terrace, this is a decent place to eat. The *spaghetti con le cozze* (spaghetti with mussels) is good value and tasty.

Getting There & Away

In summer there are at least six daily hydrofoils and a daily ferry that link the island with Stromboli to the northeast and Salina (and on to Lìpari and Milazzo) to the west. Both Siremar (☎ 090 98 30 07) and Snav (☎ 090 98 30 09) have offices along the harbour on Via San Pietro.

Getting Around

Cars are not allowed on Panarea but you don't need them as the island is small enough to get around on foot. If you find yourself missing the chaotic driving style of the mainland, you can take comfort in the fact that golf carts (the island's taxis) have well and truly arrived on Panarea, disturbing the peace whilst offering a convenient means of getting around. On some of the narrow lanes, you might want to breathe in deeply as a golf cart hurtles past. You can pick one up at the port, or call Paolo & Angela (☎ 0333 313 86 10, 24 hours). Fares are €2.60 per person one way, or you can hire one for about €26 per day (€36 in August).

To explore the small islands off its shores and some of the coves and beaches of the main island, you'll need to hire a boat. Tesoriero Roberto (☎ 090 98 30 33), on Via San Pietro, does all kinds of boat rentals, from rubber dinghies to wooden longboats with outboard motors. Expect to pay around €52 for half a day.

STROMBOLI

postcode 98050 • pop 400 • elevation 924m
Stromboli is the most captivating of all the Aeolian Islands, largely because it is the only island to have a permanently active volcano. Experts and amateurs alike are attracted by the island's unique appeal, which combines overwhelming natural beauty with the threat of the volcano's fiery rage. The Stromboli crater is the youngest in the archipelago – it was formed only 40,000 years ago. It launches periodic showers of incandescent lava accompanied by the violent emissions of sulphurous fumes and small overflows of lava. Technical volcano language, taking this kind of activity as a model, has come to include the term *attività Stromboliana* (Strombolian activity).

In recent years, eruptions have been of modest proportions and have occurred within the vicinity of the crater. A major eruption of the crater in 1930 was an additional cause of emigration to Australia of many of the island's 5000 inhabitants (residents now number around 400). The last substantial eruption was in March 1996 and, although minor, left several people injured (see the boxed text 'Facing the Volcano' later). Still, lava flow is largely confined to the Sciara del Fuoco (Trail of Fire) on the volcano's northwestern flank, leaving the villages of San Bartolo, San Vincenzo and Scari (which merge into one town) and Ginostra quite safe.

Although remote and farther away than most of the other islands, getting here is not a problem during summer, when there is a regular ferry and hydrofoil service. In winter or in bad weather, however, the service is often disrupted or cancelled altogether.

Orientation

Boats arrive at Porto Scari/San Vincenzo, downhill from the town. Accommodation is a short walk up the Scalo Scari to Via Roma, or, if you plan to head straight for the crater, follow the road along the waterfront (see Climbing the Volcano later for details).

Stromboli Town

The closest thing the island has to a tourist office is the privately owned Stròmbolania information office (☎ 090 98 63 90, W www .strombolania.it) under the Ossidiana Hotel at Porto Scari. It can help you organise accommodation as well as boat and bike rentals, and tours around the island by boat and helicopter. It opens 9am to noon and 3pm to 8pm (to 9pm in August) daily between Easter and September. A screen outside the office monitors the volcano's activity via a cable link. You can also try the volcano's own information office, Alpine Guides (☎ 090 98 62 63), just off Piazza San Vincenzo. It's nothing more than a shack and keeps irregular hours but you can get details of the state of the volcano and arrange a guide (see also Climbing the Volcano later in this chapter).

The post office (☎ 090 98 60 27) is on Via Roma. It opens 8.20am to 1.20pm Monday to Saturday. If you need to use the Internet or access your email, Totem Trekking, at Piazza San Vincenzo 4, will let you use the computer there for €5.15 per hour.

You can exchange travellers cheques and cash at the bank (with ATM) on Via Nunziante at Ficogrande, open from June to September. Another ATM is located on Via Roma, on the approach to Piazza San Vincenzo. Otherwise, exchange facilities are available at the travel agency Le Isole e Terme d'Italia (☎ 090 98 62 74), on Via Roma near the port.

There is an emergency doctor in Stromboli (☎ 090 98 60 97) and Ginostra (☎ 090 981

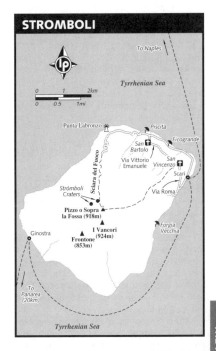

28 22). The Simone pharmacy (☎ 090 98 60 79) is on Via Roma. The carabinieri can be called on ☎ 090 98 60 21.

Around the Island

There is little to see here other than a couple of churches. Just outside the town (follow Via Roma, which then becomes Via Vittorio Emanuele), a couple of doors down on the right from Chiesa di San Vincenzo but before the Barbablù hotel, is a **pink/red house** where Ingrid Bergman and Roberto Rossellini lived during the filming of *Stròmboli* in 1949. Film buffs will be familiar with the scandal provoked by their liaison – Rossellini was a married man – which was the talk of the film world for a long time thereafter. Aside from a few ashen **beaches** on either side of the dock area (the one north of the dock is a popular spot for naturists), there is little else to do save tackle the ascent to the crater.

Climbing the Volcano

You will need heavy shoes and clothing for cold wet weather, a torch (flashlight) if you're climbing at night, food and a good supply of water. If you need any gear, **Totem Trekking** (☎ *090 986 57 52, Piazza San Vincenzo 4*) hires out a variety of well-maintained equipment, from torches to trekking boots, although supplies can run out.

Climbing to the top of the volcano without a guide has been expressly forbidden by the authorities because of the dangers, but you can go so far on your own. From the port, follow the road leading right along the waterfront, continue straight past the beach at Ficogrande. Once past the village the path heads uphill, deviating after about 20 minutes to a bar/pizzeria and observatory. Alternatively, follow it through a slightly confusing section of reeds until it ascends to the crater. About halfway up is a good view of the **Sciara del Fuoco** (Trail of Fire), although in daylight the glow of the molten lava is imperceptible. The path eventually becomes quite steep and rocky. Note the warning signs at the summit and do not go too close to the edge. The round trip from the village should take about four hours.

The climb is a totally different experience at night, when darkness throws the molten lava of the Sciara del Fuoco and volcanic explosions into dramatic relief. Under no circumstances attempt to make the climb at night without a guide.

Experienced guides can be contacted through the Alpine Guides office (see under Stromboli Town earlier in this chapter). They take groups of 15 people or more to the crater between 3.30pm and 6pm daily (depending on the time of year, weather conditions and if there are enough people to form a group), returning at around 10pm to 11.30pm (about €21 per person). Contact the office around noon to make a booking.

See Lonely Planet's *Walking in Italy* for more detailed descriptions of walks on Stromboli, both on the volcano and around the island.

Activities

La Sirenetta Diving Center (☎ *090 98 60 25, La Sirenetta hotel, Via Marina 33*) offers diving courses. Alternatively, make your way to the beach of rocks and black volcanic sand at Ficogrande to swim and sunbathe.

The **Società Navigazione Pippo** (☎ *090 98 61 35, Via Roma 47*) organises nightly **boat trips** to view the Sciara del Fuoco from the sea. The boat, named *Pippo*, leaves at 10pm from the northern port and at

Facing the Volcano

Do not attempt to climb the crater without an authorised guide. At the point where the normal climb from Punta Labronzo begins, a very visible sign (in English and Italian) warns walkers not to continue unaccompanied, while a recent mayoral ordinance has expressly forbidden it. Still, many visitors make the climb without a guide and some even pass the night at the crater, lulled by the rumblings of the eruptions, sheltered within the primitive *fortini* (forts). Many leave the area the following morning without clearing up their litter, an act of irresponsibility that not only ruins the crater's appeal but also attracts rats in their dozens; they can be seen scurrying around the crater's edge foraging through the rubbish.

Although the volcano's eruptions rarely trouble the observation posts at the Pizzo or Sopra la Fossa, their power is an uncontrollable variable that must be considered by everyone who attempts the climb. In the unlikely event that you are caught in a hail of incandescent *lapilli* (pumice) or *bombe* (larger masses of molten rock), do not turn your back and try to run, no matter what your instincts say. The best way is to deal with them head on, as they are usually travelling slowly enough to allow you to dodge them easily. If you decide to sleep at the top of the crater, remember that you are at the volcano's mercy: during the 1996 eruptions one unsuspecting visitor was hit in the head while sleeping. He survived, but he didn't need a haircut for quite a while.

10.10pm from Ficogrande. The tour costs €12.90 per person. The same company also runs two daytime trips, leaving at 10am and 3pm. Viking (for contact details see under Boat in the Getting Around section under Lìpari) offers a very good boat trip, starting in Lìpari and departing from the Stromboli ferry port for the Sciara del Fuoco at 8pm. The same boat also heads out to the Strombolicchio rock, a popular spot for underwater fishing.

Places to Stay & Eat
There's nothing much in the budget bracket on Stromboli.

Casa del Sole (☎/fax 090 98 60 17, Via Soldato Cincotta) Singles/doubles €20.65/41.30. The cheapest option is the Casa del Sole, off the road to the volcano, before you reach Ficogrande. It is popular with young people. Rates include use of the kitchen.

You will also find about half a dozen *affittacamere* (private lodgings), charging from €41 for doubles, although some are much more expensive.

Barbablù (☎ 090 98 61 18, fax 090 98 63 23, e barbablu@hpe.it, Via Vittorio Emanuele 17) Doubles with bathroom €165. This is a very pleasant guesthouse with lovely rooms. Credit cards are accepted and prices drop to about €93 in the low season.

Villaggio Stròmboli (☎ 090 98 60 18, fax 090 98 62 58, e villaggiostromboli@net net.it, Via Regina Elena) Singles/doubles with bathroom €80/134.30. This hotel is on the beachfront, with very good facilities and access to scuba diving. It also has a terrace bar/restaurant.

La Sirenetta (☎ 090 98 60 25, fax 090 98 61 24, e lasirenetta@netnet.it, Via Marina 33) Singles/doubles with bathroom €98/212, half-board €131.70 per person. La Sirenetta is perfectly located on the beach at Ficogrande in front of Stròmbolicchio, a towering rock rising out of the sea at San Vincenzo. The hotel has a swimming pool, a panoramic terrace with a restaurant and one of the best chefs on the island. It's also the home of La Sirenetta Diving Center (see the previous Water Sports entry).

La Trottola (☎ 090 98 60 46, Piazza San Vincenzo) Meals about €18. For a reasonably priced meal, try this place.

Il Conte Ugolino (Piazza San Vincenzo) Pizzas €7-9. Opposite Totem Trekking on Piazza San Vincenzo, this place stays open till midnight, which is handy for anyone descending the volcano late at night with a rumbling tummy.

Punta Lena (☎ 090 98 62 04) Meals about €20. Punta Lena, on the Lungomare, walking away from the northern port towards the volcano, has a terrace overlooking the sea and decent Sicilian dishes.

The *pizzeria* at the observatory, about 20 minutes' walk up the lower slope of the volcano, is also reasonable. There are a couple of *bars* at the port, where you can get light snacks, and the *supermarket* on Via Roma is a good place to stock up on supplies.

Getting There & Away
There are at least four daily hydrofoil and ferry connections between Stromboli and the other islands. It takes four hours by ferry to reach the island from Lìpari, 1½ to two hours by hydrofoil. Ticket offices for Snav (☎ 090 98 60 03) and Siremar (☎ 090 98 60 16) are at the port. Bear in mind the cost of the trip and the distance if you're considering a day visit – which in any case will rob you of the opportunity of a night climb up the volcano. Heavy seas can cause cancellation of ferry and hydrofoil services; bad weather will often result in boat trips or climbs being cancelled.

FILICUDI
postcode 98050 ● pop 300 ● elevation 774m
Less developed than its Aeolian neighbours to the east, disembarking at Filicudi's port gives no real indication of what a beautiful island it is. The area is a huddle of concrete houses and one large resort hotel. Most of the island's limited facilities are here, including a small post office (☎ 090 988 90 53), usually open 9am to 1pm Monday to Friday, a public phone, a general store and a pharmacy (☎ 090 988 90 77).

In a medical emergency call the doctor on ☎ 090 988 99 61. The carabinieri are on ☎ 090 988 99 42.

Things to See & Do

Once you've moved on from the port, the disappointment will definitely fade. The main road goes south towards Capo Graziano and the **prehistoric village**, a smattering of Bronze-Age huts that predate Panarea's Punta Milazzese by a few hundred years. The site, discovered in 1952, is always open. From the village you can descend to Filicudi's only real **beach**, a stony affair that offers the easiest swimming on the island – if you want to take a dip elsewhere, you'll have to clamber down some jagged rocks or rent a boat.

Just at the port via a set of steep steps is the path to the centre of the island. After about 10 minutes (just past La Canna and Villa La Rosa), the road forks. You can go north (right) to **Valdichiesa**, a little village on a hillside terrace that has great views. There's little to see here save the rather pretty church – it is a pretty unassuming place where you can rest for a few minutes before moving on, or have a look at some of the abandoned houses that may well be snapped up and restored in the coming years. Above the village is the peak of the **Fossa dei Felci** (774m), which you can

climb – just keep walking in the general direction of the peak.

Alternatively, take the road that leads south (left) at the fork and make your way down via the donkey path to the little hamlet of **Pecorini**, nothing more than a cluster of one-storey houses huddled around a church. There are a couple of restaurants here (see the following Places to Stay & Eat section) and you can swim in the water, although the rocks get *very* hot under the sun.

The best way of visiting the island, however, is by boat. There's usually someone around the port renting them out for around €21 per person during the high season for a two-hour trip, but if there isn't just ask at any of the shops around the port.

On the uninhabited western side of the island is the natural arch of the **Punta del Perciato** (Perciato Point) and the nearby **Grotta del Bue Marino** (Cave of the Monk Seal). This cavity is 37m long by 30m wide, and named after the seals that once lived here. You won't see any now, though, as the last one was harpooned in the 1960s. To the northwest is the **Scoglio della Canna** (Cane Reef), a long, thin stack of rock 71m high

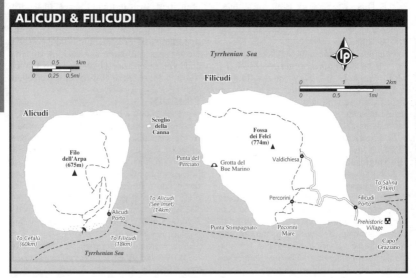

ALICUDI & FILICUDI

Aeolian-Australian Invasion

Throughout the Aeolian Islands, you'll often run into Australians whose families originally emigrated Down Under from the islands. Nowhere is this Australian presence more obvious or disconcerting than on Filicudi, where a number of houses have been rejuvenated by the return of prodigal families. It's not uncommon to hear a strong Aussie accent in any of the bars and cafes on the island, and you can even buy XXXX beer near the port. The families often come over for the Australian winter/Italian summer and stay for a few months, getting in touch with their heritage and history, and providing a bit of a boost to the local economy, which can get really quiet outside the busy summer months. They can also offer some great tips about spots to visit on the islands, especially for those visitors who don't speak Italian.

that is perhaps the Aeolian's most impressive such feature.

Places to Stay & Eat

The island has a handful of places to stay.

Hotel Phenicusa (☎ 090 988 99 46, fax 090 988 99 55, Via Porto) Singles/doubles €56.80/72.30, half-board €77.45 per person. Open May-Sept. This imposing hotel dominates the port and is quite good, but when you consider what's up the hill, you may only stay here if you need to be close to the ferries and boats or the other places are full. Some rooms have water views and the staff are friendly.

If you don't want to stay in this area, there are other options.

La Canna (☎ 090 988 99 56, fax 090 988 99 66, e vianast@tin.it, Via Rosa 43) Singles/doubles with bathroom €38.75/77.45, half-board €67.15 per person. After a lung-and-leg-busting uphill walk (10 minutes – or arrange to be picked up from the port), this place will seem like paradise, and first impressions last. A beautiful eight-room hotel with a pool, magnificent panoramic views of the sea and some of the best cooking you'll

taste on the islands, we can't recommend this charming place enough. Reservations are definitely advised.

Villa La Rosa (☎ 090 988 99 65, fax 090 988 92 91, e villalarosa@netnet.it, Via Rosa) High season doubles/triples with bathroom €62/90.40, low season about 30% less. Just beyond La Canna at the junction of Via Rosa is Villa La Rosa, a private residence that rents out lovely rooms, all with bathroom and terrace. The food is very good too, and if you're desperate for some – nay, any – type of nightlife, then the disco here is the only place to boogie.

La Sirena (☎ 090 988 99 97, fax 090 988 92 07, e lasirena@netnet.it, Via Pecorini Mare) Singles/doubles with bathroom €36.15/67.15. La Sirena is towards the sea just outside Pecorini, which is a good alternative area to stay while on Filicudi, provided you have transport. The rooms have bathroom, terrace and fan and are nicely decorated. You can also get a good home-cooked meal.

For something to eat, try *Ristorante A'Tana* (☎ 090 988 90 89). To the left as you leave the port, this is a good restaurant, with seafood dishes (meals about €28) and friendly service. You can also try the wonderful restaurant in *La Canna* or *Villa La Rosa* (see above).

Getting There & Away

Filicudi can be tricky to reach for short visits. The intermittent ferry and hydrofoil service is virtually non-existent in winter and in summer can be cancelled due to rough seas. Siremar (☎ 090 988 99 60) and Snav (☎ 090 988 99 84) both have ticket offices on Via Porto, which runs along the port. At the height of summer Filicudi is served by three hydrofoils and one ferry daily. See the Getting Around section at the beginning of this chapter for details.

ALICUDI

postcode 98050 • pop 100 • elevation 675m

When the French novelist Alexandre Dumas visited Alicudi during the 19th century, he wrote to his wife 'it is hard to find a sadder, more dismal and desolate place than this unfortunate island... a corner of the earth forgotten by creation and which has remained unchanged since the days of chaos.' The barren nature of the island clearly was not to Mr Dumas' liking, and in some respects he wasn't far wrong in his description. However, if you're looking to get away from it all and revel in some sun, sea and solitude, Alicudi is the best place for it. The flood of summer tourists to the Aeolian Islands is reduced to a mere trickle on Alicudi.

The island is as isolated a place as you'll find in the entire Mediterranean basin, with minimal facilities (one hotel and two restaurants). For a time it served as the Italian equivalent of Devil's Island, with Mafia prisoners being sent here to serve lengthy prison sentences, but that practice was phased out with the construction of maximum-security prisons on the mainland. Today it is home to a handful of farmers and fishermen who only saw the arrival of electricity and television in the 1990s. The island has no roads to speak of. There are a couple of grocery shops and a post office (☎ 090 988 99 11) by the port that keeps erratic hours; you'll just have to try your luck when you get here.

The doctor can be contacted on ☎ 090 988 99 13.

Things to See & Do

The central peak of the **Filo dell'Arpa** (String of the Harp; 672m) is climbable, a hardy, two-hour trek up a pretty rocky path with a panoramic view at the top. Be sure to wear sturdy shoes and bring plenty of water

as there is absolutely no shade along the way. There is not much else to do save potter around and find a peaceful place to sunbathe – the best spots are to the south of the port, where you will have to clamber over boulders to reach the sea. As you would expect, the waters are crystal clear and there's nothing to disturb you save the occasional hum of a fisherman's boat.

Place to Stay & Eat

Ericusa *(☎ 090 988 99 02, fax 090 988 96 71, Via Regina Elena)* Doubles €62, half-board €59.40 per person. The Ericusa is the only hotel on Alicudi, so reservations are advised. There are 12 rooms here, and it's a nice place to stay. It also has a restaurant, which you'll no doubt eat at if you choose to stay on the island. Unfortunately, it only opens from June to September, making low-season stays on the island almost impossible.

Airone *(☎ 090 988 9922)* Meals about €20. This is the other restaurant option on Alicudi.

Getting There & Away

Alicudi is the most difficult Aeolian island to reach. The intermittent ferry and hydrofoil service is virtually non-existent in winter and in summer can be cancelled due to rough seas. Both Siremar (☎ 090 988 97 95) and Snav (☎ 090 988 99 12) are on Via Regina Elena, which runs parallel to the port. At the height of summer, Alicudi is served by three hydrofoils and one ferry daily. See the Getting Around section at the beginning of this chapter for details.

The Eastern Coast

Squeezed in by the long range of the Peloritani mountains to the west and the narrow strait that separates Sicily from Italy to the east, the thin ribbon of coastline that makes up the island's eastern shore is easily Sicily's most popular tourist destination. At its northern end is Messina, the first port of call for travellers crossing the sliver of water that divides the island from the mainland.

To the south is Catania, point of arrival for many of Sicily's airborne visitors and home to a splendid collection of Baroque churches and *palazzi* (palaces). The most popular destination, however, lies between the two: the beautifully elegant resort of Taormina, a handsome medieval town that was 'discovered' in the 20th century by Europe's elite and adopted as one of their favourite summer playgrounds.

Towering above them all is the mighty peak of Mt Etna (3323m), Europe's largest and most active volcano. It rises southwest of the Peloritani mountains, where you'll find a couple of splendid hill towns that seem entirely unaffected by the advances of the modern age.

Messina & Around

MESSINA
postcode 98100 • pop 270,000
For many, Messina is their point of arrival in Sicily. From the sea, the wide curve of its beautiful harbour promises much, but once you hit dry land you realise that this is not Sicily's most beautiful city. Prosperous and industrialised, Messina is innocent of all charges of ugliness levelled against it as it has been the unfortunate victim of a series of disasters, including two major earthquakes, a few epidemics and a dose of carpet bombing in WWII. Rebuilt after each disaster, Messina is unlike other Sicilian cities that have suffered at the hands of nature and humankind, as the visionary architects and town planners weren't around for the reconstruction.

Highlights

- Play-act in Taormina's Greek Theatre – the most beautifully sited theatre in the world

- Climb marvellous Mt Etna and revel in its extraordinary power

- Wade in the invigorating Gola dell'Alcàntara

- Cross the Straits of Messina, with views of Sicily and mainland Italy competing for your attention

- Paint the town red in bar-filled Catania after a day of sumptuous Baroque sightseeing

- Snorkel, swim and sunbathe at Aci Castello

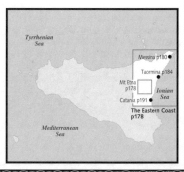

If for any reason you're stuck in Messina, don't despair – the city centre, with its wide avenues and tree-filled piazzas, is not a bad place to wander around, and there remain a couple of vestiges of happier days.

History
Founded as a Siculian settlement in 628 BC, Zankle (meaning sickle, on account of the shape of the bay) was conquered by the Greek Dionysius three centuries later, whereupon its name was changed. Strategically located at the heart of the trading

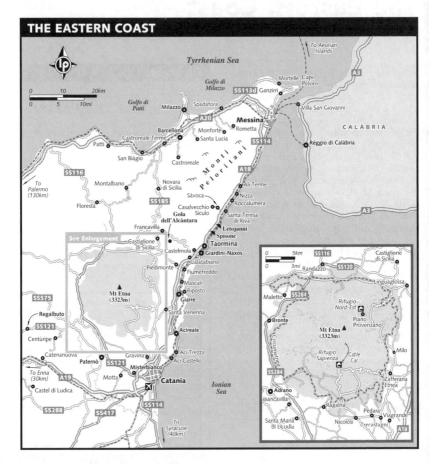

THE EASTERN COAST

routes that linked the four compass points, the city quickly prospered, its role greatly enhanced following the Roman takeover in the 3rd century BC and the construction of two main roads linking the city with Palermo and Catania. Under successive occupants the city continued to grow and, when the Spanish viceroys took charge in the 16th century, Messina was doing a roaring trade in silk, wool and leather. An ambitious building programme was undertaken, but much of the new construction came to a sorry end in 1783, when the area was devastated by an earthquake. In the 19th century

Messina tried again: a regular ferry service was established across the strait and its links with other Sicilian cities improved with the construction of new roads linking the port with Palermo, Catania and Syracuse. This new-found prosperity was short-lived: no sooner had the city reached the 20th century than disaster struck once more.

The earthquake of 1908 killed over 80,000 people and flattened the city. Deflated, demoralised and understandably panicked, city planners opted for safety over aesthetics and began rebuilding with the one objective of making everything quake-proof. Short, squat and solid were the guidelines of the 'Borzi Plan' (devised in 1911 by chief architect Paolo Borzi), and while this did nothing for the overall appearance of Messina (and generated a huge amount of indignant protest), it sought to allay the fears of those who had survived the terrible devastation.

What nature couldn't destroy, however, the human hand could: in 1943 the Allies carpet-bombed the city and once again Messina was forced to rebuild. With such a history of tragedy, it is easy to forgive the unimaginative blandness that characterises some of the city today. Hardly appealing, but safe as houses.

Orientation

The train station is on Piazza della Repubblica, at the southern end of the long waterfront. FS car and truck ferries arrive just north of here. The main intercity bus station is outside the train station, to the left on the square. To get to the city centre from Piazza della Repubblica, walk either straight across the square and directly ahead along Via I Settembre to Piazza del Duomo, or turn left into Via Giuseppe La Farina and take the first right into Via Tommaso Cannizzaro to reach Piazza Cairoli.

Those coming by hydrofoil from Règgio di Calàbria arrive about 1km north of the train station, on Via Vittorio Emanuele II, while drivers on the private car ferry from Villa San Giovanni land 3km farther on, about 500m north of the trade fair area (Fiera).

Information

Tourist Offices There are two tourist offices in Messina that are open year-round. The better-informed, better-equipped provincial APT office (☎ 090 67 42 36) is at Via Calabria 301, on the corner of Via Capra. It opens 8am to 2pm and 3.30pm to 7pm Monday to Saturday from May to October. The city tourist office (☎ 090 293 52 92) is on the 3rd floor at Piazza Cairoli 45. It keeps the same hours as the APT office.

Money There are numerous banks in the city centre between Piazza Repubblica and Piazza Cairoli – most with ATMs – and a currency exchange booth at the timetable information office at the train station.

Post & Communications The main post office is on Piazza Antonello on Corso Cavour, near the cathedral. It opens 8.30am to 6.30pm Monday to Saturday. There are public phones around town and at Piazza Cairoli.

The Paritel Telecommunicazioni centre has phones, plus email and Internet access for €4.15 per hour. It's at Via Centonze 74.

Travel Agencies The CTS student travel group has an agency (☎ 090 292 67 61) at Via Ugo Bassi 93. Lisciotto Viaggi (☎ 090 71 90 01), at Piazza Cairoli 13, can help with hard-to-get theatre tickets for performances at such venues as Taormina's Greek theatre (see Taormina later in this chapter).

Medical Services The public hospital (Ospedale Piemonte) has an emergency section (*pronto soccorso;* ☎ 090 22 43 47) on Viale Europa. There is a 24-hour pharmacy (☎ 090 34 54 22) at the corner of Via Cesare Battisti and Via Camiciotti. A booklet available at the tourist office lists pharmacies open at night on a rotation basis.

Emergency The police station (*questura;* ☎ 090 36 61) is at Via Plàcida 2. The questura for foreigners can be called on ☎ 090 36 65 19.

Things to See

The Norman **cathedral** *(duomo)*, built in the 12th century, was almost completely destroyed by the combined effects of the 1908 earthquake and the bombing in 1943. It was rebuilt virtually from scratch; the fine 15th-century doorway is one of the few original elements. The clock tower houses what is believed to be the world's largest astronomical clock – an intricate bit of machinery that is best appreciated during the noon strike, when its golden figurines put on a show.

The interior of the cathedral is massive, and there are three sets of mosaics in the apses. Only the Madonna mosaic in the left-hand apse is original. The cathedral's **treasury**

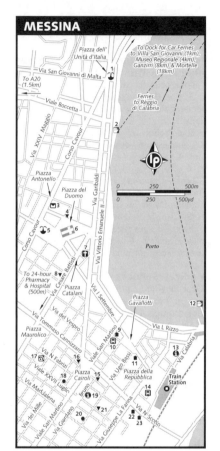

MESSINA

PLACES TO STAY
9   Hotel Cairoli
11 Grand Hotel Liberty
22 Touring
23 Mirage

PLACES TO EAT
4   Shanghai
8   Trattoria Dudù
15 Ristorante Caffè d'Italia
16 Billè
21 Ristorante Casa Savoia

OTHER
1   Fontana del Nettuno
2   Hydrofoil Dock
3   Post Office
5   Fontana di Orione
6   Cathedral
7   Chiesa della Santissima Annunziata dei Catalani
10 Giuntabus Terminus
12 Ferry Dock
13 APT Tourist Office
14 Bus Station & Office
17 Paritel Telecommunicazioni
18 Lisciotto Viaggi
19 City Tourist Office
20 CTS Travel Agency

(☎ 090 67 51 75; admission €2.60; open 9am-1.30pm & 3pm-6.30pm daily Mar-Oct, 9am-noon & 3.30pm-6.30pm daily Nov-Feb), housed to the right of the building as you enter, is a well-laid out arrangement of the cathedral's riches, including silver arms for holding reliquary, various gilt and silver chalices and the famous cloak *(manta)* made by Innocenzo Mangani in 1668, which is used to cover an image of the Madonna della Lettera. The collection's objects date from the early Middle Ages to the 20th century.

In the square facing the cathedral is the **Fontana di Orione** (Orion's Fountain), an elegant 16th-century work by Giovanni Angelo Montorsoli. Built to commemorate the construction of Messina's first aqueduct, the figures that adorn it are intended to represent the Rivers Tiber, Nile, Ebro and Camaro, while the verses carved into the stone allude to water-related themes.

Nearby in Piazza Catalani, off Via Garibaldi, is the 12th-century **Chiesa della Santissima Annunziata dei Catalani**, a jewel of Arab-Norman construction. The statue in front of it is a monument to Don John of Austria, who beat the Turks at the Battle of Lepanto in 1571. At the time of research the church was under scaffolding. Farther north, where Via Garibaldi spills into Piazza dell'Unità d'Italia, is Messina's other great fountain, the 16th-century **Fontana del Nettuno** (Neptune's Fountain).

The **Museo Regionale** *(☎ 090 36 12 92, Viale della Libertà 465; walk from cathedral or bus No 79 or 81 from train station; admission €4.15; open 9am-1.30pm Tues-Sat, 4pm-6.30pm Tues, Thur & Sat, 9am-12.30pm*

Sun) was set up in 1914 to house the works formerly kept in a monastery destroyed by the earthquake of 1908. The gallery's most famous work is the *San Gregorio* (St Gregory) polyptych by local boy Antonello da Messina, born here in 1430. Although in pretty shabby condition, the five panels of the piece are wonderfully figurative. Other highlights include a *Madonna col Bambino e Santi* (Virgin with Child and Saints) by the same artist and two splendid works by Caravaggio, the *Adorazione dei Pecorai* (Adoration of the Shepherds) and *Risurrezione di Lazzaro* (Resurrection of Lazarus). The works in the gallery are all arranged chronologically, and there are sculptures and stone fragments in the surrounding gardens and central courtyard.

Places to Stay
A couple of hotels are close to the train station.

Touring (☎ 090 293 88 51, Via N Scotto 17) Singles/doubles €20.65/36.15, with bathroom €36.15/62. Clean and well run, the Touring is not flash but it's a good base. The management insists on payment in advance.

Mirage (☎ 090 293 88 44, Via N Scotto 3) Singles/doubles €20.65/36.15, doubles with bathroom €46.50. A few doors down the street from Touring is the Mirage. Rooms here are simple and tidy, although the management's a tad gruff.

Hotel Cairoli (☎ 090 67 37 55, Viale San Martino 63) Singles/doubles with bathroom €44.40/72.30. The Cairoli is of a high standard, with good rooms and friendly management.

Royal Palace Hotel (☎ 090 65 03, fax 090 292 10 75, e royal@framon.hotels.it, Via Tommaso Cannizzaro 224) Singles/doubles with bathroom €91.95/121.90. Close to transport and Piazza Cairoli, the 106-room Royal Palace is plush and fancy in a 1970s kind of way. There's parking, wheelchair access and air-conditioning.

Grand Hotel Liberty (☎ 090 640 94 36, fax 090 640 93 40, e ricevimento.liberty@framon.hotels.it, Via I Settembre 15) Singles/doubles with bathroom & breakfast €103.30/154.95. This is the loveliest place to stay in Messina, in a renovated old building with luxurious fittings, helpful staff and all the mod-cons.

Places to Eat
Cheap eats in Messina are not a problem, although many restaurants close for a break in August.

Billè (☎ 090 71 83 11, Piazza Cairoli 5) This excellent *gelateria/pasticceria* (ice-cream/cake shop) is a great place to come, day or night for snacks and sweets. The *tavola calda* (literally 'hot table', basically a self-service counter) dishes are good value too.

Ristorante Caffè d'Italia (☎ 090 69 25 01, Piazza Cairoli 33) Meals around €10. Take the lift up to this cavernous tavola calda, where cheap meals are dished up to the ravenous hordes.

Ristorante Casa Savoia (☎ 090 293 48 65, Via XXVII Luglio 36) Meals around €24. Don't be intimidated by the swanky decor of this restaurant. There's a good €10.50 tourist menu and delicious food. It stays open throughout August, and the wine list offers an island-wide selection, plus wine by the glass.

Trattoria Dudù (☎ 090 67 43 93, Via Cesare Battisti 122) Meals around €24. Closed Sun. The decor's firmly stuck in the era when wood-panelling and cheesy art was king, but the food is fresh. A good plate of *spaghetti alle vongole* (spaghetti with clams) and some white wine soothes any aesthetic nerves.

Shanghai (☎ 090 71 35 28, Piazza del Duomo 4) Meals around €13. Shanghai is certainly not going to be the culinary highlight of your time in Sicily, but this Chinese restaurant opens throughout summer (including August) and locals seem pretty happy to eat here.

Getting There & Away
Bus Interbus (☎ 090 66 17 54) runs a regular service via either the SS114 or the A20 to Taormina (€2.60, 14 daily Monday to Saturday, three Sunday), Catania (via Taormina, Giardini-Naxos, Fiumefreddo, Giarre and Acireale; €6.20, three hours, four daily Monday to Saturday, one Sunday) and Catania's airport. The company's

JANE SMITH

Relaxing by the water on the mid-16th-century Fontana di Orione

Car & Motorcycle If you arrive in Messina by FS ferry with a vehicle (see also the Getting There & Away chapter), it is simple to make your way out of town. For Palermo (or Milazzo and the Aeolian Islands), turn right as you exit the docks and follow Via L Rizzo (which then becomes Via Vittorio Emanuele II) until you get to Piazza dell'Unità d'Italia. From there, go north along Via Garibaldi. After about 1km, turn left into Viale Boccetta and follow the green *autostrada* (motorway) signs for Palermo. To reach Taormina and Syracuse, turn right onto Via L Rizzo and then take the first left onto Via C Vettoragile, which then becomes Via Giuseppe La Farina, and follow. Messina is one Sicilian city that excels in signposting, so you should have no trouble getting in and out of town.

If you arrive by private ferry, turn right along Viale della Libertà for Palermo and Milazzo, and left for Taormina and Catania – follow the green motorway signs. You can also take the SS114 (very busy in summer).

Boat Messina is the main point of arrival for ferries and hydrofoils from the Italian mainland, only a 20-minute trip across the narrow straits. FS runs 20 hydrofoils daily from Monday to Saturday and 10 on Sunday. The 20-minute trip costs €3.10/4.65 single/return. Navigazione Generale Italiana (NGI; ☎ 0335 842 77 84) has car ferries between Messina's port and Règgio di Calàbria every two hours between 12.20am to about 11.15pm. Car tickets start at €7.75. Foot passengers need only pay €0.50.

GANZIRRI
postcode 98100 • pop 170
Only 8km north of Messina and accessible via regular bus Nos 79 and 81 (€0.65, valid for one hour 30 minutes) from Piazza della Repubblica, Ganzirri is a pleasant town that on summer evenings plays host to the crowds of youths from the city, who come to gossip and flirt in the town's bars and restaurants.

Sandwiched as the town is between the sea and a series of brackish ponds that are renowned for their mussels, it's hardly surprising that seafood dominates the menu of the many *trattorie* (small, cheap restaurants) here.

office and bus station are at Piazza della Repubblica 6, to the left as you leave the train station. Interbus also has a direct connection to Rome at 10.45am Tuesday, Thursday and Saturday (€27.40, 9¼ hours).

SAIS buses, also in Piazza della Repubblica, make the journey to Palermo (€12.40, eight daily Monday to Saturday, four Sunday) and Catania and its airport, via the A18 (€6.20, 1½ hours, approximately hourly). Giuntabus (☎ 090 67 37 82) runs a service to Milazzo (for ferries and hydrofoils to the Aeolian Islands) roughly every hour Monday to Saturday (€3.10) from Via Terranova 8, on the corner of Viale San Martino.

Train Frequent *diretto* (direct) trains connect Messina with Catania (1st/2nd class €7/4.90), Taormina (€4.05/2.85), Syracuse (€12.90/8.25), Palermo (€16.30/10.10, 3½ hours, every 30 minutes) and Milazzo (€2.32, one hour, at least 10 daily), but buses are generally faster. The train stations for Milazzo and Taormina are inconveniently located some distance from their respective town centres.

La Terrazza (☎ 090 39 36 26, Via Lago Grande 57) Meals around €18. This is a pretty good place to eat and, yes, there's a terrace.

Il Gambero Rosso (☎ 090 39 38 73, Via Consolare Pompea 143b) Meals around €18. Closed Tues. An excellent choice for those seeking fresh seafood.

MORTELLE
postcode 98100 • pop 240

A farther 10km on from Ganzirri (around the tip of the island) is the area's most popular summer resort, *the* place the Messinese go to sunbathe, hang out and eat. On summer evenings, you can hardly walk around for the number of scooters and motorcycles in the place, while during the day you'll generally have to get down to the beach early if you want to get a good spot. It only takes about 40 minutes to get here by bus from Messina (No 79 or 80 from Piazza della Repubblica).

There are plenty of *pizzerie* (pizza restaurants) and *trattorie* in town and all serve a similar menu of fish-based dishes. There's also one very well-known place with sky-high prices:

Lo Sporting da Alberto (☎ 090 32 13 90, Via Nazionale, SS113) Meals around €42. Closed Mon. Reputed to be the best restaurant in this part of Sicily, it is frequented by Messina's well-to-do crowd. Not surprisingly, it's a good idea to wear your best gear if you want to eat here.

FROM MESSINA TO TAORMINA

The road south from Messina to Taormina offers little in the way of interesting scenery until you're a good 20km out of town – then the suburbs recede, the coastline emerges into full view and on a clear day you can see right across the straits to Calabria. The towns on the coast are nothing special, but there are a couple of worthwhile excursions into the foothills of the Peloritani mountains, which trace a parallel course virtually the entire length of the coast between Messina and Taormina. Regular buses make the journey, but it is slow and laborious going; you're better off taking a train. If you have your own car, you should avoid the busy and slow state road and stick to the A18 motorway. There's a toll, but it's worth it. Beaches worth stopping at include **Spisone** and **Letojanni** – all accessible by bus from Messina or Taormina.

Sàvoca
postcode 98039 • pop 130
elevation 980m

Beautifully situated 4km inland from the grey pebble beaches of Santa Teresa di Riva is this lovely village, little more than a cluster of houses, a couple of medieval churches and the ruins of a castle. The road up to the town winds its way through lemon groves and almond stands, and from the top you have a fine view of the coastline stretched out below.

Signs in Sàvoca show the way to the **Capuchin monastery** located on the outskirts of the village. Inside the monastery, a rickety staircase takes you down to the **catacombs** *(admission by donation; open 9am-1pm & 4pm-7pm Apr-Sept, 9am-noon & 3pm-5pm Oct-Mar)* holding the eerie-looking remains of a number of 18th-century nobles and other local bigwigs who paid good money for this kind of 'immortality'. Interbus buses run between Sàvoca and Santa Teresa di Riva.

If the village seems somehow familiar it is because it was used by Francis Ford Coppola in *The Godfather*, as the setting for Michael Corleone's marriage to Apollonia. At the entrance to the town is the *Bar Vitelli*, also used in the film. This is the place to go for virtually everything in town: the keys to the churches, directions to the monastery and stories of when the Americans came to make 'that film'.

Taormina & Around

TAORMINA
postcode 98039 • pop 10,500
elevation 204m

Sicily's most picturesque town and best-known resort is spectacularly located on a terrace of Mt Tauro, dominating the sea and with views westwards to Mt Etna. A favourite playground of the European jet set, Taormina's high season goes from April through

TAORMINA

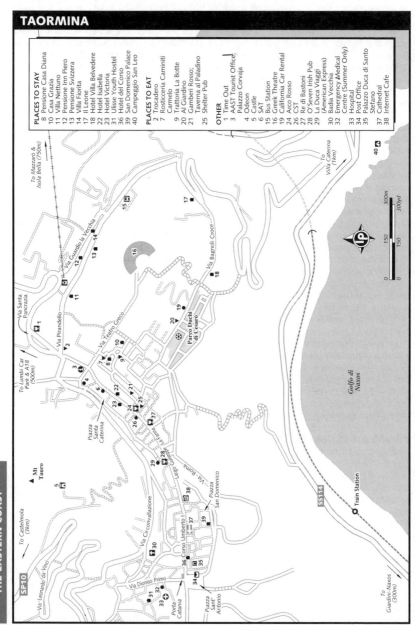

PLACES TO STAY
8 Pensione Casa Diana
10 Casa Grazia
11 Villa Nettuno
12 Pensione Inn Piero
13 Pensione Svizzera
14 Villa Fiorita
17 Il Leone
18 Hotel Villa Belvedere
22 Hotel Isabella
23 Hotel Victoria
31 Ulisse Youth Hostel
36 Hotel del Corso
39 San Domenico Palace
40 Campeggio San Leo

PLACES TO EAT
2 Trocadero
7 Rosticceria Caminiti Carmelo
9 Trattoria La Botte
20 Al Giardino
21 Gamberi Rosso;
   Taverna al Paladino
25 Shelter Pub

OTHER
1 Time Out
3 AAST Tourist Office;
   Palazzo Corvaja
4 Odeon
5 Castle
6 SAT
15 Bus Station
16 Greek Theatre
19 California Car Rental
24 Arco Rosso
26 CST
27 Re di Bastoni
28 O'Seven Irish Pub
29 La Duca Viaggi
   (American Express)
30 Badia Vecchia
32 Emergency Medical
   Centre (Summer Only)
33 Hospital
34 Post Office
35 Palazzo Duca di Santo
   Stefano
37 Cathedral
38 Internet Cafe

to October. Consequently, it can be an expensive place to visit, although its magnificent setting, Greek theatre, beautiful houses and nearby beaches remain as seductive as they were for the likes of Goethe and DH Lawrence. It's such a beautiful spot that you could be forgiven for thinking bougainvillea was created for no other reason than to adorn Taormina, and there are plenty of opportunities to feel short of breath – thanks to the steep roads and stunning vistas.

In July and August the town is *flooded* with tourists; it is difficult to find accommodation and even dining can be a problem. A good time to come is at either end of the busy season, when everything quietens down a little bit; perhaps the best time is towards the end of September, when it is still hot but not nearly as crowded.

History

From its foundation by the Siculians, Taormina remained a favourite destination for the long line of conquerors who followed. Under the Greeks, who moved in after Naxos was destroyed during colonial wars in the 5th century BC, Taormina flourished. It later came under Roman dominion and eventually became the capital of Byzantine Sicily, a period of grandeur that ended abruptly in AD 902 when the town was destroyed by Arab invaders. Throughout the subsequent periods of Norman, Spanish and French rules Taormina was an important centre of art and trade. Despite the heavy influx of tourism, Taormina today retains much of its medieval character.

Orientation

The train station (Taormina-Giardini) is at the foot of Mt Tauro, and you'll need to get an Interbus bus (€1.80 return) up to the bus station (for local and intercity buses – where you'll arrive anyway if you catch the bus from Messina) in Via Pirandello. A short walk uphill from there brings you to the old city entrance and Corso Umberto I, which traverses the town. Departures from the train station are regular (about every 30 minutes between 7.40am and 8.30pm in summer, less frequently in winter).

Information

Tourist Offices The well-stocked, well-informed and super-helpful AAST office (☎ 0942 2 32 43, Ⓦ www.taormina-ol.it) is in Palazzo Corvaja, just off Corso Umberto I, near Piazza Santa Caterina. It opens 8am to 2pm and 4pm to 7pm Monday to Saturday and 9am to 1pm on Sunday.

Money There are numerous banks with multi-language ATMs in Taormina, mostly along Corso Umberto I. You'll also find currency exchange places along the same street. Check the commissions they charge. American Express is represented by La Duca Viaggi (☎ 0942 62 52 55), Via Don Bosco 39.

Post & Communications The main post office is on Piazza Sant'Antonio, just outside Porta Catania, at the far end of Corso Umberto I from the tourist office. It opens from 8.30am to 6.40pm Monday to Saturday and 8.30am to 1.40pm Sunday. There are public telephones all over town and in many bars.

For email and Internet access, the Internet Cafe (☎ 0942 62 88 39) is at Corso Umberto I 214. Access costs €2.60 for 20 minutes and €5.15 for an hour. It opens 10am to 10pm daily.

Medical Services There is a free 24-hour medical service (☎ 0942 62 54 19) for tourists in Piazza San Francesco di Paola from 1 July to 30 September. Ospedale San Vincenzo (☎ 0942 5 37 45) is on Piazza San Vincenzo, just outside Porta Catania.

Emergency The *carabinieri* (military police; ☎ 0942 2 31 05) are at Piazza Badia 4. For an ambulance call the Ospedale San Vincenzo (see Medical Services).

Things to See

Taormina's most famous sight is undoubtedly the heavenly **Greek theatre** *(Teatro Greco; admission €4.15; open 9am-7pm Apr-Oct, 9am-4.30pm Nov-Mar)* at the end of Via Teatro Greco off Corso Umberto I. Built in the 3rd century BC, it was heavily remodelled in the 1st century AD by the

Romans, so what you see is pretty much a Roman structure. The Greeks had originally intended to make the most of the breathtaking views of Mt Etna and the Bay of Schisò, but this view was partially obscured during the rebuilding by a set of arches and columns – luckily these have largely collapsed, once again revealing the stunning panorama. Furthermore, the Romans considered the sword mightier than the pen, so the stage and orchestra pit, which once played host to the great tragedies of antiquity, were demolished and converted into a circular arena given over to gladiator fighting. The structure has been much tampered with over the centuries – the family of the Spanish Costanza d'Aragona built its home over part of the theatre (to the right as you face the stage) in the 12th century. However, it remains a most atmospheric place. In July and August the theatre hosts a well-respected international arts festival (see Special Events later in this chapter).

Parco Duchi di Cesarò, also known as the Trevelyan Garden, is a Victorian folly created for Lady Florence Trevelyan Cacciola (1852–1907). The rich flora includes magnolias, hibiscus, bougainvillaea, cacti and a variety of trees including olive, palm, cypress and cedar. A beehive-shaped aviary, a children's playground and tennis courts complete the picture. Perfect for picnicking on a summer's day, the gardens afford some glorious views over the bay below.

Back in the town centre is the **Odeon**, a small Roman theatre, badly preserved and partly covered by the adjoining Chiesa di Santa Caterina. It was discovered and excavated in the late 19th century and is believed to have been erected on the site of a Greek temple of Apollo. Taormina's **cathedral**, in the Piazza del Duomo along Corso Umberto I, was built in the early 15th century.

There are several mansions in Taormina, including the **Palazzo Corvaja**. Begun by the Arabs as a defence tower in the 11th century, it was extended several times and includes halls dating from the 14th and 15th centuries. Today it is home to the tourist office. The **Palazzo Duca di Santo Stefano**, at the other end of town, is an important example of Sicilian Gothic architecture, with a fanciful mix of Arab and Norman styles. The nearby **Badia Vecchia** (Old Abbey) is a 14th-century Gothic building, again with Norman-Arab elements.

Just wandering along the main drag, Corso Umberto I, you can see a smattering of stately old buildings, some dating from the 15th century.

The peak of Mt Tauro is adorned by the lonely, windswept ruins of the town's medieval **castle**, 500m from the town centre along the road to Castelmola (see Castelmola later in this chapter), or accessible by climbing the linking stairs. The views are great.

You can reach the beaches at **Isola Bella** and **Mazzarò** directly under Taormina by cable car (*funivia*), which runs from 8.30am to 8.15pm daily in winter and 8.30am to 1.30am daily in summer (€2.60 return) from Via Pirandello. Both beaches are largely taken up by private operators (a space with deck chairs and umbrella costs around €10.50 a day), but there is some space for free bathing. Interbus buses also connect the beaches with the upper town (€1.30).

Organised Tours

CST (☎ 0942 62 60 88, Corso Umberto I 101) CST runs good-value excursions to destinations including Mt Etna (€23.25), sunset and dinner tours to Mt Etna (€51.65), Agrigento (€36.15), Syracuse (€33.60), Piazza Armerina (with the Roman Villa, Casale and Caltagirone, €31), Palermo (with Monreale, €38.75), Randazzo (with Maniace, Bronte and Alcantara, €25.80) and Lipari and Vulcano in the Aeolian Islands (€43.90). Prices exclude admission to museums and archaeological sites.

Sicilian Airbus Travel (SAT, ☎ 0942 2 46 53, ⓔ info@sat-group.it, ⓦ www.sat-group .it, Corso Umberto I 73) This agent runs tours to Agrigento, Mt Etna, the Aeolian Islands, Palermo and Piazza Armerina for roughly the same prices as CST.

Special Events

Theatre and music concerts are organised throughout the summer during Taormina Arte, a good international arts festival that runs from July to August. Ask at the tourist office or visit the Web site (W www .taormina-arte.com). Other events worth catching are the summer concerts and plays held for Eventi d'Estati (☎ 0942 2 32 43) in August and September. You can purchase tickets from €12.90 at the booth at Piazza Vittorio Emanuele, or visit the Web site (W www.eventidestate.com – Italian only). The Reunion of Sicilian Costumes and Carts (Raduno del Costume e del Carretto Siciliano), featuring parades of traditional Sicilian carts and folkloric groups, is usually held in autumn – ask at the tourist office.

Places to Stay

Taormina has plenty of accommodation, but in summer you should definitely book in advance as rooms fill rapidly, particularly during August. In winter prices are reduced.

Camping *Campeggio San Leo (☎ 0942 2 46 58, Via Nazionale)* €4.15/14.45 per person/ tent. You can camp near the beach at this site at Capo Taormina. There are no facilities to speak of other than a spot to pitch a tent. You can get here from the train station by the bus to Taormina – the bus driver will stop at the camp site's entrance if you ask.

Hostels *Ulisse Youth Hostel (☎/fax 0942 2 31 93, Vico San Francesco di Paola 9)* Dorm bed & breakfast €14.45. This is the cheapest place to stay in Taormina's town centre, and it's a very well run place too. There are 28 beds and cheap meals (€7.75) – book ahead in August!

Private Homes & Apartments The cheapest option in Taormina is to go for a room in a private house, some of which also include breakfast in the cost. The tourist office has a full list, and can help you by calling the owner, if necessary.

Pensione Casa Diana (☎ 0942 2 38 98, Via D Giovanni 6) Doubles with bathroom €41.35. The lovely Signora Diana has only four rooms, and at these prices, they're often taken, but it's worth a try. It's close to the Greek theatre and the tourist office, plus all the shops on Corso Umberto I.

Il Leone (☎/fax 0942 2 38 78, Via Bagnoli Croce 127) Singles/doubles without bathroom €18.10/41.30. Il Leone is near the Trevelyan Garden. Some rooms have terraces and great views of the sea, although the rooms themselves are bog-ordinary, as are the bathrooms.

Casa Grazia (☎/fax 0942 24 47 76, Via Lallia Bassia 20) Singles/doubles without bathroom €18.10/41.30. Open Apr-Oct. This is a no-frills budget option and is also close to the Trevelyan Garden.

Hotels There are dozens of hotels in town to suit (virtually) every taste.

Pensione Svizzera (☎ 0942 2 37 90, fax 0942 62 59 06, e svizzera@tao.it, Via Pirandello 26) Singles/doubles with bathroom €51.65/82.65. The Svizzera, on the way from the bus station to the town centre, has simple, pleasant rooms in an unmissable pink building. Rates include breakfast and prices really drop outside summer.

Pensione Inn Piero (☎ 0942 2 31 39, fax 0942 2 32 11, Via Pirandello 20) Singles/ doubles with bathroom €51.65/72.30. This small place has simple, comfortable rooms.

Hotel del Corso (☎ 0942 62 86 98, fax 0942 62 98 56, e hoteldelcorso@itscalnet .it, Corso Umberto I 238) Singles/doubles with bathroom €82.65/123.95. A good location and attractive rooms make this a very good choice, especially in the low season, when prices drop.

Villa Nettuno (☎ 0942 2 37 97, Via Pirandello 33) Singles/doubles with bathroom €38.75/62. The Nettuno is in front of the cable car station, in a lovely building that's also very close to the bus station.

Villa Fiorita (☎ 0942 2 41 22, fax 0942 62 59 67, Via Pirandello 39) Doubles with bathroom €106. A few doors down from the Nettuno, this is one of Taormina's nicest mid-range hotels. It is well furnished and comfortable, with a garden, swimming pool, and rooms with balconies and sea views – although only double rooms are available.

Hotel Isabella (☎ 0942 2 31 55, e isabella@gaishotels.com, Corso Umberto I 58) Doubles with bathroom €132. Right in the midst of Taormina's main drag, the seriously good-looking Isabella is well fitted out for the needs of guests wanting to be pampered.

Hotel Victoria (☎ *0942 2 33 72, Corso Umberto 1 81)* Singles/doubles with bathroom €43.90/77.50. Close to everything, this friendly place has good solid rooms and reasonable prices.

Hotel Villa Belvedere (☎ *0942 2 37 91, fax 0942 62 58 30,* e *info@villabelvedere.it, Via Bagnoli Croce 79)* Singles/doubles with bathroom & breakfast €86.25/130.15. The jaw-droppingly beautiful Villa Belvedere has a great swimming pool and garden, and all rooms with balconies face Mt Etna. Even the breakfast room here is something special. Highly recommended if you plan on treating yourself.

San Domenico Palace (☎ *0942 2 37 01, fax 0942 62 55 06,* e *san-domenico@thl.it, Piazza San Domenico 5)* Singles/doubles with bathroom €242.75/413.20. If none of the above appeal you can bask in the luxury offered by the San Domenico Palace, the town's grandest and most famous hotel. The views may be unsurpassed but so are the prices, although they do drop a bit outside of 'the season'.

Villa Caterina (☎/fax *0942 2 47 09,* e *villacaterina@tao.it, Via Nazionale 155)* Singles/doubles with bathroom €43.90/ 72.30. If you want to stay near the beach at Mazzarò, try the Caterina, which has pleasant rooms and is the best one-star option for this location.

Places to Eat

Many of the cafes on Corso Umberto I charge extortionately in the high season, so if you want to sit outside with your cappuccino, have about €3 ready.

Shelter Pub (*Via Fratelli Bandiera 10)* Meals around €7.75. For a light meal and pizza try the Shelter, off Corso Umberto I.

Trocadero (*Via Pirandello 1)* Pizzas €4.65-6.70. Next to Porta Messina and a busy intersection, this is not the place for a quiet meal – however, the pizzas are excellent and well priced.

Gambero Rosso (☎ *0942 2 48 63, Via Naumachie 11)* Meals around €13. When we

popped in at 8.15pm, the place was *packed* – always a good sign. The pizza here is very good, with fast and fuss-free service. The outdoor steps are a pleasant place to dine, but the few tables tend to get taken quickly.

Taverna al Paladino (☎ *0942 2 46 14, Via Naumachie 21)* Meals around €21. With a good menu, friendly staff and a nice atmosphere, this place gets popular every night of the week in the high season.

Trattoria La Botte (☎ *0942 2 41 98, Piazza San Domenica 4)* Meals around €18. Cosy indoors and charming outdoors, this popular haunt does the Sicilian standards quickly and competently.

Al Giardino (☎ *0942 2 34 53, Via Bagnoli Croce 84)* Meals around €24. With its walls painted with flowers and a friendly, family-run atmosphere, this is a good choice if you want to avoid the bustling main street. Wine only comes by the bottle or carafe.

Rosticceria Caminiti Carmelo (*Via di Giovanni 23)* Pizza slice about €1.55. This takeaway shop has truly mouth-watering slices of pizza to go. If you want to take them back to your hotel, they'll happily wrap them up for you.

There are several gourmet *grocery shops* along Corso Umberto I and in the side streets between Via Teatro Greco and the public gardens.

Entertainment

Re di Bastoni (☎ *0942 2 30 37, Corso Umberto 1 120)* With live music, a piano, charming staff and a wicked CD collection, this place is a good spot to start, spend or finish a night.

Arco Rosso (*Via Naumachia 7)* This fantastic low-key bar mixes a mean gin and tonic, while the old-school barman whistles while he works. Delightful!

Time Out (*Via San Pancrazio 19)* This is a decent little bar and eatery, with good Guinness and a beer garden.

O'Seven Irish Pub (*Largo Giuseppe La Farina)* Snacks about €2.60-5.20. Just near the Toreo di Orologio (clock tower), this is a pleasant pub with outdoor seating – perfect for watching the *passeggiata* (evening stroll).

Shopping

You name it, Taormina's shopkeepers will sell it to you, if it's in any way Sicilian, touristy and expensive. This is where you can get everything, including high-quality ceramic goods, lace and linen tablewares, antique furniture and jewellery. Corso Umberto I is where the bulk of the shops are, but a wander through any of the streets nearby will turn up something that catches your shopper's eye. Via Teatro Greco has plenty of shops selling ceramics and lacework. Most staff in these stores have a smattering of French, German, English and Japanese. Shops in Taormina tend to stay open late (until around 10pm) and can often arrange packing and shipping to your home address (for a fee).

Getting There & Away

Bus This is the easiest means of reaching Taormina. Interbus (☎ 0942 62 53 01) services leave for Messina (€2.60, 1½ hours) and Catania (€3.90, 1½ hours) at least hourly from about 6am to 7pm. There are also numerous services to towns along the Ionian coast and the towns surrounding Taormina.

Train There are also regular trains but the awkward location of Taormina's station is a strong disincentive. If you arrive this way, catch an Interbus bus up to the town. They run roughly every 30 to 90 minutes (much less frequently on Sunday). Bear in mind that in summer, the bus pulls up close to full, so you may have to wait for the next one. Trains from Taormina to Messina depart every 30 minutes to one hour (€2.85, one hour). From Taormina to Catania is just as regular (€2.60, 45 minutes).

Car & Motorcycle Taormina is on the A18 motorway and SS114 between Messina and Catania. Parking can be a problem in Taormina, particularly in summer. The Lumbi car park (north of the town centre) is open 24 hours daily and there is a shuttle service to the centre from Porta Messina.

California (☎ 0942 2 37 69), Via Bagnoli Croce 86, rents out cars and motorcycles at reasonable prices, plus some kind added extras, such as unlimited kilometres, free child seats and hotel drop-off. A Fiat Punto with air-conditioning costs €72/328 per day/week. A Vespa 125 costs €31/194.

CASTELMOLA

postcode 98039 • pop 1120
elevation 529m

Perched above Taormina at the end of a (sometimes precipitous) 5km scenic route up the mountain, Castelmola is thought to have been the site of an ancient acropolis called the Tauromenion. The ruins of a medieval castle now stand in its place, with impressive views of the surrounding countryside, towns and sea. There is little to do here other than sample the local *vino alla mandorla* (almond wine), but the views from the tiny town are breathtaking. One eye-catching bar is the ceramic-penis-decorated *Bar Turrisi* (signposted throughout town), which is a good place to grab a drink and revel in Sicily's only antidote to the breast-obsessed Italian media.

Interbus buses make (almost) hourly runs daily from the terminal at Taormina (€1.80 return), though services stop between about 11am and 2pm, and 4pm and 7pm. If you're coming by car, you can park near the bus stop (cars are not allowed in the centre) from €1.55.

GIARDINI-NAXOS

postcode 98039 • pop 8600

This small town 5km south of Taormina is a popular alternative to the resort town for accommodation and has one of the nicest beaches on the eastern coast. The AAST tourist office (☎ 0942 5 10 10, W www.aast-giardini.naxos.it) is at Via Tysandros 54. It opens 8.30am to 2pm and 4.30pm to 7.30pm Monday to Saturday and can help you with accommodation lists and handy maps of the area.

Giardini-Naxos is also the site of the first Greek settlement in Sicily. According to legend, the Greeks had stayed well clear of the Sicilian coastline, believing it to be inhabited by monsters and savages. This belief was encouraged by Phoenicians eager to keep the Greeks away from the western Mediterranean, but when the Athenian

Theocles was shipwrecked along the eastern shore he found that the stories were untrue. He returned soon after with a group of Chalcidian settlers and the town of Naxos was founded in 735 BC. Allied to Athens, the colony did not survive an attack by the Syracusan tyrant Dionysius in 403 BC.

The ruins are not nearly as impressive as those in other Sicilian excavations. Apart from a 300m-stretch of wall, a small temple and a couple of other structures, the best part of a visit is to simply amble through the lemon groves. A small **museum** (*☎ 0942 5 10 01, Via Schisò; admission €2.10; open 9am-7pm daily*) has bits and bobs uncovered during the excavation.

Regular Interbus buses leave from the Taormina bus station on Via Pirandello for Giardini-Naxos. To get to the town from its train station, turn left as you exit the station and follow the signs for about 10 minutes.

Places to Stay & Eat
Giardini-Naxos is chock-full of accommodation. If you want to be close to the sea, try the following.

Hotel La Riva (*☎ 0942 5 13 20, fax 0942 5 13 29, Via Tysandros 52*) Singles/doubles with bathroom €46.50/56.80. Three-star La Riva is in a good waterfront position and has nice rooms with TV, fridge and air-conditioning.

Hotel Tritone (*☎ 0942 5 14 68, fax 0942 5 13 26, Via Tysandros 22*) Singles/doubles with bathroom €62/104. The three-star Tritone has water views and good rooms with air-conditioning and phone.

Giardini-Naxos is also full of cheap *restaurants*, most of which are along the waterfront.

La Cambusa (*☎ 0942 5 14 37, Via Schisò 3*) Pizza €2.60-7.75. With sea views, ocean breezes and a good list of pizzas, this is one of the town's better choices.

ALCÀNTARA VALLEY
A relatively short drive up the winding SS185 from Naxos will get you to this series of modest but interesting lava gorges known as Gola dell'Alcàntara (derived from the Arabic *al cantara*, meaning

bridge), a few kilometres short of Francavilla. You could stop off here on your way to Mt Etna. Otherwise, Interbus has buses from Taormina to Gola dell'Alcàntara and Francavilla (€4.40 return, one hour, three daily Monday to Saturday).

There is lift access and entrance to the gorges (€2.10), and you can hire wading boots (€5.15), which you'll need if you want to do anything more than peer into them or take a brief (but very invigorating) dip in the water; otherwise, take your swimming costume. The water is freezing cold here, even in summer, so prolonged immersion is not a good idea. It is also possible to reach the gorges by the stairs on the main road, 200m uphill from the lift entrance. It's ill-advised to enter the gorges from around November through to May because of the risk of unexpected floods.

Ten kilometres farther on from the Gola dell'Alcàntara (take a left at Francavilla and proceed for another 5km) is the medieval hill town **Castiglione di Sicilia** that grew up around the **Castel Leone** (Castle of the Lion), which was built by the Normans in the 12th century. The castle is wedged in a high crevice from where there are commanding views of the surrounding countryside. For the visitor unconcerned with the potential for a frontal attack, the best view is of the town itself and its many bell towers. You'll need your own transport to get here.

Catania & Around

CATANIA
postcode 95100 • pop 376,000
Sicily's second city has long been in the shadow of the capital, Palermo, and for even longer in the shadow of Sicily's most ominous natural presence, Mt Etna. Ignored and overlooked for centuries in favour of the 'other' city as the seat of power on the island, Catania has been the unwelcome focus of Etna's awesome power for thousands of years. Its role as a busy industrial and commercial city, combined with the chaotic traffic and its reputation as a centre of petty crime, has hardly done it any favours and it

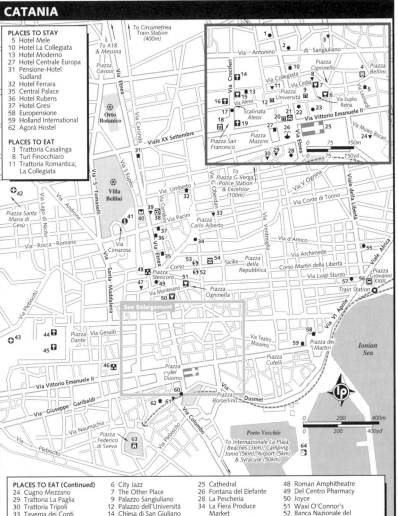

CATANIA

PLACES TO STAY
5 Hotel Mele
10 Hotel La Collegiata
13 Hotel Moderno
27 Hotel Centrale Europa
31 Pensione-Hotel
  Sudland
32 Hotel Ferrara
35 Central Palace
36 Hotel Rubens
37 Hotel Gresi
58 Europensione
59 Holland International
62 Agorà Hostel

PLACES TO EAT
3 Trattoria Casalinga
8 Turi Finocchiaro
11 Trattoria Romantica;
  La Collegiata

PLACES TO EAT (Continued)
24 Cugno Mezzano
29 Trattoria La Paglia
30 Trattoria Tripoli
33 Taverna dei Conti
39 Savia
47 Trattoria Tipica
  Catanese
61 Bar Etoile D'Or

OTHER
1 La Duca Viaggi
  (American Express)
2 CIT; Sestante Club
  Vacanze
4 Teatro Massimo Bellini

6 City Jazz
7 The Other Place
9 Palazzo Sangiuliano
12 Palazzo dell'Università
14 Chiesa di San Giuliano
15 Nievski Pub
16 Chiesa di San
  Benedetto
17 Arco di San Benedetto
18 Museo Belliniano
19 Chiesa di San
  Francesco
20 Palazzo del Municipio
21 Taxi Rank
22 Exchange Office
23 Badia di Sant'Agata

25 Cathedral
26 Fontana del Elefante
28 La Pescheria
34 La Fiera Produce
  Market
38 RAS Phone Centre
40 Post Office
41 APT Tourist Office
42 Ospedale Garibaldi
43 Ospedale Vittorio
  Emanuele
44 Chiesa di San Nicolò
  all'Arena
45 Monastero di San
  Nicolò all'Arena
46 Roman Theatre; Odeon

48 Roman Amphitheatre
49 Del Centro Pharmacy
50 Joyce
51 Waxi O'Connor's
52 Banca Nazionale del
  Lavoro & ATM
53 Deutsche Bank & ATM
54 Telecom Office
55 SAIS & Interbus-Etna
  Transporti Offices
56 Intercity Bus Station; Taxi Rank
57 AST Office
60 Porta Uzeda
63 Castello Ursino;
  Civic Museum
64 Ferry Terminal

THE EASTERN COAST

can sometimes appear an uninviting and intimidating place on arrival (the ugly location of the train and bus stations doesn't help), but it really does merit the benefit of the doubt. In the best tradition of Sicily, Catania has managed to turn disaster to its advantage, and the reconstruction that followed the devastating earthquake of 1693 heralded the building of an elegant Baroque centre using Etna's weapon as a building block: lava. Catania is also well served by hotels and *pensioni* (guesthouses), and the food is good and cheaper than at most places on the coast. Another pleasant aspect for visitors is the revelation that Catania is *not* as dangerous as some reports depict it. As long as you're mindful of your possessions on some of the more crowded public buses, you should have no problems.

History

According to Thucydides, the Chalcidians founded a settlement here in 729 BC and called it Katane. For 300 years it was engaged in a bitter rivalry with Syracuse over control of the region, before it was sacked by the Romans in 263 BC. Occupied in turn by the Byzantines (AD 535), the Saracens (878) and the Normans (1091), by the mid-17th century Catania was a relatively prosperous urban centre with a sophisticated trading relationship with its surrounding hinterland and the rest of the island. The city had been a victim of Etna's eruptions many times over the previous 2000 years, but the eruption of 1669 covered most of Catania in boiling lava and left the centre a mess of ruined streets and uninhabitable buildings. The countryside, so instrumental in providing food for the city's people, was almost completely destroyed and Catania's citizens were left virtually starving. But worse was to come. The earthquake of 1693 finished off the job begun by Mt Etna and the city was left in ruins. Disease and famine were rampant and the streets were awash with penniless refugees fighting over morsels of bread.

The following year Giuseppe Lanza, duke of Camastra, organised a committee whose brief was to rebuild the city with a view towards minimising the potential damage of another eruption. Under the supervision of architects Giovani Vaccarini and Stefano Ittar, a new street grid was created that allowed for spacious squares and streets of differing widths, all of which would provide escape routes and greater shelter when Etna stirred once more. In keeping with the dominant architectural style of the period, the new city was strictly Baroque in appearance. Despite years of neglect that have left many of Catania's elegant palaces and churches in decay, the modern city is an attractive place to wander, even if the use of the dark lava stone gives it a severe, dour look, especially in winter.

Orientation

The main train station and intercity bus terminal are a 15-minute walk east of the city centre, near the port on Piazza Giovanni XXIII. South of the square, Via Vittorio Emanuele II runs east–west through the heart of the city, while Via Etnea runs north from Piazza del Duomo. Most sights are concentrated around and west of Piazza del Duomo, while the commercial centre of Catania is farther north, around Via Pacini and Via Umberto I.

Information

Tourist Offices The APT office (☎ 095 730 62 22 or 095 31 64 07, e apt@ apt.catania.it, w www.apt.catania.it – Italian only) is at Via Cimarosa 10–12. It opens 9am to 7pm Monday to Saturday. There are branches at the train station (☎ 095 730 62 55) on platform No 1, open the same hours, and at the airport (☎ 095 730 62 66), open 8am to 10pm daily.

Money Banks are concentrated along Corso Sicilia, including the Deutsche Bank and Banca Nazionale del Lavoro, both with reliable ATMs; they open 8.30am to 1.30pm and 2.30pm to 4pm Monday to Friday. Several have currency exchange offices. There are also banks with ATMs on Via Etnea. There is a currency exchange office at the train station and another one in Piazza Università. American Express is represented by

La Duca Viaggi (☎ 095 31 61 55), Via Etnea 63–65.

Post & Communications The main post office is at Via Etnea 215, between Via Pacini and Via Umberto I. The Telecom office, Corso Sicilia 67, opens 9am to 1pm and 4pm to 7.30pm Monday to Saturday.

For email and Internet access, RAS Phone Centre (☎ 095 32 64 98), at Via Corridoni 1b, charges €5.15 per hour. It opens 9am to 7pm daily. Nievski Pub (☎ 095 715 12 84), Scalinata Alessi 15–17, has a couple of terminals that you can log on to from 7pm to 4am daily (€5.15 per hour).

Travel Agencies There is a CIT travel agency (☎ 095 31 35 77) at Via Antonino di Sangiuliano 205 and a Sestante Club Vacanze travel agency (☎ 095 31 35 17) at No 208.

Medical Services In a medical emergency, go to the Ospedale Vittorio Emanuele (☎ 095 743 54 52), Via Plebiscito 628, off Via Vittorio Emanuele II, or try the Ospedale Garibaldi (☎ 095 759 43 66), at Piazza Santa Maria di Gesù 5–7. Del Centro (☎ 095 31 36 85) is an all-night pharmacy at Via Etnea 107 and is open year-round except August. A number of chemists also open at night on a rotational basis – ask at the tourist office for details.

Emergency The police station (*questura*; ☎ 095 736 71 11) is at Piazza San Nicolella 8. The carabinieri (☎ 095 53 78 22) are at Piazza Giovanni Verga 8.

Piazza del Duomo & Around

Catania's central square was redesigned following the earthquake of 1693, replacing the original square known as the *platea magna* (main square). The city's main thoroughfares – Via Etnea and Via Vittorio Emanuele II – converge at Piazza del Duomo, which is also the centre of the Catania's ecclesiastical and political power. At its centre is the remarkable **Fontana del Elefante** (Fountain of the Elephant), designed in 1736 by Vaccarini. This curious piece combines a lava-stone elephant dating from Roman times with an Egyptian obelisk carved with hieroglyphics describing the worship of the goddess Isis. At the top is a sphere bearing the insignia of St Agatha, the city's patron. Vaccarini successfully mixes pagan and Christian symbolism in an almost humorous-looking whole, a much-needed slice of optimism considering the tragedy that had befallen the city only a few years earlier.

Vaccarini also remodelled the **cathedral** *(free; open 8am-noon & 5pm-7pm daily)*, originally built by Count Roger in the 11th century on the ruins of the Roman baths. It was a case of third time lucky for the church, as it had been destroyed by lava in 1169 and again by the earthquake of 1693. Vaccarini created an ornate Baroque facade with two orders of columns taken from the Roman amphitheatre (see Along Via Etnea later in this section). The interior is no less sumptuous and features a number of chapels, including one dedicated to St Agatha that contains all the relics paraded through the city on her feast day (5 February). Inside the main entrance, to the right, is the tomb of the city's native composer, Vincenzo Bellini (1801–35).

The northern side of the square is dominated by another Vaccarini creation, the **Palazzo del Municipio** (town hall), with the ubiquitous Baroque facade. In keeping with the square's central theme, it is also known as the Palazzo degli Elefanti. Across Via Vittorio Emanuele II from the cathedral is the **Badia di Sant'Agata** *(free; Convent of St Agatha; open 8am-5pm Mon-Fri)*, yet another Vaccarini masterpiece, whose cupola dominates the city centre. The interior was heavily ornamented after Vaccarini's death.

A few blocks northeast of the cathedral you will stumble into Piazza Bellini. The **Teatro Massimo Bellini** *(☎ 095 730 61 11, Via Perrotta 12,* W *www.teatromassimo bellini.com – Italian only)* is an eye-catching example of the city's architectural richness. If you fancy catching opera here (the acoustics are superb), ask at the tourist office or visit the theatre's Web site.

West along Via Vittorio Emanuele II, at No 266, is the entrance to the substantial ruins of the **Roman theatre**, built in the 2nd

THE EASTERN COAST

The Master of Song

In his short life (he died when he was 34) Vincenzo Bellini composed 10 operas, including the trio that made his fame: *La Sonnambula* (The Sleepwalker), *I Puritani* (The Puritans) and *Norma*. Unlike his bel canto contemporaries, Bellini refused to rely on the tried-and-tested seductive melodies that made such hits out of operas like Rossini's *Il Barbiere di Siviglia* (The Barber of Seville) and Donizetti's *Lucia di Lamermoor*. Unperturbed by the ease with which his fellow composers reeled off operas (Rossini wrote an average of one opera every two weeks!), Bellini tried to write works that didn't rely on pretty melodies at the expense of a well-crafted story. Although successful during his short career, Bellini's style fell out of favour after his death and his operas struggled for recognition until the 1950s and the revival of the bel canto style. Wagner, however, had recognised Bellini's genius and wrote that his music was 'strongly felt and intimately wound up with the words', a powerful emotional combination brought to dramatic life by Maria Callas in her 1953 performance in the title role of *Norma*.

century AD on the site of an earlier Greek theatre (so sometimes called 'Teatro Greco'). At one time it could accommodate an audience of 7000. Next door is the smaller **Odeon** *(combined admission for theatre & Odeon €2.10; both open 9am-1pm & 3pm-7pm)*, a rehearsal theatre that was used for chorus rehearsals and competitions.

Castello Ursino

If you walk south from Piazza del Duomo, through the impressive **Porta Uzeda** (built in 1696) and down to Piazza Federico di Sveva, you'll come across the imposing fortifications of this 13th-century castle built by Frederick II. The grim-looking fortress, surrounded by a moat, was once on a cliff top overlooking the sea; following the earthquake of 1693 the whole area to the south was reclaimed and the castle became landlocked. Inside is the **Civic Museum** *(☎ 095 34 58 30; admission €4.15; castle & museum*

open 9am-1pm & 3pm-6pm Mon-Sat, 9am-12.30pm Sun), which includes finds from the Roman era up to the 18th century.

Along Via Crociferì

The city's most interesting street is probably Via Crociferì, which runs north from Piazza Mazzini (west of Piazza del Duomo) alongside Via Etnea. At the southern end of Via Crociferì, on the western side of the small Piazza San Francesco, is the **Museo Belliniano** *(☎ 095 715 05 35; free; open 9am-1.30pm Mon-Sat, 9am-12.30pm Sun & hols)*, the home of Vincenzo Bellini, now a small museum with a good collection of the composer's memorabilia, including original scores, photographs and his death mask.

Opposite the museum is the 18th-century **Chiesa di San Francesco**. Just up the street is the **Arco di San Benedetto**, an arch built by the Benedictines in 1704. According to legend, the arch was built in one night as the order sought to defy a city ordnance against its construction on the grounds that it was a seismic liability. On the left past the arch is the imposing **Chiesa di San Benedetto**, built between 1704 and 1713. Inside there is some splendid stucco and marble work.

On the right-hand side about halfway up the street is the **Chiesa di San Giuliano**, designed by Vaccarini and built between 1738 and 1751. The convex central facade makes for an interesting effect. Farther on you will surely notice the notable excavations that have resulted in the whole street being closed off to traffic: here, at the crossroads with Via Antonino di Sangiuliano, a section of the old Roman road and a sizable floor mosaic have been uncovered and are in the process of being excavated. You can peer over the hoarding to take a look.

Chiesa di San Nicolò all'Arena

Directly opposite Chiesa di San Giuliano is the small Via Gesuiti, which leads west to Piazza Dante and Sicily's largest church. Commissioned in 1687, work on the building was interrupted by the earthquake of 1693 and then by problems with its size – it is 105m long, 48m wide and its cupola is 62m high. Consequently, the church was never completed. It has a sombre-looking facade, a stark contrast to the rich embellishments that adorn the city's other Baroque structures. The cavernous interior is equally devoid of frills, the long walls interrupted by a series of altars that are almost completely bare. The presbytery features a splendid organ crafted by Donato del Piano. Unfortunately, it is impossible for the time being to climb up the tambour of the cupola, which provides some of the best views of the surrounding region, including Etna and across the straits to Règgio di Calàbria.

Directly behind the church, and part of the same complex, is the old and massive Benedictine **Monastero di San Nicolò all'Arena**, built in 1703 and now part of the city's university. The monastery is currently under restoration, so you may not be able to get in to take a look at the lovely courtyards.

Along Via Etnea

The city's main north–south artery runs from Piazza del Duomo right up through the city and into the foothills of Mt Etna, but visitors need only concern themselves with the short stretch between the cathedral to the south and the elegant gardens of Villa Bellini to the north. East off Via Etnea, about 200m north of the cathedral, is Piazza dell'Università. Facing each other on the square are two buildings designed by Vaccarini, the **Palazzo dell'Università** to the west and the **Palazzo Sangiuliano** to the east. The former is the city's university.

A farther 300m north is the large and modern Piazza Stesicoro, whose western side is dominated by the sunken remains of the Roman **amphitheatre**. It doesn't look like much today, but in its heyday (around the 2nd century BC) it could seat up to 16,000 spectators and was second in size only to the Colosseum in Rome. What you see from the street is only a part of the once massive structure, which extended as far south as Via Penninello. You can explore part of the vaults and get an idea of the true size of the theatre from a diagram.

For relief from the madding crowd, continue north along Via Etnea and cut in left behind the post office for the lovely gardens of the **Villa Bellini**, with loads of trees, places to sit and a floral clock.

Special Events

Catania celebrates the feast of its patron saint, Agatha (Festa di Sant'Agata), from 3 to 5 February. During this period, one million Catanesi and tourists follow as the *fercolo* (a silver reliquary bust of the saint covered in marvellous jewels) is carried along Via Etnea. There are also spectacular fireworks during the celebrations. If you're in Catania at this time, be prepared to do a bit of walking, as public transport can seem non-existent and driving near-impossible.

Places to Stay – Budget

At the time of research, finding a single room in Catania was like a quest for the holy grail. Six hotels were in the process of renovation and many of the one- and two-star hotels have fewer than 15 rooms available at any time. You may well have to spring for a double room if travelling alone, or reserve well in advance during busy periods (early February, Easter and August).

Camping *Internazionale La Plaja* (☎ *095 34 08 80, fax 095 34 83 40, Viale Kennedy 47)* €6.20/8.80 per person/tent. Camping facilities are available at this site, with a private sandy beach, on the way out of the city towards Syracuse (take bus No 527 from Piazza Borsellino).

Camping Jonio (☎ *095 49 11 39, fax 095 49 22 77, Via Villini a Mare 2)* €5.40/11.90 per person/tent. To get here, take bus No 334 from Via Etnea. This camp site, about 5km south of the city, is close to a beautiful rocky beach and has cabins too.

Hostels *Agorà Hostel* (☎ *095 723 30 10,* e *agorahostel@hotmail.com, Piazza Currò 6)* Dorm bed with breakfast €15.50, doubles without bathroom €46.50. Almost like a classic youth hostel, with the ubiquitous reggae soundtrack, this hostel has decent rooms and staff that vary between rudely indifferent and cheerily helpful. Lock-out is between 11am and 3.30pm. Its location near La Pescheria makes it a good base for self-caterers, although the cheap dinners here get good reviews.

Hotels *Hotel Mele (☎ 095 32 75 42, Via Leonardi 24)* Single/doubles without bathroom €25.80 per person. The hilarious Mele, near Piazza Bellini, has no-frills rooms packed with dusty old antiques and plenty of atmosphere. It's situated above a horror-themed nightclub, so light sleepers should look elsewhere.

Europensione (☎ 095 53 11 52, fax 095 53 10 07, Piazza dei Martiri 8) Singles/doubles without bathroom €20.65/33.60. On the 2nd floor of a building at the northern end of Piazza dei Martiri, the Europensione offers little more than a bed and bed linen. The rooms are large and very clean, however, and the welcome is genuine and polite. It's also close to the bus and train stations.

Holland International (☎ 095 53 36 05, fax 095 746 58 92, Via Vittorio Emanuele II 8) Singles/doubles €18.10/35.10, doubles with bathroom €43.90. Near the train station and located at the back of a huge courtyard, this is popular option with budget travellers. Some rooms have some nice paintwork on the ceiling, although the furniture is a little tired. The staff are helpful.

Hotel Ferrara (☎ 095 31 60 00, Via Umberto I 66) Singles/doubles €25.30/33.60, with bathroom €32/43.90. Past its prime and not exactly friendly, this place will do if you're really in need of a quick accommodation fix.

Pensione-Hotel Sudland (☎ 095 31 13 43, Via Etnea 270) Singles/doubles €20.65/29.95, with bathroom €23.30/40.80. The Sudland is a popular choice for many budget travellers; rooms have TV and phone.

Places to Stay – Mid-Range
Hotel Gresi (☎ 095 32 27 09, fax 095 715 30 45, Via Pacini 28) Singles/doubles with bathroom €31/51.65. Near Villa Bellini, the clean and pleasant Gresi is popular with budget travellers.

Hotel Rubens (☎ 095 31 70 73, fax 095 715 17 13, Via Etnea 196) Singles/doubles €31/46.50, with bathroom €41.30/62. With only seven rooms, and a well-deserved reputation for cleanliness and hospitality, you'll do well to book in advance here. Rooms are very comfortable, with TV, air-conditioning and phone, and despite its location, it's remarkably quiet. Another bonus is the extraordinary Signor Caviezel, who knows Catania inside out and could give a masterclass on hotel management!

Hotel Moderno (☎ 095 32 65 50, fax 095 32 66 74, Via Alessi 9) Singles/doubles with bathroom €51.65/77.50. This is well-placed near Via Crociferì and in the heart of the city's nightlife. The out-of-season rates are reasonable, but in the high season the prices are poor value for the 1970s standards. The management's quite nice though.

Hotel Centrale Europa (☎ 095 31 13 09, Via Vittorio Emanuele II 167) Singles/doubles with bathroom €43.90/62. This hotel is within a hop, skip and a jump of the elephant fountain. Rooms are in good nick, although the management's a touch brusque.

Hotel La Collegiata (☎ 095 31 52 56, fax 095 32 28 48, Via Paolo Vasta 10) Singles/doubles with bathroom €43.90/62. With high ceilings and lovely furnishings, this is an excellent central choice.

Places to Stay – Top End
Central Palace (☎ 095 32 53 44, fax 095 715 89 39, Via Etnea 218) Singles/doubles with bathroom €98.15/139.45. In a supremely central location, this is five-star luxury straight from the groovy 1970s. For fans of the era, rather than connoisseurs of top hotels.

Excelsior (☎ 095 53 70 71, fax 095 53 70 15, e excelsior-catania@thi.it, Piazza G Verga) Singles/doubles with bathroom from €103.30/144.60. With every mod-con and multilingual staff, this is the flashiest hotel in the city centre. There are no single rooms as such, but you won't be charged the full double rate if you're on your own.

Places to Eat
Eating out can be pleasant and inexpensive in Catania. Aside from the usual restaurants and trattorie, the city has a number of other dining options, which involve buying Sicilian snacks and other savoury titbits from

stalls or street-facing bar counters. Don't miss the savoury *arancini* (fried rice balls usually filled with meat, cheese or tomatoes), *cartocciate* (bread stuffed with ham, mozzarella, olives and tomato) or baked onions, available for around €1.55 apiece from a tavola calda, found all over town. Stop at a pastry shop to try the mouth-watering Sicilian sweets.

Restaurants *Trattoria La Paglia (☎ 095 34 68 38, Via Pardo 23)* Meals around €15. Closed Sun. This is a great, cheap trattoria, with an in-your-face view of the action around La Pescheria.

Trattoria Tripoli (Via Pardo 30) Meals around €15. A small, bustling place, run by an extraordinary old lady who can only be described as a 'pistol' for her spark and spunk. You'll get simple pasta and fish dishes, all fresh and delicious. It's best to come in the day, when the market's buzzing.

Trattoria Romantica (Via Collegiata 9) Meals around €13. This nice little pub/restaurant/bar might not be romantic in its music choices, but it's pretty cool and popular with a young crowd.

Taverna dei Conti (☎ 095 31 00 35, Via G Oberdan 41) Meals around €20. Closed Sun. This place is great for seafood dishes, although the meat dishes are also praiseworthy (and a bit cheaper). The octopus salad or *caponata* (a sweet-and-sour dish made with tomatoes, aubergines, olives and anchovies) are from heaven.

Trattoria Tipica Catanesa (☎ 095 32 24 61, Via Penninello 34) Meals around €18. Closed Sun. This small-but-charming trattoria has great food and something indefinably sweet about it. It's also very good value.

Trattoria Casalinga (☎ 095 31 13 19, Via Biondi 19) Meals around €15. Closed Sun. This a very good place to come for a hearty, cheap meal. The *pasta alla Norma* is excellent.

Turi Finocchiaro (☎ 095 715 35 73, Via Euplio Reina 13) Meals around €18. Closed Wed. This place offers great pizza and pasta. It's best to arrive here just before 9pm, as it can get very popular, especially at the weekend.

Cugno Mezzano (☎ 095 715 87 10, Via Museo Biscari 8) Meals around €26. Closed Sun. This place, located in the old wine cellar of Palazzo Biscari, is one of the city's better restaurants. Not surprisingly, it's big on wine, but is more expensive than other eateries in Catania.

Markets, Bars and Cafes Catania is justifiably well known for its excellent *markets*. Every morning, except Sunday, Piazza Carlo Alberto is flooded by the chaos of a produce market known locally as *La Fiera*. You can pick up supplies of bread, cheese, salami, fresh fruit and all manner of odds and ends until the early afternoon. The other major fresh-produce market is *La Pescheria*, off Piazza del Duomo, which sells fresh fish. It opens until late afternoon (except Sunday) and is well worth a visit.

Students head for the area around Via Teatro Massimo and to the west of Via Etnea, where there are several sandwich bars and pubs where you can eat a pizza or a filling sandwich.

Bar Etoile D'Or (Via Dusmet 3) Open 24 hours. This handy and rather swanky-looking tavola calda has good arancini and some mouth-watering sweets. Service can be a little gruff, and so can some of the patrons, but you should try to grab a snack here at least once, as it's an institution.

Savia (Via Etnea 302) This is one of Catania's most popular and longest-standing cafes. It's a great spot to grab a coffee, a snack or a pastry and rub shoulders with the locals.

Entertainment

Not surprisingly for a busy university town, Catania's excellent nightlife is renowned throughout the island. There are *dozens* of bars, cafes and other nightspots littered throughout the city centre that offer a good mix of music, drinking and fun. Remember that most bars and nightspots are closed on Monday and opening hours are generally from around 9pm to 2am. To see what's going on (jazz, opera, theatre and puppet shows etc) in Catania while you're there, pick up a copy of *Lapis* (free; available throughout the city).

La Collegiata (☎ *095 32 12 30, Via della Collegiata 3)* Open 7pm-4am nightly. One of the city's most popular student hangouts is La Collegiata, overlooking Via Etnea. You can eat, drink and listen to live music nightly, and it's a pretty cheery place.

Nievski Pub (☎ *095 731 37 92, Scalinata Alessi 15-17)* This pub is equally popular with Catania's alternative crowd. Revolutionary posters adorn the walls, and the menu advertises the use of fresh organic produce. At night, this is a great place to hang out and chat with the young crowd, who are both friendly and welcoming. You can also surf the Internet here (€5.15 per hour).

The Other Place (*Via Euplio Reina 18-20)* Open 9pm-2am. Virtually a replica of an English pub, The Other Place serves pizzas as well as numerous kinds of draught beer, and even if you don't like 'theme' pubs, it's a great spot to unwind and get a bit social.

East of Via Etnea, in and around the lovely Piazza Santo Spirito, there are a few good spots worth checking out.

Joyce (☎ *0349 810 78 96, Via Montesano 46).* Joyce is an Irish pub where you can enjoy pints of Guinness in a pleasant courtyard. It's a very popular place (Italians think Irish culture is really glamorous) and, quite frankly, it can really go off – in a good way.

Waxi O'Connor's (*Piazza Santo Spirito 1)* Open 9pm-2am daily. The ridiculously named Waxi O'Connor's is the city's other Irish pub, but it manages to stay on the right side of cheesy. The excellent Guinness and the slices of Guinness cake are a great help.

City Jazz (☎ *0329 422 78 88, Piazza Scammacca 1b)* City Jazz is a good spot to listen to – you guessed it – jazz. Some well-known local names play here.

Getting There & Away

Air Catania's airport, Fontanarossa, 7km southwest of the city centre, has domestic services and European flights (the latter all via Rome or Milan). In summer, you may be able to dig up the odd direct charter flight to London or Paris (see the Getting There & Away chapter for more details). To get to the airport, take the special Alibus

(bus No 457) from outside the train station, although many of the services from Catania to say, Taormina, Messina, Syracuse and Catania will also stop at the airport.

Bus Intercity buses terminate in the area around Piazza Giovanni XXIII, very close to the train station. SAIS Autolinee (☎ 095 53 61 68), Via d'Amico 181–187, serves Palermo (€11.65, two hours 40 minutes), Agrigento (€9.80, three hours, 12 daily) and Enna (€5.95). It also has a service to Rome, which leaves at 8pm. A single ticket costs €38.75. AST (☎ 095 746 10 96), Via Luigi Sturzo 230, also serves these destinations and many smaller provincial towns around Catania, including Nicolosi and the cable car on Mt Etna. Interbus-Etna Trasporti (☎ 095 53 27 16), at the same address as SAIS, runs buses to Syracuse (€4.10) Piazza Armerina, Taormina, Messina, Enna, Noto, Ragusa, Gela and Rome.

Train Frequent trains connect Catania with Messina (€7, 1½ hours) and Syracuse (€440, 1½ hours); there are less-frequent services to Palermo (€15.50, 3½ hours), Enna (€4.65, 1¾ hours) and Agrigento (€10.10, four hours). The private Circumetnea train line circles Mt Etna, stopping at the towns and villages on the volcano's slopes. See Around Mt Etna later in this chapter.

Car & Motorcycle Catania is easily reached from Messina on the A18 and from Palermo on the A19. From the A18, signs for the centre of Catania will bring you to Via Etnea. Bear in mind that driving in Catania is only for the brave (or heavily insured).

Boat The ferry terminal is south of the train station along Via VI Aprile.

Virtu Ferries (☎ 095 31 67 11 or 095 53 57 11) runs express ferries from Catania to Malta. Ferries depart Catania's Molo Centrale at the port at various times, depending on the season (one departure a week March to May and four weekly departures between 24 July and 3 September). The trip takes three hours and tickets cost from €69.70/85.20 single/return and from €103 for a car.

MA.RE.SI shipping also runs ferries year-round between Catania and Malta at 7pm on Tuesday (12 hours); this service carries cars.

Adriatica Navigazione connects Catania with Ravenna (€87.80, 36 hours) on the Italian mainland. You can buy tickets at the Sestante Club Vacanze travel agency (for details see Travel Agencies earlier in this section).

Getting Around

Many of the more useful AMT city buses terminate in front of the train station. These include: Alibus, train station–airport every 20 minutes from 5am to midnight; Nos 1 to 4, train station–Via Etnea; and Nos 4 to 7, train station–Piazza del Duomo (€0.70). In summer, a special service (D) runs to the sandy beaches from Piazza G Verga.

For a taxi call CST (☎ 095 33 09 66). There are taxi ranks at the train station and on Piazza del Duomo.

ACI CASTELLO, ACI TREZZA & ACIREALE

One of the pleasant surprises for visitors to Catania is the quality swimming to be found a little north of the city. **Aci Castello** is a popular destination for swimming, sunning and snorkelling, and only 9km from the city centre (take AMT bus No 334 from Piazza Boresellino). It's a lava beach (sharp on the bum!), and in summer wooden platforms are erected for sunbathing ease. There's also a castle (hence the name) overlooking the sea.

A few kilometres north of Aci Castello is **Aci Trezza**, a fishing village and a good place to satisfy your seafood appetite. It's the setting of Giovanni Verga's 1881 novel *I Malavoglia* too. **Acireale**, about 17km north of Catania, occupies a magnificent position on the Ionic coast and has sulphur baths, Baroque architecture and a somewhat snooty atmosphere – this is definitely a place for good-looking Catanian citizens to parade themselves. To get here, take one of the regular Interbus services from Catania to Messina (about 30 minutes) and get off at Acireale's Piazza Duomo.

Mt Etna

elevation 3323m

Sicily's most prominent landmark is Europe's largest live volcano and one of the world's most active. At 3323m it literally towers over the eastern coast, dwarfing everything beneath it; its smoking peak is visible from almost everywhere on this side of the island, and is a heart-stirring (and sometimes heart-stopping!) sight. As a symbol of power, creation and destruction, it's hard to beat, and the effect on the island's psyche of this extraordinary volcano should never be underestimated.

Although today the mountain is one of the island's premier tourist attractions, the eastern coast has lived in the shadow of its unpredictable wrath for millennia. Recorded history of the region is littered with eruptions, including major ones in 475 BC, AD 1169, 1329 and 1381, all of which saw molten rock

---

Lava Boy

Mt Etna has long been a subject of fear and fascination for Sicily's inhabitants. According to the chronicler Diodonus, who wrote in the 6th century BC, the first Sicanian settlers of the island were forced west due to the volcano's activity, while the Greeks were convinced that 'the big mountain' was in fact the forge of the god Vulcan. Pindar wrote of its devastating power, having witnessed an eruption in 475 BC. But by far the most interesting of antiquity's scholars was Empedocles, the Agrigento-born scientist who saved Selinunte from the scourge of malaria in the 5th century BC. He became convinced that the crater's gases were semi-solid in form and that they were strong enough to support the weight of a human. He spent time up at the summit, making notes and taking samples to test his theory. But Empedocles was a thorough investigator of the facts and, in 433 BC, decided that the proof was in the proverbial pudding: he threw himself in. Needless to say, Empedocles was wrong and that was the end of him.

THE EASTERN COAST

flow right down to the sea. The most devastating eruption occurred in 1669 and lasted 122 days. A massive river of lava poured down its southern slope, engulfing a good part of Catania and reducing the surrounding countryside to a charred mess.

During the 20th century, eruptions occurred frequently, both from the four live craters at the summit (one, the Bocca Nuova, was formed in 1968) and on the slopes of the volcano, which is littered with crevices and old craters. Etna has claimed its fair share of victims in modern times, despite the fact that it is monitored by 120 seismic activity stations spread around the mountain and is under constant satellite surveillance. In 1971 an eruption destroyed the observatory at the summit, and another in 1983 finished off the old cable car and tourist centre (you can see where the lava flow stopped on that occasion). Nine people died in an explosion at the southeastern crater in 1979, and two died and 10 were injured in an explosion at the same crater in 1987. In 1992 a stream of lava pouring from a fissure in the southeastern slope threatened to engulf the town of Zafferana Etnea. The town was saved when the Italian Air Force dropped a pile of breeze blocks in the lava's path, but not before one family lost their home and others much of their farm land. At the time of research, Mt Etna had put on some of its most spectacular explosions in 40 years, causing immense damage to the infrastructure on the southern side of the mountain. The cable cars were not working, and the tourist office was closed.

A word of warning: access to the crater's higher slopes is restricted only by a rope (and the semi-vigilance of the guides); it would be extremely foolish to attempt to cross beyond the safety zone.

ORIENTATION & INFORMATION

The two main approaches to Etna are from the north and from the south. At the time of research, access from the southern side was difficult, due to the destruction wrought by lava flows. If your time really is limited, your best bet is to take the private Circumetnea railway from Catania (see the later Around Mt Etna section), which follows a 114km trail around the base. You'll get some great views of the mountain and the lush vegetation at its base, although it doesn't provide as great a sense of the mountain's size and power as a trip to the top does.

On the northern side of the volcano, there is a Pro Loco tourist office (☎ 095 64 30 94, Ⓦ www.prolocolinguaglossa.it – Italian only) in Linguaglossa at Piazza Annunziata 5. It has information about skiing and excursions to the craters, as well as an exhibition of the flora, fauna and rocks of the Parco Naturale dell'Etna. It is possible to hire a 4WD and guide to tour the volcano. There's also a small APT office (☎ 095 64 73 52) at Piano Provenzana, which opens 9am to 4pm Monday to Saturday.

On the southern side, there is a local tourist office (☎ 095 91 15 05) in Nicolosi at Via Garibaldi 63. It opens 8.30am to 2pm and 4pm to 7.30pm daily, April to September; mornings only from 9am the rest of the year. Pre-eruptions, organised excursions to the main craters (maximum 10 people) cost €77.50 per group, including jeep and guide. Alternatively, the tourist office in Catania can provide information.

THE CRATERS

Exploring the area around the summit is an exhilarating experience, even if you miss out on a period of violent activity. Hot lava flows almost constantly from one of the many fissures beneath the main craters, so you'll get to stand within a couple of metres of one of nature's most extraordinary shows. Even the smallest, most unthreatening flow is hot – hot enough to melt your shoes and anything in them. We cannot stress enough the importance of listening to advice from the guides or tourist offices about the safety of Mt Etna.

South

With a daily bus link from Catania via Nicolosi, the southern side of the volcano presents an easy option for an ascent towards the craters. The AST bus drops you off at the **Rifugio Sapienza**, from where SITAS (☎ 095 91 11 58) has 4WD vehicles (actually minibuses with big wheels) going up Etna for €38. The vehicles take you through the eerie lava-scape close to the 3000m level. At the time of writing, there was no cable car up the south side of Mt Etna, but services may well be active again by the time you read this, so we've included the information and an approximation of the prices, but it's probably best to check with the tourist office in Catania. From the Rifugio Sapienza, a SITAS cable car would climb to 2600m year-round from 9am to 3.30pm (around €18). In summer, the all-in price for cable car, 4WD (from 2600m to 3000m) and guide was about €36.20 return. In winter, you could ski back down (snow permitting) – there was no transport beyond the cable car. A one-day ski pass cost about €20.

Some tourists make the long climb from the Rifugio Sapienza to the top (easily 3½ to four hours on a track winding up under the cable car and then following the same road used by the minibuses), and at the time of research, this was all that was on offer. You'll need to move pretty quickly if you expect to get back down to Rifugio Sapienza for the 4.45pm return AST bus to Catania.

North

Several ski lifts operate at Piano Provenzana, snow permitting (a one-day ski pass costs around €18). From the lifts, you're looking at about an hour's walk to come close to the top – a difficult proposition on snow. Enquire about hiring a guide and the feasibility of the walk in winter at the Linguaglossa tourist office.

In summer, the lifts don't operate but 4WDs make the same journey. Again, consider a guide for the one-to-two hour scramble from where the vehicles stop.

ORGANISED TOURS

Natura e Turismo (NeT; ☎ *095 33 35 43,* ✉ *natetur@tin.it, Via R Quartararo 11, Catania)* This group organises tours of the volcano with a volcanologist or expert guide.

STAR (☎ *095 64 34 30, La Betulle hotel, Piano Provenzana)* STAR offers a 1½-hour round trip from Piano Provenzana on the northern side of Etna to 2900m with a 4WD and guide (€38).

Ferrovia Circumetnea (FCE; ☎ *095 54 12 50,* Ⓦ *www.circumetnea.it, Via Caronda 352a, Catania)* FCE has some good tours to Mt Etna and the surrounding area that are handy if you're without transport. The Catania-Giarre-Linguaglossa-Etna tour (€23.25) includes transport via air-conditioned coach to Linguaglossa and Piano Provenzana and lunch. From Piano Provenzana you can book a trip up the mountain with STAR. The tour departs from Piazza Giovanni Verga, near the Excelsior hotel, at 8am, returning to Catania at 7pm. There are also tours to Randazzo, Gola dell'Alcàntara (see earlier in the chapter) and Castello di Nelson.

PLACES TO STAY

Accommodation around Etna is scant and for the most part you're better off staying in Catania, where you get better value for money. If you do plan to stay around the mountain, be sure to book in advance as rooms are at a premium, especially in summer. All prices quoted are summer rates; these can really tumble outside the busy season.

South

Etna (☎ *095 91 43 09, fax 095 791 51 86, Via Goethe)* €6.20 per person. This camp site is an easy signposted walk from Nicolosi.

Etna Youth Hostel (☎ *095 791 46 86, fax 095 791 47 01,* ✉ *etnahostel@hotmail.com, Via della Quercia 7)* Dorm bed €12.90. Open year-round. If you don't fancy camping but need a cheap bed, this very good Nicolosi hostel is the answer to your prayers. It's close to both Catania and the volcano.

Monte Rossi (☎ *095 791 43 93, Via Etnea 177)* Singles/doubles with bathroom €20.65/31. In Nicolosi, the cheapest place to stay is the Monte Rossi, on the main road in town. Rooms are threadbare but clean.

Gemmellaro (☎ *095 91 13 73, fax 095 91 10 71, Via Etnea 160)* Singles/doubles with bathroom €46.50/72.30. The three-star Gemmellaro is a good hotel, with phone, TV and air-conditioning in the rooms.

If you have your own transport, you could stay in the nearby town of Pedara, only 5km east of Nicolosi.

THE EASTERN COAST

Bonaccorsi (☎ 095 91 53 37, fax 095 91 51 36, Via Luigi Pirandello 2) Singles/doubles with bathroom €33.60/51.65. On the western edge of town is the two-star Bonaccorsi, with well-appointed rooms with TV, fridge, phone and a pool.

North

Clan dei Ragazzi (☎/fax 095 64 36 11, Strada Marraneve 47) €3.10/9.30/2.10 per person/tent/car. Open year-round, and a couple of kilometres outside Linguaglossa, this nice camp site is surrounded by pine trees, on the way to Piano Provenzana.

Rifugio Nord-Est (☎ 095 64 79 22) Beds €20.65, half-board €33.60 per person. This refuge is at Piano Provenzana, where the accommodation generally resembles Swiss-style chalets. It's a nice place, with only 16 beds, so book in advance.

La Provenzana (☎ 095 64 33 00, fax 095 64 71 83) Singles/doubles without bathroom €25.80/43.90. La Provenzana is just before the ski lift up Mt Etna and has 15 beds. Rooms are nice, there's a decent restaurant and it's the handiest place to stay for ski-fiends.

Le Betulle (☎/fax 095 64 34 30) Singles/doubles with bathroom €46.50/77.50. This is the luxury option at Piano Provenzana, and also the biggest, with 32 rooms. It's a very good place, although not fitted-out like a chalet.

GETTING THERE & AWAY

Having your own transport will make life much easier around Mt Etna, but there are some public transport options.

South

An AST bus (☎ 095 53 17 56) for Rifugio Sapienza leaves from the car park in front of the main train station in Catania at 8.15am, travelling via Nicolosi. It returns from Rifugio Sapienza at 4.45pm. The return ticket costs €4.65. The AST office in Nicolosi (☎ 095 91 15 05) is at Via Garibaldi 63 and opens 8am to 2pm Monday to Saturday. You can also drive this route (take Via Etnea north out of Catania and follow the signs for Nicolosi and Etna).

North

SAIS and FCE buses connect Linguaglossa with Fiumefreddo, on the coast (from where other SAIS and Interbus buses run north to Taormina and Messina and south to Catania). Unless the FCE puts on a winter ski-season or summer bus to Piano Provenzana, your only chance from Linguaglossa is your thumb. If driving, follow the signs for Piano Provenzana out of Linguaglossa.

AROUND MT ETNA

Another option is to circle Mt Etna on the private FCE train line (☎ 095 54 12 50, W www.circumetnea.it, Via Caronda 352a, Catania). You can catch the metro from Catania's main train station to the FCE station at Via Caronda (metro stop: Borgo) or catch bus No 429 or 432 going up Via Etnea and ask to be let off at the 'Borgo' metro stop.

The line runs around the mountain (with some great views) from Catania to the coastal town of **Riposto**, passing through numerous towns and villages on its slopes, including Linguaglossa. You can reach Riposto (or neighbouring Giarre) from Taormina by train or bus if you want to make the trip from that end.

Catania-Riposto is about a 3½-hour trip, but you needn't go that far. If leaving from Catania, consider finishing the trip at **Randazzo** (€3.10, two hours), a small medieval town noted for the fact that it has consistently escaped destruction despite its proximity to the summit. Randazzo itself is mildly interesting, with a couple of churches to punctuate a brief stroll along a few quiet streets, some lined with Aragonese apartments. A good example of lava architecture are the walls of the Norman **Cattedrale di Santa Maria**, while the **Chiesa di Santa Maria della Volta** preserves a squat 14th-century bell tower.

An FS branch railway line connects Randazzo with Taormina/Giardini-Naxos, but services are subject to cancellation. The infrequent SAIS buses are more reliable.

Syracuse & the Southeast

The history of Sicily's southeastern corner is really the tale of two glorious epochs and one disastrous event. Settled by the Greeks, the region flourished and for nearly 500 years was considered a centre of culture, learning and political power. Nearly 2000 years later the southeast blossomed again as the birthplace of an ornate and much-lauded architectural style known as Sicilian Baroque. The region's renaissance, however, was only made possible by a devastating earthquake that flattened many towns and villages on 11 January 1693. Although separated by nearly two millennia, these three episodes have virtually defined the character and appearance of the southeast, no less so than in the region's largest and most visited city, Syracuse (Siracusa). By almost universal consent the most beautiful city on the island, Syracuse has successfully combined the glory of its ancient past with the architectural splendour of the 18th century in a unified, aesthetic whole that has few rivals in all of Italy.

Although it is tempting to devote all of your time to exploring the city only, the rest of the region deserves more than just a cursory glance. In Noto and Ragusa you will find the apogee of the Sicilian Baroque, while the traditional, mountainous interior is not just a convincing journey into a pastoral past but a field trip to some of Sicily's best-preserved and interesting archaeological digs.

SYRACUSE
postcode 96100 • pop 125,900

The cradle of Greek civilisation in Italy and at one time a rival to Athens as the most important city in the Western world, Syracuse is one of the most impressive and rewarding highlights of a visit to Sicily. Although now no more than a peripheral player in Sicilian affairs, this tidy and compact provincial capital is an unmissable repository of archaeological and architectural treasures dating back some 2700 years. Its glorious classical past now confined to ancient history, Syracuse has changed its identity many times since, no less

so than in the 17th and 18th centuries, when virtually the entire city was rebuilt following the earthquake of 1693. Today it offers an intoxicating mix of antiquity and the Baroque, with a fair amount of Byzantine and Spanish thrown in for good measure. Although it languished in the provincial backwaters for over 1000 years, the 20th century was relatively kind to Syracuse and today the city is one of Sicily's most flourishing and prosperous urban centres.

History
Syracuse's origins date to the 13th century BC, when the island of Ortygia was settled by Sicilian tribes who prospered through

203

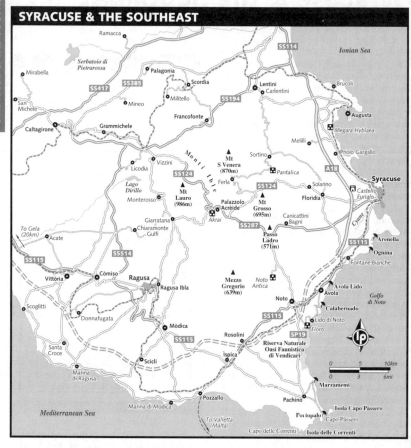

SYRACUSE & THE SOUTHEAST

trading with other settlements in the Mediterranean basin. In 734 BC the island was seized by a group of Corinthian colonists under the leadership of Archia. Four years later, the colonists expanded onto the mainland with a second town called Acradina (in the area of the Syracusan Forum). The two settlements were linked by an earth causeway and later a bridge behind the modern-day main post office. The growing city of Syracoussai derived its name from a torrential stream, called the Syrakò, which flowed nearby.

Protected on all sides and with a plentiful supply of water, Syracuse grew increasingly powerful and eventually broke its colonial relationship with Corinth and began trading in its own right, a new rival to the Mediterranean powers of Athens and Carthage. In 485 BC the 'tyrant of Gela', Gelon (540–478 BC), seized the city and ordered that the populations of all other Sicilian colonies transfer to Syracuse, triggering a sharp increase in the city's population and size. Two new quarters were created: Tyche (after the Greek goddess of Fortune) in the northeast and Neapolis (meaning 'new city') in the northwest, in the area now occupied by the archaeological park. With the help of Akragas (now Agrigento) and Gela, Syracuse inflicted a heavy defeat on the Carthaginians in 480 BC, paving the way for the city's gradual domination of the Mediterranean basin. This steady expansion was in large part due to the city's rigid political structure, which saw a series of sometimes capable but often brutal tyrant-kings maintain a totalitarian grip on the reins of power.

Threatened by this new rival to the west, in 415 BC Athens dispatched one of the largest fleets ever put together to deliver Syracuse into Athenian hands. Athenian muscle proved no match for Syracusan strategy and the fleet was almost completely destroyed. Syracuse's revenge was unmerciful: those prisoners who escaped execution were incarcerated for seven years in the city's notorious quarries, a move that drew condemnation from the Hellenistic world. Their temporary isolation from other Mediterranean powers merely spurred Syracuse to cement its dominance.

Cruel and vicious though they often were, the Syracusan tyrants were clever and vain enough to actively pursue a modicum of cultural respectability. As well as ordering an impressive programme of public works that saw the construction of mighty temples and other monuments to the gods (and put their personal stamp on the city), Syracuse's kings went to great lengths to attract the finest minds of their time to the city. Pindar and Aeschylus were invited by Hieron I, who ruled from 478 to 466 BC; it is probable that Aeschylus' masterpieces *Prometheus Bound* and *Prometheus Released* were first shown in the city's amphitheatre *(anfiteatro)*. Successive kings continued to promote Syracuse as a capital of arts and sciences; Dionysius II (who reigned 367–343 BC) was greatly taken with the 'philosopher-king' theories expounded by his tutor Plato, although when the philosopher objected to the king's more outlandish behaviour he was forced to flee lest he meet a premature end.

Following Dionysius' death the city entered an unsteady stream of alliances aimed at preserving the status quo in the face of antiquity's newest emerging power: Rome.

The tyrants became more conciliatory, and the city even underwent a short experiment in democracy. It was, however, the beginning of the end for the city's independence, and not even the ingenious defences devised by the city's most famous son, Archimedes, were enough to stave off the ransack of the city by Roman troops in 211 BC.

Under Roman rule Syracuse remained the capital of Sicily and was the seat of the praetors, but the city was in decline. It was briefly the capital of the Byzantine empire in 663 when Constans set up court here, but was sacked by the Saracens in 878 and reduced to little more than a fortified provincial town. The population fell drastically, and the next

The Man who Cried 'Eureka!'

Archimedes, arguably the classical world's greatest scientific mind, was born in Syracuse in 287 BC. Following his studies in Alexandria, he returned to his native city where he proceeded to astound the scientific world with his theories on geometry, algebra and calculus. King Hieron II was eager to put Archimedes' fine mind to use, and the story goes that he asked him to find a precise way of measuring the mass of gold. Archimedes pondered the question for a long time but could find no working solution. The scientist's wife, noting his tension and frustration, advised him to relax and take a bath. Archimedes duly did so, but no sooner had he got into the water than he jumped out and cried 'Eureka! I have found it!' Thanks to his wife, Archimedes had stumbled upon the principle of measuring mass through the displacement of water.

Loved by his fellow citizens, no less for devising a brilliant system of refractory mirrors that used sunlight to burn the Roman fleet in 212 BC, Archimedes played a key role in the defence of his city but not even his genius was enough to stop the Roman onslaught. Out of respect the Roman consul Marcus Marcellus gave a direct order that his life be spared, but an unknowing centurion burst into his house and before he had time to identify his victim he pulled out a sword and hacked him to death.

SYRACUSE

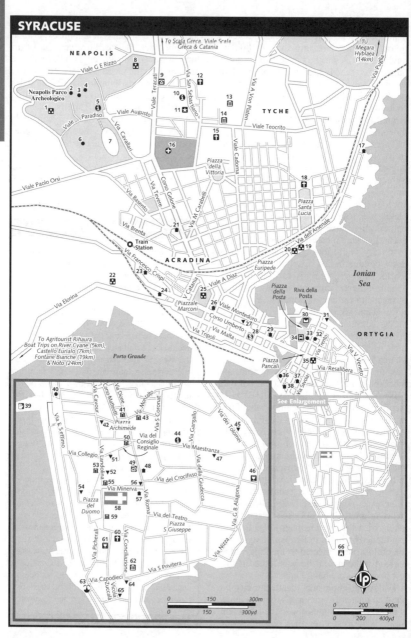

SYRACUSE

PLACES TO STAY
17 Hotel Riviera
21 Jolly
23 Aretusa; Eurailo
24 Hotel Centrale
26 B&B Casa Mia
29 Milano
37 Hotel Gran Bretagna
38 Grand Hotel
48 B&B L'Acanto
57 Roma

PLACES TO EAT
27 Pasticceria Tipica Catanese
31 Produce Market
42 Pizzeria Nonna Margherita
45 Arlecchino
47 Don Camillo
51 Trattoria Pescomare
52 Il Cenacolo
54 Gran Caffé
56 Caff%%232 Minerva
64 Trattoria la Foglia
65 Ristorante Osteria da Mariano

OTHER
1 Greek Theatre

2 Orecchio di Dionisio
3 Grotta dei Cordari
4 Latomia del Paradiso
5 APT Tourist Office
6 Ara di Ierone II
7 Roman Amphitheatre
8 Necropolis
9 Telecom Office
10 Main APT Tourist Office
11 Police Station
12 Basilica di San Giovanni;
    Catacombs
13 Paolo Orsi Archeological
    Museum
14 Museo del Papiro
15 Santuario della Madonna
    delle Lacrime
16 Hospital
18 Chiesa di Santa Lucia al
    Sepolcro; Catacombs
19 Edificio Termale
20 Arsenal
22 Train Station
23 Ginnasio Romano
25 Syracusan Forum
28 Banca Nazionale del
    Lavoror (Bank & ATM)

30 Post Office
32 Interbus Bus Ticket Office
33 AST Bus Ticket Office
34 Intercity & Urban Bus Station
35 Tempio di Apollo
36 Boccadifuoco Travel Agency
39 Selene Embarcation Point
40 Syrako Porta Marina Tourist
    Point
41 Palazzo Platamone
43 Palazzo Montalto
44 AAT Tourist Office
46 Ulysses Irish Pub
49 Web and Work
50 Palazzo Lanza
53 Palazzo Beneventano
    del Bosco
55 Palazzo Municipale
58 Cathedral
59 Palazzo Arcivescovile
60 Chiesa di Santa Lucia alla
    Badia
61 Duio
62 Museo Regionale d'Arte
    Medioevale e Moderna
63 Fontana Aretusa
66 Castello Maniace

800 years were marked by famine, plague and earthquakes. The Val di Noto earthquake in 1693, however, marked the beginning of Syracuse's renewal. Urban planners took advantage of the damage to the city to undertake a massive programme of reconstructing and restoring old buildings in the Baroque style of the day. Following the unification of 1865 Syracuse was made a provincial capital and the city began to grow once more. In the 20th century, prosperity came at the price of some rather ugly urban developments and the growth of heavy industry, but the heart of the city remains unsullied.

Orientation

Tidy and compact, Syracuse is a very manageable city to visit. The main sights are in two areas: on the island of Ortygia and 2km across town in the Neapolis Parco Archeologico (Neapolis Archaeological Park). Most accommodation is in the newer part of town, to the west (although Ortygia has some lovely, if more expensive, hotels). The best dining spots are in Ortygia.

Information

Tourist Offices The main APT office (☎ 0931 6 77 10), Via San Sebastiano 45, opens 8.30am to 1.30pm Monday to Saturday. There's also a branch office at the archaeological park in Neapolis. The AAT (☎ 0931 46 42 55) on Ortygia, Via Maestranza 33, deals specifically with Syracuse and is probably the most convenient office at which to pick up a map and hotel list. It opens 8am to 2pm and 2.30pm to 5.30pm Monday to Friday, mornings only on Saturday. If it's closed, information is still available on the notice board.

Money Numerous banks line Corso Umberto, including the Banca Nazionale del Lavoro at No 29, which has an ATM. There are others on Corso Gelone and on Ortygia. The rates at the train station exchange booth are generally poor.

Post & Communications The post office is on Piazza della Posta, to your left as you cross the bridge to Ortygia. It opens 8.30am

Making a Film You Can't Refuse

Although not particularly noted for its Mafia links, like all Sicilian cities Syracuse too has had to contend with the nefarious influence of organised crime. In the summer of 1999, one of Sicily's most distinguished sons, the filmmaker Giuseppe Tornatore (of *Cinema Paradiso*), was forced to shut down the filming of his latest work, *Malèna*, which was being shot on location in Syracuse. Some important equipment had 'disappeared' from the store rooms and it emerged that the Mafia were holding it in lieu of payment of the notorious *pizzo* or protection money. Local newspapers cried foul and expressed their disgust that one so respected as Tornatore should be a victim of this particularly Sicilian form of blackmail. A couple of days later, however, filming resumed and the story faded from the front pages. What happened is unclear, and the question remains: was the pizzo paid or was the equipment returned out of shame? The film was finished, and while Tornatore still has many fans, *Malèna* proved a disappointment to the critics and audiences who were hoping for something equal to *Cinema Paradiso*. Maybe the equipment shouldn't have been returned after all…

to 6.30pm Monday to Friday (to 1pm on Saturday).

The Telecom office, Viale Teracati 42, opens 8.30am to 7.30pm Monday to Saturday. There are plenty of public phones on the streets and in bars too.

Web and Work, at Via Roma 16 on Ortygia, has numerous terminals and a fast connection. It opens 10am to 2pm and 4pm to 10pm Monday to Friday, 11am to 2pm and 4.30pm to 9.30pm Saturday, and 6pm to 10pm Sunday. It costs €1.55 for 15 minutes, €2.60 for 30 minutes and €4.15 for an hour.

Medical Services The public hospital is at Via Testaferrata 1 (☎ 0931 46 10 42).

Emergency For medical emergencies, ring ☎ 0931 6 85 55. The police station (*questura*; ☎ 0931 46 35 56) is at Via San Sebastiano 12.

Ortygia

The island of Ortygia is the spiritual and physical heart of the city. It is a living museum of a succession of epochs – Greek, Norman, Aragon and Baroque – purposefully combined in a harmonious symmetry. Pride of place goes to the simple but utterly elegant Piazza del Duomo, one of the most beautiful Baroque squares in all of Europe, but be sure to allow plenty of time to wander in and out of the tangled maze of streets and alleyways. Centuries of neglect have certainly taken

some of the lustre off Ortygia's beauty, but in recent years city authorities have made concerted efforts to reverse the decay.

Piazza Archimede & Around This elegant square is virtually in the middle of the island. Its centrepiece is the 20th-century **fountain** (by Giulio Moschetti) depicting Artemis the Huntress surrounded by handmaidens and sirens. The square is Syracuse's 'drawing room', where locals sit around and drink coffee at the cafes that circle the square. Above them are a number of Catalan-Gothic *palazzi* (mansions), including **Palazzo Lanza** with its elegant twin-lighted mullion windows and the **Palazzo Platamone**, now home to the Banca d'Italia. If you can, take a peek at the Palazzo Platamone's courtyard, where there is a gorgeous 15th-century staircase.

To the northeast, Via Montalto gives its name to perhaps the most handsome of all of Syracuse's mansions, **Palazzo Mergulese-Montalto**. Built in 1397, it was presented to the Montalto family by Constance of Aragon, and is a clear sign of the wealth and elegance of 14th-century Syracuse. Its main features are the exquisitely crafted twin- and triple-lighted mullion windows. Unfortunately, the building is not open to the public.

Piazza del Duomo Syracusans seem to delight in amazing their visitors. Just as they have finished admiring the graceful elegance of Piazza Archimede, the unsuspecting stumble across Piazza del Duomo, one of the most wonderful public spaces in Italy. The square – which occupies the highest part of the island – is where the ancient acropolis of the Greek city once stood, giving it religious importance across 2700 years of history, and is surrounded on all sides by a series of mansions built after the earthquake of 1693.

Directly north of the cathedral is the **Palazzo Municipale** or Palazzo Senatoriale, built in 1629 by the Spanish architect Juan Vermexio, nicknamed 'Il Lucertolone' or 'the lizard'. On the left corner of the cornice is the architect's signature: a small lizard carved into a stone. Recent excavations beneath the building have uncovered the unfinished remains of an Ionic temple to Artemis. The mansion now serves as the city hall. To see the temple's remains, just ask at the gate. Attached to the cathedral's southern side is the elegant, 17th-century **Palazzo Arcivescovile** (Archbishop's Palace), which is home to a library of rare manuscripts, including a number of letters by Schopenhauer (1788–1860, a German pessimist philosopher). Visits are by appointment only; call ☎ 0931 6 79 68.

In the northwestern corner of the square is the **Palazzo Beneventano del Bosco**, which has a pretty 18th-century facade, while at its southern end is the **Chiesa di Santa Lucia alla Badia**, dedicated to St Lucy, the city's patron saint, who was martyred at Syracuse during the reign of the Roman emperor Diocletian. The church's Baroque facade is decorated with a wrought-iron balustrade. At the time of research it was closed for restoration.

The Cathedral There is no better example of Syracuse's long and distinguished mix of architectural styles than the city's cathedral *(duomo)*. Inside, traces remain of a Doric temple dedicated to Athena which date from the early decades of the 5th century BC. Below them is an even more extraordinary sight, an altar *(ara)* built by the Siculi three centuries earlier, the only surviving evidence of the island's first settlers.

The original Greek temple was renowned throughout the Mediterranean, in no small part thanks to Cicero, who visited Ortygia in the 1st century BC. The doors were adorned in gold and ivory, while the interior was lined with magnificent paintings of Agathocles fighting the Carthaginians. The roof was crowned by a golden statue of Athena that served as a beacon to sailors at sea. The temple was 'Christianised' in the 7th century and a number of alterations were made. The 36 columns that ran along the length of the interior were walled off (though 24 are still visible in the masonry) and the central nave was split into three aisles. The towers on the left side of the church's exterior were built by the Saracens, who used the building as a mosque. During the 12th century the church was adorned with mosaics, but these were destroyed during the earthquakes of 1545 and 1693, the second of which also resulted in the collapse of the facade. The great stylist of the Sicilian Baroque, Andrea Palma, drew up plans for the cathedral's restoration and a new, more impressive facade was built with statues by Marabitti.

Fontana Aretusa On the waterfront south of Piazza del Duomo along Via Picherali is the Fontana Aretusa, a 1000-year-old natural freshwater spring. Legend has it that the goddess Artemis transformed her beautiful handmaiden Aretusa into the spring to protect her from the unwelcome attention of the river god Alpheus. Undeterred and unwilling to be apart from her, Alpheus jumped into the pool. Now populated by ducks, grey mullet and papyrus plants, the fountain is a popular spot for Syracusans during their evening stroll.

Museo Regionale d'Arte Medioevale e Moderna Housed in the former monastery of St Benedict, itself located in the 13th-century Palazzo Bellomo, this gallery of medieval and modern art *(☎ 0931 6 96 17, Via Capodieci 14; admission €4.15; open 9am-2pm Tues-Sun, 3pm-7pm Wed & Fri)* has a sizable collection of sculpture and painting dating from the high Middle Ages right up to the 20th century. The gallery's most important pieces are an *Annunciazione* (Annunciation) by Antonello da Messina (1474) and *La Sepoltura di Santa Lucia* (The Burial of

St Lucy) by Caravaggio (1609). The gallery also has a number of statues by the Gagini school and a lovely collection of the applied arts such as silver- and goldsmithery, ceramics and terracotta.

Other Sights At the entrance to Ortygia, on Piazza Pancali, lies the **Tempio di Apollo** (Temple of Apollo), one of the first Greek structures built here. Little remains of the 6th-century BC Doric structure, apart from the bases of a few columns, although with a bit of imagination, it's possible to make out the basic ideas behind the place. The Byzantines used it as a church, the Saracens as a mosque and the Spaniards converted it into a barracks in the 16th century.

At the southern tip of the island is the 13th-century **Castello Maniace**, built by Frederick II as part of a massive programme of construction that more or less turned Ortygia into an island fortress. The castle is still used as a barracks and as such is off-limits.

The Mainland

Although not nearly as picturesque as Ortygia, you should still devote at least a day to exploring the mainland quarters of Syracuse. The Acradina quarter, directly across the bridge from Ortygia, is the modern city, built on the site of the ancient settlement of the same name. To the northeast in the Tyche quarter are the city's extensive catacombs and the renowned Museo Archeologico Paolo Orsi. To see the real thing, go west to Neapolis and the archaeological park.

Acradina Bombed twice during WWII (by the Allies in 1943 and then by the Luftwaffe in 1944), most of the Acradina quarter bears the unmistakable stamp of the post-war aesthetic: functional and not too pleasing on the eye. On Piazzale Marconi the old **Syracusan Forum** (Foro Siracusano), once the site of the marketplaces *(agora)*, is now bisected by a number of busy streets and overshadowed by some hideous architecture.

A few hundred yards west of the forum along Via Elorina, however, is a sight well worth visiting (though few ever seem to): the ruins of the **Ginnasio Romano** *(Roman Gymnasium; free; open 9am-1pm Mon-Sat)*, built in the 1st century. Despite the name, this was actually a small theatre at the heart of a building that also contained a large atrium and a theatre directly behind the stage.

Along the water to the east of the forum (take Via dell'Arsenale) are the fenced-off remains of the ancient **arsenal**, once a set of rectangular pits into which ships would be pulled for re-provisioning. Adjacent are the ruins of the **Edificio Termale** (Thermal Building), a Byzantine bathhouse where it is claimed the Emperor Constans was assassinated with a soap dish in 668.

North of the arsenal is one of the city's biggest squares, **Piazza Santa Lucia**, whose northern end is dominated by the **Chiesa di Santa Lucia al Sepolcro**. The 17th-century church is built on the spot where the city's patron saint, Lucy, an aristocratic girl who devoted herself to saintliness after being blessed by St Agatha, was martyred in 304. Underneath the church is a network of **catacombs** (generally not open to the public) that are the largest in Italy after those in Rome.

Catacombs of Tyche According to Roman law, Christians were not allowed to bury their dead within the city limits (which during the Roman occupation did not extend beyond Ortygia). Forced to go elsewhere, Christians conducted their burials in the outlying district of Tyche and its underground aqueducts, unused since Greek times. New tunnels were carved out and the result was a labyrinthine network of burial chambers, most of which are inaccessible except the ones underneath the **Basilica di San Giovanni** *(Via San Sebastiano; admission to church free, catacombs €2; both open 9am-12.30pm & 2pm-5.30pm Wed-Mon)*, directly opposite the tourist office. The church itself has been abandoned since the end of the 17th century and its interior is overgrown, but it once served as the city's cathedral. The first bishop of Syracuse, St Marcian, was flogged to death in 254 while tied to a pillar at the bottom of a set of steps here.

The catacombs are, for the most part, dank and a little spooky. Thousands of little niches line the walls and tunnels lead off from the main chamber *(decumanus max-imus)* into *rotonde*, round chambers used by the faithful for praying. All of the treasures that accompanied the dead on their spiritual journey fell victim to tomb robbers over the centuries except one: a sarcophagus unearthed in 1872 and now on exhibition in the Museo Archeologico Paolo Orsi.

Museo Archeologico Paolo Orsi At the top of Via Cadorna (which runs north from Piazza Euripede) is Sicily's most extensive archaeological museum *(☎ 0931 46 40 22, Via Cadorna; admission €4.15; open 9am-2pm & 3.30pm-7.30pm Tues-Sun; closed Mon morning, Tues & Thur afternoons).* Located in the grounds of the Villa Landolina, the museum (named after the archaeologist Paolo Orsi, who arrived in Syracuse in 1886 and devoted the next 45 years to uncovering its ancient treasures) contains an extremely well organised and extensive collection. At the centre of the building is a large atrium that serves as a reference point for the three sections of the museum as well as containing a wealth of information on virtually every exhibit included here.

To the left as you enter is Sector A, which begins with a geological overview of Sicily and then moves on to cover all of the arte-facts that date from the Palaeolithic period to the early Greek settlements. Sector B, at the far end of the atrium from the entrance, deals with the history of Greek settlement in Sicily, with a particular emphasis on Megara Hyblaea and Syracuse. Of note are a number of sculptures uncovered at the former, including one of the physician Sambrotidas and one of a woman nursing twins, both sculpted in the 6th century BC. Of the Syracusan finds, the most famous is the splendid copy of *Venere Uscendo dell'Acqua* (Venus Emerging from the Sea), also known as the 'Landolina Venus' (named after Saverio Landolina, who found it in 1806). Venus really does appear to be rising from the sea, tunic clinging to her curves as she strives to protect her modesty from prying eyes! Sector C, to the right of the entrance, concentrates on the Syracusan outposts of Eloro, Akrai, Kasmenai and Kamarina. There is also an interesting selection of material found in the major Doric colonies of Gela and Agrigento.

Museo del Papiro This small museum *(☎ 0931 6 16 16, Viale Teocrito 66; free; open 9am-2pm Tues-Sun)* has exhibits including papyrus documents and products. The plant grows in abundance around the River Cyane, near Syracuse, and was used to make paper in the 18th century. The museum also features some interesting papyrus canoes and a copy of the Rosetta stone.

Santuario della Madonna delle Lacrime Syracuse's most recent note-worthy building (it opened in 1994 and reaches a height of 102m), the cavernous Sanctuary of Our Lady of the Tears *(Viale Teocrito; free; open 7am-12.30pm & 4pm-7pm daily)* was commissioned to house a statue of the Virgin that allegedly wept for five days in 1953 and bestowed over 300 miraculous cures within a matter of months.

The **Museo delle Lacrimazione** *(Museum of the Lacrymation; admission €1.55; open*

The Greatest Show on Earth?

Performances in Syracuse's theatre were pretty intense affairs, particularly during the six-day Feast of Dionysus, god of wine and merriment (not to be confused with the tyrant-king Dionysius). Daily performances of a tetracycle (three tragedies and a satirical work thrown in for good measure) and no less than five comedies kept audiences glued to their seats from dawn till dusk. As the festival was essentially a hedonistic religious ceremony, the high point of the day's perfor-mance (usually during the third tragedy) saw the audience whipped into a frenzy of delir-ium described by Aristotle as 'catharsis', after which they were made to laugh for a few more hours and then sent home. After nearly 20 centuries without a festival, 1914 saw the start of a new series of productions performed every even year. See the Special Events sec-tion later in the chapter for details.

9am-12.30pm & 4pm-6pm daily), underneath the sanctuary, explains the events of the miracle and objects associated with it.

Next door, an extensive network of houses and streets from the Greek and Roman periods has been discovered.

Neapolis Parco Archeologico About 500m west of the museum off Viale Teracati is the extensive Neapolis Parco Archeologico *(Neapolis Archaeological Park;* ☎ *0931 6 62 06; admission €4.15; open 9am-2 hrs before sunset)*, Syracuse's most visited site. Indeed, the trappings of mass tourism are everywhere, from the countless beverage stands and souvenir stalls to the rows of tour buses lined up in the car park, not forgetting the hordes of visitors that in summer overrun the place. Still, the park should be on your 'not-to-be-missed' list as it contains some of the most impressive classical ruins in Sicily. There is an APT tourist kiosk just before the entrance to the park. To get there, take bus No 1, 4–6, 8, 11, 12 or 15 from Piazza della Posta to Corso Gelone/Viale Teracati. The walk from Ortygia will only takes about 20 minutes though.

Greek Theatre For the classicist, Syracuse is summed up in one image – that of the sparkling white, 3rd-century-BC Greek theatre (Teatro Greco), completely hewn out of the living rock. A masterpiece of classical architecture, the ancient theatre was commissioned by Hieron II and was built on the site of an older theatre erected 200 years earlier. Old records show that Aeschylus staged some of his later plays here, which would have been watched (most likely) by a capacity crowd of 16,000 people. When the Romans took Syracuse they made alterations to the theatre, mostly so that they could stage gladiatorial combats.

Other Ruins Near the theatre is the **Latomia del Paradiso** (Garden of Paradise), which was a limestone quarry run by the Greeks along the lines of a concentration camp, where prisoners cut blocks of limestone in subterranean tunnels for building projects. It was here that the Athenians

captured after the great sea battle of 413 BC were imprisoned and held for seven years in inhumane conditions. Most of the area remained covered by a 'roof' of earth, which collapsed during the 1693 earthquake. After this, the garden of citrus and magnolia trees was created.

A renowned curiosity at the heart of the garden is the ear-shaped man-made grotto known as the **Orecchio di Dionisio** (Ear of Dionysius). According to Caravaggio, who visited it in the 17th century, the tyrant-king Dionysius must have had it built so that he could listen in on the conversations of the prisoners, but it is most likely that the grotto, 23m high and 65m deep, was dug out as a rock quarry and later used as a sounding board for the theatre performances nearby.

Next to it is the now-closed **Grotta dei Cordari** (Rope-makers' Cave), a grotto, supported by pillars, once used in the manufacture of rope; in antiquity, humidity was an essential ingredient in rope manufacture and the cave had plenty of it.

In the northeastern tip of the park is a **necropolis** used during Roman times. Two tombs stand out, each fronted by Doric semi-columns: one of them is thought to contain the remains of Archimedes.

Back outside this area and opposite the APT tourist office you'll find the entrance to the 2nd-century AD **Roman amphitheatre**, the third-largest in Italy after the Colosseum and the amphitheatre in Verona. The structure was used for gladiator fights and horse races. Roman punters used to park their chariots in the area between the amphitheatre and Viale Paolo Orsi. The Spaniards, little interested in archaeology, largely destroyed the site in the 16th century, using it as a quarry to build the city walls on Ortygia. West of the amphitheatre is the 3rd-century BC **Ara di Ierone II** (Altar of Hieron II). The monolithic sacrificial altar was a kind of giant abattoir where 450 oxen could be killed at one time.

Organised Tours
Syrako Porta Marina Tourist Point *(☎ 0931 2 41 33, Largo Porta Marina)* Office opens 9am-1pm & 3pm-8pm. Located in the city's 15th-century gateway, this information

service/tourist guide centre can help car-less visitors wishing to see more of the province. There are tours to Castello Eurìalo and the archaeological park (€15.50), Pantalica and Noto (with lunch, €43.90), Buscemi and Palazzolo Acrèide (with lunch, €43.90), Oasi di Vendicari and Marzamemi (with lunch, €43.90) from July to September.

Selene (departs from dock near the Grand Hotel) 45-min cruise €5.15. Departs from 10am daily Apr-Oct. The *Selene* takes passengers around Ortygia in a ride that offers splendid views of the city. Specific departure times depend on demand.

Special Events

Greek Classical Drama Since 1914, in every even-numbered year, Syracuse has hosted a festival of Greek classical drama during May and June. Performances are given in the Greek theatre. Two tragedies run on alternate days for the duration of the festival; also thrown in is the occasional classical comedy. The performances have attracted some of Italy's finest actors to its stage, including Marcello Mastroianni and Vittorio Gassman. All the performances are in Italian. Tickets (€12 to €31) are available from the APT office or at a booth at the entrance to the theatre. You can telephone for information on ☎ 0931 6 74 15.

Festa di Santa Lucia On 13 December a festival to commemorate the city's patron saint begins on Piazza del Duomo, with a procession carrying a silver statue of the saint through the streets. The route winds its way through Ortygia and on to the mainland until it reaches Piazza Santa Lucia. The whole festival is accompanied by plenty of colour and fireworks, which more than make up for the sombre disposition of its participants.

Places to Stay

Camping & Hostels *Agriturist Rinaura (☎ 0931 72 12 24, on the SS115)* Bus No 21 or 22 from Corso Umberto. €4.15/11.90 per person/tent. There are camping facilities at this place, 4km west of the city on SS115, and it's pretty good for the proximity and price.

Ostello della Gioventù (☎ 0931 71 11 18, Viale Epipoli 45) Bus No 11 or 25 from Piazzale Marconi. At the time of writing, this hostel was closed for renovations, but will probably be open by the time you read this.

Hotels – Budget *Hotel Centrale (☎ 0931 6 05 28, fax 0931 6 11 75, Corso Umberto 141)* Singles/doubles €18.10/25.80, doubles with bathroom €38.75. Close to the train station, the Centrale has small, basic rooms with heating in winter but no airconditioning in summer.

Milano (☎ 0931 6 69 81, Corso Umberto 10) Singles/doubles €18.10/36.15, with bathroom €36.15/56.80. The Milano, near Ortygia, has decent rooms with air-conditioning and TV, and it's close to the bus station.

Aretusa (☎/fax 0931 2 42 11, Via Francesco Crispi 75) Singles/doubles €23.25/36.15, with bathroom €25.80/41.30. Close to the train station and with OK, albeit spartan, rooms and friendly management, this is a reasonable budget choice.

Eurìalo (☎ 0931 48 34 13 or 0931 48 34 45, Via Francesco Crispi 92) Singles/doubles with bathroom €31/51.65. Just near the Aretusa, but up the scale, is this place, which remains a budget option when you add the phone, TV, parking and heating.

Hotels – Mid-Range *Scala Greca (☎ 0931 75 39 22, fax 0931 75 37 78, Via Àvola 7)* Singles/doubles with bathroom €38.75/56.80. Scala Greca is north of the archaeological park. It is, like several other better hotels, quite a distance from the centre, but the rooms are of a good standard and there's heating and air-conditioning.

Hotel Riviera (☎ 0931 6 70 50, Via Eucleida 7) Singles/doubles with bathroom €51.65/67.15. With stunning views from a 1st-floor terrace and some of its rooms, the Riviera is a good choice. The rooms are large and elegant, and it has been recommended by some of our readers.

Hotel Gran Bretagna (☎/fax 0931 6 87 65, [e] mcapill@tin.it, Via Savoia 21) Singles/doubles/triples/quads with bathroom €69/96/120/140. Just re-opened after extensive renovations that have transformed this small hotel into a rather swanky place to stay, the Gran Bretagna has a great Ortygia location and nice management. The rooms have air-conditioning, TV and fridge – and the showers are great.

B&B L'Acanto (*☎ 0931 46 11 29, Via Roma 15*) Singles/doubles with bathroom €46.50/67.15. Right near Piazza Archimede, this small but cosy place has B&B with air-conditioning, TV and phone.

B&B Casa Mia (*☎ 0931 46 33 49,* e *dandist@tin.it, Corso Umberto 112*) Singles/doubles with bathroom €46.50/67.15. A recent arrival on the Syracusan scene, this sweetly run home-away-from-home in an old, well-located mansion is a great choice, with a nice breakfast area and tastefully furnished rooms (some named after the family members who have owned the lovely and comfortable antique beds). Definitely recommended.

Hotels – Top End *Jolly* (*☎ 0931 46 11 11, fax 0931 46 11 26, Corso Gelone 45*) Singles/doubles with bathroom €118.80/149.75. Near both the station and the archaeological park, the Jolly is a very good choice, even if the building itself is quite ugly. Rooms are fully serviced and sound-proofed, and rates can drop by 40%, so always check if any specials are running.

Roma (*☎ 0931 46 56 26, fax 0931 46 55 35,* e *info@hotelroma.sr.it, Via Minerva 10*) Singles/doubles with bathroom €123.95/180.75. Behind the cathedral and beautifully restored, this luxury hotel has excellent rooms with air-conditioning, safe, TV, fridge and phone.

Grand Hotel (*☎ 0931 46 46 00, fax 0931 46 46 11, Viale Mazzini 12*) Singles/doubles with bathroom €134.30/196.25. The Grand Hotel on Ortygia has top-class, well appointed rooms, with disabled access, parking, TV and air-conditioning – all in a beautiful location.

Places to Eat

There is no shortage of places to eat on the island, and Ortygia is the best place for it.

Il Cenacolo (*☎ 0931 6 50 99, Via del Consiglio Reginale 10*) Pizza €3.10-10.35.

Closed Wed. This place, down a tiny lane off Via Roma, is one of the cheapest restaurants on the island, with a great range of pizzas to tempt you.

Trattoria Pescomare (*☎ 0931 2 10 75, Via Landolina 6*) Meals around €20. Near the cathedral, the Pescomare serves up a pleasing selection of local fish dishes and a wide range of pizza. Grab a spot in the vine-covered courtyard and feast on the *spaghetti alle cozze* (spaghetti with mussels; €5.15).

La Foglia (*☎ 0931 6 62 33, Via Capodieci 29*) Meals around €26. This charming restaurant, decorated with art and bric-a-brac, serves delightful (often hand-picked) Mediterranean and vegetarian cuisine. Worth loosening your belt for.

Gran Caffe del Duomo (*Piazza del Duomo 18*) Tourist menu €10.35. You'd normally avoid a place like this, thinking it screams 'location + expense', but a reasonable tourist menu and prime position in this beautiful square makes it a viable option, even if only for coffee or a glass of wine.

Pizzeria Nonna Margherita (*☎ 0931 6 53 64, Via Cavour 12*) Pizza €2.60-11.35. Closed Wed. This high-ceilinged, casual pizzeria has great pizza, from simple, tasty Napolitana to more elaborate affairs. It's well known and well regarded by Syracusans.

Arlecchino (*☎ 0931 6 63 86, Via dei Tolomei 5*) Meal around €33.60. Arlecchino is near the waterfront. It is one of the city's better restaurants, so you may want to make a reservation.

Ristorante Osteria da Mariano (*☎ 0931 6 74 44, Vicolo Zuccalà 8*) Meals around €25.80. If you're looking for something other than fish, this exceptional restaurant serves good, traditional inland Sicilian fare, including a particularly delicious pasta with pine nuts *(pinoli)*. It is a small place and fills up quickly, so be sure to book ahead, especially at the weekend.

Don Camillo (*☎ 0931 6 71 33, Via Maestranza 96*) Meals around €31. Closed Sun. An upmarket restaurant with a good choice of dishes and quite formal service; this is a good choice if you want a really large selection of wine. It's very popular on Friday and Saturday night.

Caffè Minerva (Via Roma 58) This is a pleasant cafe that does typical Sicilian dessert treats and a nice, frothy cappuccino. It is also a great spot for people watching.

In the streets near the post office, there's a produce *market* until about 1pm daily, except Sunday, which is a good spot to stock up on fruit and veg.

The selection of restaurants isn't as good on the mainland, and it's best for snacks only.

Pasticceria Tipica Catanese (Corso Umberto 46) With magnificent pastries at very pleasing prices, this is a fine spot for indulging your sweet tooth.

There are several *grocery shops* and *supermarkets* along Corso Gelone.

Entertainment

As a coastal city, Syracuse has a decent social and night-time scene during the busy summer months, when out-of-town discos flourish. You can get details from the *Genia Box* pamphlets that are distributed all over town. There are also good bars on Ortygia for those who don't have a car or the desire to pay exorbitant admission charges.

Duio (☎ 0333 725 88 91, Via delle Virgini 16) With good jazz music, pavement tables and friendly service, this is a nice bar/pub to while away a few hours.

Ulysses Irish Pub (☎ 0931 46 56 15, Vicolo al forte Vigliena 3/15) The Irish theme-pub takeover has reached Ortygia. Nevertheless, this is a great place, with live music, DJs and special nights, plus a decent cocktail list and menu.

Getting There & Away

Bus Unless you're coming from Catania or Messina, you'll almost always find buses faster and more convenient than trains. Interbus buses (☎ 0931 6 67 10) leave from Riva della Posta (also known as Piazza della Posta), or near the Interbus office (☎ 0931 6 67 10) at Via Trieste 28, a block in. They connect with Catania (€4.15, 1¼ hours, at least 12 Monday to Saturday) and its airport, Palermo (€13.95, four hours), Enna and surrounding small towns, including Noto (€2.60, 55 minutes). Interbus also has a daily service to Rome, via Catania (from €32.80 one way).

AST buses leave for Catania (15 daily Monday to Saturday), Piazza Armerina (€7.25, one daily), Noto (€2.60, 12 daily Monday to Saturday), Mòdica and Ragusa from their office (☎ 0931 46 27 11) at Riva della Posta 9.

Train More than a dozen trains depart daily bound for Messina (1st/2nd class €12.90/8.25, 2½ to three hours) via Catania (€6.30/4.40, 1¼ to 1½ hours). Some go on to Rome, Turin, Milan and other long-distance destinations. There is only one direct connection to Palermo (€17.55, 6½ hours) leaving at 12.55pm. If you insist on using trains and miss this one, you'll have to go to Catania and wait there for a connection. There are several slow trains from Syracuse to Mòdica (€4.90, 1¾ hours) and Ragusa (€5.70, 2¼ hours).

Car & Motorcycle By car, if arriving from the north, you will enter Syracuse on Viale Scala Greca. To reach the centre of the city, turn left at Viale Teracati and follow it around to the south; it eventually becomes Corso Gelone. The road between Catania and Syracuse is the SS114 and between Syracuse and Noto it's the SS115. A motorway is supposed to connect the SS114 and SS115, but it starts and ends virtually in the middle of nowhere some kilometres out of Syracuse. You will need to follow the signs to get there. This road is also supposed to connect the region with Gela, but only time will tell if it gets built.

From Papyrus to Paper

The Syracuse region has long been renowned for its manufacture of papyrus, the only place in Europe where it grows wild. The slender stalk is split into long strips, which are soaked in a special vegetal solution. Once softened, they are spread out and arranged in a woven crosshatch, first vertically and then horizontally. The crosshatch is then rolled and glued together with an adhesive, also derived from the papyrus stalk. And, *voila*, paper is born!

Boat There are a number of catamaran services from Malta to Pozzallo (see that section later). For information in Syracuse, check with the Boccadifuoco travel agency (☎ 0931 46 38 66), Viale Mazzini 8.

Getting Around

If you arrive by bus, you'll be dropped on or near Piazza della Posta in Ortygia. Only a few kilometres separate the archaeological park and Ortygia, about a 20-minute walk. Otherwise, bus Nos 1 and 2 make the trip from Piazza della Posta. All city buses cost €0.75 for 90 minutes, irrespective of the number of buses you take.

AROUND SYRACUSE
Castello Eurìalo

Seven kilometres west of the city in the outlying quarter of Epipolae is the castle that was the stronghold of Syracuse's Greek defensive works *(☎ 0931 71 17 73, bus No 11 from Piazza della Posta or the archaeological park; free; open 9am-1 hr before sunset daily)*. Built during the reign of Hieron II, Castello Eurialo (Euryalus Castle) was adapted and fortified by Archimedes and was considered impregnable. Unfortunately for Syracuse, the castle was taken by the Romans without a fight. The views back to Syracuse make the trip worth it.

The River Cyane & The Olympeion

A popular diversion between May and September is a 5km longboat trip on the River Cyane, only 5km west of the city along Via Elorina. The two-hour trip brings you from the mouth of the river right up to the source pool, said to have been formed by the tears of the nymph Cyane when her mistress Persephone (Proserpina in Roman mythology) was abducted by Hades (Pluto). This is the only place outside North Africa where papyrus grows wild; the plants were originally a gift to Hieron II by Ptolemy (see the earlier boxed text 'From Papyrus to Paper'). Along the way, you can check out the ruins of the **Olympeion**, a temple from the 6th century BC. Boat rentals start at around €38.75 per boat, so the bigger the group the better (maximum 15 people). For bookings and information call ☎ 0931 6 90 76. To get there, take bus No 21, 22 or 23 from Piazza della Posta on Ortygia.

Megara Hyblaea

The area north of Syracuse is a largely unattractive sprawl of refineries and heavy industry, but right in the middle of it are the ruins of the ancient settlement of Megara Hyblaea, founded in 728 BC by Greeks from Megara. Its history is largely unfortunate: razed to the ground and all its inhabitants evicted in 483 BC by the tyrant of Gela, Gelon, it was rebuilt on the same spot by Timoleon in 340 BC but only survived until 213 BC when it was destroyed for the second time by the Roman general Marcellus, who then went on to take Syracuse. A small population continued to live there until the 6th century, but it has been abandoned ever since. You'll need your own car to get there (25 minutes north of Syracuse on the SS114).

Beaches

Good swimming is possible at some beaches south of the city. The beach at **Arenella** is accessible from Syracuse by bus No 23 (25 minutes, every 1½ hours from 7am to 8.30pm), which departs from Piazza della Posta. A bit farther south, there are the little rockpools and inlets of **Ognina**.

Fontane Bianche, 19km south of Syracuse, has a good long sandy beach with clean water, a few cheap *trattorie* (restaurants) and a camp site.

***Fontane Bianche** (☎ 0931 79 03 33) €5.70/4.15 per person/tent. Open May-Oct. It's quite big, with hot water and plenty of shaded areas, and is close to the beach. The bus from Syracuse stops right outside.*

To get to Fontane Bianche from Syracuse, take bus No 21 or 22, which run intermittently (€0.75, every 1¾ to three hours) from Piazza della Posta. The last bus to Syracuse leaves Fontane Bianche at around 8pm.

Popular local beaches south of Fontane Bianche include Àvola Lido, Calabernardo, Marzamemi and Portopalo.

The Southeast

THE SYRACUSAN INTERIOR

The mountainous interior of the province lacks the popular appeal of the coastline and is difficult to explore unless you have your own transport. The high limestone cliffs, cut through by deep gorges and valleys and topped by arid plateaus, have always served as a natural fortress against the attentions of unwelcome intruders, be it the ancient Greeks or the modern industrialists. Amid the dry-stone walls and scattered villages, however, are a couple of interesting sights that make a journey inland more than worthwhile, not least the extensive necropolis of Pantalica and the groovy little Baroque town of Palazzolo Acrèide.

Pantalica

Forty kilometres west of Syracuse lies Sicily's most important necropolis, with more than 5000 tombs of various shapes and sizes honeycombed along the cliffs that surround the barren plateau of Pantalica, settled by the Siculi in 1270 BC. The town – called Hybla – thrived until the 8th century BC and the Greek founding of Akrai (see Palazzolo Acrèide later in this chapter) in 664 BC, after which Hybla disappeared and many of the tombs were converted into cave dwellings. These were used in later centuries by Christians escaping from a wave of barbarian invasions. Of the town itself very little survives other than the **Anaktron** or prince's palace.

Getting There & Away The site is a difficult place to reach unless you have your own transport. If you don't, your best bet is to ask at the tourist office in Syracuse or at a travel agent to see if any tours of the area are available. These deals can come and go – see the Organised Tours section in Syracuse for information on Syrako Porta Marina Tourist Point.

Palazzolo Acrèide
postcode 96010 • pop 9200
elevation 670m
The archetypal Baroque answer to the earthquake of 1693, Palazzolo Acrèide was built in

the shadow of the ancient Greek settlement of Akrai, founded in 664 BC as a strategic fortress to command the Syracusan hinterland.

The handsome Baroque town is centred on the elegant Piazza del Popolo, itself dominated by the massive bulk of the 18th-century **Chiesa di San Sebastiano** and the **Palazzo Municipale**, built in 1908. The building is also home to a small tourist office (☎ 0931 88 20 00), which opens 9.30am to 1pm and 3.30pm to 6.30pm Monday to Saturday, although you might find it unstaffed. To get to Piazza del Popolo from Piazza Pretura (where buses depart and arrive), walk up Via San Sebastiano. North of the square, at the end of a tight lane, is Piazza Moro (after Aldo Moro, the Italian prime minister assassinated by the Red Brigades in 1979) and two other exquisite Baroque churches: on the northern side of the square the **Chiesa Madre** and on the southern side the **Chiesa di San Paolo**. At the top of Via Annunziata (the main road leading right out of Piazza Moro) is the fourth of the town's Baroque treasures, the **Chiesa dell'Annunziata**, with a richly adorned portal.

Off Piazza del Popolo is the **Casa-Museo di Antonino Uccello**, formerly the home of the poet and scholar (1922–79) and since 1984 a museum (☎ 0931 88 14 99, Via Machiavelli 19; free; open 9am-1pm daily) with an important and interesting collection of Sicilian folk art. Uccello devoted himself to preserving what he feared was disappearing from Sicilian life, so this is the place to go if you want to see what 18th-century farmers would have worn or how exactly they ground olives to make oil. It's a wonderful experience to wander around a traditional building with a stable, bedroom and living quarters. Only 10 people are allowed in at a time, and a custodian will escort you. Ring the doorbell to gain admission.

Akrai Although the Baroque town is definitely worth exploring, most visitors head straight for the ruins of the archaeological zone (admission €2; open 9am-7pm daily) covering the site of Akrai, a 20-minute walk southwest of the modern town along Corso Vittorio Emanuele. Syracuse's first inland colony was key to defending the overland trading route to other Greek settlements such as Akragas, and reached its apogee under the reign of Hieron II (265–215 BC). It was less important under Roman rule, and apart from a brief role as an early Christian centre it continued to decline and was eventually destroyed by the Saracens in the 9th century.

The most impressive ruin is that of the **Greek theatre**, built at the end of the 3rd century BC and subsequently altered by the Romans, who used it for sittings of the local senate. This perfect semicircle once had an audience capacity of 600 divided into three separate sections. Behind the theatre are two quarries *(latomie)*, from which stone to build the city was removed by prisoners. The quarries were later converted into Christian burial chambers, a fascinating sight, especially when you think about how many bodies were in there and the ingenious use of space. The larger of the two catacombs, the **Intagliata**, has catacombs and altars cut into its sides, while the narrower one, the **Intagliatella**, has a wonderful relief of a large banquet cut into the rock face; it is thought to date from the 1st century BC. Other remains worth noting are the hardly recognisable **Tempio di Afrodite** (Temple of Aphrodite, Venus in Roman), south of the Intagliata, and the **Tempio di Persefone** (Temple of Persephone, Proserpina in Roman), off to the west of the theatre.

South of the archaeological zone are the remarkable stone sculptures known as the **Santoni** (Holy Men). The 12 statues are set in rock and devoted to the goddess Cybele, herself depicted on a seat. The largest figurative complex devoted to this particular goddess was created sometime during the 3rd century BC. It's a five-minute walk down to the statues, but you'll need to wait for a group to go with the guide, who'll want to drive down – see if you can cadge a lift. The area around the statues is closed to the general public.

Places to Stay & Eat *Senatore (☎ 0931 88 34 43, fax 0931 88 34 44, e Largo Senatore Italia)* Singles/doubles with bathroom €38.75/56.80. This hotel is fairly modern, with comfortable air-conditioned rooms with TV and parking.

Hotel Santoro (☎ 0931 88 38 55, fax 0931 88 36 92, Via San Sebastiano 21) Singles/doubles with bathroom €36.15/57.35. Not exactly luxurious, but a hop, skip and a jump from Piazza del Popolo. The rooms have a TV, a fridge and heating. Prices can drop by about €13 in the low season.

Alfredo (☎ 0931 88 32 66, Via Duca d'Aosta 27) Tourist menu €14.45. We recommend Alfredo, just off Piazza del Popolo. The focus is on Sicilian meat dishes and the *salsiccia e costata di maiale* (sausages and roast pork chop) will fill you up and leave you happy.

Da Nunzio (☎ 0931 88 22 86, Corso Vittorio Emanuele 7) Meals around €15. Also close to town, this is good for seafood.

Getting There & Away Unless you have your own transport, the only way to get here is by AST bus from Syracuse's Piazza della Posta (€3.10, one hour, 14 daily Monday to Saturday). The last bus for Syracuse leaves Piazza Pretura at 5.30pm. You can buy tickets on board.

NOTO
postcode 96017 • pop 23,000
elevation 152m

Although a town called Noto or Netum has existed here for many centuries, the 'modern', 17th-century town of Noto dates its existence to 18 January 1693, one week after the flattening of the original Noto by earthquake. On this day the architect Giuseppe Lanza, duke of Camastra, was given the biggest commission of his life: build a town from scratch. He set about his task with a stubborn single-mindedness and a blatant disregard for the wishes of the now homeless townspeople, who were horrified when they heard that the new town was to be 15km away. Lanza was undaunted and, funded by the wealthy nobles of the area, his town was to be the highest expression of Sicilian Baroque. It is also a wonderful example of organised and coherent town planning.

Lanza's true genius, however, was in his choice of collaborators. With the help of the Flemish military engineer Carlos de Grunemberg, the master craftsman Rosario Gagliardi and the architects Vincenzo Sinatra

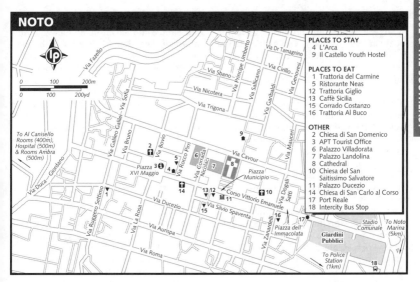

NOTO

(an ancestor of the great crooner perhaps?) and Paolo Laisi, the new Noto put into practice a revolutionary idea based on the creation of two quarters, one for political and religious administration, the other a residential area. Both quarters were built with a careful emphasis on symmetry and visual harmony; indeed, the warm gold and rose hues of the local stone soften the heavily embellished palazzi and churches, making the town very picturesque.

A few years ago, many of Noto's most important buildings were in a state of extreme disrepair – the result of decades of neglect and plenty of minor earth tremors. The town was shocked in early 1996 when the dome and roof of its splendid Baroque cathedral collapsed. Apparently local authorities knew that the dome was cracked beforehand but nothing was done to repair it. Fortunately, no-one was in the church at the time, but the absence of the dome has dramatically altered the town's skyscape. At the time of research, there was quite a bit of scaffolding on many of Noto's fine buildings – a good sign that restoration and maintenance are being taken seriously and that the money for both is actually going where it's needed!

Noto is also good for your taste buds and particularly known for its cakes and pastries. Be aware that accommodation can be a problem, as there aren't many places to stay.

Orientation & Information

Intercity buses drop you at the Giardini Pubblici (public gardens), a nice shady park that meets Porta Reale (behind scaffolding at the time of research), at the beginning of Corso Vittorio Emanuele, the town's main street. You can get a map at the APT tourist office (☎ 0931 57 37 79), along the street on Piazza XVI Maggio. It opens 8.15am to 1.50pm and 3.45pm to 6pm Sunday to Friday.

In a medical emergency call ☎ 0931 89 02 35. The public hospital is on Via dei Mille, on the way out of town towards Noto Antica.

The *carabinieri* (military police) can be contacted on ☎ 0931 83 52 02, and are located on Via Maiore, the eastern extension of Via Aurispa.

There are banks with ATMs on Corso Vittorio Emanuele, near Porta Reale.

Things to See

The collapse of the cathedral dome revealed that most previous restoration work done on the city's monuments had been very superficial – a significant problem, since the local white tufa stone is very soft and, as a building material, requires constant maintenance. The situation was so bad that several buildings remained standing only because they were held up by wooden supports. Lots of money has been allocated in the past and evaporated into the ether. Now, however, it seems that this time the authorities are serious and numerous projects are under way to restore the cathedral and other important buildings in the city centre.

Most of the important monuments line Corso Vittorio Emanuele. Overlooking Piazza XVI Maggio are the beautiful and newly cleaned **Chiesa di San Domenico** and the adjacent **Dominican monastery**, both designed by Rosario Gagliardi. A little towards Porta Reale is the **Palazzo Villadorata** (also known as Palazzo Nicolaci), on Via Corrado Nicolaci. Each of the mansion's richly sculpted balconies is different, sporting a veritable menagerie of centaurs, horses, lions, sirens and tragic masks. Once the home of the princes of Villadorata (a baronial family during the Spanish occupation), it is now partly used as municipal offices and some rooms are open to the public (free) from 9am to 12.30pm and 3.30pm to 8pm.

Across Corso Vittorio Emanuele is the **Chiesa di San Carlo al Corso**, with good views from its *campanile (bell tower; admission €1.55; open 9am-1pm & 4pm-8pm)* over Noto.

The **cathedral** stands at the top of a sweeping staircase overlooking Piazza Municipio. The facade is imposing, but less extravagant than most of Noto's other Baroque monuments. At the time of research it was hidden behind scaffolding, although a life-size picture lets you see what it looks like. Next to the cathedral is the **Palazzo Landolina**, now abandoned but belonging to the Sant'Alfano, Noto's oldest noble family. Across the square is the **Palazzo Ducezio**, Noto's town hall, which has emerged from many years behind scaffolding and is now as bright and shiny as a new tufa-pin.

Farther along the street are the **Chiesa del Santissimo Salvatore** and an adjoining **nunnery**. The church's interior is the most impressive in Noto, if only one could get inside to see it (it's closed to the public).

The nunnery was reserved for the daughters of local nobility. The fountain suspended on a wall next to it remained after Noto's streets were lowered in 1840 to facilitate the movement of carriages.

If you are interested in taking home a few pieces of Sicilian **ceramics**, there are numerous shops throughout town, with pieces from Caltagirone and Santo Stefano di Camastra.

Special Events
Noto's wonderfully colourful flower festival, Infioraci, takes place on the third Sunday in May. Artists line the length of Via Corrada Nicolaci with artwork made entirely of flower petals, a pretty cool way to greet the arrival of spring.

Places to Stay
There are only a handful of accommodation options in Noto.

Il Castello Youth Hostel (☎/fax 0931 57 15 34, e ostellodinoto@tin.it, Via Fratelli Bandiera) Dorm bed €13.50. Right in the centre of things in a beautiful old building, this place is great value for money. There are 68 beds and the open-all-day policy is a blessing.

L'Arca (☎ 0931 83 86 56, fax 0931 57 33 60, e arcarooms@notobarocca.com, Via Rocco Pirri 14/8) Singles/doubles with bathroom €41.30/62. L'Arca is close to Corso Vittorio Emanuele, has cute rooms (only four though) and chipper management.

Al Canisello Rooms (☎ 0931 83 57 93, fax 0931 83 75 70, e mazzone@polosud.it, Via Pavese 1) Singles/doubles with bathroom €51.65/62. This quiet farmhouse is at the end of Corso Vittorio Emanuele, past Piazza N Bixio. It has a lovely garden area and tastefully decorated rooms.

Rooms Ambra (☎/fax 0931 83 55 54, w www.roomsambra.com, Via F Giantommaso 14) Singles/doubles with bathroom €25.80/51.65. In a nice stone-and-concrete building, the good rooms here have been recommended by a few readers. From Corso Vittorio Emanuele, turn left at Via Duca Giordano, then right at Via Alessi and continue straight into Via F Giantommaso.

Places to Eat

The people of Noto are serious about their food, so take time to enjoy a meal and follow it up with a visit to one of the town's excellent pastry shops, where the *gelati* (ice cream) and *dolci* (cakes) are divine. **Caffè Sicilia** *(☎ 0931 83 50 13, Corso Vittorio Emanuele 125)*, which has been operating since 1892, and **Corrado Costanzo** *(☎ 0931 83 52 43, Via Silvio Spaventa 9)*, round the corner, are neck and neck when it comes to the best ice cream and cakes in Noto. Both make superb *dolci di mandorle* (almond cakes and sweets), real *cassata* cake (made with ricotta cheese, chocolate and candied fruit) and *torrone* (nougat), as well as heavenly *granite* (a drink made of crushed ice with fruit juice) – try the one made with *fragolini* (tiny wild strawberries).

Trattoria del Carmine *(☎ 0931 83 87 05, Via Ducezio 1)* Meals around €13. Closed Mon. This trattoria serves excellent home-style meals – try the *coniglio* (rabbit), an appropriate dish in this rabbit-warren of a place. Service can be as slow as a wet weekend though.

Trattoria Giglio *(Piazza Municipio 8-10)* Tourist menu €7.75. This is another good spot for home-style fare, and the prices are budget-friendly.

Ristorante Neas *(☎ 0931 57 35 38, Via Rocco Pirri 30)* Meals around €25. Closed Mon. The Neas, close to Corso Vittorio Emanuele, serves typical Sicilian fare and is a good spot to treat yourself, with excellent seafood pasta and risotto dishes.

Trattoria Al Buco *(☎ 0931 83 81 42, Via Zanardelli 1)* Tourist menu €7.75. This bustling, popular place is another good cheap option in Noto, and locals like it too.

Getting There & Away

Noto is easily accessible by AST and Interbus buses from Catania (€5.70, 2¼ hours) and Syracuse (€2.60, 55 minutes). From June to August only, buses run frequently between Noto and Noto Marina (in the winter there is a school bus service). Trains from Syracuse are frequent (€2.30, 35 minutes, 11 daily), but the station is located 1.5km south of the bus station area, so it's not as good an option for coming or going.

AROUND NOTO
Noto Marina

If you fancy a swim, there's a pleasant **beach** at Noto Marina, 15 minutes away by car or bus (although the latter only run between May and September). Hotels in Noto Marina include **Albergo Korsal** *(☎/fax 0931 81 21 19)*, which has singles/doubles for €31/49 and **President** *(☎ 0931 81 25 43)*, with a higher standard of rooms for €64.55/98.15.

Eloro

On the coast 9km southeast of Noto are the ruins of the ancient Syracusan colony of Helorus, or Eloro *(free; open 8am-2pm daily)*. The town, founded in the 7th century BC, is still in the early stages of being excavated, but so far a portion of the city walls, a small temple dedicated to Demeter (Ceres in Roman mythology) and a theatre have been uncovered. When the site is closed you can still get a look at the place through the fence. You'll need your own transport to get here, or you may fancy walking from Noto Marina. There are nice views of the coastline.

On either side of the hill where the sparse ruins lie are long, sandy beaches comparatively free of the usual crowds. Unfortunately, a storm-water drain spills into the sea at the beach to the south.

Riserva Naturale Oasi Faunistica di Vendicari

Less than 1km south of Eloro is the northern boundary of the protected Vendicari Nature Reserve *(free; open 9am-6pm daily Apr-Oct, 9am-5pm daily Nov-Mar)*, made up of three separate marshes and a splendid sandy beach. The reserve is replete with all manner of water birds, including black-winged stilt, slender-billed gull and Audoin's gull; bird-watchers are well catered for by special observatories. It is possible to reach the park by the SAIS bus connecting Noto and Pachino, or with the Interbus bus from Largo Pantheon behind the public gardens.

Àvola

With a reputation for producing excellent almonds (nicknamed *pizzuta*), Àvola is a pleasant day trip from Syracuse or Noto. Town planning buffs will appreciate the hexagonal shape of the town's design (1693), due to the need for rebuilding after the earthquake. The open and harmonious nature of its architecture and public places is pleasing – look for **Chiesa Madre San Nicolo** in Piazza Umberto I.

To get there, take an AST bus from Syracuse (€2.05, 12 Monday to Saturday, four Sunday) or Noto (12 daily Monday to Saturday, four Sunday). Buses arrive at and depart from Piazza Vittorio Veneto, about five minutes' walk from Piazza Umberto, down Corso Vittorio Emanuele. Trains connect Àvola with Syracuse and Noto, although the station is not quite as handy as the bus station.

The Cape Area

The bottom of Sicily's east doesn't offer much in the way of excitement, but the various African, Maltese and Arabic accents that pervade the area make it a sensual place to visit. **Pachino** is a wine-growing area, while **Marzamemi**, 5km nearby, is a rather lovely fishing town with an old tuna fishery and tuna-based gift/craft shops. **Portopalo di Capo Pàssero** is popular in summer and has a nightly fish market from sunset at the port. The small island off the coast is Isola Capo Pàssero, with a castle and nature reserve. **Isola delle Correnti**, at the bottom of the cape area, really *is* the end of the line, and has a charming bay, thankfully free of pollution.

Eating places aren't flash but you won't go hungry in the area and you can always buy supplies at the *markets* and *alimentari* (grocery shops).

Getting There & Away Interbus has buses to Pachino from Syracuse and Noto (11 daily Monday to Saturday, fewer on Sunday).

If you're coming by car, take the SS115 to

Noto, then follow the signs south to Pachino. Marzamemi is northeast of Pachino, while Portopalo is southeast.

MÒDICA
postcode 97015 • pop 50,500
elevation 296m

About 30km southwest of Noto, and 10km south of Ragusa, lies the town of Mòdica, with its sun-bleached colour, elegant Baroque structures, many churches and two sections: Mòdica Alta (High Mòdica) and, you guessed it, Mòdica Bassa (Low Mòdica). Mòdica has good transport links with Syracuse and is a decent choice as an alternative to Ragusa if you plan to stay in the area.

Orientation & Information

Divided into two parts, Mòdica will test your legs, but it's worth it. The train station is located just over 500m west of Corso Umberto I, past Via Vittorio Veneto. It's better to get the bus, as you'll be dropped off near the intersection of Corso Umberto I and Via Garibaldi. The bus trip is also better in terms of scenery.

The post office is on Corso Umberto I, just near Chiesa di San Domenico, while the police station is at Piazza Matteoti – call ☎ 113 for assistance.

The Pro Loco tourist office (☎ 0932 76 26 26) is at Via Grimaldi 32 and can supply you with the odd map or list.

Things to See

The highlight of a trip to Mòdica is the **Chiesa di San Giorgio** in the upper part of town (local buses run here from the lower end), easily one of the most extraordinary Baroque churches in the province. A majestic stairway sweeps up to a daringly tall facade, erected by Rosario Gagliardi in the early 18th century – it looks as if it was meant to be a tower. The interior features a polyptych by Niger. Walking down Corso Umberto I, with its many fine mansions is a pleasant experience, with the added luxury of width and some fine views.

In the lower town, near Corso Umberto I, Cattedrale di San Pietro has imposing statues of the apostles and an ornate Baroque interior.

Other noteworthy churches are Chiesa di Santa Maria di Bettem on Via Marchesa Tedeschi, Santa Maria del Carmine in Piazza Matteoti and the Chiesa di San Giovanni Evangelista, off Piazza San Giovanni.

The **Museo Civico** *(Via Mercè; free; open 9am-1pm Mon-Sat)* is located on the ground floor of Palazzo dei Mercedari, with a well-ordered display of 19th-century finds.

Places to Stay & Eat

Motel Mòdica (☎ 0932 94 10 77, Corso Umberto I 1) Singles/doubles with bathroom €43.90/59.40. Right at the start of the main drag, this is a decent hotel and worth it if you arrive in the low season, when prices drop considerably.

Bristol (☎ 0932 76 28 90, fax 0932 76 33 30, Via Risorgimento 8) Singles/doubles with bathroom €41.30/77.50. Strangely enough, the Bristol is that rare thing – almost as good value for singles as doubles. It's also a good spot to stay.

Mòdica has a few good places to eat, and you can always stock up on supplies.

Fattoria delle Torri (☎ 0932 75 12 86, Vico Napolitano 14) Meals around €28. Closed afternoon Sun & Mon. In the 'Alta' part of town, this restaurant has excellent local food and wine and is definitely worth the expense.

Getting There & Away

There are plenty of buses and trains to Mòdica from Syracuse (10 buses Monday to Saturday) and Ragusa (all under €5.15).

AROUND MÒDICA

South of Mòdica are the towns of Scicli, Pozzallo and Ìspica.

Scicli is a quiet, crumbling Baroque town, with little in the way of sights except for its main church and **Palazzo Beneventano**, an 18th-century palace decorated with grotesque sculptures (not very well maintained).

Pozzallo, on the coast, is a nice small town with a **beach** (good for swimming and very popular in summer) and a rather unfortunate industrial complex. See the Getting There & Around section later for details of the Pozzallo-Malta ferry service.

Ìspica is an 18th-century town (planned chessboard style) at the head of a 13km-long, wide gorge known as **Cava d'Ìspica** *(☎ 0932 95 11 33, admission €2.10; open 9am-1.30pm & 3pm-6.30pm daily)* that was once used in Neolithic times for burials and in Medieval times for cave-dwelling.

Getting There & Around

Scicli, Pozzallo and Ìspica are all accessible by bus and train from both Mòdica and Ragusa. If you're driving from Syracuse, take the SS115 and follow the signs to the towns.

Virtu Ferries has services between Pozzallo and Malta at around 9.30pm on Monday, Wednesday, Thursday and Saturday from 1 August to 3 September (€83/104 single/return high season, 1½ hours) and at 3pm and 9.30pm Tuesday, Friday and Sunday. Departures are less frequent at other times but run between early May and October. The Virtu office at Pozzallo (☎ 0932 95 40 62) is at Via Studi 80 (in front of Via Lungomare Raganzino). In Pozzallo, there's a free courtesy bus that will take you from the ferry dock to the town centre (to the train station it's €2.60).

RAGUSA & RAGUSA IBLA
postcode 97100 • pop 68,000
elevation 502m

Next to Noto, the best example of the Sicilian Baroque is to be found in Ragusa, the capital of the province that shares its name. Like Noto, the old town of Ragusa Ibla was flattened by the earthquake of 1693 and rebuilt in the Baroque style on a highland above the site of the original settlement. Unlike Noto, however, the old town was also rebuilt, with the result being a curious cocktail of medieval and Baroque. A rivalry developed between Ragusa Ibla and the 'new' town of Ragusa which lasted until 1927, when the Fascist authorities merged the two towns into one. Unification proved disastrous for Ragusa Ibla, whose population left in droves for the more prosperous and commercially orientated upper town. Today, people do still live here and it's a delightful place to visit.

RAGUSA & RAGUSA IBLA

PLACES TO STAY
4 Hotel San Giovanni
6 Mediterraneo Palace
10 Hotel Montreal
11 Hotel Rafael

PLACES TO EAT
1 Puglisi
14 Ristorante Duomo
17 Trattoria La Bettola
18 U Saracinù
21 La Rusticana;
    u Risuntuoriu

OTHER
2 Hospital

3 Bus Station
5 Museo Archeologico Ibleo
7 Banco di Sicilia & ATM
8 Duomo di San Giovanni
    Battista
9 Police Station
12 Post Office
13 Chiesa del Purgatorio
15 APT Tourist Office
16 Cattedrale di San Giorgio
19 Chiesa di San Giuseppe
20 Post Office
22 Chiesa di San Giorgio Vecchio
23 Chiesa di San Giacomo
24 Chiesa Sant'Agata (Convento
    dei Cappucchini)

City bus Nos 1 and 3 run from Piazza del Popolo in the upper town to Piazza Pola and the Giardino Ibleo in the lower town of Ragusa Ibla.

Orientation & Information

The lower town, Ibla, has most of the sights, but transport and accommodation are in the newer upper town. The train station is on Piazza del Popolo and the intercity bus station is on the adjacent Piazza Gramsci. From the train station, turn left and head along Viale Tenente Lena, across the bridge (Ponte Nuovo) and straight ahead along Via Roma to reach Corso Italia, the upper town's main street. Turn right on Corso Italia and follow it to the stairs to Ibla, or follow the winding road to the lower town.

The helpful tourist office (☎ 0932 62 14 21) is in Ragusa Ibla at Via Capitano Bocchieri 33 in Palazzo La Rocca. It opens 9am to 1.30pm Monday to Saturday. The main post office is in the new town at the corner of Via Ecce Homo and Via Rapisardi. There's also a post office in Piazza Pola, next to Chiesa di San Giuseppe in Ragusa Ibla. There's a Banco di Sicilia with ATM on Via Roma, opposite the Mediterraneo Palace.

The public hospital (ospedale civile; ☎ 0932 62 39 46 for the Guardia Medica), is across Piazza del Popolo from the train station. For an ambulance, call ☎ 0932 62 14 10. The police station (questura) is located next to the town hall on Via Raspardi; call ☎ 113 for assistance.

Ragusa Ibla

Despite the occasional look of decay and abandonment that pervades the lower town, it is by far the more interesting of the two. Aside from the churches mentioned below, the best thing about the town is simply to wander through its narrow streets and sun-drenched squares checking out the abandoned Baroque mansions that have been restored or are still crying out for an interested developer to take a restoring hand to them. The old town is best accessed via the *salita commendatore*, a winding pass made up of stairs and narrow archways taking you past the remains of the 15th-century Santa Maria delle Scale, from where there's a good view of Ragusa Ibla below. Keep going down and you come to Piazza della Repubblica and the **Chiesa del Purgatorio**, whose main altar features a depiction of *Anime in Purgatorio* (Souls in Purgatory) by Francesco Manno. At the time of research, it was behind scaffolding and entry was not allowed.

If you continue east along Via del Mercato (which has great views of the valley below) you'll get your first side view of palm-planted Piazza del Duomo, whose western end is dominated by the wonderful 1744 **Cattedrale di San Giorgio**, one of the best examples of the Sicilian Baroque. The brainchild of Rosario Gagliardi (of Noto fame), the church's facade is an elegant wedding-cake structure divided into three tiers, each level supported by gradually narrowing Corinthian columns and punctuated by jutting cornices. The light-filled interior is definitely not as stunning as the exterior, although there are two paintings by Dario Guerci and some other interesting bits and bobs, such as a statue of St George on horseback.

The genius of Gagliardi is also evident in the facade of the **Chiesa di San Giuseppe** on Piazza Pola, east of Piazza del Duomo on Corso XXV Aprile. Like San Giorgio, it is divided into three tiers with Corinthian columns and statues. The elliptical interior is topped by a cupola decorated with a fresco of the *Gloria di San Benedetto* (Glory of St Benedict; 1793) by Sebastiano Lo Monaco.

At the eastern end of the old town is the beautiful **Giardino Ibleo** *(open 8am-8pm daily)*, a pleasant public garden laid out in the 19th century that is perfect for a picnic lunch or a lie-down. In its grounds are the remains of three medieval churches: **Chiesa di San Vincenzo Ferrari**; **Chiesa di San Giacomo** *(1563; open 9am-1pm & 3.30pm-7pm)*, with a badly damaged but interesting painted ceiling; and **Chiesa Sant'Agata** *(Convento dei Cappuccini; open 9am-1pm*

& 3.30pm-7pm), with a noteworthy altar-piece and three great examples of painter Pietro Novelli's work *(Assumption of the Virgin, Sant'Agatha* and *Santa Caterina d'Alessandria)*. There's also the Catalonian-Gothic portal of what was once the large **Chiesa di San Giorgio Vecchio**, but is now mostly ruined. In the lunette there is an interesting bas-relief of St George killing the dragon, which is visible from the street, near the entrance to the garden.

The Upper Town

The upper town is crowned by the **Duomo di San Giovanni Battista** dedicated to John the Baptist, built between 1718 and 1778 as a lasting symbol of Ragusa's urban renewal. An elegant square fronts the ornate carved facade, made asymmetrical by a stout bell tower on its western flank.

South of the cathedral, off Via Roma, is the **Museo Archeologico Ibleo** *(☎ 0932 62 29 63, Via Natalelli; admission €2.10; open 9am-1.30pm & 4pm-7.30pm daily)*, an important archaeological museum housing finds from prehistoric times and from the Greek site at Camarina on the coast. Also of interest are the ceramics from the caravan centre of Scornavacche, including a reconstructed kiln. Don't miss the mosaic floor remains from Santa Croce Camerina, near the end of the loop around the museum. Unfortunately, if you don't read Italian, gleaning information about the finds will be a problem.

Places to Stay

All of Ragusa's accommodation is in the upper town; budget hotels are rare.

Hotel San Giovanni *(☎ 0932 62 10 13, fax 0932 62 13 94, Via Traspontino 3)* Singles/doubles €23.25/36.15, with bathroom €31/51.65. To get to this hotel from Piazza del Popolo, head down Viale Leonardo da Vinci, turn left at Via Ingegnere Migliorisi and follow it to the footbridge. It's good value and the management is amicable.

Hotel Rafael *(☎ 0932 65 40 80, fax 0932 65 34 18, Corso Italia 40)* Singles/doubles with bathroom €46.50/67.15. This is a pleasant establishment, with some very modern, minimalist decorative touches (unusual for Sicily).

Hotel Montreal *(☎ 0932 62 11 33, fax 0932 62 10 26, Corso Italia 70)* Singles/doubles with bathroom & breakfast €51.65/ 82.65. Near Hotel Rafael is the Montreal, which has good rooms and facilities in a pinker-than-pink old palazzo.

Mediterraneo Palace *(☎ 0932 62 19 44, fax 0932 62 37 99, Via Roma 189)* Singles/doubles with bathroom €82.65/108.45. The modern Mediterraneo Palace has plush rooms, right near the museum.

Places to Eat

Trattoria la Bettola *(☎ 0932 65 33 77, Largo Camerina 7)* Meals around €18. Pleasant la Bettola is downhill to the left off Piazza del Duomo, and has good local cooking.

Ristorante Duomo *(☎ 0932 65 12 65, Via Cap Bochieri 31)* Meals around €25. Next to the tourist office on Ragusa Ibla, this lovely place does a mean couscous with local lamb (€12.90).

La Rusticana *(☎ 0932 22 79 81, Via XXV Aprile 68)* Meals around €18. Try the *tonno e cippola* (tuna and onion, €9.30) at this reasonable little joint with a pleasant outdoor area.

U Risuntuoriu *(Via XXV Aprile 76)* Right next to La Rusticana, this is a pleasant 'ristopub' that's great for a drink and a snack.

U Saracinù *(☎ 0932 24 69 76, Via del Convento 9)* Tourist menu €11.35; meal around €20. Closed Wed. This eatery is off Piazza del Duomo and serves local cuisine and standard Italian dishes.

Puglisi *(☎ 0932 62 34 40, Via Dante 94)* This *tavola calda* (literally 'hot table', basically a self-service restaurant) has good basic lunches and snacks (about €3.60) and is handy in terms of transport (bus tickets are sold here and it's close to both the bus and train stations).

Getting There & Away

Ragusa is accessible by train from Syracuse (€5.70, 2¼ hours, eight daily), Noto (€4.25, 1¾ hours, eight daily) and Gela (€3.80, 1¼ hours, six daily). Interbus-Etna Trasporti (information and tickets at Puglisi, Via Dante 94), runs daily buses to Catania, Caltanissetta, Palermo and around the region.

AST (☎ 0932 68 18 18) serves Palermo (four buses Monday to Saturday, two Sunday) and runs more regularly to Noto (seven daily) and Syracuse (€5.40, 2½ hours, seven daily). An AST timetable is posted on Piazza Gramsci where AST and SAIS buses stop. Other AST destinations include Mòdica (11 Monday to Saturday) and Chiaramonte (six daily).

AROUND RAGUSA

Ten kilometres west of Ragusa, on the SS115, is the town of **Còmiso**, with plenty of Baroque buildings and churches to look at, and a rare survivor of the earthquake of 1693, the Chiesa di San Francesco (13th century). Six kilometres west of Còmiso is **Vittòria**, founded in 1603 by Vittoria Colonna, hence the name. The town has Baroque buildings and is a wine-making centre for the region.

North of Còmiso (take the SS514) is **Chiaramonte Gulfi**, with churches, decent views of the countryside and delicious ham. It was founded by Manfredi Chiaramonte, the Count of Mòdica.

Southwest of Ragusa (20km) is the **Castello di Donnafugata** *(free; open 9am-1pm Tues-Sun)*, a 19th-century building with some remnants of its 17th-century predecessor. It looks even older than that though, as it was designed in the Venetian-Gothic style – don't confuse it with the Donnafugata of *The Leopard* though! A car is definitely the best way to see these towns; although train and bus services exist from Syracuse, frequency can be a problem.

Central Sicily

Away from the tourist trails that extend their way around much of Sicily's coastline, the vast expanse of the mountainous interior is more representative of traditional Sicilian life than any other area on the island. With only a few exceptions – and despite the presence of the A19 motorway, which cuts a swathe through most of the interior between Palermo and Catania – the centre can seem isolated and forbidding. On an island whose considerable natural beauty has often been substantially damaged by overdevelopment, this is, however, a key element of its allure. Here, hilltop towns survive in splendid semi-isolation, particularly in the eastern interior. In the western half the isolation is less splendid and more desperate, as tiny villages struggle to survive in a landscape ravaged by poverty, emigration and the nefarious influence of the Mafia.

For over a decade tour operators and the Sicilian tourist authorities have been touting the areas away from the sea as the next big tourist destinations but so far nothing substantial has come of it, with most visitors still preferring the coastal cities and resorts to the mountainous inland. The problem is not the lack of interesting sights or splendid natural settings, but the deficit of tourist infrastructure, particularly budget and mid-range accommodation options. Transportation is also more problematic than on the coast, and you'll be better off with your own vehicle outside the bigger towns.

ENNA
postcode 94100 • pop 29,500
elevation 948m
Situated high on a commanding ridge in the sun-scorched centre of Sicily, Enna towers above the surrounding countryside in an enviable position that has earned it two nicknames: it is known as the *belvedere* (panoramic viewpoint) or the *ombelico* (umbilicus) of Sicily. It makes a good base for exploring the surrounding region, especially if you're visiting the region's eminent tourist

Highlights

- Stroll the medieval streets of Enna and enjoy the fine views over the surrounding countryside
- Walk above the breathtaking polychrome mosaics of the Roman Villa at Casale
- Scale the ceramic-decorated Scalinata di Santa Maria del Monte in Caltagirone

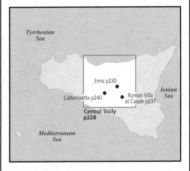

Tyrrhenian Sea

Enna p230

Caltanissetta p240 • • Roman Villa at Casale p237

Central Sicily p228

Ionian Sea

Mediterranean Sea

attraction, the extraordinary mosaics of the Roman villa at Casale. For centuries an almost impregnable fortress town, Enna has preserved much of its medieval centre in remarkably good order, which is pretty impressive when you consider that it is the capital of one of the island's poorest provinces. The beautiful approach to the town has been slightly spoilt by some ugly modern construction, particularly on its southern slope, but there is enough to see within its core to warrant at least a one-day visit. One of the most pleasant sights in town is when locals flood onto the traffic-free Via Roma for the traditional *passeggiata* (evening stroll).

History
The colony of Henna was founded on this high plateau in 664 BC by colonists from Gela eager to exploit the area's agricultural

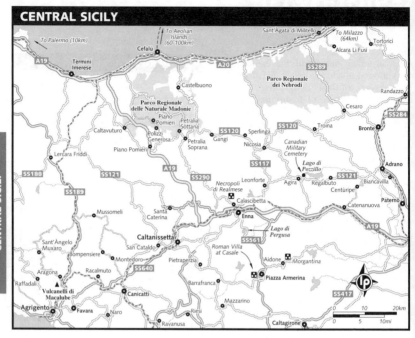

CENTRAL SICILY

resources. In 397 BC the town fell to Dionysius of Syracuse and it remained in Syracusan hands until the 3rd century BC when it entered the orbit of Roman power. The First Servile War broke out here in 135 BC under the command of the slave Eunus; the Romans eventually recaptured the town after a two-year siege. In AD 859 it was the turn of the Saracens, who had to sneak in one by one through a sewer to breach the town's hardy defences. They renamed it 'Kasr Janna' (from the Latin 'Castrum Hennae', Garrison Town of Henna) and held on until the Normans arrived in 1087. The name was then corrupted into Castrogiovanni, by which it was known until 1927, when it was changed back to Enna by Mussolini. Today the town retains its importance as an agricultural centre.

Information

The APT office (☎ 0935 52 82 88) is at Via Roma 413. The staff are helpful and you can pick up a map and information on the city and province. The office opens 9am to 1pm and 3.30pm to 6.30pm Monday to Saturday.

The post office is at Via Volta 1, just off Piazza Garibaldi. Public telephones are scattered about the town; you can try at the Grande Albergo Sicilia (see Places to Stay & Eat later), which also has a few public phones.

There are several banks with ATMs around the city centre, including the Banco di Sicilia at Via Roma 367.

For medical assistance, go to the Ospedale Civile Umberto I (hospital) on Via Trieste, or for first aid (*pronto soccorso*) in an emergency call ☎ 0935 4 52 45. The police station (*questura*; ☎ 0935 52 21 11) is at Via San Giuseppe 2.

Castello di Lombardia

Enna's most visible monument (*free; open 9am-1pm & 3pm-5pm daily*) dominates the eastern side of town. The original castle was built by the Saracens and later reinforced by the Normans; Frederick II of Aragon ordered that a powerful curtain wall be built with towers on every side. The wall is still intact but only six of the original 20 towers remain. Within the walls is a complex structure of courtyards; the closest one to the entrance (Cortile di San Martino; Courtyard of St Martin) is used in summer as an outdoor theatre (see Special Events). From the same courtyard you can climb up one of the towers (Torre Pisana), from where the view is simply breathtaking – at least when the fog (an enduring element of Enna's weather) has lifted. Across the valley is the town of Calascibetta (see that section later in this chapter) and to the distant northeast you can just about make out the towering peak of Mt Etna.

Rocca di Cerere

To the north of the castle a small road leads quickly down to the remains of the temple of the goddess of agriculture, Ceres (the Greek Demeter). Enna was the centre of an important cult of Ceres and the temple was supposedly erected in 480 BC by the tyrant Gelon, who was eager to gain favour with the goddess lest his plans for the capture of Syracuse be foiled by a couple of bad harvests. Ceres' daughter was Proserpina (also known as Persephone), whose abduction to Hades is the subject of one of the most enduring and captivating of all Roman myths; the action is supposed to have taken place 9km south of town at Lago di Pergusa (see the later boxed text 'A Devil's Bargain'). The temple's remains are not enclosed and it's a great spot for a picnic or to take in a sunrise or sunset.

Along Via Roma

Back in town, Enna's main artery is Via Roma, which extends westwards from the castle (and also down to the southwest of town) and is lined with most of the town's more important sights.

Coming from the castle, the first of these is the **cathedral** *(free; open 9am-1pm & 4pm-7pm daily)*. Founded in 1307 by Eleonora, the wife of Frederick III, the Gothic structure was destroyed by fire in 1446 and slowly rebuilt in early Baroque

style over the next 200 years. The curious facade (complete with 17th-century bell tower) covers its Gothic predecessor, while the rich interior is almost entirely Baroque in design. The dark-grey basalt columns are worth looking at for their highly ornamented bases, which are carved with a series of grotesques, such as snakes with human heads. The five paintings (dating from 1613) in the presbytery are by Filippo Paladino and feature scenes from the New Testament. Also worth checking out are the altarpieces by Guglielmo Borremans on the southern side of the church; of particular interest is the splendid painting of *Sante Lucilla e Giacinto* (St Lucy and Hyacinth).

Next door is the interesting **Museo Alessi** *(☎ 0935 50 31 65, Via Roma 465; admission €2.60; open 9am-1.30pm & 4pm-6pm Tues-Sun)*, which houses the contents of the cathedral's treasury. It was originally the property of Canon Giuseppe Alessi (1774–1837), who left the collection to his brother with the intention that he then donate it to the Church. Eager to make a tidy profit, Alessi's brother entered into lengthy negotiations with the clerical authorities who eventually bought the collection in 1860 and displayed it in 1862. A good thing, too, because some of the pieces are stunning, including a fabulous pelican-shaped jewelled ornament and a gold crown encrusted with jewels and enamels (dating from 1653) by Leonardo and Giuseppe Montalbano. Other highlights of the collection include a fascinating and well-ordered numismatic collection and a painting of the Madonna with Saints Clare and Agnes of Assisi by Giuseppe Salerno, nicknamed '*Lo Zeppo di Gangi*' (The Cripple of Gangi; see West from Nicosia later in this chapter).

On the far side of Piazza Mazzini from the cathedral is the **Museo Archeologico di Palazzo Varisano** *(☎ 0935 52 81 00; admission €2.05; open 8am-7.30pm daily)*, which has a good (if small) collection of artefacts (labelled in Italian) excavated throughout the region (Calascibetta, Pergusa, Cozzo Matrice and so on). Of particular interest is the Attic style red-and-black *krater* (drinking vessel) found in the town itself.

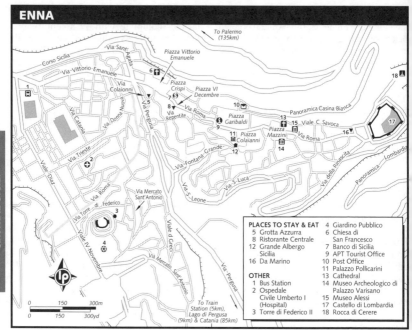

ENNA

To Palermo (135km)

To Train Station (5km), Lago di Pergusa (9km) & Catania (85km)

PLACES TO STAY & EAT	
5	Grotta Azzurra
8	Ristorante Centrale
12	Grande Albergo Sicilia
16	Da Marino

OTHER	
1	Bus Station
2	Ospedale Civile Umberto I (Hospital)
3	Torre di Federico II
4	Giardino Pubblico
6	Chiesa di San Francesco
7	Banco di Sicilia
9	APT Tourist Office
10	Post Office
11	Palazzo Pollicarini
13	Cathedral
14	Museo Archeologico di Palazzo Varisano
15	Museo Alessi
17	Castello di Lombardia
18	Rocca di Cerere

About 100m farther down Via Roma, on the southwestern side of Piazza Colaianni next to the Grande Albergo Sicilia, is the Catalan-Gothic **Palazzo Pollicarini**, one of Enna's most handsome buildings. Although it has been converted into private apartments, you can still nip in to take a peak at the medieval staircase in the central courtyard.

Towers

On Piazza Vittorio Emanuele, the most impressive element of the **Chiesa di San Francesco** is its 16th-century bell tower *(campanile)*, adorned with fine Gothic windows. The tower once formed part of the city's defence system.

Chunky **Torre di Federico II** (Tower of Frederick II), in the public gardens (Giardino Pubblico) in the new part of town, is also part of the old defences. The octagonal tower, standing 24m high, was once linked by a secret passage to the Castello di Lombardia.

Special Events

During Holy Week at Easter, Enna is the setting for colourful, traditional celebrations. On Good Friday, thousands of people wearing hoods and capes of different colours participate in a solemn procession to the cathedral.

The Feast of the Virgin of the Visitation (Festa di Maria Santissima della Visitazione), Enna's patron saint, is celebrated on 2 July. Traditionally, the saint's icon was dragged through town on a cart (called La Nave Dorata, the Golden Ship) by farmers wearing nothing but a white band over their hips; today the band has been replaced by a long, embroidered sheet. The feast is accompanied by a salvo of fireworks.

During June and July the Castello di Lombardia hosts a series of nightly plays and performances, with a medieval theme. Contact the APT office (see under Information earlier) for more information on these events.

Places to Stay & Eat
Enna itself has only one hotel and it's not cheap.

***Grande Albergo Sicilia** (☎ 0935 50 08 50, fax 0935 50 04 88, Piazza Colaianni 7)* Singles/doubles with bathroom €56.30/ 87.80. This excellent hotel has well-appointed rooms with TV, fridge, phone and good views of the surrounding countryside.

For other accommodation, you'll have to catch city bus No 5 from Piazza Vittorio Emanuele to Lago di Pergusa (see that section later in this chapter).

Dining is not a problem, however. Unlike the coast, the main staple here is meat and the local specialities usually involve some cut of mutton or beef.

***Da Marino** (☎ 0935 2 52 22, Viale C Sàvoca 62)* Meals about €13. Closed Mon. Near the castle, this no-fuss pizzeria is a good spot to get pizza and pasta dishes.

***Grotta Azzurra** (☎ 0935 2 43 28, Via Colaianni 1)* Meals about €11. Closed Sat. Down a narrow lane, the Grotta Azzurra offers cheap, simple and tasty meals.

***Ristorante Centrale** (☎ 0935 50 09 63, Piazza VI Dicembre 9)* Meals about €18. The menu of Sicilian specialities here changes daily; it's a friendly place serving good food.

There is a ***market*** every morning from Monday to Saturday on Via Mercato Sant'Antonio where you can find basics such as fresh fruit, bread and cheese.

Getting There & Around
Buses arrive at and leave from the bus station (☎ 0935 50 09 05) on Viale Diaz. SAIS Autolinee buses (☎ 0935 50 09 02) connect Enna with Catania (€5.95, 1½-two hours, six to eight daily Monday to Saturday, three on Sunday) and its airport, and Palermo (€5.95, 1¾ hours, six daily Monday to Saturday, four on Sunday). It is possible to reach Agrigento via Caltanissetta (€3.10, one hour, four daily Monday to Saturday). Regular SAIS buses also run to Piazza Armerina (€2.60, 45 minutes).

The train station is inconveniently located at the bottom of a steep hill 5km south of the town centre. Local buses (€1.30, day

pass €2.05) make the run to town hourly (except Sunday, when you might have to wait a couple of hours between buses) but you're best off not bothering with the train at all.

You can call for a taxi on ☎ 0935 50 09 05.

NORTH FROM ENNA
The winding SS121 makes its way out of Calascibetta in a northeasterly direction through some of the most splendid inland scenery on the island before it eventually reaches Catania. There are a couple of towns, such as Calascibetta and Leonforte, worth taking time to stop in, if only to get a sense of what Sicilian life is like away from the tourist trail. All of the towns mentioned are reachable by bus from Enna; check at the tourist office or the bus terminal for departure details and prices. Without a doubt, the best way to explore this area is with your own transport, as some services are non-existent after the morning and afternoon peak hours.

Calascibetta
postcode 94010 • pop 5010
elevation 691m
Just 2km north of Enna across a valley and the A19 motorway lies this hilltop town where Count Roger I camped during his siege of Enna in 1087. Seemingly ambivalent about the influence of modernism, Calascibetta is a densely packed maze of little streets above an enormous drop (on its eastern side) to the valley below. The 14th-century **cathedral** *(free; open 9am-1pm & 3pm-7pm daily)*, dedicated to St Peter, is worth popping your head into – if only for the good collection of liturgical objects.

Only 1km or so northwest of town is the well-signposted **Necropoli di Realmese,** where some 300 rock tombs dating from 850 to 730 BC have been found. The site is unenclosed and open at all times.

The town is within easy access from Enna by Sais Autolinee bus (€1.30, 11 daily Monday to Saturday, two on Sunday) from the main bus terminal; buses depart from 7.10am during school terms and from 8am Monday to Saturday otherwise.

CENTRAL SICILY

Leonforte
postcode 94013 • pop 15100
elevation 603m

A farther 18km northeast along the SS121 is this attractive Baroque town, founded in 1610 and once renowned for its horse breeding. Leonforte's most imposing building (visible from the road) is the **Palazzo Baronale**, which has a pretty, ornate facade. The town's **cathedral** houses some good wooden sculptures, but the real sight of interest is the **Granfonte**. Built in 1651 by Nicolò Branciforte, it is an ornate fountain made up of 24 separate jets against a sculpted facade. The fountain is about 300m down a small road from the cathedral (follow the signpost).

Interbus has frequent departures between Enna and Leonforte (€2.05, 35 minutes, five to 11 daily). Buy tickets on the bus or at Bar Venticinque in Leonforte.

Agira
postcode 94011 • pop 9150
elevation 650m

From a distance, Agira rises up in an almost perfect cone with the ruins of its medieval Norman castle at the top. The town was colonised by Timoleon in 339 BC and was later captured by the Romans, who added substantially to the existing Greek settlement. The Augustan historian Diodorus Siculus was born here and declared that the amphitheatre *(anfiteatro)* was matched in beauty only by that of Syracuse. Apart from a few unremarkable traces, there is little that remains of its distinguished past (the town had an important mint for 500 years) and even the town's 16th-century church is closed. Still, this is a popular stop if only because it has a hotel.

Aurora (☎ 0935 69 14 16, Via Annunziata 6) Singles/doubles with bathroom for €25.80/41.30. The rooms are bare but clean in this small hotel.

From Enna, SAIS buses make the trip to Agira (€2.85, 1¾ hours, six daily Monday to Saturday, four on Sunday). There are also three SAIS buses daily between Agira and Troina (see East from Nicosia later in this chapter).

The SS121 to Regalbuto

The road to Regalbuto (about 14km northeast of Agira) is more interesting than the town at the end of it. A couple of kilometres out of Agira (signposted to your left), atop a little hill, is a well-tended **Canadian Military Cemetery** where lie the bodies of 480 soldiers killed in July 1943. Farther on, still to your left, is a large artificial lake known as the **Lago di Pozzillo**. This is a great spot for a picnic, amid the almond trees and prickly pears. Under no circumstances try to pick one of these pears without gloves: although they look harmless enough, they are covered in tiny needles that are very difficult to remove from your skin!

Centùripe
postcode 94010 • pop 6610
elevation 730m

About 13km past Regalbuto on the road to Adrano and Mt Etna is a turn-off south for this little town, known as the Balcone di Sicilia (Balcony of Sicily) on account of its commanding position on a ridge in front of the volcano. The approach from the turn-off (you will need your own transport) brings you through 7km of lovely citrus groves and then uphill into the town, which has been fought over many times due to its strategic importance. The last battle occurred in 1943; when the Allies captured the town, the Germans realised that their foothold in Sicily had slipped and they retreated back to the Italian mainland. The town centre was partially destroyed by Allied bombs and much of it is now a collection of uninspired modern buildings, with the sole exception of the 17th-century pink-and-white **cathedral.**

Nicosia
postcode 94014 • pop 15,030
elevation 724m

This sizable town is a good base from which to begin your exploration of the region. Although it was originally a Byzantine settlement (which was later captured by the Saracens), Nicosia's glory days were during the Norman era, when it was the most important settlement of a series of fortified towns that stretched from Palermo to Messina. Although in a sometimes alarming state of decay, the private residences that line the town's streets are a good indication of its former prosperity, when wealthy Franco-German landowners competed with each other to build the most sumptuous house.

At the centre of town is the busy Piazza Garibaldi, dominated by the 19th-century **cathedral**, which was built to replace a smaller, 14th-century church and incorporated the original portal and bell tower. Of particular interest inside is a baptismal font by Domenico Gagini and a wooden crucifix by Fra Umile di Petralia, which is carried through the town on Good Friday.

At the top of the hill is the 19th-century **Chiesa di Santa Maria Maggiore** – another reconstruction as the original 13th-century church was destroyed by a landslide in 1757. In 1968 the bell tower was demolished by an earthquake and its bells re-hung on a low iron bracket – the chime you hear is electric. Inside is a lovely marble polyptych by Gagini.

Places to Stay & Eat Like so much of the island's interior, accommodation is in short supply. If you have your own transport, you can stay at one of two hotels on the outskirts of town.

Pineta (☎/fax 0935 64 70 02, Località San Paolo) Singles/doubles with bathroom €36.15/56.80. Pineta is a couple of kilometres south of town. It's clean and pretty comfortable; the rooms have phone, TV and heating, and there's parking.

Vigneta (☎ 0935 64 60 74, Contrada San Basilico) Singles/doubles €23.25/31. Vigneta is a little farther afield, about 5km south of the Pineta. This is another clean and comfortable option.

La Cirata (☎ 0935 64 05 61, SS117, Contrada Cirata) Meals about €26. Closed Mon. The cavernous La Cirata, 5km south of town on the SS117, is the best place to eat. In summer the place is a popular stop for bus tours, who come for the solid rustic cuisine, including a lip-smacking lamb roast.

There are a couple of bars on Piazza Garibaldi that can rustle up a sandwich and even a hot plate at lunch.

Getting There & Away Nicosia is served by Interbus buses from Leonforte (€2.05, 40 minutes, four daily Monday to Saturday, one on Sunday), Catania (€5.15, two hours, five daily Monday to Saturday) and other towns throughout the region. Buses arrive and depart from Piazza Marconi. You can buy your tickets from Bar del Passeggero by the bus stop.

EAST FROM NICOSIA

From Nicosia the SS120 skirts the southern border of the wide expanse of the Parco Regionale dei Nebrodi (see the Tyrrhenian Coast chapter for details), across some of the most beautiful scenery on the whole island. Before the construction of the A20 motorway (still incomplete after all these years!) along the northern Tyrrhenian coast, this was the main route between Messina and Palermo. Thankfully this is no longer the case and an air of tranquillity now prevails.

The area is not well served by public transport but has a couple of places worth checking out if you have your own wheels. About 34km along the road is the village of **Troina**, standing over 1000m high on a narrow perch. It was one of the first towns taken by the Normans from the Arabs. Count Roger I nearly suffered a humiliating defeat (which would have resulted in the complete withdrawal of his troops from Sicily) here in 1064. To commemorate his victory, Roger founded a **convent** (Convento di San Basilio), which is now in ruins.

If you are dependent on public transport, you can take an Interbus bus in Agira (€2.05, one hour, two daily) that winds its way up the narrow road from the south. There are also infrequent Interbus buses from Catania, Regalbuto, Leonforte and Enna.

WEST FROM NICOSIA

The SS120 from Nicosia heading west takes in some beautiful countryside, which is perfect for driving. There are also bus connections but it's difficult to travel through this area if you're without a car.

Sperlinga, a 15-minute bus ride or drive from Nicosia, is an interesting small town nestled underneath an impressive castle rock. The town started out as a cave-dwellers home (you can still see many of the caves) and also made a name for itself by being the only place that did not take part in the Sicilian Vespers in 1282.

The beautiful medieval hilltop town **Gangi** is definitely worth a visit if you like soaking up a quiet atmosphere. The town produced two well-known 17th-century painters, Gaspare Vazano and Giuseppe Salerno, who were both nicknamed '*Lo Zeppo di Gangi*' (The Cripple of Gangi). You can see Salerno's impressive *Last Judgement* (1629) in the town's lovely Chiesa Madre.

To get to Gangi by car, take the SS120 from Nicosia (19km) or from the Tyrrhenian Coast. Sais Autolinee has a bus connecting Gangi with Enna (via Sperlinga and Calascibetta) at 6am Monday to Saturday. From Enna to Gangi (via Sperlinga), the bus departs at 2pm (two hours).

There are some excellent establishments if you're looking to stay somewhere with more character.

Tenuta Gangivecchio (☎ *0921 64 48 04, fax 0921 68 91 91, Contrada Gangi Vecchio)* Half-board €51.65 per person. This *agriturismo* (rooms on a working farm) option is in a former 14th-century Benedictine convent just out of Gangi. Children aged under 10 aren't accommodated at Easter and New Year.

Casale Villa Rainò (☎ *0921 64 46 80, fax 0921 64 44 24,* e *villaraino@citiesonline .it, Contrada Rainò)* Singles/doubles with bathroom €46.50/67.15. Close to Gangi, this charming agriturismo is an excellent choice in the area, with a lovely family atmosphere, tastefully decorated rooms and a wonderful restaurant, all housed in a 19th-century stone building. When we visited, a swimming pool was about to be added to the list of attractions.

Pomieri (☎*/fax 0921 64 98 55, Località Piano Pomieri)* Singles/doubles with bathroom €43.90/64.55. About 3km north of Gangi at Piano Pomieri, the two-star Pomieri hotel is often cheaper and larger than hotels in the Madonie area, but not as nice.

Many hotels and agriturismo in the area have good restaurants and there's always a bar where snacks are available in the towns.

SOUTH FROM ENNA

Although the natural scenery is not nearly as spectacular as it is north of Enna, the southern part of the province has been enriched by human hand. The 17th-century town of Piazza Armerina, perhaps the most attractive of the interior's towns, is worth devoting a day to, while lovers of all things beautiful will revel in the exquisite ceramics produced in Caltagirone. The remains of the Greek city of Morgantina, east of Aidone, are considerable and worth more than the trickle of visitors they receive. The real highlight, however, is just outside Piazza Armerina at Casale, the site of one of the most extraordinary finds from antiquity and a 'must-see' attraction on any Sicilian itinerary: a sumptuous Roman villa that lay buried in mud for over 700 years until it was discovered in 1950.

Lago di Pergusa

Sicily's only natural lake lies 9km south of Enna along the SS561. Its popularity as a tourist resort since the 1950s has been its ruin: the lake is surrounded by an extremely ugly motor-racing track and a rather unattractive development, and much of the vegetation on its shores has long since disappeared, along with most of the birdlife. The brackish water laps against sandy beaches that in summer are crammed with tourists escaping from Enna. It is difficult to imagine now, but the lake plays a central role in one of Greek mythology's most enduring and heart-rending tales – the abduction of Proserpina from earth by Hades (see the later boxed text 'A Devil's Bargain').

The area around the lake has a few hotels that are a popular alternative to staying in Enna.

Miralago (☎ *0935 54 12 72, Via Nazionale, Contrada Staglio)* Singles/doubles with bathroom €25.80/36.15. This is nothing very special but it's a cheap option. It's the first place you pass on the right before entering the town proper along Via Nazionale.

Park Hotel La Giarra (☎ *0935 54 16 87, fax 0935 54 12 67, Via Nazionale 125)* Singles/doubles with bathroom €77.45/ 108.45. About 500m farther on past Miralago is this hotel with very nicely appointed rooms and all mod-cons.

To get there, take bus No 5 from Piazza Vittorio Emanuele in Enna (€1.30, every 30 minutes to hour from 7am to 9.30pm daily, to 10.30pm in summer).

Piazza Armerina
postcode 94015 • pop 22,500
elevation 697m

Set amid some of the most fertile territory on the island, this town (called simply Piazza until the 18th century) takes its name from one of the three hills on which it is built, the Colle Armerino. It is actually two towns in one: the original Piazza was founded by the Saracens in the 10th century on the slope of the Colle Armerino, while a 15th-century expansion to the southeast was redefined by an urban grid established in the 17th century.

Orientation & Information The lackadaisical AAST tourist office (☎ 0935 68 02 01) is at Via Cavour 15, in the town centre. It's uphill along Via Umberto I or Via Garibaldi from the intercity bus stops and near the cathedral, and opens 8am to 2pm Monday to Saturday. You can pick up a copy of the brochure (free) covering the Roman villa at Casale from here (often unavailable at the site itself); it explains the layout of the ruins and the mosaics.

Things to See The town itself is a collection of slightly run-down but still-handsome palazzi and churches (some in a slightly run-down state). At the heart of the old town is Piazza Garibaldi, on which you will find the elegant **Palazzo di Città** (not open to the public) and the **Chiesa di San Rocco** (also known as the Fundrò); the latter has an impressive doorway carved out of tufa stone. In between the two buildings is Via Cavour, which leads up the hill to the **cathedral**, founded in 1627. The facade dates from 1719 and the dome

A Devil's Bargain

According to myth, the god of the underworld, Pluto, had fallen in love with Ceres' beautiful daughter Proserpina but she wasn't falling for his charms. After much persistence Pluto agreed to leave her alone on the condition that she did not eat. One day, while picking flowers on the banks of Lago di Pergusa, she found a pomegranate from which she picked 12 seeds. She must have been pretty hungry because she forgot her deal with Pluto and ate six of them. Pluto, of course, being a god, hadn't forgotten. A chasm appeared in the lake and up popped Pluto, who then promptly disappeared into the lake with Proserpina in tow. A devastated Ceres began searching for her beloved daughter, ignoring her duties as goddess of agriculture and causing the corn to stop growing. Sensing disaster, Jupiter decided to intervene to settle the matter. Pluto argued his case well but Ceres would not back down. Finally, Jupiter found the solution: as Proserpina had only eaten six of the seeds, she would only have to spend six months of the year in the underworld; for the rest of the year she lived as a goddess on earth. Ceres was satisfied and the corn began to grow once more. The story makes an appearance in Milton's *Paradise Lost*:

'Not that faire field
Of Enna, where Proserpin gathring flours
Her self a fairer Floure by gloomie Dis
Was gather'd, which cost Ceres all that pain
To seek her through the World.'

Pluto purloins beautiful
Proserpina.

was added in 1768. The airy blue-and-white interior contains an altar, behind which is a copy of a Byzantine painting, *Madonna delle Vittorie* (Virgin of Victories), the original of which was supposedly presented to Count Roger I by Pope Nicholas II. The 15th-century bell tower (part of an earlier church) complements the Baroque cathedral even though the bell tower was built in the Catalan-Gothic style (look at the windows). Opposite the cathedral on the square is the baronial **Palazzo Trigona**. The statue in the middle of the square is of Baron Marco Trigona, who financed the cathedral's construction.

To the side of Palazzo Trigona, Via Floresta leads down to the ruins of a 14th-century **castle** past four beautiful Baroque residences, each in a extreme state of disrepair. From the castle you can continue walking and end up back in Piazza Garibaldi. The medieval city's most important thoroughfare was Via Monte, which descends west from Piazza del Duomo through the town's most picturesque quarter.

Special Events The Palio dei Normanni (13–14 August) is a medieval pageant celebrating Count Roger's capture of the town from the Moors in 1087. On 14 August, amid parades in traditional costume and other assorted festivities, there is an actual joust, complete with armour, lances and horses. Check with the tourist office for details.

Places to Stay & Eat Piazza Armerina is not a cheap place to stay; eating is much friendlier on the wallet.

Villa Romana (☎/fax 0935 68 29 11, Via Alcide De Gasperi 18) Singles/doubles with bathroom €51.65/77.45. This is about the cheapest accommodation in Piazza Armerina. It's a modern, well-run place and the rooms are very comfortable, with TV, phone and air-con.

Hotel Mosaici da Battiato (☎/fax 0935 68 54 53, Contrada Paratore 11) Singles/doubles with bathroom €33.60/43.90. This hotel is a few kilometres out of town (not feasible without a car) and 1km from the Roman villa's mosaics. There's a restaurant

and bar here, and (tourist groups aside) it's a nice quiet spot.

Azienda Agriturista Sàvoca (☎ 0337 88 90 52, fax 0935 68 30 78) Doubles €51.65. The Azienda Agriturista Sàvoca is also about 3km out of Piazza Armerina, on the road to Mirabella. It has very pleasant doubles with bathroom and breakfast included. Ask for a room in the older building.

Totò (☎ 0935 68 01 53, Via Mazzini 27) Meals about €16. Closed Mon. This is a typical Sicilian pizzeria/trattoria and serves good meals in an unpretentious setting.

Del Teatro (☎ 0935 8 56 62, Via Teatro 1) Meals about €16. Closed Mon. Del Teatro is just off the eastern end of Via Garibaldi. Try the *pappardelle alla Norma*.

Getting There & Away SAIS buses connect Enna and Piazza Armerina (€4.65 return, 45 minutes, five to eight daily Monday to Saturday, three to four on Sunday). Bear in mind that some of these buses depart from the bottom of Enna, not from the bus station. There is also a daily AST bus from Syracuse (€7.25, two hours).

Roman Villa at Casale

The extraordinary UNESCO World Heritage-listed Roman villa (*Villa Romana;* ☎ 0935 68 00 36; admission €4.15; open 8am-7.30pm daily) at Casale is easily the most important ruin of the Roman era in Sicily. It was the property of a Roman dignitary of some standing and wealth, possibly even Maximian (Maximianus Herculeus), co-emperor during the reign of Diocletian (AD 286–305) – hence its other name, the Villa Imperiale. Although other surviving villas testify to the magnificent lifestyles enjoyed by wealthy Romans – for example, Hadrian's villa at Tivoli and Diocletian's getaway retreat in Split, Croatia – the Casale country residence stands out for its sheer size coupled with the breathtaking extent of its polychrome floor mosaics.

The villa is made up of four connected groups of buildings, which date from the early 4th century and were built on the site of a more modest 2nd-century home (possibly a hunting lodge). Scholars believe that the buildings were maintained until about the year 1000, after which they were abandoned to local squatters and then partially destroyed. In the 12th century the entire area was covered by a landslide which left the villa under 10m of mud. The ruins were only noticed again in 1761 but it wasn't until 1881 that the first attempts at excavation were made; these were resumed in 1929 and again between 1935 and 1939. Then, in 1950, the main structure was finally exposed, as a result of a properly financed excavation. The work continues today and large parts of the estate – including the extensive slave quarters and outbuildings – remain covered. The fact that the mosaics have been concealed by mud for so long has proven to be a blessing in disguise; in 1991 they were badly damaged by a flood, which suggests that had they not been covered they would hardly have survived nearly 2000 years of inclement weather and petty vandalism.

Much of the villa has been covered with a protective structure and raised walkways carry visitors through the house's many rooms in a particular sequence. The description below follows the order of that sequence.

The **main entrance** leads through the remnants of a triumphal arch into an elegant **atrium** (forecourt). To the west are the substantial **thermae** (baths), all-important in a Roman house. The small **latrine** is a good indication of the house's elegance – it is adorned with a brick drain, a marble wash basin and rich mosaics. From the latrine you access the villa proper, walking around the western side of the massive **peristyle**, or central courtyard, where in Roman times guests would be received by the host. The paths around the courtyard are decorated with mosaics depicting animal heads draped in laurel leaves. To your left you can look down into the **palaestra** (gymnasium), with a splendid mosaic depicting a scene from the Circus Maximus in Rome (the room is also known as the Salone del Circo or Circus Room). Of the rooms on the northern side of the peristyle, the most interesting is the second-last one, depicting a hunting scene in great detail (Little Hunt). But this is merely an appetiser for what follows.

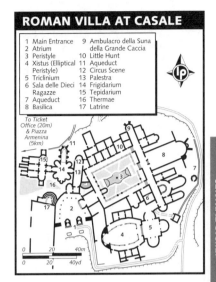

ROMAN VILLA AT CASALE

1 Main Entrance
2 Atrium
3 Peristyle
4 Xistus (Elliptical Peristyle)
5 Triclinium
6 Sala delle Dieci Ragazze
7 Aqueduct
8 Basilica
9 Ambulacro della Suna della Grande Caccia
10 Little Hunt
11 Aqueduct
12 Circus Scene
13 Palestra
14 Frigidarium
15 Tepidarium
16 Thermae
17 Latrine

To Ticket Office (20m) & Piazza Armenina (5km)

CENTRAL SICILY

A small staircase brings you to the eastern side of the peristyle and the **Ambulacro della Scena della Grande Caccia** (Ambulacrum of the Great Hunting Scene), a long corridor (64m) where the mosaics are considered to be among the finest ever found. The first figure is resplendent in a Byzantine cape and is flanked by two soldiers, most likely Maximian himself and two members of his personal legion, the Herculiani. They are overseeing an extraordinary scene which shows all kinds of animals – tigers, leopards, elephants, antelopes, ostriches and a rhino – being herded onto ships. The detail is extraordinary and inspiring.

At the far end of the corridor, steps lead south around the peristyle and the **Sala delle Dieci Ragazze** (Room of the Ten Girls), home of probably the most famous of all the villa's mosaics. The mosaic depicts ten girls, all sporting bikinis (!), and dates from the end of the 4th century. In the far left-hand corner you can see that the mosaic is laid over an earlier representation.

The walkways then lead through the rest of the house. On the other side of the long corridor is a series of apartments, whose floor illustrations reproduce scenes from

Homer, as well as mythical subjects such as Arion playing the lyre on a dolphin's back, and Cupid and Faunus wrestling. Of particular interest is the **triclinium** (dining room), with a splendid depiction of *I Labori di Ercole* (The Labours of Hercules).

Get here early if you want to avoid the large tourist groups which start arriving at around 9.30am and tend to block up the narrow passageways.

Getting There & Away The splendour of the mosaics has been matched by bus company stupidity. The decision to stop the bus that ran between Piazza Armerina and the Roman villa means that you'll either have to walk or get a taxi. The walk to the villa (signposted) is about 5km (not too strenuous – and downhill) and takes about an hour. The walk back is only steep in the last part. Taxis (parked all over town) will take you there, wait for an hour and drive you back to Piazza Armerina for about €16 – not bad value if you're in a group.

If you have your own car, head south along the SS117 – the villa is signposted. You will be charged around €1 to park your vehicle outside the entrance.

Aidone

If you're in Aidone, it's worth popping into the **Museo Archeologico** (☎ *0935 8 73 07, Convento dei Cappuccini; admission €3.10; open 8am-1hr before sunset daily*). This collection houses finds from the excavations at Morgantina (see the following section) but it's not nearly as large or significant as it should be – a staggering amount of the good stuff has been stolen from Morgantina and smuggled out of Sicily. One object worth seeing, however, is a large 3rd-century-BC bust of Proserpina.

You can get to Aidone by SAIS bus from Enna (€3.10, 50 minutes, two daily Monday to Saturday). AST buses run from Piazza Armerina to Aidone (eight daily Monday to Saturday, one on Sunday).

Morgantina

About 4km beyond the town of Aidone are the noteworthy remains (☎ *0935 8 79 55;*

admission €2.05; open 8am-6.30pm daily) of this sizable Greek colony, spread across two hills and the valley between. Morgeti, an early Sicilian settlement, was founded in 850 BC on Cittadella hill, but this town was destroyed by Ducetius in 459 BC and a new town built on the second hill, the Serra Orlando. It reached its apogee during the reign of the Syracusan tyrant Hieron II (269–215 BC). In 211 BC the town took the losing Carthaginian side during the Second Punic War and was delivered by the Romans into the unmerciful hands of a Spanish mercenary called Moericus, who promptly stripped it of its wealth. By the reign of Emperor Augustus, the town had lost all importance and was eventually abandoned. In 1955 archaeologists identified the site and began its excavation, which continues to this day.

The centre of the town is the **agora** (meeting place), spread over two levels. A trapezoidal stairway linking the two was also used as seating during public meetings. The upper level had a **market**; you can still see the walls that divided one shop from the next. The lower level was the site of the **theatre**, which has been preserved in excellent condition.

To the northeast are the **residential quarters** of the city – what must have been houses for the town's wealthier class, as testified by the ornate wall decorations and handsome mosaics in the inner rooms. Another residential quarter has been found behind the theatre and its considerable ruins are well worth checking out.

Morgantina is an easy detour if you have your own transport but a difficult proposition without. There is no way of getting there by public transport; you can get an SAIS bus from Enna to Aidone and either take a cab or walk (not tiring) the 3km along the SS288.

Caltagirone
postcode 95041 • pop 36,900
elevation 608m

The elegant Baroque town of Caltagirone is renowned throughout Sicily for the high quality of its ceramics, which have been produced here for over 1000 years. Although the town's earliest settlers were engaged in terracotta work, it was only with the arrival of the Arabs in the 10th century that the industry really took off. Not only did they give the town its name (from the Arabic *kalat* and *gerun* meaning 'castle' and 'cave') but they introduced the wide array of glazed polychromatic colours – particularly yellow and blue – that have distinguished local ceramics ever since. The town (and most of the ceramic workshops) was destroyed in the earthquake of 1693 and rebuilt in the ubiquitous Baroque style – most of the town's buildings date from the 18th-century reconstruction. The ceramics industry flourished once again in the 19th century and continues to do so today.

Orientation & Information Caltagirone is divided into an upper and lower town. All buses stop on Piazza Municipio in the upper town, where most of the town's sights are located. AST buses depart from in front of the Metropol Cinema on Viale Principe Umberto in the lower town, but stop at Piazza Municipio on the way. The train station is in the lower town, at the western end of Viale Principe Umberto, along with Caltagirone's only accommodation options. If you are travelling by bus and just planning a quick visit, you can go right up to Piazza Municipio, but if you plan on overnighting here you should get off in the lower town.

The small Pro Loco tourist office (☎ 0933 5 38 09) is at Via Volta Libertini 3, a little alley off Piazza Umberto in the upper town. It usually opens 9am to 1pm and 4pm to 7.30pm Monday to Saturday, April and September. The public hospital (☎ 0933 5 79 02) is on Via Porto Salvo in the lower town.

Things to See Caltagirone's pleasant upper town is a bustling centre of activity amid some gorgeous Baroque buildings and churches. The most evocative sight in town is a set of steps, **Scalinata di Santa Maria del Monte**, which rises up from Piazza Municipio to the **Chiesa di Santa Maria del Monte**, at the top of the town. Each of the 142 steps is decorated with hand-painted ceramics and no two are the same. On either side of the steps are rows of ceramic workshops where

you can watch local artisans and admire their handiwork (as well as buy some). The steps are the focus of the Feast of St James (Festa di San Giacomo), the town's patron saint (see Special Events for details).

In the south of the upper town, on Via Roma (which leads into the lower town), is the **Museo Regionale della Ceramica** (*Regional Ceramics Museum;* ☎ 0933 2 16 80, *Giardini Pubblici; admission €4.15; open 8am-6.30pm daily*) where you can trace the history of ceramics from prehistoric times to the present day.

Special Events During the Feast of St James (24–25 July), the Scalinata di Santa Maria del Monte is lit up by more than 4000 oil lamps for the religious procession that goes from Chiesa di Santa Maria del Monte down through the town and back again. Between 6 December and Christmas the town plays host to an exhibition of terracotta cribs. Contact the tourist office for details of both.

Places to Stay & Eat There are only a couple of hotels in Caltagirone and neither of them are cheap.

Grand Hotel Villa San Mauro (☎ 0933 2 65 00, fax 0933 3 16 61, **e** *ricevimento .vsm@framon-hotels.it, Via Porto Salvo 14)* Singles/doubles €92.95/154.95. This hotel is extremely plush, with good views of the surrounding countryside. You'll find it at the southern end of town, near Chiesa di Santa Maria di Gesù.

Monteverde (☎ 0933 5 36 82, fax 0933 5 35 33, Via delle Industrie 11) Singles/doubles with bathroom €41.30/56.80. Monteverde is on the southern outskirts of town. Walk south along Via Roma and take the first fork to the right (past the public gardens) onto Via Santa Maria di Gesù; Via delle Industrie is about 800m on, to the right. If you don't have your own transport it's a bit of a walk.

Eating is somewhat less of a problem. The upper town has plenty of small, cheap restaurants where you can get a good meal.

La Scala (☎ 0933 5 77 81, Scalinata Santa Maria del Monte) Meals about €18. Situated in Caltagirone's ceramic heart, on the long flight of steps leading to the Chiesa di Santa Maria del Monte, this is a handy place to enjoy fresh pasta and local wines.

Non Solo Vino (☎ *0933 3 10 68, Via Vittorio Emanuele 1)* Meals about €16. Closed Mon. Relax – you can get wine *and* a decent mixed grill here, the perfect cure for a hard day's ceramic shopping.

Getting There & Away Caltagirone is served by SAIS Autolinee buses from Enna (€4.15, 1½ hours, three daily Monday to Saturday) and Palermo (€9.30, three hours, three daily Monday to Saturday, one Sunday). There's an AST bus from Syracuse (€4.65, two hours, one daily Monday to Saturday) and buses from Piazza Armerina (€2.60, one hour, five daily Monday to Saturday). The town is also served by trains from Gela (€2.85, nine daily) and Catania (€4.65, 10 daily).

THE WESTERN INTERIOR

The western interior is the traditional heartland of Sicily, an area of rolling hills dotted with small villages and towns that receives fewer visitors than any other spot on the island. This is partly due to the dearth of public transport, which makes getting around almost impossible unless you have your own wheels, but the main reason is that it has been ravaged by poverty for centuries (see the later boxed text 'A Region Blighted'). The tourist authorities have done their optimistic best to promote the area for its wild and natural beauty but, without a tourist infrastructure of any kind, it is difficult to imagine anything changing for a long time. Even the interior's biggest city, Caltanissetta, is a victim: largely unattractive and industrial, it holds little appeal for the casual visitor.

Caltanissetta

postcode 93100 • pop 61,300
elevation 568m

Sitting atop a hill that gently slopes downwards into the valley, Caltanissetta was originally a Saracen settlement but was captured by the Normans in 1086. A charter was granted to the town in accordance with Count Roger's vast plan for the urbanisation of Sicily and the urban plan that is still

in evidence today was laid out. Caltanissetta is the hub of public transport in the area and makes a good base for planning your explorations, but beyond that there is little to see and do in town.

Orientation & Information The town is well-served by buses and trains coming from all corners of the island. Caltanissetta's train station is in the west of town on Piazza Roma. The bus station is close by, around the corner on Via Colojanni, where there's also a ticket office for SAIS Trasporti buses (☎ 0934 56 40 72) across the road from the bus station.

There are two tourist offices in town. The main APT tourist office (☎ 0934 53 04 11) is on Corso Vittorio Emanuele II 109. There's also a smaller tourist office (☎ 0934 2 10 89) about 300m north of the train station at the corner of Viale Testasecco and Viale Kennedy. Both open 9am to 1pm and 3pm to 6pm Monday to Saturday (to 7.30pm between June and September).

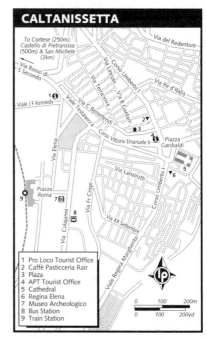

CALTANISSETTA

1 Pro Loco Tourist Office
2 Caffè Pasticceria Rair
3 Plaza
4 APT Tourist Office
5 Cathedral
6 Regina Elena
7 Museo Archeologico
8 Bus Station
9 Train Station

Things to See Sights in Caltanissetta are pretty thin on the ground. The 17th-century **cathedral** has a late-Renaissance appearance that breaks the Baroque mould that is so common in this part of the island, but substantial alterations made in the 19th century have ruined the overall effect. Inside (if you find the church open) are frescoes by Guglielmo Borremans.

The most interesting sight in town is the **Museo Archeologico** (*☎ 0934 2 59 36, Via Colajanni 3; admission €2.05; open 9am-1pm & 3pm-7.30pm daily; closed last Mon of month*), about 100m east of the train station. The displays are mostly from prehistoric times and include finds from digs conducted in the 1950s, including vases and tools from the Bronze Age and early Sicilian ceramics. Also of interest are finds from a number of necropoli spread about Caltanissetta's hinterland. One such necropolis was known by the Arabs as Gibil Habil, meaning 'mountain of death'.

To the west of town, but within easy walking distance of Piazza Garibaldi, are the ruins of the **Castello di Pietrarossa**, precariously balanced on a rocky outcrop. There isn't much left of the castle but the walk and the views from the rock are pleasant enough.

Places to Stay & Eat *Plaza* (*☎/fax 0934 58 38 77, Via B Gaetani 5*) Singles/doubles with bathroom €46.50/67.15. Not as cheap as it once was but it's close to the centre of town and the train and bus stations. Rooms are comfortable but quite uninspiring.

San Michele (*☎ 0934 55 37 50, fax 0934 59 87 91, Via Fasci Siciliani*) Singles/doubles with bathroom €67.15/98.15. A more expensive option is the flash five-star San Michele, which is northwest of town (you need your own transport).

Cortese (*☎ 0934 59 16 86, Viale Sicilia 158*) Meals about €18. Closed Mon. Cortese is an excellent restaurant serving local specialities such as *pasta con frutti di mare e funghi* (pasta with seafood and mushrooms).

Regina Elena (*Corso Umberto I 146*) Meals about €18. Closed Sun. With a

A Region Blighted

You'll get no clearer sense of the effect of poverty in Sicily than when travelling through the interior west of Caltanissetta. Unlike other parts of the island, this area has never known prosperity and has been largely ignored by Sicily's conquerors and city-builders. For centuries the rolling hills and bleached landscapes were divided into large *latifundi*, or landed estates, that were the property of absentee landlords who cared little for the fate of the peasants trying to eke out a meagre living from the difficult soil. By the end of the 19th century an avenue of escape was opened up through emigration to the United States: in 1900 Sicily was officially the chief area of emigration in the world, with nearly 1.5 million Sicilians trying their luck elsewhere. Although an island-wide problem, the effect of depopulation was greatest here, as villages were left to those too old to make the long journey across the sea. Emigration continued into the 20th century, with Argentina, Australia and, after WWII, the industrial centres of northern Italy, Switzerland and Germany attracting Sicilians in their tens of thousands.

Leonardo Sciascia captured the Sicilian desire to escape to prosperity with his stories *The Long Crossing* and *The Test*. You can find them, with other great stories about Sicily, in his collection *The Wine Dark Sea*.

It is difficult to imagine that anything substantial will be done to reverse the trend of poverty in the area. The few development projects that have been launched to much fanfare over the years have yielded few tangible benefits for the local population (a large, hideously ugly water fun-park is one of the most recent developments). A combination of mismanagement, indifference and misappropriation have ensured that the only ones who gain are the all-pervading Mafia – strongly represented here – and the bankers with whom they keep their accounts.

shocker of a portrait of Regina Elena looking over you, you can dine on well-prepared pasta dishes in quiet surroundings here.

There are a couple of great *pasticcerie* (cake shops) where you can eat some fabulous *cannoli* (cream horns).

Caffè Pasticceria Rair *(Corso Umberto I 163)* You should try the *cannolicchi alla ricotta* here, smaller versions of cannoli filled with ricotta and dusted with cinnamon, ground hazelnuts and almonds.

Getting There & Away There are SAIS Trasporti/Autolinee buses to Agrigento (€2.85, 1¼ hours, 10 daily Monday to Saturday), Catania (€4.65, 1½ hours, nine daily) and Enna (€2.58, one hour, four daily Monday to Saturday). Astra has buses to Piazza Armerina (€2.60, one hour, five daily Monday to Saturday).

There are trains to/from Agrigento (€3.87, 1½ hours, 10 daily) and also to/from Enna (€2.30, 40 minutes, seven daily). Note that you're better off getting the bus to Enna, due to the length and steepness of the road connecting Enna's train station and town centre.

If you plan on travelling into the western province from Caltanissetta, you're better off having your own transport.

WEST FROM CALTANISSETTA
Along the SS640

This road heads southwest alongside the railroad tracks that link Caltanissetta with Agrigento. About halfway between the two cities is **Canicattì**, a little market town that is the Italian Timbuktu, at least in terms of remoteness. Its name is also comically mispronounced by Italian children as 'Canigatti' or 'Cats & Dogs'. Other than that, there is nothing to see in town, although it does serve as something of a transport hub for the region.

If you're driving you can get to **Mussomeli**, northwest of Canicattì along a thin secondary road (follow the signs for Montedoro and then Bompensiere). On the far side of this little village is the imposing,

A Very Lucky Man

Mafia boss Salvatore 'Lucky' Luciano was born Salvatore Lucania in Lercara Friddi in 1897. When he was a child, his family joined the countless others on the emigrant trail to New York. In a story more than slightly reminiscent of *The Godfather II*, the young Salvatore became involved with the local Mafia and quickly rose through the ranks until he became the undisputed *Capo di tutti i Capi* (Boss of all Bosses). In 1936 his spectacular career came to an abrupt halt when he was sentenced to 30 years imprisonment for 62 counts of 'voluntary prostitution'. What saved him, however, was WWII. He was released from prison in 1943 on condition that he help the US forces during their landing in Sicily. One story tells that the troops wore yellow scarves with 'L' for 'Lucky' emblazoned on them so that the local Mafia, eager to rid the island of the Fascists, would be able to recognise them. Whatever the truth of it, Luciano's help was instrumental in allowing the Americans to take the whole island in just 39 days. His reward was extradition back to Italy, where he helped negotiate a deal between the Sicilian and American mobs that led to the creation of an international narcotics syndicate still in operation today. Luciano died, peacefully, in Naples in 1962.

14th-century **Castello Manfredonico**, built by the Chiaramonte family.

Lercara Friddi

If you keep going west past Mussomeli for about 12km you'll hit the main SS189 which links Agrigento and Palermo. About 24km north along the road is the small town of Lercara Friddi, renowned for only one reason: it is the birthplace of Salvatore 'Lucky' Luciano, one of the most notorious and important figures in Mafia history (see the boxed text 'A Very Lucky Man').

The Southern Coast

The stretch of land between Sciacca to the west and Gela to the east, commonly referred to as the Agrigentino after the region's most important town, is the least populated part of Sicily's coastline. The site of three important Greek colonies in ancient times (at Eraclea Minoa, Akragas and Gela), the southern coast today shifts between wonderful natural landscapes that bear a striking resemblance to the North African coastline and heavy industrial development at the eastern end around Gela. The main attraction here is the magnificent Valley of the Temples at Agrigento, one of the most important archaeological sites in Europe, but the town of Sciacca and the stunning beaches below the remains of Eraclea Minoa to the west should not be ignored. At the eastern end is Gela, an ugly industrial centre with a fascinating museum which boasts a stunning collection of ancient vases. Also worth visiting are the remote Pelagic Islands, a tiny archipelago 240km off the southern coast that is accessible by boat from Agrigento. Closer to Africa than to Sicily, these sun-scorched, windswept islands make a good weekend getaway.

GELA
postcode 93012 • pop 75,000
There is really only one reason for coming to Gela – to visit the archaeological museum. The town itself is a horrible mess of tangled steel and industrial mayhem. A huge petrochemical plant is responsible for the faint smell of chemicals that seems to hang in the air and, although there are beaches along the coast, the water is less than clean.

Founded in 689 BC by colonists from Rhodes, Gela quickly became one of the most important Greek cities on Sicily, rivalling even Syracuse as a centre of learning. According to legend, the playwright Aeschylus met an unfortunate end here when an eagle dropped a tortoise on his head!

Highlights

- Visit the magnificent collection of red-and-black *kraters* (vases) in Gela's archaeological museum
- Have your socks knocked off by the formidable ruins of Agrigento's Valley of the Temples
- Swim, scuba dive, sunbathe and do all things summery on Lampedusa
- Soak up the sun and sea on the coastline around Eraclea Minoa
- Enjoy the fine view from Piazza Scandaliato in Sciacca

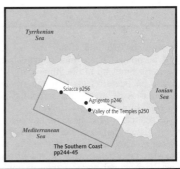

Gela was completely destroyed by Carthage in 405 BC, was refounded in 338 BC and destroyed again in 282 BC, this time by an army led by the tyrant Finzia of Agrigento. The area lay in ruins until 1230, when Frederick II ordered that a new town called Terranova be built on the site of the ancient city. The name was changed back to Gela in 1927 but that is the only resemblance between the modern city and the colony of old.

The **archaeological museum** (☎ 0933 91 26 26; admission €4.15; open 9am-12.30pm & 4pm-7pm daily; closed last Mon of month) lies at the eastern end of Gela's main drag, Corso Vittorio Emanuele. On the

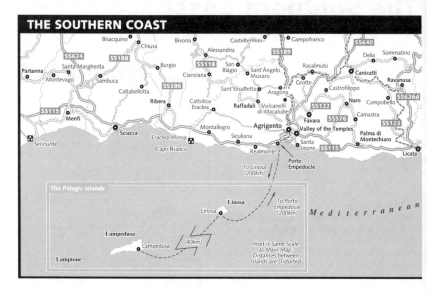

THE SOUTHERN COAST

ground floor are finds from the ancient city's acropolis. These mostly date from prehistoric times up to the 5th century BC but also include artefacts from the 4th and 3rd centuries BC, when the acropolis was converted into an artisans' district.

The best part of the museum, however, is upstairs. Here you'll find the world's largest collection of red-and-black *kraters* (vases), Gela's speciality between the 7th and 4th centuries BC. Although there are some examples of these in archaeological museums throughout Europe, the collection here is simply staggering. Also on display is part of an important collection of ancient coins minted in Agrigento, Gela, Syracuse, Messina and Athens. At one time the collection numbered over 1000 coins but it was stolen in 1976 and only about half of it was recovered.

The only other worthwhile sight in Gela is at the other end of Corso Vittorio Emanuele (turn left on Via Manzoni and follow the road to the sea; it's about a 4km walk), where you will find the remains of the ancient **Greek fortifications** *(admission €2.05; open 9am-1hr before sunset daily)*. They are in a remarkable state of preservation, most likely as a result of being covered

by sand dunes for thousands of years until they were discovered in 1948. The wind used to blow huge amounts of sand onto the town, which was dealt with in antiquity by building 8m-high protective walls. Today many of the walls are in ruins and the authorities have planted trees to act as a buffer against the encroaching sand.

Gela is easily reached by train and bus from every town on the southern coast. All buses run from Piazza Stazione, in front of the train station (ask at the Autolinee office across the street for a timetable). The journey between Agrigento and Gela takes about 1¼ hours (€3.10). SAIS Autolinee run buses between Palermo and Gela (via Enna and Piazza Armerina; 2½ to three hours, five daily Monday to Saturday) and AST has services between Syracuse and Gela (two daily Monday to Saturday). There are at least 10 trains daily from Agrigento to Gela (€4.15).

AROUND GELA

About 20km west of Gela, along the SS115, lies **Falconara**, with good swimming at its beaches and a superbly positioned 14th-century castle. **Butera**, 12km northwest of

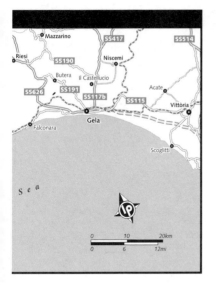

Gela on the SS191 is the most interesting and attractive town in the area around Gela, with its hilltop position and historic buildings, including its Chiesa Madre, Norman castle and town hall. **Mazzarino**, farther north on the SS191, is of little interest although it has achieved some notoriety in the past due to its Mafia-dominated history. Even Mazzarino's friars were caught up in an attention-grabbing trial in the 1960s, when they were tried and imprisoned for acting as messengers between the Mafia and the intimidated citizens of the town. Eight kilometres north of Gela, on the SS117, you'll see **Il Castelluccio**, a Norman keep that juts out of the surrounding fields. The landscape around Gela and its coast is dotted with concrete pill-box defences from WWII.

WEST TO AGRIGENTO

Licata, on the SS115 between Agrigento and Gela, is an unattractive town with a working port (it's fine to swim though). If you're a fan of the designs of Ernesto Basile, have a look at the Palazzo del Municipio (built 1936). There's also a 16th-century castle. Licata is accessible by bus from both Agrigento and Gela.

Along the SS115 from Licata (west about 18km) is the town of **Palma di Montechiaro**, famous as the town that was founded in 1637 by the *Principe di Lampedusa* (Prince of Lampedusa), an ancestor of Giuseppe Tomasi di Lampedusa, author of *Il Gattopardo* (The Leopard; see Literature in the Facts about Sicily chapter). The family's 17th-century ancestral palace has not been occupied for some time although the Chiesa Matrice still stands and can be visited.

AGRIGENTO & THE VALLEY OF THE TEMPLES
postcode 92100 • pop 55,200
elevation 230m

At first glance, the sizable town of Agrigento appears nothing more than an expanse of unremarkable modern development strewn across a hill. Obscured by the aesthetic myopia of the 1960s and '70s, however, is a lovely and compact medieval town that is deserving of more than just a cursory glance on the way to the area's main draw, the spectacular Valley of the Temples, spread out below the modern city towards the sea. Although the ruins should be on every traveller's itinerary, too many tour buses give the town a miss altogether, which is a shame considering that there are a couple of sights worth checking out.

On a negative note, Agrigento tops the list of a number of dreadful statistics. It is one of the poorest towns in Italy (although you'd never know by strolling past the elegant boutiques on Via Atenea) and unemployment statistics are grim. It's also an important centre of Mafia activity and it is reputed that Agrigento's crime families are key players in the multi-billion-dollar narcotics industry.

History

The area has been inhabited since prehistoric times but, despite claims that Agrigento was first founded by Daedalus, father of Icarus, the first organised settlement here dates from 581 BC, when a colony from Gela united with settlers from Greece to found Akragas, one of the last Greek colonies in Sicily. Strategically located halfway between Gela

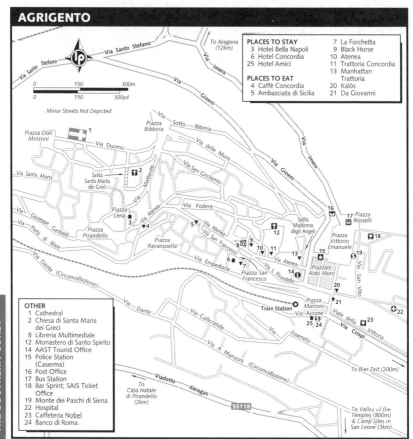

AGRIGENTO

PLACES TO STAY
3 Hotel Bella Napoli
6 Hotel Concordia
25 Hotel Amici

PLACES TO EAT
4 Caffè Concordia
5 Ambasciata di Sicilia

7 La Forchetta
9 Black Horse
10 Atenea
11 Trattoria Concordia
13 Manhattan
   Trattoria
20 Kalòs
21 Da Giovanni

OTHER
1 Cathedral
2 Chiesa di Santa Maria
   dei Greci
8 Libreria Multimediale
12 Monastero di Santo Spirito
14 AAST Tourist Office
15 Police Station
   (Caserma)
16 Post Office
17 Bus Station
18 Bar Sprint; SAIS Ticket
   Office
19 Monte dei Paschi di Siena
22 Hospital
23 Caffeteria Nobel
24 Banco di Roma

and Selinunte, the new town was conceived as a lookout post over the Mediterranean to monitor potential Carthaginian invasions. This threat was temporarily eliminated following the Battle of Himera in 480 BC and the town grew substantially in size and population. Most of the temples that you see today date from this period, a time when (it is reckoned) tyrant-ruled Akragas was home to 200,000 citizens. The Greek poet Pindar described the city as 'the most beautiful of those inhabited by mortals'.

Its good fortune came to an abrupt end in 406 BC when the old enemy Carthage finally overcame Greek resistance but it was reclaimed in 338 BC by the Corinthian general Timoleon, who instituted a liberal and democratic regime and Akragas more or less picked up where it had left off before the Carthaginian interlude. In 210 BC it was the Romans' turn to take the city. They renamed it Agrigentum and encouraged the farming and trading sectors, thus laying the foundations for the city's future as an important centre of commerce under the Byzantines.

In the 7th century the bulk of the city's inhabitants moved up the hill to the site of the modern city, virtually abandoning the

THE SOUTHERN COAST

old town of Akragas. Although experts are still at a loss as to exactly why such a shift occurred, it has been suggested that it was to fend off the island's latest conquerors from North Africa, the Saracens. Despite its best efforts, Agrigento fell to the Saracens at the start of the 9th century and for the next 200 years took on the shape of a typical Arab town, complete with elegant courtyards and narrow, twisting streets. Today the Arabic influence can also be seen in some of the town's street names, such as Via Bac Bac and Piazza Bibbiria. Under the Normans, at the end of the 11th century, the town continued as before, trading with North Africa and the rest of the island.

Agrigento did not change much until the 19th century, when the western half of the city was built. In the 20th century the urban sprawl flowed down the hill and into the valley that was hitherto the preserve of the ancient city. The period following WWII was particularly ruinous for the Valley of the Temples as construction affected the valley's appearance, leading to accusations that Agrigento's cultural and environmental heritage was being destroyed. Fortunately, there are strong signs that change is on the way (see the boxed text 'The Construction Scourge' later in this chapter). It also pays to remember that in Sicily, a powerful mix of organised crime, disorganised bureaucracy, cramped conditions and poverty have combined to create this effect – not any wilful desire to ruin the island's architectural heritage.

Orientation

All public transport (thankfully) arrives at and departs from the centre of town. Intercity buses arrive in Piazza Rosselli, just off the northern side of Piazza Vittorio Emanuele. The train station is about 300m south, on Piazza Marconi. Lying between the two is the green oasis of Piazzale Aldo Moro, situated at the eastern end of Via Atenea, the main street of the medieval town.

Information

Tourist Office The AAST office (☎ 0922 2 04 54) is at Via Cesare Battisti 15, just off the eastern end of Via Atenea. It opens 8.30am to 1.30pm and 4.30pm to 7pm Monday to Friday and 8.30am to 1pm on Saturday, although you may find it closed in the afternoon – and lacking in information.

Money Banks generally open 8.30am to 1.30pm (larger banks also open 3pm to 4pm), and the Monte dei Paschi di Siena at Piazza Vittorio Emanuele 1 has an ATM. There's a branch of Banco di Roma (with ATM) next to Hotel Amici. Out of hours, there's an exchange office at the post office and another at the train station, although the rates are mediocre.

Post & Communications The post office, on Piazza Vittorio Emanuele, opens 8.30am to 6.30pm Monday to Friday, 8.30am to 12.30pm on Saturday.

You can check email at the Libreria Multimediale, Via Celauro 7. It opens 9am to 1pm and 4.30pm to 8pm Monday to Saturday. Rates start at €1.30 for 15 minutes, €2.60 for 30 minutes and €4.65 for one hour.

Medical Services & Emergency The public hospital (Azienda Ospedaliera San Giovanni di Dio; ☎ 0922 40 13 44) is at Via Giovanni XXII. For an ambulance, call ☎ 0922 40 13 44 or ☎ 118.

The *carabinieri* (military police; ☎ 0922 59 63 22) are at Piazzale Aldo Moro 2.

The Medieval Town

Compared with the Valley of the Temples, Agrigento is comparatively modern, even though the area west of Piazzale Aldo Moro is strictly medieval. The town's main artery is Via Atenea, which is lined with elegant shops and is a popular street for a stroll with locals and visitors alike. Off Via Atenea, however, everything is quieter, and a little more run down. Still, it is fun to wander in and out of the narrow, climbing streets, where you can catch a glimpse of the lovely Arabic courtyards and get a real feel for the medieval town.

At the top of a set of winding steps north off Via Atenea is the Cistercian **Monastero di Santo Spirito** (Monastery of the Holy Spirit), founded around 1290. A handsome

Gothic portal leads inside, where there is some fine stucco work by Giacomo Serpotta and his school plus a statue of the *Madonna Incoronata* (Virgin Enthroned) by Domenico Gagini. Upstairs is a small anthropological and ethnographical museum (☎ *0922 40 14 50; free; open 9am-1pm & 4pm-7pm Mon-Sat)*, where the miscellany of objects is not very well labelled. The church is usually open the same hours as the museum but if it isn't ring the bell next door (No 2), where you can also buy cakes and pastries baked on the premises by the resident nuns (see Places to Eat later).

At the western end of Via Atenea is the small **Chiesa di Santa Maria dei Greci** *(free; open 8am-12pm & 3pm-dusk Mon-Sat)*, accessed through a lovely garden with palm trees and cypresses. It was built in the 11th century on the site of a 5th-century Doric temple dedicated to Athena. Inside are some badly damaged Byzantine frescoes and the remains of the original Norman ceiling. Opening hours are not strictly adhered to. If you find it closed, check with the custodian at Salita Santa Maria dei Greci 1 (to the right as you face the church). You might need to give a tip to the custodian for this.

About 300m west of the church (take a left and then a right onto Via Duomo) is Agrigento's magnificent **cathedral** *(free; erratic opening hours)*, built in the year 1000. It is dedicated to the town's first archbishop, the Norman San Gerlando (St Gerland). It was radically restructured over the centuries, and adjoining it is an unfinished 15th-century bell tower *(campanile)*. Inside is the saint's tomb, set in the right wing of the transept. Keep your eyes up for the wonderful Norman ceiling.

Casa Natale di Pirandello

Southwest of Agrigento, about halfway along the busy road to Porto Empèdocle in the suburb of Caos, is the birthplace of one of the great heavyweights of Sicilian literature, Luigi Pirandello (1867–1936). His early career was taken up with the writing of short stories and novels, including *Il Fu Mattia Pascal* (The Late Mattia Pascal; 1904), but he concentrated on writing for the theatre after WWI. His works include such masterpieces as *Sei Personaggi in Ricerca di un Autore* (Six Characters in Search of an Author) and *Enrico IV* (Henry IV) and are considered some of the most important plays written in the Italian language. In 1934 he was awarded the Nobel Prize for Literature.

The central themes of his work are loneliness, disillusionment and the falling away of idealism, hardly surprising considering that his private life was marked by sadness and tragedy (see the later boxed text 'Nietta Pirandello'). Nevertheless, Pirandello's legacy is a rich one. His explorations into the world of the absurd and his heavy use of irony set the tone for later playwrights such as Eugene Ionesco (author of the absurdist classic *Rinoceronte*, or Rhinoceros) and Jean-Paul Sartre, while his insightful observations into the arcane ways of his fellow Sicilians did much to inspire his two great successors, Giuseppe di Lampedusa (author of *Il Gattopardo*, The Leopard) and Leonardo Sciascia (see the boxed text 'A Sicilian Iconoclast' in the Facts about Sicily chapter).

The **villa** *(Casa Natale di Pirandello; ☎ 0922 511 102; admission €2.05; open 8am-8pm daily)* in which Pirandello was born and spent most of his summers has been converted into a museum containing a lot of memorabilia. There are also occasional exhibitions of his manuscripts and letters here, and every year there is a 'Pirandello Week' in early August when his plays are performed in a theatre near the villa (in Piazzale Caos). For information, call the AAPIT Agrigento on ☎ 0922 40 13 52.

Shh! We're in a Church!

By virtue of a remarkable acoustic phenomenon, even the faintest sound carries in Agrigento's cathedral. Two people are needed to try this little experiment: the first stands in the presbytery while the second stands at the entrance. If the first person so much as whispers, the sound is carried right through the church to the second person 85m away!

Nietta Pirandello

Overshadowed by the literary achievements of her husband, the life of Maria Antonietta Portulano, wife of Luigi Pirandello, is a particularly Sicilian tragedy. Known as Nietta, she was betrothed to Pirandello in 1894 in an arranged marriage (their fathers were business associates). The early years of their union were apparently happy and they produced three children: Stefano (who later became the writer Stefano Landi), Lietta (who moved to Chile and married writer Manuel Aguirre) and Fausto (who became a painter). After Fausto's birth in 1899, however, Nietta began to suffer anxiety attacks and fits of depression. In 1903 a landslide destroyed the sulphur mine that was Nietta's dowry and the only real source of income for the Pirandellos, and Nietta's attacks became more violent, resulting in paralysis and paranoid obsessiveness. In 1919 she was committed to an asylum, where she remained for the rest of her life.

To a Sicilian woman of the 19th century, the dowry, known as *la roba*, was a symbol of her status and importance in the world. The loss of the mine was a loss of identity made all the more damaging by the fact that she was an active, intelligent woman who saw her marriage as one based on equality. As for Pirandello, he was devastated by his wife's illness and consoled himself through writing. Apart from a dalliance with an actress called Maria Abba, he lived alone for the rest of his life.

Pirandello's ashes are kept in an urn buried at the foot of a pine tree, which lost its top half in a violent storm a few years ago.

Valley of the Temples (Valle dei Templi)

One of Sicily's premier attractions, the UNESCO World Heritage-listed complex of temples and old city walls that remain from the ancient city of Akragas are reason enough to warrant a visit to the southern coast of the island. After visiting the area, Goethe waxed that 'we shall never in our lives be able to rejoice again, after seeing such a stupendous view in this splendid valley'. While some modern construction and an enormous flyway can detract from the overall picture, he wasn't far wrong. Still, earthquakes and vandalism have done their fair share of damage and the temples in the valley (actually a ridge) are in various states of ruin.

The archaeological park *(admission €4.50, ticket including the archaeological museum €6)* is divided into eastern and western zones by the main SS118 road (Via dei Templi) that leads to the temples from town. By the entrances to the two zones is the car park, where you will also find a bar/restaurant, a newspaper kiosk and the usual assortment of souvenir stands. For information, call

☎ 0922 26 19 1 (8.30am to 1pm and 3pm to 6.30pm).

You're better off getting to the site early in the morning to avoid the crowds (and to avoid having a gawping tour group in all your photos!). The site gets boiling hot in July and August, so stock up on water and wear a hat.

In the evenings, the temples are bathed in a hue of amber light, which is a magnificent sight from any angle.

The Eastern Zone The temples that stand unfettered and unenclosed in the eastern zone *(open 8.30am-9pm daily)* are the most spectacular of all. The first of these is the **Temple of Hercules** (Tempio di Ercole), immediately inside the entrance to the right. Its origin is uncertain but it is believed to be the oldest of the lot, dating from the end of the 6th century BC. Eight of its 38 columns have been raised and you can wander around the remains of the rest.

Moving east past the remains of the ancient walls, the next temple along the path is the **Temple of Concord** (Tempio della Concordia), the only one to survive the unforgiving hands of time and history relatively intact. It was built around 430 BC and was converted into a Christian basilica in the 6th century AD; the new tenants reinforced the

THE SOUTHERN COAST

main structure, giving it a better chance of surviving an earthquake. In 1748 the temple was restored to its original form. The architect in charge of the restoration, Tommaso Fazello, gave the temple its name but it is thought that it was originally dedicated to either Castor or Pollux.

At the eastern end of the ridge, a farther 400m on, is the **Temple of Juno** (Tempio di Giunone), partially destroyed by an earthquake in the Middle Ages. Just behind the eastern end is a long altar originally used for sacrifices; the traces of red are the result of fire damage, most likely during the Carthaginian invasion of 406 BC.

The Western Zone Across Via dei Templi is the entrance to the western zone *(open 8.30am-1hr before sunset daily)*, the main feature of which is the crumbled remains of the **Temple of Jupiter** (Tempio di Giove). Covering an area measuring 112m by 56m, with columns 20m high, it would have been the largest Doric temple ever built had its construction not been interrupted by the Carthaginian sack of Akragas. (The irony is that the foundations for the temple had been laid by Carthaginian prisoners captured after the Battle of Himera nearly 100 years previously.) The incomplete temple was later destroyed by an earthquake. Lying flat on his back amid the rubble is a telamon, a sculpted figure of a man with arms raised, intended to support the temple's weight. One of several planned for the temple, the figure is 8m long.

Across the path from the ruins is a little temple set on a high base. It is known as the **Tomb of Theron** (Tomba di Therone), the Greek tyrant of Agrigento, but in fact the structure dates from around 75 BC, during the Roman occupation, nearly 500 years after the tyrant's death.

About 450m farther on is the smaller **Temple of the Dioscuri** (Tempio dei Dioscuri), also known as the Temple of Castor and Pollux. It was built towards the

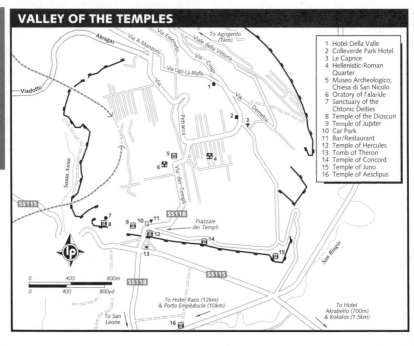

VALLEY OF THE TEMPLES

1 Hotel Della Valle
2 Colleverde Park Hotel
3 Le Caprice
4 Hellenistic-Roman Quarter
5 Museo Archeologico; Chiesa di San Nicolo
6 Oratory of Falaride
7 Sanctuary of the Chtonic Deities
8 Temple of the Dioscuri
9 Temple of Jupiter
10 Car Park
11 Bar/Restaurant
12 Temple of Hercules
13 Tomb of Theron
14 Temple of Concord
15 Temple of Juno
16 Temple of Aesclipus

end of the 5th century but was destroyed by the Carthaginians, later restored in Hellenistic style and then destroyed again by an earthquake. What you see today dates from 1832, when it was rebuilt using materials from other temples.

Just behind the temple is a complex of altars and small buildings believed to be part of the **Sanctuary of the Chtonic Deities** (Santuario delle Divine Chtoniche or, more commonly, Santuario di Demetra e Kore), which dates from the early 6th century BC.

Back at the crossroads just inside the entrance to the zone, the path south leads to the **Temple of Aesclipus** (Tempio di Esculapio), off the second fork to the left. The smallest of all the temples, it is distinguished by having solid walls instead of a colonnade.

Museo Archeologico About halfway up the road towards town from the temples is this very interesting museum *(☎ 0922 40 1 11; admission €4.15; museum & grounds open 9am-1.30pm daily plus 2pm-6pm Wed & Sat)*, housing a large collection of well-explained (in Italian and English) artefacts from the excavated site. Room *(sala)* 1 contains an archaeological plan of ancient Akragas, helpful if you want to get a sense of the scale of the old city, which covered 1400 hectares. Room 3 features a rich collection of ceramics in both black and red dating from the 6th to the 3rd centuries BC. Of particular note is the *krater*, a red ceramic chalice from 490 BC. Room 6 has a telamon standing 7.75m high (a definite highlight) and the heads of three others, plus an excellent small-scale reconstruction of their temple, which really gives the visitor a sense of how extraordinary this place would have been. Room 9 features a fine ephebus (a statue of a young boy) that was sculpted in 470 BC. The last rooms hold artefacts from around the province – be sure to check out the wonderful ceramic bowls and bronze helmets.

In the grounds of the museum is the 13th-century Cistercian **Chiesa di San Nicola**, with a fine Gothic doorway. Inside is a Roman sarcophagus (second chapel on the right) which bears a wonderful relief of the myth of Phaedra. On the church's esplanade is an

The Construction Scourge

Although unplanned and unlicensed construction is a problem throughout the Mezzogiorno (virtually all of the regions south of Rome), Agrigento can appear a particularly galling example of the scourge of irresponsible and illegal construction (widely reported as a convenient way for the Mafia to launder drug profits). The Valley of the Temples has been scarred by such construction – the products of which are known in Italian as *case abusive* (literally, abusive houses) – which has provoked the consternation and condemnation of conservationists, environmentalists and lovers of Sicily's rich cultural heritage alike. The government in Rome has been making noises about the problem since the late 1960s, but it was only in October 1999 that officials finally decided to make a decisive stand: they announced that all unlicensed houses would be demolished. Thankfully, while the views around the temples still retain some disconcertingly modern examples of Italian architecture, many of the eyesores have been demolished.

ancient Odeon called the Ekklesiasterion, built in the 3rd century BC for public meetings. Alongside it is the **Oratory of Phalaris** (Oratorio di Falaride), a temple dating from the 1st century BC that was converted into an oratory during the Middle Ages.

Hellenistic-Roman Quarter Directly opposite the museum is the Hellenistic-Roman Quarter *(Quartiere Ellenistico-Romano; free; open 8.30am-1hr before sunset daily)*, featuring a well-preserved street layout that constituted part of urban Akragas (and later, under the Romans, Agrigentum). The regular grid is made up of main streets *(plateiai)* intersected at right angles by secondary streets *(stenopoi)*, all of which were laid out towards the end of the 4th century BC. The Romans didn't alter the layout but added their own embellishments, including mosaic floors and stucco work. They were also responsible for adding water and heating

THE SOUTHERN COAST

pipes, and introduced drainage facilities for rainwater and sewage.

Organised Tours

A guide can make a tour of the temples or the town of Agrigento much more interesting and easier to understand. The AAST tourist office can provide you with a list of guides for the area and languages spoken. One excellent English-speaking guide that we can recommend for the region is Michele Gallo (☎ 0922 40 22 57 or 0360 39 37 30, ⓦ www.sicilytravel.net, Via Dante 49), who can organise individual and group itineraries according to travellers' interests. Half-day tours start at about €83, with full day tours from about €145.

Special Events

The city's big annual shindig is the Festival of the Almond Blossom (Sagra del Mandorlo in Fiore), a folk festival held on the first Sunday in February in the Valley of the Temples. The Feast of St Calògero (Festa di San Calògero) is the second big party in Agrigento, lasting a whole week from the first Sunday in July. In this festival, a statue of St Calògero (who saved Agrigento from the plague) is carried through the town while spectators throw spiced loaves of bread at the saint. For information on both festivals check with the tourist office or call ☎ 0922 2 03 91.

Places to Stay

Camping The nearest camp sites are in the small coastal town of San Leone, 6km south of Agrigento.

Internazionale San Leone (☎ 0922 41 61 21) €5.15/4.15 per person/tent. To get there, take bus No 2 (€0.75) from in front of Agrigento's train station; you'll have to walk about 1km east along the beach at San Leone.

Camping Nettuno (☎ 0922 41 62 68) €4.15/2.30 per person/car. Drive down Via dei Templi, continue along Viale Emporium towards the sea and turn left at Lungomare Akragas. About 400m farther on is this camp site which isn't as comfortable as San Leone.

Hotels – Agrigento There are a handful of cheap hotels around the medieval town. They tend to get full pretty quickly, so book early, especially around Easter or August.

Hotel Bella Napoli (☎/fax 0922 2 04 35, Piazza Lena 6) Singles/doubles/triples with bathroom €22/54/75. The Bella Napoli is uphill off Via Bac Bac. Recently renovated, it has clean, basic rooms and a friendly management.

Hotel Concordia (☎ 0922 59 62 66, Piazza San Francesco 11) Singles/doubles €15.50/24.80, with bathroom €22.70/39.75. The Concordia is in a small square just off Via Atenea. It has some good clean rooms and some that are rather depressing and dingy, and it's worth paying extra for a room with bathroom, as the communal showers are a bit yucky.

Hotel Amici (☎ 0922 40 28 31, Via Acrone 5) Singles/doubles with bathroom €43.90/72.30. This newish hotel has spotlessly clean, well-appointed rooms with TV, phone and air-con. If you want to stay close to town, this is a very good choice.

Hotels – Valley of the Temples Most of Agrigento's better hotels are out of town, around the Valley of the Temples or near the sea.

Hotel Akrabello (☎ 0922 60 62 77, fax 0922 60 61 86, Parco Angeli) Singles/ doubles with bathroom €67.15/92.95. The modern and comfortable Akrabello is in the Parco Angeli area, east of the temples. The rooms all have mod-cons and there's also a swimming pool and tennis court.

Colleverde Park Hotel (☎ 0922 2 95 55, fax 0922 2 90 12, Via Panoramica dei Templi 21) Singles/doubles with bathroom €92.95/144.60. This place is well located close to the temples (most rooms have views) and has luxurious four-star facilities and wheelchair access.

Hotel Della Valle (☎ 0922 2 69 66, fax 0922 2 64 12, Via Ugo La Malfa 3) Singles/doubles with bathroom to €92.95/ 134.30. The Della Valle has lovely rooms with all mod-cons, a pool and gardens.

Hotel Kaos (☎ 0922 59 86 22, fax 0922 59 87 70, Contrada Luigi Pirandello) Singles/

doubles with bathroom €77.45/103.30. The Kaos is by the sea, about 2km from the temples. This is a large resort complex in a restored villa and is a good choice if you have your own transport.

Places to Eat

Agrigento Eating well is not a problem in Agrigento, and you can do so without spending a fortune either.

La Forchetta (☎ *0922 59 45 87, Piazza San Francesco 9*) Meals about €12.90. Closed Sun. One of the cheapest meals in town can be found here, next door to Hotel Concordia (see Places to Stay earlier). The cramped dining room is popular with locals who come for the ever-changing daily specials.

Manhattan Trattoria (☎ *0922 2 09 11, Salita Madonna degli Angeli 9*) Tourist menu €10.35. Closed Sun. With a good tourist menu and nice outdoor tables on the stairs, this place is popular and can get crowded.

Black Horse (☎ *0922 2 32 23, Via Celauro 8*) Tourist menu €9.30. Closed Sun. Just off Via Atenea, the Black Horse serves tasty, reasonably priced fare.

Atenea (☎ *0922 41 23 66, Via Ficani 12*) Meals about €15. Closed Sun. Another fine choice with a local menu is the Atenea, positioned in a lovely ivy-covered piazzetta.

Ambasciata di Sicilia (☎ *0922 2 05 26, Via Giambertoni 2*) Meals about €18. Ambasciata di Sicilia offers typical Sicilian fare, although the pre-packaged deserts are a disappointment. If you can, get a table on the small outdoor terrace, which has splendid views of the town and the temples below.

Kalòs (☎ *0922 2 63 89, Piazza San Calògero*) Meals about €34. Closed Sun. This is a top-end restaurant close to the centre of town. The *secondi piatti* (second courses) are excellent, although the whopping service charge of 20% seems a bit rich, especially when the place can be a little funereal early in the evening.

Trattoria Concordia (☎ *0922 22 26 68, Via Porcello 8*) Meals about €18. The friendly and charming Concordia has well-priced and well-prepared local dishes.

Da Giovanni (☎ *0922 2 11 10, Piazzetta Vadalà 2*) Meals about €28.50. Closed Mon. With piazza seating, smooth service and a mind-blowing *cassata* (the famous cake made with ricotta cheese, chocolate and candied fruits), this is a great restaurant to choose if you feel like treating yourself.

Caffè Concordia (*Via Atenea 349*) This is a good breakfast stop, with decor touches from the 1950s and a nice range of pastries.

The nuns at the Monastero di Santo Spirito bake heavenly pastries and cakes, including *dolci di mandorla* (almond pastries), pistachio couscous and *bucellati* (rolled sweet dough with figs). They are expensive but it's worth it for the taste and the experience. Press the doorbell, say '*Vorrei comprare qualche dolce*' (I'd like to buy a few cakes) and see how you go.

Valley of the Temples There are some great spots to eat near the temples, especially if you can nab a table with a view of them illuminated at night.

Kokalos (☎ *0922 60 64 27, Viale Magazzeni 3*) If you have a car, head for this trattoria/pizzeria, east of the temples, where they dish up the area's best pizza to appreciative crowds. The views of the Temple of Concord are impressive too.

Le Caprice (☎ *0922 2 26 69, Via Panoramica dei Templi 51*) Meals about €28. Closed Fri. This restaurant, between the town and temples, is one of Agrigento's better places to eat (the mixed seafood grill gets the thumbs up). Take any bus heading for the temples and get off at the Colleverde Park Hotel, from where it's a short signposted walk.

Entertainment

Agrigento goes to bed pretty early. With only a few exceptions, you won't find much going on after 11pm.

Caffeteria Nobel (*Viale della Vittoria 11*) Open 6am-1am daily. This is a good place to go for a quiet drink or a late-night coffee. It's also well worth considering as a breakfast option, as many in Agrigento do.

Bier Zeit (*Viale della Vittoria 127*) Open 8pm-2am daily. This basement bar is the

Sicilian version of a German *bierkeller*. Loud music and a selection of German draught beers are the norm; during summer months this is a popular spot for visitors.

Getting There & Away

Bus For most destinations, bus is the easiest way to get to and from Agrigento. The intercity bus station is on Piazza Rosselli, just off Piazza Vittorio Emanuele, and timetables for many services are posted in Bar Sprint on the square or at the bus stops in Piazza Rossello itself. Autoservizi Cuffaro (☎ 0922 41 82 31) runs about five buses daily to Palermo (€6.70, two hours). Lumia (☎ 0922 2 04 14) has three departures daily Monday to Saturday (two on Sunday) to Tràpani (€9.30).

SAIS buses (☎ 0922 59 52 60) has a ticket office at Via Ragazzi del '99 12, just near the bus station and buses to Catania (€9.80, three hours, 12 daily), Caltanissetta (€6.20, 1¼ hours, 14 daily). There's also a bus from Falcone-Boresellino airport (Palermo) for Agrigento and Porto Empèdocle. It leaves Agrigento at 7.10am and 2.10pm daily except Sunday (€7.75. two hours and 25 minutes). Buses from the airport to Agrigento depart at 12.30pm and 8.30pm daily.

Train There are plenty of trains daily to and from Palermo (€6.70, two hours, 11 daily) and Catania (€8.80, 3½ hours). Although trains serve other destinations as well, you're better off taking the bus. The train station has a good left-luggage office, which opens 8am to 9pm (€3.10 per item).

Car & Motorcycle Agrigento is easily accessible by road from all of Sicily's main towns. The SS189 (the SS121 from Palermo) links the town with Palermo, while the SS115 runs along the coast and eventually Syracuse. For Enna, take the SS640 via Caltanissetta.

There is usually parking at Piazza Vittorio Emanuele, in the centre. Agrigento is a maze of one-way streets (often poorly signposted) so if you can get away with not driving here, do so.

Getting Around

City buses run down to the Valley of the Temples from in front of the train station. Take bus No 1, 1/, 2, 2/ or 3 (every 30 minutes) and get off at either the museum or farther downhill at the Piazzale dei Templi. Bus numbers are subject to change so it's best to ask if you're stepping on the right one! There are also regular buses (€0.75, valid for 1½ hours) running from the train station to the cathedral, for those who prefer not to make the uphill walk.

AROUND AGRIGENTO
Aragona & the Vulcanelli di Macalube

The small farming town of Aragona is 14km north of Agrigento on the SS189 (take the signposted fork to the left about 12km out of Agrigento). The town itself is unremarkable, with the exception of the interior of the 17th-century **Chiesa Madre**, which contains some fine stucco work by Giacomo Serpotta and an expertly crafted 18th-century wooden creche.

The most interesting sight, the **Vulcanelli di Macalube**, is 3km south of town in the middle of a field. To walk there, take the last left south out of Aragona (signposted) and follow the road for about 1km. At the first fork, take a left down a dirt road. When the road forks again, take a right and keep going until you reach a chain barring the way and a sign saying '*Proprietà Privata*' (Private Property). Walk 300m or so up the path. On your right is a fenced-off field. As you approach, you will notice that the field is in fact a greyish expanse of clay that looks like the surface of the moon. This is caused by a rare geographical phenomenon known as sedimentary vulcanism. Little mini-volcanoes are formed by the pressure of methane gas and sulphur pushing up through the surface. The crust is constantly bubbling and little lakes of whitish liquid are formed at the top of each 'volcano'.

Although this is private property, visitors are welcome if they stick to the path and the Vulcanelli. If you see someone on the property, it's polite to ask for permission. Try '*Le dispiace se visito i Vulcanelli?*' (Do you mind if I visit the Vulcanelli?).

The nearest train station to Aragona is Aragona-Caldare and there are intermittent services to there from Agrigento. Lattuca runs buses from Agrigento to Aragona (30 minutes); there are 16 buses a day Monday to Saturday and three on Sunday.

Racalmuto

About 13km east of Aragona off the SS189 is the signposted town of Racalmuto, an important centre for sulphur mining until the beginning of the 20th century. Since then it has survived on agriculture and rock-salt mining. Its only claim to fame is as the birthplace of Leonardo Sciascia (1921–89), widely (and deservedly) regarded as one of the best Italian writers of the 20th century. See the boxed text 'A Sicilian Iconoclast' in the Facts about Sicily chapter. You can get here on the Agrigento-Caltanissetta train (from Agrigento €2.05, 40 minutes, nine daily).

Sant'Àngelo Muxaro

This tiny town is famous for the prehistoric **rock tombs** *(tholos)* that litter the hillside on its southern side. They date from the 11th to the 5th century BC and resemble stone beehives. The largest one is known as the **Tomba del Principe** (Tomb of the Prince). Whatever treasures they once contained have long since disappeared into the display cases of Europe's museums or into private hands. The tombs are always accessible.

To get here from the north, take the SS188 west out of Lercara Friddi and turn south (towards Agrigento): Sant'Àngelo Muxaro is about 50km down the road. From Agrigento, take SS118 out of Agrigento and follow signs for the turn-off near Raffadali.

ERACLEA MINOA

A colony within a colony, Eraclea Minoa *(admission €2.05; open 9am-1hr before sunset daily)* lies about halfway between Sciacca and Agrigento, atop a wild bluff overlooking a splendid, sandy beach and the magnificent Capo Bianco cliff. Founded by Selinunte in the 6th century BC, the original colony stood on one of the most beautiful headlands in Sicily, with breathtaking views of the sea and the surrounding countryside.

The **ruins** themselves are comparatively scanty and the seating in the 4th-century theatre was once covered in moulded plastic to protect the crumbling remains, which unfortunately only aggravated the problem! At the time of research, the theatre was under cover and being restored, but was still visible to visitors.

Apart from the ruins, the main reason to come here is for the wonderful **beach**, a crescent-shaped length of golden sand that is easily one of the best on the whole island. Just behind it is a self-contained tourist village complete with a supermarket, a couple of bars and various places to stay.

Accommodation is only available between 15 June and 15 September; through the rest of the year the place is deserted.

Villagio Vacanze Eraclea (☎ 0922 84 60 23) €8.25 per person at the camp site, €62 per person with half-board at the bungalow. This well-equipped camp site is just behind the beach and a good choice for those wishing to stay in the area.

Buses running between Sciacca and Agrigento will drop you at the turn-off for Eraclea Minoa (€2.30), from where it's a 3.5km walk. In summer, buses go from Cattolica Eraclea (which can be reached from Agrigento and Sciacca) to the site.

SCIACCA
postcode 92019 • pop 40,000

One of the prettiest towns on the southern coast, Sciacca is definitely worth a flying stop, if only to check out the wonderful views of the Mediterranean from the elegant square at the centre of the old town. Although many of the older churches and buildings are in a state of disrepair, there is still enough within the walls that enclose the town to warrant a bit of sightseeing. The best time to visit is in February, as the town celebrates the Lenten period with a spectacular carnival.

History

Founded in the 5th century BC by the Greeks as a thermal spa for Selinunte, whose citizens came here to bathe in the sulphurous springs of Mt Cronio, which rises up behind the town, Sciacca itself owes its origins to the

THE SOUTHERN COAST

Saracens, who settled here in the 9th century. Although the origins of the town's name have been much debated, it is thought to have come from the Arabic word *xacca*, meaning 'water'. The Saracens built the original walls and laid out the street grid, which was later expanded by the Normans. Throughout much of the Middle Ages, the town was at the centre of a bloody feud between rival baronial families and, as is often the case, it was the citizenry that bore the brunt of the fighting: in less than 100 years over half the population was killed by one side or the other.

In the 15th and 16th centuries the town's medieval buildings were torn down to make way for grander, and sturdier, palazzi and the walls were rebuilt. In the 18th century a spate of construction gave it the Baroque look it has today.

Orientation

Sciacca still retains much of its medieval layout, which divided the town into quarters, each laid out on a strip of rock descending towards the sea. To the north of Via G Licata is Terravecchia, a maze of streets and alleyways, still largely intact, that wind their way up to the northern walls. Between Via G Licata and the town's central artery, Corso Vittorio Emanuele, is a narrow strip containing most of the town's fine buildings and churches. Below the terrace of Piazza Scandaliato (in the middle of Corso Vittorio Emanuele) is the traditional quarter of fishermen, ceramists and potters, which descends right down to the jetty.

All buses arrive at the Villa Comunale (public gardens) on Via Figuli. The town is not served by trains.

Information

The APT tourist office (☎ 0925 8 62 47) is on Corso Vittorio Emanuele 94, right on Piazza Scandaliato. It opens (supposedly) 9am to 1pm and 3pm to 7.30pm Monday to Saturday. There is also an AAST tourist office

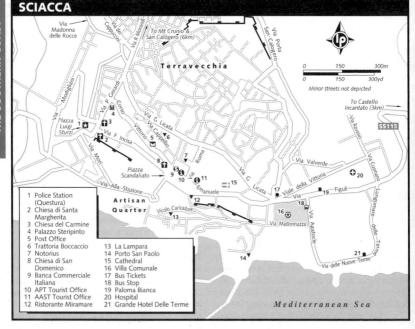

SCIACCA

0   150   300m
0   150   300yd

Minor streets not depicted

Mediterranean Sea

1 Police Station (Questura)
2 Chiesa di Santa Margherita
3 Chiesa del Carmine
4 Palazzo Steripinto
5 Post Office
6 Trattoria Boccaccio
7 Notorius
8 Chiesa di San Domenico
9 Banca Commerciale Italiana
10 APT Tourist Office
11 AAST Tourist Office
12 Ristorante Miramare
13 La Lampara
14 Porto San Paolo
15 Cathedral
16 Villa Comunale
17 Bus Tickets
18 Bus Stop
19 Paloma Bianca
20 Hospital
21 Grande Hotel Delle Terme

Still waters belie a turbulent past: Syracuse boasts a rich archaeological and cultural heritage.

You'll find the day's catch on every menu.

Sicily operates a quarter of Italy's fishing vessels.

A grand example of the Sicilian Baroque, the Cattedrale di San Giorgio dominates Ragusa Ibla's horizon.

Ride on: horses support this richly sculpted balcony of the Palazzo Villadorata in Noto.

Beautiful Noto's white tufa stone needs constant maintenance.

Magnificent Syracuse cathedral

(☎ 0925 2 27 44) down the street at No 84 which gives out free maps of the town.

The Banca Commerciale Italiana, at Corso Vittorio Emanuele 106, has an ATM. The post office is near to the APT tourist office, at Corso Vittorio Emanuele 104. The hospital (☎ 0922 9 43 76) is on Viale della Vittoria, next to the public gardens. The police station *(questura)* is at Piazza Luigi Sturzi 2, just outside the eastern gate to the old city.

Things to See

At the heart of the town is the terraced **Piazza Scandaliato**, a central meeting place for locals, with splendid views of the sea below. At the square's western end is the **Chiesa di San Domenico**, an 18th-century reconstruction of a church built in the 16th century. To the northeast off the square is the town's **cathedral** *(free; open 7.30am-noon & 4.30pm-7.30pm daily)*, first erected in 1108 and rebuilt in 1656. Only the three apses survive from the original Norman structure. The unfinished Baroque facade features a set of marble statues by Gagini.

At the western end of the old city, off Corso Vittorio Emanuele on Via F Incisa, is the small, 14th-century **Chiesa di Santa Margherita**, of which the superb Gothic portal is the only surviving original feature. Nearby is the **Chiesa del Carmine**, an interesting building with an odd-looking rose window from the 13th century and a fine dome of green majolica tiles that was added in the early 19th century. To the north is the imposing **Palazzo Steripinto**, recognisable by its diamond-point rustication and twin-mullioned windows. It was built in the Catalonian-Sicilian style at the beginning of the 16th century.

Although it doesn't look like much, the **artisan quarter** below the old town is worth checking out. The traditional artisans – mostly ceramists – live side by side with Sciacca's fishing community. The risers on the steps leading down to the port have been adorned with locally produced ceramic tiles; no one is the same as the other. Although there is nothing specific to see down here, it's worth wandering around the docks, cluttered with fishing vessels and little bars.

There are also numerous ceramics shops around the Piazza Scandaliato area, should you feel the need to fill your bags with breakables!

About 3km east of the city (take bus No 1 or 4 from the Villa Comunale) is the **Castello Incantato** *(Enchanted Castle; free; open 10am-noon & 4pm-8pm Tues-Sat)*, actually a large park with thousands of heads sculpted in wood and stone. The mind behind this bizarre collection was a local farmer-sculptor called Filippo Bentivegna, whose story is beset by woe. While living in America, he was ditched by his fiancee and later beaten up so badly that he was thought dead. He returned to his home town in 1917 and devoted the rest of his life (he died in 1967) to exorcising the memories of his American experiences through sculpture; each head supposedly represents one of his enemies. He was undoubtedly deranged, as he liked to be treated like a king, going so far as to demand that people addressed him as *'Eccellenza'* (Your Excellency).

Special Events

Sciacca's big festival is Carnevale, celebrated during the week before the beginning of Lent (February). The highlight of the festivities is the parade of bizarre figures mounted on floats, famous throughout Italy for their gaudy expressions. The whole town lends a hand in the celebrations, which involve plenty of eating and drinking.

Places to Stay & Eat

Paloma Blanca *(☎ 0925 2 51 30, fax 0925 2 56 67, Via Figuli 5)* Singles/doubles with bathroom €31/51.65. This place is on the eastern side of town and has good rooms and a rather lavish dining area. It's close to the bus station too.

San Calògero *(☎ 0925 2 10 05, Contrada Monte Kronio)* Singles/doubles with bathroom €46.50/82.65. This hotel, 6km north of town in the foothills of Mt Cronio, isn't quite 'grand' (it has the fairly ordinary rooms) but prices drop quite a bit in the low season. You'll need your own transport to get here.

Grand Hotel Delle Terme *(☎ 0925 2 31 33, fax 0925 2 17 46, Via delle Nuove*

Terme) Singles/doubles with bathroom €57.35/102.30. You can always treat yourself to a fancy room and a thermal cure at the Grand Hotel Delle Terme, set on a cliff just east of the public gardens. The rates are surprisingly affordable, especially in the low season.

The best places to eat are in and around the port, where relatively inexpensive trattorie serve up abundant menus of (mostly) seafood dishes.

***La Lampara** (☎ 0925 8 50 85, Vicolo Caricatore 33)* Meals about €18. La Lampara has a good reputation and tasty Sicilian and regional dishes.

***Porto San Paolo** (☎ 0925 2 79 82, Largo San Paolo 1)* Meals about €18. This restaurant has a nice terrace overlooking the sea.

***Notorius** (Piazza Matteotti 6)* Sandwich about €2, beer about €2.50. Close to Piazza Scandaliato, Notorius does tasty sandwiches and other bar food, and is a good spot to enjoy a beer on tap.

***Trattoria Boccaccio** (☎ 0925 8 66 77, Vicolo Capellino 24)* Meals about €16. Off Corso Vittorio Emanuele, this nice little trattoria has good dishes, although there are no views to speak of.

***Ristorante Miramare** (☎ 0925 2 60 50, Piazza Scandaliato 6)* Meals about €16. Pizza €5.15-6.20. This friendly pizzeria serves up good food and the views are superb.

Getting There & Away
There are 12 Lumia buses daily Monday to Saturday (three on Sunday and public holidays) between Sciacca and Agrigento (€7.75 return). They stop at virtually every town along the way, however, so the journey takes about two hours. There are also three daily buses Monday to Saturday (one on Sunday) between Sciacca and Tràpani (€5.15). Buses leave from Via Agatocle. Direct Gallo buses also serve Palermo (€7.25, two hours, four daily Monday to Saturday). You can buy your tickets at the small bar at Viale della Vittoria 22.

AROUND SCIACCA
Twenty kilometres northeast of Sciacca is the beautiful (often mist-shrouded) village of **Caltabellota** (850m). The highest point of interest in the town is the ruin of the Norman castle where the peace that ended the Sicilian Vespers was signed in 1302. Below the castle, there's the restored Chiesa Madre from Norman times and the Gothic Chiesa di San Salvatore. You can get here by Lumia bus from Sciacca (€2.05, 50 minutes, four daily Monday to Saturday) and Agrigento (€5.15, 3½ hours, three daily Monday to Saturday).

THE PELAGIC ISLANDS
Some 240km south of Agrigento, this tiny archipelago (Isole Pelagie) lies farther from mainland Sicily than Malta and in many respects has more in common with nearby Tunisia or Libya than Italy. Indeed, of the three islands, only Linosa is part of the Sicilian continental shelf; the other two are part of the submerged African land mass.

In July and August the archipelago's most popular island, Lampedusa, is overrun with visitors. If you want a little peace and tranquillity, you might consider skipping across the water to the small volcanic island of Linosa, where the black beaches are usually empty and the swimming is great. Tiny Lampione is little more than an uninhabited pimple and isn't even on the ferry route.

History
The Pelagic Islands (from the Greek *pelagos*, meaning 'sea') have always been largely neglected and only ever had a few inhabitants. In 1661 Lampedusa was awarded to the Tomasi family (hence Giuseppe Tomasi di Lampedusa, of *The Leopard* fame). In 1839 they tried to sell it to the British but King Ferdinand II of Naples jumped in and forked out 12 million ducats to stop the British gaining yet another strategic foothold in the Mediterranean. The islands were bombed in 1943 by the Allies and the Americans later set up a military base here, which itself was the target of a bomb attack in 1986, when Libya's Colonel Gaddafi launched a couple of wobbly missiles in retaliation for the US bombing of his country. The missiles missed their target and landed out to sea.

During the Fascist era, Lampedusa was used as a place of exile for political enemies of the regime (they were called *confinati*, from *confine*, meaning 'border'). In later years, Mafia prisoners were sent here while awaiting trial, but the Italian government yielded to pressure from the islanders and stopped the practice on account of the fact that it was damaging tourism.

Lampedusa
postcode 92010 • pop 5400

Lampedusa, a rocky, sparsely covered and, in winter, wind-whipped place, is becoming increasingly popular with Italians looking for an early tan. There is no site of any interest in the town itself and most people make a beeline straight for the sea (the water is enticingly warm) and the sand.

Orientation Whether arriving by ferry or by plane, all visitors disembark on Lampedusa, in the town of the same name. If you arrive by ferry, it's a 10-minute walk up to the old town or a 15-minute walk west to the harbour at Porto Nuovo, where you'll find many of the hotels. The airport is not much farther away on the southeastern edge of town. The bus station, handy if you want to visit beaches around the island, is on Piazza Brignone in the centre of town.

Information The archipelago's only tourist office is the Pro Loco branch (☎ 0922 97 13 90), at Via Vittorio Emanuele 89. It only opens from April to October and the hours are very erratic even then. If it is closed, try the travel agency Ente Turismo (☎ 0922 97 11 71), at Via Anfossi 3.

The Banco di Sicilia, at Via Roma 129, has an ATM, as does the Banca Popolare S Angelo, just down the street at No 50.

The post office (which also doubles as a Telecom office) is on Piazza Piave. It opens 8.30am to 1pm and 4pm to 7pm Monday to Saturday.

In an emergency, dial the *guardia medica* (first-aid station) on ☎ 0922 97 06 04. There is a pharmacy at Via Roma 26. The police station (*questura*; ☎ 0922 97 00 01) is at Via Roma 37.

Beaches Of the several beaches on the southern side of the 11km-long island, the best known is the **Isola dei Conigli** (Rabbit Island), 7km west of town. It's an easy swim away (you can even walk to it if the tide is out) and has a small nature reserve, unique in Italy in that it is the only place where Caretta-Caretta turtles lay their eggs (between July and August). You will be lucky to see one, though, as these timid creatures generally only come in when no-one's about.

Other good swimming spots on the island include the **Cala Croce**, the first bay west of the town.

Diving The waters of Lampedusa are crystal clear and brimming with different kinds of fish. Consequently, diving is very popular. **Lo Verde Diving** (☎ 0922 97 19 86, *Via Sbarcatoio*) and **Mediterraneo Immersion Club** (☎ 0922 97 15 26, *Via A Volta 8*), both on the harbour-front, organise gear rental and diving trips around the island. Expect to pay around €51.65 per day for a complete set of equipment.

Places to Stay & Eat Cheap accommodation can be hard to find and you may be obliged to stay for a minimum of three nights. The small guesthouses are often full in summer and closed in winter. The tourist office has full lists of all hotels and room rentals.

La Roccia (☎ 0922 97 09 64, fax 0922 97 33 77, e *laroccia@iol.it*) From €7.25 per person per camp site. La Roccia is a two-star facility at Cala Greca, 3km west of town past the Guitgia beach. Standards are high and it's a good choice if you have to watch your budget. There are also cabins, chalets and caravans available.

Albergo Le Pelagie (☎ 0922 97 02 11, e *info@lepelagie.it, Via Bonfiglio 7*) Half-board €88 per person. This well-appointed three-star hotel is off Via Roma, a 30-minute walk west along the waterfront from the port (alternatively, ring when you get to the port and staff will come and pick you up). Like most places, it makes at least half-board compulsory in summer, although room rates are much cheaper outside of August. There's an air-con supplement of €7.75 per room if the heat bothers you.

You'll have no problem finding somewhere to eat, even though prices tend to be more expensive than on the mainland. At night during summer, Via Roma's cafes and restaurants are chock-a-block with tourists tucking into a plethora of fish dishes and the ubiquitous couscous.

I Cuochini (☎ 0922 97 30 80, Via Vittorio Emanuele 37) Meals about €24. With a good *spaghetti alla bottarga* (spaghetti with tuna roe) and other fine dishes, this is an excellent choice if you're staying on the island.

Al Gallo d'Oro (Via Vittorio Emanuele 45) Meals about €16. Al Gallo d'Oro is a cheap and cheerful place, with a good tourist menu.

Getting Around Lampedusa is surprisingly well organised on the getting around front. You can walk into town from the airport. Most hotels and camp sites, however, arrange courtesy buses that transport passengers from the airport to their accommodation. You can also get a taxi, which cost between €2.60 and €5.15.

From June to September, orange minibuses (€1.55) run regularly from Piazza Brignone to the different beaches around the island. Although moving about on foot isn't too much of a problem, if you're pushed for time you might be better off renting a bike, scooter or even a car from one of the many rental outlets dotted around town. Licciardi Autonoleggi (☎ 0922 97 07 68), on Via Siracusa (a few steps from the docks at Porto Vecchio), rents scooters for €12.90 a day and cars from €25.80. You can also rent bicycles for €5.15 per day.

Linosa
postcode 92010 • pop 160

Linosa is essentially the summit of a dormant volcano that has been extinct for nearly 2000 years. Its black beaches and rocky coves don't attract nearly as many as visitors as Lampedusa but they are worth checking out if you fancy getting away from the crowds that flock to the larger island. In recent years Linosa has been slowly

building up its own tourist trade and today is an increasingly popular day trip from Lampedusa.

Linosa Club (☎ 0922 97 20 66, Contrada Calcarella). Doubles with half-board €82.65 per person. Closed Oct-May. This good hotel, the only one on the island, has lots of sporting facilities and a restaurant, and prices decrease outside August.

Da Errera (☎ 0922 97 20 41, fax 0922 97 20 41, Via Scalo Vecchio) Half-board €41.30 per person. This restaurant also has rooms for rent from May to November and is a pretty good choice.

Getting There & Away

Air You can fly directly to Lampedusa from Palermo. Air Sicilia (☎ 091 626 12 22 or 091 625 25 10 or toll-free 800 41 24 11) and Alitalia (☎ 848 86 56 41, W www.alitalia.it) fly twice daily to Lampedusa from Palermo (€93 single, one hour). You can buy tickets at the airport at Palermo or contact a travel agency, who might scout around for a good deal.

Air One (☎ 091 702 01 11 W www .air-one.it) also has flights between Palermo and Lampedusa from €112 return.

Boat You can get to the islands by ferry from Porto Empèdocle, 7km southwest of Agrigento. SAL Buses (€1.55) depart from Agrigento's train station every 30 minutes or so from 6.25am to 8.30pm, which is inconvenient considering the ferry departure times. You can buy tickets on the bus. The 20-minute journey brings you to Piazza Italia, on Via Roma, about 100m north of the ferry dock, along Via Quattro Novembre. Alternatively you can get a taxi from Piazzale Aldo Moro (about €5.15). Call ☎ 0922 2 18 99 or 0922 2 66 70 for a taxi.

You can buy ferry tickets from the Siremar ticket office (☎ 0922 63 66 83 or 0922 63 66 85) on the quayside, which opens 9am to 1pm, 4pm to 7pm and 9pm to midnight daily. Single fares to Lampedusa cost €33.60/30.75 (July and August/June and September) and to Linosa cost €26.60/24.55. Although you can take your car (from €49 one way), you're best advised to leave it on the mainland at a parking station near the port; you can rent vehicles pretty cheaply on Lampedusa should you need to.

The ferry leaves Porto Empèdocle at 11.59pm and gets to Lampedusa at 8.15am (Linosa at 5.45am). From Lampedusa, the ferry departs at 10.15am (12.15pm from Linosa) and arrives in Porto Empèdocle at 6pm daily. From June to September there are daily departures in both directions but the rest of the year there is no ferry out to the islands on Friday and no return ferry on Saturday. For the outward, night-time journey you should consider reserving a couchette (a fold-out bed) for €15.25 or a reclining seat (€4.40). For the return, you can get in some quality sunbathing on the deck.

Getting Around

Ustica Lines runs a hydrofoil between Lampedusa and Linosa from 15 June to 30 September (€17 return, one hour). The hydrofoil departs Lampedusa at 9.30am and 5.30pm daily and departs Linosa at 10.45am and 6.45pm daily. You can buy your ticket at the Agenzia Marittima Strazera (☎ 0922 97 00 03), at Via F Riso 1 on Lampedusa. On Linosa, tickets are available where the ferries dock.

Western Sicily

Poor Western Sicily! For decades it was written off most tourist itineraries as a remote and uninteresting corner of the island, with little to recommend it save a couple of Greek ruins and – for those fascinated by the macabre – its reputation as a hotspot of seismic instability and Mafia activity. Consequently, the area never developed the sophisticated tourist industry that attracts visitors to other Sicilian holiday centres such as Taormina and Syracuse.

But if you ignore the west, you really do risk missing out. Not only does it have some of the most beautiful stretches of coastline on the entire island and a number of towns and cities to hold your keen attention, it is also a virtual repository of Sicilian history, a region defined and shaped by the multiculturalism that has influenced the island from prehistory to the modern day. Furthermore, here it is possible to gain a meaningful insight into Sicilian life away from the larger cities and tourist resorts.

Although most of the action is concentrated along the southwestern coast, there are good reasons for not staying on the A29 as it winds its way from Palermo through the mountains around Gibellina, south to Mazara del Vallo. East of Tràpani lie the splendid ruins of Segesta, including a temple that remains virtually intact after 2500 years. Farther south are another set of ruins of an altogether more chilling nature: the Ruderi di Gibellina date from 1968 when the entire town was levelled by a powerful earthquake.

The coastline between Castellammare del Golfo and Mt Cofano (659m) is perhaps the most beautiful in all of Sicily, a promontory jutting out into the sea, distinguished by coves and rocky beaches washed by the clearest and cleanest of waters. At its heart is the Riserva Naturale dello Zingaro, Sicily's first nature reserve, stretching north for 7km from Scopello to the foot of Mt Cofano. Although none of the towns along this coast can boast any fine museums or particularly beautiful churches, they are worth stopping

Highlights

- Watch the devotion and stamina displayed during the incredible procession of I Misteri in Tràpani at Easter

- Revel in the exquisite natural beauty of Scopello and the Riserva Naturale dello Zingaro

- Wander the pretty streets of medieval Èrice while munching on some of the best pastries in all of Sicily

- Swim, snorkel and island hop on the Egadi Islands

- Get lost in Mazara del Vallo's atmospheric Casbah

- Visit the Greek theatre at Segesta, an incomparable combination of architectural elegance and nature

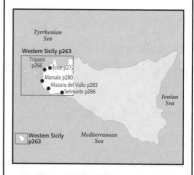

Tyrrhenian Sea
Western Sicily p263
Tràpani p266 ● ● Èrice p272
Marsala p280 ●
● Mazara del Vallo p283
● Selinunte p286
Ionian Sea
Western Sicily p263 Mediterranean Sea

in nonetheless, particularly the tiny medieval village of Scopello and the seaside town of San Vito lo Capo, home of some of the best fish couscous in Sicily.

GETTING AROUND

Western Sicily is relatively compact and easy to get around. There are regular train connections between all the towns along the coast as well as with the inland towns of Castelvetrano, Salemi and Gibellina. The

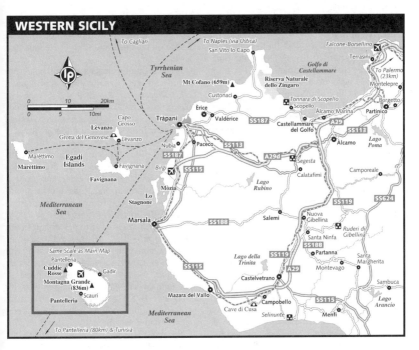

AST bus service is excellent, linking the entire province. If you're travelling by car, the A29 motorway between Palermo and Mazara del Vallo travels southward in an arc through the interior, with an offshoot going to Tràpani and Birgi airport. The coastal route SS115 links Tràpani with Marsala and Mazara del Vallo.

GOLFO DI CASTELLAMMARE
Castellammare del Golfo
postcode 91014 • pop 14,100

Hugging the coast and wholly surrounded by mountains, Castellammare del Golfo is the least attractive of the towns along the gulf, although it does have a pleasant harbour full of cafes and little restaurants.

Guarding the harbour are the remains of a 17th-century Aragonese **castle**. Away from the harbour, the town slopes upwards into the hills, a grid of narrow, uninviting streets and two-storey residential buildings. Although quiet enough today, the town has

a history of Mafia connections and bloodshed, particularly in the period following WWII, when it was reckoned to have the highest number of murders per capita of any town on the island. Not surprisingly, the town does not sit at the top of any tourist itineraries. Still, it isn't a bad place to linger for an afternoon, if only to plan your visit to the surrounding area.

There are a few accommodation options but, unless you want to camp, none are particularly cheap.

Nausicaa (☎ 0924 3 30 30, fax 0924 3 51 13, e info@nausica-camping.it, Località Forgia) €4.15 per person. This well-recommended camp site has good facilities, is close to the beach and is well-signposted on roads approaching Castellammare del Golfo.

Punta Nord Est (☎ 0924 3 05 11, fax 0924 3 07 13, Viale Leonardo da Vinci 67) Singles/doubles with bathroom €62/93. This is the cheapest hotel here, set in a big and modern building. Prices drop in the low

WESTERN SICILY

season but staying in Scopello is still a more attractive option.

Buses depart from Via della Repubblica, in the upper part of town. There are four buses daily to/from Tràpani (€3.10) and Scopello. There are also buses to Palermo, San Vito lo Capo and Segesta.

The train station is an inconvenient 3km out of town, although a shuttle bus (€1.30) takes passengers into town. There are about 13 daily trains from Palermo (€3.85, one hour 20 minutes, about 13 daily) and Tràpani (€3.10, 50 minutes).

Scopello

postcode 901014 • pop 40
elevation 106m

Blink and you'll miss it, but it would be a shame: this tiny, two-street village, delightfully placed on a ridge high above the coastline, is made up of a square in front of a *baglio* (manor house), around which the town is built. There is nothing really to do in the town except eat and explore the surrounding countryside, best done with your own transport. Still, it's only a 2km walk to the entrance to the Riserva Naturale dello Zingaro (see the following section) and only 1.5km from one of the most idyllic swimming coves on the island, by the old tuna station at the foot of the hill. If you need a bank, there's a small branch of Banco di Sicilia with an ATM at the baglio.

Tonnara di Scopello The tuna processing plant ceased operations in the 1980s, a victim of Sicily's chronic tuna malaise, but its closure has been a godsend for visitors: they are free to enter so long as they respect the site's tranquillity (no radios, no beach umbrellas – basically nothing that might disturb the appearance of the place). The place is literally perfect: an old abandoned building surrounded by rows of rusting anchors gives onto a small shingle beach lapped by waters of an incredible blue. The cove is protected by *faraglioni* (rock towers), jutting out of the sea.

Places to Stay & Eat *Baia di Guidaloca* (☎ 0924 54 12 65, fax 0924 3 04 43 Località Guidaloca) €5.40/5.15/3.10 per person/tent/

car. This is the nearest camp site to Scopello. It's near the lovely swimming hole of Cala Bianca on the bus route from Castellammare del Golfo.

All of Scopello's restaurants and hotels are within a 30-second radius of the main square.

La Tavernetta (☎/fax 0924 54 11 29, Via Armando Diaz 3) Rooms with bathroom €49 per person. This place has seven rooms and a charming restaurant underneath.

La Tranchina (☎/fax 0924 54 10 99, Via Armando Diaz 7) Singles/doubles with bathroom €41.30/61.95. Two doors down from La Tavernetta, this place has modern and comfortable rooms, plus a terrace with sea views and good food in its restaurant.

Torre Bennistra II (☎/fax 0924 54 11 28, Via Natale di Roma 19) Singles/doubles with bathroom €33.05/43.90. Around the corner from the above-mentioned places and with great food at its restaurant, this is an excellent place to stay. The owners' first establishment, at Via Armando Diaz 9, is a bit cheaper (€26.85/36.15) but not quite as nice.

You don't have to be a guest to eat at any of the restaurants. Alternatively, try *Il Baglio*, in the main square, which serves excellent pizzas. *Caffetteria Nettuno*, also in the main square, is a good spot for a beer or snack.

Riserva Naturale dello Zingaro

About 2km from Scopello is the main entrance to the Zingaro Nature Reserve *(admission €2.60, open 7am-9pm daily 16 Apr-15 Sept & 7am-6pm daily 16 Sept-15 Apr)*, 7km of pristine coastline flanked by a couple of steep mountains. Established in 1980 after protests against a planned road through the area, the reserve has a series of well-maintained paths and six beaches. Most people come for the excellent swimming but the area is rich in plant life and home to at least 40 different species of bird, including a type of eagle known as *l'aquila del Bonelli*. No kind of motorised transport is allowed in the reserve. The information/ticket booth is at the entrance.

The friendly and helpful **Cetaria Diving Centre** (☎ 0924 54 10 73, [e] cetaria@tiscalnet.it, Via Marco Polo 3) in Scopello organises dives, classes and underwater tours of the nature reserve from the Tonnara di Scopello, daily in June and August. For off-season dives, call Vittorio Ballerini (☎ 0368 386 48 08) or Fabio Centineo (☎ 0368 718 38 03).

A car is the best way to get to Scopello from Castellammare del Golfo. If you're driving from Tràpani, take the SS187.

There are four buses daily from Castellammare del Golfo to Scopello with Autoservizi Russo (☎ 0924 3 13 64) at 7.10am, 9am, 1.30pm and 4pm (€1.80/2.85 single/return). Buses from Scopello to Castellammare del Golfo depart about 30 minutes later from the communal fountain.

San Vito lo Capo
postcode 91010 • pop 3500
Occupying the tip of the promontory is the pleasant seaside town of San Vito lo Capo, full of beachcombers and sun worshippers in summer but virtually dead in winter. The town is renowned for its splendid beach (at the end of Via Savoia) and for its fish couscous, celebrated at a couscous festival every August. The most noteworthy sight is the fortress-like 13th-century **Chiesa di San Vito**, about halfway down Via Savoia. The tourist office (☎ 0923 97 24 64) is at Via Savoia 57, in the rather uninteresting Museo del Mare.

For a luxurious camp site experience, try the following place about 3km south of San Vito lo Capo.

El Bahira (☎ 0923 97 25 77, fax 0923 97 25 52, Località Makari) €6.70/17.55/118.30 per person/camp site/4-bed bungalow. It's well signposted on the roads of the area, and you can ask the bus driver to let you off if you're not coming by car.

Thàam (☎ 0923 97 28 36, Via Duca degli Abruzzi 34) Meals about €21. Closed Wed in Nov. A North African restaurant just off Via Savoia, this is a great place to eat the famous couscous.

Otherwise, Via Savoia is full of pizzerias and other restaurants all priced similarly, and there are cheap *rosticcerie* (shops selling roast meat and other prepared food) and pizza places if you're watching the budget. AST Buses to San Vito lo Capo (€3.10, 1½ hours) depart eight times daily (four on Sunday and public holidays) from Tràpani. Buses arrive at Via P Matarella, just near the beach and parallel to Via Savoia.

TRÀPANI
postcode 91100 • pop 72,500
The administrative capital of the province of the same name (which encompasses virtually all of Western Sicily), Tràpani is a largely inconspicuous, modern city with little to hint that it was – until relatively recently – a powerful and strategic trading port. The only clue to its past lies in the jumbled maze of streets that makes up the historic centre, at the tip of the thin peninsula on which the city is built. There is little here to keep you for more than a day or so, except at Easter, when the city is given over to the extraordinary celebrations known as I Misteri (The Mysteries; see the later boxed text 'I Misteri'). Still, the city is within easy striking distance of all the major points of interest (including the Egadi Islands) in the west and is the best base for visiting the region.

History
Originally a Phoenician post, Tràpani (or Drepanon, as it was called) was the key port in the Carthaginian defence of Sicily during the Punic Wars. After the sack of Èrice (Eryx) in 260 BC by Hamilcar, part of the population was moved down the hill and the port was raised to the status of a city; however, in 241 BC it was captured by the Romans and the nascent city went into decline. Subsequent conquests by the Saracens in the 9th century and the Normans 300 years later led to the rebuilding of the city and its reestablishment as a major link in the trading route that joined Tunis, Anjou and Aragon. Edward I of England stopped off here in 1272 on his return from a crusade, whereupon he learnt of his accession to the throne. Peter of Aragon landed here in 1282 to begin the Aragonese occupation of Sicily that followed the overthrow of the Angevin kings (the famous Sicilian Vespers; see History in the Facts about Sicily chapter). In recent times, Tràpani thrived on the salt and wine trades, while today it is largely a city devoted

to service industries. Extensive bombing during WWII led to the construction of some fairly ugly modern blocks which, unfortunately, dominate the city today.

Orientation

Tràpani is narrow and relatively compact, bordered on either side by the sea. The main street, Via GB Fardella, runs east–west, splitting the modern city into two neat halves. On either side a chessboard street-grid dominates as far as the historic centre, which is a confusing maze of small streets, many of which do not have signposts. All of the sights of interest are concentrated in this area, from where there is also access to the ferry terminal. The main bus station is on Piazza Montalto, in the new town, and the train station is around the corner on Piazza Umberto I. The cheaper hotels are in the heart of the historic centre, about 500m to the west.

Information

Tourist Offices The helpful and informative APT tourist office (☎ 0923 2 90 00, ℮ appt@mail.cinet.it), Piazzetta Saturno 1/2, is at the eastern edge of the historic

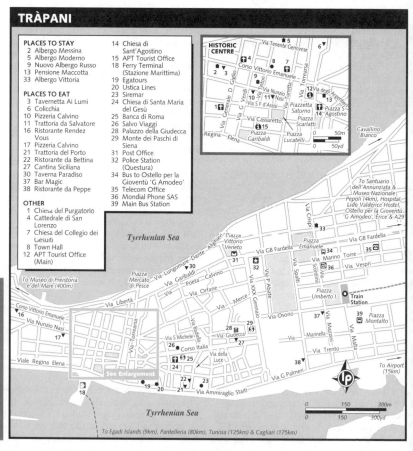

TRÀPANI

PLACES TO STAY
2 Albergo Messina
5 Albergo Moderno
9 Nuovo Albergo Russo
13 Pensione Maccotta
33 Albergo Vittoria

PLACES TO EAT
3 Tavernetta Ai Lumi
6 Colicchia
10 Pizzeria Calvino
11 Trattoria da Salvatore
16 Ristorante Rendez Vous
17 Pizzeria Calvino
21 Trattoria del Porto
22 Ristorante da Bettina
27 Cantina Siciliana
30 Taverna Paradiso
37 Bar Magic
38 Ristorante da Peppe

OTHER
1 Chiesa del Purgatorio
4 Cattedrale di San Lorenzo
7 Chiesa del Collegio dei Gesuiti
8 Town Hall
12 APT Tourist Office (Main)

14 Chiesa di Sant'Agostino
15 APT Tourist Office
18 Ferry Terminal (Stazione Marittima)
19 Egatours
20 Ustica Lines
23 Siremar
24 Chiesa di Santa Maria del Gesù
25 Banca di Roma
26 Salvo Viaggi
28 Palazzo della Giudecca
29 Monte dei Paschi di Siena
31 Post Office
32 Police Station (Questura)
34 Bus to Ostello per la Gioventù 'G Amodeo'
35 Telecom Office
36 Mondial Phone SAS
39 Main Bus Station

centre. It opens 8am to 8pm Monday to Saturday and 9am to noon on Sunday and has an excellent range of information on the province. There is also an APT tourist office (☎ 0923 54 55 11, W www.apt.trapani.it) at Via S Francesco d'Assisi 27, near Piazza Garibaldi, which keeps erratic opening hours.

Money There is no shortage of banks in Tràpani – in fact the high number of banks is one of the main tell-tale signs that this supposedly poor province obviously has more than a few profitable business ventures in the area. Among others, the Banca di Roma, at Corso Italia 38, and the Monte dei Paschi di Siena, at Via XXX Gennaio 80, have ATMs that take Visa and MasterCard plus exchange facilities.

Post & Communications The main post office is on Piazza Vittorio Veneto and opens between 8.20am and 7pm Monday to Saturday. The Telecom office at Via Agostino Pepoli 82 opens 9am to 12.30pm and 4.30pm to 8pm daily.

You can check your email at Mondial Phone SAS (☎/fax 0923 2 19 52), Via Scontrino 13, for €5.15 per hour. You can also make phone calls, photocopies and send faxes here. The Internet connection is quite slow so, if speed is of the essence, try the Internet/telephone centre on the first floor of the ferry terminal, where boats and hydrofoils dock (same prices).

Medical Services & Emergency The public hospital (Ospedale Sant'Antonio Abate; ☎ 0923 80 91 11) is on Via Cosenza, some distance from the centre of town. Dial the same number for an ambulance. For *pronto soccorso* (casualty) dial ☎ 0923 80 94 50. For the *guardia medica* (first-aid station), Piazza Generale Scio 1, call ☎ 0923 2 96 29. The police station (*questura*; ☎ 0923 59 81 11) is at Piazza Vittorio Veneto.

Things to See

The 16th-century **Palazzo della Giudecca** *(Via Giudecca 43)*, with its distinctive facade, stands out among the general decay of the old and run-down Jewish quarter. Built in the Spanish Plateresque style by the aristocratic Ciambra family, it has been extensively renovated and very little survives of the original plan, save an embossed tower and (facing the street) a series of windows adorned with lavish cornices and pillars.

Cross Corso Italia and head west to reach the **Chiesa di Santa Maria del Gesù** *(Via San Pietro)*, whose exterior has both Catalan-Gothic and Renaissance features. Dating from the first half of the 16th century, its ground plan is similar to that of the cathedral at Monreale. Inside, the chapel contains the exquisite *Madonna degli Angeli* (Madonna with the Angels), a glazed terracotta statue by Andrea della Robbia. Unfortunately, at the time of research the church was not open to visitors. On Piazzetta Saturno, near the main APT tourist office, the 14th-century **Chiesa di Sant'Agostino** *(open 8am-1pm daily)* is worth a look for its fine Gothic rose window and portal.

Head west along Corso Vittorio Emanuele, noting the **Chiesa del Collegio dei Gesuiti** *(open 8am-4pm daily)*, whose main feature is the lovely *Immacolata* (Immaculate), carved in white marble by Ignazio Marabitti, and the 17th-century **town hall**, which is closed to the public, before reaching the **Cattedrale di San Lorenzo** *(open 8am-4pm daily)*. Built in 1635 on the site of an existing church, the cathedral boasts an elegant Baroque facade and, inside, the *Crocifissione* (Crucifixion), the work of local artist Giacomo Lo Verde but often erroneously attributed to Van Dyck. Off Corso Vittorio Emanuele, the **Chiesa del Purgatorio** *(☎ 0923 56 28 82, Via Generale D Giglio; free; open 8.30am-12.30pm & 4pm-8pm daily)* houses the Misteri: 20 18th-century, life-size wooden figures depicting Christ's Passion. On Good Friday they are carried in procession (see the boxed text 'I Misteri').

At the tip of the promontory, to the west of the historic centre, is the Torre di Ligny, built in 1671 as a fortress by the Spanish viceroy. Today it is home to the **Museo di Preistoria e del Mare** *(☎ 0923 2 23 00, Via Torre di Ligny; admission €1.05; open 9.30am-1pm & 4.30pm-7pm daily)*, an excellent collection of prehistoric artefacts.

Tràpani's most important sight, however, is some distance east of the city centre. The **Santuario dell'Annunziata** (☎ *0923 53 91 84, Via Conte Agostino Pepoli; free; open 7am-noon & 4pm-8pm Mon-Sat, 7am-1pm & 4pm-8pm Sun, 7am-noon & 4pm-7pm daily in winter*) was built between 1315 and 1332. It was radically remodelled in Baroque style in 1760, when the original three aisles were made into one single nave. The only elements left from the original building are the Gothic rose window and the doorway. Behind the altar is the actual sanctuary of the church, the Cappella della Madonna, built in 1530. The large marble arch contains wonderful reliefs by Antonino and Giacomo Gagini, as well as the venerated *Madonna di Tràpani* (also known as Madonna and Child), carved, it is thought, by Nino Pisano. To get here, take bus No 24, 25 or 30 from Corso Vittorio Emanuele or Via Garibaldi and get off at Villa Pepoli.

The adjacent **Museo Nazionale Pepoli** (☎ *0923 55 32 69, Via Conte Agostino Pepoli 200; admission €4.15; open 9am-1.30pm Mon-Sat plus 3pm-6.30pm Tues-Thur, 9am-12.30pm Sun & hols*) is housed in a former Carmelite monastery. It has an archaeological collection, statues and coral carvings. Highlights are Titian's *San Francesco con Stigmata* (St Francis with Stigmata) and the *Pietà* by Roberto di Oderiso.

Special Events

Tràpani is famous throughout Italy for its Easter celebrations, the Procession of the Misteri, which begins on the Tuesday before Easter and reaches its climax on the night between Holy Thursday and Good Friday (see the boxed text 'I Misteri').

Places to Stay

Camping Located 7km north of Tràpani, on the road to Èrice, this is the nearest camp site and it's pretty good.

Lido Valderice (☎ *0923 57 30 86, Via del Dentice 15, Località Tonnara di Bonagia*) €4.15/8.25 per person/camp site. Open 1 June-30 Sept. There are six buses daily that head for Èrice from the bus station.

I Misteri

Sicily's most venerated Easter procession is a four-day festival of extraordinary religious fervour. Since the 17th century, the ordinary citizens of Tràpani – represented by 20 traditional *maestranze*, or guilds – have begun the celebration of the Passion of Christ on the Tuesday before Easter Sunday with the first procession of a remarkable, life-size wooden statue of the Virgin Mary. Over the course of the next three days, nightly processions make their way through the old quarter and port to a specially erected chapel in Piazza Lucatelli, where the icons are stored overnight. Each procession is accompanied by women following the men (who carry the statues on their shoulders) and a local band, which plays dirges to the slow, steady beat of a drum.

The high point of the celebration is on Friday afternoon, when the 20 guilds emerge from the Chiesa del Purgatorio and descend the steps of the church (in Sicilian dialect the *scinnuta*, or descent) carrying each of the statues to begin the 1km-long procession up to Via GB Fardella and back to the church the following morning. The massive crowds that gather to witness the slow march often reach a peak of delirious fervour that is matched only by that which accompanies the Easter *pasos* celebration in Seville, Spain. If you're not around for Easter, you can always see the figures in Chiesa del Purgatorio, where they are stored throughout the year. A guardian is usually on hand to explain the origins of each one.

Hostels The nearest hostel is 3km out of town.

Ostello per la Gioventù 'G Amodeo' (☎/fax *0923 55 29 64,* ℮ *scral.erice-touring @libero.it, Viale della Pineta, Contrada Raganzili*) Dorm bed & breakfast €10.85. This hostel gets a good report from its guests. Three kilometres north of town on the Èrice road, it's a 15-minute bus ride on the No 23 from Via GB Fardella to the Ospedale Villa dei Gerani. From there, turn right and then take the second right and walk about 500m uphill.

Hotels Tràpani has the best choice of hotels in the region but even then the choice isn't spectacular.

Albergo Messina (☎ 0923 2 11 98, Corso Vittorio Emanuele 71) Singles/doubles €15.50/31. The cheapest and most central hotel in Tràpani is entered via the once-grand courtyard of a 17th-century building. The nine rooms don't live up to their promise but if you like eavesdropping on loud conversations, this is the place for you!

Pensione Maccotta (☎ 0923 2 84 18, fax 0923 43 76 93, Via degli Argentieri 4) Singles/doubles €20.65/46.50, with bathroom €25.80/51.65. In an uninspiring modern building, conveniently located in the centre of town, the rooms here are good and the service is friendly.

Albergo Moderno (☎ 0923 2 12 47, fax 0923 2 33 48, Via Tenente Genovese 20) Singles/doubles with bathroom €23.25/46.50. With a wonderful old portal through which you enter and decent, simple rooms, this is a good budget choice with a warm and friendly management.

Nuovo Albergo Russo (☎ 0923 2 21 66, fax 0923 2 66 23, Via Tintori 4) Singles/doubles €25.85/51.65, with bathroom €36.15/61.95. With gilded antiques in the lobby and a classic 1950s vibe in some of the rooms, this place is clean and tidy.

Cavallino Bianco (☎ 0923 2 15 49 or 0923 2 39 01, fax 0923 87 30 02, Lungomare Dante Alighieri) Singles/doubles with bathroom €46.50/77.45. A kilometre to the northeast of Tràpani, this place is more expensive than most of the places in Tràpani but offers a better standard, with rooms overlooking the sea.

Albergo Vittòria (☎ 0923 87 30 44, fax 0923 2 98 70, Via Francesco Crispi 4) Singles/doubles with bathroom €46.50/72.30. The rooms here are spotlessly clean and have air-con, TV and swish bathrooms; it's good value and a quick walk from the train and bus stations.

Places to Eat

Sicily's Arab heritage and Tràpani's unique position on the sea route to Tunisia has made couscous (or cuscus, as they spell it here) something of a speciality, particularly when served with a fish sauce *(cuscus con pesce)* that includes tomatoes, garlic and parsley. You'll find it on the menu of every restaurant in town.

Cantina Siciliana (☎ 0923 2 86 73, Via Giudecca 32) Meals about €13. This tiled and (almost) tiny place is just near Palazzo della Giudecca and has a good, filling cuscus con pesce, served with a smile.

Trattoria del Porto (☎ 0923 54 78 22, Via Ammiraglio Staiti 45) Meals about €13. Trattoria del Porto, also known as Da Felice, has rather dour 1970s decor and a small pavement eating area. It's not the best place to eat but the pasta dishes are good and it's handy if you're about to catch a boat.

Tavernetta Ai Lumi (☎ 0923 87 24 18, Corso Vittorio Emanuele 15) Meals about €16. Closed Sun. Both the decor and the dishes are predominantly rustic at this friendly place, although you can still get a very good *spaghetti con vongole* (spaghetti with clams).

Trattoria da Salvatore (Via Nunzio Nasi 19) Meals about €13. If you can hear yourself think above the sound of the TV and the family's excited chatter, you'll enjoy yourself here. It's a simple, unflashy place with good fried calamari and local wines.

Ristorante da Peppe (☎ 0923 2 82 46, Via Spalti 50) Meals about €23. Closed Mon. With lots of stained glass, fresh seafood and a good reputation with the locals, you'll love treating yourself here.

Ristorante da Bettina (☎ 0923 2 48 00, Via San Cristoforo 5) Meals about €18. Closed Wed. A step up from the majority of places to eat near the port, this restaurant is fitted out like a hygiene-obsessed granny's living room but serves a truly superb *involtini di pesce spada* (swordfish roulade, stuffed with breadcrumbs). Sadly, the desserts are frozen.

Taverna Paradiso (☎ 0923 2 23 03, Via Lungomare Dante Alighieri 24) Meals about €31. Closed Wed. Easily one of Tràpani's eating highlights this excellent restaurant has beautiful decor and charming staff. If you want to try a Sicilian speciality, the shavings of tuna roe with olive oil and lemon *(bottarga)* are delicious.

***Ristorante Rendez Vous** (☎ 0923 2 28 66, Corso Vittorio Emanuele 191)* Meals about €18. Closed Mon. With a French feel and excellent salads, this is a good choice in the centre of town.

***Pizzeria Calvino** (Via Nunzio Nasi 77)* Closed Tues. For takeaway pizza that's been pleasing Tràpani since 1946, hotfoot it to this popular place.

***Colicchia** (cnr Via delle Belle Arti & Via Carosto)* The granita (€1.55) here is a revelation and definitely the best in Tràpani, if not Western Sicily. Many flavours are available, including old favourites such as *fragola* (strawberry) and *mandorla* (almond) but there are also more unusual choices such as the refreshing mix of carrot, lemon and orange. An essential passeggiata accessory!

***Bar Magic** (☎ 0923 2 70 39, Via Mazzini 2)* These guys can really get your heart started with their coffee (the morning techno music helps!) and the pastries are good too.

An open-air *market* is held every morning and into the early afternoon from Monday to Saturday on Piazza Mercato di Pesce, on the northern waterfront. Even if you're not buying seafood, it's a wonderful place to stroll around, taking in the sights, smells and sounds.

Getting There & Away

Air Tràpani's small national airport (☎ 0923 84 25 02) is 16km south of town at Birgi. AST buses connect Tràpani bus station and the airport (€3.10, 20 minutes).

Bus All intercity buses arrive and depart from the bus station on Piazza Montalto. Tickets can be bought from kiosks in the station. Segesta runs a service from Tràpani to Palermo (€6.70 single, two hours). Lumia (☎ 0923 2 17 54) serves Agrigento (€9.30 single, 3½ to four hours, three daily). AST (☎ 0923 2 10 21) serves Èrice (€2.85 return, 45 minutes, 11 Monday to Saturday, four on Sunday and public holidays), Castellammare del Golfo (€3.10, 1½ hours, four daily), Castelvetrano (€8.80,

1½ hours, seven daily, connections on to Selinunte), Marsala (€4.15, 45 minutes, eight daily), Mazara del Vallo (€3.85, one hour and 10 minutes, three daily) and San Vito lo Capo (€3.10, 1¼ hours, eight daily). AST also runs a bus service to Segesta (€4.15, 25 minutes, five daily June to September) and Calatafimi.

Bus frequency decreases dramatically on Sunday, public holidays and in the low season (October to May). Timetables are always posted at the bus station.

Train For general train information call ☎ 0923 2 80 71 or 0923 2 80 81. Tràpani is linked to Palermo (€5.95, two hours, 10 to 12 daily), Castelvetrano (€3.85, one hour 10 minutes, 20 daily), Marsala (€2.30, 30 minutes, 20 daily) and Mazara del Vallo (€3.10, 50 minutes, 20 daily). The left-luggage office at the station opens 8am to 9.30pm daily and costs €3.85 for 24 hours.

Boat Siremar (☎ 0923 54 54 55, **W** www .siremar.it – Italian only) runs a nightly ferry to Pantelleria from 1 June to 30 September (six times a week at other times). The high-season fare costs €22.45; car prices start at €41.30. The boat departs from Tràpani at 11.59pm, arriving at Pantelleria at 5.45am the next day. The boat leaves Pantelleria at noon during the high season (check at other times), returning to Tràpani at 4.45pm. In Tràpani, get tickets at Egatours (☎ 0923 2 17 54), Via Ammiraglio Staiti 13, at the Siremar office at Via Ammiraglio Staiti 63 or directly at the embarkation point.

Ustica Lines (☎ 0923 2 22 00, **W** www .usticalines.it – Italian only), at Via Ammiraglio Staiti 23, operates a hydrofoil service from Tràpani to Naples (€82.65), departing at 6.30am on Monday, Thursday and Saturday from 15 June to 15 September only. The service goes via Ustica (€18.60) and the Egadi Islands (from €5.15). There are also services from Tràpani directly to the Egadi Islands daily between 1 June and 30 September. Ustica Lines also has a hydrofoil to Pantelleria, departing 1.35pm daily from 1 July to 31 August (€33.60).

Tirrenia (toll-free ☎ 800 82 40 79, W www
.tirrenia.it – Italian only) runs weekly ferries
to Tunisia from Tràpani, departing at 10am
Monday June to December. Tickets for the
8¼-hour trip cost €51.40 for an airline type
seat *(poltrona)* and €63.80 for a bed in a 2nd-
class cabin (both during the high season). The
return boat leaves Tunisia at 9pm on Monday.
There is also a weekly Tirrenia service to
Cagliari (Sardinia), departing at 9pm on
Tuesday from June to December. Tickets cost
€38.20 for a poltrona and €51.65 for a bed
in a 2nd-class cabin in the high season.
Tickets can be purchased at Salvo Viaggi
(☎ 0923 54 54 55) at the ferry terminal
(stazione marittima) or at Corso Italia 48
(☎ 0923 54 54 11).

Getting Around

To/From the Airport AST buses (€3.10,
20 minutes) leave from Piazza Montalto to
coincide with flights. Segesta (☎ 0923 2 17
54) runs buses at 9am and 2.15pm Monday
to Saturday (€5.15, one hour and 10 minutes) to the main Falcone-Borsellino airport
(Palermo).

Taxis There are taxi ranks on Piazza Umberto (☎ 0923 2 28 08) and at the ferry terminal (☎ 0923 2 32 33).

ÈRICE

postcode 91016 ● pop 31,000
elevation 751m
The dramatically beautiful medieval hill
town of Èrice is about 45 minutes northeast
of Tràpani by bus and should not be missed
on any account. Settled by the Elymians, an
ancient mountain people who also founded
Segesta, it was an important religious site
associated with goddesses of fertility – first
the Carthaginian Astarte, then the Greek
Aphrodite, and finally the Roman Venus.
Today, it has become a bit of a tourist trap,
as well as a centre for international confer-
ences as it is home to the headquarters of the
Ettore Majorana Scientific and Cultural Institute. However, it still manages to maintain
a relatively authentic medieval atmosphere,
with one sore exception: the town's elevated
position has made it a prime location for

telecommunication towers, which soar
above the medieval skyline, somewhat
spoiling the whole effect.

Orientation & Information

You'll have no problems finding your way
around this small town – but be prepared for
plenty of uphill walks. The friendly and informative tourist office (☎ 0923 86 93 88)
is on Viale Conte Pepoli, near the bus terminus. There's a post office in the heart of
town, on Via Guarnotti, open 8.15am to
1.30pm Monday to Friday. The police station is at the Porta Tràpani entrance to town,
near the bus stop on Piazza Grammatico.

Things to See

This triangular-shaped town is best explored
by pottering around its narrow streets and
peeking through the doorways into courtyards. At the top of the hill stands the Norman **Castello di Venere** *(Castle of Venus;
free; open 8am-7pm daily)*, built in the 12th
and 13th centuries over an ancient temple of
Venus. Not much more than a ruin, the castle is upstaged by the panoramic vistas
northeast to San Vito lo Capo and Mt Cofano (659m), and west to Tràpani.

Of the several churches and other monuments in the small, quiet town, the **Chiesa
Madre** *(Via Vito Carvini; free; open 9.30am-
1pm & 3pm-5.15pm daily)*, just inside Porta
Tràpani, is probably the most interesting by
virtue of its separate **bell tower** *(campanile;
admission €1.05)* with mullioned windows.
Built in 1314, the interior of the church was
remodelled in neogothic style in 1865 but
the 15th-century side chapels were con-
served. Also worth paying attention to is the
ornate vaulted ceiling.

At the top of the town's main street,
Corso Vittorio Emanuele, is the heart of the
city and where you'll find the **Museo
Civico Antonio Cordici** *(☎ 0923 86 91 72,
Piazza Umberto I; free; open 8.30am-
1.30pm Mon-Fri & 2.30pm-5pm Mon &
Thur)*. The museum houses finds from the
town's necropolis, including a 4th-century
head of Venus. The other piece worth
seeing is an elegant *Annunciation* by
Antonello Gagini.

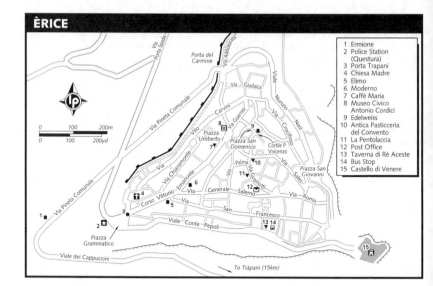

ÈRICE

1 Ermione
2 Police Station
  (Questura)
3 Porta Trapani
4 Chiesa Madre
5 Elimo
6 Moderno
7 Caffè Maria
8 Museo Civico
  Antonio Cordici
9 Edelweiss
10 Antica Pasticceria
   del Convento
11 La Pentolaccia
12 Post Office
13 Taverna di Rè Aceste
14 Bus Stop
15 Castello di Venere

Places to Stay & Eat

The number of hotels in Èrice has improved over the years but they're not at all cheap. The nearest cheap option is actually *Ostello per la Gioventù 'G Amodeo* (see Places to Stay under Tràpani earlier).

Ermione (☎ *0923 86 91 38, fax 0923 86 95 87, Via Pineta Comunale 43*) Singles/doubles with bathroom €51.65/82.65. The rooms here are a bit cramped and it's not centrally located so it's only worth staying here if you're stuck and pinching Èrice pennies.

Edelweiss (☎ *0923 86 94 20, Cortile P Vincenzo 5*) Singles/doubles with bathroom €61.95/82.63. In an ugly modern building, the rooms here are OK and quiet.

Moderno (☎ *0923 86 93 00, fax 0923 86 91 39, Via Vittorio Emanuele 63*) Singles/doubles with bathroom €77.45/113.60. This is the pick of the bunch: it's set in a lovely location, has very nice rooms and a restaurant.

Elimo (☎ *0923 86 93 77, fax 0923 86 92 52, ⓔ elimoh@comeg.it, Via Vittorio Emanuele 75*) Singles/doubles with bathroom €87.80/196.25. This good hotel charges extortionate prices in summer but reduces them to a more acceptable level in

the low season. There are only 21 rooms, so bookings are advised.

Taverna di Rè Aceste (*Via R De Martini*) Meals about €21. Closed Wed & Sun. For a decent meal at a reasonable price, try this taverna, with a lovely terrace and a long-standing reputation, in a small lane off Viale Conte Pepoli.

La Pentolaccia (☎ *0923 86 90 99, Via Guarnotta 17*) Meals about €18. Closed Tues. This atmospheric restaurant is inside a former 16th-century monastery. It can get swamped by tourist groups but the food is tasty, with *pasta con le sarde* (pasta with sardines) and other favourites featuring on the menu.

Caffè Maria (*Via Vittorio Emanuele 4 & 14*) At the No 4 location, you can get great coffee and cakes in a charming pink cafe that's open till 2am (which is incredibly late for Èrice!). At No 14, you can get eye-popping pastries – the *cannoli* (cream horns) are exquisite.

Antica Pasticceria del Convento (☎ *0923 86 90 05, Via Guarnotti 1*) With heavenly pastries and sweets, it's hard to go past this little *pasticceria* (cake shop) if you've got a sweet tooth. And since it's in an old convent, this is one time when gluttony doesn't really count as a sin.

Getting There & Away

There is a regular AST bus service to/from Tràpani (€1.80/2.85 single/return, 45 minutes), with 11 daily buses Monday to Saturday and four on Sunday. The service begins at 6.40am and ends at 7.30pm (from 9am to 6pm on Sunday). If you don't want to get stuck in Èrice, catch the last bus at 8.30pm (7.30pm Sunday). In Èrice, all buses arrive and depart from Viale Conte Pepoli.

THE EGADI ISLANDS

postcode 91023 • pop 3440

The Egadi Islands (Isole Egadi) are the most accessible of Sicily's offshore possessions. The archipelago is made up of three small islands – Favignana, Lèvanzo and Marèttimo. The islands have been inhabited since prehistoric times (as shown by the extraordinary cave paintings on Lèvanzo) and were later the site of a Phoenician-Punic settlement known as the Aegades. In 241 BC Lutatius Catulus routed the Carthaginian fleet near here and the islands came under Roman control. They eventually ended up in Spanish hands and, in the 16th century, were sold to the Pallavicino-Rusconi family of Genoa, who then sold them on to the Florio family in 1874; they were handed over to the Italian state in 1937.

In recent years they have become increasingly popular with foreign visitors, who join the thousands of Sicilian day-trippers who come here in the summer to swim and sun themselves on the beaches. Favignana, the largest of the three islands and easily the most developed, boasts a small town (of the same name) with a number of good restaurants and hotels. Lèvanzo, whose full-time population numbers 60 is, by comparison, much less developed, whereas Marèttimo, the westernmost of the three, can offer little but the wild beauty of its landscape and hidden coves.

Favignana

Windswept Mt Santa Caterina (314m) dominates the otherwise flat main island. Pleasant

to explore, it has plenty of rocky coves and crystal-clear water. Wander around the abandoned **Stabilimento Florio** tuna processing plant *(tonnara)* at the port. It was shut in 1977 due to the general crisis in the local tuna-fishing industry. Lack of funding has blocked plans to turn the building into a complex which would include a school and arts-and-crafts shops. Favignana is also famous for the *mattanza* (ritual slaughter of tuna), which takes place off the coast in May and June. See the later boxed text 'La Mattanza' for details.

There is a friendly Pro Loco tourist office (☎ 0923 92 16 47) at Piazza Matrice 8. It opens 9am to 12.30pm and 4pm to 8pm Monday to Saturday and 9am to 12.30pm on Sunday, May and September.

Favignana's post office can be found behind the cathedral, near the port.

There's a branch of the Banco del Popolo, with an ATM, on Piazza Europa, near the port.

Places to Stay & Eat There are plenty of accommodation options on Favignana but during the period of La Mattanza, and in August, you'll have trouble finding a bed without a booking. Many locals rent out rooms.

The cheapest option is to pitch a tent at one of the two camp sites.

Égad (☎ 0923 92 15 55, fax 0923 53 93 70, e camping.egad@tiscalnet.it, Località Arena) €5.70/98.15 per person/4-bed bungalow. This good camp site is on the eastern side of the island and is well-signposted.

Miramare (☎ 0923 92 13 30, fax 0923 92 22 00, e cmonach@tin.it, Località Costicella) €12.40/149.75 per person/4-bed bungalow. Smack-bang in the middle of Favignana is the fancy Miramare. Prices drop considerably in the low season.

Quattro Rose (☎/fax 0923 92 12 23, Località Mulino a Vento) Doubles with bathroom €51.65. This tourist resort is close to town and handy for access to the beaches and coves on the island's east.

Bouganville (☎ 0923 92 20 33, fax 0923 92 26 49, Via Cìmabue 10) Singles/doubles with bathroom €28.40/51.65. This is the cheapest hotel option on the island, and its

La Mattanza

A centuries-old tradition, the Egadi Islands' *mattanza* (ritual tuna slaughter) survives despite the ever-decreasing number of tuna fish swimming into the local waters each year. Schools of tuna have, for centuries, used the waters around Western Sicily as a mating ground. Locals can recall the golden days of the island's fishing industry, when it was not uncommon to catch giant breeding tuna of between 200kg and 300kg – and even the odd 500kg freak. Fish that size are rare these days and the annual catch is increasingly smaller, due to the worldwide overfishing of tuna. However, even though the island's fishing industry is in severe crisis as a result, the tradition of the mattanza goes on.

Now that the slaughter of tuna can no longer support the island's economy, it is reinventing itself as a tourist attraction. From around 20 May to 10 June, tourists flock to the Egadi Islands to witness the event. For a fee you can join the fishers in their boats and watch them catching the tuna at close hand – you'll need a strong stomach. This is no ordinary fishing expedition: the fishers organise their boats and nets in a complex formation designed to channel the tuna into a series of enclosures which culminate in the *camera della morte* (chamber of death). Once enough tuna are imprisoned there, the fishers close in and the mattanza begins (the word is derived from the Spanish word for killing). It is a bloody affair – up to eight or more fishers at a time will sink huge hooks into a (sometimes enormous) tuna and drag it aboard. Anyone who has seen Rossellini's classic film *Stròmboli* will no doubt recall the famous mattanza scene.

---

right in the centre of town, although facilities are somewhat limited. In summer, half-board here is obligatory.

Albergo Egadi (☎/fax 0923 92 12 32, Via Cristoforo Colombo 17) Singles/doubles with bathroom €31/56.80. Closed Oct-Apr. This is the best budget option on the island, rooms are good and have TV and fridge. The *restaurant* here is well regarded and proves popular in the high season. A meal will cost about €26.

There are plenty of places to eat on the island, mostly clustered around Piazza Madrice. There are also plenty of shops that specialise in tuna-related products, so you can rustle up a picnic with ease.

Getting Around A bicycle is a very good way to get around Favignana, giving you access to all the little coves and beaches dotting the island. There are plenty of places offering bikes for hire. Try Giangrasso Rosaria (☎ 0347 479 52 16), at Via Vittorio Emanuele 36. It has bikes/mountain bikes/Vespas for €3.60/5.15/25.80 per day.

Lèvanzo

The only reasons to visit Lèvanzo are to spend some time on the beach and to

examine the prehistoric cave paintings at the Grotta del Genovese. Otherwise, there's not much else to do save go for a good walk. The port area town bears a disconcerting resemblance to the Greek Islands, with its white buildings and bright blue shutters. It's a pleasant island to relax and escape the hustle and bustle, although you'll definitely need to book summer accommodation in advance.

There are three great spots to go swimming, all a healthy walk from the town (which is little more than a cluster of houses around the port). To get to **Faraglione**, take a left through the town and walk west along the road until you see a couple of rocks sticking out of the water a few metres offshore. It is about 1km. If you fancy something a little quieter, keep going until you get to **Capo Grosso**, on the northern side of the island, where there is also a lighthouse. Alternatively, take a right out of town and walk along the dirt road. Three hundred metres past the first bend the road forks; take the rocky path down towards the sea and keep going until you get to **Calo Minnola**, a small landing bay with crystal clear water and where, outside the month of August, you can swim in peace and tranquillity.

Grotta del Genovese The Upper Palaeolithic wall paintings and Neolithic incised drawings at the Genoese Cave were discovered by accident in 1949. Between 6000 and 10,000 years old, the images mostly feature animals; the later ones also include men and tuna. To get there, you can try to follow the path across the island but be warned that it is rough going on your own. You can check with the custodian, Signor Natale Castiglione (☎ 0923 92 40 32 or 0339 741 88 00, ⓔ ncasti@tin.it), who is available for guided tours on foot (€5.15) between 10am to 1pm and 3pm to 6pm. Boat trips with him cost €10.35. Alternatively, you can take the sea route by hiring one of the several sea taxis that advertise in the town's two bars: it should cost you at most €12.90 per person. These can also be hired for trips around the island.

Places to Stay & Eat There are two hotels in Lèvanzo.

Paradiso (☎ 0923 92 40 80, Via Lungomare) Singles/doubles with bathroom €23.25/43.90. This spotlessly clean and charming place also has a lovely terrace, complete with stunning views, with a restaurant.

Pensione dei Fenici (☎/fax 0923 92 40 83, Via Calvario 11) Singles/doubles with bathroom €33.60/51.65. Right behind the Paradiso (go up the stairs), this place is more expensive in the high season but of a similar standard.

There are a couple of small cafes (one is also the Ustica Lines ticket office), where you can get coffee, snacks and *gelato* (ice cream). There's also a small *alimentari* on Via Lungomare.

Marèttimo

The most westward island of the three is also the wildest and least-developed. Samuel Butler reckoned this to be the island of Ithaca, home to Ulysses, although most experts agree that this theory is a little farfetched. There are plenty of good swimming spots around the island; recommended are **Cala Sarda** and **Cala Nera**, on the southern coast. Otherwise, the island is good walking territory, especially given that there are no cars on the island.

There are no official accommodation options as such but locals do rent out rooms; ask at the cafe in the main square and expect to pay between €10.35 and €18.10. One local you can contact is *Rosa dei Venti* (☎ 0923 92 32 49). There's a *pizzeria* above the town, which opens from June to August only. Otherwise, *Trattoria Il Timone* (☎ 0923 92 31 42, Via Garibaldi 18) has a good range of seafood dishes at about €18 for a meal.

Getting There & Away

Siremar (see Getting There & Away under Tràpani for details) runs ferries and hydrofoils *(aliscafi)* to the Egadi Islands from Tràpani. A high-season single fare to Favignana or Lèvanzo costs €5.15 on the hydrofoil (20 minutes). To Marèttimo costs €11.60. In summer, hydrofoils run from Tràpani to Lèvanzo/Favignana from 7am until 7.15pm daily, with departures from Tràpani to Marèttimo at 8.15am, 3.30pm and 5.30pm (from Lèvanzo to Marèttimo at 8.35am and 4pm). Tickets are cheaper (Tràpani to Favignana from €3.10) on a slower car ferry (*mototraghetto veloce* or *tradizionale*), though departures are fewer. Ustica Lines has snazzier hydrofoils for €5.15 and frequent departures from Tràpani to Favignana/Lèvanzo from 6.30am until 10.40pm daily (from Tràpani to Marèttimo at 9.20am and 2.10pm daily).

It's also possible to get to the Egadi Islands from Marsala – see Getting There & Away under Marsala later for details.

PANTELLERIA

postcode 91017 ● pop 7400

Located 110km south of the Sicilian mainland, Pantelleria is a curious place – a giant, quasi-dormant volcano (the last eruption was in 1891) – whose culture is more African than Sicilian (Tunisia is only 70km away). The island's inhabitants are, surprisingly, less occupied with fishing than with agriculture, thanks to the rich, blackened soil nourished by the volcano. The coast is dotted with small coves and inlets that are perfect for swimming, provided the weather is good.

The island was initially settled by the Sesi, a neolithic people probably from Libya. Over the centuries it was in Phoenician, Carthaginian and Roman hands before falling to the Moors in the 8th century AD, who named it Bent-el-Rhia (Daughter of the Wind), the source of its modern name.

The 400-year Moorish occupation has left an indelible mark on this otherwise rugged island, from the typical houses known as *dammusi* to the widespread cultivation of the *zibibbo*, a grape used in the production of the local wine, Moscato di Pantelleria. Even the local dialect is laced with Arabic words, in contrast to that on mainland Italy, which is more heavily influenced by French and Spanish.

Orientation

Apart from Malta, this is the largest of the islands surrounding Sicily, so you'll need to use some kind of motorised transport to get around. Pantelleria Town occupies the northwestern tip; the airport is 6km southeast of town. Most of the island's places of interest are along the southwestern and northeastern coasts.

Information

There is a small Pro Loco tourist office (☎ 0923 91 18 38) at Via Messina 36. It opens 9.30am to 1pm and 5pm to 7pm Monday to Saturday, June to September only. Agenzia Rizzo (☎ 0923 91 11 04), on the harbour at Via Borgo Italia 12, has maps of the island. It opens 6.30am to 1pm and 5pm to 6.30pm Monday to Friday, 6.30am to 1pm on Saturday.

Things to See & Do

Pantelleria is less a place to see than to experience. Aside from the 16th-century **Castello Barabacane** *(free; open 6pm-8pm daily June-Sept)*, at the end of the harbour, there is little of interest in Pantelleria town – it was flattened during WWII and rebuilt with cube-shaped houses of little interest. More curious are the island's natural phenomena, including the 24 **cuddie**, ancient craters of red volcanic rock surrounding the main volcano – Mt Grande (836m) – which dominates the centre

of the island. Also worth checking out are the **sesi**, massive neolithic funeral cairns with low passages leading to the centre. The most impressive of them is the **Sese del Re**, about 15-minutes' walk south of the Cuddie Rosse on the northwestern coast. The island was once dotted with these mounds but over the years most were dismantled and the stones used in the construction of the Moorish dammusi dwellings, whose thick, white-washed walls and shallow cupolas keep the inside nice and cool while ridges around the top are designed to catch the rain. Also of interest are the renowned **giardini arabi**, or Moorish gardens, citrus groves built into the mountain-side and protected from the often fierce winds by high stone walls.

On the northeastern coast, an idyllic spot is the hamlet of **Gadir**, whose small harbour is perfect for swimming. Here you'll also find a number of thermal pools that are renowned for their curative powers.

Places to Stay & Eat

There is nothing cheap here, especially in the summer, when it is best to book ahead.

Albergo Myriam (☎ 0923 91 13 74, fax 0923 91 17 77, Corso Umberto I) Singles/doubles with bathroom €54.25/77.45. Better inside than appearances would suggest, this is one of the cheapest places to stay on Pantelleria, although the rooms don't have air-con.

Khamma (☎ 0923 91 26 80, fax 0923 91 25 70, Via Borgo Italia 24) Singles/doubles with bathroom €61.90/123.95. The big, waterfront Khamma has good rooms with phone, fridge and air-con. Prices drop considerably outside the high season.

Port'Hotel (☎ 0923 91 12 99, fax 0923 91 22 03, Via Borgo Italia 6, e porthotel@ pantelleria.it) Singles/doubles with bathroom €51.65/72.30. Farther along is the Port'Hotel, with good rooms and a nicely-decorated restaurant. Rooms have phone, fridge, TV and air-con.

If you're in a group of three or four, you should consider renting a *dammuso*: most bars and restaurants have notices advertising rentals, which can work out cheaper than staying in a hotel. Expect to pay about

€900 to €1000 per week for a four-person dammuso in the high season month of August.

There is no shortage of places to eat in Pantelleria.

Trattoria Dammuso *(Via Borgo Italia)* Meals about €13. This trattoria near the Port'Hotel is excellent, with great views of the harbour and a comprehensive pizza menu.

Il Cappero *(☎ 0923 91 26 01, Via Roma 31)* Meals about €21. Closed Mon Oct-Apr. Just off Piazza Cavour, Il Cappero is where you'll find the local speciality, *ravioli con menta e ricotta* (ravioli with mint and ricotta cheese).

Outside town, you'll have no problem finding somewhere to eat in the hamlets along the coast.

Zabib *(☎ 0923 91 66 17, Porto di Scauri)* Meals about €26. Closed lunch & winter. On the island's southwest, in the port of Scauri, this is a good seasonal restaurant, with simple local dishes and fresh seafood.

Getting There & Away

Pantelleria is 30 minutes by plane with Gandalf Air (toll-free ☎ 848 80 14 24, **W** www .gandalfair.it) from Tràpani. Tickets cost €77.45. Air One (toll-free ☎ 848 84 88 80) has flights between Rome and Pantelleria (from €172) and Si Fly (toll-free ☎ 800 53 55 85) has a Palermo to Pantelleria service.

All boats arrive at the port in Pantelleria town; it's a five-hour trip from Tràpani. Ustica Lines has hydrofoils departing from Tràpani daily from 1 July to 31 August at 1.35pm and arriving at Pantelleria at 4.05pm (four times weekly in June and September). Tickets cost €33.60 one way.

Plane and ferry tickets can be purchased in Tràpani at Salvo Viaggi (☎ 0923 54 54 11), Corso Italia 48, or directly at the airport. In Pantelleria, tickets can be bought from Agenzia Rizzo (see Information earlier for details).

Getting Around

Local buses (€0.75) depart from Piazza Cavour in Pantelleria town at regular intervals, daily except Sunday, servicing every village on the island. Alternatively, consider renting a moped, which allows greater mobility. Autonoleggio Policardo (☎ 0923 91 28 44), Vicolo Messina 35, just beside the Port'Hotel, rents 50cc scooters for €18/ 108.45 per day/week. During the low season, rates drop a little.

SALINE DI TRÀPANI

The coastline between Tràpani and Marsala has long been known for its salt production and travelling down the secondary road that runs west of the larger SS115 you will see the famous *saline* (saltpans). The most extraordinary features are the large mounds of salt left to dry in the sun and the Dutch-style windmills, some of them still in working order. Salt production became big business during the Norman occupation and continued during the Aragonese reign; at the end of the 19th century there were as many as 40 salt works along the coast. In recent decades production has fallen off enormously but they are still a unique and impressive sight.

At Nubia, 5km south of Tràpani, is the **Museo del Sale** *(Salt Museum; ☎ 0923 86 74 22, Via delle Saline; free; open 9am-12.30pm & 4pm-7.30pm Mon-Sat),* housed in a 17th-century salt mill. Exhibits demonstrate how the salt is extracted: water is pumped into the saltpan via a windmill and then left to evaporate in the summer sun. The salt is then removed and piled up on the pier, where it is covered in terracotta tiles to protect it from humidity. To get to the museum, take the AST bus for Marsala from Piazza Montalto in Tràpani and get off at Nubia; the museum is about 1km to the west, at the water's edge, and is well-signposted.

MÒZIA & LO STAGNONE
postcode 91025

Best reached from Marsala, the Phoenician ruins of Mòzia (also spelled Mothia or Motya) are on the small island of San Pantaleo, in the Stagnone lagoon (Lo Stagione), about 5km north of Marsala. Joseph Whitaker (the nephew of Benjamin Ingham of Marsala's wine-making trade) bought the island, where the ancient city of Mòzia was based, and built a villa there (still in his family today). Whitaker was responsible for renewing interest in the archaeological site of Mòzia and for the few excavations carried out. Mòzia was one of the most important Phoenician settlements in the Mediterranean, coveted for its strategic position and eventually destroyed by Dionysius the Elder, tyrant of Syracuse, in 379 BC. Today, it is the island's picturesque position in the saltpans that attracts visitors. Very little remains of the city, but it is interesting to follow the path around the island and visit the various excavations, including the ancient port and dry dock, as well as some ruins. Note the submerged road at the port, which connects the island to the mainland. The island is home to the **Whitaker Museum** (☎ 0923 71 25 98; admission €5.15; open 9am-1pm and 3pm-1hr before sunset); its main treasure is the *Giovinetto di Mozia*, a Phoenician statue of a young boy dating from the 5th century BC and considered by experts to be the best example of Phoenician sculpture ever found in Sicily.

The island and lagoon form part of the **Riserva Naturale dello Stagnone** (Stagnone Nature Reserve), a noted humid zone which has a large population of water birds. Swimming here is permitted but hardly encouraged: the word *stagnone* actually means large swamp! There are plans to develop better facilities for tourists, such as cycling and walking tracks, in the area of the saltpans but for now you'll have to settle for the extraordinary sunsets that prevail in the area. The Riserva Naturale dello Stagnone organises guided nature tours. The tours last for approximately one hour and are available from 9am to 6pm.

At the end of the pier is the small **Museo Saline Ettore e Inferza** (☎ 0923 96 69 36; admission €2.60; open 9.30am-6pm daily), a salt museum similar to that up the coast at Nubia (see the Saline di Tràpani earlier). It has a pretty good video (in Italian only) explaining the whole process of extracting the salt and also rents canoes (€5.15 per hour; summer only) so that you can weave your way in and out of the saltpans.

Getting There & Away

Arini e Pugliese runs a boat to the island (€2.60 return) from 9am to 1pm and 3pm

to around 6pm or 7pm (morning only in winter). The ticket includes admission to the museum. Ettore Inferza runs traditional-style boats to/from the island between 9am and 6pm daily (€2.60 return). To get to the ferry landing from Marsala, take local bus No 4 from Piazza del Popolo (€4.15, 25 minutes, Monday to Saturday).

MARSALA
postcode 90125 • pop 80,800

Best known for its sweet dessert wines and often omitted from tourist itineraries, Marsala is a surprisingly pleasant town with an interesting historic quarter. Its tidy streets and well-preserved old centre bear testimony to the town's administration, considered the most progressive in Western Sicily. If you have a car, it's a good alternative to Tràpani as a base for exploring the region, although your lodging options are far more limited than those available farther north.

History

Founded as Lilybaeon on Cape Lilibeo by Carthaginians who had fled nearby Mòzia after its destruction by Syracuse, the city was so heavily fortified (with walls 7m thick!) that it was the last Punic base to fall to the Romans. In AD 830 it was conquered by the Arabs, who renamed it Marsa Alì (Port of Ali, the Prophet Mohammed's son-in-law) or Marsa Allah (Port of God), and established it as the main port of entry for Africans landing in Sicily.

Under the Normans the city was Christianised through the construction of numerous churches and monasteries. It continued to grow and prosper until 1575, when the port was blocked in to protect it from pirate raids. It then declined in importance until the turn of the 19th century, when a group of English traders 'discovered' the local wine and began trading it as an alternative to port and Madeira. On 11 May 1860, Garibaldi and his One Thousand landed at Marsala (under the unofficial protection of a couple of English frigates), thus beginning his struggle for Italian independence.

Orientation

Marsala hugs a small promontory looking out onto the Mediterranean Sea. The old city is clustered around the tip, separated from the sea by Via Lungomare Boeo. The main entrance to the old city is through the Porta Nuova (New Gate) at the end of Viale Vittorio Veneto, which runs southeast from Via Lungomare Boeo. Alternatively, from Piazza Piemonte e Lombardo, walk north along Viale dei Mille and go through the older Porta Garibaldi. Piazza della Repubblica is at the top of Via Garibaldi. The train station is southeast of the old city.

Information

Marsala's excellent Pro Loco tourist office (☎ 0923 71 40 97) is at Via XI Maggio 100, just off Piazza della Repubblica, in the centre of town. It opens 8am to 2pm and 3pm to 8pm Monday to Saturday and there's a good range of brochures and maps in a variety of languages. An APT information kiosk beside the entrance to the Museo Archeologico-Nave Punica, on Via Lungomare Boeo, opens 9am to 2pm on Monday and 9am to 2pm and 4pm to 8pm Tuesday to Sunday, June to mid-September.

There are banks with ATMs all over town.

The post office is on Via Garibaldi, just southeast of Piazza della Repubblica. There

How Sweet It Is

Marsala wine was 'discovered' by Englishman John Woodhouse, who, after landing in the city in 1773 and tasting the local product (he already had a 'sweet nose' after time spent in Jerez, Spain), decided it should be marketed all over Europe. His first competitor was Benjamin Ingham, who established his own factory in the town and began exporting the wine to the USA and Australia. By the mid-19th century, Marsala wine was extremely popular and prestigious around the world. It varies in flavour from sweet to dry and in colour from golden amber to ruby red or brown, and is bottled only in its region of origin.

is a good bookshop, Pellegrino, just inside the Porta Nuova, at Via XI Maggio 36. It stocks a couple of English-language cookbooks on Sicilian specialities.

The public hospital (*ospedale*; ☎ 0923 78 21 11) is on Piazza San Francesco, just north of the city centre. In a medical emergency, call ☎ 0923 95 14 10.

The *carabinieri* (military police; ☎ 0923 95 10 10) are located on Via Gramsci.

Piazza della Repubblica

Most of Marsala's historical sights are in and around the central Piazza della Repubblica, the heart of the city. The elegant square is fronted on one side by the imposing **cathedral**, dedicated to St Thomas of Canterbury. Although started in 1628, the church's facade wasn't completed until 1956 (courtesy of a cash donation by a returning emigrant). The cavernous interior, divided into three aisles highlighted by tall columns, contains a number of sculptures by the Gagini brothers but little else.

On the eastern side of the square is the **Palazzo Comunale**, or town hall, formerly known as the Palazzo Senatorio (Senatorial Palace). The top floor still has its original lamps. At Via XI Maggio 89, Garibaldi fans can see where the man himself spent his first night after landing; the building now houses a bank.

Museo degli Arazzi Fiammingi

The most interesting museum (☎ 0923 71 29 03, Via Giuseppe Garraffa 57; admission €1.05; open 9am-1pm & 4pm-6pm Tues-Sun) in Marsala is just behind the cathedral. It is home to eight magnificent Flemish tapestries made in Brussels between 1530 and 1550. The Marsala-born archbishop of Messina, Antonio Lombardo (1523–95), who also happened to be ambassador to the Spanish court, received them as a gift from Felipe II and presented them to the cathedral in 1589. Representing the capture of Jerusalem from the Saracens, the tapestries have been carefully restored and are now on display across three dimly lit floors.

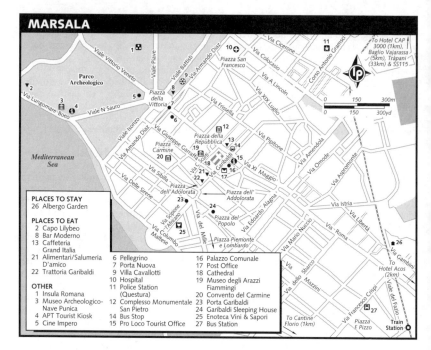

MARSALA

PLACES TO STAY
26 Albergo Garden

PLACES TO EAT
2 Capo Lilybeo
8 Bar Moderno
13 Caffeteria
    Grand Italia
21 Alimentari/Salumeria
    D'amico
22 Trattoria Garibaldi

OTHER
1 Insula Romana
3 Museo Archeologico-
    Nave Punica
4 APT Tourist Kiosk
5 Cine Impero

6 Pellegrino
7 Porta Nuova
9 Villa Cavallotti
10 Hospital
11 Police Station
    (Questura)
12 Complesso Monumentale
    San Pietro
14 Bus Stop
15 Pro Loco Tourist Office

16 Palazzo Comunale
17 Post Office
18 Cathedral
19 Museo degli Arazzi
    Fiammingi
20 Convento del Carmine
23 Porta Garibaldi
24 Garibaldi Sleeping House
25 Enoteca Vini & Sapori
27 Bus Station

Museo Archeologico-Nave Punica

On the promontory is Marsala's most popular museum (☎ *0923 95 25 35, Via Lungomare Boeo; admission €2.05; open 9am-1.30pm & 4pm-7pm Wed-Sun & hols)*, housed in the Baglio Anselmi, a typical manor house from Saracen times. Naval enthusiasts and classicists will savour the prospect of seeing the world's only recovered Punic *liburna,* or warship, discovered in 1971 by the marine archaeologist Honor Frost in the Stagnone lagoon near Mòzia. It's actually only part of the original ship, carefully reconstructed to give an impression of what it would have looked like. Manned by 68 oarsmen, the 35m-long warship is thought to have been part of a Carthaginian fleet attacked by the Romans in 241 BC at the Battle of Egadi. The find is extremely important, mainly because it has provided a valuable insight into Punic shipbuilding techniques; one of the more

intriguing puzzles is how the metal nails did not rust after nearly 1800 years under water.

The exhibit also includes objects found on board: ropes, ceramic fragments, corks from amphorae, a brush and a sailor's wooden button. In an adjacent room are two beautiful mosaics from the 3rd and 5th centuries, as well as other bits and bobs recovered from the nearby dig of the **Insula Romana**, a 3rd-century Roman villa. Access to the archaeological dig *(admission €2.05; open 9am-1pm & 3pm-1hr before sunset Mon-Sat)* is north of the museum along Viale Vittorio Veneto.

Complesso Monumentale San Pietro

This cultural complex (☎ *0923 71 62 98, Via Ludovico Anselmi Correale; free; open 8.30am-1.30pm & 3pm-8pm Tues-Sun)* is housed in a beautiful restored building and attracts locals and visitors to its three sections. A former Benedictine monastery (dating from the 16th century) in the city's Jewish quarter, it has permanent exhibitions on Garibaldi and the nationalist movement, with military regalia and paraphernalia; an archaeological section (with an interesting fragment of a sculpture of Eros catching a ride on the back of a duck) and items from Lilibeo's necropolis from the 19th-century Struppa collection. The third area is dedicated to folk traditions.

Convento del Carmine

A definite highlight for those who like to see beautiful buildings restored with care and style, this ex-convent (☎ 0923 71 16 31, Piazza Carmine; free; open 10am-1pm & 6pm-8pm Tues-Sun) of Mount Carmel was in a state of disrepair, having been used at one point as a carabinieri barracks, but has been returned to its former glory and is now in use as an art gallery and a centre for civil weddings.

Parts of the building date from 1155, when the Carmelites first came to Marsala with Roger I's widow Adelaide. The main centre of the complex dates from the 14th century, with the cloisters dating from the 18th century.

Other Things to See & Do

On the western edge of Piazza della Vittòria is the **Cine Impero** (Empire Cinema), a marvellous example of Italian futurist architecture popular during the Fascist era earlier in the 20th century. Today it's a cultural centre. Directly opposite is the **Porta Nuova**, the most recent of Marsala's gates, built in 1790 in classical Renaissance style.

If you're travelling with small children, they might enjoy a break in the **Villa Cavallotti**, a large park just outside the Porta Nuova that has a playground and acres of space for a relaxing walk.

Special Events

Marsala's most important annual religious event is the Processione del Giovedì Santo (Holy Thursday Procession). A centuries-old tradition, the procession of actors depicts the events leading up to Christ's crucifixion. Many children participate in the procession, dressed in colourful costumes as saints.

A visit to Marsala in July is a must for fans of jazz and/or wine, when the Marsala Doc Jazz Festival takes place. Contact the Pro Loco tourist office for details of events and performances.

Places to Stay

Sadly, accommodation in Marsala's centre is very thin on the ground.

Albergo Garden (☎/fax 0923 98 23 20, Via Gambini 36) Singles/doubles €23.25/43.90, with bathroom €33.55/49.05. The cheapest place to stay is the rather dreary and basic Albergo Garden, near the train station, to the southeast of town.

Hotel CAP 3000 (☎ 0923 98 90 55, fax 0923 98 96 34, Via Tràpani 161) Singles/doubles with bathroom €46.50/72.30. Outside the old centre, on the SS115 to Tràpani, this place has good rooms with phone, TV, parking and disabled access.

Hotel Acos (☎ 0923 99 91 66, fax 0923 99 91 32, Via Mazara 14) Singles/doubles with bathroom €46.48/72.30. Southeast of the train station and with well-equipped rooms, this place is a good choice if you're not relying on public transport.

Baglio Vajarassa (☎/fax 0923 96 86 28, Contrada Spagnola 176) Singles/doubles €31/46.50. A great choice if you have your own transport is the seven-bed Baglio Vajarassa, where meals can also be arranged. It's in a traditional manor house 6km north of Marsala, near Mòzia.

Places to Eat

Trattoria Garibaldi (☎ 0923 95 30 06, Piazza dell'Addolorata 5) Meals about €18. Closed Mon. Close to the action, and with tasty dishes, this place is definitely worth trying.

Caffeteria Grand Italia (☎ 0923 95 68 28, Piazza della Repubblica 3) Meals about €5. This place, directly opposite the town's cathedral, has outdoor seating and wonderful pastries. It's also a good value tavola calda (literally, 'hot table') with tasty snacks for the budget conscious.

Bar Moderno (Piazza della Vittòria) Snacks about €2. Sandwiches and other snacks are also available at Bar Moderno, just next to the Porta Nuova. In the evening, Marsala's young crowd gather here and in the square to chat and while away the hours.

Alimentari/Salumeria D'amico (☎ 0923 95 34 44, Via Garraffa 96) This is a good spot to pick up something for a picnic or cheap lunch.

Capo Lilybeo (☎ 0923 71 28 81, Via Lungomare Boeo 40) Meal about €26. Closed Mon. With very good food and some delightful ocean views, this is the place to come if you feel like treating yourself, especially on a sunny day.

Marsala's open-air fresh produce *market* is held every morning except Sunday on a square off Piazza dell'Addolorata, next to the municipal offices *(comune)*. In this small, lively marketplace, you're likely to be serenaded by a fruit vendor.

Enoteche

Marsala likes its wine (even the non-Marsala sort), and it's the best place to sample wines from the region and make a purchase. *Enoteche* (wine bars/shops) can be particularly helpful in this regard.

Cantine Florio (☎ 0923 78 11 11, Via Lungomare Florio 1) Open 9.30am-1pm & 2.30pm-5pm Mon-Thur, 9.30am-1pm Fri. Closed Aug. Tipplers should head here – the place to buy the cream of Marsala's wines. Cantine Florio opens its doors to visitors to explain the process of making Marsala wine, and to give you a taste of the goods. Fax 0923 98 23 80 to make a reservation for a guided tour. Take bus No 16 from Piazza del Popolo.

Enoteca Vini & Sapori (☎ 0923 71 82 00, Via Scipione l'Africano 25) This little enoteca, between the water and the Porta Garibaldi, offers good wines for tasting, in convivial surrounds.

Getting There & Away

Buses head for Marsala from Tràpani (AST or Lumia, €4.15, 55 minutes, seven Monday to Saturday, less on Sunday), Agrigento (Lumia, €13.15 return, 3½ hours, three daily) and Palermo (Salemi, €7.25, 2½ hours). Palermo buses arrive at Piazza del Popolo, off Via Mazzini, in the centre of town. All other buses stop in Piazza E Pizzo, in front of the train station. Buses for Agrigento generally stop at Castelvetrano, from where you can take another bus to Selinunte.

Regular trains serve Marsala from Tràpani (€2.30, 30 minutes, 20 daily) and Palermo (€6.70), although from the latter you have to change at Àlcamo Diramazione.

From June to September, Sandokan (☎ 0923 71 20 60) runs a boat service from Molo Dogana to the Egadi Islands (€6.70/13.45 single/return to Favignana).

Ustica Lines has hydrofoils to the Egadi Islands (€6.70 to Favignana and Levanza, €13.45 to Marèttimo) daily from June to September.

MAZARA DEL VALLO
postcode 91026 • pop 52,000

The African influence is most strongly felt in this charmingly dishevelled port town, one of the key cities of Saracen Sicily and the landing point for the thousands of Tunisian immigrants that arrive annually in Sicily. Many work on Mazara's fishing fleet, currently Italy's largest, and live within the labyrinth of streets informally known as the Casbah. Towering over them are the Baroque churches and fortified homes of the Norman conquest, which makes for an interesting and often elegant contrast.

History

The city, formerly Selinunte's trading port, was the site of the first Saracen landing in Sicily in AD 827. It was made capital of one of the three administrative districts *(walis, or valli in Latin)* into which they divided Sicily, hence the city's name today. In 1087 Mazara was taken by Count Roger, who ensured its continuing prosperity by declaring it an episcopal see. In 1098 the first Norman parliament sat here. Mazara's role as an important administrative and trading centre lasted another seven centuries until 1817, when it relinquished its role as provincial capital to Tràpani. Today, aside from fishing and agriculture, little remains of Mazara's former glory.

Orientation

Mazara's main street, Corso Umberto I, runs north–south from Piazza Matteotti down to Piazza Mokarta on the waterfront. The Casbah is in the old city, northwest of Piazza Mokarta; the best eateries are by the water. The train station is east of Corso Umberto I.

Information

The tourist office (☎ 0923 94 17 27) is on Piazza Santa Venerada. It opens 8am to 8pm Monday to Saturday and 9am to noon Sunday. There are two banks (Monte dei Paschi di Siena and Banco di Sicilia) with ATMs on Piazza Mokarta. The post office is on Via Garibaldi, behind the cathedral.

Things to See

For a city with such a rich history, the sights are surprisingly few and sometimes badly maintained. On Piazza Mokarta, the ruins of Count Roger's Norman **castle** don't look like much during the day but they make for a much more pleasant sight at night (when they are floodlit). Mazara's **cathedral** *(Cattedrale del San Salvatore)*, on Piazza Repubblica, was founded in 1093 but was completely rebuilt between 1690 and 1694, hence its Baroque features. Over the portal is a telling relief (from the 16th century) of Count Roger trampling a Saracen. Inside, the heavily ornamented altar features the *Trasfigurazione* (Transfiguration), a group of seven statues, dating from 1537 and sculpted by Antonello Gagini, surrounded by stuccoes by the Ferraro family.

Other buildings on the square include the elegant, two-storey **Seminario dei Chierici** (dating from 1710), which houses the Museo Diocesano *(Diocesan Museum; ☎ 0923 90 94 31, Via dell'Orologio; free; open 9am-noon Mon-Fri)*, whose library contains a number of 18th-century texts. Facing it, on the square's northern side, is the 16th-century **Palazzo Vescovile** (Bishop's Palace), remodelled in the 18th century.

From the square, Via XX Settembre leads west to Piazza Plebiscito and the **Museo Civico** *(Civic Museum; ☎ 0923 94 17 77, Piazza Plebiscito 2; free; open 9am-1pm daily, plus 3pm-6pm Tues & Thur & 4pm-7pm*

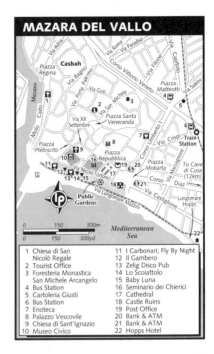

MAZARA DEL VALLO	
1	Chiesa di San Nicolò Regale
2	Tourist Office
3	Foresteria Monastica San Michele Arcangelo
4	Bus Station
5	Cartoleria Giusti
6	Bus Station
7	Enoteca
8	Palazzo Vescovile
9	Chiesa di Sant'Ignazio
10	Museo Civico
11	I Carbonari; Fly By Night
12	Il Gambero
13	Zelig Disco Pub
14	Lo Scoiattolo
15	Baby Luna
16	Seminario dei Chierici
17	Cathedral
18	Castle Ruins
19	Post Office
20	Bank & ATM
21	Bank & ATM
22	Hopps Hotel

Sat & Sun), housed in a former Jesuit college. The museum contains Roman artefacts and a series of medieval Muslim sculptures. Flanking it is the Baroque **Chiesa di Sant'Ignazio**.

To the northwest is the **Casbah** quarter – a maze of tiny streets and alleyways that were once the heart of the Saracen city, the most important of which was **Via Bagno**, the old city's main thoroughfare. Today, the area is run down but interesting, if only because it retains a strong Arabic connection through the thousands of Tunisians that live here. As you wander through the quarter you will hear Arabic mixed with Sicilian dialect and strains of North African music pouring out from the windows above. There are few sights of interest here, however, save a couple of Baroque churches that loom above the quarter, most notable of which is the small **Chiesa di San Nicolò Regale** *(free)*, at the area's western edge. Originally built in 1124, it was heavily influenced by the Saracen style. Years of renovation have paid off and it looks great, although it is simple and un-adorned inside. Make sure you don't confuse it with nearby Chiesa di San Nicolò. No opening hours were posted so try your luck.

Places to Stay & Eat

Foresteria Monastica San Michele Arcangelo (☎/fax 0923 90 65 65, Piazza San Michele Arcangelo 6) Dorm bed €20.65 per person. This is the best choice in Mazara del Vallo, for location, price and simple but kind atmosphere (it's in a monastery). Enter at the side – it opens 9.30am to 1pm and 3pm to 8pm Monday to Saturday and 9.30am to 1pm on Sunday and public holidays.

Hopps Hotel (☎ 0923 94 61 33, fax 0923 94 60 75, Via G Hopps 29) Singles/doubles with bathroom €61.45/85.25. This grand, blindingly white hotel is expensive but of a high standard, with TV, phone, car park and disabled access. It's at the eastern end of Via Lungomare Mazzini.

Eating well here isn't much of a problem. Flanking the public gardens on Via Lungomare Mazzini are these similarly priced restaurants and bars, all with terraces over-looking the water:

Il Gambero (☎ 0923 93 29 32, Via Lungomare Mazzini) Pizza about €6. Closed Thur. This is a good cheap spot to grab a pizza and watch the world go by.

Zelig Disco Pub Sandwiched between Il Gambero and Lo Scoiattolo, this is a popular bar at night-time, with beer on tap and cheap wine by the glass.

Lo Scoiattolo (☎ 0923 94 63 13, Via Lungomare Mazzini) Meals about €13. Closed Thur. You can satisfy your need for a cheap and filling fix here, and it's proximity to other bars means if you want to enjoy dessert or drinks elsewhere, you only have to stagger.

Baby Luna (☎ 0923 94 86 22, Via Lungomare Mazzini) Meals about €16. Closed Mon. This place gets very good reviews and is probably the pick of the bunch in this part of town.

I Carbonari (Via Lungomare Mazzini) If you fancy an after-dinner beer, this is the best place to go. It's got loud chart music

and is plenty of fun, and is just down the street from Il Gambero.

Fly By Night Just next to I Carbonari, this is another good place to assuage a thirst and enjoy some offshore breezes.

Another good spot to sample some of the area's wines is the *enoteca (Corso Umberto I 65)*, near the train station.

Getting There & Away

AST has three buses daily to/from Tràpani (€2.60, 1½ hours), Marsala (€1.55, 25 minutes) and Castelvetrano (€1.55, 20 minutes). The terminus is beside the train station; you can buy a ticket on the bus. Lumia has two buses daily (9.15am and 4.20pm) serving Marsala (€2.05) and Tràpani (€3.85), and three daily to Castelvetrano (€2.05), leaving from Piazza Matteotti. Buy your tickets in the Cartoleria Giusti on the square; it opens 8am to 1pm and 3.30pm to 7pm Monday to Saturday and 8am to 1pm on Sunday.

There are train connections every hour or so with Tràpani (€3.10, 50 minutes), Marsala (€2.05, 20 minutes) and Castelvetrano (€2.05, 20 minutes). Coming from Palermo, you must change at Àlcamo Diramazione, from where there are 10 trains daily (€3.10) to Mazara del Vallo.

CAVE DI CUSA

Northwest of Selinunte is the **Cave di Cusa**, the stone quarry used for the building of the city. Virtually untouched since Selinunte's destruction in 409 BC, the quarry is hardly spectacular but it is fascinating nonetheless, offering clues as to exactly how the massive stones used in the building of the temples were cut out of the rock. About 400m in from the gate are two carved columns ready for extraction. Around each is a gap of 50cm to allow the stonemason access to the column. When removed, the columns would have been transported to Selinunte across wooden logs by oxen or slaves. Archaeology aside, the site is an oasis of peace and quiet and is perfect for a picnic or a stroll.

The site is easily reached if you have your own transport. If you don't, get an AST or Lumia bus to nearby Campobello di

Mazara; it's a 3.5km walk southwest of town (follow the signposts).

CASTELVETRANO
postcode 91027 • pop 30,200
elevation 187m

On the road to Selinunte, south of Gibellina, Castelvetrano is of limited interest save for the small **Museo Civico** *(Civic Museum;* ☎ *0924 90 49 32, Via Giuseppe Garibaldi; admission €2.60; open 9am-1pm & 3.30pm-7.30pm daily)*, home of the remarkable *Efebo di Selinunte*, the bronze statue of a young man from the 5th century BC. Up the street, on Piazza Garibaldi, is the 19th-century **Teatro Selinus** *(free; open 9am-1pm & 3.30pm-7.30pm)*, built by Giovanni Battista Basile as a smaller-scale model of his Palermo masterpiece, the Teatro Massimo. It is built on the site of a hotel where Goethe stayed in 1787. The large curtain protecting the stage shows the philosopher Empedocles being thanked by the citizens of Selinunte for saving them from malaria.

Those familiar with the story of the bandit Salvatore Giuliano (see Post-War Sicily under History in the Facts about Sicily chapter) might want to check out the completely unremarkable courtyard where his body was found in 1950, which is at Via Mannone 94–100.

There are regular bus services to Castelvetrano from various places in the region and around it, including Agrigento (€4.40, two to 2½ hours, three Lumia buses daily Monday to Saturday), Selinunte (€0.75, 20 minutes, five services daily Monday to Saturday), Marsala (€2.30, one hour, three daily) and Tràpani (€4.13, 1½ hours, nine daily).

SELINUNTE
Selinunte *(☎ 0924 4 62 77; admission €4.15; open 9am-2hrs before sunset daily)* is one of the more captivating ancient sites in Italy, atop a cliff overlooking the sea. At its peak, the city had over 100,000 inhabitants and was the most advanced point of the Greek expansion into the western Mediterranean. Today, it's a huge archaeological site.

If you choose to stay round here, the area of Marinella di Selinunte is a popular haunt for Agrigento locals on holiday in summer and is a good spot to base yourself.

History
The area was first colonised by Greek settlers from Megara Hyblaea in 628 BC (according to the Greek historian Thucydides). They named their settlement Selinus, from the Greek word for celery *(selinon)*, which grows in abundance here and consequently became the symbol of the city, appearing on all its coins.

Originally allied with Carthage, it switched allegiance after the Carthaginian defeat by Gelon of Syracuse at Himera in 480 BC. Under Syracusan protection it grew in power and prestige. The city's growth resulted in a litany of territorial disputes with its northern neighbour, Segesta, which ended abruptly in 409 BC when the latter called for Carthaginian help. Selinunte's jilted former ally happily obliged and arrived to take revenge.

Troops commanded by Hannibal utterly destroyed the city after a nine-day siege, leaving only those who had taken shelter in the temples as survivors; these were spared not out of a sense of humanity but because of the fear that they might set fire to the temples and prevent their looting. In a famous retort to the Agrigentan ambassadors who sought to negotiate for the survivors' lives, Hannibal replied that as they hadn't been able to defend their freedom, they deserved to be slaves. One year later, Hermocrates of Syracuse took over the city and initiated its recovery. In 250 BC, with the Romans about to conquer the city, its citizens were relocated to Lilybaeum (Marsala), the Carthaginian capital in Sicily, but not before they destroyed as much as they could. What they left standing, mainly temples, was finished off by an earthquake in the Middle Ages.

The city was forgotten until the middle of the 16th century when a Dominican monk identified its location. Excavations began in 1823 courtesy of two English archaeologists, William Harris and Samuel Angell, who uncovered the first metopes.

Information

The archaeological site is divided into four zones – the acropolis, the ancient city, the eastern temples and the Sanctuary of Malophorus – spread out over a vast area dominated by the hill of Manuzza, site of the ancient city proper. You can access the site via two entrances: one leads to the eastern temples, while the other requires a 15-minute hike across the depression known as the Gorgo di Cottone (once the city's harbour).

You can get information about the site at the ticket office.

The Acropolis

The acropolis, the heart of Selinunte's political and social life, occupies a slanted plateau overlooking the now-filled-in harbour. It is crossed by two thoroughfares – one running north–south, the other east–west, dividing the acropolis into four separate sections. Huddled in the southeastern part are five temples (A, B, C, D and O). The northernmost is **Temple D**, built towards the end of the 6th century BC and dedicated to either Neptune or Venus. Virtually the symbol of Selinunte, **Temple C** is also the oldest temple on the site, built in the middle of the 6th century BC. The stunning metopes found by Harris and Angell were once a part of this formidable structure, as was the enormous Gorgon's mask that once adorned the pediment (both of these can be viewed in the Museo Archeologico Regionale in Palermo; see that chapter for details). Experts believe that the temple was dedicated to Apollo.

Adjacent is the smaller **Temple B**, which dates from the Hellenistic period and could have been dedicated to the Agrigentan scientist and philosopher Empedocles, whose water-drainage scheme saved the city from the scourge of malaria (a bitter irony for William Harris, who contracted the disease during the initial excavations and died soon after). The two other temples, **Temple A** and **Temple O**, closest to the sea, are the most recent, built between 490 and 480 BC. They are virtually identical in both style and size, and it's been suggested that they might have been dedicated to the twins Castor and Pollux. In front of Temple O, an area has been excavated that is believed to be a sacred spot dating from the period after the destruction of the city.

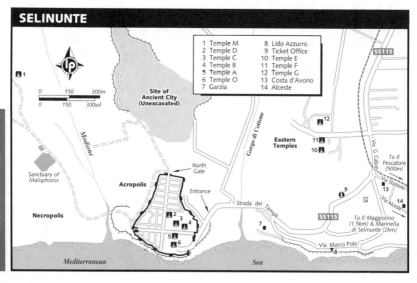

SELINUNTE

1 Temple M	8 Lido Azzurro
2 Temple D	9 Ticket Office
3 Temple C	10 Temple E
4 Temple B	11 Temple F
5 Temple A	12 Temple G
6 Temple O	13 Costa d'Avorio
7 Garzia	14 Alceste

The Ancient City

Occupying the hill of Manuzza, to the north of the acropolis, the ancient city where most of Selinunte's inhabitants lived is the least excavated of all the sites. Exploration of the area has only begun in recent years, and evidence suggests that survivors of the destruction of 409 BC may have used the city as a necropolis. Finds also suggest that the city stretched beyond the original wall to the northwest, but you can't verify this for yourself for another few years at least as the area remains a closed dig.

The Sanctuary of Malophorus

Walk west from the acropolis across the River Modione (formerly the Selinon) and up the dirt path to the hardly impressive ruins of the temple dedicated to Demeter, the goddess of fertility and harvests. The temple, renowned in antiquity, survived the Carthaginian siege and was used in later times for both Christian and Byzantine worship. Amid the debris, two altars can be made out – the larger of the two was used for sacrifices. Despite the lack of visual appeal, these are perhaps the most important finds of the whole site, as they provide a fascinating and detailed insight into the social history of Selinunte. Archaeologists remain perplexed by the votive offerings found in the area, which include steles crowned with human heads – compelling evidence that another, non-Greek, civilisation inhabited the area at the same time.

The Eastern Temples

South of the main door in the admission hall is the most visually stunning of all Selinunte's ruins, crowned by the majestic **Temple E**. Reconstructed in 1958 amid much criticism, it stands out due to its recently acquired completeness. Built in the 5th century BC, it is the first of the three temples at the eastern end of the site, close to the ticket office. The more outstanding metopes in Palermo's Museo Archeologico Regionale came from this temple and Temple C. **Temple G**, the northernmost temple, was built in the 6th century BC and although never completed was one of the largest in the Greek world. Today it is a massive pile of rubble, but evocative nonetheless.

Places to Stay & Eat

The nearest town to the ruins is Marinella di Selinunte, where you can find accommodation and a couple of reasonably priced restaurants.

Il Maggiolino (☎/fax 0924 4 60 44, e magiol@potin.it, Località Marinella di Selinunte, off the SS115) €4.65/7.75 per person/camp site. Off the SS115, and about 1.5km north of Marinella di Selinunte, this camp site has an eating area and disabled access.

Costa d'Avorio (☎ 0924 4 62 07, fax 0924 94 11 63, Via Stazione 10) Singles/doubles €20.65/41.30, with bathroom €31/46.50. Open 15 July-31 Aug. With a cheap trattoria serving simple local dishes and Sicilian staples, and rooms with facilities best described as minimal, this is the most obvious place to stay for the budget-conscious.

Alceste (☎ 0924 4 61 84, fax 0924 4 61 43, Via Alceste 21) Singles/doubles with bathroom €54.25/69.75. The upmarket, mid-sized Alceste offers its guests TV, phone, air-con, parking and disabled access.

Garzia (☎ 0924 4 60 24, fax 0924 4 61 96, Via Antonio Pigafetta 6) Singles/ doubles with bathroom €41.30/67.15. With nice rooms on the seafront and good facilities, this is the best value in its class here.

Il Pescatore (☎ 0924 4 63 03, Via Castore e Polluce 31) Singles/doubles €18.10/31. Open 1 July-31 Aug. This place offers *affittacamere* (rooms for rent) in the busy summer season. It's very spartan but the prices are low.

There are some pleasant little restaurants along the beachfront.

Lido Azzurro (☎ 0924 4 62 11, Via Marco Polo 51) Meals about €23.25. Closed Mon. At this place, also known as Baffo's, you can eat good pizza, pasta and fresh seafood virtually beside the water's edge, drinking in the view all the while.

Getting There & Away

AST buses link Marinella di Selinunte to Castelvetrano (five daily), which can be reached by Lumia buses from Agrigento, Mazara del Vallo, Marsala and Tràpani. There are also Salemi buses from Castelvetrano to Selinunte (€0.75, 20 minutes, five daily). If travelling by car, take the Castelvetrano exit off the A29 and follow the brown signposts for about 6km. If you're driving from Agrigento, take the SS115 and follows the signposts.

RUDERI DI GIBELLINA

Twenty-three kilometres southeast of Segesta (see that section later) and only accessible by car along the winding SS119, which leads off the A29 as it heads towards the southwest coast, are the disconcerting ruins *(ruderi)* of the town of Gibellina, completely flattened by an earthquake during the night of 14 January 1968. All that's left of the town are a few semi-destroyed houses and a large slab of white concrete known as **Il Cretto**. Designed by architect Alberto Burri, the concrete covers what remains of the town. Walking through the channels in the concrete (which follow the town's original street plan) is an eerie and disturbing experience, considering that no more than 30 years ago this was a busy farming town. Now silence prevails.

The second tragedy of Gibellina occurred during the resettlement of the survivors (of a population of 5000, only 541 were killed). For nearly 15 years most were kept in temporary accommodation while the authorities dallied over what to do. Eventually, the inhabitants were moved 18km west to **Gibellina Nuova**, one of the strangest towns in all of Sicily. Following a thoroughly modern (at least in the late 1970s!) urban design, the town is dotted with sculptures by renowned Sicilian and other Italian artists, intended to capture the town's suffering and survival. Despite the best intentions, however, it resembles a lifeless American suburb.

Since 1981, the ruins of the original town have been host to annual classical performances known as the **Orestiadi**, which take place in August. For information on dates call the Museo Civico in Castelvetrano (see Castelvetrano earlier for details).

SEGESTA

postcode 91013 • elevation 304m

The ancient Elymians must have been great aesthetes if their choice of sites for cities is any indication. Along with Èrice and Entella, they founded Segesta on and around Mt Barbaro (304m). The Greeks later took over and it is to them that we owe the two outstanding survivors: the theatre high up on the mountain, with commanding views out to the Castellammare del Golfo (how did spectators concentrate on the show with such a backdrop?), and the temple.

History

The history of Segesta *(admission €4.15; open 9am-1 hr before sunset daily)* is one of useful alliances. Settled by Elymians, most likely from Anatolia, the city came under Hellenic influence and sought an alliance with Athens in 426 BC. Constantly at war with Selinunte, to the south, it sought Carthaginian help in defeating its rival, and after Selinunte's destruction in 409 BC Segesta continued to benefit from the protection of Carthage against the Greeks of Syracuse (who managed to sack the city in 307 BC). The Carthaginians quickly took back the city but were repaid during the First Punic War when Segesta was the first Sicilian city to ally itself to the Romans, killing the Carthaginian garrison stationed in the city for its protection! The city went into decline during the Saracen occupation and was eventually abandoned in the 13th century.

Things to See

Time has done to Segesta what violence inflicted on Selinunte and little remains of the city. On the hill nearest the entrance is the **Doric temple**, dating from around 430 BC and remarkably well preserved. Scholars are in doubt whether the temple was ever completed (it never had a roof) or whether it was left uncovered according to the style of a local cult. It is, nevertheless, a truly wondrous site, especially considering that it has survived a number of earthquakes.

The **Hellenistic theatre** is also in a fair state of repair and is the only structure

The island's peaceful interior

The Roman Villa at Casale

Abandoned farmhouses tell a story of isolation and emigration.

The Parco Regionale dei Nebrodi, Sicily's largest park

A modern sculpture in Nebrodi

BETHUNE CARMICHAEL

The impressive 6th-century-BC Temple C, at Selinunte's acropolis

STEPHEN SAKS

Valley of the Temples

FIONN DAVENPORT

Taking it easy in the shade of Marsala's ornate cathedral...

BETHUNE CARMICHAEL

... or resting against a column

inside the old city walls to have survived intact. Built in the middle of the 3rd century BC, it is unique in that it faces north so as to make the most of the extraordinary panorama that spreads out behind the stage, of the hills and the distant Castellammare del Golfo. Nearby are the ruins of a mosque, and a castle and church built in the Middle Ages. A shuttle bus (€1.05) runs every 30 minutes from the entrance 1.5km uphill to the theatre. If you feel up to it, however, the walk up the hill is more interesting (though rather winding and tiring, especially in the heat), with splendid views of the theatre on the hill behind.

During July and August every year, performances of Greek and Latin plays are staged in the theatre. For information, contact the APT office in Tràpani.

Getting There & Away

Segesta is accessible by AST bus (☎ 0923 3 10 20) from Piazza Montalto in Tràpani (€4.15, 25 minutes). Between June and September there are buses at 8am, 10am, noon, 2pm and 5pm daily (reduced services from October to May). From Palermo, there are buses from Piazza Marina with AST at 7.50am, 2pm and 6pm Monday to Saturday (10am and 6pm on Sunday and public holidays). You can also get to Segesta by quite regular trains from Tràpani (€4.65 return, about 10 daily, 25 minutes). Get off at Segesta Tempio station (which has a small museum and a good bar/cafe/restaurant), take the road on your left, go under the autostrada and continue uphill (not difficult) for about 800m (about 20 minutes). There are signs to direct you.

Language

Although standard Italian may be Sicily's official language and is spoken almost universally on the island, most locals (over 70%) speak Sicilian among themselves. Sicilian is referred to as an Italian dialect, but is sufficiently different to warrant being termed a language in its own right; even if you're fluent in Italian, you'll find it almost impossible to understand. Luckily, Sicilians will readily revert to Italian when speaking to anyone from the mainland or abroad, although the occasional Sicilian word will still creep in.

Some Sicilians have studied English at school, but English-speakers are generally hard to find beyond the more popular tourist resorts, where staff at hotels, restaurants and tourist offices usually have a basic grasp of the language. Any attempt on your part to get to grips with Italian will endear you to the locals, no matter how many mistakes you make.

Italian

Italian is a Romance language related to French, Spanish, Portuguese and Romanian, all of which are directly descended from Latin. The Romance languages belong to the Indo-European group of languages, which includes English. Indeed, as English and Italian share common roots in Latin, you will recognise many Italian words.

Sicily has a strange relationship with the Italian language. Although it is commonly accepted that modern standard Italian developed from the Tuscan dialect, Sicilians rightly assert that the first literature in the 'common vernacular' (Italian, as opposed to Latin or Greek) was produced in Sicily (at the court of Frederick I in the 13th century).

Speaking in Tongues

Along with all Italian dialects, Sicilian belongs to the Italo-Romance language group. However, centuries of foreign occupation have exposed it to linguistic influences from many and varied sources, including Albanian, Arabic, French, Greek, Norman, Spanish and northern Italian dialects.

The grammatical structure of Sicilian is somewhat different from standard Italian: there's no single verb conjugation for the future tense – instead, Sicilian uses a form akin to 'I have (to do something)'; and the simple past (a literary form only in standard Italian) is used for the past perfect tense in everyday speech. Pronunciation is difficult, and it is commonly claimed that only a Sicilian can pronounce the double 'd' that regularly substitutes the standard Italian double 'l' – the classic Sicilian protestation of sincerity, *La bella madre e veramente* (By the beautiful mother and truly), becomes *La bedda madre e beramante*.

Sicilian is also coloured with a rich range of metaphors and proverbs, some of which date back to the days of Arabic occupation. The English 'All things in moderation' in Sicilian reads *Non essiri duci sinno tu mancianu, non essiri amaru sinno ti futanu* (Don't be too sweet lest you be eaten, don't be too sour lest you be shunned). The Sicilian way to say 'Make the most of what you've got' is *Camina chi pantofuli fino a quannu non hai i scarpi* (Walk in your slippers until you find your shoes).

Sicilians are also known for their epithets, which are used as insults of varying strength in a range of situations. If you want to call someone crazy, you refer to them as *stunato*; if there's an excess of drink involved, it's most likely that they're *scribbi di patata* – literally, taken over by the 'spirit of the potato', a reference to the distillation of some alcoholic drinks from that vegetable. If you want to curse someone, you refer to them as having *u mal'occhio* (the evil eye), and if you *really* want to slander a Sicilian man, refer to him as *cornuto* (with horns), meaning that he is a cuckold. While not an exclusively Sicilian insult, it suggests a loss of honour that is about as ignominious as it gets on the island – so be careful at whom you direct it!

Exponents of the Sicilian school of poetry, mostly court officials-turned-poets, were a source of inspiration to many of the early Tuscan writers. After the Middle Ages, works by prestigious writers from the mainland's north, such as Dante, Petrarch and Boccaccio, contributed to the steady elevation of Tuscan as the dominant written vernacular. History shows that Tuscany's status as the political, cultural and financial power base of the nation ensured that the region's dialect would ultimately be installed as the national tongue.

The Italian of today is something of a composite. What you hear on the radio and TV, in educated discourse and indeed in the everyday language of many people is the result of centuries of cross-fertilisation between the dialects, greatly accelerated in the postwar decades by the modern media.

If you have more than the most fundamental grasp of the Italian language, you need to be aware that many Sicilians still expect to be addressed in the third person formal (*lei* instead of *tu*). Also, it is not considered polite to use the greeting *ciao* when addressing strangers unless they use it first; it's better to say *buongiorno* (or *buona sera*, as the case may be) and *arrivederci* (or the more polite form, *arrivederla*). This is true of most of Italy, but in Sicily use of the informal can be considered gravely impolite – and in some cases downright insulting – especially when talking to an older person. We have used the formal address for most of the phrases in this guide. Use of the informal address is indicated by 'inf' in brackets. Italian also has both masculine and feminine forms (usually ending in 'o' and 'a' respectively). Where both forms are given in this guide, they are separated by a slash, the masculine form first.

If you'd like a more comprehensive guide to the language, get hold of a copy of Lonely Planet's *Italian phrasebook*.

Pronunciation

Surprisingly – especially after you hear the near-incomprehensible dialect – a Sicilian speaker's pronunciation of standard Italian is refreshingly clear and easy to understand, even if you have only a limited command of the language. Vowels are pronounced more openly than in mainland Italy, and there is a tendency to emphasise consonants, so that a word like *buongiorno* (good day) sounds something like 'bawn-jaw-rrno'. The French influence also means that in certain parts of Sicily, particularly the west, the 'r' is not as rolled as it is in standard Italian: locals pronounce 'Tràpani' the way an English-speaker would, without rolling the 'r'.

Setting aside the vagaries of Sicilian pronunciation and dialect, Italian is not difficult to pronounce once you learn a few easy rules. Although some of the more clipped vowels, and stress on double letters, require careful practice for English-speakers, it is easy enough to make yourself understood.

Vowels
Vowels are generally more clipped than in English:

a	as in 'art', eg, *caro* (dear); sometimes short, eg, *amico/a* (m/f) (friend)
e	as in 'tell', eg, *mettere* (to put)
i	as in 'inn', eg, *inizio* (start)
o	as in 'dot', eg, *donna* (woman); as in 'port', eg, *dormire* (to sleep)
u	as the 'oo' in 'book', eg, *puro* (pure)

Consonants
The pronunciation of many Italian consonants is similar to that of their English counterparts. Pronunciation of some consonants depends on certain rules:

c	as 'k' before **a**, **o** and **u**; as the 'ch' in 'choose' before **e** and **i**
ch	hard 'k' sound
g	as the 'g' in 'get' before **a**, **o** and **u**; as the 'j' in 'job' before **e** and **i**
gh	hard, as in 'get'
gli	as the 'lli' in 'million'
gn	as the 'ny' in 'canyon'
h	always silent
r	a rolled 'rr' sound
sc	as the 'sh' in 'sheep' before **e** and **i**; as 'sk' before **h**, **a**, **o** and **u**
sch	hard 'sk' sound
z	as the 'ts' in 'lights', except at the beginning of a word, when it's as the 'ds' in 'beds'

Note that when **ci**, **gi** and **sci** are followed by **a**, **o** or **u**, the 'i' is not pronounced unless the accent falls on the 'i'. Thus the name 'Giovanni' is pronounced 'joh-**vahn**-nee'.

Word Stress
A double consonant is pronounced as a longer, often more forceful sound than a single consonant.

Stress often falls on the second-last syllable, as in *spa-**ghet**-ti*. When a word has an accent, the stress is on that syllable, as in *cit-**tà*** (city).

Greetings & Civilities

Hello.	*Buongiorno.*
	Ciao. (inf)
Goodbye.	*Arrivederci.*
	Ciao. (inf)
Yes.	*Sì.*
No.	*No.*
Please.	*Per favore/*
	Per piacere.
Thank you.	*Grazie.*
That's fine/	*Prego.*
You're welcome.	
Excuse me.	*Mi scusi.*
	Scusam. (inf)
Sorry (forgive me).	*Mi scusi/Mi perdoni.*

Small Talk

What's your name?	*Come si chiama?*
	Come ti chiami? (inf)
My name is ...	*Mi chiamo ...*
Where are you from?	*Di dov'è?*
	Di dove sei? (inf)
I'm from ...	*Sono di ...*
How old are you?	*Quanti anni ha?*
	Quanti anni hai? (inf)
I'm ... years old.	*Ho ... anni.*
I (don't) like ...	*(Non) Mi piace ...*
Just a minute.	*Un momento.*

Language Difficulties

I (don't) understand.	*(Non) Capisco.*
Please write it down.	*Può scriverlo, per favore?*
Can you show me (on the map)?	*Può mostrarmelo (sulla carta/pianta)?*

Do you speak English?	*Parla inglese?*
	Parli inglese? (inf)
Does anyone here speak English?	*C'è qualcuno che parla inglese?*
How do you say ... in Italian?	*Come si dice ... in italiano?*
What does ... mean?	*Che vuole dire ...?*

Paperwork

name	*nome*
nationality	*nazionalità*
date of birth	*data di nascita*
place of birth	*luogo di nascita*
sex (gender)	*sesso*
passport	*passaporto*
visa	*visto*

Getting Around

What time does ... leave/arrive?	*A che ora parte/ arriva ...?*
the aeroplane	*l'aereo*
the boat	*la barca*
the (city) bus	*l'autobus*
the (intercity) bus	*il pullman/corriere*
the train	*il treno*

I want to go to ...	*Voglio andare a ...*

I'd like a ... ticket.	*Vorrei un biglietto ...*
one-way	*di solo andata*
return	*di andata e ritorno*
1st-class	*prima classe*
2nd-class	*seconda classe*

The train has been cancelled/ delayed.	*Il treno è soppresso/ in ritardo.*

the first	*il primo*
the last	*l'ultimo*
platform number	*binario numero*
station	*stazione*
ticket office	*biglietteria*
timetable	*orario*

I'd like to hire ...	*Vorrei noleggiare ...*
a bicycle	*una bicicletta*
a boat	*una barca*
a car	*una macchina*
a motorcycle	*una motocicletta*

Signs

Ingresso/Entrata	Entrance
Uscita	Exit
Informazione	Information
Aperto	Open
Chiuso	Closed
Proibitio/Vietato	Prohibited
Polizia/Carabinieri	Police
Questura	Police Station
Camere Libere	Rooms Available
Completo	Full/No Vacancies
Gabinetti/Bagni	Toilets
Uomini	Men
Donne	Women

Directions

Where is ...?	Dov'è ...?
Go straight ahead.	Si va sempre diritto.
	Vai sempre diritto (inf).
Turn left.	Gira a sinistra.
Turn right.	Gira a destra.
at the next corner	al prossimo angolo
at the traffic lights	al semaforo
behind	dietro
in front of	davanti
far	lontano
near	vicino
opposite	di fronte a

Around Town

I'm looking for ...	Cerco ...
a bank	un banco
the church	la chiesa
the city centre	il centro (città)
the ... embassy	l'ambasciata di ...
my hotel	mio albergo
the market	il mercato
the museum	il museo
the post office	la posta
a public toilet	un gabinetto/ bagno pubblico
the telephone centre	il centro telefonico
the tourist office	l'ufficio di turismo/ d'informazione

I want to change ...	Voglio cambiare ...
money	denaro
travellers cheques	degli assegni per viaggiatori

beach	la spiaggia
bridge	il ponte
castle	il castello
cathedral	il duomo/la cattedrale
island	l'isola
main square	la piazza principale
market	il mercato
mosque	la moschea
old city	il centro storico
palace	il palazzo
ruins	le rovine
sea	il mare
square	la piazza
tower	la torre

Accommodation

I'm looking for ...	Cerco ...
a guesthouse	una pensione
a hotel	un albergo
a youth hostel	un ostello per la gioventù

Where is a cheap hotel?	Dov'è un albergo che costa poco?
What is the address?	Cos'è l'indirizzo?
Could you write the address, please?	Può scrivere l'indirizzo, per favore?
Do you have any rooms available?	Ha camere libere/C'è una camera libera?

I would like ...	Vorrei ...
a bed	un letto
a single room	una camera singola
a double room	una camera matrimoniale
a room with two beds	una camera doppia
a room with a bathroom	una camera con bagno
to share a dorm	un letto in dormitorio

How much is it ...?	Quanto costa ...?
per night	per la notte
per person	per ciascuno?

May I see it?	Posso vederla?
Where is the bathroom?	Dov'è il bagno?
I'm/We're leaving today.	Parto/Partiamo oggi.

Shopping

I'd like to buy ...	*Vorrei comprare ...*
How much is it?	*Quanto costa?*
I (don't) like it.	*(Non) Mi piace.*
May I look at it?	*Posso dare un'occhiata?*
I'm just looking.	*Sto solo guardando.*
It's cheap.	*Non è caro/a.*
It's too expensive.	*È troppo caro/a.*
I'll take it.	*Lo/La prendo.*
Do you accept ...	*Accettate ...?*
credit cards	*carte di credito*
travellers cheques	*assegni per viaggiatori?*
more	*più*
less	*meno*
smaller	*più piccolo/a*
bigger	*più grande*

Time & Dates

What time is it?	*Che ora è?*
	Che ore sono?
It's (8 o'clock).	*Sono (le otto).*
in the morning	*di mattina*
in the afternoon	*di pomeriggio*
in the evening	*di sera*
When?	*Quando?*
today	*oggi*
tomorrow	*domani*
yesterday	*ieri*
Monday	*lunedì*
Tuesday	*martedì*
Wednesday	*mercoledì*
Thursday	*giovedì*
Friday	*venerdì*
Saturday	*sabato*
Sunday	*domenica*
January	*gennaio*
February	*febbraio*
March	*marzo*
April	*aprile*
May	*maggio*
June	*giugno*
July	*luglio*
August	*agosto*
September	*settembre*
October	*ottobre*
November	*novembre*
December	*dicembre*

Numbers

0	*zero*
1	*uno*
2	*due*
3	*tre*
4	*quattro*
5	*cinque*
6	*sei*
7	*sette*
8	*otto*
9	*nove*
10	*dieci*
11	*undici*
12	*dodici*
13	*tredici*
14	*quattordici*
15	*quindici*
16	*sedici*
17	*diciassette*
18	*diciotto*
19	*diciannove*
20	*venti*
21	*ventuno*
22	*ventidue*
30	*trenta*
31	*trentuna*
40	*quaranta*
50	*cinquanta*
60	*sessanta*
70	*settanta*
80	*ottanta*
90	*novanta*
100	*cento*
1000	*mille*
2000	*due mila*
one million	*un milione*

Health

I'm ill.	*Mi sento male.*
It hurts here.	*Mi fa male qui.*
I'm ...	*Sono ...*
asthmatic	*asmatico/a*
diabetic	*diabetico/a*
epileptic	*epilettico/a*
I'm allergic ...	*Sono allergico/a ...*
to antibiotics	*agli antibiotici*
to penicillin	*alla penicillina*

Emergencies

Help!	Aiuto!
Call ... !	Chiami ... !
	Chiama ... ! (inf)
a doctor	un dottore/
	un medico
the police	la polizia
There's been an	C'è stato un
accident	incidente!
I'm lost.	Mi sono perso/a.
Go away!	Lasciami in pace!
	Vai via! (inf)

antiseptic	antisettico
aspirin	aspirina
condoms	preservativi
contraceptive	anticoncezionale
diarrhoea	diarrea
medicine	medicina
sunblock cream	crema/latte solare
	(per protezione)
tampons	tamponi

FOOD

This glossary is intended as a brief guide to some of the basics and by no means covers all of the dishes you are likely to encounter in Sicily. Most travellers to the region will already be well acquainted with the various Italian pastas, which include spaghetti, fettuccine, penne, rigatoni, gnocchi, lasagne, tortellini and ravioli. The names are the same throughout Italy and no further definitions are given here.

Basics

breakfast	(prima) colazione
lunch	pranzo
dinner	cena
restaurant	ristorante
grocery shop	alimentari

What is this?	(Che) cos'è?
I would like the set menu.	Vorrei il menù turistico
Is service included in the bill?	È compreso il servizio?
I'm a vegetarian	Sono vegetariano/a

Useful Words

affumicato	smoked
al dente	firm (as all good pasta should be)
alla brace	cooked over hot coals
alla griglia	grilled
arrosto	roasted
ben cotto	well done (cooked)
bollito	boiled
cameriere/a	waiter/waitress
coltello	knife
conto	bill/cheque
cotto	cooked
crudo	raw
cucchiaino	teaspoon
cucchiaio	spoon
forchetta	fork
fritto	fried
menù	menu
piatto	plate

Staples

aceto	vinegar
burro	butter
formaggio	cheese
limone	lemon
marmellata	jam
miele	honey
olio	oil
olive	olives
pane	bread
pane integrale	wholemeal bread
panna	cream
pepe	pepper
peperoncino	chilli
polenta	cooked cornmeal
riso	rice
risotto	rice cooked with wine and stock
sale	salt
uovo/uova	egg/eggs
zucchero	sugar

Meat & Fish

acciughe	anchovies
agnello	lamb
aragosta	lobster
bistecca	steak
calamari	squid
coniglio	rabbit
cotoletta	cutlet or thin cut of

	meat, usually crumbed and fried
cozze	mussels
dentice	dentex (type of fish)
fegato	liver
gamberi	prawns
granchio	crab
manzo	beef
merluzzo	cod
ostriche	oysters
pesce spada	swordfish
pollo	chicken
polpo	octopus
salsiccia	sausage
sarde	sardines
sgombro	mackerel
sogliola	sole
tacchino	turkey
tonno	tuna
trippa	tripe
vitello	veal
vongole	clams

Vegetables

asparagi	asparagus
carciofi	artichokes
carote	carrots
cavolo/verza	cabbage
cicoria	chicory
cipolla	onion
fagiolini	string beans
melanzane	aubergines
patate	potatoes
peperoni	peppers
piselli	peas
spinaci	spinach

Fruit

arance	oranges
banane	bananas
ciliegie	cherries
fragole	strawberries
mele	apples
pere	pears
pesche	peaches
uva	grapes

Soups & Antipasti

brodo – broth

carpaccio – very fine slices of raw meat

caponata – sweet-and-sour dish of tomatoes aubergines, anchovies and olives

insalata caprese – sliced tomatoes with mozzarella and basil

insalata di mare – seafood, generally crustaceans

minestrina in brodo – pasta in broth

minestrone – vegetable soup

olive ascolane – stuffed, deep-fried olives

prosciutto e melone – cured ham with melon

ripieni – stuffed, oven-baked vegetables

stracciatella – egg in broth

Pasta Sauces

alla matriciana – tomato and bacon

al ragù – meat sauce (bolognese)

all'arrabbiata – tomato and chilli

alla carbonara – egg, bacon and black pepper

napoletana – tomato and basil

con panna – cream, prosciutto and sometimes peas

pesto – basil, garlic and oil; often with pine nuts

alle vongole – clams, garlic and oil; sometimes with tomato

Pizzas

All pizzas listed have a tomato (and sometimes mozzarella) base.

capricciosa – olives, prosciutto, mushrooms and artichokes

frutti di mare – seafood

funghi – mushrooms

margherita – oregano

napoletana – anchovies

pugliese – tomato, mozzarella and onions

quattro formaggi – with four types of cheese

quattro stagioni – like a capricciosa, but sometimes with egg

verdura – mixed vegetables

Glossary

AAST – Azienda Autonoma di Soggiorno e Turismo; local tourist office
abbazia – abbey
ACI – Automobile Club Italiano; Italian Automobile Association
aereo – aeroplane
affittacamere – rooms for rent
affresco – the painting method in which watercolour paint is applied to wet plaster
agora – (Latin) marketplace, meeting place
agriturismo – tourist accommodation on farms
AIG – Associazione Italiana Alberghi per la Gioventù; Italian Youth Hostel Association
albergo – hotel (up to five stars)
alimentari – grocery shop, delicatessen
aliscafo – hydrofoil
Alleanza Nazionale – National Alliance; neo-Fascist political party
alloggio – lodging (cheaper than a *pensione* and not part of the classification system)
alto – high
ambasciata – embassy
ambulanza – ambulance
anfiteatro – amphitheatre
Annunciazione – Annunciation
antipasto – starter, appetiser
appartamento – apartment, flat
APT – Azienda di Promozione Turistica; regional tourist office
ara – altar
arco – arch
ARTCT – Assessorato Regionale del Turismo, delle Communicazioni e dei Trasporti; the main Sicilian tourist agency
assicurato/a – insured
AST – Azienda Soggiorno e Turismo; local tourist office
atrium – (Latin) forecourt of a Roman house or a Christian basilica
autobus – bus
autostazione – bus station or terminal
autostop – hitchhiking
autostrada – motorway, freeway

badia – abbey
baglio – manor house

bagno – bathroom; toilet
bambino – child
bancomat – ATM
belvedere – panoramic viewpoint
bene – well, good
benzina – petrol
benzina senza piombo – unleaded petrol
bicicletta – bicycle
biglietto – ticket
biglietto chilometrico – kilometric card (train pass)
binario – (train) platform
borgo – ancient town or village, sometimes used to mean equivalent of *via*
Brigate Rosse (BR) – Red Brigades (terrorist group)

calcio – football (soccer)
cambio – money exchange
camera – room
campanile – bell tower
campeggio – camp site
campo – field
canto – quarter
cappella – chapel
carabinieri – police with military and civil duties
Carnevale – carnival period between Epiphany and Lent
carta – menu
carta d'identità – ID card
carta telefonica – phonecard; see also *scheda telefonica*
cartoleria – stationery shop
casa – house
case abusive – (literally, abusive houses) illegal construction usually associated with the Mafia
castello – castle, citadel
cattedrale – cathedral
cava – quarry (as in the pumice quarries at Campobianco)
cena – evening meal
cenacolo – refectory
centro – centre
centro storico – historic centre
chiave – key

chiesa – church
chiostro – cloister; covered walkway, usually enclosed by columns, around a quadrangle
cin cin – cheers (a drinking toast)
Circumetna – private train line circling Mt Etna
CIT – Compagnia Italiana di Turismo; Italian national travel agency
città – town, city
clientilismo (politico) – system of political patronage
codice fiscale – tax number
colazione – breakfast
colonna – column
comune – equivalent to a municipality or county; town or city council; historically, a *commune* (self-governing town or city)
consolato – consulate
contorno – side dish
contrada – district
convalida – ticket stamping machine
coperto – cover charge in restaurants
corso – main street, avenue
cortile – courtyard
Cosa Nostra – alternative name for the Mafia
Crocifissione – Crucifixion
CTS – Centro Turistico Studentesco e Giovanile; Centre for Student and Youth Tourists
cuccetta – couchette
cupola – dome
Cupola – Mafia commission

decumanus – (Latin) main street
Democrazia Cristiana (DC) – Christian Democrats; centre-right political party
deposito bagagli – left luggage
digestivo – after-dinner liqueur
diretto – direct; slow train
distributore di benzina – petrol pump
dolce – sweet, dessert
duomo – cathedral

elenco – list
elenco degli alberghi – list of hotels
ENIT – Ente Nazionale Italiano per il Turismo; Italian Tourist Board
enoteca – wine bar
ephebus – (Latin) statue of a young boy
espresso – express mail; express train; short black coffee

fangho – mud bath
faraglione – rock stack
farmacia (di turno) – pharmacy (open late)
fermo posta – poste restante
Ferragosto – Feast of the Assumption, 15 August
ferrovia – train station
festa – festival
fiume – river
focaccia – flat bread
fontana – fountain
forno – bakery
foro – forum
fortezza – fortress
fortino – fort
Forza Italia – Go Italy; centre-right political party
fossa – pit, hole
francobollo – postage stamp
fresco – see *affresco*
FS – Ferrovie dello Stato; State Railway
funivia – cable car

gabinetto – toilet, WC
gasauto or **GPL** – liquid petroleum gas (LPG)
gasolio – diesel
gelateria – ice-cream parlour
gelato – ice cream
gola – gorge
golfo – gulf
granita – drink of crushed ice flavoured with lemon, strawberry, coffee and so on
grappa – grape liqueur
grotta – cave
guardia di finanza – fiscal police
guardia medica – emergency doctor service

IC – Intercity; fast train
interregionale – long-distance train that stops frequently
isola – island
IVA – Inposta di Valore Aggiunto; valued-added tax of around 19%

lago – lake
largo – (small) square
latifondo – large landed estate
latomie – small quarries

lavanderia – laundrette
lavasecco – dry-cleaning
lido – beach
locale – slow local train
locanda – inn, small hotel
loggia – covered area on the side of a building; porch; lodge
lungomare – seafront road, promenade

mafioso – member of the Mafia
mare – sea
mattanza – ritual slaughter of tuna (in Favignana)
menù del giorno – menu of the day
mercato – market
merceria – haberdashery shop
mescita di vini – wine outlet
mezza pensione – half board
Mezzogiorno – literally, midday; name for the south of Italy
monte – mountain
moschea – mosque
motorino – moped
mototraghetto veloce/tradizionale – car ferry
municipio – town hall, municipal offices
museo – museum

Natale – Christmas
nave – large ferry, ship
necropoli – (ancient) cemetery, burial site
Novecento – 20th century
numero verde – toll-free phone number

oggetti smarriti – lost property
Ognissanti – All Saints' Day, 1 November
omertà – code of silence used by the Mafia
oratorio – oratory
ospedale – hospital
ostello per la gioventù – youth hostel
osteria – snack bar, cheap restaurant

Pagine Gialle – Yellow Pages; phone directory
pala – altarpiece
palazzo – palace or mansion; large building of any type, including an apartment block
palio – contest
panetteria – bakery
panino – bread roll with filling

paninoteca – sandwich bar
parco – park
Pasqua – Easter
passeggiata – traditional evening stroll
pasta – cake; pasta; pastry or dough
pasticceria – shop selling cakes, pastries and biscuits
Partito Comunista Italiano (PCI) – Italian Communist Party; political party
Partito Democratico di Sinistra (PDS) – Democratic Party of the Left; political party
pedaggio – toll
pensione – small hotel, often with board
pensione completa – full board
permesso di lavoro – work permit
permesso di soggiorno – residence permit
pianta della città – city map
piazza – square
piazzale – (large) open square
pinacoteca – art gallery
pinoli – pine nuts
polizia – police
poltrona – airline-type chair on a ferry
polyptych – altarpiece consisting of more than three panels
pomice – pumice stone
ponte – bridge
porta – gate, door
portico – portico; covered walkway, usually attached to the outside of buildings
porto – port
posta – post office
posta aerea – airmail
pranzo – lunch
prigione – prison
prima – first; starter (meal)
Pro Loco – local tourist office
pronto soccorso – first aid; casualty ward
pullman – (English) long-distance bus

Quattrocento – 15th century
questura – police station

rapido – fast train
reale – royal
regionale – slow local train
rifugio – mountain hut
riserva naturale – nature reserve

rocca – fortress; rock
ronda – roundabout
rosso – red
rotonda – round chamber
ruderi – ruins

sagra – festival (generally dedicated to one food item or theme)
sala – room
saline – saltpan
salumeria – delicatessen
santuario – sanctuary
scalinata – staircase, steps
scheda telefonica – phonecard; see also *carta telefonica*
servizio – service charge in restaurants
sindaco – mayor
soccorso stradale – breakdown service
sopra – over, above
sotto – under
spiaggia (libera) – (public) beach
stazione – station
stazione di servizio – petrol or service station
stazione marittima – ferry terminal
strada – street, road
strada provinciale – main road; sometimes just a country lane
strada statale – main road; often multi-lane and toll free
superstrada – motorway; highway with divided lanes
supplemento – supplement, payable on a fast train

tabaccheria – tobacconist's shop
tavola calda – literally, 'hot table'; prepared meat, pasta and vegetable selection, often self-service
teatro – theatre
tempio – temple
terme – thermal baths
tholos – rock tomb
tonnara – tuna-processing plant
tonno – tuna
torre – tower
torrente – stream
torrone – type of nougat
traghetto – ferry, boat
tramezzino – sandwich
trattoria – cheap restaurant
treno – train
triptych – painting or carving on three panels, hinged so that the outer panels fold over the middle one; often used as an altarpiece

ufficio postale – post office
ufficio stranieri – foreigners bureau
uffizi – offices

vacanza – holiday, vacation
via – street, road
via aerea – by airmail
viale – avenue
vico – alley, alleyway
vigili del fuoco – fire brigade
vigili urbani – traffic police; local police
villa – town house or country house; also the park surrounding the house
vinai – wine bar or shop
vino alla mandorla – almond wine

zona rimozione – vehicle removal zone

LONELY PLANET

You already know that Lonely Planet produces more than this one guidebook, but you might not be aware of the other products we have on this region. Here is a selection of titles that you may want to check out as well:

Italy
ISBN 1 86450 352 1
US$24.99 • UK£14.99

Rome
ISBN 1 86450 311 4
US$15.99 • UK£9.99

Milan, Turin & Genoa
ISBN 1 86450 362 9
US$14.99 • UK£8.99

Florence
ISBN 1 74059 030 9
US$17.99 • UK£8.99

Tuscany
ISBN 1 86450 357 2
US$17.99 • UK£10.99

Venice
ISBN 1 86450 321 1
US$15.99 • UK£8.99

Walking in Italy
ISBN 0 86442 542 2
US$17.95 • UK£11.99

World Food Italy
ISBN 1 86450 022 0
US$12.95 • UK£7.99

Italian phrasebook
ISBN 0 86442 456 6
US$5.95 • UK£3.99

Europe on a shoestring
ISBN 1 86450 150 2
US$24.99 • UK£14.99

Western Europe
ISBN 1 86450 163 4
US$27.99 • UK£15.99

Europe Phrasebook
ISBN 1 86450 224 X
US$8.99 • UK£4.99

Available wherever books are sold

LONELY PLANET

ON THE ROAD

Travel Guides explore cities, regions and countries, and supply information on transport, restaurants and accommodation, covering all budgets. They come with reliable, easy-to-use maps, practical advice, cultural and historical facts and a rundown on attractions both on and off the beaten track. There are over 200 titles in this classic series, covering nearly every country in the world.

 Lonely Planet Upgrades extend the shelf life of existing travel guides by detailing any changes that may affect travel in a region since a book has been published. Upgrades can be downloaded for free from **www.lonelyplanet.com/upgrades**

For travellers with more time than money, **Shoestring** guides offer dependable, first-hand information with hundreds of detailed maps, plus insider tips for stretching money as far as possible. Covering entire continents in most cases, the six-volume shoestring guides are known around the world as 'backpackers bibles'.

For the discerning short-term visitor, **Condensed** guides highlight the best a destination has to offer in a full-colour, pocket-sized format designed for quick access. They include everything from top sights and walking tours to opinionated reviews of where to eat, stay, shop and have fun.

CitySync lets travellers use their Palm™ or Visor™ hand-held computers to guide them through a city with handy tips on transport, history, cultural life, major sights, and shopping and entertainment options. It can also quickly search and sort hundreds of reviews of hotels, restaurants and attractions, and pinpoint their location on scrollable street maps. CitySync can be downloaded from **www.citysync.com**

MAPS & ATLASES

Lonely Planet's **City Maps** feature downtown and metropolitan maps, as well as transit routes and walking tours. The maps come complete with an index of streets, a listing of sights and a plastic coat for extra durability.

Road Atlases are an essential navigation tool for serious travellers. Cross-referenced with the guidebooks, they also feature distance and climate charts and a complete site index.

LONELY PLANET

ESSENTIALS

Read This First books help new travellers to hit the road with confidence. These invaluable predeparture guides give step-by-step advice on preparing for a trip, budgeting, arranging a visa, planning an itinerary and staying safe while still getting off the beaten track.

Healthy Travel pocket guides offer a regional rundown on disease hot spots and practical advice on predeparture health measures, staying well on the road and what to do in emergencies. The guides come with a user-friendly design and helpful diagrams and tables.

Lonely Planet's **Phrasebooks** cover the essential words and phrases travellers need when they're strangers in a strange land. They come in a pocket-sized format with colour tabs for quick reference, extensive vocabulary lists, easy-to-follow pronunciation keys and two-way dictionaries.

Miffed by blurry photos of the Taj Mahal? Tired of the classic 'top of the head cut off' shot? **Travel Photography: A Guide to Taking Better Pictures** will help you turn ordinary holiday snaps into striking images and give you the know-how to capture every scene, from frenetic festivals to peaceful beach sunrises.

Lonely Planet's **Travel Journal** is a lightweight but sturdy travel diary for jotting down all those on-the-road observations and significant travel moments. It comes with a handy time-zone wheel, a world map and useful travel information.

Lonely Planet's eKno is an all-in-one communication service developed especially for travellers. It offers low-cost international calls and free email and voicemail so that you can keep in touch while on the road. Check it out on **www.ekno.lonelyplanet.com**

FOOD GUIDES

For people who live to eat, drink and travel, **World Food** guides explore the culinary culture of each country. Entertaining and adventurous, each guide is packed with detail on staples and specialities, regional cuisine and local markets, as well as sumptuous recipes, comprehensive culinary dictionaries and lavish photos good enough to eat.

LONELY PLANET

OUTDOOR GUIDES

For those who believe the best way to see the world is on foot, Lonely Planet's **Walking Guides** detail everything from family strolls to difficult treks, with 'when to go and how to do it' advice supplemented by reliable maps and essential travel information.

Cycling Guides map a destination's best bike tours, long and short, in day-by-day detail. They contain all the information a cyclist needs, including advice on bike maintenance, places to eat and stay, innovative maps with detailed cues to the rides, and elevation charts.

The **Watching Wildlife** series is perfect for travellers who want authoritative information but don't want to tote a heavy field guide. Packed with advice on where, when and how to view a region's wildlife, each title features photos of over 300 species and contains engaging comments on the local flora and fauna.

With underwater colour photos throughout, **Pisces Books** explore the world's best diving and snorkelling areas. Each book contains listings of diving services and dive resorts, detailed information on depth, visibility and difficulty of dives, and a roundup of the marine life you're likely to see through your mask.

LONELY PLANET

OFF THE ROAD

Journeys, the travel literature series written by renowned travel authors, capture the spirit of a place or illuminate a culture with a journalist's attention to detail and a novelist's flair for words. These are tales to soak up while you're actually on the road or dip into as an at-home armchair indulgence.

The range of lavishly illustrated **Pictorial** books is just the ticket for both travellers and dreamers. Off-beat tales and vivid photographs bring the adventure of travel to your doorstep long before the journey begins and long after it is over.

Lonely Planet **Videos** encourage the same independent, tough-minded approach as the guidebooks. Currently airing throughout the world, this award-winning series features innovative footage and an original soundtrack.

Yes, we know, work is tough, so do a little bit of deskside dreaming with the spiral-bound Lonely Planet **Diary** or a Lonely Planet **Wall Calendar**, filled with great photos from around the world.

TRAVELLERS NETWORK

Lonely Planet Online. Lonely Planet's award-winning Web site has insider information on hundreds of destinations, from Amsterdam to Zimbabwe, complete with interactive maps and relevant links. The site also offers the latest travel news, recent reports from travellers on the road, guidebook upgrades, a travel links site, an online book-buying option and a lively travellers bulletin board. It can be viewed at **www.lonelyplanet.com** or AOL keyword: lp.

Comet, our free monthly email newsletter, is loaded with travel news, advice, dispatches from authors, raging debates, travel competitions and letters from readers. To subscribe, click on the newsletters link on the front page of our Web site or go to: **www.lonelyplanet.com/comet/**.

Planet Talk is a free quarterly print newsletter, full of travel advice, tips from fellow travellers, author articles, news about forthcoming Lonely Planet events and a complete list of Lonely Planet books and other products. It provides an antidote to the being-at-home blues and helps you dream about and plan your next trip. To join our mailing list contact any Lonely Planet office or email us at: talk2us@lonelyplanet.com.au.

Lonely Planet Guides by Region

Lonely Planet is known worldwide for publishing practical, reliable and no-nonsense travel information in our guides and on our Web site. The Lonely Planet list covers just about every accessible part of the world. Currently there are 16 series: Travel guides, Shoestring guides, Condensed guides, Phrasebooks, Read This First, Healthy Travel, Walking guides, Cycling guides, Watching Wildlife guides, Pisces Diving & Snorkeling guides, City Maps, Road Atlases, Out to Eat, World Food, Journeys travel literature and Pictorials.

AFRICA Africa on a shoestring • Botswana • Cairo • Cairo City Map • Cape Town • Cape Town City Map • East Africa • Egypt • Egyptian Arabic phrasebook • Ethiopia, Eritrea & Djibouti • Ethiopian Amharic phrasebook • The Gambia & Senegal • Healthy Travel Africa • Kenya • Malawi • Morocco • Moroccan Arabic phrasebook • Mozambique • Namibia • Read This First: Africa • South Africa, Lesotho & Swaziland • Southern Africa • Southern Africa Road Atlas • Swahili phrasebook • Tanzania, Zanzibar & Pemba • Trekking in East Africa • Tunisia • Watching Wildlife East Africa • Watching Wildlife Southern Africa • West Africa • World Food Morocco • Zambia • Zimbabwe, Botswana & Namibia
Travel Literature: Mali Blues: Traveling to an African Beat • The Rainbird: A Central African Journey • Songs to an African Sunset: A Zimbabwean Story

AUSTRALIA & THE PACIFIC Aboriginal Australia & the Torres Strait Islands •Auckland • Australia • Australian phrasebook • Australia Road Atlas • Cycling Australia • Cycling New Zealand • Fiji • Fijian phrasebook • Healthy Travel Australia, NZ & the Pacific • Islands of Australia's Great Barrier Reef • Melbourne • Melbourne City Map • Micronesia • New Caledonia • New South Wales • New Zealand • Northern Territory • Outback Australia • Out to Eat – Melbourne • Out to Eat – Sydney • Papua New Guinea • Pidgin phrasebook • Queensland • Rarotonga & the Cook Islands • Samoa • Solomon Islands • South Australia • South Pacific • South Pacific phrasebook • Sydney • Sydney City Map • Sydney Condensed • Tahiti & French Polynesia • Tasmania • Tonga • Tramping in New Zealand • Vanuatu • Victoria • Walking in Australia • Watching Wildlife Australia • Western Australia
Travel Literature: Islands in the Clouds: Travels in the Highlands of New Guinea • Kiwi Tracks: A New Zealand Journey • Sean & David's Long Drive

CENTRAL AMERICA & THE CARIBBEAN Bahamas, Turks & Caicos • Baja California • Belize, Guatemala & Yucatán • Bermuda • Central America on a shoestring • Costa Rica • Costa Rica Spanish phrasebook • Cuba • Cycling Cuba • Dominican Republic & Haiti • Eastern Caribbean • Guatemala • Havana • Healthy Travel Central & South America • Jamaica • Mexico • Mexico City • Panama • Puerto Rico • Read This First: Central & South America • Virgin Islands • World Food Caribbean • World Food Mexico • Yucatán
Travel Literature: Green Dreams: Travels in Central America

EUROPE Amsterdam • Amsterdam City Map • Amsterdam Condensed • Andalucía • Athens • Austria • Baltic States phrasebook • Barcelona • Barcelona City Map • Belgium & Luxembourg • Berlin • Berlin City Map • Britain • British phrasebook • Brussels, Bruges & Antwerp • Brussels City Map • Budapest • Budapest City Map • Canary Islands • Catalunya & the Costa Brava • Central Europe • Central Europe phrasebook • Copenhagen • Corfu & the Ionians • Corsica • Crete • Crete Condensed • Croatia • Cycling Britain • Cycling France • Cyprus • Czech & Slovak Republics • Czech phrasebook • Denmark • Dublin • Dublin City Map • Dublin Condensed • Eastern Europe • Eastern Europe phrasebook • Edinburgh • Edinburgh City Map • England • Estonia, Latvia & Lithuania • Europe on a shoestring • Europe phrasebook • Finland • Florence • Florence City Map • France • Frankfurt City Map • Frankfurt Condensed • French phrasebook • Georgia, Armenia & Azerbaijan • Germany • German phrasebook • Greece • Greek Islands • Greek phrasebook • Hungary • Iceland, Greenland & the Faroe Islands • Ireland • Italian phrasebook • Italy • Kraków • Lisbon • The Loire • London • London City Map • London Condensed • Madrid • Madrid City Map • Malta • Mediterranean Europe • Milan, Turin & Genoa • Moscow • Munich • Netherlands • Normandy • Norway • Out to Eat – London • Out to Eat – Paris • Paris • Paris City Map • Paris Condensed • Poland • Polish phrasebook • Portugal • Portuguese phrasebook • Prague • Prague City Map • Provence & the Côte d'Azur • Read This First: Europe • Rhodes & the Dodecanese • Romania & Moldova • Rome • Rome City Map • Rome Condensed • Russia, Ukraine & Belarus • Russian phrasebook • Scandinavian & Baltic Europe • Scandinavian phrasebook • Scotland • Sicily • Slovenia • South-West France • Spain • Spanish phrasebook • Stockholm • St Petersburg • St Petersburg City Map • Sweden • Switzerland • Tuscany • Ukrainian phrasebook • Venice • Vienna • Wales • Walking in Britain • Walking in France • Walking in Ireland • Walking in Italy • Walking in Scotland • Walking in Spain • Walking in Switzerland • Western Europe • World Food France • World Food Greece • World Food Ireland • World Food Italy • World Food Spain **Travel Literature:** After Yugoslavia • Love and War in the Apennines • The Olive Grove: Travels in Greece • On the Shores of the Mediterranean • Round Ireland in Low Gear • A Small Place in Italy

Lonely Planet Mail Order

Lonely Planet products are distributed worldwide. They are also available by mail order from Lonely Planet, so if you have difficulty finding a title please write to us. North and South American residents should write to 150 Linden St, Oakland, CA 94607, USA; European and African residents should write to 10a Spring Place, London NW5 3BH, UK; and residents of other countries to Locked Bag 1, Footscray, Victoria 3011, Australia.

INDIAN SUBCONTINENT & THE INDIAN OCEAN Bangladesh • Bengali phrasebook • Bhutan • Delhi • Goa • Healthy Travel Asia & India • Hindi & Urdu phrasebook • India • India & Bangladesh City Map • Indian Himalaya • Karakoram Highway • Kathmandu City Map • Kerala • Madagascar • Maldives • Mauritius, Réunion & Seychelles • Mumbai (Bombay) • Nepal • Nepali phrasebook • North India • Pakistan • Rajasthan • Read This First: Asia & India • South India • Sri Lanka • Sri Lanka phrasebook • Tibet • Tibetan phrasebook • Trekking in the Indian Himalaya • Trekking in the Karakoram & Hindukush • Trekking in the Nepal Himalaya • World Food India **Travel Literature:** The Age of Kali: Indian Travels and Encounters • Hello Goodnight: A Life of Goa • In Rajasthan • Maverick in Madagascar • A Season in Heaven: True Tales from the Road to Kathmandu • Shopping for Buddhas • A Short Walk in the Hindu Kush • Slowly Down the Ganges

MIDDLE EAST & CENTRAL ASIA Bahrain, Kuwait & Qatar • Central Asia • Central Asia phrasebook • Dubai • Farsi (Persian) phrasebook • Hebrew phrasebook • Iran • Israel & the Palestinian Territories • Istanbul • Istanbul City Map • Istanbul to Cairo • Istanbul to Kathmandu • Jerusalem • Jerusalem City Map • Jordan • Lebanon • Middle East • Oman & the United Arab Emirates • Syria • Turkey • Turkish phrasebook • World Food Turkey • Yemen **Travel Literature:** Black on Black: Iran Revisited • Breaking Ranks: Turbulent Travels in the Promised Land • The Gates of Damascus • Kingdom of the Film Stars: Journey into Jordan

NORTH AMERICA Alaska • Boston • Boston City Map • Boston Condensed • British Columbia • California & Nevada • California Condensed • Canada • Chicago • Chicago City Map • Chicago Condensed • Florida • Georgia & the Carolinas • Great Lakes • Hawaii • Hiking in Alaska • Hiking in the USA • Honolulu & Oahu City Map • Las Vegas • Los Angeles • Los Angeles City Map • Louisiana & the Deep South • Miami • Miami City Map • Montreal • New England • New Orleans • New Orleans City Map • New York City • New York City City Map • New York City Condensed • New York, New Jersey & Pennsylvania • Oahu • Out to Eat – San Francisco • Pacific Northwest • Rocky Mountains • San Diego & Tijuana • San Francisco • San Francisco City Map • Seattle • Seattle City Map • Southwest • Texas • Toronto • USA • USA phrasebook • Vancouver • Vancouver City Map • Virginia & the Capital Region • Washington, DC • Washington, DC City Map • World Food New Orleans **Travel Literature**: Caught Inside: A Surfer's Year on the California Coast • Drive Thru America

NORTH-EAST ASIA Beijing • Beijing City Map • Cantonese phrasebook • China • Hiking in Japan • Hong Kong & Macau • Hong Kong City Map • Hong Kong Condensed • Japan • Japanese phrasebook • Korea • Korean phrasebook • Kyoto • Mandarin phrasebook • Mongolia • Mongolian phrasebook • Seoul • Shanghai • South-West China • Taiwan • Tokyo • Tokyo Condensed • World Food Hong Kong • World Food Japan **Travel Literature:** In Xanadu: A Quest • Lost Japan

SOUTH AMERICA Argentina, Uruguay & Paraguay • Bolivia • Brazil • Brazilian phrasebook • Buenos Aires • Buenos Aires City Map • Chile & Easter Island • Colombia • Ecuador & the Galapagos Islands • Healthy Travel Central & South America • Latin American Spanish phrasebook • Peru • Quechua phrasebook • Read This First: Central & South America • Rio de Janeiro • Rio de Janeiro City Map • Santiago de Chile • South America on a shoestring • Trekking in the Patagonian Andes • Venezuela **Travel Literature:** Full Circle: A South American Journey

SOUTH-EAST ASIA Bali & Lombok • Bangkok • Bangkok City Map • Burmese phrasebook • Cambodia • Cycling Vietnam, Laos & Cambodia • East Timor phrasebook • Hanoi • Healthy Travel Asia & India • Hill Tribes phrasebook • Ho Chi Minh City (Saigon) • Indonesia • Indonesian phrasebook • Indonesia's Eastern Islands • Java • Lao phrasebook • Laos • Malay phrasebook • Malaysia, Singapore & Brunei • Myanmar (Burma) • Philippines • Pilipino (Tagalog) phrasebook • Read This First: Asia & India • Singapore • Singapore City Map • South-East Asia on a shoestring • South-East Asia phrasebook • Thailand • Thailand's Islands & Beaches • Thailand, Vietnam, Laos & Cambodia Road Atlas • Thai phrasebook • Vietnam • Vietnamese phrasebook • World Food Indonesia • World Food Thailand • World Food Vietnam

ALSO AVAILABLE: Antarctica • The Arctic • The Blue Man: Tales of Travel, Love and Coffee • Brief Encounters: Stories of Love, Sex & Travel • Buddhist Stupas in Asia: The Shape of Perfection • Chasing Rickshaws • The Last Grain Race • Lonely Planet ... On the Edge: Adventurous Escapades from Around the World • Lonely Planet Unpacked • Lonely Planet Unpacked Again • Not the Only Planet: Science Fiction Travel Stories • Ports of Call: A Journey by Sea • Sacred India • Travel Photography: A Guide to Taking Better Pictures • Travel with Children • Time & Tide: The Islands of Tuvalu

Index

Text

Bold indicates maps.

Boxed Text

MAP LEGEND

BOUNDARIES

▬ ▬ · ▬ · ▬ · ▬ ....International
▬ · · ▬ · · ▬ · ....Provincial, State
▬ · ▬ · ▬ · ▬ ....Regional, Suburb

HYDROGRAPHY

................................Coastline
................................River, Creek
................................Lake
................................Canal

................................Building
................................Urban Area

ROUTES & TRANSPORT~

....................Freeway
....................Highway
....................Major Road
....................Minor Road
= = = = = = : ....Unsealed Road
....................City Freeway
....................City Highway
....................City Road
....................City Street, Lane

AREA FEATURES

❀ ....Park, Gardens
....................Cemetery

....................Pedestrian Mall
⫩⫥⫩⫥⫩⫥ ....Tunnel
●━━●━━ ....Train Route & Station
━━━ ❶ ━━ ....Metro & Station
▪▪▪▪▪▪🅣▪▪▪ ..Tramway & Tram Stop
ᚼ—ᚼ—ᚼ—🅒—ᚼ—.... Cable Car or Chairlift
— — — — — — — ....Walking Track
· · · · · · · · · · · · · · · ....Walking Tour
— — — — —🄹— — Ferry Route & Terminal

....................Market
⌃⌃⌃⌃⌃ ⌃⌃ ....Mountain Range

MAP SYMBOLS

✪ **FLORENCE**	Large City	🛪	Airport	▲	Mountain or Hill
⊙ **Lucca**	City	⌒⌒	Ancient or City Wall	🏛	Museum
⊙ Miniato	Large Town	⊠	Archaeological Site	🏕	National Park
⊙ Galleno	Town or Village	⦵	Bank	🏛	Palazzo
		↗	Beach	🅿	Parking
•	Point of Interest	🚏 🚌	Bus Stop, Station	★	Police Station
◼	Place to Stay	🏰	Castle or Fort	▣	Post Office
⛺	Camp Site	⌂	Cave	⚹	Ski Field
🚐	Caravan Park	🏩 ▬▬	Church or Cathedral	🏊	Swimming Pool
🏠	Hut or Chalet	⊞	Cinema	🕍	Synagogue
▼	Place to Eat	📷	Embassy	☎	Telephone
⬛	Pub or Bar	⚓	Fountain	🎭	Theatre
⊛	Picnic Area	⊕	Hospital	❶	Tourist Information
		🅐	Internet Cafe	🏃	Trail Head

Note: not all symbols displayed above appear in this book

LONELY PLANET OFFICES

Australia
Locked Bag 1, Footscray, Victoria 3011
☎ 03 8379 8000 fax 03 8379 8111
email: talk2us@lonelyplanet.com.au

USA
150 Linden St, Oakland, CA 94607
☎ 510 893 8555 TOLL FREE: 800 275 8555
fax 510 893 8572
email: info@lonelyplanet.com

UK
10a Spring Place, London NW5 3BH
☎ 020 7428 4800 fax 020 7428 4828
email: go@lonelyplanet.co.uk

France
1 rue du Dahomey, 75011 Paris
☎ 01 55 25 33 00 fax 01 55 25 33 01
email: bip@lonelyplanet.fr
www.lonelyplanet.fr

World Wide Web: www.lonelyplanet.com *or* **AOL keyword: lp**
Lonely Planet Images: lpi@lonelyplanet.com.au